Robert S. Leventhal
Making the Case

Interdisciplinary German Cultural Studies

―

Edited by
Irene Kacandes

Volume 25

Robert S. Leventhal
Making the Case

Narrative Psychological Case Histories
and the Invention of Individuality in Germany,
1750–1800

DE GRUYTER

ISBN 978-3-11-076343-0
e-ISBN (PDF) 978-3-11-064346-6
e-ISBN (EPUB) 978-3-11-064279-7
ISSN 1861-8030

Library of Congress Control Number: 2019939360

Bibliographic Information published by the Deutsche Nationalbibliothek
The Deutsche Nationalbibliothek lists this publication in the Deutsche Nationalbibliografie;
detailed bibliographic data are available on the Internet at http://dnb.dnb.de

© 2021 Walter de Gruyter GmbH, Berlin/Boston
This volume is text- and page-identical with the hardback published in 2019.
Cover image: Théodore Géricault: *Portrait of a Demented Woman*
or *The Monomaniac of Envy* (also named *The Hyena of the Salpêtrière*).
Courtesy of Musée des beaux-arts de Lyon
Typesetting: Integra Software Services Pvt. Ltd.
Printing and binding: CPI books GmbH, Leck

www.degruyter.com

For Joseph C. Miller (1939–2019), a true friend and fellow sailor, who on our many voyages and adventures shared with me his passion for historical research and incredible range of learning, listened and responded to the ideas and arguments presented in these pages.

Preface

This book has been a long time in the making. When I returned to teaching and research in 2004 after a ten year hiatus, I became interested in the psychological case-history before Freud, and began with the nineteenth-century case histories in the forensic medicine of Johann Ludwig Casper (1796–1864) and the clinical psychiatry of Carl Westphal (1833–1890). For two summers, I was able to pursue this research thanks to two Summer Grants from The College of William and Mary and the hospitality of the Institut für die Geschichte der Medizin at the Humboldt Universität, Berlin. In particular, several workshops led by Volker Hess and Eric Engstrom helped me hone my ideas about the psychological case-history developed and expanded in these pages. In 2009 and 2010, I was fortunate to receive a research grant at the Herzog-August-Bibliothek in Wolfenbüttel to get to the primary sources in the eighteenth century. I would like to specifically thank Dr. Jill Bepler, who made my and all of the fellows' stay that year so wonderfully rich in conversation and exploration. At the College of William and Mary, my Chairs Silvia Tandeciarz and Maryse Fauvel, my Deans Carl Strikwerda and Kate Conley always lent a hand to make possible research trips or attendance at conferences in Europe, as did the Vice Provost for Research Dennis Manos and The Reves Center for International Study.

In addition to the institutions mentioned, I would like to thank many colleagues who helped me clarify my thinking and writing about the narrative psychological case-history along the way: Lorna Martens, Joachim Gessinger, Robert Sackett, Sander Gilman, Giulia Pacini, Christof Wingertszahn, Carsten Zelle, Alexander Košenina, Ron Schechter, Liliane Weissberg, Wolfert von Rahden, Michael Prince, Jerome McGann, and Joel Black. Further back, Ian Hacking and David Wellbery were both instrumental in shaping the contours of my thinking about how individuals and individuality were made. Many very dear friends over the years helped in ways they probably cannot even imagine: Jeff Bokor, Jay Field, Joe Miller, Ernstfriedrich Jünger, Lawrence Fischman, John Wade, and Rafael Triana. I would also like to express deep gratitude to Maurice Apprey, whose wisdom and insight were crucial in my return to university teaching and research.

Some of the work presented here is revised and expanded from articles I published 2008–2012. An earlier version of the Schiller chapter appeared as "The Aesthetics of the Case: Schiller's Juridical-Psychological Contribution" in *The Aesthetics of Modernity from Schiller to Marcuse*, edited by Jerome Carroll, Steve Giles and Maike Oergel (New York/Berlin: Peter Lang, 2011), 69–92. I would like to thank Jerome Carroll in particular for his editorial assistance with that piece. "Die Fallgeschichte zwischen Ästhetik und Therapeutik," in *Fakta, und kein moralisches Geschwätz: Die Fallgeschichten im Magazin zur Erfahrungsseelenkunde* (1783–1793), ed. Stefan Goldmann, Sheila Dickson, and Christof Wingertszahn (Göttingen: Wallstein, 2011), 63–81, was a talk delivered at a conference in Potsdam bearing the title of the volume. "Vorstudien zur Hysterie: Marcus Herz's Etwas Psychologisch-Medizinisches. Moriz Krankengeschichte (1793)," in: *Kulturen des Wissens. Studien zum 18. Jahrhundert*, ed. Ulrich Johannes Schneider (Berlin and New York: de Gruyter, 2008), 431–440 was a presentation at the Deutsche Gesellschaft zur Erforschung des achtzehnten Jahrhunderts Conference in Halle in 2010. Last but not least, some of the material of chapter 1 appeared in "Kasuistik, Empirie und Pastorale Seelenführung: Die Entstehung der modernen psychologischen Fallgeschichte, 1750–1800," in *Jahrbuch Literatur und Medizin*, ed. Bettina von Jagow und Florian Steger (Heidelberg: Carl Winter, 2008), 13–40. Thanks to all the readers and editors for their detailed comments and suggestions, and to the publishers for giving me permission to rework and re-present this work in what I hope to be a coherent form with a sustained argument.

I would also like to express my thanks to the two readers at de Gruyter who offered many constructive criticisms and suggestions, and helped me to sculpt the original manuscript into a more unified and coherent book. The series editor, Irene Kacandes, was incredibly supportive and enthusiastic of my effort. Sam Brawand brought a sharp eye in the phase of copyediting and proofreading, and prepared the basic index which I then expanded and filled out.

I would like to express my special gratitude to my daughters Alethea, Chelsea, and Miran, and to Janet Warren, my best friend and soulmate, who encouraged and assisted me every step of the way, always ready to lend an ear or a kind word.

R. L.
Castelmuzio (SI), Italy
May 2017

Contents

Preface —— VII

List of Figures —— XI

A Note on Translations —— XIII

Introduction —— 1

1 Historicizing the Psychological Case History —— 21

2 Theorizing the Psychological Case History —— 69

3 Disciplining the Human Soul: German Empirical Psychology in the Eighteenth Century from Christian Wolff to Kant —— 107

4 Ethnicity, Gender, Religion, and Madness in Mid-Eighteenth-Century Germany: A Case History of Demonic Possession in Lower Saxony, 1744 —— 147

5 The First Modern Psychological Case History: Marcus Herz's *Psychological Description of His Own Illness* (1783) and the Construction of the Modern Soul —— 191

6 Friedrich Schiller: The Juridical-Psychological Case History as a Literary Work of Art —— 219

7 A Doctor's Worst Fear: Marcus Herz's Case History of Karl Philipp Moritz *Etwas Psychologisch-Medizinisches. Moriz Krankengeschichte* (1793) —— 247

8 The Case History, Therapeutics, and the Dietetics of the Soul: Aesthetics and Empirical Psychology in the Work of Karl Philipp Moritz —— 273

9 Towards an Epistemology of the Individual Case: Stance and Deviation in the Philosophy of Marcus Herz —— 309

Conclusion: Becoming a Culture of Individual Cases —— 339

Bibliography —— 363

Index —— 391

About the Author —— 409

List of Figures

Figures 1 and 2 Felix Platter's portrait (fig. 1) and the title page of Book III of his *Observationes* (1614) (fig. 2), the most widely recognized collection of medical case histories in early modern Europe —— **24**

Figures 3 and 4 Carl Wilhelm Jerusalem (fig. 3) and the request for Kästner's *Reisepistole* (fig. 4), which provided Goethe with a "true" case-history for his famous psychological novel *Die Leiden des jungen Werther* (1774) —— **31**

Figures 5, 6 and 7 *Sturm und Drang* dramatist Johann Michael Reinhold Lenz, 1751–1792 (fig. 5), who became the subject of Pastor Johann Friedrich Oberlin's (fig. 6) case-history, and the physician and playwright Georg Büchner, 1813–1837 (fig. 7), who read Oberlin's case-study and whose novella *Lenz* (written 1835–1836) is often regarded as one of the first truly modern literary texts —— **33**

Figure 8 Albrecht Wolfgang Graf zu Schaumburg-Lippe (1699–1748) —— **156**

Figure 9 The "Conversation with the Spirit" from the Protocol of the Case-History of Grendel, the Jewish girl whose father requests that a Rabbi be allowed to perform an exorcism, 1744 —— **170**

Figure 10 Engraving of "On the Narrative 'The Criminal because of Lost Honor,' by Schiller" —— **220**

A Note on Translations

Unless otherwise noted in the text or the footnotes, translations are mine. I have attempted to remain very close to the original German, allowing the nuances of the text to shine through, while making the texts as stylistically and grammatically accessible as possible. In the case of the protocol contained in chapter 4, which presented significant difficulties of translation both because of the type of text and the archaic locutions contained in the case-history, I have tried to render the core meanings, style, and rhetoric of the interrogation as accurately as possible, but I have modernized the text in many instances in order to increase its intelligibility to a contemporary audience. Where a term or phrase in Latin or German has a very specific historical purport and use that might have been lost in English translation, I have left them in the original language.

The German term *Erfahrungsseelenkunde,* usually rendered as "empirical psychology," poses a special problem of translation. I have decided upon *empirical-experiential psychology* in order to emphasize both the rejection of top-down, rationalist *a priori* models, and the strong reliance on direct human observation and experience, both one's own and that of others. As there are various types of empiricism, some concerned with statistics and mere facts, while the new discipline in eighteenth-century Germany prized above all else narratives of lived-experience, I believe this manner of phrasing *Erfahrungsseelenkunde* is most appropriate.

German has a number of terms for "case history." In the eighteenth century, the term *Krankengeschichte,* essentially a transcription of the *historia morbi* of early modern Europe, appears in Adelung's *Grammatisch-kritisches Wörterbuch der Hochdeutschen Mundart* (1774–1786): "bey den Ärzten, die Erzählung von dem Ursprunge und den Abwechselungen einer Krankheit, so wohl überhaupt, als bey einzelnen Kranken." It is used widely in texts of the eighteenth century. And while variants containing the root *Fall* in the sense of *casus* (*Fallgeschichte, Fallstudie, Fallbeschreibung, Fallbeispiel, Fallerzählung*) only appear in the twentieth century,[1] short texts concerning an individual "case" utilizing the term *Fall,* as in "the strange case," "a case of child murder," "a criminal case," "a noteworthy case," and "description of a case" proliferate

---

[1] Stefan Goldmann, "Kasus –Krankengeschichte – Novelle," in *"Fakta und kein moralisches Geschwätz": Zu den Fallgeschichten im "Magazin zur Erfahrungsseelenkunde" (1783–1793),* ed. Sheila Dickson, Stefan Goldmann and Christof Wingertszahn (Göttingen: Wallstein 2011), 33–64.

in the second half of the eighteenth century. My choice of "case history" with the qualifiers "narrative" and "psychological" to denote the narrative texts – medical-psychological and literary – of the second half of the eighteenth century seems to me justified in light of their attempt to excavate and document the deeper forces at work in the narrative construction of the individual.

Introduction

> I propose to augment Foucault's two poles, anatomo- and bio-. What is missing seems pretty obvious. It is the mind, the psyche, the soul.
> Ian Hacking, *Rewriting the Soul*[1]

Making the Case is an attempt to articulate how and why the narrative *psychological case history* emerged as a medical, psychological, and literary meta-disciplinary genre in Germany in the second half of the eighteenth century. In particular, we are interested in how it served as a medium of scientific-scholarly exchange about the "self" and its vicissitudes for the burgeoning literate public; how it created a very specific way of thinking and writing about individuality; and how it functioned as part of a pastoral apparatus. The *narrative psychological case history* must be distinguished from physicians' diaries in early modern Europe, the medical case history (*Krankengeschichte, historia morbi*), the *consilia* and *consultatoria* of doctors, the juridical case history, and the moral case in theological casuistry. Rather than subsuming the individual under an established medical classification, moral precept, category, or type, the narrative psychological case history that appeared in the second half of the eighteenth century endeavored to articulate the individual in its very individuality – a unique self, conceived in its irreducible singularity. It provided *psychological* reasons for an anomalous event or series of occurrences by linking the external circumstances, symptoms, expressions of an individual with that individual's inner world of emotion, feeling, thoughts, fears, and world-understanding. In the present study, the term *case history* will be used to refer to this narrative psychological genre rather than "case study" to mark the difference between the case as *exemplum* or mere *Beispiel* and the more introspective attempt to establish the subliminal connections between the patient's suffering and history.

The book begins with a reconstruction of the discipline of empirical psychology in the work of Christian Wolff, which he regarded as "the science that establishes principles through experience, whence reason is given for what occurs in the human soul."[2] Empirical psychology, with its imperative to

---

[1] Ian Hacking, *Rewriting the Soul: Multiple Personality and the Sciences of Memory* (Princeton, NJ: Princeton University Press, 1995), 215.
[2] Christian Wolff, *Psychologia empirica, methodo scientifica pertractata, qua ea, quae de anima humana indubia experientiae fide constant, continentur et ad solidam universae philosophiae practicae ac theologiae naturalis tractationem via sternitur* (Francofurti and Lipsiae: officina libraria Rengeriana, 1732, 1738), §1.

observe through apperception or introspection what occurred in the human soul, served as the disciplinary framework in eighteenth-century Germany for a discursive medium to describe, as accurately as possible, the representations of the mind. In the late Enlightenment, roughly 1770 to 1800, the narrative psychological case history proved to be precisely such a medium. The origins of this uniquely modern genre are then traced from the psychologically-minded physicians at the Universität Halle around 1750 – Johann Gottlob Krüger (1715–1759), Johann August Unzer (1727–1799), Ernst Anton Nicolai (1722–1802), and Johann Christian Bolten (1727–1757) – to Andreas Elias Büchner's (1701–1769) insistence on narrative (*Erzählung*) in a well-written case history and Johann Georg Zimmermann's (1728–1795) treatise on "experience" in the early 1760s to the first journal of empirical-experiential psychology, *Gnothi Sauton oder Magazin zur Erfahrungsseelenkunde*, edited by Karl Philipp Moritz (1783–1793). Friedrich Schiller's edition and translation of François Gayot de Pitaval's (1673–1743) *causes célèbres* and his *Criminal from Lost Honor* (1786), and Marcus Herz's (1747–1803) insightful psychological case histories of 1780–1793 and his articulation of an epistemology of "case" round out the study. Collectively, this body of work created the discursive conditions of the possibility of a specifically modern, "small" anthropological-psychological genre that proved decisive to literature and the human sciences.

The book draws on a wide range of recent interdisciplinary work in the history of science, medicine, and literature in the eighteenth century, and on influential theoretical work by John Forrester, Ian Hacking, Michel Foucault, and Niklas Luhmann. Foucault alerted us to the individualizing power of the case, the role that the case played in a classificatory system of surveillance and subjection, and the pastoral apparatus of "care" and "concern" directed at the guidance of souls in the latter part of the eighteenth century.[3] Forrester's seminal article of 1996 opened the way for what has become a vast literature on case studies.[4] In a number of studies, Hacking directed our attention to the ways in which subjects are *made*. In *Rewriting the Soul*, he went so far as to argue that the sciences of memory emerged in the years 1874 to 1886 as a secular "science of the soul."[5] For his part, the German sociologist Niklas Luhmann interrogated the individuality of individuals, showing it to be a *function* of increasing differentiation and incomparability within the emerging modern social system during and after the collapse

---

3 I distinguish three different determinations of the "case" in Foucault's work in chap. 1.
4 John Forrester, "If p, then what? Thinking in Cases," *History of the Human Sciences* 9.3 (1996): 1–25.
5 Hacking, *Rewriting the Soul*, 209–218.

of traditional hierarchical society based on family, class, and *Stand*.[6] The book also takes into account recent historical-philosophical metanarratives such as Charles Taylor's *Sources of the Self* and Jerold Seigel's *The Idea of the Self* regarding the construction of individuality in modernity. Offering an addition to the accounts of the ways in which modern individuality was crafted, *Making the Case* challenges the still widely accepted emphasis on the novel as the genre *par excellence* of modern individuality.[7] With its narrow focus, it seeks to show how this "small" psychological-anthropological genre shaped our modern notion of the individual. In the second half of the eighteenth century in Germany, a particularly modern species of individuality was forged in and through the proliferation of narrative psychological case histories, a genre that created the literary, stylistic, and narratological framework for the exposition of a unique individual *self*. This is not to suggest that it was an exclusively German invention by any means, or that other concepts of individuality – associationist, atomist, mechanist, animist, expressivist, autonomous – did not co-exist with the notion that became dominant in the German territories of the period I discuss. In fact, the broad impact of the rise of modern "experience" and reasoning based on empirical observation in the late seventeenth and early eighteenth century across Europe laid the groundwork of the psychological narrative case histories.[8] Interpretation of specific cases and programmatic writings with regard to their publication, discussion, and ultimate utility is supplemented by close readings of philosophical texts that dealt with reasoning and writing in cases at the time. I also document how the case history became a valuable and widely-used literary communication medium in a "pastoral apparatus" of proto-psychologists, priests and preachers, teachers and professors, superintendents and other civil authorities concerned with the care, direction, and guidance of the self in the late Enlightenment.

---

6 Niklas Luhmann, "Individuum, Individualität, Individualismus," in *Gesellschaftsstruktur und Semantik. Studien zur Wissenssoziologie der modernen Gesellschaft* (Frankfurt: Suhrkamp, 1989), vol. 3, 149–258.
7 Ian Watt, *The Rise of the Novel: Studies in Defoe, Richardson and Fielding* (Berkeley: University of California Press, 1957). Both Taylor and Seigel cite the novel as the genre in the eighteenth century that modeled our modern notion of the individual self.
8 Notwithstanding the debate concerning the "scientific revolution" in Europe generally, and the nature and role of induction more specifically, it is generally accepted now that the second half of the seventeenth century was a watershed moment in the shift in the notion of "experience" and the understanding of the decisive function of empirical observation. On this, see Peter Dear, *Discipline and Experience: The Mathematical Way in the Scientific Revolution* (Chicago: University of Chicago Press, 1995); and Lisa Jardine, *Ingenious Pursuits: Building the Scientific Revolution* (New York: Anchor, 2000).

There are many compelling reasons to study the modern narrative psychological case history. As the historian of science Gianna Pomata has written, case histories constitute an *epistemic genre*; they give "literary form to an intellectual endeavor and in so doing they shape and channel the cognitive practice of attention"; they provide "a framework for gathering, describing and organizing the raw materials of experience."[9] The study of these case histories also allows us to do the history of medicine and psychology, as Roy Porter suggested, "from below."[10] Rather than dealing only with lofty scientific, medical, and philosophical theory, we encounter, often in the form of first-hand reports, in-depth narratives, and "ego-documents," the internal world of the subjects. Through such narratives one can discover not merely the diagnosis, etiology, course, treatment, and outcome of an illness as in earlier medical case histories (*Krankengeschichte, historia morbi*), but also how the illness is experienced, felt, and represented by the subject herself, the discrepancies between the lived-experience of the illness and its material and institutional inscription by physicians, pastors, educators, philosophers and civil administrators, and, in turn, between such inscriptions and the literary works they inspired. Finally, as a *model* and *modeling* of individuality, the case history serves a critical function in what Foucault called the *history of subjectivization* – that is, how the soul is made a "self," how the individual is engendered as a *subject* of a specific form of knowledge.[11]

For something to count as a "case" in the first place, it must be – in the eighteenth century as now – *interesting*, worthy of consideration, unique, compelling, as Karl Philipp Moritz stated in 1783, *interessant*, or *denkwürdig*. It has to stand out. The modern narrative psychological case explored in these pages differs from the cases known to early modern medicine in a significant way: the psychological case is not an *example*, an attempt to shore up a specific theory or confirm a method of treatment; its entire point is its *deviation* from typical cases that preceded it. Such *interesting cases* must be distinguished, I would argue, not only from the curiosities and monstrosities of the fifteenth and sixteenth centuries, but also from the collections of medical case

---

9 Gianna Pomata, "Observation Rising: Birth of an Epistemic Genre, 1500–1650," in *Histories of Scientific Observation*, ed. Lorraine Daston and Elizabeth Lunbeck (Chicago: University of Chicago Press, 2011), 46.
10 Roy Porter, "The Patient's View: Doing Medical History from Below," *Theory and Society* 14.2 (1985): 175–198.
11 Michel Foucault, "The Subject and Power," in *Power*, ed. James D. Faubion (New York: New Press, 2000), 326, where he states his objective "to create a history of the different modes by which, in our culture, human beings are made subjects."

histories of the great physicians Felix Platter, Hermann Boerhaave, Thomas Sydenham, Georg Ernest Stahl, and Friedrich Hoffman in the seventeenth and early eighteenth centuries, whose *consilia* and *consultatoria medica* were disseminated in books, collections, appended to treatises, and later republished in learned journals as models. Their cases exemplified a specific type of illness and were used to provide an example of a *type*, or to show the effectiveness of a specific therapy. The modern psychological case as it emerged in the second half of the eighteenth century, by contrast, existed on the threshold of the incomprehensible; it was a case for which, analogous to aesthetic experience according to Immanuel Kant, no adequate concept or category could be found; it was an *exception* that defied classification.[12] As André Jolles noted in the first genre-theoretical consideration of the "case" in 1930, rather than merely subsuming a particular under a given rule or prescribed norm, the "case" sets us the task of a decision (*Entscheidung*) in which judgment must discern whether there is a fitting rule for the particular, or whether the particular initiates or calls for a consideration or questioning of the rules or norms themselves. The "case" poses a *question*, and does not provide the solution. Jolles writes, "The unique character of the form 'case' consists in the fact that it poses a question, but cannot provide the answer; that it tasks us with the duty of a decision, but does not contain the decision itself. What is realized in the 'case' is the weighing, but not the result of the weighing."[13] This concurs with the more recent argument of Carlo Ginzburg, who has issued a *plaidoyer* for a renewed consideration of the case. For Ginzburg, the case is a provocation, an argument for a normative or theoretical transformation, calling existing norms into question or suggesting a new paradigm of thought and writing.[14]

My study is rather narrowly focused on the German tradition for several reasons. First, as Fernando Vidal has pointed out, empirical psychology as a discipline flourished particularly in Germany in the eighteenth century as a result of the refusal to abandon metaphysics in general and the "soul" in particular.[15] While I disagree with Vidal that the empirical or, as I prefer,

---

12 Giorgio Agamben, *Homo Sacer: Sovereign Power and Bare life*, trans. Daniel Heller-Roazen (Stanford, CA: Stanford University Press, 1998), 15.
13 André Jolles, *Einfache Formen* (Halle [Saale]: Niemeyer, 1930; Tübingen: Niemeyer, 1968), 179, 191.
14 Carlo Ginzburg, "Ein Plädoyer für den Casus," in *Fallstudien: Theorie – Geschichte – Methode*, ed. Johannes Süßmann et al. (Berlin: Trafo, 2007), 29–48.
15 Fernando Vidal, *The Sciences of the Soul: The Early Modern Origins of Psychology*, trans. Saskia Brown (Chicago and London: University of Chicago Press, 2011), 110: "German philosophers and psychologists, contrary to their counterparts in England and in France, refused to reduce metaphysics to a sensualist theory of the origin of knowledge and pursued research

experiential psychology (what was referred to as *Erfahrungsseelenkunde*) in late eighteenth-century Germany sought first principles or universal concepts,[16] it is true that most of the preeminent writers, philosophers, critics, aestheticians, and physicians in Germany rejected the anti-metaphysical approach to psychology prevalent in England and France during the Enlightenment.[17] Empirical or experiential psychology was perfectly compatible with the idea of a human soul. Second, unlike the nosological and nosographical model that flourished in France in the work of Jean-Étienne Dominique Esquirol (1772–1840) and Philippe Pinel (1745–1826), primarily concerned with the classification of illness, or the nominalist, associationist empiricism that dominated psychological-medical thinking in England, a distinctly *narrative* approach to medical psychology emerged in Germany around 1750–1800. Several rather heterogeneous currents converged in the German-speaking territories to make this unique genre possible: the inner-directed tendency of German Pietism; the explosion of aesthetics and the significance it accorded to the so-called lower faculties (emotion, imagination, sensation, and experience) beginning with Alexander Baumgarten and Georg Friedrich Meier; the nascent theory of the novel (Blanckenburg, 1774) as "the inner history of a human being" ("die innere Geschichte eines Menschen")[18]; Wieland's novel *Geschichte des Agathon* (1765–1766)[19]; the ascendency of the genre of autobiography or what is referred to as "life-descriptions" (*Lebensbeschreibungen*); the "psychological" novel (Goethe, Moritz); and finally, the "anthropological turn" in the German *Aufklärung*, which wrote off Cartesian dualism in favor of the idea of the entire human being (*der ganze Mensch*).[20] It is

---

into first principles. The deductive schemas and 'geometric method' were abandoned, but not the imperative to arrive at fundamental universal concepts."

16 In fact, all of the programmatic writings warn against reasoning from first principles, *a priori* reasoning, or universal assumptions. The collection, dissemination, and discussion of case-histories served to gradually lead to an ever more precise systematic science.

17 Kurt Danziger has referred to the "national style" of psychology and psychiatry. See *Naming the Mind: How Psychology Found Its Language* (London: Sage, 1997), and other work by him. Danziger specifically refers to the strange pairing of experimental physiology, narrative psychiatry, and forensic psychopathology in the German-speaking areas in the nineteenth century.

18 Christian Friedrich von Blanckenburg, *Versuch über den Roman* (Leipzig und Liegnitz: David Siegerts Witwe, 1774).

19 Lorna Martens, "Constructing Interiority in Eighteenth-Century Narrative Fiction: Wieland's *Geschichte des Agathon*," *German Quarterly* 81.1 (2008): 49–65.

20 Hans-Jürgen Schings, ed., *Der ganze Mensch. Anthropologie und Literatur im 18. Jahrhundert.* (Stuttgart and Weimar: J. B. Metzler, 1994); Carsten Zelle, *Vernünftige Ärzte. Hallesche Psychomediziner und die Anfänge der Anthropologie in der deutschsprachigen Frühaufklärung* (Tübingen: Niemeyer, 2001); Alexander Košenina, *Literarische Anthropologie: Die Neuentdeckung des Menschen* (Berlin: de Gruyter, 2008).

within this German tradition, within this unique constellation, I argue, that the narrative psychological case history achieved its modern defining form and structure, probing the inner world of the subject and connecting, for the first time, individual disposition, character, and personal memory and history with illness, suffering, trauma, and criminal behavior.

Other reconstructions of the modern "self," specifically Taylor's *Sources of the Self* and Seigel's *The Idea of the Self*, while intellectually rigorous and equally compelling, chart the emergence of the self, with different emphases and anchors, on the battleground of ideas and issues – in a word, in the domain of *philosophy*. I have taken a somewhat different approach. By looking at one of the key scriptural media for the construction of individuality in modernity, I have also questioned the hegemony of the novel as the exemplary "genre of modern individuality" common to both Taylor and Seigel, a view that can be traced to Ian Watt's *Rise of the Novel*.[21] While the modern novel from Samuel Richardson (1689–1761) onward certainly explored the internal workings of an individual soul, it did so within the parameters of a socialization process, always regarding the individual as a figure on the larger canvas of family, class, and society; the "private" sphere of the individual was always disclosed over and against the backdrop of a "public" sphere of *habitus*, convention, virtue, expectation, honor, and obligation. In this sense, one might say the novel was always *inter-subjective*. Its topic was in fact the *bourgeois private sphere*, and its "object" was the individual as the medium through which the conflicts, rifts, and incongruities between the "private" and "public" spheres could be exposed and articulated, and sometimes reconciled.[22] Even a novel so radically "psychological" and focused on the internal world of the individual such as Goethe's *The Sorrows of Young Werther* (1774) did not fail to frame Werther's internal fragmentation and disintegration within the context of the rules, conventions, *mœurs* and morals, and strictures of bourgeois society.[23] The psychological case history, by contrast, exhibited a laser-like focus *exclusively* on the inner world of the specific, one might say *idiopathic* individual, her unique thoughts and ideas, emotions, imaginings, hopes and

---

21 Watt, *Rise of the Novel*. Watt argued that the uniqueness of the novel, its "primary criterion was truth to individual experience – individual experience which is always unique and therefore new." (13) The new "realism" Watt discerned in the novel of the eighteenth century was viewed to be part and parcel of a shift from universals to the "*immediate facts of consciousness.*" (15; emphasis mine)

22 Franco Moretti, *Distant Reading* (London and New York: Verso, 2013), 17.

23 It is interesting to note that the "case histories" of the *Bauernburschen* and the young girl embedded in Goethe's novel both deal with individuals as they rub up against the stifling and repressive structures of society.

fears, history, and memory. It eschewed moral considerations, social conventions, and traditional scripts. As a "small" or "minor" narrative prose form, it made up in depth and the attention to detail for what it lost in breadth and scope.

The first two chapters analyze the ways in which the case history has become an object of historical research and theoretical concerns. In chapter 1, the extended diachronic arc of the medical case from classical antiquity to early modern Europe demonstrates an enduring concern for writing and transmitting individual cases. In the eighteenth century, this medical concern with the individual case converges with the new discipline of empirical psychology, based on introspection and description of the mind's representations. In the second half of the eighteenth century, literary and psychological texts register a recognition of an inscrutable and irreducible, enigmatic individual that must be deciphered and articulated. In chapter 2, the most significant theoretical voices and discussions surrounding the case history in the last thirty years are presented and critiqued with an eye toward the specific contribution made by the philosophical physicians and psychologically motivated writers of the German eighteenth century. In these two chapters, the scope and purport of the study, its argument, the key issues, the theoretical work that has informed it, and the existing research are laid out. The question as to why the narrative psychological case history matters to modern German and, more broadly, European literary and cultural history receives a preliminary justification, setting the stage for the specific arguments put forward in the rest of the book.

Chapter 3 concerns the birth and evolution of the discipline of empirical psychology (*psychologia empirica*) from Christian Wolff to Immanuel Kant. Proceeding chronologically through the various iterations of empirical psychology allows us to grasp the transformation of the discipline from a theory of knowledge of the human soul conceived in general terms to a study of the "lower" faculties – sensate cognition, "dark" and "obscure" ideas – through the aesthetic turn in Alexander Baumgarten and Georg Friedrich Meier around 1750. With its emphasis on observation, individual experience, and the specific processes of the individual mind, empirical psychology provided the disciplinary framework for the philosophical physicians in Halle around 1750 and the experiential psychology (*Erfahrungsseelenkunde*) of the last two decades of the eighteenth century. Through an analysis of key texts by Wolff, Baumgarten, the Halle physicians, Johann Georg. Sulzer, Zimmermann, Jacob Friedrich Abel, Johann Gottfried Herder, Ernst Platner, Marcus Herz, and Kant, the distinct arc of empirical psychology in Germany is elucidated from its origin in Wolff's text of 1738 to Kant's scathing critique of the discipline in his *Metaphysical Foundations of Natural Science* (1786) and his *Anthropology from a Pragmatic Point of View* (1798; 1800).

During the entire eighteenth century, empirical psychology served as the underlying "discourse" for treatises, essays, and books on the mind until Kant questioned its very scientific validity. Kant argued that the very *practice* of empirical psychology would have debilitating effects for both practitioner and patient.

Chapter 4 presents the case history of a young Jewish woman in Schaumburg-Lippe allegedly afflicted with what was referred to as demonological possession in 1744. Influenced by enlightenment values and precepts, but prior to the development of a truly psychological conceptualization of mental illness, this case, the protocol of which comprises some 120 pages, demonstrates how, in the first half of the eighteenth century, cases concerned with mental illness became a grave concern of the civil authorities and the state. It also shows that despite an "enlightened" attitude and intention to ascertain the real basis of the affliction, and even with sustained interviews and interrogations of a diverse array of educated interlocutors, the early Enlightenment simply lacked a language and method for plumbing the depths of a psychological malady. What would have been summarily dismissed and remanded to the Jewish community just decades earlier summoned all of the investigative and interpretive capabilities of the entire court. With the demise of the Galenic theory of humors and vapors, and an enlightened suspicion regarding superstition and demonology, all of those involved – the family, the Jewish community, the rabbi, priests, court physicians, privy councilors, and even the Duke himself – struggled to find a reasonable explanation and a proper, humane treatment. To be clear, this case is *not* a narrative psychological case history. However, it deserves a place in this study because it offers a clear example of the kinds of juridical case protocols concerning psychological phenomena absent a properly psychological idiom and explanatory matrix, even while it exemplifies the new enlightened, rational approach to mental illness. Despite their best attempts to extract the truth, the physicians, privy councilors, and court administrators concerned with Grendel's case could not achieve any resolution regarding her condition, not because they lacked charity and sympathy, but because they had no category or concept in terms of which they could understand her ravings. In 1744, demonological possession was already a fiction of superstition and irrational belief. And yet all the expertise, medical knowledge, and pastoral techniques were unable to get at the true nature and cause of Grendel's illness. Her case is notable as it alerts us to a liminal historico-cultural situation in which the Galenic theory of the humors and vapors had already been eclipsed, rational, enlightened ideals and precepts were operative, but unable yet to address mental illness – specifically a mental illness that involved an alleged habitation of the body by an evil spirit.

Chapter 5 offers an in-depth reading of the first narrative case history in which the qualifier "psychological" is actually contained in the title: Marcus

Herz's *Psychologische Beschreibung seiner Krankheit* (*Psychological Description of His Illness*, 1783), which appeared in Karl Philipp Moritz's *Gnothi Sauton oder Magazin zur Erfahrungsseelenkunde*, the first journal of empirical-experiential psychology.[24] Remarkably, Herz's case history does not concern a psychological or mental illness, but a serious "fever" Herz contracted in the normal execution of his everyday obligations and duties as a practicing physician in Berlin. His attention to and interpretation of his own thought processes, feelings, fantasies, day dreams, and hallucinations during the three-week ordeal and the surprising connections he makes between his character, profession, personality, and disposition and what he experienced during the illness make this an extraordinary example of the genre.

Chapter 6 is a new reading of the poet and philosopher Friedrich Schiller's engagement with the case history as a psychological-juridical genre crucial to an understanding of the individual and humanity. Trained as a physician, Schiller had an astute awareness of both the individual "case" and the genre of the case history as special medium for narrating the origins of mental illness and criminal behavior. Interested in nothing less than a "dissection of the soul" and an "autopsy of vice," phrases he used in his suppressed preface to his drama *Die Räuber (The Robbers)* of 1781, Schiller must be considered one of the key philosophers of the case. Here, Schiller's case history of his fellow cadet Grammont's severe depression at the Karlsschule reveals only the beginning of a life-long engagement with the psychological case. His writing concerning the epistemological, historical, and humanitarian value of the writing and communication of individual cases in his *Aesthetic Letters* (1795), as well as in the introduction to his edition and translation of François de Gayot Pitival's *Causes célèbres, and* his literary case history *Criminal of Lost Honor* (1786), attest to his advocacy of the case as a key medico-philosophical genre. Schiller had learned of this case first-hand from his mentor Jacob Friedrich Abel (1751–1829), whose father had apprehended and produced a case history of Friedrich Schwan, the "Sonnenwirth" Christian Wolf in Schiller's novella. In our reading of Schiller's *Criminal of Lost Honor*, we are concerned with the differences, discrepancies, and incongruities between his literary work and Abel's text, which in rhetoric and procedure follows the standard protocol of the classical moral-juridical case history. Schiller's narrative, in stark contrast, engages the subject on an

---

24 Moritz famously changed the name from *Experimentalseelenkunde* to *Erfahrungsseelenkunde* on the recommendation of Moses Mendelssohn. The former had been employed by Johann Gottlob Krüger, one of the psychologically minded physicians in Halle at mid-century. Mendelssohn pointed out that the type of psychology Moritz was practicing lacked a properly "experimental" basis, as one did not "experiment" with or on human beings.

entirely different level, seizing on the inner experience of the Sonnenwirth, his shame, rage, sense of loss, and failure, his feelings of uselessness, and his envy and jealousy.

Chapter 7 returns to Marcus Herz and his posthumous case history of his friend and patient Karl Philipp Moritz, specifically, the strained relation (today we would say transference and countertransference) between physician and patient. Following his trip to England in 1782, Moritz contracted a serious illness, the first signs of the tuberculosis that would eventually claim his life. Yet aside from his very real suffering and symptoms, Moritz quickly exhibits a hysterical-hypochondriacal mania of sorts that puts him at odds with his friend and physician. Herz's in-depth psychological case history of Moritz is a wonderful tale of the *agon* of treatment and therapy, the conundrums of the philosophical physician, and the resistance of a patient who is struggling to come to terms with his own finitude. The bold and cunning intervention Herz devises for Moritz to wrest him from his tortured state points both backward to Bolton's notion of "philosophical pathology" and call for a psychical cure of 1751 and forward to Johann Christian Reil's (1759–1813) *Rhapsodies* of the early nineteenth century.

Chapter 8 shows parallels between the aesthetic attitude, which requires a move beyond the empirical self and fixed concepts, and the position of the caregiver of the soul (*Seelensorger*) in the programmatic writings on experiential psychology of Karl Philipp Moritz of the 1780s. It also expands on the oft-noted parallel between aesthetics and the "case" in the absence of an adequate concept or category. Five years before Kant's *Kritik der Urteilskraft* (1790), Moritz developed an aesthetics of autonomy that presages much of what Kant argued in his aesthetics, and this chapter shows the close relation between aesthetics, psychology, the "case" and therapeutics in Moritz's work. Moritz's advocacy of the narrative psychological case history is read as making explicit and concrete Foucault's braiding of *gnothi sauton* ("know thyself," contained in the title of Moritz's journal, *Magazin zur Erfahrungsseelenkunde*) and *epimeleia heautou*, the care of and concern for the self, in his late work on the hermeneutics of the subject, governmentality and the "pastoral apparatus."[25] Moritz's "dietetics of the soul" (*Seelendiätätik*), the aim of which is to preserve the soul in the equilibrium of all of its powers, provides us with a concrete historical instance of the "care of the self" in the late eighteenth century.

Finally, chapter 9 addresses Marcus Herz's sophisticated philosophy of the "case" and the two central terms of this medical-psychological theory: stance

---

[25] Michel Foucault, *Hermeneutics of the Subject: Lectures at the Collège de France, 1981–82*, ed. Frédéric Gros, trans. Graham Burchell (New York: Picador, 2001), 4–5.

(*Haltung*) and deviation (*Abweichung*). This chapter represents a new reading of the work of Herz, wresting him from the shadow of his mentor Kant and the rigid rationalism often ascribed to him. Against an *a priori* determination of the purview and limits of the medical art, Herz is shown to be a philosopher of the individual case, how attention to particular stance and deviation means the difference between a subtle and nuanced understanding of an illness and a simplistic, generalizing explanation that misses the mark. His importance not only for evolution of the genre but also for late eighteenth-century medicine, psychology, and philosophy in general has been seriously underestimated.

My concern in this study is a history of the emergence of the *narrative* psychological case history, to be distinguished from mere chronicles, observations, notes, descriptions, and other written forms that might contain psychological content. This begs the question of narrative itself. For the purposes of this study, I rely on a development in narrative theory and narratology over the last two decades which foregrounds what Monika Fludernik has referred to as "the representation of experientiality," by which she means a linguistic representation "at whose center there are one or several protagonists of an anthropomorphic nature who are existentially anchored in a temporal and spatial sense [...] It is the *experience* of these protagonists that narratives focus on, allowing readers to immerse themselves in a different world and in the life of the protagonists."[26] The focus on the subjects' *experience*, inscribing both the invitation to inhabit the other's world while also the boundary or limit of such a hermeneutical endeavor, as such experience is only available to us in language, constitutes the horizon within which the psychological narrative case history must be understood. Other narratologists, particularly Algirdas Julien Greimas and Tzvetan Todorov, have insisted – rightly, I think – on a continuant subject and the constitution of a "whole," by which they mean at least the attempt to supply not just bits and pieces, but an overarching sense of the experience of that subject.[27] I am also working with and indebted to a notion of "narrative psychology" as developed by Jerome Bruner. In his decisive article of 1991, Bruner put forth the fundamental thesis that "we organize our experience and our memory of human happenings mainly in the form of narrative."[28] In his elaboration of ten distinct features of narrative, I particularly want to draw attention to Bruner's insistence on the tension between canonicity and *breach*, the idea that a narrative story "must be

---

[26] Monika Fludernik, *An Introduction to Narratology*, trans. Patricia Häusler-Greenfield and Monika Fludernik. (London: Routledge, 2009), 6, emphasis mine.
[27] Gerald Prince, *Dictionary of Narratology* (Lincoln and London: University of Nebraska Press, 1987), 58.
[28] Jerome Bruner, "The Narrative Construction of Reality," *Critical Inquiry* 18.1 (1991): 4.

about how an implicit canonical script has been breached, violated or deviated from in a manner to do violence to what Hayden White calls the legitimacy of the canonical script."[29] In other words, a narrative is not simply a diachronic telling of an event; it must in some way tell something significant, meaningful, or decisive; it must break with staid scripts and well-rehearsed commonplaces and tell us something unique not just about a subject as another "phenomenon" existing as yet another object, but something distinctive and unique about *how that subject experiences the world*. It is this sense of narrative as *breach*, as offering vital, new information – at once experiential and psychological – that I assume in the following.

Two developments make 1800 a fitting closure of the present book. First and foremost, the emergence of the discipline of *psychiatry* and its institutions in the first quarter of the nineteenth century.[30] Johann Christian Reil (1759–1813), the most important physician of the mind in Germany around 1800, published his *Rhapsodies Concerning the Application of the Psychical Cure Method on Mental Illness* (*Rhapsodieen über die Anwendung der psychischen Curmethode auf Geisteszerrüttungen*, 1803),[31] according to Robert Richards "the most influential work shaping psychiatry before Freud."[32] A student of Marcus Herz in Berlin, Reil founded the journal *Archiv für die Physiologie* in 1795 with the explicit purpose of making medicine a scientific (*wissenschaftlich*) discipline. In 1797–1798, he became deeply influenced by the *Naturphilosophie* of Friedrich Wilhelm Joseph Schelling. Mental illness, which he understood in contrast to Pinel as a disturbance of the basic representational functions of the mind – *Selbstbewusstsein, Besonnenheit,* and *Aufmerksamkeit* – became his central focus. Reil coined the term "psychiatry" in *Beyträge zur Beförderung einer Curmethode auf psychischem Wege*, a journal he began with Johann Christian Hoffbauer in 1808.[33] Between 1810 and 1830, the discipline of *psychiatry* flourished in Germany; the first chair

---

29 Bruner, "Narrative Construction of Reality," 11.
30 Otto M. Marx, "German Romantic Psychiatry. Part 1," *History of Psychiatry* 1 (1990): 351–381; and "German Romantic Psychiatry. Part 2," *History of Psychiatry* 2 (1991): 1–25.
31 Johann Christian Reil, *Rhapsodieen über die Anwendung der psychischen Curmethode auf Geisteszerrüttungen* (Halle: Curtsche Buchhandlung, 1803; Zweite Ausgabe, 1818).
32 Robert J. Richards, *The Romantic Conception of Life: Science and Philosophy in the Age of Goethe* (Chicago: University of Chicago Press, 2002), 263.
33 Johann Christian Reil, "Ueber den Begriff der Medicin und ihre Verzweigungen besonders in Beziehung auf Berichtigung der Topik der Psychiaterie," in *Beyträge zur Beförderung einer Curmethode auf psychischem Weg*, by Johann Christian Reil and Johann Christoph Hoffbauer (Halle: Curtschen Buchhandlung, 1808), 153–160. See Albrecht Koschorke, "Poiesis des Leibes. Johann Christian Reils romantische Medizin," in *Romantische Wissenspoetik. Die Künste und*

of psychiatric medicine established at a Germany University was occupied by Johann Christian August Heinroth at the Universität Leipzig (1827).[34] The first journals of "psychiatry" proper appeared, such as Friedrich Nasse's *Zeitschrift für psychische Ärzte* (1818–1824). But the proto-psychiatrists in the first decades of the nineteenth century in Germany such as Reil, Hoffbauer, Nasse, and Heinroth were highly critical of the eclectic, seemingly arbitrary and disordered collections of narrative psychological case histories that had characterized German experiential psychology (*Erfahrungsseelenkunde*) of the 1780s and 1790s and its interlocutors.[35] Such a casuistry, no matter how refined or nuanced, could never, according to the new psychiatrists, amount to real *science* – the systematic knowledge of *Wissenschaft*.

Why is there a rather sudden shift toward psychiatry and scientific psychology at the beginning of the nineteenth century? As Kurt Danziger has shown in his excellent study of the emergence of experimental psychology circa 1860, it took a while for Germany to emerge from the hangover of Kantian philosophy and his critique of psychology. Kant had made a sharp distinction between the general *a priori* conditions of psychic organization in terms of which such inner mental life must be constituted if we are to make sense of it whatsoever – rational psychology – and mental life as it appears to and can be described by the individual subject and outside observers – empirical

---

die Wissenschaften um 1800, ed. Gabriele Brandstetter and Gerhard Neumann (Würzburg: Königshausen & Neumann, 2004), 259–272.

34 See the work of H. Steinberg, "Creation of the First University Chair in Psychiatry: Johann Christian August Heinroth in Leipzig," *Nervenarzt* 75.3 (2004): 303–307; and Steinberg, "Johann Christian August Heinroth (1773–1843): The First Professor of Psychiatry as a Psychotherapist," *Journal of Religion and Health* 51.2 (2012): 256–268.

35 See especially Johann Christian Reil and Johann Christian Hoffbauer, "Nachschrift der Herausgeber," in *Beyträge zur Beförderung einer Kurmethode auf psychischem Wege* 1.1 (1808): 153–160, esp. 157. Reil and Hoffbauer acknowledge the importance of Moritz's case-histories for the general public interested in what they refer to as the "culture of psychology," (158) but agreed with the Scottish physician Alexander Crichton's criticism that they were absolutely useless for the physician. See Alexander Crichton, *An Inquiry into the Nature and Origin of Mental Derangement* (London: Cadell, Junior, and W. Davis, 1798), vol. 1, preface, v–vi: "In this work (Moritz's *Magazin*, R. Leventhal), I have found what I had not yet met with in any other publication, a number of well-authenticated cases of insane aberration of mind, narrated in a full and satisfactory manner, without a view to any system whatsoever [...] It is, indeed, to be lamented that by far the greatest number of cases contained in this work are uninteresting to the physician." While Crichton credits the *Magazin* with having given "fresh vigour to his studies," he is quite critical of its method, the eclectic collection of cases, and the absence of any systematic theory.

psychology.³⁶ The latter, according to Kant, would never amount to anything but a set of contingent (and therefore highly variable) rules – "a kind of natural history of the mind."³⁷ It could never achieve the status of *Wissenschaft*. Kant's influence on the development of psychology in Germany was profound: "The result was that, in the nineteenth century German Universities, the question of psychology as a field of study became problematized in methodological terms. Three issues dominated this debate: introspection, mathematization, experimentation."³⁸ The "philosophical physicians" of the late eighteenth century who developed a "medical psychology," the practitioners of experiential psychology (*Erfahrungsseelenkunde*), had relied on introspection, narrative description, intuitive understanding, and interpretation in their case histories to plumb the vexing problems of the human soul. If psychology were to be any more than a collection of individual cases, their interpretation and commentary, the study of the mind would have to become truly *scientific*, and this meant that it had to dispense with introspection, intuition, and reasoning in and by cases and to become rigorously experimental, quantitative, and mathematically precise. Kant deemed this impossible.

Johann Friedrich Herbart (1776–1841) argued in his *Psychology as Exact Science* (*Psychologie als Wissenschaft*) (1824) that Kant was fundamentally mistaken in his skepticism and advocated for precisely such a truly scientific psychology. For Herbart, the mathematization of psychology was possible, at least in principle. Herbartian psychology remained an extremely influential school in Germany until the end of the nineteenth century.³⁹ Herbart's rigorous medical-scientific approach attacked the critical philosophy of Kant, the idealism of Fichte and Schelling, and Romantic *Naturphilosophie*. It renounced the experiential psychology or *Erfahrungsseelenkunde* of the second half of the eighteenth century that constitutes the center of my study. Eschewing intuition, introspection, reasoning in and arguing from individual cases, Herbart wrote:

---

[36] On the distinction, see Gary Hatfield, "Empirical, Rational, and Transcendental Psychology: Psychology as Science and as Philosophy," in *Cambridge Companion to Kant*, ed. Paul Guyer (Cambridge: Cambridge University Press, 1992), 200–227; and more recently, Corey W. Dyck, *Kant and Rational Psychology* (Oxford: Oxford University Press, 2014).
[37] Kurt Danziger, *Constructing the Subject: Historical Origins of Psychological Research* (Cambridge: Cambridge University Press, 1990), 21.
[38] Danziger, *Constructing the Subject*, 22.
[39] On Johann Friedrich Herbart, see David E. Leary, "The Historical Foundation of Herbart's Mathematization of Psychology," *Journal of the History of the Behavioral Sciences* 16.2 (1980): 150–163.

I will clearly have to distance myself from those who wish to ground a theory of nature in any form of internal intellectual intuitions. Their theory of nature is not the fitting analogy for psychology; their "intuitions" are subject to and suspicious as self-delusion [...] The so-called empirical psychology that emerges from such a treatment of its object is well-known enough, some still tinker with it here and there, even though the interest in it has, for the most part, disappeared.[40]

Taking up Kant's challenge, Herbart countered the casuistic experientiality heralded by Herz, Schiller, and Moritz, seeking to bring the discipline of psychology to a scientific rigor and systematicity he found lacking in the narrative case approaches of the eighteenth century. Brought to the precision of a thesis, we might therefore argue: in the first quarter of the nineteenth century, qualitative experiential psychology (*Erfahrungsseelenkunde*) based on narrative psychological case histories was displaced by scientific psychology and psychiatry, with claims of experimental rigor, quantification methods, and more objective, verifiable knowledge that could be empirically validated, unlike the introspective or purely descriptive narratives and analogical correlation of individual cases.

The second reason 1800 marks a significant threshold is that, by the turn of the century, the template for narrative psychological case histories had been firmly established; it had become a widely recognized, enthusiastically discussed, extremely popular and sought-after "small" literary, medical-psychological genre. Moritz's journal *Magazin zur Erfahrungsseelenkunde* marked only the first such collection in a vast series, one might even say a tidal wave of narrative criminal-juridical[41] and psychological case study publication: Abel's *Sammlung und Erklärung merkwürdiger Rechtsfälle* (1787)[42]; Schiller's edition of the Pitaval,

---

[40] Johann Friedrich Herbart, *Psychologie als Wissenschaft, neu gegründet auf Erfahrung, Metaphysik, und Mathematik* (Königsberg: Unger, 1824), 2. Also in *Johann Friedrich Herbart's Sämmtliche Werke*, ed. G. Hartenstein (Leipzig: Leopold Voss, 1850), vol. 5, 198–199: "Von den Meinungen derer, die auf innere, auf intellectuale Anschauungen eine Naturlehre gründen, werde ich freilich mich weit entfernen müssen. Ihre Naturlehre ist nicht das passende Gleichniß für die Psychologie; ihre Anschauungen sind der Selbsttäuschung mehr als verdächtig [...] Die sogenannte empirische Psychologie, welche aus solcher Behandlung des Gegenstandes entsteht, ist bekannt genug, es wird noch jetzt hie und da daran gekünstelt, obgleich das Interesse dafür sich grossentheils verloren hatte."
[41] On the history and typology of juridical-criminal case-studies, see Jörg Schönert, ed., *Kriminalität erzählen. Studien zu Kriminalität in der deutschsprachigen Literatur (1570–1920)* (Berlin: de Gruyter, 2015).
[42] Jacob Friedrich Abel, *Sammlung und Erklärung merkwürdiger Rechstfälle* (Frankfurt and Leipzig, 1784–1790).

Unerhörte Kriminalfälle: eine Sammlung berühmter und merkwürdiger Kriminalfälle (1792)[43]; J. D. Mauchart's *Allgemeines Repertorium für empirische Psychologie und verwandte Wissenschaften* (1792)[44]; Karl Müchler's *Kriminalgeschichten. Aus gerichtlichen Akten gezogen* (1792)[45]; Karl Friedrich Pockels's *Denkwürdigkeiten zur Bereicherung der Erfahrungsseelenkunde und Charakterkunde* (1794); in a more popular register and tone, Christian Heinrich Spiess's *Biographien der Wahnsinnigen* (1795–1796); Paul Johann Anselm Feuerbach's *Merkwürdige Rechtsfälle* (1808)[46]; and, finally, in 1842, *Der neue Pitaval*, edited by Julius Hitzig and Georg Wilhelm Heinrich Häring (Willibald Alexis), which had a run of 60 volumes. While these vast collections lacked the attention to detail and the nuance of the intensive eighteenth-century case examined in this study, they continued a tradition focused on the aberrant, the anamalous, the enigmatic, the unheard of – that which could not be easily subsumed under an existing concept, the rule, or the law. And while the publication of popular collections of psychologically-minded case histories flourished in the first half of the nineteenth century, the only real ground-breaking formal, rhetorical, and narratological innovations, probing the inner world of their subjects, are to be found in literature's "special cases," most notably Georg Büchner's *Lenz* (1836) and *Woyzeck* (1839), Edgar Allan Poe's *The Facts in the Case of M. Valdemar* (1845), Gerhard Hauptmann's *Bahnwärter Thiel* (1887), Robert Louis Stevenson's *The Strange Case of Dr. Jekyll and Mr. Hyde* (1886), Franz Kafka's *The Judgment* (1912) and *The Metamorphosis* (1915), Alfred Döblin's *The Two Girlfriends and their Murder by Poisoning* (1924) and, of course, in psychoanalysis itself, in Sigmund Freud's famous case studies starting in the late 1880s. The genre of the narrative psychological case history, which emerged in the 1780s in the work of Herz, Moritz, and Schiller, had been firmly established in the German literary public sphere and cultural imaginary; it became the stencil for an entire array of physicians, educators, pastors,

---

43 Friedrich Schiller, "Vorrede zu dem ersten Theile der merkwürdigsten Rechtsfälle nach Pitaval" in *Merkwürdige Rechtsfälle als ein Beitrag zur Geschichte der Menscheit. Nach dem französischen Werke des Pitaval durch mehrere Verfasser ausgearbeitet*, ed. Friedrich Schiller, (Leipzig: Crusius, 1792–1795), in 4 parts.
44 J. D. Mauchart, *Allgemeines Repertorium für empirische Psychologie und verwandte Wissneschaften*, ed. Mauchart and others (Nürnberg: in der Felseckerschen Buchhandlung, 1792).
45 Karl Müchler, *Kriminalgeschichten. Aus gerichtlichen Akten gezogen* (Berlin: Friedrich Vieweg, 1792) and *Kriminalgeschichten. Ein Beitrag zur Erfahrungsseelenkunde* (Berlin: W. Natorff, 1828–1833).
46 Paul Johann Anselm Feuerbach, *Merkwürdige Rechtsfälle vorgetragen und herausgegeben von Paul Johann Anselm Feuerbach* (Giessen: Tasché and Müller, 1808; 1811).

psychologists, councilors, superintendents, and civil administrators interested in charting the individual psyche and creating a "science of the soul." In a word, the truly path breaking work had been done. Rather than simply a feature or aspect of modern sensibility and culture regarding individuality, my argument is that the culture and cult of individuality was "invented" – in a manner parallel to but distinct from the socializing, more integrative function of the novel – in and through the production, review, exchange, dissemination of, and encounter with such "interesting cases."

With the emergence of a new scientific culture of "norm" and "normalization," the "deviant" and "deviation" from such norms around 1800,[47] the appearance of Adolphe Quetelet's (1796–1874) "social physics" around 1830,[48] the application of statistics to the social world – what Hacking has referred to as the avalanche of printed numbers 1820–1840[49] – and finally, the call for a *scientific psychology* of experimentation and validation, the narrative individual case-history lost its scientific legitimacy, relevance, and critical novelty in the new crusade for scientific rigor and the vast sea of "facts" and "data." It lived on in literature and as a genre of popular magazines and of low-brow collections which fed on the prurient reading interests of a new mass society. It also enjoyed a brief resurgence in the forensic medicine of Johann Ludwig Casper (1796–1864) and the psychiatry of Carl Westphal (1833–1890) in the last quarter of the nineteenth century,[50] both of whom used their own narrative case histories, until it

---

[47] This, of course, is one of the key arguments of Georges Canguilhem's groundbreaking study of 1943 *The Normal and the Pathological* (New York: Zone, 1991). See also: Michel Foucault, *Security, Territory, Population: Lectures at the College de France, 1977–1978*, ed. Michael Senellart (New York: Palgrave Macmillan, 2007), 56–57; Werner Sohn, "Bio-Macht und Normaliserungsgesellschaft – Versuch einer Annäherung," in *Normalität und Abweichung: Studien zur Theorie und Geschichte der Normalisierungsgesellschaft*, ed. Sohn und Herbert Mertens (Opladen und Wiesbaden: Westdeutscher Verlag, 1999), 9–30. Nicolas Pethes, *Literarische Fallgeschichten. Zur Poetik einer epistemischen Schreibweise* (Konstanz: Konstanz University Press, 2016), makes the point that with the proliferation of *modern series of cases* in popular media, and the concomitant trivialization, the individual case has lost its critical, epistemic function.

[48] Lambert Jacques Adolphe Quetelet, *Treatise on Man and the Development of his Faculties*, trans. R. Knox, ed. T. Smibert (Cambridge: Cambridge University Press, 2013). See also Ian Hacking, *The Taming of Chance* (Cambridge: Cambridge University Press, 1990), 105–128.

[49] Ian Hacking, "Biopower and the Avalanche of Printed Numbers," *Humanities in Society* 5 (1982): 279–295.

[50] Johann Ludwig Casper was a forensic physician and pathologist, and author of *Practisches Handbuch der gerichtlichen Medizin, nach eigenen Erfahrungen* (Berlin: Hirschwald, 1857–1858). Carl Friedrich Otto Westphal became the Director of the *Klinik für Psychiatrie und Nervenkrankheiten* at the Charité in Berlin after the death of Wilhelm Griesinger in 1868,

was rehabilitated by Freud around 1890 as a genre *par excellence* for the transmission of psychoanalytic knowledge and technique, and as the ideal medium for linking in narrative the history of individual suffering and the symptoms of an illness.

---

and became famous for his essay on homosexuality, "Die conträre Sexualempfindung: Symptom eines neuropathischen (psychopathischen) Zustandes," *Archiv für Psychiatrie und Nervenkrankheiten* 2.1 (1869): 73–108.

1 Historicizing the Psychological Case History

> Individual cases are so infinitely various that no systematic knowledge of them is possible.
> Aristotle, *Rhetoric*, 1356b

> Nature is nowhere accustomed more openly to display her secret mysteries than in cases where she shows traces of her workings apart from the beaten path; nor is there any better way to advance the proper practice of medicine than to give our minds to the discovery of the usual law of nature, by the careful investigation of cases of rarer forms of disease.
> William Harvey, "Letter to Physician John Vlackveld of Harlem," 1657[1]

> *Casus* is precisely what one calls a symptom, an occurance, and this in a specific place. Concerning this it is also called by the physicians a total description and history of an illness.   Zedler's *Universallexikon aller Wissenschaft und Künste*, 1736[2]

> Casuistry is neither a science nor a part of any science, for that would be dogmatism; it is neither a teaching of how something can be discovered or ascertained, nor a practice of how the truth should be sought. It is purely fragmentary, not systematic.
> Kant, *The Metaphysics of Morals* (1797), AA 4:411[3]

The case history has a rich and venerable tradition in Western literature and medicine, reaching back to the Hippocratic corpus and the *Epidemics*.[4] In mapping out this history, and identifying the critical junctures within it, intermittent forays into contemporary readings become necessary in order to tease out what is salient for the overall argument. Moving between the history of the case itself and some of the ways in which this history has been presented and appropriated will also provide some degree of insight into how such a history has in fact shaped the historical understanding of the genre, and the entwinement of the case history and its interpretation in history.

In classical antiquity, Hippocrates (460–377 BCE), whom Aristotle referred to as "the great Hippocrates, the wise physician" in the *Politics* and who is still referred to as the "father of medicine," developed the science of medicine

---

1 William Harvey, "Letter to Physician John Vlackveld of Harlem," in *The Works of William Harvey*, trans. Robert Willis (London: Sydenham Society, 1847), 614.
2 "Casus ist eben, was Symptoma, ein Zufall, davon an seinem Orte. Ueber dieses heist es auch bey denen Medicis so viel als eine ganze Beschreibung und Historie einer Kranckheit." Johann Heinrich Zedler, *Universallexikon aller Wissenschaft und Künste* (Halle and Leipzig: Verlag Johann Heinrich Zedler, 1736), vol. 5, 1391.
3 Immanuel Kant, *The Metaphysics of Morals*, Akademie Ausgabe (AA) 4:411.
4 Volker Langholf, *Medical Theories in Hippocrates: Early Texts and the Epidemics* (Berlin: de Gruyter, 1992), 73–231.

https://doi.org/10.1515/9783110643466-002

consisting of three components: (1) knowledge of the nature of the human being (anatomy and physiology); (2) the documentation of patterns of illness and pathology; and (3) medicine and therapeutics. In the earliest case histories contained in the Hippocratic corpus, Hippocrates drew on observations by himself and from other physicians, and established the fundamental structure of the case history: *anamnesis, present status, epicrisis,* and *prognosis.* He insisted that the observations be written down in the form of a journal or diary, consisting of day-by-day detailed observations of fever, color and consistency of urine and stool, breathing and pulse, sleep, sweat, pain, condition of the skin, and behavior.[5] Not only did this signal a significant shift from traditional oral transmission of knowledge. It set an important precedent for the discipline of medicine as a whole, which Hippocrates understood as progressing precisely through the analysis and comparison of cases. While the short, epigrammatic cases particularly of the *Epidemics* might have been used for teaching purposes, Hippocrates inaugurated the practice of written testimony, recollection, and discrimination of medical cases as an integral part of the medical art.[6]

As Hippocrates emphasized and Volker Hess has noted, medicine as an art and practice was and is first and foremost concerned not with disease or diseases, but with the individual sick person and their treatment.[7] In the history of medicine, the radical shift from the dogmatic scholasticism that governed medical thought and practice since the eleventh century with its reliance on textual authority, deduction, rhetoric, and mere hypothesis to an empirical model based on careful observation and experiment can be attributed to Theophrastus Bombastus von Hohenheim (Paracelsus) (1493–1591). With the phrase *experimenta ac ratio auctorum* as his battle cry, often expressed in his lectures during his brief stint as the city physician of Basel, Paracelsus urged his students to take nature – direct experience, experiment, and actual contact with the patient – as their guide.[8] The empirical, experimental ethos of early modern medicine extends and amplifies the renewed urgency of observation and documentation. The discovery of the circulation of the blood by William Harvey (1578–1657) constituted not merely a decisive contribution to physiology, but reflected the massive transformation

---

[5] K. Böhm, C.O. Köhler, and R. Thome, *Historie der Krankengeschichte* (New York and Stuttgart: F. K. Schattauer Verlag, 1978), 37.
[6] Laurence Totelin, *Hippocratic Recipes. Oral and Written Transmission of Pharmacological Knowledge in Fifth- and Fourth-Century Greece* (London: Brill, 2008).
[7] Volker Hess, "*Observatio* und *Casus*: Status und Funktion der medizinischen Fallgeschichte," in: *Fall – Fallgeschichte – Fallstudie. Theorie und Geschichte einer Wissensform,* ed. Susanne Düwell and Nicolas Pethes (Frankfurt/New York: Campus, 2011), 34–59.
[8] K. Böhm et al., *Historie der Krankengeschichte,* 63–64.

from scholastic hypothesis to an empirically-based medical science during the first half of the seventeenth century. In the *New Organon* of 1620, Francis Bacon required that all scientific observation and experience be written down to achieve and insure its very scientific legitimacy:

> Yet up to now the role of thought has been more prominent than that of writing in the work of discovery; no *written experience* has yet been developed, though we should not approve any discovery unless it is in writing. When it shall come into use, we may expect more from experience finally made literate.[9]

Bacon's *New Organon* and its demand for written documentation should not be considered in isolation, but rather as part of a more widespread attempt to give the sciences a firm foundation on the basis of which new discoveries could be verified, communicated, and subjected to criticism. Such a program fit nicely with what Stephen Toulmin has argued in *Cosmopolis*, namely that the quest for such a foundational scientific "method" at the beginning of the seventeenth century was informed by the search for transcendent norms and values resistant to the factionalism, strife, and dogmatic claims of the various religious sects.[10]

While *psychology* or a psychological mode of consideration *per se* does not explicitly figure in the early modern case history, one can, with subtle interpretation, discern at least a nascent interest specifically in mental illness or illnesses of the mind apart from theological-religious concerns in Germany from the early modern period on.[11] The earliest use of the medical case history with such a specific interest in mental maladies in the German speaking territories can be traced to the work of Felix Platter (1536–1614). Chief Physician of the City of Basel and Professor at the University of Basel from 1571 until his death, his *Observationes* stand out for their explicit empirical methodology.

Platter was one of the first medical doctors to consider mental illness from a scientific, physiological standpoint rather than as the result of supernatural causes, or within the religious framework of sin and "the dark soul." Remarkably, in Platter's *Observationes*, we find early modern case histories of obsession,

---

9 Francis Bacon, *The New Organon*, ed. Lisa Jardine and Michael Silverthorne (Cambridge: Cambridge University Press, 2000), 82.
10 Stephen Toulmin, *Cosmopolis: The Hidden Agenda of Modernity* (Chicago: University of Chicago Press, 1990).
11 On the early uses of the term and the emergent discipline, see: Wolfgang Riedel, "Erster Psychologismus: Umbau des Seelenbegriffs in der deutschen Spätaufklärung," in *Zwischen Empirisierung und Konstruktionsleistung: Anthropologie im 18. Jahrhundert*, ed. Jörn Garber and Heinz Thoma (Tübingen: Niemeyer, 2004), 1–18; and Fernando Vidal, *The Sciences of the Soul: The Early Modern Origins of Psychology*, translated by Saskia Brown (London and Chicago: University of Chicago Press, 2011), 110–111.

Figure 1

Figures 1 and 2: Felix Platter's portrait (fig. 1) and the title page of Book III of his *Observationes* (1614) (fig. 2), the most widely recognized collection of medical case histories in early modern Europe. Platter's text also included case-histories of madness. Portrait courtesy and with permission of Kunstmuseum Basel; photograph by Martin Bühler. Title page courtesy of the Bayerische Staatsbibliothek, Münchener Digitalisierungszentrum, Med.g. 374, urn:nbn:de: bvb:12-bsb10085871-6 .

mania, melancholy, hypochondria, alcoholism, and envy.[12] Thomas Sydenham (1624–1689), clearly influenced by Bacon's demand, formalized the medical case

---

12 On Platter see: P. E. Pilet, "Felix Platter" in *The Dictionary of Scientific Biography*, ed. Charles C. Gillispie (New York: C. Scribner, 1975), vol. 11, 33; and Oskar Diethelm and Thomas F. Heffernan, "Felix Platter and Psychiatry," *Journal of the History of the Behavioral Sciences* 1.1 (1965): 10–23.

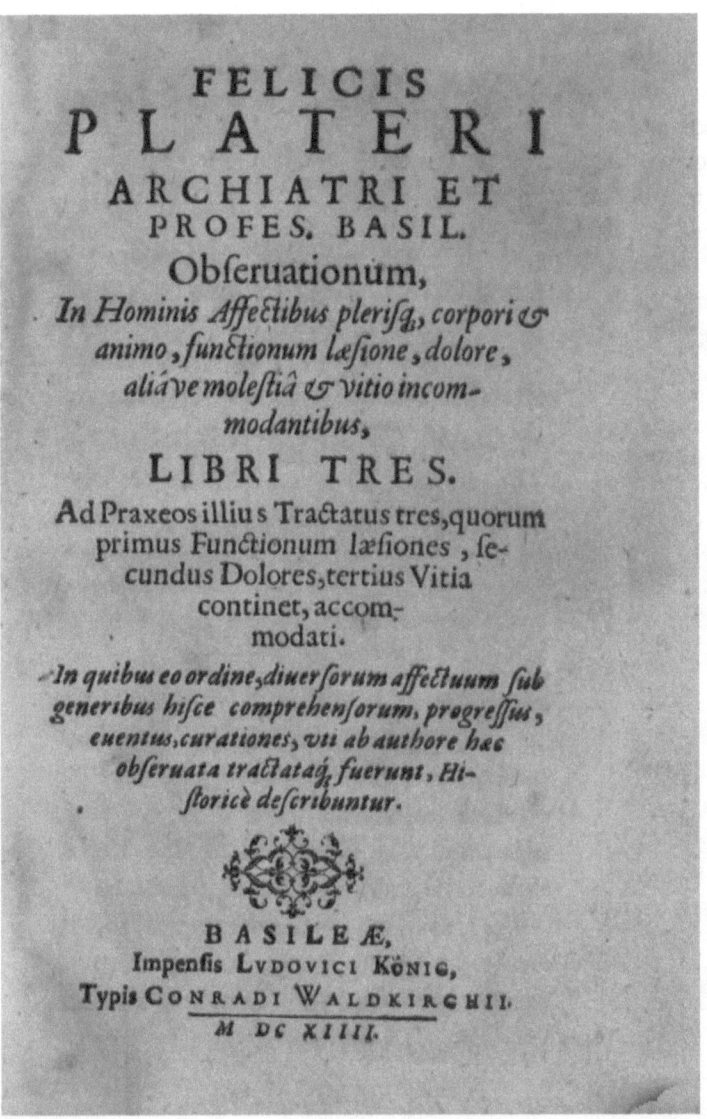

Figure 2

history as the *documentation* of the precise observation of the symptoms, course of illness, the various remedies and therapies applied, the reaction of the patient, and the outcome. Sydenham's extensive and exact case histories and his therapeutic medicines or remedies, documented and empirically vetted in several cases, served as a model for practicing physicians and were often used by the physicians of the late seventeenth and early eighteenth centuries. Also formative in the new experiential, empirical, and experimental medicine of early modern Europe were Herman Boerhaave (1668–1738) and his famous clinic at the University of Leiden, where he instructed his students at the bedside of the patient and underscored the importance of exact observation and direct experience, while also stressing the importance of the autopsy. Although we only have two case histories from Boerhaave himself, his statements concerning what constitutes a proper *Krankengeschichte* reveal the extent to which direct experience and precise description combine to produce a casuistry through which *a case of the same kind* might be recognized and treated in the future:

> I will try very hard to paint the picture of the terrible illness with the liveliest colors, so that a case of exactly the same kind that later comes to the fore can be recognized, or at least, if there is doubt concerning the essence of an enigmatic illness, we might have a certain advantage to consider this as a possibility.[13]
>
> For in my opinion it is absolutely necessary in every case history composed by and for physicians according to anatomical principles to first impart the natural disposition of the body, the previous illnesses, the way of life and the healing methods which have been applied before one begins to report about the illness to which the patient has succumbed.[14]

As we know from the texts of Albrecht von Haller and Andreas Elias Büchner, Boerhaave, his clinic, and his method were held in the highest esteem in Germany in the eighteenth century, revered as the very model of scientific medicine. The case history provided an *example* that could be used for future treatments, an analogue that linked one instance or iteration of an illness or disease to another, and became a part of a reliable communication-network between physicians. As such, the case formed the basis of a series or repository, a medical casuistry that functioned as a trans-generational reference network

---

13 Margarete Blank-Panitzsch, "Eine Krankengeschichte Herman Boerhaaves und ihre Stellung in der Geschichte der Klinik," *Archiv für Geschichte der Medizin* 27.1–2 (1934): 63: "Ich werde mir Mühe geben, das Bild der schrecklichen Krankheit mit so lebhaften Farben zu malen, daß der Fall genau derselben Art, der vielleicht später einmal eintritt, danach erkannt werden könne, oder wenigstens beim Zweifel über das Wesen einer rätselhaften Erkrankung der Vorteil geboten wäre, eine Möglichkeit in Betracht zu ziehen."
14 Blank-Panitzsch, "Eine Krankengeschichte Herman Boerhaaves," 66: "Denn meiner Meinung nach ist es in jeder nach anatomischen Grundsätzen von Ärzten geschriebenen und für Ärzte bestimmten Krankengeschichte unbedingt nötig, zuerst über die natürliche Körperanlage, die vorhergegangenen Krankheiten, die Lebensweise und die angewandten Heilmethoden Mitteilung zu machen, ehe man von der Krankheit zu berichten beginnt, der der Patient erlegen ist."

for research, dissemination, and practice; it was one of the essential ways medical knowledge got transmitted. Previous research on the emergence of the psychological case history had concentrated on the juridical case and the *species facti* of the juridical case history in early modern Europe, but as Stefanie Retzlaff has recently shown, the medical case history truly provides the missing link between the case histories of the sixteenth and seventeenth centuries, and the narrative psychological case histories of the second half of the eighteenth century.[15]

In addition to the medical case history, two other disciplines and their respective institutions hosted the case from the late middle ages to early modern Europe. The Catholic Church had for centuries developed a vast system of moral-theological casuistry, the adjudication of difficult individual cases under canon law. Theological casuistry spurred a massive negative reaction among the educated and scientifically minded literate of the late seventeenth-century public as hair-splitting, hopelessly contingent, and hypocritical. In the seventeenth century, for example, the Jansenist mathematician and physicist Blaise Pascal (1623–1662) famously attacked casuistry or "reasoning from cases" in his *Provincial Letters* (1656).[16] Directed primarily against the Jesuits, Pascal's critique not only decried the complete lack of principle and moral rigor, but sought to point out the degradation of all moral reasoning as a direct consequence of using individual cases as the basis for any argument whatsoever. This form of skeptical critique continued well into the twentieth century, until Albert Jonsen and Stephen Toulmin published their powerful rebuttal in *The Abuse of Casuistry: A History of Moral Reasoning* (1988), in which they exposed the essential difference between "mere" casuistry and rhetorical moral reasoning.[17] While the case long served in jurisprudence and legal theory as a limiting instance, an exception, or even as "special" or "unique" event that could not be handily decided, the Anglo-American legal school of the nineteenth century established the "case" as testing ground, as precedent, as the very embodiment of legal reasoning and as the preferred pedagogical tool. John Forrester pointed out exactly how, in the late nineteenth century, Oliver Wendell Holmes's critique of legal formalism went hand in hand with the identification and analysis of particular cases not merely as a heuristic practice, but as the way in which legal issues

---

[15] Stefanie Rezlaff, *Observieren und Aufschreiben. Zur Poetologie medizinischer Fallgeschichten (1700-1765)* (München: Wilhelm Fink, 2017), 12.
[16] Blaise Pascal, *The Provincial Letters of Blaise Pascal*, ed. O. W. Wright (Boston: Houghton, Osgood, 1880), 194–200.
[17] Albert Jonsen and Stephen Toulmin, *The Abuse of Casuistry: A History of Moral Reasoning* (Berkeley, Los Angeles, London: University of California Press, 1988).

were decided in the application of the law. "Concrete cases are not solved by general statements,"[18] Holmes wrote. His perceptive dictum hit on something crucial about the individual case that has been accentuated by recent theory, namely, *that it cannot be decided simply through recourse to a general rule, norm or law.* As Lauren Berlant perceptively stated in her introduction to a special issue of *Critical Inquiry* in 2007: "As genre, the case hovers about the singular, the general, and the normative. It organizes publics, however fleeting. It expresses a relation of expertise to a desire for shared knowledge."[19]

It was not until the late eighteenth century, however, that a genuine systematic approach in the ordering and evaluation of case histories together with a more thorough, fully historical documentation of the anamnesis occurred. After Sydenham, physicians influenced by the Swedish zoologist, botanist, and physician Carl Linneaus (1707–1778) pursued a method of classification of the various illness types with the goal of bringing the vast repository of case histories to a nosological system. As Director of the Medical Clinic in Vienna, Johann Peter Frank (1745–1821) established a more fully documented history of the patient from the earliest childhood illnesses combined with a thorough documentation of the treatments and their results, a detailed journal of the daily developments, and finally a protocol of the results of the autopsy as the standard of a complete medical case history of the patient. Very different from the nosological-nosographical classificatory system being advanced after Sydenham and Linneaus, Frank, the author of the multi-volume *Complete System of Medical Policy* (1779–1821), instructed his students to keep detailed notes on each patient, observe, and report on their present status at regular intervals, culminating in an exhaustive narrative and summary (*epicrisis*) without assumptions regarding pathogenesis, until the entire course of the illness, all of the facts of the patient's history, and the autopsy could be considered as a whole.[20]

An important thread in the argument of this book is that the narrative psychological case history came of age in the mid-eighteenth century in a scientific, cultural, intellectual milieu fascinated with the reciprocal influence of mind and body, the causes of mental illness, and the condition and guidance of individual souls. While these concerns are in evidence in the period 1750–1770 in the writings of the psychological physicians, they become acute around 1770. Johann Wolfgang Goethe's blockbuster novel *The Sorrows of*

---

18 Oliver Wendell Holmes, *The Common Law* (1882), cited in John Forrester, "If p, then what? Thinking in Cases," *History of the Human Sciences* 9:3 (1996): 16.
19 Lauren Gail Berlant, "On the case," *Critical Inquiry* 33.4 (2007): 664.
20 Christian Probst, "Johann Peter Frank als Arzt am Krankenbett," *Sudhoffs Archiv* 59.1 (1975): 20–53.

Young Werther (1774) narrated a case of obsessional love and suicidal depression in epistolary form that had to "completed" by the editor – who becomes the narrator – as Werther's internal world begins to fall apart. *The Sorrows of Young Werther* has been rightly named the first truly *psychological* novel in German literature.[21] According to Johann Kasper Lavater, Goethe himself referred to it as a *Krankengeschichte*, explicitly appropriating and transforming the classical *historia morbi*, imbuing it with – as Werther himself calls for in the novel – a history of the "inner circumstances of an action" (*innere Verhältnisse einer Handlung*)[22] – as a psychological style or form.[23] Werther was not merely itself a case history of Werther's own "suffering"; as Rüdiger Campe has recently shown, the first version of the novel (1774) reiterates the classical "case" in the form of traditional casuistry – Werther as the enthusiastic letter-writer who becomes a "type" – while the second version of 1787 profiles the individual himself as a special "case."[24]

And it is not just Werther himself; the novel included several other case histories that were used as examples by Werther as indices and justification of his own suffering, as "proof" of the injustice of the world, and as the mitigation of individual responsibility.[25] In Werther's letter of August 12, for example, he narrates in conversation with Albert the *Fallgeschichte* of young girl who, spurned by a lover on whom she had placed her hopes for marriage, and in a state of desperation, committed suicide, and described it as a *case of illness*: "ist das nicht der Fall der Krankheit?"[26] In addition, there is the case of the peasant lad

---

21 Karl Viëtor, "La Maladie du siècle," in *Goethe: A Collection of Essays*, ed. Victor Lange (Englewood Cliffs, NJ: Prentice Hall, 1968), 31. On the various "psychological approaches" to *Werther*, see Bruce Duncan, *Goethe's Werther and the Critics* (Rochester, NY: Camden House, 2005), 39–71.
22 Johann Wolfgang Goethe, *Die Leiden des jungen Werthers*, in *Sämmtliche Werke in 40 Bänden* (Frankfurt: Deutsche Klassiker Verlag, 1994), vol. 8, 94.
23 Lavater claimed that, in conversation, Goethe had called the novel an *historia morbi* or *Krankengeschichte*. See Johann Caspar Lavater, *Vermischte Schriften* (Winterthur: Heinrich Steiner, 1781), vol. 2, 128: "Historiam morbi zuschreiben, ohne unten angeschriebenen Lehren, a. b. c. d. – sagte mir eins Göthe, da ich ihm einige Bedenklichkeiten über Werther an's Herz legte." See also: Christiane Frey, "'Ist das nicht ein Fall der Krankheit?' Der literarische Fall am Beispiel von Goethes *Werther*," *Zeitschrift für Germanistik* 19.2 (2009): 317–329; and Alexander Košenina, *Literarische Anthropologie: Die Neuentdeckung des Menschen* (Berlin: de Gruyter, 2008), 76: "Tatsächlich lässt sich der Roman als eine kunstvolle ausgeführte Krankengeschichte von psychologisch bestechender Finalität lesen."
24 Rüdiger Campe, "Von Fall zu Fall: Goethes *Werther*, Büchners *Lenz*," in *Was der Fall ist: Casus und Lapsus*, ed. Inka Mülder-Bach, Michael Ott (München: Fink, 2014), 46–48.
25 See Frey, "Ist das nicht der Fall der Krankheit?" 317–329.
26 Goethe, *Die Leiden des jungen Werthers*, in *Sämmtliche Werke*, vol. 8, 100.

in love with his widowed employer, who is fired by the widow's brother after assaulting her, and ends in killing his rival.[27] Werther also became obsessed with the case of Heinrich, a scribe employed by Lotte's father, who fell deeply in love with Lotte, suddenly became extremely ill with a fever and went insane, spending a year in an asylum. Case histories thus proliferate in and circle around the novel as examples of human beings gone awry, as pathographies, and even perhaps as premonitions of Werther's own fate.

Psychological case histories have often served as the actual historical basis of important works of modern literature. As was noted shortly after the appearance of *Werther*, Goethe fictionalized the actual case history of a friend from his days as a student of law in Leipzig, Carl Wilhelm Jerusalem. In September 1772, Goethe completed a practicum at the *Reichskammergericht* in Wetzlar, where Jerusalem had fallen madly in love with an older married woman – Elizabeth Herd – and committed suicide one month later on October 30, 1772. The day before the deed, Jerusalem made a written request to his friend, Johann Christian Kestner, for his *Reisepistol*, just as Werther asks for Albert's in Goethe's novel. A copy of *Emila Galotti* supposedly lay open on Jerusalem's desk, as was the case with the fictitious Werther in Goethe's novel. And, like Werther, Jerusalem did not succumb immediately to the self-inflicted gunshot wound, but lay in agony until his death the following day. Kestner expanded his diary entries of the days following Jerusalem's suicide to a report (*Bericht*) most likely at the request of Goethe, who wrote Kestner immediately after he had heard the news: "Poor Jerusalem. The news was terrible and unexpected [...] it was ghastly [...] the poor young lad!"[28]

On November 19, 1772, after a short visit in Wetzlar, Goethe wrote to Kestner and asked him to send the report.[29] In the novel, especially the final description of the suicide scene, Goethe appropriated entire sentences verbatim from Kestner's report,[30] interjecting that material testimony into his own

---

[27] Alexander Košenina, "Es 'ist also keine dichterische Erfindung': die Geschichte vom Bauernburschen in Goethes *Werther* und die Kriminalliteratur der Aufklärung," *Goethe Jahrbuch* 124 (2007): 189–197.
[28] Johann Wolfgang Goethe, *Briefe. Historisch-Kritische Ausgabe*, ed. Elke Richer and Georg Kurscheidt (Berlin: Akademie Verlag, 2008), vol. 1.1, 24: "Der unglückliche Jerusalem. Die Nachricht war mir schröcklich und unerwartet [...] es war grässlich [...] der arme Junge!"
[29] Goethe, *Briefe*, vol. 1.1, 244: "schicken Sie mir doch die Nachricht von J. Todte."
[30] Beautifully documented in Carl Wilhelm Jerusalem, "...*Kein Geistlicher hat ihn begleitet*": *Dokumente aus dem Nachlass von Johann Christian Kestner über den Selbstmord Carl Wilhelm Jerusalems am 30. Oktober 1772 in Wetzlar*, ed. Michael Wenzel (Wetzlar: Michael Imhof Verlag, 2015), 16–17.

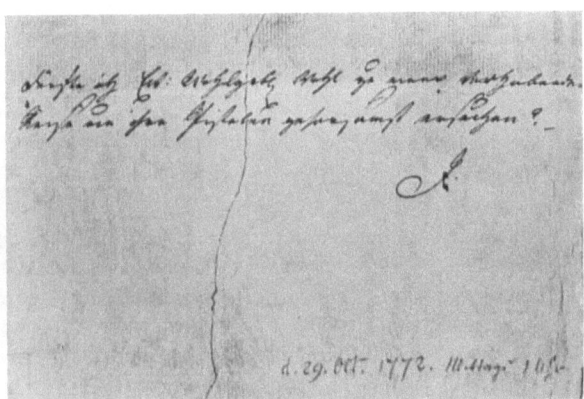

Figures 3 and 4: Carl Wilhelm Jerusalem (fig. 3) and the request for Kästner's *Reisepistole* (fig. 4), which provided Goethe with a "true" case-history for his famous psychological novel *Die Leiden des jungen Werthers* (1774). Portrait with permission of the Stiftung Klassik Weimar, Bereich Museen. Billet of Jerusalem with permission of Goethe- und Schiller Archiv, 29/264, I, 1. Photo: Klassik Stiftung Weimar.

narrative fiction. To further complicate the relation between fact and fiction in the novel, Goethe had himself fallen in love with Kestner's future wife, Charlotte Buff, but had been rejected. *Werther* should thus be read as a double fictional-historical hybrid case history, or an early instance of *faction*, braiding the narratives of Jerusalem's suicide as documented in Kestner's report and Goethe's own unrequited love for Kestner's future wife Charlotte Buff into the first truly psychological novel in Western literature.

Another famous example of the psychological case adapted and translated into literature is *Lenz*. In 1777, the *Sturm und Drang* German poet and dramatist Johann Michael Reinhold Lenz (1751–1792) was banished from the Court of Weimar, to which Goethe had introduced him. Lenz suffered from severe mental illness, and Goethe in his account only elliptically alludes to the behavior that caused his expulsion. Lenz traveled to Steinthal in Alsace, where, suffering from what most historians and critics categorize as a form of severe psychosis, he came under the care of the pietist social reformer and clergyman Johann Friedrich Oberlin. Oberlin wrote a detailed diary, what amounts to a case history of Lenz during his stay.[31] In 1836, the German physician and dramatist

---

[31] Johann Friedrich Oberlin, "Der Dichter Lenz, im Steinthal," [ed. August Stöbel], in *Georg Büchner: Werke und Briefe*, ed. Karl Pörnbacher et al. (München: DTV, 2001), 520–530. A more replete manuscript version of Oberlin's report is available: Hartmut Dedert, Hubert Gersch, Stephan Oswald, and Reinard Spiess, "J.-F. Oberlin: Herr L..... Edition des bisher unveröffentlichter Manuskripts. Ein Beitrag zur Büchner- und Lenz-Forschung," *Revue des*

Georg Büchner composed the novella *Lenz*, transforming Oberlin's case history of Lenz (1777–1778) into a psychological case history as an aesthetic, literary text, published by Karl Gutzkow in 1839 after Büchner's death. However, the precise relation between Oberlin's case report and Büchner's literary text is anything but clear. As Helmut Müller-Sievers has argued:

> Despite the Marburg editors' desperate efforts, the seams between Oberlin's diary and Büchner's "own" text cannot be clearly retraced, although there are areas where the density of quotation is higher and others where no immediate sources can be identified. Rather than remaining identifiable as two strata, quoted and unquoted material grow into one another and foil every attempt to separate them.[32]

Oberlin's "original" diary and Büchner's literary stylization are nearly indistinguishable at certain points in the text. Büchner lifted specific phrases, sentences, even entire passages from Oberlin's diary/case history. Compare the following passage from Oberlin's notes in the diary recounting one of Lenz's rants about his beloved Friederike Brion, with whom Goethe also had a brief love affair, to the corresponding passage in Büchner's *Novella*.

> O! Is she dead? Does she still live? – The angel, she loved me – I loved her, she was worthy of it – o the angel – cursed jealousy! I sacrificed her – she loved another – but she loved me as well – even deeply – sacrificed – I had promised her my honor – then abandoned – o cursed jealousy! – o good mother! She, too, loved me – I am your murderer etc. etc.

> Oh she is dead! Does she still live? You angel, she loved me – I loved her, she was worthy of it, oh you angel. Cursed jealousy, I sacrificed her – she loved another – I loved her, she was worthy of it – O good mother! even she loved me. I am a murderer.[33]

Langues Vivants 42 (1976): 357–385. On Georg Büchner's appropriation of Oberlin's case history of Johann Michael Reinhold Lenz, see: H. P. Pütz, "Büchners Lenz und seine Quelle: Bericht und Erzählung," *Zeitschrift für deutsche Philologie* 84 (1965): 1–22; and Wolfram Schmitt, "Psychisch Kranke und ihre Helfer am Ende des 18. Jahrhunderts. Pfarrer Oberlin und der Dichter Lenz," *Jahrbuch Literatur und Medizin* 2 (2008): 41–60.

[32] Helmut Müller-Sievers, "Reading without Interpreting: German Textual Criticism and the Case of Georg Büchner," *Modern Philology* 103.4 (2006): 515–516.

[33] Hubert Gersch, *Der Text, der (produktive) Unverstand des Abschreibers und die Literaturgeschichte: Johann Friedrich Oberlins Bericht "Herr L…" und die Textüberlieferung bis zu Georg Büchners "Lenz"-Entwurf* (Berlin: de Gruyter, 1998), 17. In Oberlin's diary, we read: "Ach! Ist sie tot? Lebt sie noch? – Der Engel, sie liebte mich – ich liebte sie, sie war's würdig – o der Engel – Verfluchte Eifersucht! Ich habe sie aufgeopfert – sie liebte noch ein andern – aber sie liebte mich – ja herzlich – aufgeopfert – die Ehre hatte ich ihr versprochen – hernach verlassen – o Verfluchte Eifersucht! – O gutte Mutter! Auch die liebte mich – ich bin euer Mörder &c &c." In Büchner's *Lenz*, this passage is transcribed as: "Ach sie ist tot! Lebt sie noch? Du Engel, sie liebte mich – ich liebte sie, sie war's würdig, o du Engel. Verfluchte Eifersucht, ich habe sie aufgeopfert –

Figure 5   Figure 6

Figures 5, 6, and 7: *Sturm und Drang* dramatist Johann Michael Reinhold Lenz, 1751–1792 (fig. 5), who became the subject of Pastor Johann Friedrich Oberlin's (fig. 6) case-history, and the physician and playwright Georg Büchner, 1813–1837 (fig. 7), who read Oberlin's case-study and whose novella *Lenz* (written 1835–1836) is often regarded as one of the first truly modern literary texts. Engraving of Lenz by Georg Friedrich Schmoll, 1776. Public domain. Jean Gottfroid Gerhardt: Portrait of Johann Friedrich Oberlin, circa 1790. Courtesy and with permission of Musée Alsacien de Strasbourg; Photo Musées de Strasbourg. Portrait of Georg Büchner by Philipp August Joseph Hoffmann courtesy and with permission of the Stadtarchiv Gießen, Bildersammlung.

The fragmentary nature of the original is maintained, yet Büchner's text alters the crucial possessive pronoun to an indefinite article, making Lenz a case. Oberlin's paratactic recitation of Lenz's madness becomes condensed and compressed in Büchner. Büchner's use of Oberlin's actual case history does not simply reflect a commitment to realism, materiality, and the empirical precision and detail of Oberlin's text as some critics have suggested; rather, it enacts or performs an aesthetic-literary stylization and construction of Lenz's psychopathology that blurs the very distinction between fact and fiction, between material-factual "basis" and literary "invention," between history and literature itself. The textual situation with regard to Büchner's *Woyzeck* (published posthumously in 1839) is quite similar; Büchner studied all of the many psychiatric experts' reports on a series of soldier-murderers (Schmolling, Diess, and Woyzeck) and incorporated snippets of

---

sie liebte einen anderen – ich liebte sie, sie war's würdig – o gute Mutter, auch die liebte mich. Ich bin ein Mörder."

Figure 7

testimony – especially the psychological determinants such as nighttime anxiety, shaking, and paranoia (*Wahn der Verfolgung*), dreams and voices with the call to murder, fantasies of previous lovers – into the various versions of the text.[34]

If the actual breakthrough signaling the rise of a new genre and manner of observing and writing about human beings can be dated to around 1770, one should query what precedents – medical, juridical, scientific – created the historico-philosophical conditions of the genre's possibility.

At the University of Halle at the end of the seventeenth century and beginning of the eighteenth century, the medical case histories of Georg Ernest Stahl and Friedrich Hoffmann produced the "template" for the medical-psychological case history that was to be employed by the psychologically-minded physicians of the mid-eighteenth century. One can delineate a direct arc from Stahl to the so-called rational physicians (*vernünftige Ärzte*) in the mid-eighteenth century in Halle: Johann August Unzer (1727–1799), Johann Gottlob Krüger (1715–1759), Ernst Anton Nicolai (1722–1802), and Johann Christian Bolten (1727–1757), all of whom were

---

[34] Georg Büchner, *Woyzeck. Texte und Dokumente*, kritisch herausgegeben von Egon Krause (Frankfurt: Insel Verlag, 1969), 160–203.

influenced by Stahl's psychological approach to the etiology of disease.[35] Unzer's *Thoughts on the Influence of the Soul on the Body* (*Gedanken vom Einfluß der Seele in ihren Körper*, 1746) stands squarely in the tradition of Stahl's influential influxionist, animist treatise *Concerning the Manifold Influence of the Movements of the Mind on the Human Body* (*Über den mannigfaltigen Einfluss der Gemütsbewegungen auf den menschlichen Körper*, 1695). Like Stahl, Unzer criticizes speculative metaphysics and insists on Stahl's method of strict scientific observation.[36] And, like Stahl, Unzer rejected purely materialistic, mechanistic accounts of the relation between soul and body. At this time, the so-called lower faculties – sensation, feeling, and specifically the affective passions – became an important topic in scientific-philosophical discussions.[37] Krüger's *Attempt at an Experimental Psychology* (*Versuch einer Experimentalseelenlehre*, 1756) postulated a psychophysical unity of the human being with the assumption of an active soul.[38] In the plan for the *Journal of Empirical Psychology* (1783–1793), Karl Philipp Moritz takes Krüger's concept of experimental psychology (*Experimentalseelenlehre*) and transforms it, with the guidance of Moses Mendelssohn, who suggested the shift in terminology, to experiential psychology (*Erfahrungsseelenkunde*). As Carsten Zelle has pointed out, one reason for the transformation of *Experimental* to *Erfahrung* in the title of Moritz's journal had to do with the fact that the very notion of *Erfahrung* harbored a very specific meaning at the time.[39] According to Krüger,

---

35 Carsten Zelle, ed., *Vernünftige Ärzte. Hallesche Psychomediziner und die Anfänge der Anthropologie in der deutschsprachigen Frühaufklärung* (Tübingen: Niemeyer, 2001). On Krüger, see: Wolfram Mauser, "Johann Gottlob Krüger. Der Weltweise als Arzt. Zur Anthropologie der Frühaufklärung in Deutschland," in '*Vernünftig Ärzte*,' ed. Zelle, 48–67. On the connection between these physicians and the "anthropological turn" see: Carsten Zelle, "Erfahrung, Ästhetik und mittleres Maß: Die Stellung von Unzer, Krüger und E.A. Nicolai in der anthropologischen Wende um 1750" in *Reiz – Imagination – Aufmerksamkeit*, ed. Jörn Steigerwald and Daniela Watzke (Würzburg: Königshausen & Neumann, 2003), 203–224.
36 Johanna Geyer-Kordesch, *Pietismus, Medizin, und Aufklärung im Preußen im 18. Jahrhundert* (Tübingen: Niemeyer, 1996), 243f.
37 Hans Adler, "Fundus Animae – Grund der Seele. Zur Gnoseologie des Dunklen in der Aufklärung," *Deutsche Vierteljahrsschrift für Literaturwissenschaft und Geistesgeschichte* 62.2 (1988): 197–220.
38 Especially helpful in this regard is the work of Gabriele Dürbeck, *Einbildungskraft und Aufklärung. Perspektiven der Philosophie, Anthropologie und Ästhetik um 1750* (Tübingen: Niemeyer, 1998), 124–130.
39 Karl Philipp Moritz, "Vorrede zum Magazin für Erfahrungsseelenkunde," in *Karl Philipp Moritz. Die Schriften in dreißig Bänden*, ed. Petra Nettelbeck and Uwe Nettelbeck (Nördlingen: F. Greno, 1986), 8: "Nach dem Vorschlage des Herrn Moses Mendelssohn werde ich die Eintheilungen in der Arzneiwissenschaft auf die Erfahrungsseelenkunde anzuwenden suchen." Concerning the shift from "Experiment" to "Erfahrung," see: Carsten Zelle, "Experiment,

Erfahrung consists of perceptions and observations *as well as* experience one was able to gather in experiments. The case history, according to Krüger, was to function in empirical psychology precisely as the "experiment" in physiology; instead of: the case history therefore served as a replacement or proxy for actual scientific experimentation, which Krüger deemed unworthy and inappropriate for human subjects,[40] a second reason for Mendelssohn's suggestion.

Unzer and Krüger intensify Stahl's and Hoffmann's requirement of observation – *Beobachtung* – (as a form of "experience" or *Erfahrung*) and transform this methodological principle[41] into a new form of scientific evidence and a new medium of writing about individual cases. These "psychological" or "rational" physicians at mid-century in Halle maintained a reciprocal relation between body and soul, *physis* and *psyche*, but their actual case-descriptions remain very much indebted to and within the tradition of Boerhaave and Hoffmann. Thus, in the second volume of *Attempt at an Experimental Psychology*, which contains all of the case histories, Krüger utilizes the term perceptions (*Wahrnehmungen*) to designate the case-historical examples and to convey the supposedly direct, objective and unmediated character of the texts.[42] These case histories contain neither psychological indices for the explanation of the illness nor any subjective statements that impart the actual experience of the illness by the patient.[43] Even

---

Experience and Observation in Eighteenth-Century Anthropology and Psychology – the Examples of Krüger's *Experimentalseelenlehre* and Moritz's *Erfahrungsseelenkunde*," *Orbis Litterarum* 56.2 (2001): 93–105; Zelle, "Experimentalseelenlehre und Erfahrungsseelenkunde" in *Vernünftige Ärzte*, 174–185; and Matthew Bell, *The German Tradition in Psychology in Literature and Thought, 1780–1840* (Cambridge: Cambridge University Press, 2005), 94. Lorraine Daston has also discussed the transformation of the notion of experience, albeit in a different context in her "Strange Facts, Plain Facts, and the Texture of Scientific Experience in the Enlightenment," in *Proof and Persuasion. Essays on Authority, Objectivity and Evidence*, ed. Suzanne Marchand and Elisabeth Lunbeck (Brussels: Brepols, 1996), 59. We move, pace Daston, from experience as "granular, bumpy, and singular" to experience as "smooth, woven and regular."

40 Johann Gottlob Krüger, *Versuch einer Experimentalseelenlehre* (Halle and Helmstedt, 1756), §§6–7, 13–15, 16, and 18–21. Carsten Zelle has shown how Krüger shifts from "Experiment" to "Beobachtung" (*observation*) because of the violation of the dignity of the human being. See Zelle, "Experiment, Experience and Observation," 93–105.

41 Johanna Geyer-Kordesch, "Medizinische Fallbeschreibungen und ihre Bedeutung in der Wissensreform des 17. und 18. Jahrhunderts," *Medizin, Gesellschaft, Geschichte* 9 (1990): 13.

42 Krüger, *Versuch einer Experimentalseelenlehre*, vol. 2, 1: "Mein Zweck ist hierbey kein anderer gewesen, als den Philosophen, welche keine Ärzte sind, den Nutzen zu zeigen, welchen ihnen die Arzneygelahrtheit in der Seelenlehre verschaffen kann, und die angehängten Wahrnehmungen sind nichts anders, als Rätsel, welche niemand leichter auflösen wird, als wer sie am wenigsten aufzulösen vermögend ist."

43 Krüger, *Versuch einer Experimentalseelenlehre*, §7, 21.

Ernst Anton Nicolai, whose *Thoughts of the Effects of the Imagination on the Human Body* (*Gedancken von den Würckungen der Einbildungskraft in den menschlichen Körper*, 1744; second edition 1751) sought to link the emerging discipline of aesthetics inaugurated by Alexander Baumgarten and Georg Friedrich Meier as the science of the "lower" faculties with medicine, employed case histories that he had taken from Albrecht von Haller's edition of Boerhaave's academic lectures, and, as Gabriele Dürbeck points out, remained completely wed to the tradition of casuistry and the practice of uncritically appropriating existing case-examples in order to shore-up and embellish his medical theory.[44] In a word, the quite innovative anthropological theory of the unity and totality of the human being advanced in the medical texts of the psychological physicians of the mid-eighteenth century in Halle did not find a commensurate praxis of narrative psychological case-taking and -writing; they relied upon the traditional case-examples and -descriptions of the late seventeenth and early eighteenth century as could be found in the texts of Stahl and Hoffmann. The nascent anthropology would first find the new discursive means appropriate to the narrative of the entire human being in its irreducible singularity after the psychological revolution forged by Goethe and Johann Gottfried Herder in the early 1770s and the convergence of discursive, institutional, and disciplinary factors that made the narrative psychological case history possible.

Two epistemological figures – narrative and experience – intervene directly in the years before the emergence I am interested in. Both are exemplified in the writings of two physicians, the first being Andreas Elias Büchner (1701–1769), the second Johann Georg Zimmermann (1728–1795). Between 1762 and 1765, Büchner, professor of medicine and philosophy at the University of Halle-Wittenberg, published a two-volume teaching handbook for young physicians on how to formulate, order, and communicate case histories, the title of which betrays his indebtedness to both rhetorical tradition and the philosophy of the Enlightenment: *Der in schweren und verwirrten Krankheiten vernünftig rathende und glücklich curirende Medicus, oder Gründlicher Unterricht, wie in solchen wichtigen Fällen besonders von jungen Ärzten Consilia medica am sichersten können theils eingeholet, theils auch fürnemlich nach Hofmannischen und Boerhaavischen Grundsätzen klüglich*

---

44 Gabriele Dürbeck, "Physiologischer Mechanismus und ästhetische Therapie: Ernst Anton Nicolais Schriften zur Psychopathologie," in *Vernünftige Ärzte*, ed. Zelle, 104–119, here esp. 111–112; and Dürbeck, *Einbildungskraft und Aufklärung*, 10: "Von Bedeutung ist, daß um 1750 zwar ein großes Interesse an merkwürdigen und pathologischen Phänomenen der Einbildungskraft bestand, ohne daß dies bereits die Beobachtung von Einzelfällen und Lebensgeschichten [...] bedeutete."

*ertheilet werden.*⁴⁵ Büchner provided his reader with a manual for the proper structuring and composition of a complete history of an illness (*Krankheitsgeschichte, historia morbi*) in the section *Von der ordentlichen Einrichtung und Aufzeichnung einer vollständigen Krankheits-Geschichte, und denen sämtlichen dazu erforderlichen Stücken*.⁴⁶ Büchner's two principles of reason and experience provide the framework for his modeling of the case: "Reason and experience are the two sources, from which all human knowledge flows, especially that of which the physicians pride themselves."⁴⁷ Using the language of "distinctness" (*Deutlichkeit*) derived from Descartes, Gottfried Wilhelm Leibniz, and Christian Wolff, and the idiom of observational empiricism stemming from Bacon and John Locke, Büchner defines the "history of an illness" for his readers:

> The history of an illness consists properly understood in a clear and cohesive narrative of all of the circumstances, changes and contingencies which have been perceived from the very beginning of the illness, whether they derive from the illness itself, from the medications utilized, or from specific, coincidental causes.⁴⁸

What stands out in this definition of the case history is the explicit linkage between the case history and narration (*Erzählung*). Büchner compares the medical case history with the criminal case history (*juristische Fallgeschichte*), especially with its emphasis on the small details that might appear meaningless at first

---

45 Andreas Elias Büchner, *Der in schweren und verwirrten Krankheiten vernünftig rathende und glücklich curirende Medicus*. 2 vols. (Erfurt: Weber, 1762, 1765).

46 Andreas Elias Büchner, *Von der ordentlichen Einrichtung und Aufzeichnung einer vollständigen Krankheits-Geschichte, und denen sämtlichen dazu erforderlichen Stücken*, in *Der in schweren und verwirrten Krankheiten vernünftig rathende und glücklich curirende Medicus, oder Gründlicher Unterricht, wie in solchen wichtigen Fällen besonders von jungen Ärzten Consilia medica am sichersten können theils eingeholet, theils auch fürnemlich nach Hofmannischen und Boerhaavischen Grundsätzen klüglich ertheilet werden*, by Andreas Elias Büchner (Erfurt: Weber, 1762–1765), vol. 1, 33–92. I am indebted to Carsten Zelle for introducing me to Büchner's fascinating text. See Carsten Zelle, "'Die Geschichte bestehet in einer Erzählung': Poetik der medizinischen Fallerzählung bei Andreas Elias Büchner 1701–1769," *Zeitschrift für Germanistik* 19.2 (2009): 301.

47 Büchner, *Der in schweren und verwirrten Krankheiten vernünftig rathende und glücklich curirende Medicus*, vol. 2, 136.

48 Büchner, *Von der ordentlichen Einrichtung und Aufzeichnung einer vollständigen Krankheits-Geschichte*, §5, 43: "Die Geschichte einer Krankheit bestehet ordentlicher Weise in einer deutlichen und zusammenhangenden Erzählung aller derjenigen Umstände, Veränderungen und Zufälle, welche von Anfang derselben sind wahrgenommen worden, sie mögen nun der Krankheit selbst, oder von denen gebrauchten Arzneimitteln, oder von besondern zufälligen Ursachen herrühren."

sight.[49] The proper subject of such a history is twofold: (1) the ill person him/herself and everything which pertains to his/her physical constituency and mental sensibility ("der Kranke an und vor sich selbst [...], mit allen dem, was zu seiner ganzen Leibes= und Gemüths=Beschaffenheit gehöret"), and (2) the actual emergence and course of the illness with which the person is burdened ("womit derselbe [der Kranke] behaftet ist, deren sämtliche Zufälle, Abwechselungen und Veränderungen"), and all of its contingencies, alterations and changes over time. As to the former, Büchner names gender and age (*Geschlecht und Alter* [§ 6]), constitution of the body (*Leibes-Constitution* [§ 7]), a physiological description of the person's temperament (*physiologische Beschreibung des Temperaments* [§ 8 and § 9]), a psychological description of the constitution of the mind (*die moralische, oder die Gemüthsbeschaffenheit des Patienten* [§ 9]); attention to the first appearance of the illness and the actual manner in which it was first manifest; attention to the lifestyle and class, office and profession of the patient; and finally, attention should be given to the unnatural things (*unnatürlichen Dinge* or *res non naturales*), matters of diet and life-order (*Diät bzw. Lebensordnung* [§ 12]).[50] As to the latter, Büchner requires a "thorough, clear, and orderly historical narration of all of those circumstances, changes, and contingencies perceived concerning the illness from the beginning;"[51] the origins and circumstances of the illness, and whether it had a felicitous or deadly outcome. Büchner demands concentration on matters of significance, rational thinking in terms of what is typical and customary, and meticulous attention to any and all medications used in the treatment. He admonishes the student to observe "the sick person in and for themselves, and with everything that has to do with their bodily constitution and

---

49 Büchner, *Von der ordentlichen Einrichtung und Aufzeichnung einer vollständigen Krankheits-Geschichte*, §5, 43: "wie eine sogenannte *Species Facti*, welche von redlichen Advokaten zum Grund eines zu erhebenden Processes geleget wird..."; "das ist, sie muß sich auch bis auf Kleinigkeiten erstrecken, die vor und bey dem Anfang, auch ferneren Fortgang der Krankheit, vorgefallen sind, und nichts von allem dem weglassen, was nur irgend einiger massen als ausserordentlich und im gesunden Zustande ungewöhnlich kann angesehen werden" (43).
50 Büchner, *Von der ordentlichen Einrichtung und Aufzeichnung einer vollständigen Krankheits-Geschichte*, §18: "Aer (Licht und Luft), d.h. Umwelt, 2) Cibus et potus (Essen und Trinken), 3) Motus et quies (Bewegung und Ruhe), 4) Somnus et vigilia (Schlafen und Wachen), 5) Excreta et secreta (Stoffwechsel), 6) Affectus animi (Gemütsbewegungen)." As Zelle notes, these were the constituent elements of *Lebens=Dietätik* from Galen. See Zelle, "'Die Geschichte bestehet in einer Erzählung,'" 316.
51 Büchner, *Von der ordentlichen Einrichtung und Aufzeichnung einer vollständigen Krankheits-Geschichte*, §5, 43: "einer deutlichen und zusammenhangenden Erzählung aller derjenigen Umstände, Veränderungen und Zufälle, welche von Anfang derselben sind wahrgenommen worden."

their mental state."[52] As the title of the work suggested, directions for writing a well-structured case history followed the examples of the great physician Boerhaave of Leyden and Hoffmann at the University of Halle. What is significant in Büchner, however, as Carsten Zelle has pointed out, is the shift from a mere description of the facts of the case and the history of the illness (*species facti, historia morbi*) to the narration of the state of mind of the patient (*Gemüthsbeschaffenheit des Patienten*).

Büchner did not write his own case histories, but rather appropriated those of Hoffmann[53] and Boerhaave[54] as *case-examples* in order to show the young aspiring physicians what a well-constructed and well-written case history looked like. He was essentially modeling the case history, trying to impart the know-how necessary to write a well-formed *Krankheits=Geschichte*. In his manual, several historical medical-scientific "languages" intersect and overlap: first and foremost, the insistence on the experimentalism of Bacon, Isaac Newton, Locke, and Robert Boyle in the form of strict, precise observation (*Beobachtung*); second, the remnants of traditional "psychology" from classical antiquity (Aristotle), the theory of animal spirits and the theory of the four temperamental humors of Galen (melancholic, sanguine, choleric, phlegmatic); third, the juridical language of the *species facti*, the legal case history embedded in and deriving from the rich tradition of Roman Law; fourth, the moral-theological case stemming from the casuistry of the Christian tradition; and finally, the emerging sense, typical of the leading physicians and professors of medicine and philosophy in the mid-eighteenth century, of a reciprocal and interactive relation between the body and the mind, the physiological and the psychological, the physical and the spiritual.[55]

Büchner's text did not target mental illness specifically, but his insistence that a well-written case history consisted chiefly in a narrative (*Erzählung*), presenting a clear, orderly story/history (*Geschichte*) of the patient, distinguishes his narratological approach from precise description or nosological categorization that became prominent in France, and the method of strict analysis and the physiological materialism that dominated English writing on madness at the end of eighteenth

---

52 Büchner, *Von der ordentlichen Einrichtung und Aufzeichnung einer vollständigen Krankheits-Geschichte*, §5, 45.
53 Friedrich Hoffmann, *De modo historias morborum recte consignandi et ad usum applicandi* (Diss., Halle, 1721).
54 Hermann Boerhaave, *Sylloge Epistolarum cum responsis* (Göttingen: Vandenhoeck, 1744). Although we only have two cases directly from Boerhaave himself, there are numerous case histories attributed to him by his students, one of whom was Albrecht von Haller (1708–1777). Boerhaave also wrote a precise definition of the ideal case history (*Krankengeschichte*). See Blank-Panitzsch, "Eine Krankengeschichte Herman Boerhaaves," 51–86.
55 Zelle, ed., *Vernünftige Ärzte*.

and the beginning of the nineteenth century. As to the former, the groundbreaking work of Philippe Pinel (1745–1826), *Traité medico-philosophique sur l'aliénation mentale, ou la manie* (1801), influenced by Locke and Étienne Bonnot de Condillac, paved the way for a "moral," fully naturalized treatment of the insane that became the starting point for German psychiatry of the nineteenth century.[56] The latter, exemplified in Alexander Crichton's (1763–1856) *Inquiry into the Nature and Origin of Mental Derangement* (1798), which influenced Pinel, was informed by the physical psychology of Thomas Reid, who held that the mind was a kind of alchemist, synthesizing and transforming what the senses had offered up into cogent ideas and rational thought. As Stephanie Kiceluk has pointed out, a profound tension persisted between the narrative, historical-interpretive and the visual, purely descriptive modes of understanding mental illness, highlighted by Michel Foucault in his *Birth of the Clinic* (1963), especially in Pinel's work.[57] According to Foucault, the emergence of the clinic created the institutional space of a medical semiological gaze, scanning and surveying the surface of the patient for the telltale signs of the disease lurking underneath, making possible a decidedly individual approach to (mental) disease, its causes, symptoms, etiology and treatment. Such an approach individualized disease and illness, making it an individual *case*.

Büchner, writing in 1765, was on the threshold of a profound transformation – one might even say crisis – in thinking about and documenting individual cases of mental illness. With the waning of the ancient Galenic medical model of humors and vapors and the increasing emphasis placed on the nervous system and the brain as the site of mental disturbances in the second half of the eighteenth century, the traditional explanatory framework for the ordering and categorization of such illness began to falter. Yet there was no singular medical-scientific paradigm to take its place. Two essential ingredients were missing from Büchner's scientific lexicon and grammar in 1765 to form the modern, specifically psychological case history, both of which were to appear in German literature and letters of the 1770s: first and foremost, a semantics of individuality and the invention of "interiority," the enigmatic inner-life of a unique individual as a historically constituted "self," constructed through its own experience and the memories of that experience, irreducible to moral, normative criteria and expectations.[58] As the sociologist Niklas

---

56 Klaus Dörner, *Madmen and the Bourgeoisie: A Social History of Insanity and Psychiatry*, trans. Joachim Neugroschel and Jean Steinberg (Oxford: Basil Blackwell, 1981), 128.
57 Stephanie Kiceluk, "The Patient as Sign and Story: Disease Pictures, Life Stories, and the First Psychoanalytic Case History," *Journal of Clinical Psychoanalysis* 1.3 (1992): 335–368.
58 Fotis Jannidis, "'Individuum est ineffabile'. Zur Veränderung der Individualitätssemantik im 18. Jahrhundert," *Aufklärung* 9.2 (1996): 77–110. According to Renate Heydebrand, "Innerlichkeit," in *Historisches Wörterbuch der Philosophie*, ed. Joachim Ritter and Karlfird

Luhmann argued, this is a "self" that is characterized by its *exclusion from* rather than its *participation within* society.⁵⁹ Second, conditioned by this new semantics, a new genre of self-reflexive autobiography emerges with its unique combination of introspection, childhood memory as a determinant of character, and the project to get at what is essentially unique and different about the self as is evident in Jean-Jacques Rousseau's *Confessions* (1765–1769; published 1782).

In Germany, this project is most evident in the work of Herder, Goethe, Friedrich Schiller, and Moritz in the 1770s and 1780s, whose writing and texts helped to establish and popularize this specifically modern, psychological conception of the self. There is virtually no plot in Goethe's *Werther* (1774), which is focused almost entirely on Werther's "inner world," his emotions and very personal, one might say psychological-pathological readings of and reactions to external events. Moritz subtitled his novel *Anton Reiser* (1781–1785) a "psychological novel" (*ein psychologischer Roman*), the first such designation in the history of literature. His *Gnothi Sauton, Magazin zur Erfahrungsseelenkunde* (1783–1793) was the first journal of experiential psychology, and contained in its ten-year run over one hundred psychologically-minded case histories. As will be more fully spelled out in chapter 6, Schiller, who studied at the Karlsschule in Stuttgart under Jakob Friedrich Abel, famously edited a collection of case histories known collectively as the Pitaval – the *Causes célèbres et interessantes* of the French jurist François Gayot de Pitaval (published 1734–1743 in 18 volumes). As is evident in his early drama *The Robbers* (1781), Schiller was fascinated by aberrant human behavior and the psychological composition of vice. His controversial Preface to that drama reveals a latent psychology; in the character of Franz Moor, Schiller claims to have unfolded "vice together with its entire machinery," and to have articulated "the complete mechanism of his system of vice."⁶⁰ While at the Karlsschule, Schiller wrote a detailed case history of his fellow cadet Grammont, underscoring the socio-psychological determinants – pietistic rigidity, harsh control of emotion, tightly regulated affect, and metaphysical enthusiasm.⁶¹ He developed a psychological theory of the specific criminalization of a person in his

---

Gründer (Basel: Schwabe, 1976), vol. 4, 386–388, the German term for interiority (*Innerlichkeit*) is first used by the poet Friedrich Klopstock in 1779.

59 Niklas Luhmann, "Individuum, Individualität, Individualismus," in *Gesellschaftsstruktur und Semantik. Studien zur Wissenssoziologie der modernen Gesellschaft* (Frankfurt: Suhrkamp, 1989), vol. 3, 149–258.

60 Friedrich Schiller, *Sämmtliche Werke*, ed. Gerhard Fricke and Herbert Göpfert (München: Hanser 1958–1959), vol. 2, 16: "[d]as Laster [...] mit sammt seinem ganzen innern Räderwerk);" "die vollständige Mechanik seines Lastersystems."

61 Friedrich Schiller, "Über die Krankheit des Eleven Grammont," in *Werke. Erzählungen/ Theoretische Schriften* (1967), vol. 5, 268–280.

opening remarks to *Criminal of Lost Honor* (1786), based on the actual case history of Johann Friedrich Schwan, to which he had been introduced by the philosopher-psychologist Abel, whose father, the country commissioner and bailiff Konrad Ludwig Abel, captured Schwan on March 7, 1760.

The convergence of distinctly psychological discursive practices and writing techniques with the steady thematization of the unique, anomalous, and enigmatic individual provides the underlying conditions of the modern psychological case history. As is clear from Büchner's "list" of contributing circumstances, the "register" of facts, and the "conditions" of the patient, he was still writing within the discourse of early modern medicine in 1765, with its emphasis on an intrinsic, immutable "temperament" and the fundamental "constitution" of the patient. As Zelle has observed, however, Büchner's valuable contribution lies precisely in its move away from mere description of the deed or the illness itself and its distinctly narratological imperative: a well-written case history consists in the *story* of the illness.[62] Notwithstanding this narrative impetus, what is striking about Büchner's text is not its familiarity, its modernity, but precisely its traditional, even classical style and rhetoric, especially given the date of its publication in 1765. Certainly, we can easily understand the scientific drive to codify and formalize the writing of cases. It is less clear why, in 1765, a physician would write a two-volume manual on how to write a medical case history specifically concerning "difficult and confusing cases," as Büchner's title announces, given the fact that the structure, style, and rhetoric of the case history had already been firmly established by the physicians whose case histories he himself used as examples. Why then devote a textbook to a practice which had already been institutionalized in countless case history collections, compendia of every conceivable illness and every possible permutation of any of the then designated mental and physical maladies since the late sixteenth century? After all, since Platter[63] and Sydenham[64] and then certainly with Hoffmann and Stahl,[65] *Observationes* were ubiquitous in medical literature. And, as Barbara Duden has demonstrated in her account of the Eisenach physician Johann Storch in the first

---

62 Zelle, "Die Geschichte bestehet in einer Erzählung," 301–316.
63 Felix Kettilby, *Observationes. Krankheitsbeobachtungen in drei Büchern* (1614), trans. Günther Goldschmidt, ed. Heinrich Buess (Bern and Stuttgart: H. Huber, 1963).
64 Thomas Sydenham, *Observationes medicae* (London: Kettilby, 1676).
65 Friedrich Hoffmann, *Medicina Consultatoria* (Leipzig: Leipzig: Halle im Magdeburg, Renger, 1721–1738); and Georg Ernest Stahl, *Collegium causuale magnum*, ed. and trans. Johannes Storch (Leipzig, 1733). On Hoffmann and Stahl in particular, see: Geyer-Kordesch, "Medizinische Fallbeschreibungen," 7–19; and Geyer-Kordesch, *Pietismus, Medizin, und Aufklärung*. On Stahl, see the insightful article by L. J. Rather, "G.E. Stahl's Psychological Physiology," *Bulletin of the History of Medicine* 35.1 (1961): 27–49.

half of the eighteenth-century, the case history had already evolved beyond the classical medical case history or *Krankengeschichte* of Stahl and Hoffmann; patients' words were recorded by the practicing physician in the vernacular. Storch embedded first-person accounts in many of his case histories to convey how the illness was experienced by the patient.[66] What could have been the underlying function and purpose of Büchner's manual, and why at this particular junction in the history of medicine? Further, why does it become so important to instruct young physicians in the "rhetoric" of case history writing, the invention, ordering, and exposition of the medical case history in "difficult" and "obscure" cases? What is the motivating force behind this concern and how does it "respond" to larger cultural-historical issues concerning the construction of "difficult" afflictions, mental illness, or "diseases of the soul"? How does the "case" aid in the invention, codification, and institutionalization of the intimate sphere of interiority, the enigmatic yet formidable power of the soul – *die Seele* – one of the most prominent figures in the unfolding of late eighteenth-century thought and writing?

My interpretive hypothesis is that precisely at this historical moment the relation between the general and the particular, the rule and the individual case, and the norms governing the mapping or correlation of the two, had become deeply problematical. Only in this way can we understand Büchner's emphasis precisely on *difficult, obscure*, and *confusing* cases. With its insistence on a good narration or *Erzählung*, Büchner's text might be read as an effort to shore up what had in fact been standard procedure since the great *Observationes* of his scientific mentors Hoffmann and Boerhaave in an era of the erosion of classical Galenic medical theory, increasing uncertainty as the causes of mental illness, and the emergence of a new, anthropological model of thinking about the individual human being. At precisely this historical moment, the entire rhetorical structure of type, code, register, and formula, indeed *rhetoric itself*, begins to lose its power as a new vocabulary of individual sensibility (*Empfindsamkeit*), feeling and emotion take center stage in literary culture. The Galenic model of humors

---

66 The pathbreaking work on the Eisenach physician Johannes Storch by Barbara Duden, *Geschichte unter der Haut. Ein Eisenacher Arzt und seine Patientinnen um 1730* (Stuttgart: J. B. Metzler, 1987). The English translation is *The Woman Beneath the Skin: A Doctor's Patients in Eighteenth-Century Germany*, trans. Thomas Dunlap (Cambridge, MA: Harvard University Press, 1998). Duden's work is a wonderful affirmation of Roy Porter's plea, "The Patient's View: Doing Medical History from Below," *Theory and Society* 14.2 (1985): 175–198. On the significance of "narrative medicine" in contemporary medicine, which involves the ability to recognize, interpret, and be affectively moved by patients' stories of their illnesses, see Rita Charon, *Narrative Medicine. Honoring the Stories of Illness* (Oxford: Oxford University Press, 2008).

and vapors was ceding to the new discourse of the "nerves," the "brain," and the interdependency of mind and of body. The unique human being in its enigmatic individuality begins to announce itself as an object of discourse.[67] In the case of A. E. Büchner in 1765, we are right on the cusp of the new empirical psychology and its unit of evidence – the narrative case history – yet still under the influence of and seeking to reinforce the classical *Krankengeschichte*, a *historia morbi*, the structure and rhetoric of the classical medical case history and traditional casuistry. In 1765, as Foucault suggested in *Discipline and Punish*, the threshold between the "classical" case as it had been transmitted in moral casuistry, medicine, and in jurisprudence and the "modern" case had not yet been crossed. The "classical" case referred to the totality of circumstances that qualify a deed and justify or legitimize the application of certain "rules" or "statutes," whereas the modern case instantiated the *individual itself*, how it could be measured, described, compared with others and, if necessary, corrected, modified, or guided.[68] Less than a decade later – some would argue as early as 1770 – a new paradigm appears.

Another decisive intervention – a reformulation of the notion of experience (*Erfahrung*) – was introduced by the Swiss physician Johann Georg Zimmermann (1728–1795). Zimmermann was regarded as one of the most influential physicians and popular philosophers of his time, shown by the number of editions of his work and his extensive correspondence with the most influential scientists, writers, and intellectuals of his time: Albrecht von Haller, Samuel-Auguste Tissot, Johann Jakob Bodmer, Isaac Iselin, Johann Jakob Breitinger, Friedrich Nicolai (and through him Mendelssohn and Gotthold Ephraim Lessing), Lavater, Johann Georg Sulzer, and Christoph Martin Wieland, whose novel *History of Agathon* (1766–1767) was directly influenced by Zimmermann's theory of experience.[69] He was received by Fredrick the Great, and achieved applause and the designation of knight from the Empress Katharina II for his four-volume magnum opus

---

67 Already with Christoph Martin Wieland's novel *Agathon* (1766–1767), we can see the cracks and fissures of the old rhetorical edifice and the beginnings of a unique subjectivity concerned with itself: secularized interiority. Wieland read and corresponded with Johann Georg Zimmermann, whose *Von der Erfahrung in der Arzneykunst* has appeared in 1763. On the introduction of "interiority" in Wieland, see Lorna Martens, "Constructing Interiority in Eighteenth-Century Narrative Fiction: Wieland's *Geschichte des Agathon*," *German Quarterly* 81.1 (2008): 49–65; and Bernhard Greiner, "'that until now, the inner world of man has been given ... such unimaginative treatment': Constructions of Interiority around 1800," in *Rethinking Emotion. Interiority and Exteriority in Pre-Modern, Modern and Contemporary Thought*, ed. Rüdiger Campe and Julia Weber (Berlin: de Gruyter, 2014), 137–171.
68 Foucault, *Discipline and Punish: The Birth of the Prison* (New York: Random House, 1979), 191.
69 See Martens, "Constructing Interiority in Eighteenth-Century Narrative Fiction," 49–65.

Concerning Loneliness (1784–1785). But it is for his *Concerning Experience in Medicine* (1763–1764) that he remains so significant for the history of science and medicine, for this text spelled out a theory of experience (*Erfahrung*) as "knowledge which emerges from well-made observations and experiments,"[70] and linked experience to historical knowledge, without whose pre-understanding, Zimmermann reasoned, one would not even know what to look for. As I show more extensively in chapter 3, Zimmermann was absolutely central to the discussion concerning the status of "experience" at the very moment a new sensibility of interior intuition and inner life were being articulated, and just as a clear distinction is being drawn between observation, experiment, and experience.

The first explicit treatment of the "case" as a *literary genre* we owe to André Jolles and his book *Simple Forms* of 1930.[71] Jolles distinguished the "case" from the illustrative instance or example (*Beispiel*), noting that the latter is merely a token of a prescribed type; the relation of the example to that which it seeks to exemplify is clear. Not so with the case, he argued. The case puts into motion a *weighing* not merely of the applicability of the individual or particular to the norm, but of the norms themselves. Rather than merely subsuming a particular under a given rule or prescribed norm, the "case" sets us with the task of a decision (*Entscheidung*) in which judgment must discern whether there is a fitting rule for the particular, or whether the particular initiates or calls for a consideration of the rules or norms themselves. According to Jolles, the "case" poses a *question*, and does not provide the solution.

> What appears before us in its contradictory parts shows the real sense of the case: in the mental process which presents the world to us as something that is judged by norms and values, [the case] not only measures actions with respect to norms, but even more importantly, norm is increasingly judged against norm.[72]

> The unique character of the form "case" consists in the fact that it poses a question, but cannot provide the answer; that it tasks us with the duty of a decision, but does not contain the decision itself. What is realized in the "case" is the weighing, but not the result of the weighing.[73]

---

70 Zimmermann, *Von der Erfahrung in der Arzneykunst*, 46.
71 André Jolles, *Einfache Formen* (Halle [Saale]: Niemeyer, 1930; Tübingen: Niemeyer, 1968).
72 Jolles, *Einfache Formen*, 179: "Das, was in diesem Ganzen der widersprechenden Teile vor uns liegt, zeigt den eigentlichen Sinn des Kasus: in der Geistesbeschäftigung, die sich die Welt als ein nach Normen Beurteilbares und Wertbares vorstellt, werden nicht nur Handlungen an Normen gemessen, sondern darüber hinaus wird Norm gegen Norm steigend gewertet."
73 Jolles, *Einfache Formen*, 191: "Das Eigentümliche der Form Kasus liegt nun aber darin, daß sie zwar die Frage stellt, aber die Antwort nicht geben kann, daß sie uns die Pflicht der Entscheidung auferlegt, aber die Entscheidung selbst nicht enthält – was sich in ihr verwirklicht, ist das Wägen, aber nicht das Resultat des Wägens."

While Jolles was on to something important about the case, his is a genre-theoretical study which did not provide a complete history of the form. I would historicize Jolles's claims about the case by asserting that the *question* (without definitive answer) he identifies as defining for the case, the *weighing* (without result) he attributes to the case, and the conflict of norm versus norm he sees enacted in the case is actually a specifically modern phenomenon; this *questioning, weighing,* and *conflict* of norms becomes acute in the second half of the eighteenth century as the *ancien régime*, the society of castes and class (*Stände*), the religious, social, and political order, and the established forms of conferring, embodying, and representing meaning and identity begin to collapse. What Jolles discerned as a mere formal, genre-theoretical type was, in other words, actually a historical *rupture*. Only when the norms, values, rules themselves began to quiver and quake does the "case" emerge in the full sense of Jolles's theory.

The subject of the present study, the *psychological* case history, has become a significant area of research in recent years. The scholarship on this important discursive and scriptural communication medium of knowledge-transfer of the late Enlightenment[74] that provides the link between the nascent modern empirical psychology of the eighteenth century and the psychiatry of the nineteenth is vast; there have been no less than five major volumes of articles in the last five years alone.[75] Yet there has been no attempt to create a systematic, theoretically articulated history of the emergence of this genre.[76] Rather, as I have written

---

74 Hans-Joachim Schrimpf, "Das Magazin zur Erfahrungsseelenkunde und sein Herausgeber," *Zeitschrift für deutsche Philologie* 99 (1980): 161–187.
75 Rudolf Behrens and Carsten Zelle, eds. *Der ärztliche Fallbericht. Epistemische Grundlagen und textuelle Strukturen dargestellter Beobachtung* (Wiesbaden: Harrassowitz, 2012); Inka Mülder-Bach and Michael Ott, eds., *Was der Fall ist. Casus und Lapsus* (München: Wilhelm Fink, 2014); Susanne Düwell and Nicolas Pethes, eds., *Fall Fallgeschichte Fallstudie: Theorie und Geschichte einer Wissensform*, (Frankfurt and New York: Campus, 2014); Carsten Zelle, ed. *Casus. Von Hoffmanns Erzählungen zu Freuds Novellen. Eine Anthologie der Fachprosagattung 'Fallerzählung'* ed. (Hannover: Wehrhahn, 2015); *Fallgeschichten. Text- und Wissensformen exemplarischer Narrative in der Kultur der Moderne*, ed. Lucia Aschauer et al. (Würzburg: Königshausen & Neumann, 2015); and the monograph by Nicolas Pethes, *Literarische Fallgeschichten. Zur Poetik einer epistemischen Schreibweise* (Konstanz: Konstanz University Press, 2016).
76 A start was made by Andreas Gailus, "A Case of Individuality: Karl Philipp Moritz and the Magazine for Empirical Psychology," *New German Critique* 79 (2000): 67–105; and "Anton Reiser, Case History, and the Emergence of Empirical Psychology," in *A New History of German Literature*, ed. David Wellbery et al. (Cambridge, MA: Harvard University Press, 2005), 409–414. Gailus (2000) argues that "the genre of the psychological case history did not emerge from the simple extension of medical discourse to mental problems but from the complex crossings of

elsewhere, the case history itself has become yet another "case," or, more precisely, it has experienced a "disintegration" or dispersion into a *series of cases*, a "collection" of histories, each looking at its theory and practice at various historical junctures,[77] lacking coherence and clear delineation. Even the rich interdisciplinary research regarding the anthropology of the German Enlightenment has only recently started to approach the question of the origins and emergence of this important form.[78] The modern psychological case history stands in a complex constellation of literary forms and genres, scientific disciplines, and new emerging discourse forms and media within the public sphere. In the literary sphere, one immediately thinks of the confession, autobiography, the criminal story, and the psychological novel.[79] In terms of governing scientific disciplines, the case history found its justification in Philosophy, Medicine, Psychology, Anthropology, Pedagogy, and the Law. Finally, the new forms of communication and publication, above all the "journal," "collections" of case histories, and medical monographs that often contained appendices with exemplary case histories, created the possibility of the dissemination of such case histories to a broader public beyond the boundaries of the academic and literary public sphere. Whereas previously one could read case histories contained in an apparatus to be referred to while reading the main text of a medical book as a series of illustrative *exempla*, in the second half of the eighteenth-century case histories take on a medial existence of their own and become a subject in their own right. However, the complexity and difficulty of the history of the case should not become a warrant for a plethora of discontinuous and disparate histories. In order to understand the peculiarity of the modern psychological case, I argue that we must discern exactly how these disparate cultural forces, media, and disciplines converged to create the conditions of the possibility of this uniquely modern genre.

---

medical thought, (auto)biographical traditions, and juridical narratives" (73). According to Gailus, Moritz's journal was "the birthplace of the psychological case history" (69).

77 Robert Leventhal, "Der Fall des Falls: Neuere Forschung zur Geschichte und Poetik der Fallerzählung im 18. Jahrhundert," *Das Achtzehnte Jahrhundert* 41.1 (2017): 94–102.

78 Geyer-Kordesch, "Medizinische Fallbeschreibungen," 7–19; Doris Kaufmann, *Aufklärung, bürgerliche Selbsterfahrung und die Erfindung der Psychiatrie in Deutschland 1770–1850* (Göttingen: Vandenhoeck & Ruprecht, 1995), 41; Jutta Heinz, *Wissen von Menschen und Erzählen vom Einzelfall. Untersuchungen zum anthropologischen Roman der Spätaufklärung* (Berlin and New York: de Gruyter, 1996). On the crime story, see Holger Dainat, "Der unglückliche Mörder: Zur Kriminalgeschichte der deutschen Spätaufklärung," *Zeitschrift für deutsche Philologie* 107 (1988): 517–541; and Alexander Košenina, "'Tiefere Blicke in das Menschenherz': Schiller und Pitaval," *Germanisch-romanische Monatsschrift* 55.4 (2005): 383–395.

79 Each of these has a rich literature, which I can only point to summarily.

The psychological case history has been interpreted alternately as the representation of an "instability" or "exception" on the way towards normativity,[80] or as the oppositional figure in the struggle against the putative Enlightenment assumption of universal, objective binding laws of a generalized notion of what constitutes human being; as an expression and outbreak of unmediated intimacy and the private-sphere as a bourgeois counter to the vertical rigidity of *Ständegesellschaft*; as the "publication" of the private[81]; as a symptom of the individual as a "unique" and "irreducible" force to be reckoned with against the supposedly arid and cold insistence on reason in the Enlightenment; as an "escape into interiority"[82] or as a compensation for the loss of the life-world in an increasingly institutionalized, bureaucratic and policed world of norms, standards, and regulations[83]; as a prophylactic and warning against religious *Schwärmerei*,[84] unproductive introspection, idle musing, and the obsessive reading of novels and romances, a kind of scientific defense against "religious melancholic illness."[85]

There are, however, other, deep-structural reasons why it was "good to think" the psychological case history at this particular time in Germany, why thinking and writing in individual cases, and this in a distinctively *psychological* manner, made good sense. During the second half of the eighteenth century, at the moment when the first explicitly *psychological* case histories appear, the canonical model of the four humors and wandering vapors within Galenic medicine that had held sway since its rediscovery in the sixteenth century – the idea that mental illness is the result of an imbalance or disruption of

---

[80] Stephen Greenblatt, "Fiction and Friction," in *Reconstructing Individualism: Autonomy, Individuality and the Self in Western Thought*, ed. Thomas C. Heller et al. (Stanford, CA: Stanford University Press, 1986), 30–52, has alerted us to the danger of Jakob Burckhardt's thesis of the emergence of "individuality" in der Renaissance.

[81] Jean Marie Goulemot, "Literary Practices: Publicing the Private," in *A History of Private Life*, ed. Roger Chartier and Philippe Ariès, trans. Arthur Goldhammer (Cambridge: Cambridge University Press, 1989), vol. 3, 364–392.

[82] Wolf Lepenies, *Melancholie und Gesellschaft* (Frankfurt: Suhrkamp, 1972), 83.

[83] Odo Marquard, "Der angeklagte und der entlastete Mensch in der Philosophie des 18. Jahrhunderts," in *Studien zum Achtzehnten Jahrhundert*, ed. Bernhard Fabian (München: Fink, 1980), vol. 2–3, 193–209.

[84] As Niklas Luhmann has shown, pietistic inwardness is qualitatively different from the enigmatic individual soul that surfaces in the psychological case history. See Luhmann, "The Individuality of the Individual: Historical Meanings and Contemporary Problems," in *Reconstructing Individualism: Autonomy, Individuality and the Self in Western Thought* ed. Thomas C. Heller et al. (Stanford, CA: Stanford University Press, 1986), 315–316: "Salvation presupposes something to be saved, whereas an individual, in the literal sense, is a being with an indivisible, indestructible soul."

[85] Kaufmann, *Aufklärung*, 62–74.

the equilibrium of the four humors and the emission of certain toxic "vapors" from the organs – was supplanted, beginning in the late seventeenth century, by a more rigorous scientific, experimental procedure, more precise anatomo-physiological investigation, the theory of the nervous system, and, most importantly for our purposes, a recognition of mental illness (mania, melancholia, hysteria, and hypochondria) as *Gemütskrankheiten* – illnesses of the *mind*. As madness is robbed of its religious interpretation and the "new science" of Boyle, Harvey, Thomas Willis, Sydenham and Newton gradually displaces the canonical humoral-vaporal model, the problem of the causes of mental illness – illness for which one can find no organic basis – became acute. While physicians of the early-late seventeenth and early eighteenth century in Germany as in Holland and England still paid homage to the ancient model, by 1760 this "canon" had been virtually eclipsed. Even the new model of the nervous system as a structure of fibers, tubes, juices and "animal spirits" introduced by Willis in his groundbreaking *Pathologiae cerebri, et nervosa generis specimen* (*The Anatomy of the Brain and the Description of the Use of the Nerves*, 1667), and the advance of the iatro-mechanical view of illness did not stop the philosophically-minded physicians of the eighteenth century in Germany influenced by Stahl's animism from developing a *psychological* theory of the "corruption" or deleterious "infiltration" of the "nervous substance." The power of Stahl's theory in Germany cannot be overstated. The notion that madness was *individual*, that all illness was related to the psycho-physical constitution of the individual soul, that it was caused by something in the individual's life or personality, and its specific expression and trajectory was linked to the individual's mind, emotions, and imagination is the very hallmark of the German psychology of the eighteenth century.

In the last quarter of the eighteenth century, an intensive debate raged in Germany concerning the autonomy of the soul, whether the soul had an independent existence apart from the material chain of cause and effect of natural phenomena. This philosophical controversy regarding the metaphysics of the soul was being carried out in the disciplines of medicine, specifically physiology, in the newly emergent discipline of anthropology, in philosophy, and as part of the discussion concerning the empirical psychology. Increasingly, materialists and advocates of a radical empirical experimentalism were striking at the very core of one of the most entrenched and unquestioned assumptions of the Western tradition: the transcendent character of the *soul*.[86] To be sure, the

---

[86] Michael Hißmann, *Psychologische Versuche, ein Beitrag zur esoterischen Logik* (Frankfurt and Leipzig, 1777), is a paradigmatic example for this new psychology, oriented completely

soul never ceased being a part of the scientific discussion of the eighteenth century, even within the framework of naturalistic empiricism and its insistence on strict observation and direct experience; Stahl's physiological psychology in Halle continued to exercise considerable influence, as we have noted in the example of the psychologically-minded physicians at mid-century.[87] The new empirical materialism of the second half of the eighteenth century wished to make the mind-body connection exclusively an object of empirical-scientific research; the metaphysical soul was, on this view, *persona non grata*. But the soul did not die easily, and powerful proponents of the soul such as Mendelssohn, Herder, Marcus Herz, Moritz, Sulzer, and Schiller continued to adduce arguments for mind, spirit, *Geist* – the existence of the human soul quite distinct from that of material things. The soul could not be reduced to a purely material entity strictly determined by the law of cause-and-effect. They postulated the soul in a twofold manner: first, as the ground and seat – "*Grund*" and "*Sitz*" – of the human capacity for representation and language, human sensibility, and feeling that would never be available to strict empirical analysis; and second, as the enigmatic, deep "character" of the person, a "true" self, one influenced by, but not reducible to, milieu, experience, family history, and social environment.

There were, of course, differences within the metaphysical camp itself, specifically regarding the exact nature of the mind-body interaction, and here, the old models of influxionism and interactionism continued to be weighed and debated. But all of these figures held fast to a metaphysics of the soul. This fundamental remnant of Western metaphysics, this "ground" of human being, was not mere ideology or idle chatter. For the figures of the late Enlightenment in Germany, the soul was an absolute requirement and unconditional principle of human dignity, respect, responsibility, freedom, human right and law, societal order, accountability, and sociability. The final editor of Moritz's *Magazin zur Erfahrungsseelenkunde*, the post-Kantian Jewish philosopher Salomon Maimon, who Kant said was the most astute reader and critic of his philosophy, wrote in his contribution to the journal

---

toward an empirical concept of experience and extremely critical of all metaphysics, see Nicolai Merker, *Die Aufklärung in Deutschland* (München: C. H. Beck, 1982), 227–229; and Kaufmann, *Aufklärung*, 29–30 and Udo Thiel, "Hißmann und der Materialismus," in *Michael Hißmann (1752–1784): Ein materialistischer Philosoph der deutschen Aufklärung*, ed. Heiner F. Klemme, Gideon Stiening, Falk Wunderlich (Berlin: de Gruyter, 2015), 25–41.

87 L. J. Rather, "G.E. Stahl's Psychological Physiology," *Bulletin of the History of Medicine* 35.1 (1961): 27–49.

"Über den Plan des Magazins zur Erfahrungsseelenkunde" in 1791 the following:

> I remark that, even notwithstanding the more precise relation between the soul and the body, the soul is active in and of itself, that is, it brings forth modifications which do not correspond to any bodily modifications. The effects of the so-called higher faculties of the soul and of the free will are of this type [...] these the effects of free will are not merely independent of the effects of the organs, they are actually *opposed* to them [...] Health of the soul is that condition of the soul in which the effects of the free will can be executed without interference, just as disease or illness of the soul consists in the exact opposite condition.[88]

For Maimon, the emphasis on observation and experience as Moritz had urged in his original call for papers of 1783 retreats at the very moment an explicit metaphysics of the soul guarantees the freedom of the human being as a measure of its *Seelengesundheit* – its very health.[89] Even in the various debates concerning the relative merits of mechanism and vitalism of the 1790s and still more surprisingly with the emergence of the discipline of biology around 1800, the soul persists: *Pneuma, spiritus, die Seele* – the soul transforms itself and adapts to become a principle of "life," and organic life, as Michael Sonntag has argued, "becomes a distinct object of positive knowledge."[90] Thus, instead of an "eclipse" of the soul, instead of its demise, we see the transformation of the concept of the soul as an *organic life-force*, as Sonntag has articulated: "The organic is from now on that which breathes, nurtures, grows, and generates itself forth on the basis of specific characteristics."[91] G.S. Rousseau has characterized this astonishing rehabilitation

---

88 Salomon Maimon, "Über den Plan des Magazins zur Erfahrungsseelenkunde," *Magazin für Erfahrungsseelenkunde* 8.3 (1791): 12: "Ich bemerke aber, daß ohngeachtet dieser genaueren Verbindung zwischen Seele und Körper, die Seele auch in sich selbst würkt, d.h. Modifikationen hervorbringt, denen keine körperliche Modifikationen entsprechen. Von dieser Art sind die Würkungen der sogenannten höheren Seelenkräfte und des freien Willens [...] Diese nämlich die Würkungen des freien Willens sind nicht nur von den Organenwirkungen unabhängig, sondern sogar denselben entgegengesetzt. [...] Seelengesundheit ist nehmlich derjenige Seelenzustand, wo die Würkungen des freien Willens ungehindert ausgeübt werden können; so wie die Seelenkrankheit in dem entgegengesetzten Zustand besteht."
89 Kaufmann, *Aufklärung*, 108–109; and Gailus, "A Case of Individuality," 91.
90 Michael Sonntag, "Die Seele und das Wissen vom Lebenden. Zur Entstehung der Biologie im 19. Jahrhundert," in *Die Seele. Ihre Geschichte im Abendland*, ed. Gerd Jüttemann (Göttingen: Vandenhoeck & Ruprecht, 1991), 294–318, at 302: "wird selbst zum eigenständigen Gegenstand eines positiven Wissens."
91 Sonntag, "Die Seele und das Wissen vom Lebenden," 302: "Das Organische ist von nun an das, was aus sich selbst heraus, aufgrund seiner besonderen Eigenschaften, atmet, sich ernährt, wächst, und sich fortpflanzt."

of the soul, so ridiculed by many Enlightenment figures, particularly those of a materialist bent, in the following way: "That 'mind' which the Enlightenment set out to expose as a 'fiction' fought back and reasserted itself, in surprising and troublesome fashions [...] coming to recognize that lunacy was not just seated in the blood, nerves, the brain, but was an authentically *mental* disorder, requiring to be treated by moral means."[92] Notwithstanding the enormous force of the epigenetic theory put forth by Caspar Friedrich Wolff and Johann Friedrich Blumenbach at the time in Germany, which formed the basis of subsequent embryology, organic life – in opposition to materialistic reductionism – came to be viewed as a *formative principle* (*Bildungstrieb* or *Nisus formativus*): as Blumenbach wrote, "a drive (or tendency or striving, however one wants to call it) that is to be distinguished from the general characteristics of the body in general."[93] Such a view was not only entirely consistent with a sense of the "soul" as a higher, organizing principle of *human* life; it also supported the intelligibility of illness as a curve or swerve away from the natural "programming" inherent in human life.

On the other side of this battle, advocates of a radical empiricism and strict materialism – Julian Offray de La Mettrie (1709–1751) and Paul Henri Tiery (Baron) d'Holbach (1723–1789) – dismissed as nonsense the very notion of the human soul. One of the most formidable opponents of Mendelssohn and his metaphysics was the Göttingen philosophy professor Michael Hißmann (1752–1784), who was strongly influenced by Hume's empiricism and skepticism.[94] In his *Psychological Essays* of 1777, he wrote that that one should take "the only correct path, the path of experience," and that if one followed this path consistently, one would not even come upon the idea that there is some spiritual essence or soul that resides "inside" of the human being.[95] According to Hißmann, whom I use here merely as one example of this strong anti-metaphysical tendency, the soul is an "improbable fiction" (*unwahrscheinliche Fiktion*), or worse, something "entirely made-up" (*eine Erdichtung*): "No thought strikes me as stranger and

---

92 G.S. Rousseau, "Introduction," in *Languages of the Psyche. Mind and Body in Enlightenment Thought*, ed. Rousseau (Berkeley and Oxford: University of California Press, 1990), 33.
93 Johann Friedrich Blumenbach, "Über den Bildungstrieb (*Nisus formativus*) und seinen Einfluss auf die Generation und Reproduktion," *Göttingsches Magazin zur Wissenschaft und Literatur* 1.5 (1780): 247–266, at 250.
94 For more in Hißmann, see the volume, Heiner F. Klemme, Gideon Stiening, and Falk Wunderlich, eds., *Michael Hißmann (1742–1784): Ein materialistischer Philosoph der deutschen Aufklärung* (Berlin: de Gruyter, 2013).
95 Hißmann, *Psychologische Versuche* (1777), qtd. by Merker, *Die Aufklärung in Deutschland*, 227. See also: Heinz, *Wissen von Menschen*, 37–38: "den einizg richtien Weg, den Weg der Erfahrung."

more incomprehensible as the thought of a simple essence that lives in the human being."[96] One could cite many others. Christian Gottlob Selle, Director of the Charité in Berlin, a staunch critic of the metaphysics of the soul and one of Herz's opponents, announced a new epoch of medicine in his *New Contributions to Natural and Medical Science* (1782–1786); the era of "theorizing," he argued, was finished, and a new medical science grounded in rigorous observation – ironically, Selle uses the same term Moritz had frequently used in his Journal – *Beobachtung* – without any metaphysical trappings and absent the very idea of a soul, had begun.[97] For Herz, as for Mendelssohn, Herder, and Moritz, the interest remained the "Verbindung und wechselweise[n] Veränderung von Seele und Körper"[98] – the connection and reciprocal change(s) of soul and body. The controversy was intense enough to challenge even the charitable reading of texts. In his review of Ernst Platner's *Anthropologie für Ärzte und Weltweise* (1772), a treatise which sought to research "body and soul in their reciprocal relations, delimitations and connections,"[99] Herz was so intent about maintaining the autonomy and integrity of the soul that he actually misunderstood Platner's text and project:

> Herr Platner seems to us to go too far when he maintains that outside of the connection with the body all thinking and volition would have to cease. For the inner consciousness of ourselves, for the idea, which each person has of their own "I", the body seems to be totally dispensable.[100]

Platner had indeed located the seat of the soul in the brain (*Gehirn*), and he actually did identify deviant, irrational and illogical representations and dreams as

---

96 Hißmann, *Psychologische Versuche* (1777), 249: "So kömt mir kein Gedanke, der je von einem Menschen gedacht worden, sonderbarer und unbegreiflicher vor, als der Gedanke von einem einfachen, im Menschen wohnenden Wesen."
97 Christian Gottlob Selle, *Neue Beiträge zur Natur und Arzenei-wissenschaft* (Berlin: Mylius, 1782–1786): "Es war eine Zeit, wo nichts als Theorien galten. Jetzt ist das Zeitalter der Beobachtungen."
98 Marcus Herz, *Versuch über den Schwindel* (Berlin, 1786), 1.
99 Ernst Platner, *Anthropologie für Ärzte und Weltweise* (Leipzig 1772), Vorrede xvi: „Körper und Seele in ihren gegenseitigen Verhältnissen, Einschränkungen und Beziehungen,"
100 Marcus Herz, Review of Dr. Ernst Platners *Anthropologie für Ärzte und Weltweise* (Leipzig 1772), *Allgemeine Deutsche Bibliothek* 20.1 (1773): 25–51, here 38–39: "Herr P[latner] scheint uns hierin offenbar zu weit zu gehen, wenn er behauptet, daß außer der Verbindung mit dem Körper alles Denken und Wollen aufhören müßte. Zu dem inneren Bewußtsein unserer Selbst, zu der Idee, die ein jeder von seinem eigenen Ich hat, scheint der Körper ganz entbehrlich zu seyn."

"monstrosities of fantasy" and as illnesses (*Krankheiten*),[101] but Platner continued to believe in the concept of the soul as an existing reality (*realexistierend*), yet as something immaterial: he used the terms *Ich, Identität,* and *Bewusstseyn* as synonyms to refer to the soul. However, a striking difference between this view and that of the staunch metaphysicians persisted: for Platner, soul is a *substance* (in the Cartesian sense of substance, thinking substance), and this substance must stand in a relation to materiality. The health of the soul was thus directly linked for Platner to the quality of the brain, dependent on the sensations of the body, and existing in an empirically verifiable relation to objects and people in the world.[102] But Herz was not the only one to misread Platner's anthropology in this way. In a review of Platner written in 1772, the psychologically-minded physician in Halle Johann August Unzer wrote:

> Who can doubt, that the soul can do something without being conscious of it? That the soul has influence into the movements of the heart even if it does not have complete control over it through the will? Don't all the passions alter the movement of the heart, and aren't passions in the soul?[103]

According to Herz – in stark contrast to Platner – there is, in the human soul, "the consciousness of itself," which constitutes the character of the human being, and this is the condition of the possibility of distinct knowledge: "It is on the basis of consciousness alone that we are capable of distinct knowledge."[104]

---

101 Ernst Platner, *Anthropologie für Ärzte und Weltweise* (Leipzig: Dyckischen Buchhandlung, 1772), par. 501, 165. Platner calls representations that do not have their ground in previous representations or experience "diseased" (*krankhaft*).
102 See Rita Wöbkemeier, *Erzählte Krankheit. Medizinische und Literarische Phantasien um 1800* (Stuttgart: Metzler, 1990), 163–165. Compare also Udo Thiel, "Das Gefühl 'ich': Ernst Platner zwischen empirischer Psychologie und Transzendentalphilosophie," in *Aufklärung: Interdisziplinäres Jahrbuch zur Erforschung des 18. Jahrhunderts* (Hamburg: F. Meiner, 2007), vol. 19, 139–161.
103 Johann August Unzer, Review of "Briefe eines Arztes an seinen Freund," by Ernst Platner, in *Allgemeine Deutsche Bibliothek* 14.1 (1771): 86: "Zu dem, wie kann man wohl in Zweifel ziehen, daß die Seele etwas thun könne, ohne sich dessen bewußt zu seyn? Daß die Seele einen Einfluß in die Bewegungen des Herzens habe, ob sie gleich durch den Willen keine Herrschaft darüber hat? Verändern nicht alle Leidenschaften die Bewegung des Herzens, und sind wohl die Leidenschaften nicht in der Seele?"
104 Marcus Herz, Review of *Anthropologie für Ärzte und Weltweise*, by Dr. Ernst Planter (Leipzig, 1772), *Allgemeine Deutsche Bibliothek* 20.1 (1773): 38: "das Bewusstsein ihrer selbst, welcher den Charakter des Menschen ausmacht," and: "Vermittels des Bewusstseins allein sind wir der deutlichen Erkenntnis fähig." It is evident that Herz reduces Platner's theory of self-consciousness. For a much more nuanced and charitable interpretation, see: Thiel, "Das Gefühl 'ich'"; and Werner Euler, "*Commercium mentis et corporis*? Ernst Platners medizinische

Here, the difference between Platner's anthropological view and Herz's psychological-physiological theory becomes clear; while Platner reverted back to the soul as a distinct type of *substance* – a remnant of Cartesian metaphysics – Herz defended the autonomy of the human soul as the *sine qua non* of human dignity, responsibility, autonomy, and self-determination. Today, suspicious of metaphysical suppositions, we speak of *agency*.

What does this argument about the soul have to do with the psychological case history? Put simply, the psychological case history that definitively emerges around 1780 opened the way for a new, "secular" metaphysics of the soul with the appearance of scientificity, with the apparent claim of direct, scientific "experience" and observation, with the putative precision of "description" and "facts." To paraphrase Forrester, it was a matter of *making the soul scientific*.[105] The psychological case histories, according to Moritz, were supposed to be the result of rigorous attentiveness, attunement, and experience; all speculation, moral judgment, textbook learning and transmitted scholarship were to be cast aside. Moritz wanted "*Fakta*, not moral prattle." By seeking to find the elusive unity of the person, the case history became a metaphysics of the soul by other means.[106] Rather than metaphysical speculation, the soul could now be graphed using narrative history. The psychological case history confirmed what was viewed to be the necessary continuity and coherence of the soul by decoupling religion (sin) and mental illness and effectively linking mental illness to a person's history and experience. It produced the required integrity of the spiritual self precisely in the confrontation with its rupture – psychic or mental illness; it "documented" quite literally the persistence of the soul, and, by focusing on the mental state (*Zustand*) of the patient, the culpability of the human being.[107] As a form of scientific writing, it endeavored to grasp

---

Anthropologie in der Kritik von Marcus Herz und Immanuel Kant," in *Aufklärung: Interdisziplinäres Jahrbuch zur Erforschung des 18. Jahrhunderts* (Hamburg: F. Meiner, 2007), vol. 19, 21–68.

105 Forrester, "If p, then what? Thinking in Cases," 10.

106 In his article on Schiller's *Verbrechen aus Infamie* Alexander Košenina writes of the human soul as the discursive object of the psychological case history. See: Košenina, "'Tiefere Blicke in das Menschenherz,'" 391. As Košenina emphasizes, with Schiller it is not simply a matter of the individual case itself, but with universal human knowledge of the soul, the assumption, "daß dabei die Einheit der Menschennatur außer Frage steht." See also Harald Neumeyer, "'Schwarze Seelen'. Rechts-Fall-Geschichten bei Pitaval, Schiller, Niethammer und Feuerbach," *Internationales Archiv zur Sozialgeschichte der deutschen Literatur* 31.1 (2006): 101–132. The importance of the German reception of the French Pitaval has only recently been truly recognized.

107 In disagreement with Neil Vickers's take on the Moritzian ideal psychological case history as a rejection of all claims to consistency: Neil Vickers, "Coleridge, Moritz and the

the enigmatic "interior" of the human being, "das Innere des Menschen," the individual soul as a singular and unique case – as an *Einzelfall* – but always with the goal of returning to, and, if possible, restoring the humanity of that soul, its dignity and integrity. Ultimately, such cases would invariably lead to ever more universal knowledge concerning the human being. In sharp contrast to the case as example as in the casuistical thinking of the late seventeenth and early eighteenth century, and in distinction to the medical case-descriptions in the sense of the classical *observationes, medicina consultataria, consilia*, the psychological case history exhibited both a unique structure and served a very distinct function. The convergence of experimentalism and psychological reflection, of careful observation, recording and linking was designed to invent the enigmatic individual case as comprehensible, intelligible, communicable: it thereby transformed encounters with the darkest and most incomprehensible moments of the human soul into states of mind that could be articulated and explained in terms of the inner workings of the individual's mind, and the hidden forces of the individual's soul. The psychological narrative case history started a tradition of writing about "the intimate relation between the history of suffering and the symptoms of an illness," as will become clear in chapter 2 in our discussion of Sigmund Freud's use of the genre.

The psychological case history thus proffered an articulation of the "soul" of the Other, or *as* Other, and allowed the humanity of this Other to appear precisely at the point where it was most vulnerable and challenged.[108] The case history fulfilled a significant *pastoral* function as well, identifying and thematizing, evaluating and judging the individual as a stray, as an exception. Foucault's "individualizing power of the pastoral"[109] tells of a unique form of socialization and integration – very different from the disciplinary dimensions

---

'Psychological' Case History," *Romanticism* 13.3 (2007): 271–280, especially 271 and 277. Vickers does see in Moritz's project an interest in the "shaping of the self" (277).

108 In the "repressed" preface of *Die Räuber*, and in his reception and edition of Pitaval (1792), and finally in the preface to his story *Der Verbrecher aus verlorener Ehre* (1786; 1792), Schiller is always interested in pointing out the constitutive knowledge-interest and the possible epistemological traction to be gained from the publication and reading of such psychological case histories. Schiller is not primarily concerned with the uniqueness of the case itself, but rather what the case can provide in terms of general knowledge of human beings and behavior – "die geheimen Bewegursachen menschlicher Handlungen." See: Košenina, "'Tiefere Blicke in das Menschenherz': Schiller und Pitaval," 383–395, esp. 388–392.

109 Michel Foucault, *Geschichte der Gouvernementalität I: Sicherheit, Territorium, Bevölkerung. Vorlesung am College de France 1977–1978*, ed. Michel Senellart, trans. Claudia Brede-Konersmann and Jürgen Schröder (Frankfurt: Suhrkamp, 2004), 191–193.

of "terror and coercion of fear-incusing force" (*Schrecken und Zwang oder von furchterregender Gewalt*).¹¹⁰ In the *pastoral apparatus*, it is a matter of gently guiding the conscience and soul of the individuals without having to discipline the body explicitly and directly.¹¹¹ The psychological case history had the transformative purpose of bringing order to the apparently coincidental and enigmatic case, making it something that can be described, analyzed, and used for further moral and pedagogical purposes. It enables the shepherds – read the philosophical or "moral" doctors, priests, officers, counselors, teachers, professors, "sisters," nurses and mothers – to reintegrate those who have gone astray back into the bourgeois order precisely through the reading, exchange, dissemination, and compilation of case histories. In this we can see a renewed sense of the traditional moral-theological casuistry, of course with a fundamentally different spin: here it is not so much a matter of instilling fear of the "monstrous" or the "defective" Other, the morally impaired or the sinner of conscience. Rather, the point was the education of literate, cultivated individuals who could be brought to recognize in this new Other an inherent possibility of themselves.

The psychological case history emerges in Germany in a constellation of thinking and writing about how to capture the unique story of the individual soul in the process of its becoming, from its early development, in its evolution, its sensibility, its socialization process, and, where applicable, how it went astray or deviated from a healthy, productive life. As the rigid, hierarchical society of castes (*Ständestaat/Ständegesellschaft*) begins to fall apart in the second half of the eighteenth century, the question of personal identity is posed at the individual and the societal level: new forms of subjectivity become possible, while others become highly problematic if not unviable.¹¹² In this rapidly changing society, what it *meant* to be who one was, apart from the societal designations and classifications, roles and functions, was very much at stake. In the tumult of this social upheaval, it begins to matter how individuals came to be what they are, and how they can be understood in terms of their history, their constitution, their childhood, and their life trajectory. Care for the

---

110 Foucault, *Geschichte der Gouvernementalität I*, 191.
111 Compare also Zelle, "Erfahrung, Ästhetik, und mittleres Maß," 214–215, where he sees the convergence of Baumgarten, Meier, Krüger, and Johann Christian Bolten in the following: "dass die Affekte [...] nicht unterdrückt, sondern vielmehr geleitet werden sollen," and, quoting Baumgarten, "eine sichere Führung nötig haben." (215) Zelle mentions the "Hinwendung zum Einzelfall und zur Fallgeschichte, d.h. den Einbezug narrativer bzw. literarisiernder Verfahren in die Anthropologie" (209), but does not elaborate further.
112 On this crisis, see Reinhard Koselleck's pathbreaking work *Kritik und Krise: Eine Studie zur Pathogenese der bürgerlichen Welt* (Freiburg and München: K. Alber, 1959).

individual life was increasingly becoming the responsibility of the state,[113] part of a bio-politics that was directed at the rational, moral construction of a strong, healthy, lawful, productive population by a "caring" state, and this meant that one would have to ascertain how individuals become what they are, how and why they become ill or criminal, and how various therapeutics – medical, pedagogical, pastoral, juridical – might mitigate such deviations. In addition to case histories, one discursive medium for the production of the understanding of a unique individual and her unique trajectory was the genre of *autobiography*. The other decisive genre for such an understanding in the eighteenth century was the *novel*.

While there were many previous historical examples (Gerolamo Cardano, Michel de Montaigne, Benvenuto Cellini) of autobiography or self-representations in early modern Europe,[114] self-generated life-stories, or *Lebensbeschreibungen*, became an especially beloved and privileged genre in the late 1760s and 1770s, with numerous examples both in Europe as a whole and in the German-speaking territories in particular.[115] One detects a radical shift from the spiritual and educated autobiographies of the sixteenth and seventeenth centuries to the increasingly psychologically-structured and -oriented narratives of the eighteenth century. Beginning with Adam Bernd's famous life-history of 1738, the pace and volume of publication of such narratives increased exponentially in the second half of the century: thus, in a short period of time, Johann Georg Hamann's *Gedanken über mein Lebenslauf* (1758), Lavater's *Geheimes Tagebuch. Von einem Beobachter seiner selbst* (anonymously published 1771), Jung-Stilling's *Heinrich Stillings Jugend* (1772), Johann Salamo Semler's *Lebensbeschreibung* (1781–1782),[116] Ullrich Bräker's *Lebensgeschichte und Natürliche Abentheuer des Armen Mannes im Tockenburg* (1789, 1792), Schubart's *Leben und Gesinnungen* (1778–1779), Rousseau's *Confessions*, written 1764–1766, but first published in 1782 (in Germany, 1785), Maimon's *Lebensbeschreibung* (1792), and Moritz's *Anton Reiser* (1785–1790), a roman á clef, were viewed as significant, even pathbreaking literary innovations, as signs of a new authenticity and sincerity, imparting intimate details of a unique individual's life in a seemingly direct, unmediated fashion. The tradition of Montaigne's *Essays* – to give voice to one's self, "for it is myself that

---

113 Most forcefully evident in Johann Peter Frank's *System einer vollständigen medizinischen Polizei* (Wien: Carl Schaumberg, 1793–1827).
114 Ralph-Rainer Wuthenow, *Das erinnerte Ich: Europäische Autobiographie und Selbstdarstellung im 18. Jahrhundert* (München: C.H. Beck, 1987).
115 Helmut Pfotenhauer, *Literarische Anthropologie: Selbstbiographien und ihre Geschichte am Leitfaden des Leibes* (Stuttgart: Metzler, 1987).
116 *Johann Salamo Semlers Lebensbeschreibung von ihm selbst abgefasst* (Halle, 1781–1782).

I portray"[117] – found an intensifying echo in the second half of the eighteenth century in Germany. Semler wrote in the Preface to his *Lebensbeschreibung*: "Without any artifice, and without any falsity I have written my history."[118] Rousseau had also promised a narrative *intus et in cute* ("inside and under the skin," the motto of both volumes of Rousseau's *Confessions*), famously writing "Myself alone. I feel my heart and I know men. I am not made like any I have seen; I venture to believe that I was not made like any that exist."[119] Critics have pointed out that Rousseau's text is still marked by a moral apologetics, but clearly the tendency of the late eighteenth century was towards the complete, authentic revelation and disclosure of the self, without any theological trappings, and without the moral undertones still present in Rousseau.

It was also not merely a matter of the autobiographies themselves, but an entire literature on the writing, value, and meaning of such life-descriptions emerges in the popular writings of the late Enlightenment: Johann Joachim Eschenburg, Herder, Christian Garve, and Sulzer all discuss the importance of life-descriptions and theorize these life-descriptions as part of the anthropological interest of gaining knowledge of the human being. Eschenburg's *Outline of a Theory and Literature of the Beautiful Sciences* (*Entwurf einer Theorie und Literatur der schönen Wissenschaften*, 1783) names the autobiography as a particularly significant genre and asserts that life-descriptions are both *lehrreich* and *interessant*. Herder's *On Cognition and Sensation of the Human Soul* (*Vom Erkennen und Empfinden der menschlichen Seele*, 1774;1775;1778) famously recommended three paths to research the vital connection between psychology and physiology in the individual case: life-descriptions, remarks of physicians and friends, and works of literature. His models were Cardanus, Montaigne, and Rousseau. Only through the study of such texts are we able, according to Herder, to come to know the most entwined pathology of the soul (*die verflochtenste Pathologie der Seele*), to disclose the deep particularities (*tiefen Besonderheiten*) of a life, and to learn to understand the dark indications (*dunklen Anzeigungen*) of the total person.[120]

---

117 Michel de Montaigne, *Essays and Selected Writings*. Trans. Donald M. Frame (New York: St. Martin's Press, 1969), 3.
118 Semler, *Lebensbeschreibung*, "Vorrede," unpaginated: "Ohne alle Kunst, ohne alle Untreue, habe ich meine Historie geschrieben."
119 Jean-Jacques Rousseau, *Confessions*, trans. Angela Scholar (Oxford: Oxford University Press, 2000), 5.
120 Johann Gottfried Herder, "Vom Erkennen und Empfinden der menschlichen Seele" (1778), in *Werke in zehn Bänden*. ed. J. Brummack and M. Bollacher (Frankfurt: Deutsche Klassiker Verlag, 1994), vol. 4, 342.

Herder's is certainly one of the most incisive contributions to the theory of autobiography. In 1802, Daniel Jenisch even published a theory of such *Lebensbeschreibungen* in which he distinguished between "poetic-ideal" and "historical-real" life-descriptions,[121] and divided biography into simply historical, narrative, and pragmatic.[122]

One of the most important autobiographical narratives of the early German Enlightenment was that of Adam Bernd (1676–1748) in 1738.[123] By examining Bernd's autobiography, one can begin to discern the shift from a primarily moral-religious-centered narrative of the "fall" into madness toward the psychologically minded narratives of the late eighteenth century. The origin of his suffering is identified in the early parts of his life description. He attributed his thick and black blood (*dickes und schwarzes Blut*) to the trauma of the Silesian wars as he lay in his mother's womb. Instead of a form of protection, the womb becomes a place of trauma, an incubator of suffering, and a determinant in his ongoing suffering and illness. "For in the years in which my mother held me under her heart began the incursion of Sweden into Pomerania against Silesia, and the inhabitants of Silesia fell under fear and terror."[124] Here the external war and its trauma identify the causes of his disease, the historical circumstance viewed as the etiology of the illness. Listen to Bernd's description of his youth:

> the whole house was filled with such fear, rage, misery, anxiety and apprehension and despair that I couldn't help but think that they would kill me out of rage [...] the hard words, as they were expressed against me, the evil wishes, the prophecies concerned my soul for a long time afterwards, as I feared a curse and malediction by God himself concerning my future life in this world.[125]

---

121 Daniel Jenisch, *Theorie der Lebensbeschreibung* (Berlin: Frölich, 1802).
122 See Gunter Niggl, *Geschichte der deutschen Autobiographie im 18. Jahrhundert* (Stuttgart: Metzler, 1977), esp. 168–170.
123 Adam Bernd, *Eigene Lebensbeschreibung samt einer aufrichtigen Entdeckung und deutlichen Beschreibung einer der größten, obwohl grossen theils noch unbekannten Leibes- und Gemüths-Plage* (Leipzig: J. S. Heinsius, 1738).
124 Bernd, *Eigene Lebensbeschreibung*, 19.
125 Bernd, *Eigene Lebensbeschreibung*, 73–74: "so war das ganze Haus und alles mit solcher Furcht, Zorn, Jammer, Angst und Zagen und Verzweifelung angefuellt, daß ich nicht anders meinte, sie würden mich vor Zorn tödten [...] die harten Worte, so sie gegen mich ausgestossen, die bösen Wünsche, und Prophezeiungen [..] haben eine lange Zeit hernach meine Seele aufs Höchste bekümmert, indem ich lauter Fluch und Unsegen von mein zukünftiges Leben in der Welt deshalben von Gott befürchtete."

This history of "sin" or *Sündengeschichte* begins when Bernd becomes a member of a circle of juvenile delinquents who drink and visit prostitutes. His becomes a story of transgression and then of grace and resurrection: "The terrible example of a human being who had given himself over to the devil, and is wretchedly brought back to the right path."[126] He describes in fine detail the melancholia which overtakes not merely his mind, but his body, expressing itself in overheated and thick blood and constipation in the bowels: "The affliction of the mind had also, for all appearances, corrupted my body, as much as it had seemed healthy to me, so that now the melancholy found a basis and place in the heated and thick blood in which the constipated viscera resided, which had been caused by the peristent anxiety."[127] The additional trauma of the death of his father and youngest sister in December of 1695 precipitated a strengthening of his Christianity: "that these two instances of death contributed to the strengthening of my new virtuous way of thinking."[128]

Rhetorically, Bernd's work exhibits a distinctive formal-demonstrative structure; he seeks to show the etiology of certain forms of psychic illness: "How the blood is, so too are the life-spirits, the nerve-fluids."[129] The real culprit is the miserable constitution of the body (*die elende Beschaffenheit des Leibes*), the bodily determination which carries within itself the possibility of the illness and the origins of the disease when triggered by external circumstance – happenstance and accidents [*Zufälle, Unfälle*]. However, the narrative is still framed within Christian eschatology and the story of redemption and salvation (*Erlösungsgeschichte*); how the soul is led astray by the body, the flesh; driven to pathological forms of fantasy and imagination through inner constitution and external accident or chance (the war of Sweden against Silesia, the death of the Father and the Sister), and, through crisis and grace, able to return to a state of health through renewed piety. Weak souls, especially those of *Melancholici* and *Hypochrondriaci*, are particularly subject to a sickly imagination (*kränkliche Einbildungskraft*), vulnerable to attacks and illnesses of the mind. Indeed, Bernd fears that the reader will become ill by

---

126 Bernd, *Eigene Lebensbeschreibung*, 115: "Das schreckliche Exempel des Menschen, der sich dem Teufel verschrieben, und kuemmerlich wieder zu rechte gebracht worden."
127 Bernd, *Eigene Lebensbeschreibung*, 18: "Die Gemüthsplage hatte auch, allem Ansehen nach, meinen Leib, so gesund auch derselben meinem Beduenken nach war, verderbet, so dass jetzt die MELANCHOLIE auch einen Grund und Stuetze in dem hitzig und dicken Gebluete in denen verstopften Vsceribus fand, welche durch die anhaltende Angst waren verursachet worden."
128 Bernd, *Eigene Lebensbeschreibung*, 25: "daß diese zwei Todes-faelle in meinem Christentum zur Befestigung der neuen guten Gemuethsart ein grosses beigetragen."
129 Bernd, *Eigene Lebensbeschreibung*, Vorrede: "Wie das Gebluete ist, so sind auch die Lebensgeister, oder der Nervensaft."

reading what he has written in his autobiography, and stresses the necessity of the bourgeois values of natural pleasure (*natürliches Vergnügen*), great courage (*großer Muth*), heart (*Herz*), bravery (*Tapferkeit*), steadfastness (*Standhaftigkeit*), honor (*Ehre*), and especially friendship (*Freundschaft*). He attacks the new naturalism, i.e., the scientific materialism of the *Gelehrten*, saying that it is like a cancer that has infected the scholars' way of writing: "The desperate naturalism has, like a cancer, eaten around itself to such an extent that the writing style of the learned have been infected by it."[130]

I have cited Bernd's *Lebenbeschreibung* at length not to draw a connection between this autobiographical narrative and the modern psychological case history, but rather to show a discontinuity, their historical difference with respect to form, procedure, and purpose. Bernd's *Lebenbeschreibung* does not concern the uniqueness or the individuality of the case; rather, it enlists a rather typical religious, specifically Christian framework to plot his fall into mental illness, the crisis that leads to a renewed Christian faith, and the resulting rejuvenation of the "healthy soul." In short, it relies on and is framed within a meta-narrative of salvation.[131] Instead of describing the experience through direct observation and narration, it draws on two discourses in particular that had powerful currency in the early Enlightenment in Germany: first, the medical discourse of the "nerve fluids" (*Nervensaft*) and the brain (*Gehirn*) as the "seat" of the human soul, and secondly, the critique of the inwardly directed stringent Pietism that dictated a withdrawal from the world and a return to a more fundamental, more rigorous, internal religiosity.[132] As apparently antithetical as these might seem to us now, they were perfectly compatible in Early German Enlightenment thinking regarding mental illness. In opposition to the Deism prevalent in England and the materialism characteristic of the radical Enlightenment in France, the German Enlightenment, at least a significant strand of it, was perfectly comfortable with a strong, albeit, unorthodox and

---

130 Bernd, *Eigene Lebensbeschreibung*, Vorrede: "Der verzweifelte Naturalismus hat, wie der Krebs, so weit um sich gefressen, dass auch die Schreibart der Gelehrten damit angestecket worden." On Bernd's attack on materialism, see also Roy Porter, *Patients and Practitioners: Lay Perceptions of Medicine in Pre-Industrial Society* (Cambridge: Cambridge University Press, 2003), 200–201.
131 Here, I rely on Hayden White, *Metahistory: The Historical Imagination in Nineteenth Century Europe* (Baltimore: Johns Hopkins University Press, 1973), specifically, the very idea of "emplotment."
132 Barbara Thums, *Aufmerksamkeit. Wahrnehmung und Selbstbegründung von Brockes bis Nietzsche* (München: Wilhelm Fink, 2008), 82–83 seeks to show a premonition of an aesthetic appreciation of the sensate cognition of people and things in Bernd's text.

unconventional religious belief and scientific models of the nervous system and the mind.

Other autobiographies, such as Maimon's *Lebensgeschichte* or the autobiographical novel à clef *Anton Reiser* by Moritz, could be enlisted for an argument that the autobiography is just as, if not even more significant in, Foucault's "history of subjectivization." There is, however, a central and decisive difference between the two genres. While there might be and often is psychologically salient content in these autobiographies, their true purpose is to draw the larger arc around a life, to show continuity, to connect the individual moments and create a unified or unifying trajectory of a self, not to address a particular *event* (illness, mental or otherwise) with the expressed aim of uncovering the psychological reasons for the event. This is precisely what narrative psychological case histories do. On this view, autobiographies are directed at totality, closure, and general meaning-endowment, whereas cases, as Jolles already suggested in 1930, "*pose a question.*"[133] They challenge norms, categories, and conceptual frameworks. Cases involve an "I" or "self" that has experienced something unique, particular, "unheard of," *how* it has experienced it, and how that experience has *impacted* that I or self in a significant way. If this is so, the psychological case history uniquely poses the question of selfhood itself, as it is solely concerned with a unique, defining event or occurrence that calls for psychological or "depth" interpretation and understanding. In the following, I argue that such a model begins in Germany in the second half of the eighteenth century.

The early authors and advocates of psychological case histories, Moritz, Herz, and Schiller in particular, absorbed such autobiographical writing, as well as the theory of the novel advanced by Christian Friedrich von Blanckenburg in his *Versuch über den Roman* (1774), which seized on the psychological and anthropological dimensions of the novel as an "inner history of a human being" (*innere Geschichte des Menschen*).[134] According to Blanckenburg, the central object of the novel was the concrete, real existence of a person (*Seyn des Menschen*), the internal world of the individual (*inneren Zustand[es]*). The whole point of the genre is to represent this internal history of the individual, her unique thoughts and sensibilities. For this, Blanckenburg argued, one would have to examine the self-emergence of this individual, his or her *self-formation* or *Bildung* – how the individual develops to become what she truly is. This study suggests that while the novel and the autobiography represent two historically

---

133 Jolles, *Einfache Formen*, 191.
134 Christian Friedrich von Blanckenburg, *Versuch über den Roman* (Leipzig und Liegnitz: David Siegerts Witwe, 1774), in *Romantheorie. Dokumentation ihrer Geschichte in Deutschland 1620–1880*, ed. E. Lämmert (Köln and Berlin: Kohlhammer, 1971).

significant forms of self-constitution, the psychological case history possesses a special importance because of its laser-like focus on the individuality of the individual and a life-altering (or shattering) event, its bracketing-off of the broader social-historical canvas in order to concentrate on the specific vicissitudes of the soul at a singular synchronic moment.

In the introduction, we noted how, following Kant's devastating critique of empirical psychology, scientific psychology, and nascent psychiatry essentially displaced *Erfahrungsseelenkunde* and its essential "evidence" – the individual psychological case history – in the first decades of the nineteenth century. Demands of scientific rigor and even quantification became ubiquitous. Johann Friedrich Herbart (1776–1841) found Kant's critique of a "scientific" psychology to be misguided and advocated for precisely what Kant had deemed impossible: the application of quantitative methods in studying the human mind. In the emerging discipline of psychiatry, Johann Christian Reil (1759–1813), Friedrich Nasse (1778–1851), the jurist Johann Christoph Hoffbauer (1766–1827), and Johann Christian August Heinroth (1773–1843) all sought to place the study of the mind and mental illness on firmer scientific ground. It would be erroneous, however, to say that the narrative psychological case history was simply eclipsed or superseded by the scientific psychology, psychiatry, and the forensic science of the nineteenth century. Nasse's *Zeitschrift für psychische Ärzte* (1818–1824) contained approximately ten narrative psychological "cases" each year. As he wrote in the opening report of the first issue of 1818:

> In order to continue what has already been suggested and put forward, to impart that which is communicable, and to disclose that which has been locked up – that is what our journal is going to concern itself with. It will therefore be engaged in presenting scientific investigations, observations brought forward by psychologists and physicians concerning mental illness, narratives of individual strange cases of illnesses, and their attempted cures, with or without success, and reports of autopsies of the mentally ill.[135]

---

[135] Friedrich Nasse, "Vorbericht" in *Zeitschrift für psychische Ärzte*, ed. Friedrich Nasse in Verbindung mit den Herren von Schenmacher, Grohmann, Haindorf, Hayner, Heinroth, Henke, Hoffbauer, Hohnbaum, Horn, Maass, Pienietz, Ruer, Vering, und Weiss herausgegeben von Fr. Nasse. (Leipzig: Carl Cnobloch, 1818–1824), 1.1 (1818): 13–14: "Das Angeregte fortzuleiten, das Mittheilbare zur Mittheilung zu bringen, das Verschlossene zu öffnen, soll nun unsere Zeitschrift bemüht sein. Sie wird daher wissenschaftliche Untersuchungen, von Psychologen und von Ärzten angestellte Beobachtungen über das psychische Krankseyn, Erzählungen von einzelnen merkwürdigen Krankheitsfällen mit oder ohne Erfolg der versuchten Heilung, Berichte von Leichenöffnungen irre gewesener Personen, zu solchem Endzweck darzubringen habe."

In the second issue of that year, we read titles of narrative psychological case histories such as "Example of a mania that was the result of a chronic disease of the lungs," "three cases of madness in children," "observation of a case in which a woman became black during the night as a result of a serious vexation," "a case of melancholy and mania with a felicitous outcome." The terms and phrases employed here in the first "psychiatric" journal – *Krankengeschichte, Geschichte eines Falles, Beobachtung, Beispiel, Fallstudie* – echo both the vocabulary and the ethos of the empirical psychology of the late eighteenth century. However, the discourse strikes a decidedly scientific tone: "the researcher ought to grasp mental illness itself" (*der Forschende soll den Wahnsinn ergreifen*) writes Nasse,[136] and the *abnormality* of case is radically juxtaposed to the "principle of *organic life*, and the regularity with which we designate the healthy state, which has been interrupted or destroyed."[137] This is not to say that the journal did not sometimes indulge in odd reflections, bizarre speculations, and even admit articles that remind one of an earlier era – one such contribution by Dr. L. Valentin read "Beobachtungen über die Wirkung des glühenden Eisens zur Heilung des Irrenseyns" (*Observations on the Effect of the Glowing Hot Rod in the Healing of Madness*).[138] The discourse of "normality" and "abnormality," and the "deviation" from the norm, however, appears regularly in the pages of the journal, distinguishing the new scientific horizon of expectation of the new psychiatry from the empirical-experiential psychology of Moritz, Herz, Schiller in the late eighteenth century.[139]

Later in the nineteenth century, Johann Ludwig Caspar's *Klinische Novellen zur gerichtlichen Medicin: nach eigenen Erfahrungen* of 1863, a key work in forensic psychiatry, presented a *Casuistik* of "examples" for each of the conditions and crimes enumerated.[140] In the preface to this work, Caspar cited Michael Bernhard Valentin's *Corpus juris medico-legale* of 1722 and its accompanying quarto volume

---

136 Nasse, "Vorbericht," in *Zeitschrift für psychische Ärzte* 1.1 (1818) 15: "der Forschende soll den Wahnsinn ergreifen."
137 Johann Haslam, "Über die psychische Behandlung der Wahnsinnigen," *Zeitschrift für psychische Ärzte* 2.1 (1819): 105.
138 Dr. L Valentin, "Beobachtungen über die Wirkung des glühenden Eisens zur Heilung des Irrenseyns," *Zeitschrift für psychische Ärzte* 4.1 (1821): 189.
139 Georges Canguilhem, *The Normal and the Pathological* (New York: Zone Books, 1991), first charted this territory. It is further articulated precisely by Werner Sohn, "Bio-Macht und Normaliserungsgesellschaft – Versuch einer Annäherung," in *Normalität und Abweichung: Studien zur Theorie und Geschichte der Normalisierungsgesellschaft*, ed. Werner Sohn und Herbert Mertens (Opladen und Wiesbaden: Westdeutscher Verlag, 1999), 9–30.
140 Johann Ludwig Caspar, *Klinische Novellen zur gerichtlichen Medicin: nach eigenen Erfahurngen* (Berlin: Hirschwald, 1863).

Novellae medico-legales as his models for the term *Novellen* with the following justification:

> For I, too, intend in the following work to offer scientifically annotated experiences through casuistic observations which, without diminishing the purpose and the scope of the handbook, could not be considered either at all or not in the volume as their importance demanded.[141]

Caspar emphasized the originality of the observations and cases in his handbook. This lent evidentiary credibility to his undertaking. Carl Westphal, Wilhelm Griesinger's successor as the director of the psychiatric and neurological clinic at the Charité in 1869 and the founder of the first out-patient clinic for nervous disorders, also employed his own narrative, psychologically-minded case histories in his revolutionary article on homosexuality "The Contrary Sexual Sensation: Symptom of a Neuropathic [Psychopathic] Condition," which appeared in the *Archiv für Psychiatrie und Nervenkrankheiten* in Berlin in 1869.[142] In 1857, the forensic physician Ferdinand Hauska, Professor for State Medicine at the Medical-Surgical Josephina in Wien, published his *Compendium der gerichtlichen Arzneikunde* (*Compendium of Forensic Medicine*),[143] in which he developed a model and prescription for the examination/investigation of the "mental state of the individual" (*Geisteszustand eines Individuums*). With its emphasis on the speaking subject, language, and narrative, this text bears all of the marks of the psychological case history traced in the following pages. In the place of the empirical, visual method centered on observation, the forensic physician was to become a kind of *biographer* of the accused, keeping a diary or journal focused on the *language and expression* of the patient.

> The examination protocol of the investigation concerning someone who is mentally ill takes the form of a *diary* in which the observing physicians enter everything that they observe on a daily basis of the corporeal and psychic symptoms, along with the exact word-for-word citation of meaningful expressions of the ill person.[144]

---

141 Johann Ludwig Caspar, Preface, in *Klinische Novellen*, iv: "Denn auch ich beabsichtige in den nachfolgenden Arbeiten wissenschaftliche, durch casuistischer Beiläge eigener Beobachtungen erläuterte Erfahrungen zur Erörterung zu bringen, welche im Handbuch ohne dem Zweck und Umfang eines solchen zu schaden, theils gar nicht, teils nicht in dem Maße, erwogen werden konnten, wie es deren Wichtigkeit erfordert."
142 Carl Friedrich Otto Westphal, "Die conträre Sexualempfindung: Symptom eines neuropathischen (psychopathischen) Zustandes," *Archiv für Psychiatrie und Nervenkrankheiten* 2.1 (1869): 73–108.
143 Ferdinand Hauska, *Compendium der gerichtlichen Arzneikunde* (Wien: Braumüller, 1857); 2nd revised ed. (Wien: Braumüller, 1869), 173.
144 Hauska, *Compendium der gerichtlichen Arzneikunde* (1869), 172: "Das Untersuchungsprotokoll über einen Geisteskranken bekommt die Form eines *Tagebuches*, in welches die beobachtenden

Caspar and Hauska both renew and continue the genre of the narrative psychological case history born in the last decades of the eighteenth century with its emphasis on language, narrative, and a description of the lived-experience of the patient. Hauska goes so far as to recommend that the physician assign essays for the patient to write. The way of writing, the punctuation, the grammatical structure, and the choice of expressions of the patient provide "a deep insight" for Hauska into the "mental constitution of the individual."[145] The point was to bring the individual and the illness – the individual in its uniqueness, precisely in its deviation from the norm – to language; to induce him or her speak/write about his/her own mental constitution, with the hope that this would reveal something about the origin, causes and development of the condition. Simultaneously, we see how, in the solicited acts of writing and speaking, in the very act of articulation demanded by the protocol, the individual constitutes *itself* and in this manner becomes a *case*.

Ärzte Tag für Tag alles eintragen was sie von den körperlichen und psychischen Symptomen beobachtet haben, mit wörtlicher Citierung bedeutungsvoller Äusserungen des Kranken."
145 Hauska, *Compendium der gerichtlichen Arzneikunde* (1869), 171: "einen tiefen Einblick in die geistige Verfassung des Individuums gestatten."

2 Theorizing the Psychological Case History

> It still strikes me myself as strange that the case histories I write should read like *novellas* and that, as one might say, they lack the serious stamp of science.
>
> Freud, *Studies in Hysteria*[1]

> The case is no longer, as in casuistry or jurisprudence, a set of circumstances defining an act and capable of modifying a rule; it is the individual as he may be described and judged, measured, compared with others, *in his very individuality*.
>
> Foucault, *Discipline and Punish*[2]

In 1986, the philosopher Ian Hacking published an essay with the provocative title "Making Up People."[3] What he meant, of course, was not that people are chimerical, simply invented "fictions" or, even worse, mere fantasies. He was pressing for what he called a *dynamic nominalism*, the position that "human beings and human acts come into being hand in hand with our invention of categories labeling them."[4] Hacking was neither alone nor the first to propose such a view. Michel Foucault, who influenced both Hacking and Arnold Davidson's view that the categories, terms, classifications, and labels employed at certain moments in history for specific purposes have everything to do with how a person is seen and how a person sees *themselves*, had already espoused such a theory in *The History of Sexuality* of 1978. Hacking said he thought there was no general story to be told about "making up people." "Each category has its own history," he wrote, meaning that we have to look at each individual category, rubric, statistical grouping, and social "labeling" historically, and then examine its purported intention, classificatory sweep, and effects. However, both he and Foucault proposed that we look carefully at two "vectors" in each case: "One is the vector of labeling from above, from a community of experts who create a 'reality' that some people make their own. Different from this is the vector of the autonomous behavior of the person so labeled."[5] He also made explicit Foucault's distinction in *The History of Sexuality* between an "anatomo-politics of the body,"

---

[1] Sigmund Freud, *Studies on Hysteria* (New Tork: Basic Books, 2000), 160–161.
[2] Michel Foucault, *Discipline and Punish: The Birth of the Prison*. Trans. Alan Sheridan (New York: Random House, 1979), 191.
[3] Ian Hacking, "Making Up People," In *Reconstructing Individualism: Autonomy, Individuality and the Self in Western Thought*, ed. Thomas C. Heller et al. (Stanford, CA: Stanford University Press, 1986), 222–236.
[4] Hacking, "Making Up People," 235.
[5] Hacking, "Making Up People," 233.

centered on the individual as a living, speaking, working, socially interacting entity, and the "biopolitics of the population," concerned with macro-analyses of the "sciences of the state": birth, death, marriage, crime, disease, famine, deviant behaviors, education, unemployment, and the other facts that become the grist of statisticians, civil institutions, and government bureaucracies.[6] Taken together, the discipline of bodies and the regulation of populations formed for Foucault a useful way of understanding the exercise of power in modernity, roughly since the eighteenth century. The individual "case" and its scriptural medium, the case history or case study (in German, *Fallgeschichte, Krankengeschichte, Fallerzählung, Fallstudie*)[7] constituted for Foucault a vital aspect of this power apparatus: the attempt of a scientific study and systematic knowledge of the human in its many forms became the key to both a grasp of the individual in its individuality (and, by extension, deviance, aberration, anomaly) and the analysis required by the new "science of the state." As Roy Porter put it when writing about the emerging new model of madness as a *psychological condition* in the eighteenth century: "The case history approach this entailed demanded the transformation of the old craft of minding the insane into the pursuit of systematic psychological observation."[8]

This brief exposé might give us a glimpse into why one might want to study narrative psychological case histories, a "minor" psychological-anthropological genre, as it emerges in the second half of the eighteenth century. As the historian of science Gianna Pomata has written about case histories in general, they constitute what she calls an *epistemic genre*; they give "literary form to an intellectual endeavor and in so doing they shape and channel the cognitive practice of attention"; they provide "a framework for gathering, describing and organizing the raw materials of experience."[9] The psychological case history is a meta-genre

---

[6] Michel Foucault, *The History of Sexuality. An Introduction*, trans. Robert Hurley (New York: Random House, 1978), vol. 1, 139.

[7] Stefan Goldmann has noted that the term *Fallgeschichte* does not appear in the eighteenth century, and has argued that it is anachronistic to speak of *Fallgeschichten* at this time. However, a survey of the journals of the late eighteenth century shows that members of the educated, literate public were in fact thinking and writing about *Fälle*, with at least forty-three entries concerning the narration of individual cases, specifically using the term *Fall*. Furthermore, the term *Krankengeschichte* is a transliteration of *historia morbi*, and this term refers back to the very traditional medical case history. See Stefan Goldmann, "Kasus – Krankengeschichte – Novelle," in *Fakta, und kein moralisches Geschwätz*, ed. Sheila Dickson et al. (Göttingen: Wallstein, 2011), 33–64.

[8] Roy Porter, *Madness. A Brief History* (Oxford: Oxford University Press, 2002), 129.

[9] Gianna Pomata, "Observation Rising: Birth of an Epistemic Genre, 1500–1650," in *Histories of Scientific Observation*, ed. Lorraine Daston and Elizabeth Lunbeck (Chicago: University of Chicago Press, 2011), 45–80.

that crosses traditional scientific, literary, historical, and philosophical disciplinary boundaries: history and fiction, science and literature, medicine and narrative, law and psychology, and cultural and intellectual history.

Apart from the significance for the literary production of the period, we find a number of other compelling reasons to explore the emergence of early modern psychological case histories. The study of case histories allows us to do the history of medicine "from below," as Porter suggested.[10] We encounter, often in the form of first-hand reports and descriptions, and sometimes in ego-documents or first-person narratives written by the patient, the psychologically-minded physicians, or criminals themselves, how the illness is constituted, construed, felt, and represented. We learn how it is *experienced*, and the discrepancies between the "lived-experience" of the illness and its material and institutional inscription, and, in turn, between such narratives and the literary works they gave birth to. As noted in the introduction, narrative in this sense is conceived not simply as a chronicling of events or emplotment, but as the "representation of experientiality"[11] and the essential difference, rupture, or breach the individual's narrative introduces with respect to the ordinary, expected, and predictable.[12]

Prior to exploring the various theoretical contributions that have been brought to bear on the case, one should consider first how an event, incident, or circumscribed experience is constituted such that it becomes apt or fitting as being a "case" whatsoever. For something to count as a case – at least since the eighteenth century – the most basic criteria seems to have been that it must be *interesting*, or, as Karl Philipp Moritz stated in 1783, *interessant*, or *denkwürdig*, "worthy of thinking about," something that catches our interest, provokes thought and raises questions. It has to *stand out*, be suggestive or extraordinary, unique or peculiar. Such a determination immediately differentiates the "case" from an *example* (*Beispiel*) or a mere token; its entire point is its deviation from *typical* cases that preceded it. Such *interesting cases* must be distinguished, I would argue, not only from the curiosities and monstrosities of the fifteenth and sixteenth centuries, but also from the short medical case histories or *Krankengeschichten* of the great physicians of early modern Europe in 1600–1750: Felix Platter, Thomas Sydenham, Herman Boerhaave, Friedrich Hoffmann, and Georg Ernest Stahl. Their cases exemplified a specific type of illness; they were used heuristically to provide an example of a *type*, to shore up a theory, or to

---

10 Roy Porter, "The Patient's View: Doing Medical History from Below," *Theory and Society* 14.2 (1985): 175–198.
11 Monika Fludernik, *An Introduction to Narratology*, trans. Patricia Häusler-Greenfield and Monika Fludernik (London: Routledge, 2009), 6.
12 Jerome Bruner, "The Narrative Construction of Reality," *Critical Inquiry* 18.1 (1991): 4.

demonstrate the success of a specific therapeutics or treatment.[13] The modern case as it emerges at the end of the eighteenth century, on the contrary, existed on the cusp of the unintelligible; it was an *individual* case for which, in a manner analogous to aesthetic experience in Immanuel Kant, no adequate concept, category, or theory could be found. For this very reason, cases can tell us much about what a specific historical culture posits as being *interesting, compelling, worthy of study and scientific discussion,* what a specific historical culture constitutes as an *object of truth or inquiry*. It is no coincidence that the very notion of "the interesting" (*das Interessante, das Interessierende*) appears as an *aesthetic category* in the writings of Johann Georg Sulzer, Christian Garve, and Friedrich Schlegel precisely at the time that forms the focal point of the present study: individual, historically situated and -constituted unique human behavior and action that defies concepts and categories became the object not merely of medical and juridical writing, but of aesthetic literary works as well.[14]

*

As we begin to probe why and how a particular sub-genre of the case history, the *narrative psychological case history*, emerged as a model and *modeling* of individuality in the eighteenth century, we must confront the question as to why this specific development takes place in Germany. There are several reasons why the preponderance of books, collections, discussions, journals, and the theory of this genre occurred in the German territories. First, as Fernando Vidal has pointed out:

> In the eighteenth century, psychology blossomed particularly in Germany. This can be attributed to the history and pedagogical requirements of the Protestant Universities, in which prevailed a tradition of metaphysical investigation; many German philosophers

---

13 This goes back to the fourteenth century, when the new genre of the collection of medical *consilia* became the staple of physicians exchanging information on therapies and remedies. This genre was then expanded in the fifteenth and sixteenth centuries to include medical epistles and *consultatoria*. See Nancy Siraisi, *History, Medicine, and the Traditions of Renaissance Learning* (Ann Arbor: University of Michigan Press, 2007), 67–68.
14 Christian Garve, "Einige Gedanken über das Interessierende" (1779), in *Philosophische Schriften über literarische, ästhetische, und gesellschaftliche Gegenstände*, ed. Kurt Wölfel (Stuttgart: Metzler, 1974), vol. 1, 161–348. On the history of this category and concept, see: Aurel Kolnai, "On the Concept of the Interesting," in *Aesthetics in the Modern World*, ed. Harold Osborne (London: Thames & Hudson, 1968), 166–187; Kurt Wölfel, "Interesse/interessant," in *Ästhetische Grundbegriffe*, ed. Karlheinz Barck (Stuttgart and Weimar: Metzler, 2001), vol. 3, 138–174; Altrud Dumont, "Das Interessante – Theorie und narrative Praxis. Friedrich Schlegel und E.T.A. Hoffmann," *Weimarer Beiträge* 38.3 (1992): 430–447; and finally Eberhard Ostermann, "Das Interessante als Element ästhetischer Authentizität," in *Authentizität als Darstellung*, ed. Jan Berg et al. (Hildesheim: Universitätsverlag, 1997), 197–215.

and psychologists, contrary to their counterparts in England and in France, refused to reduce metaphysics to a sensualist theory of the origin of knowledge and pursued research into first principles. The deductive schemas and "geometric method" were abandoned, but not the imperative to arrive at fundamental universal concepts. Empirical psychology could provide the starting point for this kind of research, even if not its outcome.[15]

While we disagree with Vidal's assessment of empirical psychology – specifically that it "pursued research into first principles" and sought to arrive at "universal concepts" – it is true that, in Germany, with very few exceptions, metaphysics was not "banned" or "shunned." In fact, the belief in the inner soul was viewed as perfectly compatible with the project of knowledge of that soul based on empirical observation, introspection, reflection, and precise description. Second, the strong tradition of Pietism in Germany created fertile ground for an inwardly directed, self-examining attitude with its imperative of the self-cultivation of inner piety, one which witnesses a depth and complexity of the concern for the *narration* of the individual.[16] Third, the theory of the novel as presenting the unique "inner history of a human being," the emergence of the "psychological" novel in particular (Goethe's *Werther* [1774] and Moritz's *Anton Reiser* [1785–1790]) aimed at the inner life and emotional world of a unique person, and the theory of the novella all contributed to a new sensibility regarding the possibilities and function of narrative. Finally, the corpus of psychological medicine, centered in Halle and inflected there by the discipline of aesthetics, deepened and focalized the inquiry of empirical psychology. It is within this specifically German constellation that the narrative psychological case history achieves its modern defining form and structure, introducing a unique, vital style and rhetoric into the construction of modern literature that has proven to be powerful and enduring. It is in the German tradition that the psychological case history explicitly emerges both as an aesthetic phenomenon and as a literary model for the construction of the "unique" – and often pathological – individual.

*

When Freud, one hundred years after the texts and figures analyzed in this study and drawing on the narrative psychiatric case-histories of the nineteenth

---

15 Fernando Vidal, *The Sciences of the Soul: The Early Modern Origins of Psychology*, trans. Saskia Brown (Chicago and London: University of Chicago Press, 2011), 110.
16 Kurt Danziger has referred to the "national style" of psychology and psychiatry. See *Naming the Mind: How Psychology Found Its Language* (London: Sage, 1997), and other work by him. Danziger specifically refers to the strange pairing of experimental physiology, narrative psychiatry, and forensic psychopathology in the German-Speaking areas in the nineteenth century.

century, chose the genre as the vehicle for presenting much of his most incisive clinical work, he implicitly drew on its reflective capability and narrative stance. Freud's psychoanalytic case histories have captured the imaginations and incurred the wrath of writers, critics, and philosophers alike. They are the subject of an extensive literature.[17] Freud's cordoning-off of the "case history" in *Studies in Hysteria* (1892) in particular has led to much speculation on the truth status of Freud's narrative case histories or *Krankengeschichten*.[18] "It still strikes me myself as strange," Freud wrote, "that the case histories I write should read like short stories and that, as one might say, they lack the serious stamp of science."[19] Freud's case histories were not *chronicles*, mere notes or

---

[17] Anthony Clare, "Freud's Cases: The Clinical Basis of Psychoanalysis," in *The Anatomy of Madness: Essays in the History of Psychiatry. People and Ideas*, ed. W. F. Bynum et al. (London and New York, 1985), vol. 1, 271–88; Frank Sulloway, "Reassessing Freud's Case Histories: The Social Construction of Psychoanalysis," *Isis: Journal of the History of Science* 82.2 (1991): 245–275; repr. *Freud and the History of Psychoanalysis*, ed. Toby Gelfand and John Kerr (London and Hillsdale, NJ: Taylor & Francis, 1992), 153–192; Sander L. Gilman, *The Case of Freud. Medicine and Identity at the Fin de Siécle* (Baltimore: Johns Hopkins University Press, 1993); Steven Marcus, "Freud and Dora: Story, History, Case History," in *Freud and the Culture of Psychoanalysis: Studies in the Transition from Victorian Humanity to Modernity* (Englewood Cliffs, NJ: Prentice Hall, 1987); Charles Bernheimer and Claire Kahane, eds., *In Dora's Case: Freud, Hysteria, Feminism* (New York: Columbia University Press, 1985); Gisela Steinlechner, *Fallgeschichten: Krafft-Ebing, Panizza, Freud, Tausk* (Wien: WUV-Universitatsverlag, 1995); Ulrike Hoffmann-Richter and Asmus Finzen, "Die psychiatrische Krankengeschichte – eine vernachlässigte Quelle," *BIOS* 11 (1998): 280–297; and Jan E. Goldstein, *Console and Classify: The French Psychiatric Profession in the Nineteenth Century* (Chicago: University of Chicago Press, 2002).

[18] Dorrit Cohn, "Freud's Case Histories and the Question of Fictionality," in *Telling Facts: History and Narration in Psychoanalysis*, ed. Joseph Smith (Baltimore: Johns Hopkins University Press, 1992), 21–47; repr. in *The Distinction of Fiction* (Baltimore: Johns Hopkins University Press, 2000). At the most critical end of the spectrum, Frank Sulloway has urged that Freud's case histories were little more than narrative excuses for Freud to expound his psychoanalytic theory: "Freud's case histories are rampant with censorship, distortions, highly dubious 'reconstructions,' and exaggerated claims.... The destruction of history was an essential part of becoming and remaining a great hero in the eyes of posterity. Freud actively cultivated the 'unknowable' about himself in order to set himself apart from the non-heroic component of humanity." Sulloway, "Reassessing Freud's Case Histories," 245–275.

[19] Sigmund Freud and Joseph Breuer, *Studien über Hysterie* (Frankfurt: Fischer Verlag, 1991), 180: "Ich bin nicht immer Psychotherapeut gewesen, sondern bin bei Lokaldiagnosen und Elektroprognostik erzogen worden wie andere Neuropathologen, und es berührt mich selbst noch eigentümlich, dass die Krankengeschichten, die ich schreibe, wie Novellen zu lesen sind und daß Sie sozusagen des ernsten Gepräges der Wissenschaftlichkeit entbehren." Freud continues that he consoles himself with the fact that it is the nature of the object itself, and not his preference, that makes it so.

observations, not exact reports or recordings, as he himself admitted, but rather highly stylized "stories," narratives that not only presented the history of the clinical signs of the illness, the course of therapeutic intervention or treatment (*Behandlungsgeschichte*), but also the history of the pathogenic trauma, the gradual unfolding of the illness and its resolution, and perhaps more importantly, the interjections, commentary, reflections, and speculations of the analyst. They are replete with digressions, theoretical observations, interpretations, hypotheses, suggestions, and queries. Indeed, Freud often shifts narrative stances from that of the observing psychoanalyst to the *focalized perception* of the subject of the case history him or herself at the primal scene.[20] At the imaginary primal scene of the psychoanalytic case history, in other words, we already have multiple narrative stances, layers of storytelling, and the implied closure of the resolution, in which the pathogenic "kernel" or "knot" is, if not unraveled, at least set to language, and through this process, the symptom(s) "lifted."

Freud's case histories also contain later versions or retrospective commentary, making the case history itself a tiered, archival historical document. Such "case histories," Freud writes in the same paragraph, ought to be judged as *"psychiatric case histories"*[21] with the difference that *his* case histories have the advantage that they display "the intimate relation between the history of suffering and the symptoms of illness."[22] Freud experienced his decisive turn towards psychiatry in Paris as a student of Jean-Martin Charcot's. He was, like most neuropathologists of the time, trained in neurology. To be sure, Charcot utilized the case history as an instrument to present his treatment of hysteria and epilepsy; his case histories and their iconography have all the trappings of science. Charcot employed sequential still photography as part of his case histories to render the symptomology of hysteria *visible*; no doubt he also used this same photography[23]

---

20 Joel Black, *The Reality Effect: Film, Culture and the Graphic Imperative* (New York: Routledge, 2002), 72. A wonderful example of this is Freud's seminal essay "A Child is Being Beaten – A Contribution to the Study of the Origins of Sexual Perversions," *International Journal of Psychoanalysis* 1 (1920): 371–395.
21 Freud and Breuer, *Studien über Hysterie*, 180: "wie psychiatrische Krankengeschichten"; emphasis mine.
22 Freud and Breuer, *Studien über Hysterie*, 180: "die innige Beziehung zwischen Leidensgeschichte und Krankheitssymptome."
23 Jean-Martin Charcot had studied Muybridge's experimentation with still sequential photography and used it in *Iconographie photographique de la Salpêtriere*. See: D. M. Bourneville and P. Regnard, *Iconographie photographique de la Salpêtriere, 1875–81* (Paris: Progrès médical – A. Delahaye, 1875–1881) and the study by Georges Didi-Huberman, *Invention of Hysteria: Charcot and the Photographic Iconography of the Salpêtriere* (Cambridge, MA: MIT Press, 2004).

and the photographic image to lend his case histories the authority of strict observational, empirical-scientific medicine. Beginning with Charcot, they also powerfully fixed such images of the mentally ill in the public imaginary, and incarcerated their "subjects" into reified types, allegorical figures.[24] They are the attempt, *par excellence*, to represent, in as much detail as literally and as physically possible, not only what mental illness *is*, but what it is *like* to be mentally ill, and how it *looks*: the gaze, the gesture, the bodily comportment. As Hacking has written: "Charcot was the great master of the use of the case, especially of an ideal type exemplifying a disorder in a heightened state."[25]

Freud, by stark contrast, used the *narrative case history* to articulate the *aetiology* of neurosis, to spell-out the *pathogenic core* or the *traumatic origin* of neuroses, to establish the discipline of psychoanalysis, which is grounded in narrative, story-telling, communication, and transference from the very beginning.[26] Rather than exemplifying an ideal type, Freud's case histories tell a story of the analysis of a unique individual neurosis. In doing so, he appropriated and transformed a long, rich history of the case history from the medical case descriptions of the seventeenth and eighteenth centuries, the criminal case of the eighteenth and nineteenth century, the narrative psychological cases studied in this book, and the psychiatric case histories of the nineteenth century. In a sense, this book is a genealogy of precisely Freud's claim to disclose, as he put it in *Studies in Hysteria*, "the intimate relation between the history of suffering and the symptoms of illness," his quest to discover and articulate the "pathogenic core" within the field of signs and symptoms displayed by the individual, to track the forms of description, interpretation, and narrative that have governed the writing of psychological case histories.

The pre-history of Freud's psychoanalytic case histories is to be found in the genre of the narrative psychological case history that emerges in the 1780s in Germany, which in turn became the discursive basis of an important genre in literature in the nineteenth century: the *Novella*. The connection to the *Novella*

A very substantial collection of the *Iconographie photographique* is available on the web at http://charcot.bum.jussieu.fr/matiere.php?NF=7

24 Suzanne Regner, *Visuelle Gewalt: Menschenbilder aus der Psychiatrie des 20. Jahrhunderts* (Bielefeld: Transcript Verlag, 2010).

25 Ian Hacking, *Rewriting the Soul: Multiple Personality and the Sciences of Memory* (Princeton, NJ: Princeton University Press, 1995), 187.

26 Freud's case histories are supposed to capture what Charcot's photographs could not: the very historicity, emergence, aetiology of the illness, the therapeutic interventions, and also the resolution of the symptoms.

was established, as we have just noted, by Freud himself when he asserted that his case histories were to be read as novellas.[27] The English translation often renders this as "short-stories," yet Freud knew well and understood the precise genre of the *Novella* to which he was referring. It was a genre with a distinct poetics – Johann Wolfgang Goethe famously said "for what is a novella other than an emergent, unheard of occurrence"[28] – and an incredibly well-established, rich tradition championed by Goethe and others in German literature of the late eighteenth and nineteenth centuries.[29] With a temporally focalized purview and the "unheard of," distinctive, unique event (*Begebenheit*) as its object, the novella became a sister genre to the case history, often enlisting and even cribbing from actual case histories to realize its task. In our reading of Schiller's *Criminal of Lost Honor* (1786), we will return to this genre in our effort to show how the psychological case history is formalized, stylized, and canonized as an integral discursive component of the exploration of a problematic individuality in literature.

The narrative psychological case history, a discursive and scriptural communication, publication and knowledge medium of the late Enlightenment[30] in Germany, provides the link between the nascent modern empirical psychology of the eighteenth century and the psychiatry of the nineteenth.[31] Yet there has

---

27 Freud and Breuer, *Studien über Hysterie*, 180.
28 Johann Peter Eckermann, *Gespräche mit Goethe in den letzten Jahren seines Lebens*, ed. Fritz Bergemann (Frankfurt: Insel, 1981), vol. 1, 207: "denn was ist eine Novelle anders als eine sich ereignete unerhörte Begebenheit."
29 As documented in the rich body of research on the genre: Benno von Wiese, *Novella* (Stuttgart: J. B. Metzler, 1963); John M. Ellis, *Narration in the German Novella* (London and New York: Cambridge University Press, 1974); Martin Swales, *The German Novelle* (Princeton, NJ: Princeton University Press, 1977); Henry H. H. Remak, *Structural Elements of the German Novella from Goethe to Thomas Mann* (New York, Bern, Berlin, and Frankfurt: Peter Lang, 1996).
30 Hans-Joachim Schrimpf, "Das Magazin zur Erfahrungsseelenkunde und sein Herausgeber," *Zeitschrift für deutsche Philologie* 99 (1980): 161–187.
31 Rudolf Behrens and Carsten Zelle, eds., *Der ärztliche Fallbericht. Epistemische Grundlagen und textuelle Strukturen dargestellter Beobachtung* (Wiesbaden: Harrassowitz, 2012); Inka Mülder-Bach and Michael Ott, eds., *Was der Fall ist. Casus und Lapsus* (München: Wilhelm Fink, 2014); Susanne Düwell and Nicolas Pethes, eds., *Fall- Fallgeschichte – Fallstudie. Theorie und Geschichte einer Wissensform* (Frankfurt and New York: Campus, 2014); Carsten Zelle, ed., *Casus. Von Hoffmanns Erzählungen zu Freuds Novellen. Eine Anthologie der Fachprosagattung 'Fallerzählung'* (Hannover: Wehrhahn 2015); Lucia Aschauer et al., eds., *Fallgeschichten. Text- und Wissensform exemplarischer Narrative in der Kultur der Moderne* (Würzburg: Königshausen & Neumann, 2015); and the monograph by Nicolas Pethes, *Literarische Fallgeschichten. Zur Poetik einer epistemischen Schreibweise* (Göttingen: Konstanz University Press, 2016).

been no attempt to create a systematic, theoretically articulated history of the emergence of this genre.[32] Rather, the "case" of the case history has devolved into a mere series of cases, a "collection" of discrete histories, each looking at its theory and practice at various historical junctures.[33] Even the rich interdisciplinary research regarding the anthropology of the German Enlightenment has only recently started to approach the question of the origins and emergence of this important form.[34] The modern psychological case history stands in a complex constellation of literary forms and genres, scientific disciplines, and new emerging discourse forms and media within the public sphere in the eighteenth century. In the literary sphere, one immediately thinks of the confession, autobiography, the criminal story, and the psychological novel.[35] In terms of governing scientific disciplines, we would name Philosophy, Medicine, Psychology, Anthropology, Pedagogy, and the Law. Finally, the new forms of communication and publication, above all the "journal" and book "collections" of case histories created the possibility of the dissemination of such case histories to a broader public beyond the boundaries of the academic and literary worlds. Whereas previously case histories appeared either in compendia or were appended to books – an apparatus to be referred to while reading the main text – case histories in the second half of the eighteenth century became

---

32 A start was made by Andreas Gailus, "A Case of Individuality: Karl Philipp Moritz and the Magazine for Empirical Psychology," *New German Critique* 79 (2000): 67–105; and *"Anton Reiser*, Case History, and the Emergence of Empirical Psychology," in *A New History of German Literature*, ed. David Wellbery et al. (Cambridge, MA: Harvard University Press, 2005), 409–414. Gailus (2000) argues that "the genre of the psychological case history did not emerge from the simple extension of medical discourse to mental problems but from the complex crossings of medical thought, (auto)biographical traditions, and juridical narratives." (73) According to Gailus, Moritz's journal was "the birthplace of the psychological case history." (69)
33 Robert Leventhal, "Der Fall des Falls: Neuere Forschung zur Geschichte und Poetik der Fallerzählung im 18. Jahrhundert, " *Das Achtzehnte Jahrhundert. Zeitschrift der Deutschen Gesellschaft zur Erforschung des 18. Jahrhunderts* 41.1 (2017): 94–102.
34 Johanna Geyer-Kordesch, "Medizinische Fallbeschreibungen und ihre Bedeutung in der Wissensreform des 17. und 18. Jahrhunderts," *Medizin, Gesellschaft, Geschichte* 9 (1990): 7–19; Doris Kaufmann, *Aufklärung, bürgerliche Selbsterfahrung und die Erfindung der Psychiatrie in Deutschland, 1770–1850* (Göttingen: Vandenhoeck & Ruprecht, 1995), 41; Jutta Heinz, *Wissen von Menschen und Erzählen vom Einzelfall. Untersuchungen zum anthropologischen Roman der Spätaufklärung* (Berlin and New York: de Gruyter, 1996). On the crime story, see Holger Dainat, "Der unglückliche Mörder: Zur Kriminalgeschichte der deutschen Spätaufklärung," *Zeitschrift für deutsche Philologie* 107 (1988): 517–541; and Alexander Košenina, "'Tiefere Blicke in das Menschenherz': Schiller und Pitaval," *Germanisch-romanische Monatsschrift* 55.4 (2005): 383–395.
35 Each of these has a rich literature, which I can only point to summarily.

a regular entry in journals, appeared in edited collections, and constituted a subject in their own right. However, in order to understand the peculiarity of the modern psychological case history – after all, that's what the modern case history is all about, *peculiarity* – it is necessary to see how these disparate forces converge to create the conditions of the possibility of this uniquely modern genre.

In 1996, the historian of science John Forrester lamented that there was still no comprehensive history of the modern "case history,"[36] and underscored the difficulty of writing such a history. He began with the startling insight that we still do not really have a precise and reliable definition of this form, and that even the criteria for such a history of the genre are still lacking. Forrester outlined the philosophical-historical terrain of the "case" from the Aristotelian *phronesis* to John Stuart Mill's "practical reasoning," but stated that the very category or "style of reasoning" we associate with the modern case history had still not been clearly delineated.[37] With the posthumous appearance of Forrester's long-awaited book in 2016, *Thinking in Cases*, we are no closer to a history of the case, despite several excellent "examples" or "cases" Forrester offered in lieu of such a history. Forrester did, however, provide certain guideposts, above all, that the modern "case" and the modern "case history" stand in opposition to *normative thinking*. The "case history" seeks to present something unusual, different, peculiar, specific, and unique; the modern case history raises a *claim of singularity*. Simultaneously, however, "cases" are valued precisely because of their *exemplary, representative* character, their ability to point up something that *might* define a type. The very idea of the case and its presentation in the case history presupposes that this case might function as an exemplary instance of an event or a state-of-affairs from which we can learn. Similar to the way in which models function, the case is supposed to grasp the individual in its individuality while at the same time bringing it to a level of an example or typical, analyzable instance that can serve *scientific knowledge*. It is this tension between the unique and the typical, the individual and the

---

36 John Forrester, "If p, then what? Thinking in Cases," *History of the Human Sciences* 9:3 (1996): 1–25.
37 Ian Hacking, *The Taming of Chance* (Cambridge: Cambridge University Press 1990), 6; Ian Hacking, "Styles of Reasoning," in *Postanalytic Philosophy*, ed. John Rajchman and Cornel West (New York 1985), 145–164. Hacking follows A. C. Crombie, *Styles of Scientific Thinking in the European Tradition. The History of Argument and Explanation Especially in the Mathematical and Biomedical Sciences and Arts* (London: Duckworth, 1994), vol. 2, who had identified six "styles of scientific reasoning," to which Forrester adds a seventh: "Reasoning in cases" (Forrester, "If p, then what? Thinking in Cases," 2).

exemplary that must be explored historically: how, in a specific historical field, is this tension constituted, structured, articulated?

Forrester named four basic functions and characteristics of the case history in his article: first, it is marked by the research into and disclosure of the "interiority of a person," probing of the "intimate" or "private" sphere of an individual.[38] Second, the modern case history is the medium for the expression and communication of very specific, unique "facts."[39] Third, the modern case history functions as a scientific and literary communication medium, as a public form or presentation and interaction– and this presentation is to endow the case history with a certain degree of scientific legitimacy and validity. Forrester refers to this aspect of the case history as "making it scientific."[40] Finally, the case history serves as a documentation and recording medium: "the idea of the case appears to be closely linked with the very idea of the *compilation of a dossier*."[41] We might well extend this further by asserting that the case history and the compilation of a dossier constitute a part of and are inextricably linked to an archive.

With the mention of the "dossier" and the "archive," the work of Michel Foucault immediately comes to mind, specifically the scriptural mechanisms or writing technologies through which individuals are constituted in their individuality. For the Foucault of *Discipline and Punish*, the case history was a form of corporeal power of individuation in which individuals are *made* "as a reality fabricated by this specific technology of power that I have called 'discipline.'"[42] Let us recall that passage from Foucault's text where he describes the modern "case":

---

[38] Charles Taylor, *Sources of the Self: The Making of the Modern Identity* (Cambridge: Cambridge University Press, 1992), makes the argument that English Deists of the early eighteenth century already developed a "proto-discourse" of "interiority." The same might also be said of the Pietists in the eighteenth century in Germany. With subtle interpretation one can see modern "individuality" and "interiority" emerging. But it requires no interpretation whatsoever to get the sense of a discourse of the self around 1760 in England, with the publication of Adam Smith's *A Theory of Moral Sentiments* (Edinburgh: Millar, Kincaid, J. Bell, 1759), and in Germany with the emergence of the new discourse of "intimacy." On this, see Niklas Luhmann, *Love as Passion: The Codification of Intimacy* (Stanford, CA: Stanford University Press, 1985); and Albrecht Koschorke, "Alphabetisation und Empfindsamkeit," in *Der ganze Mensch. Anthropologie und Literatur im 18. Jahrhundert*, ed. Hans-Jürgen Schings (Stuttgart and Weimar: Metzler, 1994), 605–628.
[39] Forrester, "If p then what? Thinking in Cases," 10.
[40] Forrester, "If p then what? Thinking in Cases," 11.
[41] Forrester, "If p then what? Thinking in Cases," 11; emphasis in the original.
[42] Foucault, *Discipline and Punish*, 194.

> The examination, surrounded by all its documentary techniques, makes each individual a case [...] the case is no longer, as in casuistry or jurisprudence, a set of circumstances defining an act and capable of modifying a rule; it is the individual as he may be described and judged, measured, compared with others, *in his very individuality*.[43]

In contrast to the "case" in the moral-theological domain of casuistry or in jurisprudence, the modern case renders the individual as a subject-object that can be analyzed or described, *not*, as Foucault emphasizes, classified or made an example, reduced to certain characteristics, as the naturalists sought to do. The case rather intends, according to Foucault, "to maintain the individual in his individual features, in his particular evolution, in his aptitudes or abilities, under the gaze of a permanent corpus of knowledge."[44] This is the disciplinary power of the case history, one technology of power among several in the arsenal of modernity "for constituting individuals as correlative elements of knowledge and power."[45] Forrester took this opportunity to point out the ambiguity in Foucault's specification of the "case": on the one hand, the "case" in jurisprudence and law in which the decisive similarities are utilized in order to establish a liability under a more general rule, while, on the other, the "case" in psychoanalysis and the clinical sciences in which the case is meant precisely to maintain its unique character or peculiarity over and against any type, concept, or norm.[46]

Forrester remarks a significant shift or displacement in the history of the "case" at the end of the eighteenth and beginning of the nineteenth century: "reasoning in cases" moves from being a subject of casuistry for the instructional aggregation of iterations or instances in the service of the establishment of the "typical" or "norm" – either for pedagogical or moral-theological purposes – to the *psychological case*, which narrates an "unheard of" series of events, a unique and peculiar person with a unique history and an extraordinary outcome. Such a definition immediately recalls the *Novella* mentioned above and its classical definition as the narrative of an "unheard of incident or occurrence" (*unerhörte Begebenheit*). Then, around 1870, Forrester identifies a new, modern casuistry, especially in law, in which case functions as an

---

[43] Foucault, *Discipline and Punish*, 191; emphasis mine.
[44] Foucault, *Discipline and Punish*, 190.
[45] Foucault, *Discipline and Punish*, 194.
[46] Norm, normative thinking and "normality" actually appear first around 1800. See Werner Sohn, "Bio-Macht und Normalisierungsgesellschaft – Versuch einer Annäherung," in *Normalität und Abweichung: Studien zur Theorie und Geschichte der Normalisierungsgesellschaft*, ed. Werner Sohn and Herbert Mertens (Opladen and Wiesbaden: Wesdeutscher Verlag, 1999), 9–30; Friedrich Kittler, "Das Subjekt als Beamter," in *Die Frage nach dem Subjekt*, ed. Manfred Frank et al. (Frankfurt: Suhrkamp, 1988), 401–420.

example for the elucidation of a principle.[47] Forrester puts forth the plausible thesis that, since the end of the nineteenth century and into the present, we are dealing with a new form of casuistry, particularly in Bio-Ethics and in jurisprudence.[48] Forrester is skeptical that Foucault's splitting between casuistry and the clinical case was ever truly achieved, and the return of casuistry in which the individual case is now being utilized as the "test-case" for questions of ethics and medicine in the search for reasonable principles appears to have at least some validity.[49]

There is another source of confusion that makes a theory and history of the case history from a Foucauldian standpoint difficult. In his writings on governmentality,[50] Foucault identified yet another form of power alongside the purely disciplinary (hard) power he had identified in *Discipline and Punish*, a form of power that he referred to as the ensemble of mechanisms and practices that constitute the *Sicherheitsdispositiv* or "security apparatus" of modernity: in these writings, Foucault discussed the "case" as a central category of modern organization next to "security," "danger," "risk," and "crisis." In the context of bio-politics in the late eighteenth century, the "case" resurfaces not as the "individual" case, but as an instrument for grasping the distribution of a disease or other anomaly in a specific population, time and place.

> the result is that the disease no longer appears in this solid relationship of the prevailing disease to its place or milieu, but as a distribution of cases, in a population circumscribed in time and space. Consequently, the notion of case appears, which is not the individual case, but a way of individualizing the collective phenomenon of the disease, or of collectivizing the phenomena, integrating individual phenomena within a collective field, but in the form of quantification and of the rational and identifiable.[51]

---

[47] Forrester, "If p, then what? Thinking in Cases," 15–18, where he talks about the introduction of "case law."
[48] Stephen Toulmin, "How Medicine Saved the Life of Ethics," *Perspectives in Biology and Medicine* 25.4 (1982): 736–750; and K. Danner Clouser, "Bioethics and Philosophy," *Hastings Center Report* 23.6 (1993): 10–11.
[49] See Albert R. Jonsen and Stephen Toulmin, *The Abuse of Casuistry: A History of Moral Reasoning* (Berkeley and Los Angeles: University of California Press, 1988). However, this new casuistry is anything but unproblematic. See James F. Childress, "Narrative(s) Versus Norm(s): A Misplaced Debate in Bio-Ethics," in *Stories and their Limits: Narrative Approaches to Bioethics*, ed. Hilde Lindemann Nelson (New York and London: Routledge, 1997), 252–271.
[50] Michel Foucault, *Geschichte der Gouvernementalität I: Sicherheit, Territorium, Bevölkerung. Vorlesungen am College de France 1977–1978*, ed. Michel Senellart, trans. Claudia Brede-Konersmann and Jürgen Schröder (Frankfurt: Suhrkamp, 2004).
[51] Michel Foucault, *Security, Territory, Population: Lectures at the Collège de France, 1977–1978*, ed. Michel Senellart (New York: Palgrave MacMillan, 2007), 60.

It is therefore all the more curious that, in the context of his writings on governmentality, Foucault seeks to write a history of what he refers to as the *pastoral* as an "individualizing power."⁵² In addition to the anatomo-politics of body in *Discipline and Punish*, or the bio-politics of populations concerned with birth, death, education, imprisonment, disease, war, and starvation that characterizes much of Foucault's middle period, the late writings on governmentality articulated the *pastoral* and the *pastoral apparatus* as a form of *Seelenführung* oder *Gewissensleitung* – a type of the moral guidance or counseling of the soul – in contradistinction to the direct, corporeal control of the body, or the surveillance of populations.⁵³

The Pastorate has to do first and foremost with the "direction of souls."⁵⁴ Extending back to Greek antiquity, this form of power, unlike the more explicit and direct anatamo-politics of the body, "operates to do good." It is, according to Foucault, a "power of care."⁵⁵ The figure of the good shepherd keeps a vigilant eye on the flock, watching for possible evils, but more importantly perhaps, for the possible misfortunes that may threaten the weakest, the most unfortunate of its members. As opposed to the fear and terror of the force of violence issued by sovereign power and executed by the state apparatuses, pastoral power does not impose a set of teachings of general principles, but rather gently advocates the modulation of the soul, through observation, counsel, and supervision. Foucault goes to great lengths to discern pastoral power from politics, rhetoric, and even pedagogy; as the conveyor of "spiritual direction," or the "direction of conscience." It is, as Foucault states, "a form of individualization that will not be acquired through the relationship to a recognized truth, but will be acquired instead through the production of an internal, secret and hidden truth."⁵⁶ The consequences of such a modality of subjection and individualization for the history of the subject, for the shaping of souls and the conduct of individuality, prove to be enormous. For it means not only the perpetual intervention into the life of the individual, the continual *management*

---

52 Foucault, *Geschichte der Gouvernementalität I*, 191.
53 Pastoral power reaches back to early Christianity and precedes the disciplinary power that definitively emerges in the sixteenth and seventeenth centuries. The appropriation and deployment of pastoral power in the eighteenth century exists alongside Foucault's "disciplinary power," and contributes to both the bio-politics of populations as well as anatomo-politics of the body (training, dietetics, etc.).
54 Foucault, *Security, Territory, Population*, 123.
55 Foucault, *Security, Territory, Population*, 127.
56 Foucault, *Security, Territory, Population*, 181.

of lives, but the very constitution of the individual as a subject first objectified and made a concern as such by the community and the State. Foucault writes:

> What the history of the pastorate involves, therefore, is the entire history of procedures of human individualization in the West [...] the history of the subject. [...] *The pastorate is a prelude to governmentality, through the constitution of a specific subject, of a subject whose merits are analytically identified, who is subjected in continuous networks of obedience, and who is subjectified through the compulsory extraction of truth.*[57]

The distinction between direct disciplinary and the more indirect pastoral power opens up an avenue for considering how, in the late eighteenth century, the "psychological case" provides an individuating instance of "subjectification," that is, how patterns of action, sets of behaviors, tendencies, inclinations, impulses, fears, aversions, denials, and frustrations become organized into certain identifiable "types" or analyzable "instances," and therefore provide the basis for governmentality. "Pastoral power," Foucault wrote, "is an individualizing power."[58]

To make the matter of Foucault and the "case" even more complicated, his work on the emergence of the "clinical gaze" in *Birth of the Clinic* proposed a slightly different account of the history of the case. In this text, it is the clinic itself as the historico-spatial condition of the possibility of a so-called objective science of experience that first makes the properly *clinical* case history at all possible.[59] According to the nosological-nosographical model, the complexity and uniqueness of individual case can be reduced by *analogy*; what is unique is not the disease or illness itself, but the various *circumstances*, different degrees of *intensity*, and different *combinations* of factors.

> Consequently, the complexity of individual cases could no longer be attributed to those uncontrollable modifications that disturb essential truths, and force us to decipher them only in an act of recognition that neglects and abstracts; it may be grasped and recognized in itself, in a complete fidelity to everything it presents, if one analyses it according to the principles of a combination, that is, if one defines all the elements that compose it and the form of that composition.[...] The medicine of species and classes also made use

---

57 Foucault, *Security, Territory, Population*, 184–185; emphasis mine.
58 Foucault, *Security, Territory, Population*, 128.
59 Michaela Ralser, *Das Subjekt der Normalität: Das Wissensarchiv der Psychiatrie. Kulturen der Krankheit um 1900* (München: W. Fink, 2010), 31: "Die Klinik stellt im allgemeinen Sinn die Bedingung erst her, durch die der Kranke zum Fall wird. Zu einem Fall von Krankheit. [...] Das Besondere des Einzelfalls [...] erhält seine Bedeutung zuallererst durch sein Verhältnis zum Allgemeinen, in unserem Fall zum Allgemeinen der Geisteskrankheit."

of them in the decipherment of pathological phenomena: the resemblance of disorders could be recognized from one case to another.⁶⁰

This led Foucault to write about a profound duality in late eighteenth-century medicine: "It never ceased to hesitate between a *pathology of phenomena* and a *pathology of cases*."⁶¹ The abundance of references to Étienne Bonnot de Condillac and the nosology/nosography from Boissier de Sauvages to Philippe Pinel should alert us, however, to the fact that the direction in transmission is *always* one from what is *perceived* in the clinical gaze to the *written* case, from the visible to language, from the signs and symptoms of illness and disease to its discursive truth and narrative: "The clinic brings into play what, for Condillac, was the fundamental relation between the perceptual act and the element of language. The clinician's description, like the philosopher's analysis, proffers what is given by the natural relation between the operation of consciousness and the sign."⁶² Such a reconstruction necessarily precludes precisely the kind of narrative case history I have in mind in this study. For Foucault, at least the Foucault of *Birth of the Clinic*, precisely what was at stake in the narrative case studies I shall consider – the *individuality of the individual* – was largely irrelevant: "Medical certainty is based not on the *completely observed individuality* but on the *completely scanned multiplicity of individual facts*."⁶³ The "scanned multiplicity of individual facts" converge in an identity of perceived signs and discursive language-structures that transcribe, clearly and accurately, what is seen.

> The clinician's gaze and the philosopher's reflexion have similar powers, because they both presuppose a structure of identical objectivity, in which the totality of being is exhausted in manifestations that are its signifier-signified, in which the visible and the manifest come together in at least a virtual identity, in which the perceived and the perceptible may be *wholly restored in a language whose rigorous form declares its origin*.⁶⁴

Foucault's choice of textual sources, the nosological-nosographical medical model, and its authors and practitioners, not to mention the omnipresence of Condillac's epistemology as the underpinning for much of what he writes about perception and language, not only reflects a bias in his research; it precludes

---

60 Michel Foucault, *The Birth of the Clinic: An Archeology of Medical Perception*, trans. A. M. Sheridan Smith (New York: Random House, 1979), 99–100.
61 Foucault, *Birth of the Clinic*, 103; emphasis in the original.
62 Foucault, *Birth of the Clinic*, 95.
63 Foucault, *Birth of the Clinic*, 101; emphasis in the original.
64 Foucault, *Birth of the Clinic*, 96; emphasis mine.

other models and moves us in an entirely different direction, away from the narrative psychological case history that is the subject of this study.⁶⁵

At the very least, therefore, there are three different determinations of the "case" in Foucault and, *mutatis mutandis*, three different (his-)stories, or three *kinds* of histories to be written. In *Discipline and Punish*, the emphasis was clearly on demarcating the modern "case" as part of a power-apparatus aiming at individualization und subjection, placing the "case" squarely within the power mechanisms that operated on the body to individualize and specify that individuality for the distinct purpose of saturating the individual body with power. In *Birth of the Clinic*, by contrast, the clinical case illustrates a pathology and opens up a certain way of training the gaze of the clinician to pathological phenomena to be studied under the strict regimen of decipherment, recognition, and resemblance. Finally, in the later writings on governmentality, the "case" figures as one "practice" in the security-apparatus (*Sicherheitsdispositiv*) alongside "security," "danger," "risk," and "crisis," as a medium and method of guiding and leading the soul, persistently directing it back into the mentality and behavior of the community and society.

In what follows, we will suggest that there is a good deal of purchase specifically in Foucault's later notion of the *pastoral* for an analysis of the psychological case history in the late eighteenth century; it becomes the genre of choice for pastors, psychologists, pedagogical reformers, philosophers, teachers, physicians, counselors and civil servants for the guidance and direction of souls. In his public invitation to contribute to his newly founded journal for empirical-experiential psychology 1782–1793 (*Magazin zur Erfahrungsseelenkunde*), Moritz calls on parents and educators to share their "experiences" and "observations" of how souls have lost their way, and the methods used to bring them back to a "virtuous life":

> May I therefore receive many contributions from parents, educators and school personel or other persons, for whom the well-being of mankind is close to their heart, wherein extensive and specific reports are given, through which means someone perhaps succeeded in bringing back to a state of virtue one who had gone astray, or at least to pull him away gradually from a well-entrenched vice.⁶⁶

---

65 To be sure, the nosology and nosography dominant in medical psychology in France did not preclude the use of narrative "observations." See Sabine Arnaud, *On Hysteria. The Invention of a Medical Category between 1670 and 1820* (Chicago: University of Chicago Press, 2015), 177.

66 Karl Philipp Moritz, "Grundlinien zu einem ohngefähren Entwurf in Rücksicht auf die Seelenkrankheitskunde," in *Werke in zwei Bänden. Dichtungen und Schriften zur Erfahrungsseelenkunde*, ed. Heide Hollmer and Albert Meier (Frankfurt: DKV, 1999), vol. 1, 812–816: "Möchte ich doch viele Beiträge von Eltern, Erziehern und Schulleuten, oder andern

Promising anonymity, Moritz sought interesting and thought-provoking cases – particularly on illnesses of the soul (*Seelenkrankheitskunde*) and comprehensible to the general reading public – as the first stage of a more comprehensive empirical psychology. This request for interesting and thought-provoking cases represents a qualitatively new discursive social, cultural, and political project. It derives some of its qualities from earlier medical, moral-theological, and juridical models, but distinguishes itself in several key respects. Under the conditions of the emerging disciplines of experimental psychology (*Erfahrungsseelenkunde*) and anthropology in the mid-eighteenth century, and in the context of a fierce debate concerning the metaphysics of the soul, the modern psychological case history becomes a part of a *pastoral apparatus* designed to insure the integrity, educability, stability, accountability, freedom, and dignity of the human soul.

Since Forrester's article and in addition to Foucault's interventions there have been numerous important contributions and approaches that have significantly added to the conversation concerning the history of the case history, the psychological case history in particular. The literature on the case history is enormous, and I restrict myself in the following to the work specifically on the psychological case history that has been decisive for the present study.

In 1988, Hans Adler made a decisive contribution when he interpreted the case history as the unique and powerful genre that provides access to the dark "foundations" of the soul: if what was previously seen as "deviant" human modes of behavior were suddenly viewed to have their very basis in the human soul itself and not as something "foreign" that entered and destroyed it from without, then the existing norms became very much at stake and the "case" took on an important corrective, modulating function.[67] Shortly after Adler, Rita Wöbkemeier's *Erzählte Krankheit* read the modern case history as the result of a turn towards empiricism in anthropology and psychology.[68] Then, in 1995,

---

Personen, denen das Wohl der Menschheit am Herzen liegt, erhalten, worinn ausführliche und specielle Nachrichten gegeben werden, durch welche Mittel es jemanden gelungen ist, irgend einen Verirrten nach und nach auf den Weg der Tugend wieder zurückzubringen, oder ihn von diesem oder jenem eingewurzelten Laster allmählig abzuziehen."

67 Hans Adler, "Fundus Animae – Grund der Seele. Zur Gnoseologie des Dunklen in der Aufklärung," *Deutsche Vierteljahrsschrift für Literaturwissenschaft und Geistesgeschichte* 62.2 (1988): 197–221.

68 Rita Wöbkemeier, *Erzählte Krankheit. Literarische und Medizinische Phantasien um 1800* (Stuttgart: Metzler, 1990), 159: "Die Erforschung des Menschen als Ensemble von Körper und Seele, die sich die Anthropologie zur Aufgabe machte, hatte – in mehr oder minder unklarer Abgrenzung zur empirischen Psychologie der 'Erfahrungsseelenkunde' – mit der Sammlung von Einzelfällen begonnen."

Julia Epstein's *Altered Conditions* performed the important task of situating the case history within the history of medicine, arguing that "taking" case histories "did not become systematic and were not flagged as playing a role in diagnosis or therapeutics until physicians such as Bellers and Clifton began calling for a more formal approach to record-keeping in the first half of the eighteenth-century."[69] Thomas Browman's study of German academic medicine in the eighteenth century cogently argued how the case history enables the reader to be "co-present" with the physician in the treatment of the patient, to occupy with the physician a space so as to provide a meaningful narrative context for the manifold historical details of the case.[70] Matthew Bell, writing on the German tradition in psychology, persuasively argued that we find "the root of the modern psychological case history" in Moritz's *Magazin zur Erfahrungsselenkunde* (1783–1793), but he did not pursue further the psychological case history *per se* in his analysis.[71] Jason Tougaw has convincingly noted the moment of the "inexplicable" as a defining aspect for the modern case history in his work on the case history and the British novel,[72] and has related this genre to the "wonder books" of the seventeenth century.[73] Margaret Ann Kennedy's dissertation of 2005 then demonstrated the rhetoric of the "curious" to be operative in the ongoing struggle between scientific experimentalism of the eighteenth century deriving from Francis Bacon, John Locke, Isaac Newton, and Robert Boyle, and the challenge that the peculiar, the anomaly, and the strange posed for such classificatory systems.[74] However, in an earlier decisive contribution from 1989, Thomas Laqueur, using two case histories of Boerhaave, noted that the early modern case recording or reporting needed to

---

[69] Julia Epstein, *Altered Conditions: Disease, Medicine and Storytelling* (New York and London: Routledge, 1995), 51.

[70] Thomas H. Broman, *The Transformation of German Academic Medicine, 1750–1820* (Cambridge: Cambridge University Press, 1996), 138–139.

[71] Matthew Bell, *The German Tradition of Psychology in Literature and Thought, 1780–1840* (Cambridge: Cambridge University Press, 2005), 103.

[72] Jason Daniel Tougaw, *Strange Cases: The Medical Case History and the British Novel* (New York: Routledge, 2006), 2: "The case history emerged in the seventeenth century and flourished in the eighteenth specifically to provide a public forum for the discussion of medical phenomena that could not be explained or cured with the tools and the knowledge of the period's medical science."

[73] Tougaw, *Strange Cases*, 34: "If case histories have ancestors, they are the 'wonder books' of the late 17th century in which strange cases and miraculous events are told with a degree of narrative detail that lends them plausibility."

[74] Margaret Kennedy, *A Curious Literature: Reading the Medical Case History from the Royal Society to Freud* (PhD. Diss., Brown University, 2000).

make its truth-claims credible precisely by *disassociating* itself from the popular tradition of sensationalist "tall-tales," the spectacles of the hideous, the monstrous, and the merely odd.[75]

In a series of articles emphasizing "distant reading" and focused on the case in early modern Europe, Gianna Pomata has traced the shift from the use of the case as *exemplum* – the case as the universal made concrete from the medieval period to the *consilia* of the early sixteenth century – to the emerging sense of case in the later sixteenth and early seventeenth century as a *historia medica*, a medical case history based on first-hand empirical observations.[76] What becomes central for Pomata at the end of the sixteenth century is a new understanding of the case in which particularity and singularity – "selective attention to whatever is rare, exceptional, and unheard of" – become the defining qualities of observation and the writing of the case history of illness. She writes: "A case seems noteworthy precisely when its singularity is so extreme that it challenges classification: the rare and the odd is the epitome of individuality. An instance of the unforeseeable, the odd case proves the complexity and the mysteriousness of nature."[77]

To be sure, Pomata is very careful *not* to attribute to the *historia medica* of the late sixteenth century an anachronistically modern, psychological sense; her point is rather that medical observation makes a stunning movement in this period from *experimentum* to *curatio* to *observatio/historia*. Herein lies the latent modernity of the case: the unexpected and unaccountable, that which defies classification could "steal in," as she puts it, to become the selective focal point(s) for medical discourse.[78] Pomata has shown the epistemological import for medical case studies as an *epistemic genre*; they give, she has written, "literary form to an intellectual endeavor and in so doing they shape and channel the cognitive practice of attention"; they provide "a framework for gathering, describing and organizing the raw materials of experience."[79] More recently, using Franco Moretti's technique of "distant reading," she has carefully demonstrated how cases flourish in times of scientific transformation or

---

75 Thomas W. Laqueur, "Bodies, Details, and Humanitarian Narrative," in *The New Cultural History*, ed. Lynn Hunt (Berkeley: University of California Press, 1989), 176–204.
76 Gianna Pomata, "*Praxis Historialis*: The Uses of *Historia* in Early Modern Medicine," in *Historia: Empiricism and Erudition in Early Modern Europe*, ed. Gianna Pomata and Nancy G. Siraisi (Cambridge and London: MIT Press, 2005), 105–146.
77 Pomata, "*Praxis Historialis*," 131.
78 Pomata, "*Praxis Historialis*," 136.
79 Gianna Pomata, "Sharing Cases: The *Observationes* in Early Modern Medicine," *Early Science and Medicine* 15.3 (2010): 197.

crisis, when the operative concepts and categories are questioned or simply deemed inadequate.[80]

What has been absent in all of this important work is a clear distinction between the medical and the *psychological case history*. Even less clear is precisely what constitutes a specifically *narrative* psychological case history. Even if, as Nicholas Pethes argues, a strict definition of the genre apart from its historical-literary function is not possible, one is justified in trying to discern precisely how narrative works in such case histories.[81] As my reading of Marcus Herz's psychological description of his own illness of 1782 demonstrates, the psychological case history need not be about psychological or mental illness, and case histories concerning mental illness or disturbance are not always composed in a narrative, psychological fashion. Rather, in its form and structure, the narrative psychological case history seeks to connect significant aspects of character and personality to the aetiology and unfolding of an illness, psychological or not. It endeavors to construct an overarching narrative that in some way accounts for why a particular person became ill in a specific way, how the nature of the "self" contributed to the history of the illness and its outcome, how a traumatic history or past contributed to or even caused the illness, and how the illness tells us something about the "individuality" of the individual. Finally, it most often includes moments in which reflection, interpretation, or commentary "interfere" with or impinge upon a strict chronological account or recital of mere facts, the course of the illness, diagnosis and prognosis, and the remedies or therapies applied.

Regarding the psychological case history in particular, and within the German tradition, Alexander Košenina has done compelling research on the modern psychological case history in Moritz and Friedrich Schiller. He has articulated what he refers to as a performative representation of expressions of the soul (*performative Repräsentation des Seelenausdrucks*): from the protocol-like *species facti* of the case in jurisprudence to the "history behind the history," the modern psychological case history follows the anthropological interest to enter into the inner motivations of the delinquent or patient and to plumb the depths of his thoughts (*Quellen seiner Gedanken*).[82] As a paradigmatic example of the psychological case history in the last quarter of the eighteenth century, Košenina analyzes "Aus K...s Papieren" by Moritz (1786) and concludes that the psychological case history is

---

[80] Gianna Pomata, "The Medical Case Narrative: Distant Reading of an Epistemic Genre," *Literature and Medicine* 32.1 (2014): 1–23.
[81] Nicholas Pethes, *Literarische Fallgeschichten. Zur Poetik einer epistemischen Schreibweise* (Konstanz; Konstanz University Press, 2016), 19–35.
[82] Košenina, "'Tiefere Blicke in das Menschenherz': Schiller und Pitaval," 388–392.

"not a simply chronological protocol of a case of illness, but rather a small 'inner history of a human being' in the sense of Christian Friedrich von Blanckenburg's *Theory of the Novel*,"[83] thereby placing it in direct proximity to the theory and history of the novel. The decisive moment, according to Košenina, is that "with precise focus on the hidden mental mechanisms and causes, a history of the person's suffering is presented."[84] Such a focus on the internal mechanisms and causes of a "history of suffering" has three dimensions: first, the gradual manufacture of psychological thoughts and concepts in the "study" of psychological material; second, a kind of instruction for aspiring philosophically-minded physicians and bourgeois readers with a "psychological" interest; and finally, a moral-pedagogical endowment of empathy: "Through this structure of a non-chronological movement between documents and commentary, the reader herself is placed into the role of philosophical physician."[85] The performative nature of such case histories – the creation of the empathic reader capable of placing herself in the role of the philosophical physician – aligns perfectly with Moritz's stated objectives for his journal. Košenina's conjugation of Blanckenburg's theory of the novel – widely circulated in Germany at the time, and praised by Christoph Martin Wieland and Goethe – and Moritz's program for experiential psychology is fully justified, except for one important difference; Blanckenburg's text emphasized the novel of *character and action* over and against what he called the novel of *incident* – he uses the terms *Begebenheit* and *Vorfall* – thereby bracketing off or at least demoting precisely the field that would be of interest for the elucidation of the specific event or "case," or what we might term the "event character" of the case.[86]

Andreas Gailus has also placed Moritz at the center of his concerns and has identified in Moritz's *Journal of Experimental Psychology* the origin of the modern psychological case history: "It is thus precisely Moritz's casuistic approach to the writing of the soul that opens up the conceptual space for a new notion

---

83 Alexander Košenina, *Karl Philipp Moritz. Literarische Experimente auf dem Weg zum psychologischen Roman* (Göttingen: Wallstein, 2006), 12: "kein bloß chronologisches Protokoll einer Krankengeschichte, sondern eine kleine 'innere Geschichte des Menschen' im Sinne von Friedrich von Blanckenburgs *Versuch über den Roman*."
84 Košenina, *Karl Philipp Moritz*, 12: "mit genauem Blick auf die verborgenen seelischen Mechanismen und Ursachen die Leidensgeschichte eines Menschen präsentiert wird."
85 Košenina, *Karl Philipp Moritz*, 103.
86 Christian Friedrich von Blanckenburg, *Versuch über den Roman* (Leipzig and Liegnitz: David Siegerts Witwe, 1774), 354–355. Blanckenburg clearly distances himself from the "event" and the "incident," conflating an interest in the "inner" world of the human being with character and action, and aligning this with a *philosophical* rather than a *historical* ordering of the novel.

of the individual: the individual, understood not as a member of a species, but as a self shaped by a particular life history."[87] Gailus refers to the erasure of the firm distinction between the healthy and the ill, resulting in what he refers to a "shared existential ground" between the physician and the patient.[88] This is particularly useful in thinking about cases of hysteria and hypochondria, in which the entanglement of the patient with the physician, specifically the transference of the patient's anxiety onto the physician (and her inability to effectively treat the patient) becomes, as we shall see in the case of Herz's treatment of Moritz, the therapeutic key.

Most recently, *Literary Case Histories* (2016) by Nicolas Pethes has rightfully problematized the very possibility of a genre-historical or narratological definition of the case history in favor of what he terms a *functional-historical* determination of this epistemic form of writing (*epistemische Schreibweise*). Thus the emphasis is placed on how someone or something becomes a case in a particular discursive practice, and how this individual then becomes a subject for juridical, educational, medical and psychological power.[89] Strongly influenced by Foucault, in particular the Foucault of *Discipline and Punish* and *Birth of the Clinic*, Pethes shows the literary case history as disciplinary technic across two centuries concerned with the linguistic codification, communication, archivization, and recording of *constructions of individuality*. By eschewing such generic and narratological definitions, Pethes is able to broaden the scope to include a wide range of historical instances from Gotthold Ephraim Lessing's *Treatise on the Fable* to Jakob Michael Reinhold Lenz's *Zerbin, or the Recent Philosophy,* from Moritz's *Magazin* to Spieß' *Biographies of the Insane*, and from these eighteenth-century examples to recent incarnations of the literary case history in texts by Thomas Bernhard (*Verstörung, Frost*), Ingeborg Bachmann (*Der Fall Franza*), Reinald Goetz (*Irre*), and Peter Handke (*Der große Fall*). Pethes is exactly right that the case history is not simply another genre among genres, but a transmedial, transdisciplinary, and transinstitutional form that cuts across multiple discourses, reflecting upon its own foundations and assumptions as it unfolds its own discursive and medial potentional. Key for Pethes is the double role of the literary case history: first, to construct internal or interior views into the individuality of the individual (how the individual is *made* as such), and, second, to reflect on its own mediality and construction. Pethes is able to

---

[87] Gailus, "Case of Individuality," 79.
[88] Gailus, "Case of Individuality," 91: "if the sick soul is merely the healthy soul thrown off-balance, then the psychologist and his object are not so much distinct entities as individual variations arising from a shared existential ground."
[89] Pethes, *Literarische Fallgeschichten*, 15, 23.

show how this new epistemic genre equipped with a strong empirical-observational procedure goes hand in hand with the emergent autonomy aesthetics of the late eighteenth entury: both reject rhetorical patterns and models, pre-conceived aesthetic norms and standards, and both effect a realism aimed at the individual instance or case in its individuality, precisely as something *constructed* or *made*.[90] The difficulty with this type of approach, however, is that with the enormous scope and historical breadth, we lose some of the historical specificity on precisely wherein the *ceasura* of the late eighteenth century consists, how the case history becomes *psychological*, with the result that the case history itself becomes merely a series, or perhaps an archive, of literary cases in which the historical function, particularly at the watershed moment at the end of the eighteenth century, relinquishes some of its precison.

Nevertheless, certain common arguments and readings surface from the substantial reservoir of historical research that has appeared over the last fifteen years. The first concerns the relation of the modern psychological case history to the literature of the "curious" and "strange" of the early modern period. Tougaw's and Kennedy's emphasis on the "strange" and the "curious" respectively, while identifying an important piece of this trajectory – Kennedy in particular goes to great lengths to show the "curious" not merely as a physical-physiological but also a psychological category – does not, in my view, sufficiently distinguish between the categories of "curious" and "strange," prevalent in early modern Europe, from the categories of the *interesting* (*das Interessante, das Interessierende*), and worthy of consideration (*denkwürdig*), which become of tremendous importance for the psychological discourse of the late eighteenth century, specifically in Germany.[91] Košenina singles out the *Histoires tragiques* of the seventeenth century and François Gayot de Pitaval's *Causes célèbres* of the eighteenth as the basis for Schiller's interest in crime literature, but notes that the eighteenth-century appropriation of these genres alters the focus from that which defies classification to what is psychologically interesting or significant in the particular case.[92]

---

90 Pethes, *Literarische Fallgeschichten*, 73, 129.
91 Christian Garve, "Einige Gedanken über das Interessierende," (1779), vol. 1, 161–348. On the history of this category, see: Kolnai, "On the Concept of the Interesting," 166–187; Wölfel, "Interesse/interessant," vol. 3, 138–174; Dumont, "Das Interessante – Theorie und narrative Praxis," 430–447; Robert S. Leventhal, *The Disciplines of Interpretation: Lessing, Herder, Schlegel and Hermeneutics in Germany 1750–1800* (Berlin: de Gruyter, 1994), 260–265. The "interesting" also becomes a fundamental category of the eighteenth-century novel, appearing in Samuel Richardson's "Preface" to *Clarissa* (1747–1748), and his Postscript of 1759.
92 Košenina, "'Tiefere Blicke in das Menschenherz': Schiller und Pitaval," 383–384.

Second, as Julia Epstein has argued, the writing up of cases "did not become a formalized or systematic procedure until it became connected with clinical schools and institutions and their need to produce and codify a professional discourse."[93] In particular, the work of Boerhaave and Sydenham in forging the profession and institution of medicine in the seventeenth century is essential to any genealogy of the case history. Experimentalism derived from Bacon's *Novum Organum* (1620) served as the modern scientific method which made exact direct experience, observation, and careful recording the *sine qua non* of medical knowledge. However, these late seventeenth- and early eighteenth-century physicians also demanded a return to classical models, Hippocrates in particular, as when Francis Clifton, in his *The State of Physick, Ancient and Modern* (1731), laments the "discontinuance of the useful method of Hippocrates, in writing narratives of particular cases."[94] Third, the shift from learned Latin – the language of the academies, universities and science until the eighteenth- century – to the vernacular marks the opening to a more public and less formal-academic practice of case writing and publication. This is particularly interesting in the German tradition, as Barbara Duden has documented in her study of the Eisenach physician Johannes Storch, who recorded the descriptions and experiences of his patients in their own words in his case histories from the 1720s to the 1740s. Finally, Schiller's translation of Pitaval's *Causes célèbres* into German (1786), the teeming discourse of "interesting and unusual cases" in medicine and jurisprudence, and the consultation of case histories in Johann Peter Frank's successful and widely-read *Complete System of a General Medical Policy* (1779–1821) – perhaps the most important work on statecraft of the late Enlightenment in Germany – all of these fueled the interest in and the penchant for the case history beyond the generic boundaries of the medical case history.

The theories that have been put forward to account for the emergence of the "psychological" in the late eighteenth century reveal a tendency to move from the specificity of a semantics of the "individual" to general framing conditions of society, education, and culture, often without sufficient mediation of or attention to the actual, concrete philosophical, medical-scientific, institutional and cultural institutions, debates and practices of this emergence. In attempting to bridge this divide between theory and practice, the systems-theoretical approach of sociologist Niklas Luhmann has been one of the most ambitious, suggestive and provocative arguments that proposes an overarching account of

---

93 Epstein, *Altered Conditions*, 38.
94 Francis Clifton, *The State of Physick, Ancient and Modern* (London: W. Bowyer, 1731), 131.

the "individuality of the individual" in modernity.[95] The increasing differentiation, or the intensification of difference in modern society, not simply a more rigorous division of "labor," reaches a climax in the mid-eighteenth century, an era in which, according to Luhmann, a thoroughgoing modalization and temporalization of the individual occurs; it becomes the subject of its very own "project," the object of its own self-referentiality, of "information" concerning itself,[96] and therefore becomes engaged, for the first time, in a struggle of identity and difference, caught in the agonistics of the general and the particular.[97] One way this struggle is "managed" or adjudicated for Luhmann is through aesthetics or, more specifically, the aesthetic experience.[98] In aesthetics, it is argued, a sphere is opened up in which the necessarily disastrous opposition, the radical disconnect of the general (ideal) and particular (real) in society, is resolved in a unique type of experience which, at least provisionally, offers a mediation of the two. The other way this conflict or dissonance between the universal and the particular is managed, according to Luhmann, is the equation of "subject" and "individual." No longer simply a species of a general type, an "instance" or "deficient mode" of a more universal "concept," or a "token" of prescribed modes of sociability and behavior, the "individual" in the new discourse of the eighteenth century claims "rights," possesses the principle of its own individuation/individuality in itself, and bears the weight of its own uniqueness and incomparability, its "difference" or incommensurability.[99] The new semantics of "individuality" in the eighteenth century emerges precisely in and through the tension between the general and the particular, and the fact that they do *not* coincide: "The individual achieves its individuality precisely as a parasite of the difference between the general and the particular, and the fact that these do not coincide."[100] To place these reflections and arguments in a more concrete, and for our purposes more historical, medical-psychological context, the writing of the case history itself, particularly in the times of crisis

---

95 Niklas Luhmann, "Individuum, Individualität, Individualismus," in: *Gesellschaftsstrukur und Semantik. Studien zur Wissenssoziologie der modernen Gesellschaft*, by Luhmann (Frankfurt: Suhrkamp, 1989), vol. 3, 149–258.
96 Luhmann, "Individuum, Individualität, Individualismus," vol. 3, 194.
97 Luhmann, "Individuum, Individualität, Individualismus," vol. 3, 205–207.
98 Luhmann, "Individuum, Individualität, Individualismus," vol. 3, 200.
99 Luhmann, "Individuum, Individualität, Individualismus," vol. 3, 186. It is of course precisely this "difference" or "incommensurability" of the individual that fuels the literature of late eighteenth century, but this is equally true of the psychological cases considered here.
100 Luhmann, "Individuum, Individualität, Individualismus," vol. 3, 207: "Das Individuum gewinnt, als Parasit der Differenz von Allgemeinen und Besonderem, und daraus, das diese *nicht* übereinkommen, seine Individualität."

when it flourishes,[101] presents a questioning of the relation between individual/particular and general/universal theory, or, more strongly put, questions the very relation between the unique, enigmatic specific instance and the supposedly explanatory, general model.

No study of the emergence of the narrative psychological case history as a particularly fruitful epistemic genre concerning the self in the late eighteenth century would be complete without a consideration of two meta-narratives concerning the evolution of the "self" in the Western tradition that have been useful in providing us with a more complete understanding of how this notion developed. The first is Charles Taylor's *Sources of the Self* (1989); the second is Jerrold Seigel's *The Idea of the Self* (2005).

Subtitled *The Making of Modern Identity*, Taylor's book was and is still today considered a major breakthrough in philosophical-historical understanding of the stages or phases of the emergence of our modern notion of selfhood.[102] Beginning from what he viewed as an inescapable presupposition, namely that our modern notion of selfhood – that is, what it means to be a human agent, a person, a self – has everything to do with certain "background" assumptions regarding morality – autonomy, dignity, respect – Taylor persuasively argued that the moral world of modernity constitutes the fundamental conditions of what we now think of as being a *self*. Respect and dignity, he argued, are inextricably linked to *autonomy*, and the modern sense of the self necessarily involves freedom and self-control, the avoidance of suffering, and the notion that human beings ought to lead productive social and familial lives.[103] The very idea that we define who we are on the basis of where we stand with respect to certain key issues of value and morality, by our orientation toward the "good" and what we believe is right, is for Taylor evidence that the modern notion of the self is essentially a *moral concept*. From the nascent awakenings of individual conscience in Augustine's *Confessions* to Montaigne's *Essays*, from Romantic individuality to Martin Heidegger's existentials of temporality, historicity, being-in-the-world, "care," and human "projects," Taylor creates a broad canvas in which each node fulfills a certain strategic reflection in an ongoing search for and story of the self-realization of autonomy. Even when it is most powerfully contested or challenged, such a notion remains absolutely central to our modern understanding of what being a self entails.

---

101 Gianna Pomata makes the case that cases flourish either when the medical canon is in crisis, or there is no consensus. See Pomata, "Medical Case Narrative," 1–23.
102 Taylor, *Sources of the Self*.
103 Taylor, *Sources of the Self*, 19–33.

To be sure, Taylor's notion of autonomy is not that of an isolated individual, constituted apart from history, memory, interaction, but rather one that fully recognizes its operation within human language and within a community of interlocutors. Taylor presents an astounding array of examples from Plotinus's "the inner is the soul"[104] to Augustine's act of radical reflexivity in his turn towards away from the world of things towards the self (*in interiore homine habitat veritas*),[105] from the Cartesian ideal of the subject as a human agent "able to remake himself by methodical and disciplined action,"[106] to Locke's explication of the self as "punctual"[107]; from Montaigne's "inauguration of a new kind of reflection which is intensely individual, a self-explanation , the aim of which is to reach self-knowledge,"[108] to the eighteenth-century radicalizations of these views in Shaftesbury, Hutcheson, and the "expressivist" turn in Jean-Jacques Rousseau and Johann Gottfried Herder. This "expressivist" self is then heightened and intensified in Romanticism as *self-invention*: "that each individual is different and original, and that this originality determines how he or she ought to live."[109] Taylor's meta-narrative does not offer another "idealist" historical explanation; rather, he successfully shows precisely what was *at stake* in the notion of the modern self, the origins of which are to be found in with Descartes and Locke, and why this new sense of modern identity, "disengaged" and "punctual," has held sway. The moment of what Taylor refers to as "radical reflexivity," a "turn to the self as a self"[110] introduces a radical distinction, the move towards a "first-person" stance or perspective; the disengaged (Cartesian) and punctual (Lockean) selves install a radical difference with respect to classical models by making the first-person perspective the condition of the possibility of all third-person, "objective" perspectives and narratives:

> The subject who can take this kind of radical stance of disengagement to himself or herself with a view to remaking, is what I want to call the "punctual" self. To take this stance is to identify oneself with the power to objectify and remake, and by this act to distance oneself from all the particular features which are the objects of potential change.[111]

---

104 Taylor, *Sources of the Self*, 129.
105 Taylor, *Sources of the Self*, 131.
106 Taylor, *Sources of the Self*, 159.
107 Taylor, *Sources of the Self*, 171.
108 Taylor, *Sources of the Self*, 181.
109 Taylor, *Sources of the Self*, 375.
110 Taylor, *Sources of the Self*, 176.
111 Taylor, *Sources of the Self*, 173.

What is of particular interest for us with regard to the psychological case history is Taylor's interpretation of the turn, in the late eighteenth century, to the "particular," which he reads as a powerful reversal of the abstract, universalist/generalist mode of thinking that governed Western thought since antiquity: "the general or typical now emerges out of the description of particular, situated people in their peculiarity," Taylor writes, "we have to scrutinize the particular to arrive at the general."[112] The turn toward the specific, the particular at the end of the eighteenth century is, as it were, the exact opposite of the "punctual," "disengaged" self insofar as, in this new mode of self-narration and –presentation, one is precisely *unable* to distance oneself from all of the above mentioned "particular features." The ground of the impartial, objective "I" erodes under the pressure of a historicity that impinges not merely on its representation from without, but its self-constitution from within. At this point in Taylor's argument, he discusses the importance of the modern novel: "The new modern novel stands out against all previous literature in its portrayal of the particular. It departs from traditional plots and archetypal stories and breaks with the classical preference for the general and the universal."[113] Taylor situates this peculiarly modern form of radical self-narration – against models, archetypes, and prefigurations – in the autobiographies of Rousseau and Goethe; and as the evidence of this modern self-narration he invokes the intrinsic "formal realism" of the novel, the premise, according to Ian Watt, that the novel is "a full and authentic report of human experience."[114] Yet if the eighteenth-century autobiography is, as has been forcefully suggested, more of an instance of self-staging and self-production than it is the "realistic" and authentic portrayal of the inner life of the individual, we might ask as well whether the novel really fulfilled even the "formal realism" as Watt claimed. As many critics have suggested, however, Watt's "formal realism" stresses empirical objectivity *at the expense* of self-conscious reflexivity, and aligns itself with classical *mimesis* and representation in the formal manner in which it seeks to specify the unique formal qualities of narrative in the novel. Taylor – perhaps uncritically – inherits both the preference for the novel as the key modern genre of self-narration and Watt's argument for a "formal realism." It is interesting to note that Locke's theory of personal identity in the *Essay* (1690) figures in both texts as the philosophical underpinning. In contrast to Taylor (and implicitly to

---

112 Taylor, *Sources of the Self*, 287.
113 Taylor, *Sources of the Self*, 287.
114 Ian Watt, *The Rise of the Novel. Studies in Defoe, Richardson and Fielding* (Berkeley: University of California Press, 1957), 34–35.

Watt as well), I shall argue that the psychological case history at the end of the eighteenth century fuses the mimetic desire for *authenticity* (in the figures I am concerned with, a particular emphasis on the "true" or "real" self beneath social conventions, norms, and appearances), now focused on the interior of the self, with both a *scientific claim* to precise observation, experience, documentation of evidence and knowledge, *and* a subjective reflexivity that seeks to hermeneutically disclose internal, psycho-dynamic connections and cross-references. Such reflexivity, however, enters into a sustained tension with precisely such a demand for scientific, objective "representation." The birth of the modern "disengaged" and "punctual" self is in a sense both registered and countered in the psychological case history insofar as this new medium seeks to reestablish hidden and obscure linkages between illness and selfhood, history and self-representation, memory and agency, in order to demonstrate underlying, unconscious mechanisms that tie disparate moments or elements into a coherent, if not fully unified and absolutely consistent, narrative.

Jerrold Seigel's *The Idea of the Self* (2005)[115] takes issue with Taylor's meta-narrative on a number of points,[116] but particularly with Taylor's reading of Descartes and Locke, the "disengaged" and "punctual" self, and with Taylor's account of reflexivity, which Seigel sees as rather weak in Taylor's account and absolutely essential to the story of the self in Western thought. For Seigel, there are three dimensions of selfhood that need to be historically reconstructed and examined: *bodily, relational*, and *reflective*. Against recent attempts to deconstruct or utterly historicize the self, specifically Derrida and Foucault, Seigel argues that the reflective aspect of the self cannot be reduced to, absorbed within, or folded into the relational or socio-cultural construction of the self. In this sense, Seigel's study operates within the intellectual terrain of the new philosophy of the subject being put forth by the "Heidelberg School," whose central expositors Dieter Henrich and Manfred Frank return to Johann Gottlieb Fichte and the Early German Romantics (Friedrich von Schlegel, Novalis [Friedrich von Hardenberg], and Friedrich Hölderlin in particular) respectively for their meta-narratives of the history of the self, a "deep" historical, constructivist subjectivity very far indeed from Locke's and Taylor's "punctual" self. Within this tradition, Seigel sees his

---

115 Jerrold Seigel, *The Idea of the Self: Thought and Experience in Western Europe since the Seventeenth Century* (Cambridge: Cambridge University Press, 2005).
116 Taylor, *Sources of the Self*, 42.

study as a "historical hermeneutic," as an "aid to understanding and interpreting the legacy of thinking about the self."[117]

Seigel pays a good deal of attention to the different national and cultural contexts of the development of the idea of selfhood, and to the specific literary genres – the novel and the epistolary novel in particular – in which modern self-formation achieved expression. Adam Smith's theory of self-fashioning in his *Theory of Moral Sentiments* (1760) is granted "a signal place in the history of modern self-reflection."[118] In Smith, Seigel sees the transformation of the stoic imperative of self-command being carried through by writers such as Voltaire, Richardson and Pierre de Marivaux, giving new force to Jean de La Bruyère's theory of "putting oneself in the place of others" (*se mettre à la place*), Denis Diderot's reading of Richardson (1761), which extols the virtue and educational value of empathetic identification, and heralds the novel as the exemplary genre capable of producing such "empathetic understanding." Arguing against what he sees as a reductionism in Taylor's account, however, Seigel states that Smith and the other eighteenth century British figures he considers did not "regard the self as fully integrated, homogeneous, without tensions or fissures,"[119] that "each saw the persistence of rifts and strains in selfhood as unavoidable and as an incitement to the continuing project of personal integration."[120] Seigel shares with Taylor the assignation of the novel as the privileged modern literary genre that becomes the medium par excellence for this type of self-fashioning: "Whatever its other sources may have been, one operative one was in literary practice. The rise in the production and reading of fiction in the eighteenth century took place especially around novels of sentiment and sensibility, which drew readers into the lives of fictional characters in ways earlier writing seldom had."[121] As in Taylor's meta-narrative, the novel is the modern genre that captures individuality in a unique, singular manner. It is important to note that this singling out of the novel as the genre *par excellence* has resonated in German scholarship as well. One of the most astute readers of Schiller's psychological-anthropological case history *Criminal of Lost Honor*, Wolfgang Riedel, underscores the novel as uniquely situated as a "discourse of the human,"[122]

---

117 Seigel, *Idea of the Self*, 17.
118 Seigel, *Idea of the Self*, 139.
119 Seigel, *Idea of the Self*, 167.
120 Seigel, *Idea of the Self*, 167.
121 Seigel, *Idea of the Self*, 160.
122 Wolfgang Riedel, "Literarische Anthropologie: Eine Unterscheidung," in *Wahrnehmen und Handeln: Perspektiven einer Literaturanthropologie*, ed. Wolfgang Braungart et al. (Bielefeld: Aisthesis, 2004), 360.

a "medium of the study of mankind," capable of revealing the "internal existence of the individual."[123]

In his examination of the German tradition, Seigel argues that what characterizes its unique contribution to the discourse of the self in the late eighteenth century was "the emergence there of a new and specifically modern form of the sense that society and the self shared a basic structure, and that they were homologous and isomorphic;"[124] "Such an image of the world infused with inner purpose had a particular significance for the ways of thinking about the self that developed in Germany," Seigel writes, "it depicted a world and the individuals who make it up as homologous or isomorphic, that is, as having corresponding or parallel structures."[125] Here, Gottfried Wilhelm Leibniz serves as his point of departure. The world was, according to Seigel, for the tradition stemming from Leibniz's *Monadology*, infused with an inner purposiveness. The self participated in, according to Seigel, this notion of an immanent, intrinsic teleology. The apparent paradox raised by Taylor and others of competing "autonomous" (Kant, Fichte) and "expressivist" (Herder) theories of self within the German tradition is thus rendered moot; for Seigel, both relied on and extrapolated from the fundamental purposiveness of nature, one underscoring the individual's self-imposed adherence to the moral law, the other insisting that in its very unfolding, the self would in any case "realize," express, and make objective and visible the actual purpose always already contained within it. Based on the teleological underpinning common to both nature and self, society and the individual, autonomy and *Bildung* or self-formation, Seigel argues: "The two forms of selfhood were thus internally related to each other."[126] Seigel's reading of the German tradition – Kant, Herder, Humboldt, Fichte, and Hegel – remarks this parallel of self and society as its distinguishing feature, and once again, it is the genre of the novel which embodies this particular iteration of selfhood. The novel functions in Seigel's view to engender an *expanded sociability*. He uses Goethe's *Wilhelm Meisters Lehrjahre* as a paradigmatic vehicle for the representation of what he sees as this specifically German idea of selfhood.[127] The isomorphism of self and society in the texts of Herder and Goethe serves as a guarantor of the activity of the self being an "undistorted

---

123 Wolfgang Riedel, "Anthropologie und Literatur in der deutschen Spätaufklärung. Skizze einer Forschungslandschaft," *Internationales Archiv für Sozialgeschichte der deutschen Literatur*. Sonderheft 6.3 (1994): 111, 133.
124 Seigel, *Idea of the Self*, 38.
125 Seigel, *Idea of the Self*, 297.
126 Seigel, *Idea of the Self*, 299.
127 Seigel, *Idea of the Self*, 351.

manifestation of the individual's inner nature because the world where the action takes place is isomorphic with the individual life-forms that together constitute it."[128]

While Seigel's reading of the German tradition of autonomy and *Bildung* acknowledges the heterogeneous and multifarious aspects of selfhood, the insistence on isomorphism and homology disavows precisely the more problematical moments of fissure, conflict, strain and difference exhibited in every meaningful act of self for the writers of the late eighteenth century in Germany. The imperative of *Bildung* or self-formation can be debilitating, even crushing. Recall Werther's scathing indictment of the educated and *Bildung* in *The Sorrows of Young Werther*: "We educated – miseducated and oversophisticated for nothing!"[129] The claim of homology and isomorphism also reproduces the ideology of romantic self-formation precisely by ignoring or denying the serious discrepancy between the imperative to individuate and the demand to conform, between a progressive theory of the self in its intrinsic development and the very real regressive, inhumane, and often brutal conditions the self was forced to confront – especially evident in the psychological novel such as Goethe's *Werther* (1774) and the novel of self-formation (*Bildungsroman*) such as *Anton Reiser* (1781–1785), but also present in the less psychological *Bildungsromane* of the age 1770–1830 – above all *Wilhelm Meisters Lehrjahre* (1795) – on the path of its supposed "self-realization."[130] It is precisely in the confrontation and encounter with, and the interactive differentiation between, the always-in-process self and the often difficult Other(s) – be they a factual situation, an aspect of the self itself, or another human individual – that the self performs acts of self-rendering, against and in terms of which it supposedly reaches an ever greater understanding of its own mechanism, and through which it learns to question, even give up, the absolute stability and unity of the "self." The use of Goethe's *Wilhelm Meister* is especially auspicious, as Goethe's

---

128 Seigel, *Idea of the Self*, 359–360.
129 Goethe, *Sämmtliche Werke in vierzig Bänden*, vol. 16, 50: "Wir Gebildeten – zu Nichts Verbildeten!"
130 The central contradiction contained within the romantic ideology of individuality finds its most precise articulation in Gerald N. Izenberg, *Impossible Individuality: Romanticism, Revolution, and the Origins of Modern Selfhood, 1797–1802* (Princeton, NJ: Princeton University Press, 1992), 50: "All of them put the unique individual – and more specifically, their own histories – at the center of experience, all of them believed that individuality demanded the expansion of the self towards infinity, and all of them insisted that this was not only compatible with, but dependent on, a fusion with totality conceived, or at least named, as a finite entity – nature, woman, form, Absolute, God, state."

particular use of irony is directed precisely at the tentative and transient constructions of self revealed at each point along the journey of *Bildung* as instances or "cases" of misprision or error. Rüdiger Campe has recently shown how the injection of the *Confessions of a Beautiful Soul* – *Bekenntnisse einer schönen Seele* – into the novel, a "case" literally derived from a psycho-pathological collection of a physician, is a case history of the *failure* of self-formation (*Bildung*), one that disrupts both the ideology of self-formation and the generic expectation of the novel.[131] Herder, as I have sought to show elsewhere, was particularly aware of the multiple voices, texts, "languages" and "disciplines" that make up any one iteration of the self, any one formation at any given point in time.[132] In this sense, Seigel's "undistorted manifestation of the individual's [true and authentic] inner nature" would itself have to be an invention, a distortion or misconstrual of the self in its never-ending, deferred, distorted, tentative, and preliminary process of self-formation. Seigel's book, one can argue, accepts the meta-narrative of *Bildung* and intrinsic teleology at face value, without ever seriously questioning either the more difficult vicissitudes of the self (specifically mental illness and criminality) or the importance of other media besides the novel of the eighteenth century – such as autobiography and the psychological case history – forms which clearly influenced our modern conception of the self. In the German tradition, the failure or destruction of *Bildung*, the fissures opened up in the interval of self-reflexivity, and the errant interpretations and readings constituting genuine threats to self-formation become even *more significant* in the years after 1775. Goethe's *Werther* (1774), which contains within it two case histories of murder, is only one instance of a radical questioning of the *Bildung*-paradigm.[133] And while the Romantics revive and appropriate *Bildung* in the 1790s, it is a paradigm of self-formation that includes, to paraphrase the young Friedrich Schlegel, a continual, radical dismantling, deconstruction, or "undoing" of the self, a constant addition (*Anbildung*) or transformation (*Umbildung*) through the introduction of and the confrontation with a radical Other (for the later Romantics, madness in particular) in its ceaseless, and oftentimes misguided, quest for the Absolute. The narratives of Ludwig Tieck, Jean Paul, and E.T.A. Hoffmann only serve to further problematize this romantic ideology of self-reflexivity and progressive *Bildung*.

---

131 Rüdiger Campe, "Von Fall zu Fall. Goethes *Werther*, Büchners *Lenz*," in *Was der Fall ist. Casus und Lapsu*, ed. Inka Mülder-Bach and Michael Ott (München: Fink, 2014), 34.
132 Leventhal, *Disciplines of Interpretation*, 138–204.
133 Christiane Frey, "'Ist das nicht der Fall der Krankheit?' Der literarische Fall am Beispiel von Goethes *Werther*," *Zeitschrift für Germanistik* 19.2 (2009): 317–329.

Understood broadly, "literature" as a discursive force has fueled and informed the writing of psychological and psychoanalytic case histories. Case histories often enlist rhetoric, in particular metaphoric displacement, metonymic condensation, and allegorical enframing to achieve their effect. Freud himself acknowledges his debt to the "stories," "novellas" and "fictions" of the nineteenth century, and famously became one of the foremost exegetes of some, most notably perhaps E.T.A. Hoffmann's *Der Sandmann* in particular. We have also noted how actual psychological case histories – both in terms of their structure and actual content – have been used, either explicitly or implicitly, as the material basis for literary works. The psychological case history has powerfully impacted German literary history; psychologically-minded case histories have been appropriated and recycled for literary purposes. In the cases of Schiller's *Verbrecher aus Infamie. Eine wahre Geschichte* (1786)[134] and Georg Büchner's *Lenz*,[135] the psychological case history is stylized and formalized into a literary construct, relying heavily on the actual case histories for their "story" and also their specific rendition of the "state of affairs," but also transforming the psychological case history into public, affective literary discourse, where it could be discussed, criticized and, of course, emulated. One of the most famous, intriguing psychological case histories of the early nineteenth century, the story of the foundling Kaspar Hauser, spawned many literary and cultural "works,"[136] producing an enigma[137] that is still the subject of controversy to

---

[134] Jacob Friedrich Abel, *Sammlung und Erklärung merkwürdige Erscheinungen aus dem menschlichen Leben* (Frankfurt and Leipzig, 1784–1790), vol. 2, 1787. For a discussion of Abel's influence on the young Schiller, see: Frederick C. Beiser, *Schiller as Philosopher: A Re-Examination* (Oxford: Oxford University Press, 2005), 17–18. An edition of Abel's writings at the Karlschule where Schiller was his student, including his epistolary novel *Ein Beitrag zur Geschichte der Liebe aus einer Sammlung von Briefen* (1778) is available: Jacob Friedrich Abel, *Karlschul-Schriften. Eine Quellenedition zum Philosophieunterricht an der Stuttgarter Karlschule (1773–1782). Mit Einleitung, Übersetzung, Kommentar und Bibliographie*, ed. Wolfgang Riedel (Würzburg: Königshausen & Neumann, 1995).
[135] Wolfram Schmitt, "Physisch kranke und ihre Helfer am Ende des 18. Jahrhunderts: Pfarrer Oberlin und der Dichter Lenz," ed. Bettina von Jagow and Florian Steger, *Jahrbuch Literatur und Medizin* 2 (2009): 41–60.
[136] For an overview, and all of the essential documents pertaining to the case, see Jochen Hörisch, ed., *Ich möchte ein solcher werden wie...: Materialien zur Sprachlosigkeit des Kaspar Hauser* (Frankfurt: Suhrkamp, 1979).
[137] See: Gerd Gemünden, "The Enigma of Hermeneutics: The Case of Kaspar Hauser," in *Reading after Foucault: Institutions, Disciplines, and Technologies of the Self in Germany, 1750–1830*, edited by Robert S. Leventhal (Detroit: Wayne State University Press, 1994), 127–150. For the incredible reception-history of this case, see: Ulrich Struve, ed., *Der imaginierte Findling: Studien zur Kaspar-Hauser-Rezeption* (Heidelberg: Carl Winter, 1995).

this day. Despite the many protocols, interviews, the autobiographical writings, representations of contemporary jurists, criminologists, philosophers, counselors, and psychologists from his appearance in Nuremberg in 1828 until his murder in 1834, Kaspar Hauser serves as stunning example of how all the "expertise" and guidance brought to bear on the individual by the pastoral apparatus results in an abysmal failure – not only of the individual, but of hermeneutical understanding itself.

Since its origins in the eighteenth century, the psychological case history has operated as a powerful discursive medium of self-production and self-construction, a form of popular, public disclosure of intimate, interesting and often deviant details of a specific individual soul. When thinking about this form of the literary appropriation of actual case histories, some interesting questions emerge: what makes a specific psychological case history attractive or "interesting" for literary stylization? How is the psychological case related to the discipline of aesthetics, and how does the case become an *aesthetic* phenomenon, as it clearly does for Herz, Moritz, Goethe, Schiller, and Büchner? What underlying discursive features does it share with the aesthetic, and wherein does such an aesthetic quality of the case consist? Our aim is to illuminate this fascinating tradition and some of its most enduring cultural artifacts and effects, placing it next to the better-known and more highly researched genres of the novel, the autobiography, and the memoir as one of the formative genres of *modern individuality*. At the intersection of various disciplines – psychology, pedagogy, anthropology, criminology, philosophy, physiology, literature, and biology – and implementing, at least in theory, various methods – observation, interpretive hermeneutics, experience, analogy, collection, commentary, and as a vehicle for "scientific" dissemination, discussion, and debate – the psychological case history opens up a vast, still largely uncharted terrain of inquiry for cultural studies.

On a philosophical-historical level, the narrative psychological case appears as one of the key instruments of the *pastoral apparatus* in Foucault's sense; it is favored, employed, collected, and read by pastors and priests, police and court officials, jurists, teachers and educators, physicians, psychologists, and the new civil servants in Prussia and the German states.[138] As a feature of governmentality, it created a scriptural power of documenting, tracking, and

---

[138] An announcement regarding the interesting case of the foundling Kaspar Hauser in 1828 makes this audience and the circulation of cases abundantly clear. See Hörisch, ed., *Ich möchte ein solcher werden wie*, 25: "Ärzte, Lehrer, Erzieher, Psychologen, Polizei- und Gerichtsbeamte, die scharfsinnigsten Beobachter aus allen Ständen" writes the mayor of Nürnberg Binder.

adjudicating anomalous and aberrational behavior and conduct. It provided insight into the construction of mental illness, the criminally insane, and was thought to be the "evidence" for a full-blown empirical psychology, an imagined "science of the soul." Empirical-experiential psychology and the narrative psychological case history created a "scientific apparatus" as well as the new subjectivities concerned with the guidance of souls, forming a constellation of practices, therapies, and media directed at the general health of the individual, society, and the state. Johann Peter Frank's *Complete System of a Medical Policy* (1779–1821) advocated the writing, deliberation, and dissemination of case studies as a key element of late eighteenth- and early nineteenth-century biopolitics: a significant tool in the emerging scientific policing of the state. Collections of interesting cases proliferated, and the reading public was confronted with an avalanche of "interesting cases" for edification, education, learned debate, and, yes, increasingly for sheer entertainment. It was also a component of juridical-political structure of ongoing sovereignty and authority: as Agamben has argued, the "case" is both *exception* and *example* to/of the general rule, "that which cannot be subsumed,"[139] a procedure and instance of exclusion, as that which is simultaneously "banned" and presented as a paradigm of transgression, assigned to a place on the margins and simultaneously often held up as a representative instance or sample of a form of psychological pathology. Case histories as the ones presented here *invented* the individual, defined it as a *case* to be studied, compared, adjudicated, evaluated, used as example and evidence, collected and communicated, and mobilized as a technique of mitigation and modulation, as a method for the guidance and direction of souls. It was also employed as an object of aesthetic pleasure and edification in literature. The individual who escaped classification and categorization could henceforth be grasped not according to some generalizing scheme, but rather precisely in its individuality. As such, the psychological case history deserves a prominent place in what Foucault termed the history of *subjectification*: "This form of power applies itself to immediate everyday life which categorizes the individual, marks him by his own individuality, attaches him to his own identity, imposes a law of truth on him which he must recognize and which others have to recognize in him. It is a form of power which makes individuals [into] subjects."[140]

---

[139] Giorgio Agamben, *Homo Sacer: Sovereign Power and Bare life*, trans. Daniel Heller-Roazen (Stanford: Stanford University Press, 1998), 15.
[140] Michel Foucault, "The Subject and Power," *Critical Inquiry* 8.4 (1982): 781.

3 Disciplining the Human Soul: German Empirical Psychology in the Eighteenth Century from Christian Wolff to Kant

> Our psychology has still not advanced very far beyond its childhood, when it continues along its path of conclusions and hypotheses in an attempt to get at the most familiar things, what all human souls have in common, without noticing the specificities of individual subjects with the precision with which the natural scientist analyzes the bodies of animals in order to sneak into the inner workshop of nature.
>
> J.G. Herder, *Über Thomas Abbts Schriften* (1768)[1]

The modern discipline of Psychology in eighteenth-century Germany emerged in an intricate historical context of secularization, natural philosophy, natural law, and German Enlightenment or *Aufklärung*.[2] Throwing off superstition, transmitted learning, bookish authority, and the uncritical reliance on Galenic and Hippocratic medical models in favor of the new natural-scientific demand for empirical evidence, rigorous observation, and experimentation, German psychology in this period deposed the Aristotelian theory of the soul contained

---

[1] Johann Gottfried Herder, *Über Thomas Abbts Schriften. Der Torso von einem Denkmal, an seinem Grabe errichtet*, in *Werke in zehn Bänden. Schriften zur Ästhetik und Literatur, 1767–1781* (Frankfurt: Deutsche Klassiker Verlag, 1994–2010), vol. 2, 571: "Immer ist unsere Psychologie noch nicht weit über die Kindheit hinaus, wenn sie blos nach dem Bekanntesten, das alle menschliche Seelen gemeinsam haben, ihren Weg durch Schlüsse und Errathungen fortsetzt, ohne auf die Besonderheiten einzelner Subjekte mit der Genauigkeit zu merken, mit welcher der Naturforscher die Körper der Thiere zergliedert, um sich in die innere Werkstätte der Natur einzuschleichen."

[2] Most recently, Matthew Bell's *The German Tradition of Psychology, 1740–1800* (Cambridge: Cambridge University Press, 2005) has argued a move away from Christian Wolff around 1770 in Germany: "In the 1770s the creeping movement away from Wolffian Psychology and towards French and especially British Models becomes noticeable" (59). Bell pegs Wolff as a rationalist, omitting that Wolff essentially founded the discipline of empirical psychology, arguing it was the basis for a rational psychology. John H. Zammito follows the same line of reasoning in his *Kant, Herder, and the Birth of Anthropology* (Chicago: University of Chicago Press, 2002), 241: "Locke and Hume carried German Psychology away from its rational elaboration in Wolff and Baumgarten towards a physiological-observational psychology, or *Erfahrungsseelenkunde*." I will suggest here that there is more of a direct line of transmission and tradition from Wolff's *empirical* psychology to the developments of the later eighteenth century than has been recognized thus far, and that it is less the French and British influence than the expansion and enhancement of Wolff's empirical psychology. See also: David E. Leary, "The Philosophical Development of the Conception of Psychology in Germany, 1780–1850," *Journal of the History of the Behavioral Sciences* 14.2 (1978): 113–121.

https://doi.org/10.1515/9783110643466-004

in *De anima*. The metaphysical and theological apparatus that had governed thinking about the human soul since antiquity began to give way to a natural-scientific understanding of the human being as a unity of mind and body, as a physiological-psychological hybrid, what has been referred to in the literature as "the anthropological turn,"[3] a turn at least as powerful as Kant's "Copernican Turn," if not more so. The primacy of *experience – Erfahrung –* became the new standard for medicine and psychology alike.[4] But "experience" in the German tradition of psychology of the eighteenth century was not atomistic, momentary, or merely sequential; it encompassed induction from actually observed cases, self-observation and retrospection, attention to empirical facts, and self-reflection of the mind's activity. More importantly, as we shall see in the case of Johann Georg Zimmermann, "experience" included the written narratives or case histories of other respected physicians of the early modern period such as Herman Boerhaave, whose observations, descriptions, and recommendations could be trusted. This enhanced or expanded notion of "experience" was to set the stage for the avalanche of actual psychological case-histories, autobiographies, and psychological novels beginning in the last three decades of the eighteenth century.

If empirical psychology is indeed the disciplinary pre-condition to the modern narrative psychological case history, as we have suggested in the previous historical rendering, then one must first identify the historical emergence and development of German empirical psychology. First, through close readings of Wolff, Baumgarten, Stahl and the psychological physicians at Halle, Mendelssohn and Sulzer, Zimmermann, Platner, Abel and Kant, we will trace the trajectory of empirical psychology. Second, the profound differences between German empirical psychology and the developments in England and France have to be made explicit; empirical psychology in Germany represents a very different field of inquiry than the atomistic, "punctualist," associationist psychology of John Locke or the materialism and metaphysical skepticism of the *philosophes* in France. In particular, Stahl's psycho-dynamic model of medicine informed later thinking about the reciprocal relation between mind and body, and laid the groundwork for the anthropological turn at the University of Halle around 1750. Third, it must be shown how the *soul*, both as a representational power/activity and as the "seat" of the emotions, affects, and passions, was of the utmost importance to eighteenth

---

[3] Hans-Jürgen Schings, ed., *Der ganze Mensch. Anthropologie und Literatur im 18. Jahrhundert* (Stuttgart and Weimar: J. B. Metzler, 1994).
[4] Thomas H. Broman, *The Transformation of German Academic Medicine in Germany, 1780–1820* (Ann Arbor: University of Michigan Press, 1996). Broman locates the empirical turn in medicine in Seydenham's *De arte medica* (1669).

century thought and literature. Philosophers and physicians became fascinated by the "dark" and "obscure" aspects of the human soul, and began to attempt a scientific understanding of the so-called "lower" faculties. Finally, we have to indicate how the individual psychological case history emerged in this context of interest in a science of the soul as the most appropriate response to a specific requirement for original, authentic, empirical, observation-based reports and narratives that would provide the evidentiary corpus necessary for a systematic study of the entire human being as psycho-physical unity.[5] Case histories, case studies, and case narratives became the "evidence" for a "new science" of the soul.

How did psychology in this modern sense get started? What discursive and disciplinary transformations contributed to the formation of psychology as a modern natural-scientific discipline? Foucault's history of madness provided numerous clues as to why and how psychology became a key discipline in the "classical era," mostly having to do with new forms of discipline and governmentality, but he gave us very little on the specificity of German psychology. Doris Kaufmann made a very convincing case in the mid-1990s that the "invention" of the *psychiatry* of the nineteenth century was a direct result of what she referred to as the "bourgeois experience of a self" as something "endangered" or "in play" in the eighteenth century. In the German Enlightenment discourse of the science of the soul, certain fears and sufferings become thematized, and Kaufmann sought to show exactly how these fears and anxieties concerning the fate of the soul became articulated in the bourgeois discourse and academic-scholarly discipline of *Seelenkunde*. According to Kaufmann, the Enlightenment's critique of the metaphysical soul sparked the interest in precisely what forms of internal and external disruptions and obstacles to reason threatened the soul's very health and existence.[6] More recently, Fernando Vidal's otherwise excellent *The Sciences of the Soul: The Early Modern Origins of Psychology* offers a broad canvas from the early modern psychologies of the sixteenth century to the modern texts of empirical psychology of the eighteenth

---

[5] The "anthropological turn" of the eighteenth century became one of the most important and fruitful research areas in the 1990s, above all through the work of Hans Jürgen Schings and Helmut Pfotenhauer. See: Schings, ed., *Der ganze Mensch*; and Helmut Pfotenhauer, *Literarische Anthropologie. Selbstbiographien und ihre Geschichte – Am Leitfaden des Leibes* (Stuttgart: Metzler, 1987).

[6] Doris Kaufmann, *Aufklärung, bürgerliche Selbsterfahrung und die 'Erfindung' der Psychiatrie in Deutschland, 1770–1850* (Göttingen: Vandenhoeck & Ruprecht, 1995), esp. 49: "Die erfahrungsseelenkundlichen Zeitschriften wie das Moritzsche *Magazin* bildeten eine neue Form und ein wichtiges Forum für die bürgerlichen Schichten, die Ängste und Unsicherheiten ihrer Bewusstseins- und Gefühlslage zum Ausdruck zu bringen."

century,⁷ but fails, in my view, to adequately account for the decisive transformation which occurs in the German tradition, specifically during the period 1750 to 1780. Vidal stages the specific emergence of empirical psychology in the eighteenth century in Germany within the battle between Locke's empirical, observational method and the rationalistic (*raisonnierende*) method of the French and Gottfried Wilhelm Leibniz,⁸ stating that while psychology in the German *Aufklärung* "did not form a homogeneous whole, it generally resisted Locke's ascendency."⁹ Yet it was precisely Locke's and Isaac Newton's insistence on empirical study and their rejection of speculative hypotheses that in fact informs much of the methodological preference for rigorous observation (*Beobachtung*), direct experience, and arguing from actual cases in Germany. This is most powerfully evident in the work of Johann Nicolas Tetens (1736–1807) and Karl Philipp Moritz (1759–1793). It is during this period, and in the German territories that the most salient methodological and stylistic components – literary, philosophical, critical – of the modern discipline of empirical psychology as a science of the soul converge and become articulated explicitly.

Kurt Danziger has located the emergence of scientific psychology in the laboratory of Wilhelm Wundt and in the experimental psychology of the nineteenth century.¹⁰ Moving against historical accounts that seek to identify the roots of psychology in the early modern dichotomy between the extended mechanical world of matter and the world of the mind, Danziger noted that the "inner world of the isolated individual mind" might well have surfaced in the early modern era as a *potential* object of specialized scientific investigation,¹¹ but that the actual institutionalization and professionalization of the discipline does not occur until the nineteenth century, according to Danziger, when Wilhelm Wundt's properly experimental procedure and method of introspection became the scientific model for the study of human psychology.

As John Forrester has pointed out, however, Danziger's history was aimed at experimental scientific psychology as a probabilistic-statistical discipline. Here, one must be careful to distinguish between empiricisms. A very different strand of psychology emerges in eighteenth-century Germany that has a strong influence on the special character that psychiatry was to assume in

---

7 Fernando Vidal, *The Sciences of the Soul: The Early Modern Origins of Psychology*, trans. Saskia Brown (Chicago: University of Chicago Press, 2011).
8 Vidal, *Sciences of the Soul*, 109–112.
9 Vidal, *Sciences of the Soul*, 112.
10 Kurt Danziger, *Constructing the Subject: Historical Origins of Psychological Research* (Cambridge: Cambridge University Press, 1990).
11 Danziger, *Constructing the Subject*, 21.

nineteenth century Germany; this other, "experiential" psychology was not concerned with statistics or statistical knowledge, and did not employ nosographical tables, but rather specific *cases*.[12] This specific "style"[13] of psychology derived from two sources: first, as already indicated, the "anthropological turn," articulated by scholars such as Hans-Jürgen Schings, Wolfgang Riedel, Carsten Zelle, and Alexander Košenina, that occurs in Germany in the middle of the eighteenth century; second, experiential psychology – what was referred to as *Experimentalseelenkunde* – as it was theorized by the psychologically-minded physicians in Halle around 1750 – Johann August Unzer, Johann Gottlob Krüger, Johann Christian Bolten, and Ernst Anton Nicolai – and then by Zimmermann in 1763 in his *Concerning Experience in Medicine*. We find an explicit connection between this mode of psychological inquiry with its emphasis on direct observation, introspection, and case narratives, and *experiential or empirical psychology* – Krüger's *Experimentalseelenlehre*, or Moritz's *Erfahrungsseelenkunde*. In the eighteenth century, in other words, experiential psychology – a psychology interested in the rigorous observation and description of the representational processes of the mind – is institutionalized in Halle by the psychologically-minded physicians who had been influenced by Stahl's psycho-dynamic concept of illness. This tradition is carried forth in the second half of the eighteenth century – what is often referred to as the late Enlightenment (*Spätaufklärung*) in Germany – by figures such as Friedrich Schiller, Marcus Herz and Karl Philipp Moritz.[14] Without question, this new discipline and discourse of empirical-experiential psychology transformed the literature and philosophy of the late eighteenth and early nineteenth centuries.

---

12 John Forrester, "If p, then what? Thinking in Cases," *History of the Human Sciences* 9.3 (1996): 4.
13 I use the term in the sense of A.C. Crombie's *Styles of Scientific Thinking in the European Tradition: The History of Argument and Explanation Especially in the Mathematical and Biomedical Sciences and Arts* (London: Duckworth, 1995), vol. 2; and Ian Hacking, "Styles of Reasoning," in *Postanalytic Philosophy*, ed. John Rajchman and Cornel West (New York: Academic Press, 1985), 145–164.
14 Moritz changed the name of his project from *Experimentalseelenlehre* (Krüger's term) to *Erfahrungsseelenkunde* on the recommendation of Mendelssohn, who pointed out that psychology lacked the actual strict scientific "experiments" of the natural sciences and had to rely instead on observation, introspection, and, at best, *Versuche*, which, unlike scientific experiments, do not *alter* or physically affect the subject, but merely attempt to discern how individuals respond to certain types of physical stimuli or other "influences." On this, see Carsten Zelle, "Experiment, Experience and Observation in Eighteenth-Century Anthropology and Psychology – the Examples of Krüger's *Experimentalseelenlehre* and Moritz' *Erfahrungsseelenkunde*," *Orbis Litterarum* 56.2 (2001): 93–105.

Relying on philological and textual evidence, recent accounts place the emergence of modern experiential psychology in the metaphysical divide that opens up in the early modern period. The term "psychology" appears from the neo-Latin usage in the sixteenth century as a "theory of the soul," as one can read in the primal text of European psychology, Melanchthon's *De anima* of 1540, a commentary on Aristotle's text of the same name.[15] The first text containing the word *psychologia* in Germany is Otto Casmann's *Psychologia anthropologica sive animae humanae doctrina* of 1594.[16] The ontological two-world structure that dominated thought in the sixteenth century – a finite, mortal earthly-material world (*mundus sensibilis*) and a transcendent, immortal world of the soul (*mundus intelligibilis*) – was to become philosophically legitimated and canonized, secularized, and made philosophically "scientific" in René Descartes's dualism of *res extensa* and *res cogitans*. Psychology in early modern Europe was a study of the human soul, the immortal, "spiritual" substance as the exact opposite of sensuous, bodily, earthly existence. This "cordoning off" of the soul as a substance diametrically opposed to all corporeal being, an onto-theological spiritual sphere utterly devoid of any trace of material, earthly existence, dominated philosophical discourse until the rise of early modern medicine. At the end of the sixteenth century, based on Galenic doctrine, medicine turned towards "physiology" as the teaching and theory of the human body, its organs and their function; "psychology" was merely a parallel study, the spiritual, *mental* correlate and mirror of this world of material bodily function. It was a *physics of the soul*.[17] The question as to the interaction between the two now became paramount, and became the contest of any number of theories.

At the beginning of the eighteenth century in Germany, two distinct, yet parallel intellectual-academic transformations occurred that exerted significant influence on subsequent psychological thought. First, from the field of medicine, the Professor of Medicine at the University of Halle Georg Ernest Stahl

---

[15] Eckhart Scheerer, Article "Psychologie," in *Historisches Wörterbuch der Philosophie*, ed. Joachim Ritter (Basel: Schwabe, 1971), vol. 7, 1599–1653.

[16] Bell, *German Tradition of Psychology*, 12.

[17] Hobbes is paradigmatic for this view. For Hobbes, in his *De Corpere* of 1655, psychological states are the result of physical motions; to understand the perturbations of the mind, we have to understand the perturbations of the material body. We also have, according to Hobbes, not only rational knowledge of the motions of the mind, but also "the experience of every man who takes the pains to observe those motions within himself." Thomas Hobbes, *The Elements of Law Natural and Politic*, edited with an introduction by J.C.A. Gaskin (Oxford: Oxford University Press, 1999), 199.

(1660–1734) pioneered a psychological theory of the influence of the mind on the body, a psycho-dynamic explanation of the unity of the human being. The terms "influxionism" and "animism" are frequently employed to categorize Stahl's psycho-dynamic account of illness and disease and to distinguish it from the iatro-mechanical model of his colleague and sometime adversary at Halle, Friedrich Hoffmann (1660–1742). Second, in philosophy, Christian Wolff (1679–1754) founded the discipline of an *empirical psychology* (*psychologica empirica*) and thereby paved the way for an observational, evidence-based science of the soul relying on introspection and reflection, rather than on purely speculative metaphysics.[18] While Wolff recognized the distinction between the introspective attention to the soul and the observable evidence of empirical science, self-reflection as the method of empirical psychology still counted for Wolff as an *empirical* undertaking. It is just this discursive sense of "empirical," encompassing both external observation as well as inward self-reflection, that distinguishes German psychology in the eighteenth century. This expansion of what it means to count as "empirical" runs parallel to the enhancement of the concept of "experience" (*Erfahrung*) which we find in the German eighteenth century, beginning most explicitly with Zimmermann's influential work *Concerning Experience in Medicine* (*Von der Erfahrung in der Arzneykunst*) in the early 1760s.

The center of academic medicine in Germany at the end of the seventeenth and beginning of the eighteenth century was the University of Halle, established in 1694 by Frederick I, Elector of Brandenburg. Halle rapidly became the most prestigious medical institution in Germany. The two chairs in Medicine were held by Stahl and Hoffmann, who were both influenced by the new scientific method of Francis Bacon, and rejected scholasticism.[19] They developed an enormous body of case-histories (*observationes medicae*) based on their own

---

18 Kant famously rejected the entire Wolffian psychology, claiming in the *Critique of Pure Reason* (1781; 1787) that knowledge of the soul, or the "I," is beyond the power of human reason, and, in his *Metaphysical Foundations of Natural Science* (1786), that psychology as an empirical undertaking could never become a natural science proper. On this, see: Leary, "Philosophical Development of the Conception of Psychology," 113–121. I deal with Kant's critique later in this chapter.

19 See the work of Johanna Geyer-Kordesch, *Pietismus, Medizin, und Aufklärung in Preußen im 18. Jahrhundert* (Tübingen: Niemeyer, 1996); and Geyer-Kordesch, "Georg Ernest Stahl's Radical Pietist Medicine and Its Influence on the German Enlightenment," in *The Medical Enlightenment of the Eighteenth Century*, ed. Andrew Cunningham and Roger French (Cambridge, New York, and Melbourne: Cambridge University Press, 1990), 67–87. Geyer-Kordesch stresses the connection between Stahl's medical ideas and the reform movement of the Pietists in Halle.

clinical experience.[20] But while Hoffmann adhered to a rigid mechanistic, material-causal theory of the relationship between the mind and the body, Stahl developed a psycho-dynamic theory of the relationship in which the soul was ultimately the causal basis for all bodily changes. Instead of explaining the movements of the soul as the flow of nervous fluids through nervous tubes or canals, Stahl proposed a "string" model of the nerves and the psycho-dynamic concept of animism, *influxus animae*, whereby the soul has a sufficient idea of and is synergistically linked to the body.[21] The human being becomes a functional unity according to Stahl only through the activity of the soul. Passions play a decisive role in the etiology of disease, as Stahl wrote in 1695: "Passions, which are incited from within and not simply through external objects, are usually the most repercussive and mediate causes of illness."[22] Stahl singled out depressive states and mourning in particular as "viscous" passions likely to cause the most chronic illnesses by bringing about stagnation of the life-forces.[23] According to historian of medicine L. J. Rather, the essence of Stahlian medicine was that the soul "arouses, sustains, controls and directs all bodily movements, and this *anima* is immaterial, regulative, and purposeful."[24]

As both Sulzer and Georg Wilhelm Friedrich Hegel later recognized, Christian Wolff was the first philosopher to clearly recognize and articulate the importance of the separate discipline of empirical psychology.[25] "Psychology"

---

20 Geyer-Kordesch, "Medizinische Fallbeschreibungen und ihre Bedeutungen in der Wissensreform des 17. Und 18. Jahrhunderts," *Medizin, Gesellschaft, Geschichte* 9 (1990): 7–19.
21 Gabriele Dürbeck, *Einbildungskraft und Aufklärung: Perspektiven der Philosophie, Anthropologie und Ästhetik um 1750* (Tübingen: Niemeyer, 1998), 119–155. See also: Richard Toellner, "Medizin in der Mitte des 18. Jahrhunderts," in *Wissenschaft im Zeitalter der Aufklärung*, ed. Rudolf Vierhaus (Göttingen: Vandenhoeck & Ruprecht, 1985), 194–217.
22 Georg Ernest Stahl, *De passionibus animi corpus humanum varie alterantibus* (Halle, 1695), trans. as *Über die mannigfaltigen Einfluss der Gemüthsbewegungen auf den menschlichen Körper*, in *Georg Ernest Stahl*, by Bernward Josef Gottlieb (Leipzig: Johann Ambrosius Barth, 1961), 27: "Leidenschaften, die mehr von innen her, nicht nur von äußeren Objekten erregt werden, pflegen meist die rückwirkenden und unmittelbaren Ursachen von Krankheiten zu seyn."
23 Stahl, *Über den mannigfaltigen Einfluss*, 32: "Niedergeschlagenheit und Trauer als zähflüssige Leidenschaften verursachen meist chronische Krankheiten."
24 L. J. Rather, "G.E. Stahl's Psychological Physiology," *Bulletin of the History of Medicine* 35.1 (1961): 27–49.
25 See Johann Georg Sulzer, *Kurzer Begriff aller Wissenschaften und anderer Theile der Gelehrsamkeit* (Leipzig: Johann Christian Langenheim, 1759), §206, 158; Georg Wilhelm Friedrich Hegel, *Vorlesungen über die Geschichte der Philosophie. Teil 4*, ed. Pierre Garniron and Walter Jaeschke (Hamburg: F. Meiner, 1986), 136–140. See also: Robert J. Richards, "Christian Wolff's Prolegomena to Empirical and Rational Psychology: Translation and Commentary," *Proceedings of the American Philosophical Society* 124.3 (1980): 227.

in Wolff's philosophy was divided into two parts: *rational psychology*, the theory of the *soul* as the exact opposite of material being, and *empirical psychology*, which was thought to corroborate and demonstrate in the realm of experience what had been exposed theoretically in rational psychology. Wolff's philosophical psychology, contained in his *Psychologia rationalis* (1734; 1740) and *Psychologia empirica* (1732; 1738), were standard textbooks throughout the eighteenth century and emblematic for the German *Frühaufklärung* and its reliance on reason (*Vernunft*) as the ultimate guarantor of knowledge. But Wolff was far from a dogmatic rationalist as has often been argued. He actually opened the way for the discipline of empirical-experiential psychology that was to take charge in central Europe during the second half of the eighteenth century.

For Wolff, the soul was a simple substance – immaterial, indivisible, and immortal – outside of the causal chain of material events; it was fundamentally *representational activity*. Precisely because of its ontological uniqueness as an immaterial substance or being, it guaranteed two fundamental precepts: the *immortality* of the soul and *human freedom*. However powerful the insistence on rational demonstrability in Wolff's psychology, the empirical component – empirical psychology or *psychologia empirica* – was not simply an auxiliary discipline in the service of rational psychology.[26] Wolff parsed out the structure of perceptual experience as having two components: the *representing activity of the mind* and the *represented content*.[27] To be sure, empirical psychology was to verify through introspection, experiment, observation, and case-studies what rational psychology could already establish in a purely deductive, speculative fashion in theory. Empirical psychology had the advantage, however, for Wolff, of being the "area" in which such inquiries would occur, by virtue of its proximity to the immediate data provided by the "introspection" and direct observation of mental phenomena. For his primary instrument of "introspection," Wolff mobilized the notion of "apperception"[28] contained in the work of

---

[26] See Robert J. Richards, "Christian Wolff's Prolegomena to Empirical and Rational Psychology," 227–239.

[27] Christian Wolff, *Psychologia Empirica, methodo scientifica pertractata, qua ea, quae de anima humana indubia experientiae fide constant, continentur* (Francofurti and Lipsiae: officina libraria Rengeriana, 1732, 1738), §24. It is astonishing to remark the similarities of this type of theory to that of Husserl's phenomenology. The history of these "disciplines" would suggest a historico-cultural continuity from the experiential or empirical psychology of the eighteenth century to Brentano and Husserl. This includes, but is not limited to, the reliance on "apperception" of the relation between representational activities of the mind and the represented content or *Inhalt*.

[28] Vidal, *Sciences of the Soul*, 92–93, 160.

Leibniz; the mind could, through an intentional act, attend to the mental operation itself, i.e., how the representing activity and the represented content are related, and thus progressively bring obscure or vague perceptions to increased levels of clarity and distinctness. In the introductory paragraphs of the *Psychologia empirica*, Wolff states that apperception "is attributed to the mind, inasmuch as the latter is conscious of its own perceptions,"[29] that "we come to acknowledge of the mind, if we pay attention to our thoughts; and if further we attribute to the mind all that has been gathered by legitimate reasoning."[30] Later in the text, Wolff tells us that "the faculty of reflecting is the faculty of directing one's attention at will to the things contained in the thing perceived."[31] Leibniz of course had already recognized the existence of obscure (*dunkle*) representations, and had distinguished between those representations which are obscure because of the matter itself and those which are obscure due to the present, and therefore temporary, limitations of human knowledge (and could theoretically be clarified in time). It was simply an anthropological fact for Leibniz and Wolff that human beings not only had limited knowledge, but that certain things in themselves would never achieve clarity *in principle*, and would therefore remain relegated to the realm of obscure representation: sensations such as tastes and smells, and the perception of colors could never be brought to level of clear knowledge. They did not believe that one could mathematize things like desires, emotions, passions, feelings, premonitions, or dreams. Wolff's very dualism, however, specifically his authoring of a text on empirical psychology, prepared the way for later developments which increasingly recognized the significance and power of *obscure* (*dunkle*) representations in the human soul precisely by placing such obscure representations within the purview of empirical psychology, and even going so far as to say that obscurity was an inescapable part of the human soul itself.[32] If that is true, empirical psychology would be the indispensable discipline to cull the results of these observations, in addition to becoming the framing method by which questions pertaining to psychopathology, dreams, imaginative projections, feelings, and

---

29 Wolff, *Psychologia Empirica*, §5.
30 Wolff, *Psychologia Empirica*, §8.
31 Wolff, *Psychologia Empirica*, §142.
32 Christian Wolff, *Psychologia Empirica*, in *Gesammelte Werke* II, Abteilung, ed. H. Arndt and J. Ecole. Hildesheim: G. Olms, 1962–), vol. 5, §50. Also, in the *Deutsche Metaphysik*, Wolff wrote: "[...] dass unser Verstand niemals ganz reine ist, sondern bei der Deutlichkeit beständig noch viel Undeutlichkeit und Dunkelheit übrig bleibt."

passions would be articulated. In his *German Metaphysics*,[33] Wolff states that obscure (*dunkle*) representations – that is, sensations, feelings, intuitions and "senses" lacking clarity and distinction – are an unavoidable part of human cognition. As the eighteenth century in Germany unfolded, these obscure representations became a gold-mine for aesthetics, anthropology, and psychology.[34] Such "dark" or "obscure" representations became a font for a unique form of knowledge, a sensual knowledge, a knowledge that lacked the logical discursive rigor of clear and distinct judgments, but was more immediate, more intuitive, and "closer" to the actual experience of the world in its repleteness.[35] Wolff's dichotomy between rational and empirical psychology was not merely the forerunner to German experiential psychology of the later eighteenth century; he paved the way for the methodology of empirical or experiential psychology – introspection, observation, and experiment – as it was to replace a fully rational psychology of *a priori* principles and theoretical speculation. Thus, in Wolff's *Psychologia empirica*, we read in the first paragraphs that empirical psychology "is the science that establishes principles through experience, whence reason is given for what occurs in the human soul."[36] Wolff argues that "we come to know the subjects dealt with in empirical psychology by attending to those occurrences in our souls of which we are conscious;"[37] and finally, in the most astonishing defense of the empirical branch of psychology, Wolff asserts that "empirical psychology supplies principles for rational psychology; in rational psychology, reason is given for what occurs in the human soul. But empirical psychology establishes principles whence reason is given for what occurs in the human soul."[38] Indeed, Wolff goes so far as so say that empirical psychology "provides principles for *natural law*."[39] Rational psychology seeks to give *reasons* for what is presented in empirical-psychological "studies" and "research." Wolff was therefore no strict rationalist when it

---

33 Christian Wolff, *Vernünftige Gedanken von Gott, der Welt und der Seele des Menschen, auch allen Dingen überhaupt* [*Deutsche Metaphysik*] (Halle, 1719), §285. Wolff states here that the faculty of understanding is never absolutely "pure" and that there always remains indistinction (*Undeutlichkeit*) and obscurity (*Dunkelheit*).
34 Hans Adler, "'Fundus Animae – Grund der Seele.' Zur Gnoseologie des Dunklen in der Aufklärung," *Deutsche Vierteljahrsschrift für Literaturwissenschaft und Geistesgeschichte* 62.2 (1988): 197–220.
35 On this, see David E. Wellbery, *Lessing's Laocoon: Aesthetics and Semiotics in the Age of Reason* (Cambridge: Cambridge University Press, 1984).
36 Wolff, *Psychologia empirica*, §1.
37 Wolff, *Psychologia empirica*, §2.
38 Wolff, *Psychologia empirica*, §4.
39 Wolff, *Psychologia empirica*, §6; emphasis mine.

comes to psychology; in fact, he often seems to privilege empirical psychology and its direct method of *introspection* as supplying the most important data for the study of the human soul, specifically, the relationship between the *representing activity of mind* and the *represented content* or objects of such activity.

Alexander Baumgarten (1714–1762) is perhaps better known for his *Aesthetics* (1750), but his *Metaphysics* (1739) was used as an introduction to the field throughout the eighteenth century. Kant used the fourth edition of the *Metaphysics* (1757) as a textbook in his lectures on the subject, and Baumgarten's metaphysics – his theory of the soul in particular – served as a foil against which Kant was to formulate his theory of self-consciousness in the Transcendental Dialectic section of the *Critique of Pure Reason*.[40] While certainly based on Wolff's theory and sharing a number of underlying assumptions with it, Baumgarten's empirical psychology in the *Metaphysics* makes some interesting observations that underscore the more general shift away from rational psychology to empirical psychology in the middle of the eighteenth century. For Baumgarten, empirical psychology deduces its assertions "based upon experiences that are nearest to hand."[41]

Baumgarten shares with Wolff the basic notion of the mind as an intentional, fundamentally representational activity – meaning it is directed at some real or imagined object. In part 3, chapter 1, Baumgarten "deduces" the existence of the soul in the following manner: "If there is something in a being that can be conscious of something, that is a SOUL. Something exists in me that can be conscious of something. Therefore, a soul exists in me (I, a soul, exist)."[42] Because specific thoughts are "accidents" of the soul, some of which have their sufficient ground in the soul itself, the soul is a power, and because thoughts are not simply arbitrary, but representations of *something*, the soul is a *power for representing*.[43] But the soul always thinks about, represents *something*, and this "something" is the universe and the bodies contained within it. Now the soul thinks about some bodies and their alterations more than others, and it thinks most about the alterations of one body in particular most of all: one's own body. Baumgarten writes: "My body is the one whose changes I think

---

[40] Compare Udo Thiel, "The Critique of Rational Psychology," in *A Companion to Kant*, ed. Graham Bird (New York: John Wiley, 2009), 207–221.
[41] Alexander Baumgarten, *Metaphysics: A Critical Translation with Kant's Elucidations, Selected notes, and Related Materials*, trans. and ed. Courtney D. Fugate and John Hymers (London, New Delhi, New York: Bloomsbury, 2013), 198.
[42] Baumgarten, *Metaphysics*, §504, 198.
[43] Baumgarten, *Metaphysics*, §505, 198.

more about than I do those of any other body."⁴⁴ The body has a determinate position, place, age and situation in the world, and therefore the soul represents according to *the position of the body*.⁴⁵ Some of these representations are clearer and more distinct than others; we conceive of some things more clearly and distinctly, and others – those things that are given to us through the senses – more confusedly and obscurely. The faculty of knowing something obscurely and confusedly is for Baumgarten an inferior cognitive faculty, what he refers to as *sensate representation or cognition*. However, this form of representation or cognition can be more lively and stronger than a perception that is clearer and more distinct, and therefore has value in and of itself. Baumgarten calls the science of such sensate cognition or representation *aesthetics*: "The science of knowing and presenting with regard to the senses is aesthetics."⁴⁶

Baumgarten followed Wolff's reading of Leibniz in the notion that the states of the soul follow one another as the representations themselves follow one another, but he departs from Wolff in three essential ways. First, he opens up the possibility of sensate (obscure/confused) cognition having a far more significant role in the constitution of the soul precisely by affording the soul a more lively, richer, more replete form of cognition which could be considered on its own terms and theorized in a science dedicated solely to this form of cognition – aesthetics. Second, Baumgarten emphasizes the positionality of the *body*, its situatedness in the world, and its determinative power in the constitution of all cognition: my body is the standpoint through which I perceive and represent, and while I can certainly abstract from such perspectival and bound representation, the body and its position remain determinate in my apprehension of the universe and the bodies within it. Finally, Baumgarten's notion of the *association of ideas* as a law of the imagination, what he also refers to as *nexus*,⁴⁷ is intended to bring that which is cognized less clearly and distinctly to a higher level of comprehension by contextualizing it, and providing a linkage between singular sensations, some of which have occurred in the past, other sensations, and the field within which they occur: "Imagination and sensation are of singular beings, and hence of beings located within a universal

---

44 Baumgarten, *Metaphysics*, §508, 199.
45 Thus, the prominent idea of the "point of view" or *Sehepunkt* of the subject, which Leibniz developed in the *Monadology* (written 1714, published after his death in 1720 [German], 1721 [Latin]) becomes one of the underlying epistemological figures of German Enlightenment. See Robert S. Leventhal, *The Disciplines of Interpretation: Lessing, Herder, Schlegel and Hermeneutics in Germany 1750–1800* (Berlin: de Gruyter, 1994), 50–51.
46 Baumgarten, *Metaphysics*, §533, 205.
47 Baumgarten, *Metaphysics*, §561–563.

nexus."[48] This lends a specifically historical dimension to representation and sensation. The greater the nexus, the clearer and livelier the representation becomes: "Those things I have sensed and reproduced more often are parts of more total ideas than those that I have sensed or reproduced more rarely. Therefore, the images of the former are perceived in a greater nexus with many more ancillary notes than the images of the latter and hence they are extensively clearer, and much livelier."[49] This privileging of contextualized and historicized representation and sensation, and the placement of *nexus* as a determinative force, alongside positionality or bodily perspective, provided the groundwork for a more sustained and robust theory of empirical psychology; it was to have a strong influence on the philosophical physicians of the latter half of the eighteenth century, Herz in particular, who studied with Kant in Königsberg and used Baumgarten's text as his introduction to empirical psychology.

In the mid-eighteenth century, a group of psychologically-minded professors of medicine and physicians in Halle expanded and enhanced this terrain that had been prepared by Stahl, Wolff, and Baumgarten: Johann Gottlob Krüger (1715–1759), Johann August Unzer (1727–1799), Ernst Nicolai (1722–1802) and Johann Christian Bolten (1727–1757).[50] Although there were significant differences between them, all of the psychologically-minded medical professors and doctors at Halle rejected a mute materialism and were fascinated by the reciprocal influence of the mind and the body. They all certainly read Stahl and Wolff carefully. But they were by no means uncritical of the animistic influxionism – the soul as the animating force and cause of the body and illness – put forth by Stahl, or the seemingly dogmatic and rationalistic system of Wolff, at least as it was being disseminated by his students. One of the key players in this constellation, the physician and later editor of the journal *Der Arzt* (1759–1764), Unzer, wrote a text that was heavily indebted to Stahl: *Thoughts on the Influence of the Soul on its Body* (*Gedanken vom Einfluß der Seele in ihren Körper*, 1746). But Unzer took Stahl to task in his "Considerations about Stahl's Theoretical Fundamental Principle in Medicine" (*Betrachtungen über des seligen Herrn Hofraths Stahls theoretischer Grundsatz in der Arzneywissenschaft*) of 1753. Despite his respect for Stahl and his theory, Unzer sought to question the – in his view unwarranted and unexamined – assumption that *all* movements of the body are, without exception, "effects of the soul." Unzer claimed

---

[48] Baumgarten, *Metaphysics*, §561, 212.
[49] Baumgarten, *Metaphysics*, §563, 212–213.
[50] Carsten Zelle, ed., *Vernünftige Ärzte. Hallesche Psychomediziner und die Anfänge der Anthropologie in der deutschsprachigen Frühaufklärung* (Tübingen: Niemeyer, 2001).

that even Stahl himself did not provide an adequate account of the relation between body and soul in his theory of influxionism. The psychological harmonists who claimed an "ideal" influence of the soul on the body like Stahl were guilty, according to Unzer, of what he called a "one-sided" influxionism, denying that the body could in turn affect the soul. In his review of Stahl's contribution, Unzer wrote: "he considers the body as a merely passive, suffering clump that could not possibly have an effect on the soul."[51] Unzer differentiated his version of influxion from Stahl in his *Gedanken vom Einfluß der Seele in ihren Körper* of 1746:

> A Stahlian is an absolute influxionist; however, as far as I understand it, he does not maintain that the body does not act at all insofar as the soul effects something in the body [...] The influxionists to which I belong maintain that with the emergence of a specific change in the soul, to a degree the power of the soul, in part the power of the body is effectual; that the effect is partly ideal, and partly physical.[52]

The two fundamental propositions of Stahl – that the soul has a *real* influence on the body and that the body itself is an active, fully alive entity and not merely a passive thing – had not, in Unzer's view, been sufficiently distinguished. Unzer and the other psychologically minded physicians of the mid-eighteenth century affirmed the influence of the soul on the body, but rejected the view that the body itself was simply a passive, inactive, material "thing," receiving all direction, control and change from the soul. Citing Boerhaave and Albrecht von Haller, who had "reconstituted the body as an active organism" and as a "masterpiece of nature,"[53] Unzer argues for a reciprocal influence of soul and body, the theory of *Wechselwirkung*, "that the body and the soul consistently and reciprocally effect one another."[54] Unzer's point is that the largely

---

51 Johann August Unzer, "Betrachtungen über des eligen Herrn Hofraths Stahls theoretischer Grundsatz in der Arzneywissenschaft," *Hamburgisches Magazin* 10.4 (1753): 407–408: "er betrachtet den Körper als einen bloß leidenden Klumpen, der also nicht einmal in die Seele wirken könnte."
52 Johann August Unzer, *Gedanken vom Einfluss der Seele in ihren Körper* (Halle: Hemmerde, 1746), 118: "Ein Stahlianer ist ein vollkommener Influxionist; allein, so viel als ich davon verstehe, behauptet er nicht, daß der Körper gar nicht handle, indem seine Seele in ihm würkt [...] Die Influxionisten, zu denen ich gehöre, behaupten, daß bey Entstehung einer gewissen Veränderung in der Seele theils die Kraft der Seele, theils auch die Kraft des Körpers wirksam sey; mit einem Wort: daß die Würckung theils idealisch, theils physikalisch sey."
53 Johann August Unzer, "Betrachtungen über des eligen Herrn Hofraths Stahls theoretischer Grundsatz in der Arzneywissenschaft," 410.
54 Unzer, "Betrachtungen über des eligen Herrn Hofraths Stahls theoretischer Grundsatz in der Arzneywissenschaft," 420–421: "daß Leib und Seele beständig wechselweise in einander wirken."

theoretical debate regarding the influence of the mind on the body is superfluous; the real issue for the practicing physician is precisely *how* the reciprocal relation between that two actually occurs in any specific instance. For Unzer, Stahl had merely posited what he referred to as the *ideal* influence of the soul on the body; the actual influence remained to be demonstrated. It should be noted that Unzer's appraisal of Stahl misses the mark; Stahl did not, in fact, subscribe to the view of the human body as a merely passive, inert clump of matter.[55] Unzer probably exaggerated Stahl's animism in order to give greater profile to his theory of reciprocal influence.

Krüger was one of the key figures in the anthropological psychology that emerges around mid-century, a student of Wolff's, and Professor of Medicine and Philosophy at the Universities of Halle and Helmstedt. As Tanja van Hoorn has shown, Krüger sought to forge a reconciliation between the iatromechanical and animistic models of medicine.[56] His departure from Stahl's particular variant of animism is already visible in his *Grundriß eines neuen Lehrgebäudes der Artzneygelahrtheit* of 1745. Rejecting a metaphysical "positing" of the soul, and the essential faculty of the soul as reason, Krüger's interest was to research the soul scientifically, as a "feeling machine,"[57] thus bridging the gap between Stahl and Hoffmann and making the case for what Krüger envisioned would be a truly *empirical* psychology. Krügers *Versuch einer Experimentalseelenlehre* (1756)[58] essentially took what Wolff had laid out and

---

[55] Georg Ernest Stahl, *Dissertatio inauguralis medica de medicina medicinae curiosae* (Halle, 1714), where Stahl suggests a much more nuanced notion of the living human body (*Leib*) as a specific kind of body capable of adaptation and receiving "instruction." This goes against the recent assessment of John H. Zammito, *The Gestation of German Biology. Philosophy and Physiology from Stahl to Schelling* (Chicago: University of Chicago Press, 2017), 23: "For all of his emphasis on clinical outcomes, Stahl *was* a theorist. He set out from the ontological posit that matter was passive – *inert* in the strict Cartesian sense"; emphasis in the original.

[56] Tanja van Hoorn, *Entwurf einer Psychophysiologie des Menschen. Johann Gottlob Krügers Grundriß eines neuen Lehrgebäudes der Artzneygelahrtheit (1745)* (Hannover-Laatzen: Wehrhahn, 2006), 32.

[57] van Hoorn, *Entwurf einer Psychophysiologie des Menschen*, 100.

[58] There is now a significant amount of work on Krüger. Especially good are: Gabriele Dürbeck, "'Reizende und reizbare Einbildungskraft': Anthropologische Ansätze bei Johann Gottlob Krüger und Albrecht von Haller," in *Reiz – Imagination – Aufmerksamkeit: Erregung und Steurung von Einbildungskraft im klassischen Zeitalter*, ed. Jörn Steigerwald and Daniela Watzke (Würzburg: Königshausen & Neumann, 2003), 225–245; Wolfram Mauser, "Johann Gottlob Krüger. Der Weltweise als Arzt. Zur Anthropologie der Frühaufklärung in Deutschland," in *'Vernünftige Ärzte': Hallesche Psychomediziner und die Anfänge der Anthropologie in der deutschsprachigen Frühaufklärung*, ed. Carsten Zelle (Tübingen: Niemeyer, 2001), 48–67; Zammito, *Kant, Herder, and the Birth of Anthropology*, 241f. Zammito argues that "Locke and Hume carried German

created an "experimental" science of the soul. By equating psychology with the theory of soul (*Seelenlehre*), and requiring active experimentation as proof, he essentially taught psychology as a discipline at the intersection of physiology and experimental natural science (*Experimentalphysik*).[59] His project, evident in his inaugural lecture of 1751,[60] was an anthropology of the whole human being as a spiritual-material unity. Medicine should seek precisely to examine the various aspects of the relation between the mental and the physical, the effects of the world on the soul (*influxus physicus*) and the soul's internal operations and "mechanics" and how they in turn affected the body. As empirical psychology gained the upper hand, Krüger's sober and down-to-earth assessment of the human soul poses a stark contrast to Wolff's still quite theoretical approach. Krüger's psychology was descriptive rather than prescriptive; his whole point was to depict the human soul *as it is*, not as it *should be*.[61] As such, Krüger rejected the speculative theory of the soul put forth by Wolff and his disciples. He believed instead that the physician should base his practice on reasonable observations of actual life experiences and phenomena. For Krüger, a reciprocal relation or *Wechselwirkung* between the soul and the body existed whereby each exerted influence on the other through a complex process of sensation, perception, neural transmission,[62] affect and ideation. As Gabriele Dürbeck has noted: "Krüger conceives of the connection between soul and

---

Psychology away from its rational elaboration in Wolff and Baumgarten towards a physiological-observational psychology" (241). He mentions Krüger. However, I would argue that this development is more closely indebted to Wolff's *empirical psychology* and its methodology than Zammito would like to admit.

59 Krüger defined *Experiment* as Wolff did, as the procedure of placing something in such circumstances without which it would not have come about. See: Johann Gottlieb Krüger, *Versuch einer Experimentalseelenlehre* (Helmstedt, Halle: Hemmerde, 1756), vol. 1, 15. On this, see Tanja van Hoorn and Yvonne Wübben, "Zwischen Experimentalphysik und Experimentalseelenlehre," in *'Allerhand nuetzlicher Versuche': Empirische Wissenskulturen in Halle und Göttingen (1720–1750)*, ed. van Hoorn and Wübben (Hannover: Wallstein, 2009), 7–20, esp. 9.

60 Johann Gottlieb Krüger, *Zuschrift an seine Zuhörer von der Ordnung, in welcher man Arztneygelahrtheit erlernen müsse* (Halle: Carl Hermann Hemmerde, 1752).

61 Krüger, *Versuch einer Experimentalseelenlehre*, vol. 1, unpaginated preface: "die menschliche Seele so zu schildern, wie sie ist, aber nicht wie sie seyn soll."

62 Krüger, like most of his contemporaries, had adopted a neural model of sensation and perception whereby bodily sensations were conducted along neural paths – be they tubes, strings, or canals – and ultimately transmitted to the brain (*Gehirn*), which was seen as the *seat of the soul*. This was the center of the soul's representational activity, its "theater." Here, sensations were received, taken up and transformed into human perception and feeling, upon which thought reflected and on the basis of which a certain input of elemental data was "processed" by the soul's representation powers (*Kräfte*).

body in natural philosphy as well as in his experimental psychology as a reciprocal-effect relationship."[63] Krüger stresses in his *Naturlehre* "the soul affects the body and body the soul."[64] He explains this relation in terms of the excitation of the nerve surfaces and the proportionality between the intensity of the sensation and the movement of nerve-surfaces and the resulting sensations of the body, which in turn produce specific representations in the mind; these representations form part of a feedback-loop in which the bodily affect is also codetermined by the representations of the mind. Alternating between mechanistic and animistic models, Krüger sees both contributing to a general theory of sensation, excitation, and ultimately illness: powerful sensations and stimulations lead to a tensing of the nerve-surfaces and nerve-tubes which produce an excess or a constriction of the flow of nerve-fluids, and these in turn give rise to powerful and often violent or turbulent ideas in the mind: "The representations are all the more lively," wrote Krüger in his *Naturlehre*, "the greater the force of the nervous fluid in the brain."[65] In his *New Theory of the Movements of the Mind* (*Neue Lehre von den Gemüthsbewegungen*, 1746), Krüger departed from the theory of the humors and humoral pathology and seeks to explain various emotions and passions such as love, shame, hope, fear, anger, rage, ambition, envy, and hatred as affects related to the manner in which the soul processes the various sensations and perceptions.[66] The difference between sensation and imagination, *Empfindung* and *Einbildung*, is for Krüger ultimately quantitative; when a sensation becomes so powerful in the mind it drifts into imagination, the mind has difficulty separating the actual sensation from what it imagines, and this can lead to a "crisis of the system" which can only be "corrected" or "set right" by therapy: "the only means to assist people out of their error is to place them into the condition of such sensations that quite obviously conflict with their own imaginative thoughts, so that they are able to conclude from the resulting contradictions that these imaginings are foolish."[67] The only

---

[63] Dürbeck, "'Reizende und reizbare Einbildungskraft,'" 231n28: "Den Zusammenhang von Seele und Körper konzipiert Krüger sowohl in der Naturlehre als auch in seiner Experimental-Seelenlehre als ein Wechselwirkungsverhältnis."
[64] Johann Gottlob Krüger, *Naturlehre. Zweiter Theil, welcher die Physiologie oder Lehre von dem Leben und der Gesundheit der Menschen in sich fasset* (Halle: Carl Hemmerde, 1748), vol. 2, §315, 586: "die Seele in den Leib und der Leib in die Seele würket."
[65] Krüger, *Naturlehre*, vol. 2, §86, 82: "Die Vorstellungen sind desto lebhafter je größer die Gewalt des Nervensaftes im Gehirn ist."
[66] Krüger, *Neue Lehre von den Gemüthsbewegungen* (Halle: Carl Hemmerde, 1746).
[67] Krüger, *Naturlehre*, vol. 2, §429, 727: "das einzige Mittel, solchen Leuten aus ihren Irrthum heraus zu helfen, ist dieses, dass man sie in den Zustand solcher Empfindungen setze, welche

means of helping a person from such untethered imaginings that have gained the upper hand is to return them to the sensations themselves that are at odds with such representations, and, through the contradiction between the two, they would thus be able to see the folly of their imagination. Of course, this presupposes a rational mind capable of recognizing the contradiction, but Krüger does not seem to be concerned about that. He simply presupposed a rational kernel within the person capable of grasping the contradiction between actual sensation and imagination.

Another of the psychologically-minded physicians and later Professor of Medicine at Jena (1758), Ernst Anton Nicolai (1722–1802) studied experimental physics with Wolff, applied mathematics and natural science under Krüger at the University of Halle, and advanced to Doctor of Medicine in 1742 under Hoffmann with a dissertation concerning pain. Influenced also by Hoffmann's insistence on empirical evidence and observation, Nicolai became increasingly interested in the anthropological question of the "entire human being." He discussed the effects of the imagination on the human body in his *Wirkungen der Einbildungskraft in den menschlichen Körper* of 1744 and 1751. Whereas in the first edition he aligned himself with Newton and Wolff, in the second edition one sees the increasing influence of Georg Friedrich Meier's *Anfangsgründe aller schönen Wissenschaften* of 1748. Meier, student and then colleague of Baumgarten's who taught philosophy and aesthetics at the University of Halle, gave the psychologically-minded physicians the notion of imagination they mobilized for their writings on the effects of imagination on the body. Nicolai established a link between imagination and the power of poetry, indeed, between imagination and the capacity of the soul to create new representations from aspects of existing representations and ideas. This marks the shift from a merely reproductive to a productive sense of imagination that becomes commonplace in the second half of the eighteenth century and the basis for much of Romanticism. Nicolai identified the power of poetry as "a capacity to distinguish various imaginative associations and from these parts and the remnants of these associations to put together and create new representations."[68] Human imagination is capable of bringing about significant changes in the body and has, according to Nicolai, the most profound effect on the health or sickness of

---

ganz offenbar mit ihren Einbildungen streiten, damit sie aus dem daraus erfolgenden Widersprüchen schliessen können, dass ihre Einbildungen thöricht sind."

68 Ernst Anton Nicolai, *Wirkungen der Einbildungskraft in den menschlichen Körper* (Halle: Carl Hermann Hemmerde, 1744), §13, 24: "ein Vermögen [...] die Einbildungen zu theilen und aus Theilen und Trümmern verschiedener Einbildungen neue Vorstellungen zusammenzusetzen und zu erschaffen."

the individual: "Imagination is capable of bringing forth changes in the human body and has a very strong influence on the healthy and ill condition of the human being."[69] He developed an entire theory of medical-philosophical pathology whereby psychic phenomena such as disgust, fear, homesickness, and madness became mental effects of the imagination. For his examples, however, Nicolai did not produce a significant body of original work, but relied instead on the case-histories that Haller had published from the academic lectures of Boerhaave.[70] His originality was therefore not in empirical work or in the narrative of concrete individual cases, but in his elaboration of the theoretical connection between medicine, psychopathology, and the discipline of aesthetics.

In this regard, the last of our psychologically-minded physicians from the Halle constellation around the middle of the eighteenth century is perhaps also the most interesting. Johann Christian Bolten was the younger brother of Johann Friedrich Bolten, city physician of Hamburg. Often designated as the founder of *psychotherapy*, Bolten emerged out of the aforementioned constellation of psycho-medicine and anthropology at Halle, was promoted to Doctor of Medicine under Unzer at Halle in 1750, and later became the city-physician in Hamburg/Altona. He published his *Thoughts concerning Psychological Cures* (*Gedanken von psychologischen Curen*) in 1751. Bolten's purpose in writing the book was to identify what a psychological cure is, to establish the usefulness, indeed the necessity of such cures for specific types of illness, and to teach others how to go about curing mental illness or illnesses of the soul (*Kranckheiten der Seele*) through psychological therapy. The influence of Unzer, Krüger and above all Meier is immediately and explicitly apparent. Citing Meier's *Anfangsgründe*, Bolten states that Meier has provided the most important means for psychological cures, that aesthetics as Meier has outlined it establishes the laws and rules of the "lower" knowledge-faculties and is therefore in an even better position than psychology itself to develop the actual *means* of psychological cures.[71] Bolten then proceeds to present his variation of Nicolai's

---

[69] Nicolai, *Wirkungen*, §27, 49: "Die Einbildung kann Veränderungen im menschlichen Körper hervorbringen und hat einen starken Einfluss in den gesunden und den krancken Zustand eines Menschen."

[70] On this, see Gabriele Dürbeck, "Physiologischer Mechanismus und aesthetische Therapie: Ernst Anton Nicolais Schriften zur Psychopathologie," in *Vernünftige Ärzte. Hallesche Psychomediziner und die Anfänge der Anthropologie in der deutschsprachigen Frühaufklärung*, ed. Carsten Zelle (Tübingen: Niemeyer, 2001), 104–119, n25.

[71] See Zelle's excellent discussion of Bolten in his preliminary remark to his edited volume *Vernünftige Ärzte*, 19–20.

philosophical pathology,⁷² whose aesthetic component teaches how one can activate and control the movements of mind: "Philosophical pathology is the theory of the affects, the aesthetic part of which teaches how one can incite, suppress and gain control over the movements of the mind."⁷³ The "aesthetic" component of this philosophical pathology "provides the rules by which one can stir up, increase, hinder and repress the fluctuations of the mind [...] this part of science is the one that a person must master if they are to be able to apply such a science for the treatment of illness."⁷⁴ Aesthetics, which emerges as a distinct "discipline" or theory of the beautiful in the eighteenth century, is cast here in the role of a system of guidance and control of the "lower" faculties of the soul, the movements of the mind connected with sensation, emotion, and perception. For Bolten, mental illness or illnesses of the soul are located in the soul itself – its capacities of desiring and knowing – and, therefore, the sciences which concern themselves with these aspects of the soul – namely aesthetics, logic, philosophical pathology, and morality – are the sciences one should use in attempting to cure the soul of such illness: "All illnesses of the soul have their seat in the representational and desiring capacities of the soul [...] and therefore these sciences are sufficient to be able to cure the illnesses of the soul."⁷⁵ But these "sciences" only provide the theoretical basis for the particular application of each psychological cure; each particular psychological illness is the result of a particular overpowering emotion or passion, and will require a special set of rules for the specific psychological cure according to Bolten. Bolten thus merged his theoretical belief that there were general characteristics of mental illness, that they could be understood and cured, with the practical belief that one had to attend to the specificities of each individual case. Bolten's "psychological cure," however, turns out to be something less than what the modern sense of that phrase might suggest; the idea was to transform a will of vice into one of virtue, to alter the will of the patient: "The

---

72 Johann Christian Bolten names Nicolai explicitly in his *Gedancken von den psychologischen Curen* (Halle: Carl Hermann Hemmerde, 1751) in §1, 15, and §34, 61.
73 Bolten, *Gedancken von den psychologischen Curen*, 62: "Die philosophische Pathologie ist die Lehre von den Affekten, deren ästhetischer Theil lehret, wie man die Gemüthsbewegungen erregen, unterdrücken und in seiner Gewalt haben soll."
74 Bolten, *Gedancken von den psychologischen Curen*, 86: "gibt die Regeln an die Hand, wie man Gemüthsbewegungen erregen, vermehren, hindern und unterdruecken soll [...] dieser Theil der Wissenschaft ist es, den man insbesondere lernen muss, wenn man diese Wissenschaft bey den Kranckheiten wieder anbringen will."
75 Bolten, *Gedancken von den psychologischen Curen*, §35, 63: "Alle Kranckheiten der Seele haben ihren Sitz in den Erkenntnis- und Begehrungskräfte der Seele [...] folglich sind diese Wissenschaften hinreichend, die Kranckheiten der Seele daraus kurieren zu lassen."

most despicable diseases are effects of the darkest vices, and to prevent them in most cases is simply to alter the will [...] what does making a person better mean other than to make someone of vice virtuous, to better his will by means of a psychological cure."[76] Psychological cures work on the will of the individual, transforming dark desires and imaginings into virtuous thoughts.

Johann Georg Sulzer (1720–1779) was professor of mathematics and philosophy first in Switzerland and then at the Berlin-Brandenburg Academy of Sciences 1775–1779, but much of his written work concerned aesthetics and psychology.[77] In his *Kurzer Begriff aller Wissenschaften* of 1759, Sulzer regards empirical psychology as the single most important scientific discipline.[78] One of his more interesting contributions to the ongoing conversation concerning empirical psychology was his essay "On Consciousness and its Influence on Our Judgments" (*Von dem Bewusstseyn und seinem Einfluss in unsere Urtheile*) of 1757. In the tradition of Wolff and Leibniz, Sulzer defines consciousness as *apperception*, "the specific act of the soul on the basis of which we distinguish our essence from the ideas that we are concerned with, and therefore also distinctly cognize what we are doing and what is happening in and around us."[79] While consciousness requires by definition a clear idea of itself, Sulzer fully acknowledges the fragility of our cognition of ourselves: we never have a distinct and complete idea of our individuality; this "idea" we have of ourselves is subject to circumstances and contingencies that vary. He was interested in the "obscure" (*dunkle*) representations which make up a good deal of our sense of the self.[80] The idea of the "self" is a *sensible idea* that is inseparably connected to a *body*. As such, it does not permit of distinctness or completeness, and even loses its clarity in instances of overpowering emotions or passions, or when the brain is affected by external trauma.

---

76 Bolten, *Gedancken*, §53, 90: "Die schändlichsten Krankheiten sind Würkungen der schwärzesten Laster und ihnen vorzubeugen, ist in denen mehresten Fällen nichts anders, als den Willen bessern [...] Was heisst einen Menschen bessern, einen Lasterhaften tugendhaft machen, anders als seinen Willen durch eine psychologische Cur bessern."
77 On Sulzer, see Guido Naschert, "Kurzbiographie: Johann Georg Sulzer (1720–1779)" in *Aufklärung. Interdisziplinäre Jahrbuch zur Erforschung des 18. Jahrhunderts* (Hamburg: F. Meiner, 2007), vol. 19, 379–382.
78 Sulzer, *Kurzer Begriff aller Wissenschaften und anderer Theile der Gelehrsamkeit*, §206, 158–159.
79 Johann Georg Sulzer, *Von dem Bewusstseyn und seinem Einfluss in unsere Urtheile* (1757), in *Vermischte Philosophische Schriften*, by Sulzer (Leipzig: Weidmanns Erben and Reich, 1773), part 1, 199–224, here 200: "diejenige Handlung des Geistes, wodurch wir unser Wesen von den Ideen, welche uns beschäftigen, unterscheiden, und also deutlich wissen, was wir thun und was in uns und um uns vorgeht."
80 Vidal, *Sciences of the Soul*, 111.

> It is with the idea which we have of ourselves as with all ideas of sensible things: it is subject to the exact same contingencies.[81]
>
> This idea of our selves, I say, is exactly as all the others, sometimes more, sometimes less clear or apparent [...] we do not have a complete idea of an individual.[82]
>
> One must notice that the idea of ourselves, which belongs to consciousness, as it is the idea of an individual, must necessarily be quite incomplete. We never see ourselves with all of the determinations that constitute our individuality.[83]

To shore up his argument, Sulzer presents two case-histories, one of a man whose pistol blew up and damaged his brain. The man recovered and recited his own story always as if it had happened to someone else. The second case history was from Sulzer's own personal experience. He awoke in the night and heard the clock strike a particular hour, and had two very different ideas accompany this experience: the first of the clock itself striking the hour, the other of someone, an anonymous "I," hearing the clock striking. From these "cases" Sulzer concludes that we tend to gravitate toward a very general, abstract sense of the "I," apart from specific and multiple coincidental and contingent determinations or modalities, precisely because the actual, real "I" is so beleaguered by a whole range of extraneous and confused perceptions, and often unable to synthesize them adequately. The presence of "obscure" representations due to the multiplicity and variability of such determinations constantly threatens the sense of the "I." Sulzer likens these obscure or confused ideas to sirens, whose enchantment affects the mind directly, without any mediation of the senses: "The confused ideas, when they are taken together, contest the felicitous presence of the mind the most; they are sirens, but all the more dangerous sirens as one feels the effect of their spells without seeing or hearing them."[84]

---

[81] Sulzer, *Von dem Bewusstseyn*, 201: "Es verhält sich mit der Idee, die wir von uns selbst haben eben so, wie mit allen Ideen von sinnlichen Dingen: sie ist eben denselben Zufällen unterworfen."

[82] Sulzer, *Von dem Bewusstseyn*, 206–207: "Diese Idee von uns selbst, sage ich, ist so wie alle übrige, bald mehr, bald weniger klar oder auffallend [...] Wir haben keine vollständige Idee von einem Individuo."

[83] Sulzer, *Von dem Bewusstseyn*, 207: "Nun muss man bemerken, dass die Idee von uns selbst, welche zum Bewusstseyn gehöret, da es die Idee von einem Individuo ist, nothwendig sehr unvollständig seyn muss. Wir sehen uns selbst niemals mit allen den Bestimmungen, welche unsere Individualität ausmachen."

[84] Sulzer, *Von dem Bewusstseyn*, 224: "Die verworrenen Vorstellungen, wenn sie zusamengesetzt sind, widersetzen sich dieser glücklichen Gegenwart des Geistes am meisten; sie sind Sirenen, aber um so viel fürchterlichere Sirenen, da man die Wirkung ihrer Bezauberungen empfindet, ohne sie zu sehen und zu hoeren."

It is only through the most disciplined vigilance that we are able to focus our attention (*Aufmerksamkeit*) sufficiently so as to guard against the onslaught of these "sirens" as Sulzer calls them, and maintain a (more or less) clear idea of the self. To remedy the intrusion of "obscure" representations, Sulzer urges the development of *a science of the discipline of the soul*: "these remarks can provide us with the fundamental propositions concerning the most important of all sciences, by which I mean that of the discipline of the soul, which makes such a discipline superior to all of the impressions of the senses and all of passions that conflict with the thetic intentions of its behavior."[85] The science or discipline of the soul requires for Sulzer attention and concentration, allowing sufficient time for reflection on one's impressions and thoughts, not adding or subtracting anything to or from such observation, so that one might be able to achieve a better sense of the connection between impressions, experience, and the associated thoughts. Such attention allows the "I" to thematize precisely what is governing this connection.

Johann Georg Zimmermann (1728–1795) studied medicine in Göttingen and became the Royal Physician to George III in Hannover. His main work – *Concerning Experience in Medicine* (*Von der Erfahrung in der Arzneykunst*, 1763–1764) – achieved a great deal of notoriety in Europe. Zimmermann's work displays the same concern for empirical observation as the Halle constellation, but is more narrowly focused on the central methodological issue of "experience." At this time, a distinction was made between three forms of experience (*Erfahrung*) in natural philosophy: observation (*Beobachtung*), experiment (*Experiment*), and a scientific trial (*Versuch*).[86] All of these were seen to contribute to medical knowledge (*Erkenntnis*) and the art of the medical practice, although most of the physicians we have discussed viewed experiments on human beings as a violation of the dignity of man. Zimmermann's key

---

[85] Sulzer, *Von dem Bewusstseyn*, 218: "ich halt mich also nicht länger dabey auf, und füge nur noch überhaupt hinzu, dass diese Anmerkungen Grundsätze von der wichtigsten aller Wissenschaften abgeben könnten, ich meyne die Theorie derjenigen Disciplin *der Seele*, welche sie allen Eindrücken der Sinne und allen mit dem festgesetzten Entwürfe ihres Verhaltens streitenden Leidenschaften überlegen machet."
[86] At the same historical moment, Johann Heinrich Lambert, *Neues Organon* (Berlin: Akademie-Verlag, 1764), distinguishes these three types of "experience." On the differentiation of "experience" (*Erfahrung*) from "observation," "experiment" in the mid-eighteenth century, see Zelle, "Experiment, Experience and Observation in Eighteenth-Century Anthropology and Psychology," 93–105. Curiously, Zelle does not mention Zimmermann, who it seems to me forms the bridge between the Halle physicians and Moritz. The link has been carefully provided by Stefanie Retzlaff, *Observieren und Aufschreiben*, 50–51. Retzlaff's emphasis is on how observation (*Beobachtung*) informs experience in Zimmermann.

contribution to this conversation was his enhancement and expansion of the notion of "experience" itself. He begins *Concerning Experience* with a general account of his subject:

> We attain our knowledge through the senses and the understanding. The senses grasp as much as they can upon the great stage of the world and the infinite number of objects [...] I name this collection of sensible and simple ideas the raw material [...] the understanding compares, orders and connects these sensible ideas, it sees their relation and creates from these more composite ideas, and from these, principles and conclusions.[87]

Experience (*Erfahrung*) is then generally defined as "the knowledge of something that emerges through the frequent intuition of the same."[88] Zimmermann then points out the confusion that has resulted from identifying experience with experiment, observation, and trial. His task was to single out "experience" from this complex construction and provide an account of "experience" itself.

Zimmermann then described the function of experience in medicine in the following way: "a learned, achieved capability, acquired through observations and experiments, in the art of protecting the human being from illness."[89] Careful to distinguish his notion of "experience" from that of the empiricists, he claimed that the "experience" of the empiricists was always incomplete, false, or misleading because it lacked a hermeneutical component: "The experience of the empiricists is always false, for they execute their art without understanding it."[90] Experience without *understanding* is impossible. Most importantly, Zimmermann *historicized* the notion of experience. Experience always presupposed an historical pre-structure or *Vorwurf*, a knowledge that guides the physician: "Now this experience presupposes the historical cognition of its project, for without this knowledge one would not know what to look for [...] learnedness

---

[87] Johann Georg Zimmermann, *Von der Erfahrung in der Arzneykunst* (Brugg and Zürich, 1763–1764), 6: "Wir gelangen in unserer Erkenntnis durch die Sinne und den Verstand. Die Sinne fassen auf dem grossen Schauplatz der Welt von der unendlichen Menge der Gegenstände so viel als sie fassen können [...] ich nenne diese Sammlung der sinnlichen und einfachen Ideen den rohen Stoff. [...] Der Verstand vergleicht, ordnet und verbindet diese sinnlichen Ideen, er sieht ihre Beziehungen und macht aus denselben zusammengesetzten Ideen, aus diesen Grundsätze und Schlüsse."
[88] Zimmermann, *Von der Erfahrung*, 6.
[89] Zimmermann, *Von der Erfahrung*, 46: "Erfahrung (*experientia*) in dem menschlichen Leben, in der Kriegskunst, in der Arzneykunst, ist überhaupt, die aus guten Beobachtungen und Experimente erlangte Fertigkeit in der Kunst, den Menschen vor Krankheiten zu bewahren."
[90] Zimmermann, *Von der Erfahrung*, 13: "Die Erfahrung der Empiriker ist immer falsch, weil sie ihre Kunst ausüben, ohne sie zu verstehen."

gives us precisely this historical cognition."[91] Bringing scholarship or learnedness back into the loop of "experience," Zimmermann actually includes the "experience" of others as written down and communicated in case-histories. The "experience" of others, especially that of a gifted physician, is often far more instructive than the phenomena themselves:

> The experience of others is usually contained in cases that have often come before us in a manner different from our own experience. To have the description of an illness according to Boerhaave firmly in one's head is, for a physician who is not a first-rate observer, often better than having one's own experience of the illness [...] the lively narrative of a series of occurrences is often more informative and educative than the occurrences themselves.[92]

Zimmermann not only historicizes the notion of "experience," he counts the study and appropriation of well-written and -observed cases by other renown physicians to be on a par with, and often surpassing, one's own observations of a case: "with the science of one's predecessors one also has their experience."[93] Both Zimmermann and A. E. Büchner departed from a naïve or limited empiricism relying solely on the personal direct observation of facts or first-hand accounts, and created a space of "reasons" outside of the individual physician's own range of experience. According to Büchner, observation becomes experience transmitted from one physician to the next through the case history:

> Otherwise a well-ordered history of an illness [*Krankheits=geschichte*, RL] is based on the experience of others and takes into consideration what other famous and credible physicians have already observed and written down as a result of yearlong practice in our healing art.[94]

---

91 Zimmermann, *Von der Erfahrung*, 47: "Nun setzet diese Erfahrung die historische Kenntnis ihres Vorwurfs zum Grunde, weil man ohne diese Kenntnis nicht wüßte, worauf man zu sehen hat [...] die Gelehrsamkeit giebt uns die historische Kenntnis."
92 Zimmermann, *Von der Erfahrung*, 131–132: "Anderer Erfahrung ist zuweilen in Fällen, die wir doch oft unter Augen gehabt als unsere eigene Erfahrung. Eine Krankheit nach Boerhaaves Beschreibung im Kopf haben ist für einen Arzt, der nicht ein Beobachter vom ersten Range ist, besser als sie nach eigener Erfahrung im Kopf haben [...] Die geistvolle Erzählung einer Reihe von Begebenheiten ist oft unterrichtender als die Begebenheiten selber."
93 Zimmermann, *Von der Erfahrung*, 130: "Mit der Wissenschaft seiner Vorgänger hat man auch ihre Erfahrung."
94 Büchner, *Der in schweren und verwirrten Krankheiten vernünftig rathende und glücklich curirende Medicus*, vol. 2, 34–35: "andern Theils aber auch sich auf fremde Erfahrungen gründet, und dasjenige mit zu Hulfe nimt, was andere berühmte und glaubwürdige Aerzte bereits in einer vieljahrigen Ausübung unserer heilsamen Kunst beobachtet und zum besten derer Nachkommen aufgezeichnet haben."

Recent histories of "experience" have, I think, underestimated this significant shift in the understanding of "experience" in the mid-eighteenth century. Lorraine Daston and Peter Dear are absolutely correct that experience lost some of its uneven texture and variability in the shift from the multi-tiered perception of the world of the seventeenth century to the enlightened, more uniform and rational eighteenth.[95] However, we must note an important rupture in the notion of "experience" in the 1760s, especially as regards the historicity of experience and its indebtedness to previous (and current) case-histories. The expansion of the notion of "experience" to encompass written case-histories and life-descriptions proved to be decisive. What traction did this new concept of "experience" provide? In a word, it made, once again, the knowledge gained from the "experience" contained in the case history an essential instrument in the toolbox of the physician, and also a respected and legitimate object of public enlightened conversation, yet in an entirely different manner than its predecessor in the corpus of Stahl and Hoffmann. From this point on, the case history becomes a source of new and interesting knowledge, a medium of scientific and social interchange, and the subject of interesting conversations about the nature of human being, aesthetics, physiology, morals, logic, and metaphysics. Rather than an example of pre-fabricated theory, the case history was not merely an "epistemic genre,"[96] as Gianna Pomata has forcefully shown for the sixteenth and seventeenth centuries, but also became a form of human scientific *evidence*, the actual *material* of the new science of empirical psychology, and a medium of bourgeois self-understanding, self-differentiation, and self-construction.

Johann Gottfried Herder (1744–1803) understood the transformation underway in the 1770s in the production and dissemination of case-histories and life-descriptions as contributing not only to psychology and an understanding of

---

[95] Lorraine Daston, "Strange Facts, Plain Facts, and the Texture of Scientific Experience in the Enlightenment," in *Proof and Persuasion. Essays on Authority, Objectivity and Evidence*, ed. Suzanne Marchand and Elisabeth Lunbeck (Brussels: Brepols, 1996), 59. Daston persuasively argues that "experience" shifts from being "granular, bumpy, and singular" in the early modern period to "smooth, woven and regular" in the enlightened eighteenth century, with its claims of regularity and uniformity, while Peter Dear, *Discipline and Experience: The Mathematical Way in the Scientific Revolution* (Chicago: University of Chicago Press, 1995), argues that experience in the seventeenth century moved from indicating "a general statement about how things habitually behave" (as in the Aristotelian/Scholastic sense) to "statements describing specific events," 24–25, 85–92, 125. In both cases, "experience" experiences a leveling, disciplined regularization and homogenization in the eighteenth century.

[96] Gianna Pomata, "Sharing Cases: The *Observationes* in Early Modern Medicine," *Early Science and Medicine* 15.3 (2010): 193–236.

the individual, but to a general history of mankind and to cultural history. Usually recognized for his contributions to literary criticism, aesthetics, and the philosophy of language and of history, Herder was also an astute observer of the human soul. His *On Knowledge and Sensation of the Human Soul* (*Vom Erkennen und Empfinden der menschlichen Seele*, 1774; 1775; 1778), a *Preisschrift* submitted to but not awarded by the Berlin Academy, must certainly be counted as one of the most important essays of the decade. Herder, already deeply influenced in the early 1770s by Spinoza's monism[97] – the view that mind and body are just two aspects or "attributes" of substance, and that the individual human being is a unified psycho-physical "mode" of the one substance – "God or nature" as Baruch Spinoza put it – develops a startling holistic view of the human being as an historical individual imbricated in the world and striving to interpret its position in and through language. Herder recommended three paths by which one could research the vital connection between psychology and physiology in individual cases: life-descriptions or autobiographies, written observations (*Bemerkungen*) of physicians and friends of those afflicted, and literature, what he referred to as the "prophecies of the poets." Herder noted that only through these textual documents would we be able to know "the most entangled pathology of the soul,[98] to be able to discern "the deepest specificities" of an individual life, the "dark indications" of the whole person. Herder's examples are Petrarch, Augustine, Gerolomo Cardano, and Michel de Montaigne, but he could easily have chosen Jung-Stilling, Rousseau, Lavater, and J. S. Semler, as Moritz did, as paradigms of self-writing and self-explication.[99] Writing about autobiographies, diaries, and written cases, Herder notes: "It is strange how autobiography can show the whole man even from those sides that he doesn't want to show himself [...] and one sees in cases of this kind that everything in nature is a whole, that one cannot deny oneself

---

[97] On Herder's monism and Baruch Spinoza's influence, see Michael Förster, "Herder und Spinoza," in *Spinoza and German Idealism*, ed. Eckhart Förster and Yizak Malamed (Cambridge: Cambridge University Press, 2012), 59–84; Claas Cordemann, *Herders Christlicher Monismus. Eine Studie zur Grundlegung von Johann Gottfried Herders Christologie und Humanitätsideal* (Tübingen: Mohr-Siebeck, 2010), 96–101 and more recently, my "'Eins und Alles': Herders Spinoza-Aneignung in *Gott, einige Gespräche*," *Publications of the English Goethe Society* 86.2 (2017): 67–89.
[98] Johann Gottfried Herder, *Vom Erkennen und Empfinden der menschlichen Seele* (1778), in *Werke in zehn Bänden*, by Herder, ed. Jürgen Brummack and Martin Bollacher (Frankfurt: Deutscher Klassiker Verlag, 1994), vol. 4, 342: "die verflochtenste Pathologie der Seele."
[99] Karl Philipp Moritz, "Vorschlag zu einem Magazin einer Erfahrungsseelenkunde," *Deutsches Museum* 1 (1782): 485–503.

precisely in such obscure references and investigations."[100] As Schings pointed out, Herder forges nothing less than a new form of literary criticism and theory with this text: a program of a psychological literary science that advocates the analysis and critique of literary works from the specifically *psychological* viewpoint of a unique, singular individual.[101] Herder was instrumental in framing, on the theoretical-philosophical level, what Moritz and Schiller were to realize in literary practice in the 1780s: making the *individuality of the individual an object of scientific-critical study.*

Ernst Platner (1744–1818) was first Professor of Medicine, then of Physiology, and finally of Philosophy at the University of Leipzig. His *Anthropology for Physicians and Philosophers* (*Anthropologie für Ärzte und Weltweisee*, 1772) is the first instance in which the very term "anthropology" is used in the vernacular in the title of a German book in its modern meaning. It is also a wonderful example of the difficulties and paradoxes of the "anthropological turn" of the German *Spätaufklärung*. In this work, Platner sought to demarcate the discipline of anthropology as the science of the entire human being, as the meeting ground of physiology and psychology, as the discipline of the reciprocal influence of the relations, connections, and limitations of the body and the soul. As Platner explains in his Preface:

> The knowledge of human being would, I think, be divided into three sciences. One can first of all consider the parts and operations of the machine without looking at the restrictions that these movements receive from the soul or that the soul suffers from the machine; this is anatomy and physiology. One can secondly investigate in this way the powers and characteristics of the soul itself, without however considering the cooperation of the body or the changes which issue from the machine: this would be psychology, or what is one and same, logic, aesthetics and a large part of moral philosophy. Finally, one can consider body and soul in their reciprocal relations and constraints, and that is what I call anthropology.[102]

---

100 Herder, *Vom Erkennen und Empfinden* (1778), 342: "Es ist sonderbar, wie eine eigene Lebensbeschreibung den ganzen Mann auch von Seiten zeigt, von denen er sich eben nicht zeigen will [...] und man sieht aus Fällen dieser Art, dass Alles in der Natur ein Ganzes sei, dass man sich gerad'eben in dunklen Anzeigungen und Proben, vor sich selbst am wenigsten verleugnen könne."
101 Hans-Jürgen Schings, *Melancholie und Aufklarung: Melancholiker und ihre Kritiker in Erfahrungsseelenkunde und Literatur des 18. Jahrhunderts* (Stuttgart: Metzler, 1977), 32.
102 Ernst Platner, *Anthropologie für Ärzte und Weltweisee* (Leipzig: Dyckischen Buchhandlung, 1772), xv–xvii: "Die Erkenntnis der Menschen wäre, wie mir dünckt, in drei Wissenschaften abzutheilen. Man kann erstlich die Theile und Geschäfte der Maschine allein betrachten; ohne auf die Einschränkungen zu sehen, welche diese Bewegungen von der Seele empfangen; oder welche die Seele wiederum von der Maschine leidet; das ist die Anatomie und Physiologie. Zweitens kann man eben auf diese Art die Kräfte und Eigenschaften der Seele untersuchen,

The "self" for Platner is a persistent self-conscious identity; in the tradition of Leibniz and Wolff, Platner understands apperception as the very definition of conscious human activity. As he puts it, "That which is conscious of itself, this I is called my soul [...] I and soul are the identical."[103] However, contrary to Herder's Spinozist monism according to which mind and matter are merely two aspects of the one substance, Platner remained a strict dualist. To be sure, anthropology is the science of the relation between the soul and the "machine" as he refers to it, but the soul and the body are two distinct substances: "Therefore the soul is a substance, a substance distinct from the entire body, and always precisely this soul."[104] And yet contrary to the Cartesian tradition, Leibniz and Wolff, Platner argues that the essence of the soul cannot be known through the faculty of reason (*Vernunft*), but only through *experience (Erfahrung)*. "The essence of the soul," he writes, "can only and ever be known from experience, not from reason alone."[105] This is an important departure from the Cartesian tradition and those elements of Leibniz and Wolff which relied on a purely speculative, immediate grasp of the soul through reason or the *lumen naturale* alone, and it once again underscores the importance of the new notion of "experience" circulating around Germany in the 1760s. In fact, for all of the rhetoric of an anthropological consideration of the "entire human being," Platner remained quite materialistic in his account of the precise intersection of the physical and the mental, or of physiology and psychology. The brain, or that part of the brain whose injury results in death of the disruption or destruction of human understanding, is for Platner, very much like Krüger, actually the place where the soul resides: "The brain is the seat of the soul."[106] In his early work, self-consciousness gives credence to the *reality* of the immateriality of the soul; in his later work, specifically in his *Philosophische Aphorismen* of 1793, Platner rejects that argument; the sense of a "self" – "that I am the

---

ohne allezeit die Mitwirkung des Körpers oder die daraus in der Maschine erfolgenden Veränderungen in Betrachtung zu ziehen: das wäre Psychologie, oder welches einerley ist, Logik, Ästhetik, und ein großer Theil der Moralphilosophie [...] Endlich kann man Körper und Seele in ihren gegenseitigen Verhältnissen, Einschränkungen und Beziehungen zusammen betrachten, und das ist, was ich Anthropologie nenne."
103 Platner, *Anthropologie*, 16. "Das, was sich bewußt ist, dies Ich heisst meine S e e l e [...] Ich und Seele ist einerley."
104 Platner, *Anthropologie*, 16: "Also ist die Seele eine Substanz, eine von dem ganzen Körper verschiedene Substanz, und immer die nämliche Seele."
105 Platner, *Anthropologie*, 33: "Das Wesen der Seele läßt sich nicht aus der Vernunft, sondern einzig und allein aus der Erfahrung erkennen."
106 Platner, *Anthropologie*, 47.

identical subject that has both the present and past representations of my life"¹⁰⁷ – only gives rise to the *thought* of the soul as immaterial, spiritual essence distinct from matter. It does not suffice to prove the *actuality* of the immortality of the soul.¹⁰⁸

Platner's anthropology thus presented a complicated and at times incoherent argument. On the one hand, he remained firmly within the Leibniz-Wolffian discourse which identified apperception or self-consciousness as the defining characteristic of the human soul. On the other hand, he departed from Leibniz and Wolff by arguing that reason in itself was insufficient, and insisting that the only way to gain knowledge of the soul was through experience (*Erfahrung*). Unlike Herder, a monist who adopted Spinoza's sense of the individual as a mode of the one absolute substance, with two "aspects" or "attributes" (conceived of as "thought" and "extension"), Platner remained a philosophical dualist for whom mind and body represented two distinct substances. Platner's anthropology as the discipline linking the two realms of inquiry – physiology/anatomy and psychology – thus promised more than it delivered; his dualism prevented him from adequately explaining the precise relations and connections between the two substances. Platner did, however, succeed in avoiding the reductionism of many of his contemporaries. The representations of the soul for him did not follow a strict causality and could not be simply reduced to the mechanisms of the body; nor were modifications of the body merely the results or effects of the movements or fluctuations of the mind.

Jacob Friedrich Abel (1751–1829) was a Professor of Philosophy and Schiller's mentor at the *Hohe Karlsschule* in Stuttgart from 1776–1780. Unlike the critical philosophy of Kant and the turn towards transcendentalism, Abel's philosophy was a strange mixture of empiricism, practical wisdom, and eighteenth-century anthropology. As Riedel puts it: "His foundation of philosophy in the theory of the soul, in 'empirical psychology,' is representative for the new philosophical orientation of the German Enlightenment after the end of the scholastic tradition."¹⁰⁹ Influenced by Platner, Johannes Nikolaus Tetens,

---

107 Ernst Platner, *Philosophische Aphorismen* (Leipzig: Schwickertschen Verlage, 1793), §143, 87: "daß ich dasselbe Subjekt bin, welches die gegenwärtigen, und die vergangenen Vorstellungen meines Lebens hatte."
108 Udo Thiel, "Das Gefühl 'ich': Ernst Platner zwischen empirischer Psychologie und Transzendentalphilosophie," in *Aufklärung: Interdisziplinäres Jahrbuch zur Erforschung des 18. Jahrhunderts* (Hamburg: F. Meiner, 2007), vol. 19, 139–161.
109 Jacob Friedrich Abel, *Karlsschul-Schriften. Eine Quellenedition zum Philosophieunterricht an der Stuttgarter Karlsschule (1773–1782). Mit Einleitung, Übersetzung, Kommentar und Bibliographie*, ed. Wolfgang Riedel (Würzburg: Königshausen & Neumann, 1995), 6: "Seine Grundlegung der Philosophie in der Seelenlehre, in der 'empirischen Psychologie', darf als

Christian Garve, Christoph Meiners, Johann Augustus Eberhard, and the empirical, anthropological turn of the 1770s, Abel eschewed the metaphysical tendencies of Kant and insisted on a psychology of the human soul on an empirical basis. Explaining the difference of his approach to psychology from that of Kant, he wrote in the *Introduction to the Theory of the Soul* (*Einleitung in die Seelenlehre*) of 1786:

> I cannot omit saying something about a book that is too noteworthy that everyone who writes about psychology now must give it some thought. Because the psychology which I am presenting is simply empirical, and I have avoided every metaphysics of the soul, I was only able to find Kant in my own manner, namely, that psychology provides the basis for metaphysics; in the origin and the deduction of aesthetic and transcendental concepts concerning this area, I have really ventured my own opinion. which differs from Kant; but the metaphysical application of these concepts and especially that of the soul was too far from my own position that I was unable to use Kant's great discovery, and could only treat these matters empirically.[110]

Abel identified his empirical psychology as a natural science that begins with the collection of individual appearance (we might read observations or *Beobachtungen* here, although Abel himself uses the term *Erscheinungen*), gradually leading to the construction of more general "laws," which are then used for the explanation of these "appearances" and for the invention of "new rules":

> The method of the theory of the human being is the one that is customary with research concerning nature: first individual appearances are collected, then from these general laws are constructed, which are then used to bring forth explanations of the phenomena and for the invention of new rules, through whose application new products are

---

charakteristisch gelten für die philosophische Neuorientierung der deutschen Aufklärung nach dem Ende der scholastischen Tradition."

[110] Jacob Friedrich Abel, *Einleitung in die Seelenlehre* (Stuttgart: Metzler, 1786; repr. photmech. Nachdruck: Hildesheim, Zürich, New York: Georg Olms, 1985), vii: "Ich kann nicht unterlassen, noch etwas wegen eines Buchs hinzuzusetzen, das zu merkwürdig ist, als dass nicht jeder, der gegenwärtig über Psychologie schreibt, desselben gedenken muss. Da diese Psychologie blos empirisch ist, und ich absichtlich Metaphysik über die Seele vermieden, so konnte ich Kanten nur da auf meinem Wege finden, wo Psychologie den Grund der Metaphysik legt: in dem Ursprung und in der Deduktion der ästhetischen und transzendentalen Begriffe und über diesen Gegenstand habe ich wirklich meine eigene von Kant verschiedene Meinung gewagt; aber die metaphysische Anwendung dieser Begriffe überhaupt und die metaphysische Behandlung der Seele insbesondere war zu sehr ausser meinem Wege, als dass ich Kants grosse Entdeckung benutzen, und diese Gegenstände anders als empirisch behandeln konnte."

produced. [...] The spirit of the psychologist is therefore that of a scientific researcher. For because the psychologist observes what transpires in himself, and because the theory of man, by means of vague, difficult and artificial tests, contains concepts not so easily verifiable as in physiology, the education of the psychological researcher is more difficult, but also much more important.[111]

The method and spirit of the researcher of the human soul is identical to that of the researcher of nature. The only difference is that the psychologist observes what is in himself, and the human soul does not permit of the forms of artificial experiments and verifiable concepts as that of the body. However, the study of the human soul is the basis of all human sciences, all sciences which have as their object *der Mensch*: "The usefulness of the theory of man, which flows partially from specific knowledge of the human being, partially from the psychological spirit contained therein, extends to all sciences whose object is the human being."[112] Abel was sensitive to the difficulties confronting the researcher of the human soul, the challenge of attending not merely to the *objects* of consciousness, but to the *conscious acts* themselves. But he believed, as did Leibniz, Wolff, and all of the empirical psychologists we have considered thus far, that the soul possessed a capability of reflection, apperception or differentiation, and that precisely the *duration* or *persistence* of the consciousness of the object enabled one to attend to the operations of the mind itself as it was affected by sensation and as it entertained its object, allowing the human researcher to focus on the conscious acts themselves rather than simply the content of those acts:

> But the former duration of the impression we have described renders us capable in this regard. For as it persists in us for a time, so can and must we concentrate on the unique nature of the impression, the unique condition of our attention and of the condition of our soul, and even the intentions, at least as the impression lasts, that we observe,

---

111 Abel, *Einleitung in die Seelenlehre*, xxxi: "Die Methode der Menschenlehre ist die bey Erforschung der Natur überhaupt gewöhnliche: Erst individuelle Erscheinungen zu sammeln, dann aus denselben allgemeine Gesetze zu bilden und endlich diese theils zu Erklärung der Erscheinungen, theils zu Erfindung neuer Regeln, durch deren Anwendung aufs neue gewisse Produkte hervorgebracht werden sollen, anzuwenden [...] Auch der Geist des Psychologen ist also überhaupt der Geist des Naturforschers. Nur da der Psychologe das in ihm selbst Vorgegangene beobachtet, und die Menschenlehre unbildliche, feinere, schwerere und durch künstliche Proben nicht so leicht prüfbare Begriffe als die Körperlehre enthält, so ist die Bildung des psychologischen Geistes schwerer, aber auch viel wichtiger."
112 Abel, *Einleitung in die Seelenlehre*, xxxi: "Der Nutzen der Menschenlehre, welche theils aus den bestimmten Kenntnissen vom Menschen, theils aus dem dadurch erhaltenen psychologischen Geist fliesst, erstreckt sich unmittelbar auf alle Wissenschaften, deren Gegenstand der Mensch ist."

distinguish and differentiate it from all others, from behind as it were, and, if it begins to threaten to escape us, we turn our attention back to it. Through this process it receives such a status with respect to all others, that it awakens a unique, distinct feeling quite different from all others that not only induces the soul to its own apperception, but actually gives rise to it.[113]

The fundamental difference of Platner and Abel to Leibniz and the empirical psychology of Wolff is that this capability of the soul to reflect on its own activity and to attend to its own operations is not given innately, immediately, or *a priori*, but is rather precisely a function of the *experience of objects*. It is thus empirically accessible, experientially grounded, and cannot be simply deduced according to laws of pure reason.

If Wolff had already distinguished between rational and empirical psychology, and placed the latter as the primary access to the human soul, even attributing to it a foundational role, Kant sought to show that empirical psychology could never rise to the status of science (*Wissenschaft*) in his *Metaphysical Foundations of Natural Science* (*Metaphysische Anfangsgründe der Naturwissenschaft*) of 1786.[114] In "The Paralogisms of Pure Reason" chapter of the first *Critique* (1781), Kant had already demonstrated the fatal flaw in the very constitution of rational psychology from Descartes to Leibniz and Wolff: making the "I think" an *object* (*Gegenstand*) of knowledge in the strict sense.[115] If the "I think" were to be such an actual object of cognition, there would have to be an *empirical intuition* of such an object. However, human beings can have no such empirical intuition of what is in fact the very foundation for any cognition whatsoever; the "ich

---

113 Abel, *Einleitung in die Seelenlehre*, §316, 121: "Aber jene oben beschriebene Fortdauer des Eindrucks macht uns hiezu fähig. Da er nämlich eine Zeit lang in uns fortdauert, so können und müssen die eigene Natur der Eindrucke, der eigenthümliche Zustand unserer Aufmerksamkeit und unseres Seelenzustandes und nachmals auch Absichten, wenigstens auf diesen Nacheindruck so hinziehen, dass wir ihn vor allen andern, und zwar von hinten zu, beobachten, herausheben und absondern, ja wenn er uns zu entwischen droht, die Aufmerksamkeit auf ihn zurückbeugen. Hierdurch bekommt er eine solche Stellung gegen alle übrige, dass er ein eigenes, von jedem vorherigen noch zu unterscheidendes Gefühl erweckt, das nicht nur die Seele zu seiner Gewahrnehmung lockt, sondern auch diese wirklich erzeugt."
114 For the historical development of Kant's critique of empirical psychology in great detail, see Thomas Sturm, *Kant und die Wissenschaften am Menschen* (Paderborn: Mentis Verlag, 2009), 184–260.
115 For this discussion of Kant's critique of rational psychology in the *Critique of Pure Reason*, I have drawn on three main sources: Karl Ameriks, *Kant's Theory of Mind: An Analysis of the Paralogisms of Pure Reason* (Oxford: Oxford University Press, 1992; 2000); Rolf-Peter Horstmann, "Kant's Paralogismen," *Kant-Studien* 84.4 (1993): 408–425; and Patricia Kitcher, "Kant's Paralogisms," *Philosophical Review* 91.4 (1982): 515–547.

denke" – that is, *subjectivity itself* – is the very condition of the possibility of any such knowledge, indeed of any representation whatsoever. It cannot therefore simultaneously be an *object* (*Gegenstand*) of such knowledge.

> But the I which I think must always be valid and be able to be considered in thought as a *subject*, not merely something which, as a predicate, is simply attributed to thought; it is an apodictic and self-identical judgment; but this does not mean that I, as an object, am a persistent essence or substance that actually exists for me.[116]

Kant is extremely circumspect in his wording of how we are able to even conceive of this "Ich denke," what he refers to as the "text of rational psychology,"[117] without hypostatizing it into a "thing," "essence," or "substance," that is, without making the categorical error of thinking it as a cognizable object as any other, or as a distinct substance or essence. To do so would be to fall into an uncritical metaphysics. He cautiously says we do not even have a *concept* (*Begriff*) of it, but merely a *consciousness* (*Bewusstsein*) of it as *accompanying all of our thoughts*:

> As the basis of such a transcendental theory of the soul we can place nothing other than the simple and, what concerns content, complete empty representation: I, of which one cannot even say that it is a concept, but rather only a consciousness (*Bewusstsein*) that accompanies all concepts.[118]

But this was by no means Kant's last word on psychology. If one were not to use this "Ich denke" as the basis of psychology, as Descartes, Leibniz, Wolff, and Baumgarten had mistakenly done according to Kant, and if one were instead to seek to derive knowledge of the human being as a thinking being through observations (*Beobachtungen*) and natural laws (*Naturgesetze*), then an empirical psychology would be possible, at least in principle. The question then is only whether such an empirical psychology could ever achieve the status of a *science*.

---

116 Immanuel Kant, *Akademie-Ausgabe* (Berlin: G. Riemer, 1902-), vol. 3, 267, emphasis mine: "Daß aber Ich, der ich denke, im Denken immer als Subjekt, und als etwas, was nicht bloß wie Prädikat dem Denken anhänge, betrachtet werden kann, gelten müsse, ist ein apodiktischer und selbst identischer Satz; aber er bedeutet nicht, daß ich, als Objekt, ein, für mich, selbst bestehendes Wesen, oder Substanz sei."
117 Kant, *Akademie-Ausgabe*, vol. 3, 264: "Ich denke, ist also der alleinige Text der rationalen Psychologie, aus welchem sie ihre ganze Weisheit auswickeln soll."
118 Kant, *Akademie-Ausgabe*, vol. 3, 265: "Zum Grunde derselben können wir nichts anderes legen, als die einfache und für sich selbst an Inhalt gänzlich leere Vorstellung: Ich, von der man nicht einmal sagen kann, daß sie ein Begriff sei, sondern ein bloßes Bewußtsein, das alle Begriffe begleitet."

After debunking the very basis of rational psychology in the first *Critique*, Kant sets his sights on empirical psychology in the Preface of the *Metaphysical Foundations of Natural Science* (1786). In this text, Kant issued the two essential criteria for something to be considered a science: the *warrantability* of its claims to truth, and its *systematicity*. If a body of knowledge (*Wissen*) is based on pure principles, then it has the chance to become true knowledge (*Erkenntnis*), and if such knowledge can be rendered systematic, it can become science (*Wissenschaft*); if, however, it is merely based on experience, observation and the "laws of experience," then Kant states we can merely establish a systematic "art" (*systematische Kunst*), but never *science* in the strict sense. Empirical psychology fails the test of true science for Kant on two accounts: first, it cannot be mathematized, i.e., rigorously quantified, relying as it does on experience and examples; second, it cannot even achieve the status of chemistry – a protoscience, what Kant refers to as an analytical art (*Zergliederungskunst*) or experimental teaching (*Experimentallehre*)[119] – as it is based solely on introspection and subjective observation; the results of its research cannot be verified through any controlled experimentation. As Kant states in *Metaphysical Foundations of Natural Science*:

> It [psychology] can never become more than a historical, and, as such, as much as possible, a systematic natural theory of internal sense, that is, a natural description of the soul, but not a science of the soul, indeed, not even a psychological experimental theory.[120]

Empirical psychology, based as it is on inner observation (*innere Beobachtung*) or introspection, or a case by case observation of others, can only discern the elements of thought as they unfold in real time; it can never hold or maintain them (*aufbehalten*) for further analysis, nor can it intentionally rearrange or connect them in an experimental fashion to determine what is the actual cause of any single representation. Still less can one systematically analyze another thinking subject with the intention of understanding the connections of thoughts and feelings. In both cases – introspection and observation of another subject – the observation itself invariably *alters* and *distorts*, according to Kant,

---

[119] Kant, *Akademie-Ausgabe*, vol. 4, 471: "Sie (die Psychologie, RL) kann daher niemals etwas mehr als eine historische und, als solche, so viel möglich systematische Naturlehre des inneren Sinnes, d.i. eine Naturbeschreibung der Seele, aber nicht Seelenwissenschaft, ja nicht einmal psychologische Experimentallehre werden."
[120] Kant, *Akademie-Ausgabe*, vol. 4, 471.

the state of the object under observation (*den Zustand des beobachteten Gegenstandes alteriert und verstellt*).[121]

Kant's critique of empirical psychology as a discipline escalates in his *Anthropology*. Up to this point, psychology has merely been considered from a purely *philosophical* and *theoretical* standpoint. From this standpoint, it fails to meet the most basic criteria of science. However, first as a "physiology of internal sense," and second as a *pragmatic anthropology*, the questions of psychology are taken up and analyzed as a general theory of human being as a thinking and freely-acting being.[122] And although it can never attain the status of a true science for Kant, he seems to suggest at times it is a genuinely useful and, for the human being, enriching area of study, despite the various pitfalls he enumerates in the Preface.

The most basic problem, Kant observes in the chapter "On the Observation of Oneself" in the *Anthropology*, is that in attempting to concentrate on the processes of one's representations and feelings, one finds oneself implicated, one might say entangled or entwined, in the process by a sense of awkwardness (embarrassment or shame) or affected in some way, which of course immediately problematizes the objectivity and validity of precisely those very observations. What strikes one in Kant's discourse of self-observation is that he ultimately views it as a reversal (*Verkehrung*) of the natural order of things. Specifically, he explicitly connects incessant self-observation to mental illness, unbridled enthusiasm, what was called (perjoratively) *Schwärmerei* at the time – fanaticism. The observation of oneself, "which provides the material in the diary of the self-observer, and easily leads to fanaticism and madness,"[123] signifies a reversal in the sense that it occurs *prior* to reasonable thought, prior to the rational consideration of such processes, and is therefore either already a sickness of the mind (*Krankheit des Gemüts*), or leads to such illness, madness, and to the asylum.[124] Thus, excessive or compulsive introspection, when undertaken without the guidance of the understanding, not only causes mental illness, but can induce extreme, fanatical ways of thinking such as Illuminatism or Terrorism.[125] In the section "Vom inneren Sinn," Kant argues

---

121 Kant, *Akademie-Ausgabe*, vol. 4, 471–472.
122 Immanuel Kant, *Anthropologie in pragmatischer Hinsicht*, in *Werke in zehn Bänden*, by Kant, ed. Wilhelm Weischedel (Darmstadt: Wiss. Buchgesellschaft, 1983), vol. 10, 399.
123 Kant, *Anthropologie*, vol. 10, 413–414: "welche den Stoff zum Tagebuch eines Beobachters seiner Selbst abgibt, und leichtlich zu Schwärmerei und Wahnsinn hinführt."
124 Kant, *Anthropologie*, vol. 10, 416: "oder führt zu derselben und zum Irrenhaus."
125 On Kant's tortuous inner regime of defense, renunciation, fear of the Other, repudiation of the sensual world and rejection of all forms of heteronomy, see: Harmut Böhme and Gernot

that we do have an inner intuition of the play of our own thoughts, and calls such an "inner Experience" (*innere Erfahrung*) a psychological rather than an anthropological phenomenon. He even goes as far as to state that one could *say* that the soul is the organ of internal sense.[126] Yet here again, Kant links inner sense to the predisposition toward *Schwärmerei* and *Geisterseherei* – and refers to both as mental illness (*Gemütskrankheit*). The tendency to turn inward is viewed by Kant as a preface to madness; the only way to "bring order" is to *direct the person back to the external world*, as Kant says, to the "order of things" (*Ordnung der Dinge*).[127] Psychology as a theory or teaching (*Lehre*) is therefore not only demoted in Kant's estimation, robbed of every possibility of ever becoming a science; Kant viewed the very practice of psychology as a path to deception, mistake, error, emotional indulgence, fanaticism, and possibly madness itself.

The history of empirical psychology in Germany from Wolff, Baumgarten, and Meier, the Halle physicians to Herder, Platner, Abel, and finally Kant tells us something important about the ways in which "subjects" were increasingly imbricated and interpellated in the course of the eighteenth century. While Wolff admitted to constitutive, "dark" or "obscure" representations of the soul that resisted rational explanation, he simultaneously sought to advocate for an empirical psychology as the foundation for rational psychology or any rational account of the human soul; the principles derived from empirical psychology could guide the way forward to a more comprehensive understanding of the operations of the mind. Wolff's decisive move was to articulate the methodology of empirical or experiential psychology – *introspection, observation*, and *experiment* – in order to undergird a fully rational psychology of *a priori* principles and theoretical "reasons." Wolff not only founded empirical psychology as a distinct discipline; he elevated it to the level of an experiential science. Baumgarten appropriated much from Wolff, but deviated from him significantly; as we were able to show, Baumgarten's notion of the *association of ideas* as a law of the imagination, what he also refers to as *nexus*,[128] sought to bring that which is cognized less clearly and distinctly to a higher level by contextualizing it and offering a linkage between singular sensations, some of

---

Böhme, *Das Andere der Vernunft: Zur Entwicklung der Rationalitätsstrukturen am Beispiel Kants* (Frankfurt: Suhrkamp, 1983).

126 Kant, *Anthropologie*, vol. 10, 457: "Da gibt es alsdann nur Einen inneren Sinn; weil es nicht verschiedene Organe sind, durch welche der Mensch sich innerlich empfindet, man könnte sagen, die Seele ist das Organ des inneren Sinnes."
127 Kant, *Anthropologie*, vol. 10, 457–458.
128 Baumgarten, *Metaphysics*, §561–563.

which have occurred in the past, other sensations, and the *field within which they occur*: "Imagination and sensation are of singular beings, and hence of beings located within a universal nexus."[129] This, we argued, brought in, for the first time, a specifically *historical* dimension to representation and sensation. With Zimmermann and the psychologically-minded physicians in Halle around 1750 – Krüger, Unzer, Nicolai, and Bolten – contextualization, positionality, and historical derivation take center stage in the construction of the individual "case." Sulzer (1757) put forth the idea of the "self" as a *sensible idea* that is inseparably connected with a *body*. As such, it does not permit of distinctness or completeness, and even loses its clarity in instances of overpowering emotions or passions. Zimmermann (1762) championed experience (*Erfahrung*) as the antipode to *a priori* rational psychology; but his is a rich, textured empiricism that includes the experience of others – both in orally communicated narratives and in written case-histories – counting as part of a more communicative, interactive theory of how one ought to approach and analyze the disturbances of the soul. In his seminal *On Knowledge and Sensation of the Human Soul* (1775; 1776; 1778), Herder radicalizes this historicity by juxtaposing the self-identity of Lockean "puctualism" with his Spinoza-influenced monist theory of the intersection of various "substantial forces" (*substanzielle Kräfte*). Platner's anthropology, by contrast, reverts back to a dualism in which mind and body occupy equal territory on a plane of material causes and relations. Kant's *Anthropology* (1798; 1800) marked a profound rejection of empirical psychology as unworthy of the name of science and as fostering the pathological tendency toward errant introspection and even mental illness. Finally, we saw how Abel (1786), Schiller's teacher and mentor at the Karlsschule in Stuttgart, distanced himself from Kant's critique of psychology and fully recognized the pitfalls of the empirical path, which he nevertheless defended and embraced as the only true approach to a knowledge of the human soul.

As we have traced the path of German empirical psychology in the eighteenth century, one can discern the contours of an emergent theory of the individuality of the individual, an attempt to develop a more scientific, systematic discipline of a *specific* human soul, and perhaps more importantly, an attempt to discipline the very thinking about the soul. For if the soul harbors dark, obscure, and pathological ideas and passions, not only must one study and understand the mechanism of such deviation, one must develop appropriate therapeutics to contain, ameliorate and when possible eliminate them as well. The very possibility of a psychological cure (Nicolai and Bolten) is thus

---

129 Baumgarten, *Metaphysics*, §561, 212.

inscribed in this "discipline" of the soul at precisely the historical moment when this "individual" is constructed as the enigmatic and problematical source of dangerous emotion, passion, imagination, enthusiasm, and fanaticism, forms of self-expression deemed sick, diseased, or corrupted. Bourgeois individuality, which never ceases to proclaim, represent, project, and ensure its own individuality by every means, and every medium, available at the time – autobiography, diary, the novel, and the case-history – required a "scientific discipline" to identify, collect, disseminate, and treat wayward *cases*. Such a science was the *Erfahrungsseelenkunde* of the last quarter of the eighteenth century in Germany.

4 Ethnicity, Gender, Religion, and Madness in Mid-Eighteenth-Century Germany: A Case History of Demonic Possession in Lower Saxony, 1744

> Whether or not a human being is possessed by an evil spirit is so very difficult to ascertain, for it remains concealed from the eyes.[1]
>
> Salvation presupposes something to be saved, whereas an individual, in the literal sense, is a being with an indivisible, indestructible soul.
> Luhmann, "The Individuality of the Individual"[2]
>
> What seems almost impossible is to speak always of the specter, to speak to the specter, to speak with it, therefore especially to make or let a spirit speak.
> Derrida, *Specters of Marx*[3]

Empirical Psychology created a new vocabulary for speaking and writing about an inner world of subjects – an inner world that could be accessed by apperception, introspection, rigorous observation, and precise description. Yet, its emergence in the eighteenth century occurred at a moment when advances in experimental science, experience and documentation, physiology, and anatomy were transforming medicine, displacing the model of the human body as a site of humors and vapors. William Harvey (1578–1657) and Marcello Malpighi (1628–1694) had exposed the circulation system beyond the heart and the lungs, extending it out to the entire body, including the brain. Antonie van Leeuwenhouk (1632–1723) and Robert Hooke (1635–1703) had opened new worlds in microscopy. But despite such advances, the early Enlightenment in Germany witnessed a profound conflict in the field of medicine, with animism, influxionism, and the iatro-mechanical model all vying for supremacy. The translation of modern medicine into everyday practice was anything but straightforward, and the emerging discipline of empirical psychology did not

---

[1] *Niedersächsisches Staatsarchiv Bückeburg*, Dep. 22, Nr. 360_Bl. 45–118. Hereafter *NSB* with the sheet number. *NSB*, Blatt 87: "Ob ein Mensch mit einem bösen Geist besessen sey, ist so schwer zu erörtern, als selbiger denen leiblichen Augen verborgen ist."
[2] Niklas Luhmann, "The Individuality of the Individual: Historical Meanings and Contemporary Problems," in *Reconstructing Individualism: Autonomy, Individuality and the Self in Western Thought*, ed. Thomas C. Heller et al. (Stanford, CA: Stanford University Press, 1986), 315.
[3] Jacques Derrida, *Specters of Marx* (New York and London: Routledge, 1994), 11.

immediately inform, much less govern, even the most enlightened centers of learning overnight. To be sure, the most general principles of Gottfried Wilhelm Leibniz, Christian Wolff, and Christian Thomasius powerfully influenced intellectual life in the German principalities, and Georg Ernst Stahl and Friedrich Hoffmann reigned unchallenged in medicine in the first part of the century. Yet by 1740, the power of the mind to effect the body, interactionism, or a theory of "reciprocal influence" of spirit and matter/mechanism seemed to win general acceptance. In 1750, the "Halle School" of psychologically-minded physicians discussed in the previous chapter reflected this new anthropological concept of *der ganze Mensch*. For the practicing physician, the medical councilor, and other subjects of the pastoral order, older rhetorical learnedness in medicine, reliance on sources, and the application of what were believed to be effective methods, the network and exchange of *consilia* and *consultatoria* continued, although inflected by the new imperative of "rational medicine" and careful observation, void of superstition, occult forces, and blind obedience to theological judgment.

The quarrel in medicine between the ancients and the moderns was most evident in specific cases that pushed traditional medical practices, diagnostics, treatments, and cures to their limit. One such "test case" was the alleged possession by an evil spirit or demon, which continued well into the eighteenth century. Demonology and demonic possession in early modern Germany are typically considered in a Christian, surprisingly Lutheran, context.[4] However, possession and exorcism exhibit a rich tradition in Judaism as well, reaching back to one of the first "cases" in the Old Testament, that of Saul, whose melancholy is ascribed to an evil spirit:

> Now the Spirit of the Lord departed from Saul, and a harmful spirit from the Lord tormented him. And Saul's servants said to him, "Behold now, a harmful spirit from God is tormenting you. Let our lord now command your servants who are before you to seek out a man who is skillful in playing the lyre, and when the harmful spirit from God is upon you, he will play it, and you will be well." (1 Samuel 16:14–16)[5]

---

[4] The overwhelming majority of published cases of demonic possession in Germany in this period were from central and northern Germany, predominantly in Protestant principalities and territories. See H.C. Erik Midelfort, *A History of Madness in Sixteenth-Century Germany* (Stanford, CA: Stanford University Press, 1999), 55–67, esp. 61. The majority of cases of demonic possession 1560–1650 occurred in Saxony, Brandenburg, Thuringia, and Hessen. Witchcraft, on the other hand, was far more prevalent in Catholic ecclesiastical territories.
[5] *The English Standard Version Bible: Containing the Old and New Testaments with Apocrypha* (Oxford: Oxford University Press, 2009).

Possession by an evil spirit and exorcism became subjects of increased interest in rabbinic literature during the sixteenth century. Specifically, tales of demonic possession and exorcisms by a rabbi appear in the late sixteenth century – the first two cases documented in 1571 in a letter and then circulated by Rabbi Elijah Falco – based upon the Kabbalistic notion of the *gilgul* or transmigration of souls.[6] These two accounts of exorcism from the Galilean town of Safed, the center of Kabbalistic mysticism in the sixteenth century led by Rabbi Isaac Luria and his disciples, can be found in the *Mayse-bukh*, a collection of stories, folktales, sagas, and legends handed down from generation to generation, published in Basel in 1602 and translated into German in 1612.[7] According to J. H. Chajes, Rabbi Eliezer Ashkenazi (1512–1585) was the first recipient of the broadsheet from the Safed detailing a dramatic case of demonic possession from the 1570s. In his *Ma-asei ha-Shem* of 1583, he stated: "It has been explained that to become demons (*shedim*) is the punishment and ultimate destiny of evil people."[8]

In the eighteenth century, with the emergence of Hasidism, the use of the term *Dybbuk*[9] to describe an evil spirit, the spirit of a dead person who would inhabit the soul of someone living, became common practice. It was believed that this evil spirit was of a person who either had a criminal history or had led a particularly (sexually) sinful life, and for this reason was a *wandering soul* who could not be properly assigned to the afterlife or find an everlasting resting place.[10] The *Shivhe ha-Besht* (1760), the famous hagiography of the founder of Hasidism, the Jewish Mystical Rabbi ben Eliezer (1700–1760), known as *Baal Shem-Tov*, contains two possession/exorcism stories. As Harold Fisch has written concerning the discourse and practice of possession in Judaism at this time, "stories of possession and exorcism were a by-product of sixteenth- and

---

6 Raphael Patai, "Exorcism and Xenoglossia among the Safed Kabbalists," *Journal of American Folklore* 91.361 (1978): 823–835.
7 Collected, edited and published by Jacob ben Abraham of Mezhirech. On the transmission of the tales of possession and exorcism from the Safed to the *Mayse-Bukh*, see Morris M. Faierstein, "The *Dibbuk* in the *Mayse Bukh*," *Shofar: An Interdisciplinary Journal of Jewish Studies* 30.1 (2011): 94–103.
8 J. H. Chajes, *Between Worlds: Dybbuks, Exorcists, and Early Modern Judaism* (Philadelphia: University of Pennsylvania Press, 2005), 11.
9 *Dybbuk* is an abbreviation of the phrase *dibbūq mē-rūaḥ rā'ā*, "a cleavage of an evil spirit," or דיבוק מן החיצונים *dibbūq min ha-ḥiṣonim*, or "dibbuk from the outside." *Dybbuk* itself comes from the Hebrew word ד־י־ב־ק *dibbūq*, which means "the act of sticking" and is a nominal form derived from the verb דָּבַק *dāḇaq*, "to adhere" or "to cling." Cf. *The Jewish Encyclopedia* (New York: Funk & Wagnalls. 1901–1906), article "Exorcism," 5. 5, 305–306.
10 Although based on very different sources, the obvious connection to the legend of the *Ahasverus* or the "wandering Jew," rampant during the seventeenth century, should be explored.

seventeenth-century Kabbalists."[11] Regarding demonic possessions in seventeenth- and eighteenth-century Jewish communities in Western Europe, Zwi Mark has stated:

> One of the widespread explanations given in seventeenth and eighteenth century Jewish society for certain varieties of madness was the demonic account. Madness was understood as the result of a person's bodily possession by a spirit, shade, or departed soul. Phenomena that are today termed hysteria, schizophrenia, epilepsy, possessions of various sorts, or flagrant transgression of social and religious norms were all considered well explained by demonic interpretations of spirit possession.[12]

Thus, Jews of the early to mid-eighteenth century who were connected to Hasidism or steeped in Yiddish folklore and the literature of the Kabbalistic renaissance of the late sixteenth and seventeenth centuries would have been familiar with several stories of demonic possession and exorcism. At the very latest by 1700, the template for possession by an evil spirit and exorcism by a rabbi had been forged in the Jewish popular imaginary.

The possibility of arriving at some sense of what the supposedly "demonically possessed" subject might have been actually *experiencing* has been a subject of some debate. The historian H. C. Erik Midelfort has claimed that, through a close examination of the source materials, it may be possible to understand what the possessed individual actually experienced. Alternatively, through close attention to the direct reporting of statements by the allegedly demon-possessed, one might be able to understand what possession must have *seemed like* apart from the authorial voices of the rabbis, priests, and other authorities who presided over and reported such cases.[13] "By taking the shape and color of the lens into account," Midelfort wrote, "we may yet be able to say something of what demon possession was like to the demon-possessed."[14]

---

[11] Harold Fisch, "The Messianic Politics of Menassah ben Israel," in *Menasseh Ben Israel and His World*, ed. Yôsēf Qaplan et al. (London: Brill, 1989), 228.

[12] Zwi Mark, "*Dybbuk* and *Devekut* in the *Shivhe ha-Besht*: Toward a Phenomenology of Madness in Early Hasidim," in *Spirit Possession in Judaism: Cases and Contexts from the Middle Ages to the Present*, ed. Matt Goldish (Detroit: Wayne State University Press, 2003), 257.

[13] Although one cannot rule out, as Midelfort, *History of Madness*, 14, has noted, "the Protestant or materialist suspicion that demoniacs were being coached by their exorcists and confessors on how best to appear if possessed."

[14] H. C. Erik Midelfort, "The Devil and the German People: Reflections on the Popularity of Demon Possession in Sixteenth-Century Germany." *Religion and Culture in the Renaissance and Reformation, Sixteenth Century Essays and Studies* 11 (1989): 119. Also in: Midelfort, *History of Madness*, 58.

While researchers may not be able to know precisely *what* possessed individuals experienced, Midelfort makes the case that "we might be able to catch glimpses of what these girls actually said and obtain some impression of how they understood and experienced their mental and spiritual troubles, as distinguished from the theological and polemical interpretation imposed upon their words and behaviors."[15] Getting at the original experience of the demonically possessed required recognizing the bias of the accounts of the time and rendering them transparent.

By contrast, the work of Michel de Certeau persuasively argues that the exorcist essentially makes the inchoate utterances and behaviors of the possessed conform to the rules of rhetoric and language, and that in doing so, the actual experience and voice of the possessed are subjugated to the ruling norms and conventions of their interlocutors. No meaningful distinction can therefore be made between "what the possessed or demoniac woman is stating and what is stated by demonological treatises or exorcists who witness demonology."[16] For de Certeau, the voice/discourse of the possessed ceases to exist; there is no "hidden treasure to be exhumed from under the interpretations piled over it [...] This situation excludes the possibility of tearing the possessed woman's true voice away from its alteration."[17] This view seems corroborated by the fact that analyses of case histories of demonic possession we have from the sixteenth and seventeenth centuries provide ample evidence that the language and expression of the possessed subject seems to have been *learned*, for they contain an abundance of biblical tropes, *topoi* or typical phrases associated with demonology and possession, and well-known and well-rehearsed modes of "demonic behavior." In sharp contrast to the case presented here, two things are worth noting: first, de Certeau was analyzing a mass-possession of nuns at the Ursuline convent at Loudun in 1634, and, second, his critique is directed at the well-known genre of the demonological treatise, which only sought to further the belief in the actuality of demonic possession, and to condemn and control such occurrences.

Demonic possession in the early modern period has also claimed the interest of feminist, social, and cultural historians who see in the archive of cases one of the few vehicles of female expression in an era in which possibilities for the voicing of feminine sexuality, religiosity, feeling, and emotion stood under both internal/implicit and external/explicit suppression. These inquiries stress

---

15 Midelfort, *History of Madness*, 57.
16 Michel de Certeau, *The Writing of History* (New York: Columbia University Press, 1992), 247.
17 de Certeau, *Writing of History*, 248.

not what such case histories say about women so much as the mere fact that they *document* both what women experienced and the "aberrant" or "transgressive" modes of comportment *ascribed* to them. Rather than viewing such possessed women simply as subjects of a hostile inquisition of rabbis, physicians, councilors, and fathers, recent interpretations of this idiom have indicated the possibility of uncovering – beneath the disciplinary, bio-political, and punitive agency of the male interrogators and exorcists and their respective institutions – the voices of pneumatic women who crossed normative social and cultural boundaries.[18] While there are only slightly more documented, published instances of the demonic possession of women than men in the "long" sixteenth century (1480–1620), many of these types of cases, especially in rural areas, remained undocumented and unpublished, and only truly special cases, particularly compelling, "curious" or "strange" cases achieved the level of interest and importance required for substantive documentation or publication. The feminist cultural-social historical line of inquiry, focused on what the primary accounts of such cases might be able to tell us about the lived experience of historical subjects, is exemplified in recent histories written "from below," in cultural history and the history of medicine in particular, from the perspective of the patient.[19] The intent here is to discern what case histories of behaviors of women considered to be "abnormal" or "transgressive" at the time might be able to contribute to a more general history of gendered cultural practices.

In writing about demonic possession in the early modern period, one must be careful to distinguish between cases of demonic possession and instances of witchcraft. Whereas it is true that a "witch" could curse someone to become possessed by a demon or even the devil himself, witchcraft was understood primarily as a collective *practice*, rarely a singular phenomenon. According to Lutheran doctrine, demonic possession was a horrible punishment inflicted by God on a person who had sinned. More importantly, demonic possession

---

18 Midelfort, *History of Madness*, 14: "I think it likely that demonic possession provided troubled persons with the means of expressing their often guilty and morally straining conflicts, a vocabulary of gestures, grimaces, words, voices, and feelings with which to describe their sense that they were not fully in charge of their lives or their own thoughts." Midelfort is not a feminist historian by any means, but does view "demonic possession" in the sixteenth and early seventeenth centuries as an expression of conflict, normative constraint, and sexual concerns.

19 Roy Porter, "The Patient's View: Doing History from Below," *Theory and Society* 14.2 (1985): 175–198. One of the best examples of this in the history of medicine is Barbara Duden's wonderful *The Woman Beneath the Skin: A Doctor's Patients in Eighteenth-Century Germany*, trans. Thomas Dunlap (Cambridge: Harvard University Press, 1998).

happened to people, whereas witchcraft was allegedly sought out, one could say *embraced* by those who engaged in its rituals. As Lyndal Roper has perceptively noted, "When a person became possessed, trembling and rolling in fits or speaking in tongues, this was because the devil had inhabited his or her body. In witchcraft, by contrast, the witch intentionally made a pact with the devil and went on to harm others."[20] Even the "clusters" of demonic possession 1580–1650 in Hessen, Thuringia, Saxony, and Brandenburg mapped by Midelfort must be differentiated from witchcraft and the witch trials of the early seventeenth century.[21] Such chains or outbursts of demonomania – in some cases one can even speak of small "epidemics" such as in Brandenburg at the end of the sixteenth century – seem to have struck particularly pious and observant young Christians; unlike the "pact" of witchcraft, the rhetoric of possession consisted of being "struck," "overtaken," or "commanded." For the theologians, scholars, physicians and jurists, and for the literate authors who composed the pamphlets, *Flugblätter*, and broadsides, and those who published them, witchcraft and demonic possession were viewed to be quite distinct.

Since the revival of Galenic Medicine in the mid-sixteenth century and until the scientific-empirical breakthroughs of the late seventeenth century, illness in general and mental illness in particular was viewed to be, with slight variation and emphasis, as an imbalance of the four humors – sanguine (blood), choleric (yellow bile), phlegmatic (phlegm), and melancholic (black bile) – and as "vapors" emanating or issuing from various organs of the body. Madness in the form of melancholia was considered to be the overabundance, the "corruption," or stagnation of, and, in extreme cases, the "roasting" or even "burning" of "black bile"; mania could be either the result of a corrupt choler or phlegm, while a mania characterized by constant sadness or anxiety would be ascribed to an overabundance of black bile as well. This corpus of medical doctrine exhibited an astonishing adaptability and staying power; accidents, lineage, fevers, and physical environment (damp or dry, hot or cold, and the combinations thereof) could all influence this tenuous equilibrium of the humors and the rise of certain vapors. Physicians of sixteenth and early seventeenth century in Germany had no difficulty in allowing Christian demonology to coexist alongside this model of pathology. Even a careful observer such as Felix Platter (1536–1614), the city

---

20 Lyndal Roper, *Witch Craze: Terror and Fantasy in Baroque Germany* (New Haven, CT: Yale University Press, 2004), 240. See also Midelfort, *History of Madness*, 76: "Witches consciously and voluntarily entered into a pact with the devil, while the possessed passively and involuntarily endured his external and internal assaults."
21 Midelfort, *History of Madness*, 62–66.

physician of Basel famous for his *Observationes* (1614), perhaps the best example of a case history book in the early seventeenth century, recognized that there were two types of madness: natural and supernatural, the former with purely natural causes and the latter caused by the devil himself or the demonic influence of his surrogates.[22] With the rise of empirical observation, careful description, comparison, the writing and dissemination of detailed *consilia, consultationes medicae, observationes*, and the sharing of cases in medical practice in the seventeenth century, the phenomenon of demonic possession subsided, but did not vanish.[23]

The case presented here occurred in the era of the early German Enlightenment, and is thus all the more striking as it appears at an historical moment that witnessed the rejection of mystical, occult, and demonic forces, and thereby the abandonment of "demonic possession" as a valid explanation of a mental illness.[24] Two leading philosophers of the early German Enlightenment, Christian Thomasius (1655–1728) and Christian Wolff (1679–1754), while very different in both temperament and beliefs, consistently argued for a purge of all prejudgments, superstitions, and unwarranted beliefs. This case also occurs at a time of a revolution in medicine: the older model of humoral pathology – the theory of the humors and the vapors – is gradually displaced by the "new science" emerging in the work of Robert Boyle, William Harvey, and Isaac Newton: a rigorous, rational empiricism

---

[22] On Platter, see: Oskar Diethelm and Thomas F. Heffernan, "Felix Platter and Psychiatry," *Journal of the History of the Behavioral Sciences* 1.1 (1965): 10–23. This departs significantly from the view of P. E. Pilet, "Felix Platter," in *The Dictionary of Scientific Biography*, ed. Charles C. Gillispie (New York: C. Scribner, 1975), vol. 11, 33, who stated that Platter did not consider the possibility of mental disturbances being caused by demons. On this, see Midelfort, *History of Madness*, 175.

[23] See the work of Gianna Pomata, "Observation Rising: Birth of an Epistemic Genre, 1500–1650," in *Histories of Scientific Observation*, ed. Lorraine Daston and Elizabeth Lunbeck (Chicago: University of Chicago Press, 2011), 45–80; and Pomata, "Sharing Cases; The *Observationes* in Early Modern Medicine," *Early Science and Medicine* 15.3 (2010): 193–236. Midelfort, *History of Madness*, 61, documents a peak in published cases 1580–1600, and a sharp decrease 1600–1650, but cases of demonic possession can be found as late as the 1760s and 1770s, for example, in Catholic Swabia, where Johann Joseph Gassner was performing exorcisms. On this, see H. C. Erik Midelfort, *Exorcism and Enlightenment: Johann Joseph Gassner and the Demons of Eighteenth Century Germany* (New Haven, CT: Yale University Press, 2005).

[24] As Lennard J. Davis notes, in Britain, an act of Parliament in 1736 actually banned "demonic possession" as a valid medical diagnosis. See Davis, *Obsession: A History* (Chicago: University of Chicago Press, 2009), 33.

based on meticulous observation and experimental verification.[25] The new empiricism was absolutely formative at the University of Halle when it was founded in 1694. Under the leadership of the physicians Hoffmann and Stahl, the medical faculty in Halle combined pietistic religiosity with the new science,[26] and became the most important institution of medical education in Germany. In the mid-eighteenth century, as madness is gradually decoupled from religion, Halle was the vibrant center of the great "psychological physicians": Johann August Unzer, Johann Gottlob Krüger, Ernst Anton Nicolai, and Johann Christian Bolten.[27] As the Galenic model of humoral pathology recedes due to the discoveries in anatomy and physiology, specifically the nervous system, the accepted medical canon entered a crisis. As Gianna Pomata has suggested, "Case-knowledge thrives in those situations in which either there is no canon or the dominant canon is being questioned."[28] The mid-eighteenth century is precisely such a breaking point, a period of a massive paradigm shift in thinking about madness: the collapse of the age-old humoral-vaporal model and the emergence of neurophysiology and –pathology as the real basis of mental illness.[29] In Germany, Stahl

---

[25] On the gradual demise of humoral pathology, see: Jürgen Helm, "'observatio' and 'experientia' – Fallgeschichten in der Medizin des 18. Jahrhunderts," in *'Aus Gottes Wort und eigener Erfahrung gezeiget': Erfahrung – Glauben, Bekennen und Gestalten im Pietismus*, ed. Christian Soboth and Udo Sträter (Halle: Harrasowitz, 2009), 361–376; and Stanley W. Jackson, "Melancholia and the Waning of Humoral Theory," *Journal of the History of Medicine and Allied Sciences* 33.3 (1978): 367–376.
[26] Hoffmann had traveled to Belgium, the Netherlands and England 1686–1688 and met Herman Boerhaave, Thomas Sydenham, and Robert Boyle personally. Stahl was particularly influenced by Sydenham.
[27] On these "psychological physicians" see: Carsten Zelle, ed. *Vernünftige Ärzte. Hallesche Psychomediziner und die Anfänge der Anthropologie in der deutschsprachigen Frühaufklärung* (Tübingen: Niemeyer, 2001); and Zelle, "Erfahrung, Ästhetik und mittleres Maß: Die Stellung von Unzer, Krüger und E.A. Nicolai in der anthropologischen Wende um 1750," in *Reiz – Imagination – Aufmerksamkeit*, ed. Jörn Steigerwald and Daniela Watzke (Würzburg: Königshausen & Neumann, 2003), 203–224. See my discussion of the psychologically minded physicians: Robert S. Leventhal, "Kasuistik, Empirie und Pastorale Seelenführung: Die Entstehung der modernen psychologischen Fallgeschichte, 1750–1800," *Jahrbuch Literatur und Medizin* 2 (2008): 13–40, esp. 22–24.
[28] Gianna Pomata, "The Medical Case Narrative: Distant Reading of an Epistemic Genre," *Literature and Medicine* 32.1 (2014): 13.
[29] Specifically, the work of Thomas Willis (1621–1675) *Pathologiae Cerebri et nervosi generis specimen* (Oxonii: Excudebat Guil, 1667). On this medico-epistemic rupture, see: G. S. Rousseau, *Enlightenment Crossings: Pre- and Post-Modern Discourses. Anthropological* (Manchester and New York: Manchester University Press, 1991), 130–131; Albrecht Koschorke, *Körperströme und Schriftverkehr. Mediologie des 18. Jahrhunderts* (München: W. Fink, 1999), 54–112.

and his animist disciples, who had certainly read Thomas Willis, used the new model of the nervous system as one of fibers, tubes, nervous "juices" and "animal spirits" to make the case for a fluid, seamless relation between the mind and body, and, contrary to the purely mechanistic view, madness came to be viewed predominantly as a *Gemüthskrankheit*, an illness of the *mind*. As Midelfort notes regarding the sixteenth century, however, cases of possession were often "the product of popular fears, fancies, and images of the devil or other spirits," and such attitudes were "completely strange to the biblical, classical or medical minds of the literate."[30] Such a gap between popular belief and superstition among the common people and enlightened, skeptical attitudes among academics, scholars, and physicians became even more pronounced in the eighteenth century.

Figure 8: Albrecht Wolfgang, Graf zu Schaumburg-Lippe. From the private collection and courtesy of Prince Alexander of Schaumburg-Lippe. I am grateful to the Niedersächsisches Landesarchiv Bückeburg and Stefan Brüdermann for both the reference and securing permission.

---

30 H. Erik Midelfort, "The Parliament and the German People," in *The Witchcraft Reader*, ed. Darren Oldridge (New York: Psychology Press, 2002), 241–242.

Our case history concerns an eighteen-year-old Jewess in Schaumburg-Lippe, in Lower Saxony, Germany, [31] in 1744, whose father asked permission of the Graf Albrecht Wolfgang (ruled 1728–1748) to allow him (and the Jewish community) to employ the services of a rabbi to perform an exorcism on his daughter, who, he wrote, suffered from pain in all of her extremities, moaning and groaning, screaming and crying, bodily contortions, fits, and facial grimaces.[32] First discovered by the German linguist Joachim Gessinger[33] in the Niedersächsisches Landesarchiv in Bückeburg, it offers us a remarkably complete dossier of a case of demonic hysterical possession from the mid-eighteenth century, from the first letter of appeal to the detailed interrogations of the rabbi asked to perform the exorcism, the mother, witnesses from the community, statements by privy councilors to the Count, and the Priest, testimony by physicians and the Court Superintendent, and the responses of Albrecht Wolfgang himself. Under the general heading *Ecclesiastica generalia*, we read *Possessed Souls, exorcism of the evil spirit of the possessed person* (<u>Besessene</u>, *Austreibung des bösen Geistes des Besessenen*). In the file, the specific "case" appears simply as:

In Specie
The permission sought by the Jew Bendix Moses,
To have an evil spirit exorcized from his daughter by a rabbi.
1744.[34]

Why might the case of an allegedly possessed Jewish girl have commanded the attention of an entire court, the ensemble of councilors, physicians, priests and community leaders, and elicited the consideration of Albrecht himself? Might it not have simply been dispensed with through an executive order, handled as were no doubt numerous cases in the course of the seventeenth and first half of

---

[31] To contextualize the case, it is important to note that the principalities of Schaumburg and Lippe had been the site of some of the fiercest witch hunts of the late sixteenth and early seventeenth centuries. It is estimated that in the period between 1580 and 1630, there were 250–300 executions. See Bengt Ankerloo et al., eds., *Witchcraft and Magic in Europe. The Period of the Witch Trials* (London: Athlone Press, 2002), vol. 4, 28. On the Jews of Schaumburg-Lippe, see Hans-Heinrich Hasselmeier, *Die Stellung der Juden in Schaumburg-Lippe von 1648 bis zur Emanzipation* (Bückeburg: Verlag Grimme, 1967). There were approximately 150–200 Jews living in the principality in the first half of the eighteenth century, with only brief expulsions in 1705 and again in 1717.
[32] *NSB*, Dep. 22, Nr. 360_ Bl. 45–118.
[33] Joachim Gessinger, "Das Mädchen, der Arzt, und der böse Geist, " *Osnabrücker Beiträge zur Sprachtheorie* 37 (1987): 161–192.
[34] *NSB*, Blatt 45: "In Specie [...] Die vom Juden Bendix Moses Aus Cappel nachgesuchte 1744 Erlaubniß, durch einen Rabbiner einen bösen Geist aus seiner Tochter aus=treiben zu lassen."

the Eighteenth century? What was at stake in such an investigation? Why, in a word, had this case become of particular interest to the state authority? We might adduce several reasons for this interest in the case. First and foremost, the Enlightenment required that reason and rational explanation be deployed in the study of man. Enlightened physicians demonstrated a keen interest in the workings of the mind, the relationship between the mind and the body, and a desire to understand and treat madness in its own "right" one might say, as an illness of the mind rather than to simply dismiss it and/or lock it away. By the mid-eighteenth century, the psychologically-minded physicians mentioned above influenced by the psycho-physiological theory of Georg Ernst Stahl (1660–1734), Professor of Medicine at Halle, explored the reciprocal relation of body and soul, moving away from the iatro-mechanistic model of Herman Boerhaave and Hoffmann.[35] This spurred an intense debate concerning the etiology and the treatment of mental illness.[36] Second, the mid-eighteenth century saw the emergence of *Polizeywissenschaft*, or the science of state policy, and principalities and territories with enlightened rulers began to take greater interest in the welfare and care of their subjects. Jewish populations in particular – the protected Jews as well as the traveling Jews who traversed Lower Saxony with or without permission – came under increased scrutiny as their numbers increased steadily in the eighteenth century. In the instance of this case history, the state authority demonstrated an extraordinary interest in the treatment of this Jewish female subject, and, if we are to believe the text, sought to "rationally" investigate and adjudicate her case; the court proved sensitive to the issue of a possible resolution through the Jewish community itself.

My interest here is not whether Grendel's Jewish identity was absolutely determinative in the handling of the case, but rather in the "overdetermination" of the case – the various social and cultural forces that converge and intersect in Grendel. As a young woman, she becomes the object of the male gaze with many of the stereotypes often ascribed to women in early modern Europe: unfettered fantasy, a corrupt imagination, emotionality, sexual frustration, and uncontrollable sexual desire, physical and mental weakness. The "evil spirit" of the deceased woman from Bielefeld whose spirit possesses her bears the

---

35 On Stahl, see L. J. Rather, "G.E. Stahl's Psychological Physiology," *Bulletin of the History of Medicine* 35.1 (1961): 37–49; as well as Johanna Geyer-Kordesch, *Pietismus, Medizin und Aufklärung in Preußen im 18. Jahrhundert: Das Leben und Werk Georg Ernst Stahls* (Berlin: de Gruyter, 2000).
36 On the debate between Hoffmann and Stahl, see: Francesco Paolo de Ceglia, "Hoffmann and Stahl: Documents and Reflections on the Dispute," *History of Universities* 22 (2007): 98–140.

name *Gütel* ("little good one"), and thus shares with *Grendel* phonemically both the beginning letter and the diminutive/diminishing ending (*-el*). One could also point to the broken semantic-moral code of "good," or "goodness" (*Gut, Gute, Gütel*) that occurs with the differentiated and differentiating *ü*-sound of this diminutive. In the popular imaginary, women were projected both as the most modest, pious, obedient, and therefore most "protected" of souls, as well as easy targets for demonological forces, and it is precisely this radical ambivalence which also rendered them particularly susceptible *and* dangerous. Grendel therefore also becomes the site of the adjudication and subjugation of the subaltern. As a Jewess, she easily functions as a paradigmatic example of what Zygmunt Bauman has referred to as *allosemitism*; she is the incomprehensible, "strange" body whose otherness threatens the very order of the evangelical consistory and state of early enlightened Absolutism; she is the dangerous figure who, using Bauman's words, "does not fit the structure of the orderly world, does not fall easily into any of the established categories, emits therefore contradictory signals as to the proper conduct – and in the end blurs the borderlines which are to be kept watertight."[37] Finally, as "demonically possessed," she contests the claims of the new medical-psychological theory and practice – empiricism, observation, reason, and rational explanation – as we shall see, "stifling" and "frustrating" the medical, theological, and juridical attempts to provide a clear resolution.

On June 2, 1744, the *Schutzjude* or "protected Jew" Isaac Solomon from Stadthagen appears at the Residenz-Schloss in Bückeburg on behalf of the supplicant, the "protected Jew" Moses Bendix of the town of Cappel, bringing a letter of appeal to Graf Albrecht, asking his permission to have a rabbi from the neighboring town of Wahrendorf brought in to exorcize a spirit that had presumably taken possession of his daughter Grendel. Solomon testifies that the patient had been possessed by the evil spirit for several years and that all means possible had been employed by the Jewish community itself and experienced physicians to no effect, so that the father knew of no other remedy than to call for a rabbi residing in nearby Wahrendorf known for having successfully carried out an exorcism in Detmold to perform the ritual on his daughter. Bendix requested a quick resolution from the consistory as the matter required immediate attention. In his letter of petition (*Bittschrift*), Bendix mentions that the rabbi to be called in to perform the exorcism had consented

---

[37] Zygmunt Bauman, "Allosemitism: Premodern, Modern, Postmodern," in *Modernity, Culture, and "the Jew,"* ed. Bryan Chenette and Laura Marcus (Cambridge: Polity Press, 1998), 143–156.

to allow all those who would be interested to observe the exorcism to be present at the ritual.

> I appeal to the high imperial count mercifully to allow me to have a rabbi come here who has committed himself to exorcizing a spirit who has apparently possessed my daughter. The rabbi has obliged himself to allow all observers who wish to do so to be present at such exorcism; I remain the high imperial count's servant Bendix Moses, Protected Jew in Cappel.
> Bückeburg
> 3rd June
> 1744
>
> Hoch Reichs gräffl. Exelentz grenchen gnädigst zu erlauben, daß ich einen Rabiener hier her kommen laße, der sich unter standen meine Tochter welche mit einem Geist besessen, wieder denselben abzutreiben hat sich der Rabiener obligihrt alle zu schauer die belieben haben solches an zu sehen dar beÿ zu laßen; ich verharre
>
> €d: Hoch Reichs gräffl. Exelentz
>   Unter Knecht
> Bückeburg Bendix Moses
> 3te Juny   Schutz Jude zu Cappel, 1744[38]

The supplicant already stipulates that his daughter has been possessed by a spirit, but curiously avoids the term evil in his appeal. The claim that the rabbi has committed to having an "open" exorcism in which members of the court could attend simultaneously recognizes the liminality of the procedure itself, as well as the precarity of the request in an age of dismissive skepticism regarding such superstitious phenomena.

The position of Graf Albrecht is evident from the beginning of the proceeding; he directs his councilors to proceed rationally in this case – the term *vernünfftig* is used no fewer than three times in Graf Albrecht's initial response – and to allow the Medical Councilor (*Medizinalrat*) Rabe and others to examine and interrogate her, and to have the Rabbi himself testify as to his understanding of the girl's affliction. Graf Albrecht states that this is best way to achieve a rational explanation and understanding of the girl's condition: "as through such reasonable means something reasonable can be gained from this person most reliably and conveniently."[39] As the matter is deliberated in

---

38 *NSB*, Blatt 48.
39 *NSB*, Blatt 49: "da durch vernünfftige Mittel diese Persohn Vernünfftiges angeben gewiß am sichersten und convenabelsten zu haben seyn wird."

the consistory, the councilors voice little concern about the ritual itself; mention is made of the fact that this practice is fully in accordance with the principles of Judaism (*Principiis Judaismi*), and also that exorcisms are even still common in the Protestant provinces of Germany: "because the act which is being sought is consistent with Jewish principles and therefore tolerated, and, on the other hand, because exorcism even today is practiced by Protestants in some provinces."[40] The exorcism itself does not seem to raise any eyebrows; it is only a matter whether the girl, the Rabbi, the mother and father are telling the *truth*, or whether this is a deception, a case of malingering, or some form of conspiracy with an ulterior motive.

The actual investigation/examination of the young woman's case begins almost immediately, with four members of Albrecht's cabinet present: the Consistory Advisor Dr. Prof. de Lehenen, Medical Councilor Rabe, Superintendent Hauber, and Advisor Wolbrecht. On the 22nd of June 1744, the Rabbi from Wahrendorf, Moses Bendix, and his daughter arrived in Bückeburg at the Residenz-Schloss. A preliminary investigation creates skepticism as to the authenticity of the alleged "possession" – the language here is of *impostura* or *glaucomata* – and for this reason, it was deemed appropriate and reasonable to delay the exorcism until all involved could be properly questioned through an official interrogation (*Verhör*). At this point, other councilors from the court, in addition to the ones already mentioned – Frederking, Colson, and most importantly the Court Preacher le Maitre – are called on to take part in the proceedings. The entirety of the principality's apparatus has been brought to bear on Grendel's case not because of the alleged possession itself, but because of the suspicion of fraudulent activity on the part of the family or the Jewish community of Schaumburg-Lippe.

The Rabbi (Samuel, sixty years old, from Vienna, residing in Wahrendorf) was the first to be interviewed. Asked how he had come to be in Bückeburg, he replies that he had been summoned by the family of the patient in order to gain a consensus concerning the presence of a spirit and, if necessary, with permission of the authorities, to exorcize the spirit from the young woman. He stated he met the patient and the family halfway to Wahrendorf four weeks earlier where he had a chance to speak with the patient. He is then asked about the details of the exorcism he had performed in Detmold. Significant here is the

---

[40] *NSB*, Blatt 51: "weil der nachgesuchte actus mit den *Principiis Judaismi* so doch überhaupt toleriret würden übereinkäme, und anderntheils weil der Exorcismus auch so gar noch heutiges Tages den Protestanten selbst in einigen Provincien exerciret würde."

question put to the Rabbi whether or not he would be allowed to practice the exorcism without the consultation with and approval of the State/Land authority:

9.) ob die Juden nach ihrer Religion ohne oder mit Consens der Landes Obrigkeit dergleichen Austreibung der Geister veranstalten durfften?	Rs. Nein! Sie dürffte[n] solches nicht ohne Consens veranstalten.[41]
9.) whether the Jews according to their religion without or with the consent of the authority of the land may carry out such an exorcism?	Rs. No! They may not arrange such an exorcism without the consent of the authorities.

Because the Rabbi did not first obtain the permission of the authorities to conduct the exorcism in Detmold, the members of the family of the boy of twelve years on whom the exorcism had been performed had been punished. The Jewish community must first seek the approval of the state/land authority (*Landes Obrigkeit*) in order to be able to carry out such an exorcism. When asked by the councilors and advisors why he would need such an approval if the act is in accordance with the law and principles of Judaism, the Rabbi responds: "in order to avoid suspicion and other unfortunate vexating, troublesome consequences."[42]

When asked how he had been able to recognize the presence of an evil spirit in the case of the twelve year-old boy in Detmold by the name of Kalman, the Rabbi simply responded: "by his incantations and conjurations and through the holy name of God, with which he demanded of the evil spirit that it reveal itself to him."[43] And when questioned how he knew that this Jewish girl was also possessed with an evil spirit, he states that the girl exhibited the

---

41 *NSB*, Blatt 57.
42 *NSB*, Blatt 58: "Rs. um nur Verdacht und Verdrieslichkeiten zu vermeiden, müsten sie von der Obrigkeit vor hero Consens ausbringen." Rs. Refers to *Responsa*. As part of the rhetorical structuring of the protocol, *Reponsa* refers to any commentary or answers to questions posed by the consistory. It is interesting to note that *Responsa* also have a long history in Rabbinic literature as commentary on the Bible, the Mishnah, and the Talmud.
43 *NSB*, Blatt 58: "Rs. durch Beschwehrungen [*Beschwörungen*] und durch die heilige Nahmen Gottes, wodurch er den Geist genötiget sich zu entdecken."

identical typical indications, at which point he placed a sign with the word of God on her, and the spirit had then revealed itself to him.[44]

As to the procedure of exorcism itself, the Rabbi communicated to the advisors and councilors that he primarily used the 91st Psalm of David and other psalms as well as additional *Media und Formalitäten* to drive out the evil spirit. Included in the "media" and "formalities" were passages from the Kabbalah that he would not be able to explain adequately: "It was cabbalistic secrets which he would not be able to explain to everyone."[45] With regard to how the evil spirit had let itself be known and the origins of the *böser Geist* itself, the spirit called itself *Gütel*, the name of a deceased woman in Bielefeld who lived one hundred years ago. This woman had done so many evil things in her life, and had not followed the law of God; her spirit had been wandering about in the world before she had entered the girl's soul and taken possession of it.

The Superintendent le Maitre then begins his part of the interrogation, enquiring as to the basis in Judaism that such spirits enter the souls of human beings. The Rabbi responds that it is in the Talmud itself, especially the 22nd chapter of the 1st Book of Kings, that such a justification can be found. The passage referred to from Kings 1:20–23 reads as follows:

> And the LORD said, who shall persuade Ahab,
> That he may go up and fall at Ramothgilead.
> And one said on this manner, and another said
> on that manner.
>
> And there came forth a spirit, and stood before
> the LORD, and said, I will persuade him.
> And the LORD said unto him, Wherewith? And
> He said, I will go forth and I will be a *lying spirit*
> In the mouth of all his prophets. And he
> said, Thou shalt persuade him, and prevail also:
> go forth, and do so.
>
> Now therefore, behold, the LORD hath put a
> lying spirit in the mouth of all these thy
> prophets, and the LORD hath spoken evil
> concerning thee.

---

44 *NSB*, Blatt 58: "Rs. auf gleiche Art, und hätte er derselben die heil(igen) Worte angehängt worauf sich der Geist zu erkennen gegeben."
45 *NSB*, Blatt 59: "Es waren kabbalistische Geheimnisse, welche (er) einem jeden nicht erklären könte."

The Talmud provides evidence justifying the Rabbi's belief that such evil spirits inhabit the souls of humans, and that such spirits possess the soul of the afflicted, controlling their speech and action, causing them great distress and vexation, and threatening family and communal life. When questioned as to the belief that the evil spirit is the soul of a dead person, the Rabbi responds that the Spirit is mentioned by name; in the *Book of Kings*, it was the spirit of *Naboth* who reappeared. Naboth owned a vineyard close to Ahab's fortress and refused to relinquish it even with compensation because it had been gifted to him by his father and could therefore not be disappropriated from the family. Ahab informed his wife Jezebel of Naboth's refusal, at which point she intrigues a mock trial sentencing Naboth to death and naming Ahab as the rightful heir of all of his property. Rabbi Samuel is then asked to come to the chambers of the Superintendent later that afternoon to be questioned further.

Bräunchen, from Petershagen and previously from Cappel, about fifty years old, testified that the "patient" (in the text, the Jewish girl is continually referred to as the *Patientin*) was in fact her daughter. The mother states that she had been sick (*krank*) for a long time and that they had tried every conceivable medical treatment, every possible cure, in vain, until "she perceived from her daughter's strange (*wunder[lichen]*) behavior that she was possessed by an evil spirit, which was then later confirmed by the Rabbi."[46] The physicians summoned by the family to examine the girl had been unable to form a unified diagnosis; one thought they were symptoms of the *Gicht* that had been afflicting many in the area; the other that these were signs of a pregnancy (*Mutter Erscheinungen*). The mother is then asked whether in these attacks the patient had not spoken or stated that she was possessed by an evil spirit. She replies that her daughter had only recently said that she was possessed by such a spirit, and that this spirit was of a woman who had sinned a great deal. The first statement from the patient that she was possessed by an evil spirit had occurred shortly before Easter, before she had met with the Rabbi. Finally, the mother is asked whether the spirit had always spoken, to which the mother replies in the affirmative and adds that she had not seen any change during the last several months. Due to the suspicion of malingering, or of conspiracy hovering above the case, the key question for the consistory was precisely when, and from whom, the idea of possession by an evil spirit became the explanation of the young woman's symptoms. The supposed contradiction perceived by the consistory is clear: the mother's testimony stated that Grendel herself had expressed being possessed by an evil spirit prior to the meeting with the Rabbi,

---

46 *NSB*, Blatt 60.

while the Rabbi stated that the evil spirit had first "presented itself" using the common conjuring techniques at their first meeting.

The Rabbi is called before the consistory again and asked whether such an evil spirit could itself be known prior to a Rabbi evoking it by placing the words of God on the patient. He responds that this may occur, but that *in this instance that had not been the case*; he testifies the evil spirit had not let itself be known until they had a tried several medications about a half year ago (which proved ineffective) for the treatment of what they then believed was a case of severe melancholy. It was only after these medications had failed to produce any results that the father returned to the Rabbi in April, and *the father* had first put forth the idea that the young woman might be possessed by an evil spirit. The father's hypothesis had resonated with him, and he then prescribed certain medicines (about two months prior to their arrival in Bückeburg) for the treatment of an evil spirit. The Rabbi then prescribed a medicine for possession by an evil spirit, which had led to the evil spirit revealing itself. Asked whether an evil spirit would reveal itself before being called forth, the Rabbi replies:

> Rs. it could well happen, but in this case the spirit had not revealed itself before he had administered the aforementioned medication; that he had sent one or the other medications for melancholy approximately a half a year ago, but seeing that such medication had not had the desired effect, he was advised when the father had returned and only then, through his telling of the circumstances, had he come to the idea that the daughter was possessed by an evil spirit, at which point he prescribed and sent medications+ specifically against such a possession of the spirit, and that these had had the effect that the spirit presented itself.
> +about two months ago

> Rs. es könne wol geschehen, aber in diesem Fall hätte der Geist sich eher nicht kund gegeben alß biß die vorhin benannte Mittel gebrauchet; indem er vor ohngefehr einem halben Jahr ein oder ander gegen die Melancholie dienliche Mittel zugesandt, alß aber auch solche beÿ ihr nicht verfangen wollen, so wäre er auf Wiederkunft des Vatters, und desselben Erzehlung erst auf die Gedanken gerathen, daß das Mensch mit einem bösen Geist beseßen, worauf er ihr die vorhin deponierte Mittel⁺gegen die Beseßung des Geistes zu gesandt, die so viel effektuiret, daß sich der Geist darauf zu erkennen gegeben.
> +vor ohngefehr zweÿ Monathen[47]

The mother is called before the commission once again, and asked if the evil spirit had let itself be known prior to meeting the Rabbi. The mother responds that her daughter herself had informed her that she had been possessed by

---

47 *NSB*, Blatt 61.

a spirit, and that this spirit was that of a woman from Bielefeld. She thus denies that the explanation of possession by an evil spirit was the suggestion of the Rabbi, or that the father had arrived at the conclusion that the girl was possessed by an evil spirit. The Rabbi, the mother testifies, had merely affirmed what the family already believed, and had treated her accordingly.

The girl is then led by two gendarmes before the consistory. Unable to stand or walk on her own accord, and refusing to sit in the chair assigned to her, she is brought before the inquiry making grimaces with her face and stamping with her feet. As the evil spirit is then threatened to be whipped with the rod, the "evil spirit" itself began to "speak" according to the protocol:

> Thus, she was dragged by two guards, whereby the evil spirit who had been surging up in her forced her not being able to either stand or walk; she was then placed in a chair, but the supposed spirit desired that she only be allowed to sit on the floor whereupon she with much ado slid down from the chair to the floor and began to to make all sorts of grimaces and to stamp with her feet, and as the supposed spirit was threatened, stated that he could be lashed with a rod, began to say, I am the evil spirit and one cannot do me harm, one can whip me as much as one wishes *et quo talia*...

> so wurde dieselbe durch zweÿ Mousquetiers herauf geschleppt, indem der angeb(liche) beÿ ihr aufgewallete böse Geist vorgab; wie die Patientin nicht gehen, noch stehen könte hierauf wurde dieselbe auf ein Stuhl gesetzet die Patientin aber oder ihr vermeintl:(liche) böser Geist begehrte, sie nur auf den Fußboden sitzen zu laßen, worauf die selbe mit zimlicher Addresse vom Stuhl auf die Erde sich nieder sezte und anfing allerleÿ grimaces zu machen mit den Füßen zu stampfen und alß der vermeintl: (ichen) Geist gedrohet wurde; wie er schon mit Ruthen heraus gepeitscht werden könte, zu sagen, ich bin der böse Geist, man kann mir nichts zu leide thun; man mag mich schlagen, so viel man will *et quo talia*...[48]

Notes were tied to her fingers by her parents, but Grendel claims not to have known what the little notes meant or that she was possessed, nor finally that the evil spirit was named *Gütel*. The Patient is again implored to tell the truth, and asked whether she is engaged in a conspiracy or deceit, but she remains absolutely steadfast.[49]

The Rabbi is brought before the consistory again and asked why he had claimed that the patient had been brought to him in Wahrendorf, of which the patient knew absolutely nothing, to which he replied: "What the spirit speaks through her, she of course cannot know anything about."[50] The mother of the patient is then confronted with the Rabbi and told that in her deposition she

---

48 *NSB*, Blatt 61–62.
49 *NSB*, Blatt 63.
50 *NSB*, Blatt 65.

had claimed that her daughter had already claimed to be possessed by an evil spirit *before* the encounter with the Rabbi, and that the spirit had said it was the spirit of a woman from Bielefeld. The Rabbi however had claimed that this had occurred only after he had given her a prescription that had revealed the spirit:

> At this point, the mother of the patient was confronted with the Rabbi, and they were warned that the mother had stated that her daughter had given to understand that she was possessed by an evil spirit even *before* the Rabbi had been brought in, but that the Rabbi had maintained that this had first occurred when he had given her the suitable medications. The Rabbi* however wanted to explain this apparent contradiction with the fact that the patient's mother had not traveled with him the entire journey, but had met him and brought the patient to him halfway in Wahrendorf.
> *this contradiction
>
> Hierauf ist der Patientin Mutter mit dem Rabbi konfrontiret und ist ihnen vorgehalten, daß jene *ad interri* gesaget, daß ihre Tochter schon vorher ehe sie zu dem Rabbi gebracht, zu erkennen gegeben, daß sie mit einem Geist beseßen, der Rabbiner aber vorgegeben gestalten dieses allererst sich zugetragen, alß er ihr seine Mittel ad hibiret. Es wollte sich aber der Rabbiner* mit dieser Erläuterung entschuldigen, daß der Patientin Mutter nicht mit gereiset alß ihre Tochter auf den halben Weg nach Wahrendorf ihn zugebracht worden.
> *diese Contradiction [51]

The patient's mother is implored once again to tell the truth regarding the entire matter, what she knows about it, and to dispense with any hidden intentions or disguises in order to get money or favor. The mother remains completely resolute that she knows nothing but what she has previously testified: "she fervently remained with her assertion, that she knew and believed nothing other than what she had already testified how the matter occurred."[52]

An extraordinary consistory session was then convened, in which the participants concluded that, despite all of the precise questioning and interrogation, they have been "unable to get at the truth," specifically, whether or not the patient is malingering or there has been a conspiracy to extract money or favor from the court. As the patient is too weak to undertake the exorcism, and the Rabbi cannot remain in Schaumburg-Lippe, the mother is declared free to take her daughter back to Stadthagen, to the physician Isaac Solomon, who can prescribe medicines, and to allow the Rabbi to return when and if the patient gets stronger. The Rabbi responds that he will probably not be able to return, but,

---

51 *NSB*, Blatt 65.
52 *NSB*, Blatt 65: "sie blieb aber beständig dabeÿ, wo sie nichts anders wüste und glaube, alß daß die Sache so wie sie angegeben, sich verhielte."

more importantly, that the case would become shameful for the Jews (the exorcism not having been performed; the young woman returning without a cure): "that the rabbi would in all likelihood not be able to return, and that therefore the matter would remain unresolved to the shame of the Jews."[53] The mother is once again called before the consistory and told that any charitable interpretation of depositions would suggest that there is a deceit or a conspiracy at hand. She is admonished once again to tell the truth. If she were to admit that there had been "other intentions," the councilors inform the mother that she and her daughter would not be punished, but rather that all of the means possible would be brought to bear to try to help her daughter and the costs paid by the state. The mother sticks by her statements, reasserts that she believed her daughter to be sick, that everything possible had been tried to offer her remedy, and that, by and by and without any improvement of her condition, she had finally been convinced that her daughter was possessed by an evil spirit. In this phase of the testimony, the mother significantly does *not* repeat her previous assertion that her daughter herself had told her she was possessed by an evil spirit. She seeks, if the sovereign authority would consent and allow, having her daughter's detainment rescinded, or for her daughter to be placed under the care of the state, but that she should be allowed to see her daughter and care for her while she is in custody. In addition, she testifies on her honor that the Pastor Hoff at Cappel also had thorough knowledge of her daughter and her situation, and would be able to attest to her condition and the history of the illness.[54] It is then resolved to write to Pastor Hoffe to report back in writing what he knew of the patient's life, transformation, and illness.

On June 23rd, Graf Albrecht notes that even though all in attendance had the sense of a simulation or other deceit, nothing could be definitively proven, that the number of inconsistencies or contradictions had only increased, and because the said exorcism could not be carried out immediately, it is resolved that the protocol and questioning should be continued until the other supporting documents arrived. On the suspicion that the mother has not been truthful under questioning, Albrecht orders that the mother and the daughter should be kept in custody in the barracks until such time as they tell the truth, without anything untoward happening to them or them having to want of anything or suffer in any way: "to lead them back to the barracks, without anything malicious happening to her or her daughter and without them having to do without

---

[53] *NSB*, Blatt 67: "daß der Rabbi wohl schwerl(ich) wieder kommen mögte, mithin die Sache dadurch selbst zur Beschämung der Juden würde erlegen bleiben."
[54] *NSB*, Blatt 69.

whatever is necessary."⁵⁵ Letters are then sent to von Hoffe and Doctor Müller in Detmold asking for information regarding the patient and her illness. In the case of the Doctor, he is requested to provide a *Certificat* that the patient had in fact been under his treatment, and the precise nature of the illness.⁵⁶

Medical Councilor Rabe visits Grendel to further interrogate her. He asks her specifically about her history, whether she had her *menses* at regular intervals, whether she had been of good cheer prior to the attacks, whether she had dreamt, had slept peacefully, whether she had been able and willing to work. Rabe asked how long she had known that a spirit was within her, to which she replies that he should please not utter the "word," obviously referring to the evil spirit: "Rs. she asked that I not mention the word, that I would not mention it if I knew how much a sense of unease and distress she feels at the very mention of it."⁵⁷ Rabe then fires off a series of questions concerning the spirit itself: whether the spirit is more peaceful when she is happy, enjoys something good to eat or drink, whether the spirit had suggested marriage to her, whether the spirit was more a friend or foe, whether it would lead her astray, whether it showed itself unwilling to be discovered or to be exorcised, whether it could bear her being questioned, where the spirit resides in her body, and whether it could reveal itself. To all of these she replies that she has no knowledge about it other than that she has pains and often headache, and that she knows nothing about a "spirit" other than what had been told to her. At this point the "evil spirit" reveals itself.

The next section of the protocol bears the title "with the spirit" (*Mit dem Geist*), the section in which Medical Councilor Rabe questions the evil spirit itself: how it had come to possess this girl, whether it could possess a person with a cross, whether it wanted to do good or evil to the girl (to which it of course replies evil, for it is an evil spirit); whether it could lead the girl astray to do evil things (to which the spirit replies that she can do nothing that (s)he, the evil

---

55 *NSB*, Blatt 72: "dieselbe darauff wieder *ad* cascerne zu führen, ohne daß da Ihr und ihre Tochter übles zuzufügen werde oder einige Mangel am nothwendigsten gelitten wurde."
56 *NSB*, Blatt 73: "Alß habt Ihr zu Cappel, von der Patientin, ihren Umständen ihres Übells ihrer Familie und von allem was man daselbst von ihren angebl(ichen) Übell wissen mogte (und in Erfahrung bringen) so fort alle mögl(iche) Informationes; daneben auch muß von dem Dr (r.) Müller zu Detmold ein *Certificat* zu verschaffen, ob es wahr seÿ oder nicht, daß diese Patientin ihrer Mutter gethane Außage, ihm jemals in die Cur gelieffert worden, ingleichen was jenenfalls für Umstände ihres Übells an ihr sich geäußert worden."
57 *NSB*, Blatt 77: "sie bäte mich, ich möchte doch das Wort nicht nennen, ich würde es auch nicht thun, wenn ich wüste, was sie vor Mishagen und Ungemach sie dabey empfände."

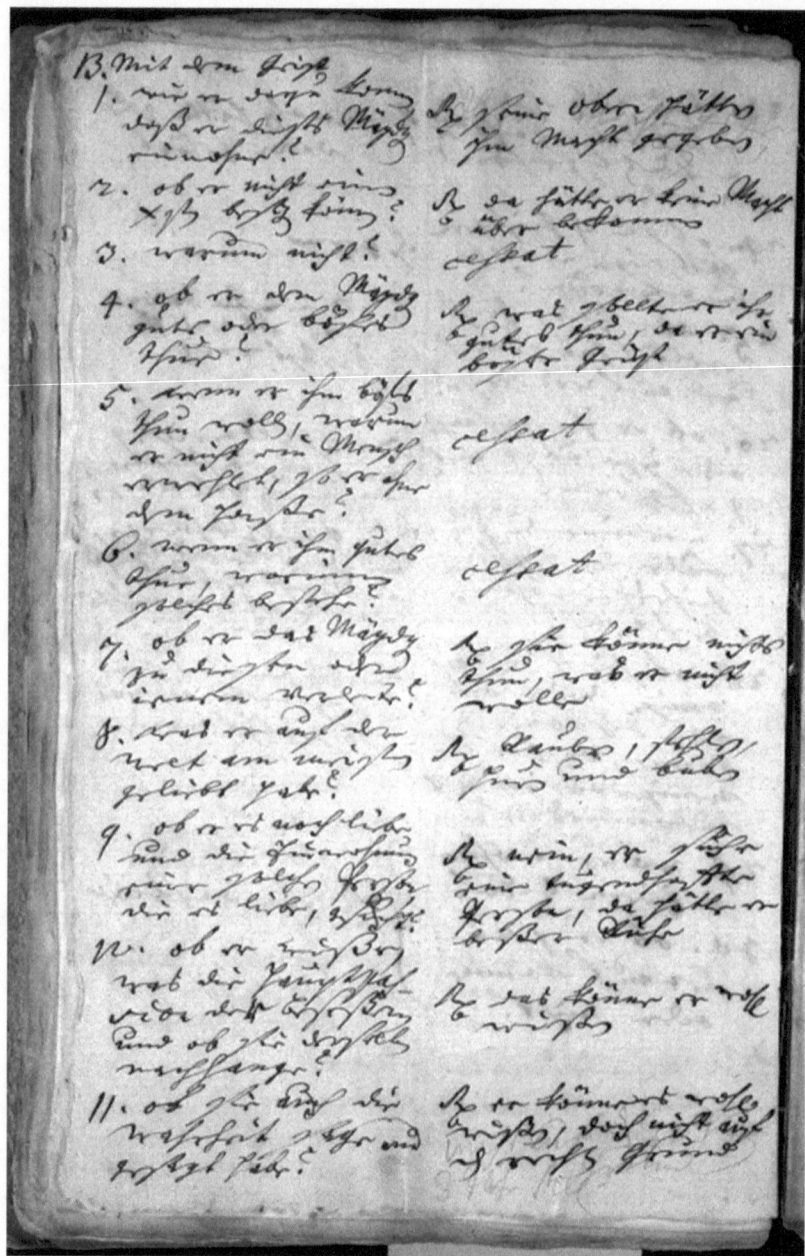

Figure 9: The "Conversation with the Spirit" from the Protocol of the Case-History of Grendel, the Jewish girl whose father requests that a Rabbi be allowed to perform an exorcism, 1744. NLA Staatsarchiv Bückeburg Dep 22 _Blatt 57. Courtesy and with permission of the Niedersächsisches Landesarchiv Bückeburg.

spirit, does not want); what it loved the most in this world (to which the spirit replies robbers, stealing, whores and young boys); how it chooses a person to possess. The spirit states that it had been quiet for four years, but that the Rabbi had compelled her to come forward. The fifty five questions of this protocol interrogation directed to the evil spirit I reproduce here, first in English translation, then in the original German.

---

13. *With the spirit*

1. How it occurred that he had Come to possess this young girl?	R[esponsa]. His masters had given him power
2. Whether he could possess [someone] With a cross?	Rs. for this he hadn't received the power
3. Why not?	Rs. *Cessat*
4. Whether he wanted to do good or evil spirit	Rs. why should he do good as he was an evil the girl?
5. If he wanted to do evil, why handn't he shosen a different human he could call witthout here?	Rs. *Cessat*
6. If he wanted to do good, what would this be?	Rs. *Cessat*
7. Whether he wanted to lead the girl to This or that?	Rs. she could not do what he did not want
8. What he had loved most in this world?	Rs. robbers, stealing, whores, and young boys
9. Whether he still loves it and had sought to reside?	Rs. no, he sought a virtuous person, for there he could remain more easily
10. whether he knows the main passion of of the one possessed and whether she remained committed to it?	Rs. that of course he could know
11. Whether she was speaking and had spoken the truth?	Rs. he could of course know it, but not on the correct basis.
12. Whether he paid attention to what she does or speaks?	Rs. she could not do anything without his willing it, as one admitted yesterday
13. Whether he likes to see her sad or happy?	Rs. it doesn't matter to him
14. Whether he is her friend or enemy?	Rs. why would he want to be her friend?
15. Whether he had revealed himself or had been discovered by another?	Rs. he had not revealed himself; rather the Rabbi had forced him to reveal himself; he had lived quietly in her for four years, had been in possession of her five years.

(continued)

16. How long [ago] this had been?	Rs. about a quarter of a year
17. Whether or not the Rabbi had discovered him?	Rs. *Cessat*
18. Whether he hated the Rabbi	Rs. of course
19. Whether he had imparted something to the Rabbi	Rs. he told him that he would gladly leave, but that his masters wouldn't have it
20. Whether he came from Bielefeld?	Rs. yes
21. Whether he had come to Cappel by chance?	Rs. his masters had given him the power
22. Whether he remembers anything that happened to his body in Bielefeld?	Rs. he did not have permission from his masters to say; it would also not help me, why would I ask.
23. What type of ruler governed the land?	
24. Whether Bielefeld is in a mountainous or a flat reigion?	Rs. he is not permitted to say, and I should not ask
25. Whether there is a castle there or nearby?	
26. Whether the spirit after death had remained there?	Rs. he hovered around the whole world
27. What he had sought or wished for?	Rs. he had wandered around restlessly
28. Whether he feels better now or outside of a body?	Rs. yes, he now had peace and didn't need to wander about anymore
29. Why?	
30. Whether he hates the cross in the person more than in life?	Rs. doesn't matter
31. Whether he had, after his death, seen souls that had the cross, and how he felt at those moments	
32. What other kinds of spirits he had been aware of and how they had encountered him?	Rs. they weren't any of his business; the evil spirits such as he was, also didn't matter to him; they just float around in the dark; but those spirits that contained much light, i.e. those that were pious, saw much
33. Whether or not he had encountered good spirits in the realm of death?	Rs. that is friendship, whereas the evil spirits only trouble each other
34. Whether or not he could see what occurs among the living?	Rs. Negat

(continued)

35. Whether there was war or peace in Germany at the present time?	Rs. negat
36. Whether or not he knew something of the future?	Negat
37. Whether or not he knew what stood before him in the future?	Negat
38. Whether or not he knew that he ought to to leave the young girl?	Rs. yes
39. Whether that would be not to his wishes, and why?	Rs. of course, then he would have to hover about again
40. Whether that would happen or not?	Rs. here in prison it could not happen, but in the Synagogue it could; but it would not happen, for the Rabbi is away
41. Whether he hates those who wish to drive him out, but loves those who are opposed to driving him out?	Rs. goes without saying, but he loves no one
42. Whether he requests that he be left undisturbed?	Rs. if he could obtain it by requesting it
43. How one could perhaps soothe him, or that he would cause the girl less or no harm?	Rs. he needs nothing
44. Whether the girl gushes over him and would like to be left with him?	Rs. she can and may do nothing without his willing it so
45. Whether he knows what the girl thinks, or speaks and does?	Rs. yes
46. Whether it matters to him at all, what she thinks or does?	Rs. yes
47. Whether he could bring the girl to pray?	Rs. yes, once in a while, but now he doesn't allow it
48. Whether she is pious in her prayer?	Rs. yes
49. Whether the Rabbi is a pious man?	Rs. yes
50. Whether the spirit of this girl would lead her to be disobedient against state authority?	Rs. concerning 50, it depends on him what the girl does
51. Whether he has any pity when the girl is hit by him or by another?	Rs. what does he care about pity?
52. Whether he knew me, loves or hates me?	Rs. no, why would he even be concerned about me?

(continued)

53. Whether he tolerates being questioned by me in this manner?	Rs. yes, I should only continue
	Respondi, he must have been a real talker during his life; me: I am too.
In closing, I also asked the spirit:	
Whether it is true, what I had asked the girl previously?	Rs. yes, it was all true. I would have also asked the same thing, I would of course know that she wouldn't want to say it; that he could stop if he wanted to. And then I asked the spirit:
Where in the body do you dwell?	Rs. he has no specific place, could dwell in all parts of her body; the girl knows nothing of this.

13. *Mit dem Geist*

1. Wie er dazu komme, daß er dieses Mägden einwohne?	Rs. seine Obere hätte ihm Macht gegeben
2. ob er nicht einen Xses[58] beseßen könne?	Rs. da hätte er keine Macht über bekommen
3. warum nicht?	Cessat
4. ob er dem Mägden gutes oder böses thun?	Rs. was sollte er ihr gutes thun, da er ein böser Geist
5. wenn er ihm böses thun wolle, warum er nicht ein Mensch erwehlet, so er ohne dem heiße?	Rs. cessat
6. wenn er ihm gutes thue, worinnen solches bestehe?	cessat
7. ob er das Mägden zu diesem oder ienem verleite?	Rs. sie könne nichts thun was er nicht wolle
8. was er auf der Welt am meisten geliebt habe?	Rs. Räuber, stehlen, Huren und Buben

---

58 Kreuz (cross).

(continued)

9. ob er es noch liebe und die Einwohnung liebe, gesuchet?	Rs. nein, er suche eine solchen Person die aus tugendhafte Person, da hätte er besser Ruhe
10. ob er wiße, was die Haupt passion der Beseßne und ob sie derselben nach hange?	Rs. das könne er wohl wißen
11. ob sie auch die Wahrheit sage und gesagt habe?	Rs. er könne es wohl wißen, doch nicht auf den rechten Grund
12. ob er acht darauf habe, was sie thue oder rede?	Rs. sie könne ohne seinen Willen nichts thun, wie man gestern gestehe
13. ob er sie lieber traurig oder fröhlich sehe?	Rs. das sey ihm gleich viel
14. ob er ihr Freund oder Feind sey?	Rs. was wolle er ihr Freund seyn
15. ob er sich selbst verrathen habe, oder ob er von anderen entdeckt sey?	Rs. habe sich nicht selbst verrathen, sondern der Rabbi habe ihn genöthigt; derer 4 Jahr sey er in dem Menschen stille gewesen, also besetze er es schon 5. Jahr
16. wie lange dieses sey?	Rs. ad sb. ohngefahr 1/4 Jahr
17. ob ihn der Rabbiner entdeckt habe?	Cessat
18. ob er den Rabbiner haße?	Rs. allerdings
19. ob er dem Rabbiner was weiß gemacht habe?	er habe ihm theils weiß gemacht, daß er gutwillig heraus wolle, es hätte aber auch die Obern nicht haben wollen
20. ob er von Bielefeld?	Rs. ad 20. ia.
21. wie er nach Cappel komme, ob von ohngefehr?	Rs. ad 21. Die Oberen hätten ihm Macht gegeben
22. ob er sich nichts erinnere, was ehemahls bey seinem Leib in Bielefeld passiret sey?	Rs. er habe von seinen Obern nicht Erlaubniß, es zu sagen, es würde mir auch nichts helfen, warum ich doch darnach fragte
23. was vor ein Herr das Land regiret?	
24. ob Bielefeld auf Berge oder in der Ebene lieget?	Rs. das dürffte er nicht sagen, ich möchte doch nicht darnach fragen.
25. ob ein Schloss darinne oder dabey?	
26. ob sich der Geist nach dem Tode nicht dasselbst aufgehalten?	Rs. er habe in der ganzen Welt herum geschwebt
27. was er gesucht oder gewünscht habe?	Rs. in der Unruhe sey er herum vagirt
28. ob er sich iezo besser besinnt als außer einem Cörper?	Rs. ja, er habe nun Ruhe und brauchte nicht zu schweben
29. warum?	

(continued)

30. ob er die Xsten noch als sp. haße, als beym leben?	Rs. das wäre gleich viel
31. ob er nicht nach seinem Tode Xsten Seelen gesehen und wie es ihm ergehe?	
32. was er sonst vor Geister gewahr worden und Sie ihm begegnet?	Rs. die gingen ihm nichts an, die bösen Geister, als er wäre, auch nicht, sondern schwebten im Duncklen. Die Geister aber, so viel Licht hätten, od. fromm wären, sähen viel
33. ob er nicht gute Geister im Reich der Tod angetroffen?	Rs. da wäre die Freundschaft, denn die bösen Geister plagten einander
34. ob er nicht sehen könne, was unter den Lebenden geschehe?	Rs. negat
35. ob Krieg oder Frieden in Deutschland sey?	Negat
36. ob er nichts vom zukünftigem wiße?	Negat
37. ob er selbst wiße, was ihm bevorstehe?	negat
38. ob er wiße, daß er solle ausgehen?	Rs. ja
39. ob ihm solches zuwider und warum?	Rs. Allerdings, so müsse er wieder schweben
40. ob es geschehe werde oder nicht?	Rs. hier in carcere könne es nicht geschehen, aber in der Synagoge; es werde aber nicht geschehen, denn der Rabbi weg wäre
41. ob er die haße, die ihn delogieren wolle und hin gegen die liebe, die dargegen sich setzen?	Rs. ad 41. das verstehe sich, indeßen liebe er niemand
42. ob er bitte, daß man ihn ungestört laße?	Rs. wenn er es mit Bitten erhalten könte
43. wodurch man ihn besänftigen könne, daß er dem Mägde weniger oder keine Graaf anthun?	Rs. er habe nichts vonnöthen
44. ob ihm das Mägden ergehen sey und sich gerne laße?	Rs. sie dürffe und könne ohne seinen Willen nichts thun
45. ob er alles wiße, was das Mägden denkt oder spricht und thut?	Rs. ia
46. ob ihm alles gleich viel, was sie denkt oder thut?	Rs. ia
47. ob er könne, daß das Mägden bete?	Rs. ia, bißweilen und auch iezo ließe er sie nicht darzu
48. ob sie andächtig in ihrem gebet sey?	Rs. ia
49. ob der Rabbiner ein frommer Mann?	Rs. ia

(continued)

50. ob er der Geist dieses Mägdens zum Ungehorsam gegen die Obrigkeit verleite?	Rs. ad. 50. es dependire von ihm, was das Mägden thue
51. ob ihm denn gar nicht erbarme, wenn das Mägden von ihm odern anderen geprahlet werde?	Rs. was soll ihm das erbarmen?
52. ob er mich könne und liebe oder haße?	Rs. nein, und was ihm an mir gelegen seyn könte?
53. ob er es wohl vertragen könne, daß er befragt werde?	Rs. ia, ich möchte nur continuiren:
	Respondi, so muste im Leben eine rechte Plaudertasche gewesen seyn; illa: das bin ich auch gewesen.
Zuletzt habe den Geist noch gefragt:	
Ob es wahr, was ich vorher das Mägden gefragt hätte?	Rs. ia, es wäre alles wahr. Ich hätte auch noch gefragt, ich werde es wohl wißen, sie hätte es nicht gern sagen wollen, /: das wäre N.Z.:/ das könte er, der Geist, aufhalten wenn er wolle.
Hier nächst fragte ich noch:	
wo er sich im Leibe aufhalte?	Rs. er habe keinen gewißen Ort, könne sich in allen Gliedern aufhalten, daß Mägden wiße davon nichts.[59]

Highlighting the most significant questions of the interrogation of the "evil spirit," we should mention the following: when asked how she came to possess this particular girl, the spirit replies that his masters had given him/her power (1); whether it could lead the girl astray, it replies that she (Grendel) could not do anything that s/he (the evil spirit) did not want (7). Questioned whether it had revealed itself or was discovered by others, the spirit replies that it had not revealed itself, rather that the Rabbi had *demanded* that it come forth (15), that it had lived in the girl peacefully for four years until the Rabbi had called her forth. Asked if it knows what will happen to it if it were to leave the girl, the "evil spirit" replies that it will have to hover or float (*schweben*) again (39); that it understood she would have to leave the girl's body, but that this could not occur in incarceration, but only in the Synagogue, and could not occur without the Rabbi (40), presumably only through an exorcism. The evil spirit is asked

---

[59] *NSB*, Blatt 78–81.

whether it might lead the girl to disobedience against the authority, to which she replies that it depends solely on him/her what the girl does, and how she acts (50). When asked whether it could stand being interrogated, the spirit replies, yes, that it would like to continue, the spirit must have been a "real talker" (*Plaudertasche*) in actual life, and still is now (53). When asked where, specifically, it resides in the girl's body, the spirit replies that it has no specific "place," that it could reside in all parts of the body; the girl knows nothing of this and has no control over the matter. The conversation with the "evil spirit" signifies the climax of the proceeding and recognizes, at least to some degree, the possibility of a possession, even if it does not assert this outright.

The consistory requests a report from E. L. von Hoffe, the Pastor in Cappel, who, when asked whether he thought there might be deceit or trickery or conspiracy underway, testifies that he had often visited the home of the family and had never heard of a demonic possession or an exorcism (*Geisttreibung*), but that the girl had appeared ill (a *patient*). The family itself consisted of honest Jews (*redliche Juden*), about whom he could only say good things:

> So I have to say, as it has been gossiped that the speech of the girl had been prefabricated, that I very often had gone into the house [of the family] with others present, or had asked while passing by how the girl was doing, but never heard anything about an exorcism, but viewed her as a patient [as being ill,]; the girl had also been in my house many times and I had never gotten a sense of an abortion. In the matter of the family life and the circumstances of their living, one can only say only good things about them, that during my presence there that they were honest, hard-working Jews.
>
> So muß wegen des ersteren sagen, daß, da die Rede gieng das Mägden wäre befohlen, ich etliche mal unter Vormund anderer Ursachen selbst in das Haus getreten, oder im Vorbeÿgehen gefragt, wie es dem Mägden ginge, habe aber niemals etwas von Geisttreibung gesehen noch gehört, wol aber es als eine Patientin angesehen; auch ist es etlichemal selbst in meinem Haußse gewesen, aber nie etwas von Abbruch an ihnen gespüret. Was aber der Familie-leben und Wandell anlangt, so kan von ihnen doch als redlichen Juden, in Zeit meines Daseÿn, nichts anders als Gutes sagen.[60]

The Pastor not only shores up the previous accounts of Grendel's illness, testifying that there had been no talk of possession of an evil spirit and that he had simply believed the girl was ill. He provides a very charitable recommendation of both Grendel and her family.

Two further witnesses are brought before the consistory, one of whom was the widow of a provincial judge, who testified that Grendel had suffered for the last two years from a severe bodily weakness (*Leibes-Schwachheit*), and would

---

60 *NSB*, Blatt 82–83.

begin to shake and convulse, open her mouth very wide and scream so that it would disturb the neighbors with ridiculous behaviors and sounds like a sheep, with sweats, which would often last up to three weeks. The other witness is Johann Christoff Nieman from Cappel, who states that the family of Jews in question had lived in the area for more than twenty years, had been industrious and had earned a good living and, as subjects, had lived in good relations with the administrative offices there. Regarding Grendel, Nieman testifies that he would often find the patient with her fingers in her mouth, but unable to bring up anything. Other times he would ask her how she was doing and she would answer quite rationally that she experienced a great lameness as if there were gout in her entire body, with no appetite and debilitating weakness. Nieman also testifies that the father Moses Bendix had contacted not merely Dr. Müller in Detmold but also the Regiment-Surgeon Imhof in Lemgen, all of whom confirmed that the girl had been quite ill, in the greatest agitation and fear, and had been acting very strangely for the past two years. The testimonies from these additional witnesses not only confirm the persistence of Grendel's affliction over several years, thus effectively eliminating the early suspicion of malingering, imposture, or conspiracy; they attest to a particularly enlightened and tolerant understanding of the Jewish community in Schaumburg-Lippe.

Privy Medical Councilor Rabe crafts the response on behalf of the consistory. As the epigraph at the beginning of the chapter demonstrates, Rabe is acutely aware of the difficulty of answering the question whether or not a human being is *in fact* possessed by an evil spirit. The theologians, he writes, cannot specify any distinguishing characteristics, and are especially incapable of stating the difference between a "good" and "evil" spirit. The physicians, he writes, understand as little as the theologians about demonic possession; they, too, are also unable to specify the distinguishing characteristics and provide a rational explanation. Instead, they contradict all of the alleged signs of possession, no matter how horrible or terrifying, and seek to explain such attacks from natural causes, but in so doing they themselves provide no proof or explanation of the phenomenon whatsoever. Rabe then summarizes the apparent contradictions contained in the depositions of the Rabbi, the Mother, and the girl, but concludes that there must be some cause other than deceit or conspiracy:

> One is therefore required to think of a cause other than deception and this could of course be a corrupted imagination to which the girl herself might have been prepared according to numbers 9 and 23 of my interrogation, through the narrative concerning the exorcism which had occurred in Detmold, and the Rabbi's prognosis and his sending of the medications for such a condition, there might indeed obtain a cunning that is common to everyone, that they seek to represent their fantasy, as would appear to have been the case here and there with the supposed assertions of the spirit.

> so ist man doch genöthigt, auf eine andere mögliche Ursache als einen Betrug zu dencken und diese kan allerdings eine verdorbene Imagination seyn, worzu das Mägdgen nach n. 9 und 23. meiner Befragung, und durch Erzehlung der Detmoldischen Austreibung, auch der Prognosis des Rabbi bey Ertheilung der Mittel zu ihrem eigenen Zustande vorbereitet seyn kan zu so einer verdorbenen Imagination, welche die Lebhafftigkeit der Leute reget, kan sich allerdings eine Schlauigkeit, die alle Ohren gemein ist, gestellen, daß sie ihre Phantasie zu vertreten suchen, wie hie und wieder durch die vermeintliche Außage des Geistes geschehen zu seyn scheint.[61]

A corrupt imagination (*verdorbene Imagination*), for Rabe the probable cause of Grendel's suffering, invokes a well-rehearsed *topos* of early modern European mentality concerning women and madness: they are subject to flights of fantasy, an overabundance of emotion and feeling, and the absence of rational control. However, the appearance of such a corrupt imagination might also present itself as a ruse through which the young woman projects the presence of the evil spirit. After citing several sources (Detharding and Bayle), Rabe repeats the obligation of the authority to examine and interrogate the young woman, and to discover if there has been such a deceit, but he doubts whether further examination and interrogation will prove fruitful, and he declares therefore that a remedy of the case must be handled *extra iudiciale* – outside of the legal structure and norms – and in a timely fashion. Rabe concludes that this is a matter for the Jewish religion and community, concerning which the state authority has no jurisdiction:

> At the same time, what is important is that this act is solely an action of the Jewish religion, to which the civil authority's power does not extend, such power having exerted its sole power and carried out is obligation in the matter of the disclosure of whether or not a deception or fraud had occurred.
>
> Zugleich daran haftet und dieser Actus lediglich eine Handlung der Jüdischen Religion ist, über welche sich die obrigkeitliche Gewalt nicht erstrecket, als die nur in Ansehung der Entdeckung eines vermutheten Betrugs das Ihre gethan...[62]

Rabe affirms the limits of state action; her illness is deemed an "action of the Jewish religion," over which state authority has no jurisdiction, except to investigate a criminal act. He concludes that the state reserves the right to intervene and to punish should a deceit or conspiracy be discovered in the future. In view of the fact, however, that no deceit or fraud had been established after rigorous interrogation and depositions, Rabe consigns the case to the Jewish community.

---

[61] *NSB*, Blatt 88–89.
[62] *NSB*, Blatt 91.

He recommends allowing the Rabbi to proceed with the exorcism, with the argument that it is not unheard of for superstition itself to be expelled by superstition,[63] and that while according to existing "enlightened" principles any "power" accorded to an exorcism must be ascribed to the imagination alone, he is convinced that such a ceremony would indeed have the hoped-for effect. While he is in complete agreement with Rabe's assessment of the case, Dr. De Lehenen interjects that allowing the ritual of exorcism to proceed runs the risk of affirming superstition, giving it some form of legitimacy, making it appear that demonic possession truly exists, thus strengthening the people – it is not specified whether Jewish, Christian, or both – in their irrational beliefs: "in this manner, the arrangement of such a ceremony might well even provide the people the opportunity that they are encouraged in their prejudices, and some will even conclude that there is something to possession after all."[64] De Lehenen therefore recommends that the mother and daughter should be permitted to leave Bückeburg and have the "cure" carried out elsewhere by the Rabbi or someone else. Under the principle of freedom of conscience (*Gewißensfreyheit*), subjects should be allowed to pursue the remedies that are within the bounds of their religion as long as no crime has been committed, and the proposed remedy does not exercise a damaging influence on the state and its authority:

> At the same time it would be allowed for such an alegedly possessed person, if they let themselves be exorcised, that such a process be – now as then – free for them to choose. But it is probably the case that the Rabbi will not be able to return, and that the family will also go back to their community, and that they retain, according to the judicial, legal matter at hand, that for them and others of another religion, their freedom of conscience remains unhindered, according to which one is allowed to believe what one wishes according to their religion, just as long as their beliefs do not result in actions or unintended examples that have a harmful effect on the civil state or undermine the same.
>
> sogleich wäre aber angeblich beseßnen Person zu erlauben, daß, wenn sie sich noch exorcisiren laßen, ihr solches nach als vor annoch freÿ gestellt bliebe. Es ist doch zu vermuthen, daß der Rabbi nicht wieder hieher kommen und die Leute wieder wegziehen werden, da denn auf solche Art *fides judicialis* beÿbehalten und denen Person anderer Religion ihre Gewißensfreyheit ungekränkt gelaßen wird, welchen man dasjenige er nach

---

[63] *NSB*, Blatt 95: "daß der Aberglauben durch Aberglauben können vertrieben werden." Rabe thus invokes a practice recommended even by Stahl of curing such mental illness through fear and terror. See Stahl, *Über den mannigfaltigen Einfluß von Gemüthsbewegungen*, 33: "Furcht und Schrecken können unter gewissen Umständen auch Erleichterung für den Kranken bringen."

[64] *NSB*, Blatt 96: "mithin dürfte nunmehr die Verstattung solthaner caeremonie Gelegenheit geben, die Leute in ihren Vorurtheilen desto mehr zu bestärken [...] viele den Schluß machen dürfften, daß es mit der Besetzung seine Richtigkeit habe."

ihrer Religion zu glauben freÿ laßen muß, in so ferne ihre Glaubens Lehren nicht in Handlungen und ohngeahndete Beÿspiele aus brechen die schädliche Influenz in *statum civile* haben und denselben unterbauen.[65]

In the dossier, there are several pages bearing the title Diary of the Jewish-Girl from Cappel (*Diarium des Juden=Mägdgens von Cappel*). These contain essentially a series of reports, observations, remarks describing Grendel's comportment, statements, sleeping and eating habits, and the number of "attacks" (*Anfälle*). There seem to be two reasons for collecting such information: first and foremost, such written notes serve as "evidence" in the event of a judicial proceeding, specifically, in the event a deceit or conspiracy is discovered. Second, Medical Councilor Rabe in particular seems intent on getting to the root of the matter and discovering the true cause of the woman's suffering. The *Diarium* also contains further questions that must be read as a continuation of the formal interrogation of the consistory by other, less formal, and more intimate means. By isolating Grendel from the influence of her mother and the Rabbi, and under strict interdiction of any discourse concerning demons or possessions, Rabe appears optimistic not only that a rational explanation of her suffering will be found, but that the symptoms and "attacks" (*Anfälle*) will also disappear. However, under observation of a corporal and the Christian woman assigned to her, the diary merely confirms that the paroxysms, pain throughout her body, and convulsions continued unabated throughout her internment.[66]

On the 29th of June, Graf Albrecht writes his final response.[67] Although he concurs with the consistory that one must seek to fight superstition with superstition, he voices concern (with Lehenen) that allowing the exorcism to proceed will simply empower superstition; to destroy such superstition is, according to Albrecht, "one of the most noble duties of state authority wherein God's honor is advanced."[68] He is convinced that the idea of demonic possession was introduced by the Rabbi, that "the mother as well as the daughter would not have arrived at the idea of madness through possession if the Rabbi had not said this to them."[69] Albrecht concludes that any rational consideration of the case would lead one to believe that Grendel suffers from a mental illness (*gemüth*

---

[65] *NSB*, Blatt 97.
[66] *NSB*, Blätter 104–108.
[67] I am grateful to Joachim Gessinger, who assisted me in the transcription of this most difficult passage.
[68] *NSB*, Blatt 107: "eine der vornehmsten pflichten der obrigkeiten [ist] wodurch Gottes Ehre am wahrhafftigsten befordert wird."
[69] *NSB*, Blatt 107: "das sowohl Mutter als Tochter muss auff den Wahn der Beßeßung würden gekommen, wan ihnen nicht der *Rabiner* solches gesaget."

krankheit) and the nerves that have been affected by such an illness: "the illness of the girl is more reasonably to be ascribed to a mental illness and affected nerves than any ordinary causes."⁷⁰ He orders that she be moved to a room in the castle, that a "rational" woman be assigned to her for her assistance and benefit, and that she be placed in the care of Medical Councilor Rabe for further observation.

> For the young woman everything is to be done that can be done at my expense. For the felicitous Maintenance of this purpose, and because it is mainly a matter of a cure of the mind, I remand her to the care of the authorities, that she be brought to an already appropriately prepared room in the castle, that a reasonable woman for her care and attention be found, and that she be placed in the care of the Medical Councilor Rabe.
>
> So soll derselben hinzu auff meiner kosten aller nur erdenkliche vorschub geschehen. Zu desto besserer erhaltung dieses zweckes u<nd> da es auff die Chur des gemüths haubtsachig ankomt dieselben das Amt erlaßen, in ein sie auff dehm schloß albereit aptirtes zimmer gebracht, ihr eine vernunfftige frau zur beyhülffe und auffwartung aus gesuchet werden, dieselben ganzlicher *dinction* des raht Raben übergeben werde.⁷¹

The girl's mother is to be permitted to see Grendel once more in Rabe's presence (presumably to avoid any further talk of demonic possession, the evil spirit) before she returns to Petershagen. Albrecht further states that his interest and concern should be communicated to the mother:

> I further order that she be told that my interest is for her daughter to be cared for, that everything must be applied for her health to be restored [...] [Medical Councilor] Rabe has my full trust and he will cooperate with her [the mother] in this what is so worthy for humanity and the common good of us all, I will spare no effort and truly attempt to provide everything to restore this poor person in mind and in body.
>
> dabey ihr mein Interesse wie vor ihre Tochter sollen gesorget und alles muß zu ihrer gesundheit angewendet werden [...] Zu dehm Raht Rabe habe übrigens das feste vertrauen er werde mit mir eifrigst cooperiren in dieser der *humanitaet* so würdigen als dehm gemeinen besten unzriger/ werde keine mühe sparen und wahrlich versuchen alles / was der arme Mensch am Gemüthe und Leibe wieder herstelen möge.⁷²

Care, health, trust, humanity, communal well-being (i.e., *gemeinen Besten unzriger, Gemeinwohl*), the rehabilitation of body and soul constitute the very discourse of enlightened medicine and "rational policy," and the core of pastoral

---

70 *NSB*, Blatt 107: "die Kranckheit des Mädgens einer gemüth kranckheit und *afficierten nerven* viel vernünfftiger als eyner *ordinairen* uhrsachen zuzuschreiben."
71 *NSB*, Blatt 107.
72 *NSB*, Blatt 107.

therapeutics. Albrecht appears as the benevolent sovereign and the pastoral leader, taking on the care of one of his own, even a Jew, providing a room in the castle and the necessary medical care. Both the father and mother appeal to Albrecht to release the girl into their custody, but he repeats his resolution that she be kept in the *Residenz-Schloss* for observation and treatment for two months. Her detainment is viewed as necessary to attempt to determine whether, without the influence of the Rabbi, the Jewish community, and particularly the mother, Grendel's illness can in fact be treated. This concludes the dossier. We have nothing further to indicate whether or not Grendel continued to be kept in custody at the castle, or finally returned to her family and the Jewish community.

The "case" has often been conceptualized as a marker for conflict or contested knowledge and disparate scientific views. In his study of 1930, *Einfache Formen*, André Jolles remarked concerning this most essential aspect of the "case": "The unique character of the form 'case' consists in the fact that it poses a question, but cannot provide the answer; that it tasks us with the duty of a decision, but does not contain the decision itself. What is realized in the 'case' is the weighing, but not the result of the weighing."[73] According to Jolles, cases ask a question, but do not provide the answer; a weighing (*Wägen*) of possibilities, but not the result. Such a view aligns nicely with Pomata's argument mentioned previously that cases flourish in times of uncertainty, shifting paradigms, or unstable knowledge. More than merely *exempla* for already existing theory and models, cases convey the strife or contest of their historical moment; they serve as the decisive test-cases for validation of a not-yet-fully articulated or accepted theory.[74] Cases require *judgment*, not simply entering a variable into an equation or subsuming an instance under a general rule.

The case explored here from mid-eighteenth-century Germany meets this generic description exactly; for the consistory and the Count, it posed the problem of an alleged demonic possession in an era of increasing secular rationality – a remnant of supersitition and unfounded belief in the Age of Enlightenment. For the contemporary reader, it poses questions regarding gender, science, superstition, ethnicity, and mental illness. And while it does provide a kind of

---

[73] André Jolles, *Einfache Formen* (Halle [Saale]: Niemeyer, 1930; Tübingen: Niemeyer, 1968; Berlin: de Gruyter, 2010), 191.
[74] This has been shown beautifully in the case of journals publishing case history "collections" in the German Enlightenment. See: Susanne Düwell and Nicolas Pethes, "Noch nicht Wissen. Die Fallsammlung als Prototheorie in Zeitschriften der Spätaufklärung," in *Literatur und Nicht-Wissen: Historische Konstellationen 1730–1930*, ed. Michael Bies and Michael Gamper (Zürich: Diaphanes, 2012), 131–148.

resolution – the young woman is kept in the care of the Count, a "Christian woman," and his medical privy-councilor Rabe – there were clearly no definitive answers to the questions raised, and perhaps more importantly, the precise reasons for the state or states of mind that could be labeled as demonic possession in the age of Enlightenment in Germany.

Foucault's *History of Madness* provided a general account of the forms, experiences, and institutions of madness in the "classical age" (roughly 1650–1800).[75] While this monumental study increased our knowledge of the ways in which physicians, theologians, jurists, artists, state authorities, and sovereigns framed, conceptualized, categorized, and imagined madness in all of its various forms, objections of schematic oversimplification, loose periodization, and theoretical generalization have been voiced by historians.[76] What is certain is that "demonic possession" does not figure in Foucault's account of madness in this period; neither "demons" nor "demonic," neither "possession" nor "demonic possession" nor "exorcism" occur in the index; dementia, mania and melancholy, and the "illnesses of the nerves" – hysteria and hypochondria – constitute the "figures of madness" in Foucault's "classical age."[77] In addition, one finds very few examples of actual instances of madness written from "below," and Foucault offers very little on how madness and its treatment are inflected by ethnicity and race, religion, and gender.[78] While his argument was intended to be of a more general nature and did not seek to exhaustively treat all of the different examples of madness and their social-cultural contexts, the absence of "demonic possession" is telling, especially in the Early

---

[75] Michel Foucault, *History of Madness*, ed. Jean Khalfa, trans. Jonathan Murphy and Jean Khalfa (London and New York: Routledge, 2006).
[76] See Midelfort, *History of Madness*, 7–9, 229; H. C. Erik Midelfort, "Madness and Civilization in Early Modern Europe: A Reappraisal," in *Michel Foucault: Critical Assessments*, ed. Barry Smart (London and New York: Routledge, 1995), vol. 4, 117–133; Allan Megill, "The Reception of Foucault by Historians," *Journal of the History of Ideas* 48.1 (1987): 117–141. On Foucault's (faulty) periodization of the "Great Confinement," see: Roy Porter, "Foucault's Great Confinement," *History of the Human Sciences* 3.1 (1990): 47–54. Also pushing against Foucault's periodization, Jan E. Goldstein places the "great confinement" in the nineteenth century in *Console and Classify: The French Psychiatric Profession in the Nineteenth Century* (Chicago: University of Chicago Press, 2002).
[77] Foucault, *History of Madness*, 277–286.
[78] Except in the case of hysteria, which is coded "feminine" as a commonplace in the eighteenth century. See Foucault, *History of Madness*, 192. There are of course other descriptions of the women incarcerated, the dangers of novel reading and theater for women, and nervous illnesses in women in Foucault's study, but it is near impossible to discern an actual argument concerning women and madness in the book.

Enlightenment in Germany. It is as if possession had been erased from central Europe with the scientific-medical advances of the late seventeenth and eighteenth century. That it is not simply a matter of "demons out, nerves in" in the Enlightenment and the revolution in medical science 1700–1800, that demonic possession does not simply disappear with the demise of humoral pathology and the emergence of diseases of the nerves and mental illness is, as our case history shows, amply demonstrated by the persistence of a discourse of and on demonic possession well into the eighteenth century, one compelling enough to warrant an extensive investigation and the involvement of the complete state apparatus.[79] The court remains skeptical concerning Grendel's affliction as a case of possession, but nevertheless concedes that this is a belief-structure that still persists in religious communities, and that the shock of an exorcism might be precisely what is necessary in order to return her to reason.

The case history presented here clearly indicates the ongoing presence of such "superstitious" and "irrational" instances of demonic possession – at least among the rural Jewish population – at a time when the precepts of Enlightenment were widely held and practiced, not simply as topics of philosophical discourse, in theoretical essays or learned treatises, but in and by provincial courts and consistories, by the privy councilors, physicians, legal advisors, educators, and proto-psychologists and at least some of the priests and rabbis who were called upon to investigate such cases. The case also provides a corrective, in my view, to Foucault's suspicion that power, domination, control, and subjugation lurked everywhere in the eighteenth century, even (or precisely) in the most enlightened, secular-humanist practices. A close reading of the dossier compels us to conclude that Graf Albrecht and the consistory were honestly attempting to dispel the proliferation of superstitious, irrational belief; to bring common sense and care of the soul to bear on the young woman in the hope of mitigating her suffering and – in Albrecht's own words – under the banner of *humanitaet*, "to restore her in mind and body," not by harsh treatment or imprisonment, not by "hard" discipline, but by a form of "soft" power, a type of *pastoral care*. One could perhaps read the Graf's order to move Grendel into a room in the Residenz-Schloss under the care of a reasonable woman and privy-medical-councilor Rabe simply as a guise for the desire of control and surveillance, and yet the document is quite clear in its rejection of punitive, disciplinary measures, premature assumptions, and the capricious use of power. Enlightened principles such as respect for the freedom of conscience (*Gewissensfreyheit*), rational treatment, recognition of the limits of jurisdiction and state action in

---

79 See the balanced argument of Davis, *Obsession: A History*, 33–35.

religious matters, careful empirical observation and due diligence all figure prominently in the case history. While originally skeptical and suspicious of her motives, Albrecht and the Consistory seek neither to demonize/vilify her, nor do they wish to be complicit in a superstitious ritual and the identification of a form of mental illness – "possession by an evil spirit" – in which they clearly do not believe. Such a diagnosis remains for them a function of the Rabbi's suggestion, the family's susceptibility, religious superstition within the Jewish community, and counter to every reasonable explanation.

This is not to say that such enlightened principles and practices completely diminished or eliminated the force of prejudice, assumptions of ethnicity, religion, and gender that render Grendel such a compelling case to be reckoned with by the entire court at Bückeburg. Stereotypical concerns and prejudices about "Jews" – their influence and increasing numbers, mobility and evasiveness, cunning, and deceit – are clearly present; the consistory and Albrecht suspect deceit and imposture, or even worse, conspiracy. But they are quite rigorous in their examination, and, due to the actual evidence presented by numerous witnesses, ultimately admit that they are unable to discern such a *dolus* or *impostura*. The focus of the interrogation on the mother, the daughter, and the Rabbi invites conjecture that the case constructs a triangular, patriarchal web of assignation and ascription of the "possessed woman." The "evil spirit" itself is grammatically and semantically gender-split, as "spirit" in German (*Geist*) is masculine, and therefore designated with *er* in the interrogation, but the evil spirit possessing Grendel, *Gütel*, is female. And, to be sure, an alleged "danger" to state authority becomes palpable when the evil spirit is asked whether it has the power to lead the young women astray to act in defiance or disobedience of such authority and rulership (*Obrigkeit/Herrschaft*).[80] As a Jewish "madwoman," Grendel is doubly determined as embodying a disturbing illness. Because of their "weakness," women were supposedly more susceptible to such diseases of the mind (*Gemüthskrankheit*). A sinful female spirit inhabiting one of their own, as well as contributing to the embarrassment of the Jewish Community as a whole – a blemish or stain on the *Gemeinde* itself – reveals a sense of shame expressed by the Rabbi, her father, and her mother should the exorcism prove unsuccessful, or in the event she would return to Petershagen with her madness unabated. The "concern" of the parents and the push to appeal for the exorcism through the intercession of the Count seems to have been equally motivated by genuine concern for their daughter as well as the "social concern" for the "integrity" and approbation of the Jewish community.

---

[80] *NSB*, Blatt 80, question 50.

Yet it would be false to see in this case merely another instance of Christian, male patriarchal "hard," disciplinary power bearing down on, and thus "inventing," a voiceless, pneumatic Jewish woman and bringing her inchoate madness to clear and cogent expression. In fact, the case summons the entire state apparatus in an effort to rationally adjudicate Grendel's illness and to remove her from an environment believed to be reinforcing the superstitious idea of possession by an evil spirit. Remarkably, Grendel's case is not marked either by virulent anti-Judaism or anti-Semitism, but rather a concern that the Jewish community suffers from irrational beliefs and the absence of rational, medical guidance. What is at stake in Grendel's illness and her treatment by the Consistory and Graf Albrecht is much more akin to what Foucault later described as "pastoral power" as a prelude to governmentality. As he wrote in *Security, Territory, Population*, "pastoral power […] is only concerned with individual souls insofar as this direction (*conduite*) of souls also involves a permanent intervention in everyday conduct (*conduite*), in the management of lives […] It concerns not only the individual, but also the community."[81] Multiple power centers and different "agencies" – all implicated and interpellated by gender, ethnicity, religion, and medical-scientific knowledge – determine the "individuality" of this case. Especially, the supplication of the family, the Rabbi "authorized" to perform the ritual, the pressure of the community and the testimony of neighbors, physicians, state and sovereign authorities, the testimony of priests and preachers – all of these together form the ensemble of forces converging in the consideration of Grendel's case. The case exhibits conflicting religious and scientific-medical beliefs, and the profound inability of the physicians and advisors to form a rational explanation or reach a clear conclusion. At the very moment when Enlightenment appears radiant in Central Europe, the attempt to adjudicate legally and psychologically a case of "demonic possession" in an age of rational procedure and practice turns out not to be clear cut at all, but rather fraught with strife, contradiction, and conflict. The conversation with the evil spirit presents us with a stunning example not of artifice or malingering, nor a cunning stratagem on the part of the medical establishment or state authority to ensnare or entrap Grendel, but a key fissure or rupture in enlightenment discourse expressing and documenting the suffering of a young Jewish woman in Lower-Saxony, Germany in the mid-eighteenth century. The voices of the consistory in fact do little to stifle or obliterate Grendel's suffering; in point of fact, they elicit the "conversation with the

---

[81] Michel Foucault, *Security, Territory, Population: Lectures at the Collège de France, 1977–1978*, ed. Michel Senellart (New York: Palgrave Macmillan, 2007), 154.

spirit," entering into a discourse that blatantly contradicts their own rational precepts. Nor can or should we either prematurely dismiss or anachronistically assign an explanation to her suffering and the vexation it caused the court, the ensemble of community officials – secular and religious – her family, and the Jewish community of Schaumburg-Lippe.[82] Finally, despite the extraordinary depth and breadth of the document we have, including the numerous narratives of the history, hearings, testimonies, witnesses, reports, opinions, recommendations of the consistory, and the resolutions of the Graf, one must conclude that it is not clear what, precisely, was afflicting Grendel, not to mention what she must have *experienced*. Besides her *responsa* in the context of the official interrogations, we only have the reported "I"–statements contained in the so-called diary. In these statements, we putatively have her own words, which tell us quite clearly and simply that she hoped she would get well once again; that she had not done anything evil and wanted to be able to return home. Her neighbors all confirmed that she had been ill for some time and had been seen by many physicians, none of whose efforts had been able to cure her. The testimonies concur that she had not been able to work, suffered attacks at regular intervals, had felt alternating terrible pain and weakness in all the parts of her body, and, finally, that she wished to be among her people once again.[83] Despite all of the "reasonable" efforts to uncover the true causes of her affliction, and all of the medical, juridical, and religious expertise brought to bear, Grendel's case defied the early Enlightenment's call for reason and the classificatory power of the title under which it was subsumed.

---

82 For example, by attempting to assimilate demoniacs into the history of hysteria, as in G. S. Rousseau, "'A Strange Pathology': Hysteria in the Early Modern World, 1500–1800," in *Hysteria beyond Freud*, ed. Sander L. Gilman et al. (Berkeley and Los Angeles: University of California Press, 1993), 91–221.
83 *NSB*, Blatt 93.

5 The First Modern Psychological Case History: Marcus Herz's *Psychological Description of His Own Illness* (1783) and the Construction of the Modern Soul

> Pastoral power is only concerned with individual souls insofar as this direction (*conduite*) of souls also involves an intervention in everyday conduct (*conduite*), the management of lives...
> Foucault, *Security, Territory, Population*[1]

In the first volume of the journal *Deutsches Museum* of 1782, Karl Philipp Moritz, the author of the self-proclaimed "psychological novel" *Anton Reiser* (1784–1786), published a call for papers for his new project *Gnothi Sauton oder Magazin für Erfahrungsseelenkunde* (1783–1793), often seen as the first journal of empirical-experiential psychology.[2] "Suggestion for a magazine of experiential psychology,"[3] with its subtitle "To all followers and supporters of knowledge and sciences beneficial to the general good," explained Moritz's intention to spread truth and happiness among mankind (*Wahrheit und Glückseligkeit unter den Menschen zu verbreiten*).[4] According to Moritz, what was sorely missing in his time was a theory and teaching of the illnesses of the soul – what he referred to as a theory of mental illness (*Seelenkrankheitslehre*). Such a theory and practical teaching proves difficult precisely because it requires an

---

[1] Michel Foucault, *Security, Territory, Population: Lectures at the College de France, 1977–1978*, ed. Michel Senellart (New York: Palgrave MacMillan, 2007), 154.

[2] Moses Mendelssohn famously suggested to Karl Philipp Moritz that he change his originally planned title of *Experimentalseelenlehre*, a term used by the philosophical physicians in Halle around the middle of the eighteenth century, especially Johann Gottlob Krüger, *Versuch einer Experimentalseelenlehre* (Halle: Carl Helmstedt, 1756), in 2 vols., to *Erfahrungsseelenkunde*. The distinction between *Experiment* and *Erfahrung* is significant because it marks the boundary between science or *Wissenschaft* that actually has "experiments" or "trials," and science that relies on the experience of "true observers of the human being." On this, see: Carsten Zelle, "Experiment, Experience and Observation in Eighteenth-Century Anthropology and Psychology," *Orbis Litterarum* 56.2 (2001): 93–105; Carsten Zelle, ed. "Experimentalseelenlehre und Erfahrungsseelenkunde," in *Vernünftige Ärzte. Hallesche Psychomediziner und die Anfänge der Anthropologie in der deutschsprachigen Frühaufklärung* (Tübingen: Niemeyer, 2001), 174–185; and Matthew Bell, *The German Tradition of Psychology in Literature and Thought, 1780–1840* (Cambridge: Cambridge University Press, 2005), 94.

[3] Karl Philipp Moritz, "Vorschlag zu einem Magazin einer Erfahrungsseelenkunde," *Deutsches Museum* 1 (1782): 485–503.

[4] Moritz, "Vorschlag," 485.

enormous reservoir of observations and experiences rather than the simplistic, universal theories and treatment methods available at the time: "it presupposes a thousand times more observations and experiences."[5] The root causes of this cultural-scientific *desideratum* were nothing other than religion, which had subsumed all the deviations of the soul under one concept – madness – and a medical science prone to see mental illness as either a result of a physical aberration or as a primordial, irrevocable "corruption" of the soul which could only be treated through the most primitive methods of bleeding, purgatives, baths, and terror. Moritz lamented that this situation of "identifying so many different illnesses of the soul with a single name"[6] systematically reduced, simplified, and misunderstood the complexity and depth of psychological illness. Because of the hold religion had on the culture at large, and because medicine had not taken the time and trouble to inquire into the specific nature and constitution of particular mental illnesses – "to engage more precise investigations concerning the nature and constitution of mental illness"[7] – the very possibility of a *Seelenkrankheitslehre* had been sabotaged. Moritz hoped to receive from physicians, preachers and priests, teachers, officers, jurists, philosophers, and writers of literature life-descriptions or observations concerning themselves – "Lebensbeschreibungen oder Beobachtungen über sich selber"[8] – and named Johann Heinrich Jung-Stilling, Johann Caspar Lavater, Johann Salamo Semler, and Jean-Jacques Rousseau as paradigmatic examples of such introspection and self-observation already extant and available to the reading public.[9] Authenticity, truthfulness to nature, and sincerity were on the agenda: "first

---

5 Moritz, "Vorschlag," 486: "noch tausend mal mehr Beobachtungen und Erfahrungen voraussetzt."
6 Moritz, "Vorschlag," 486: "so mannigfaltig verschiedenen Gebrechen der Seele mit einem einzigen Namen benannte."
7 Moritz, "Vorschlag," 487: "über die Natur und Beschaffenheit der Krankheit selbst genauere Untersuchungen anzustellen."
8 Moritz, "Vorschlag," 488.
9 Compare Johann Gottfried Herder, "Vom Erkennen und Empfinden der menschlichen Seele (1778)," in: Herder, *Werke in zehn Bänden*, ed. Jürgen Brummack and Martin Bollacher. Jürgen Brummack and Martin Bollacher (Frankfurt: Deutsche Klassiker Verlag, 1994), vol. 4, 342. Herders text recommends three paths to explore the lively relation between psychology and physiology in the individual case: biography or *Lebensbeschreibungen*, remarks of physicians and friends (*Bemerkungen von Ärzten und Freunden*) and the insights of poets (*Weissagungen der Dichter*). Only through such texts are we in a position to grasp the *most complicated pathology of the soul* (*die verflochtenste Pathologie der Seele*), the deep particularities (*tiefen Besonderheiten*) of the individual, and the "dark indications" (*dunklen Anzeigungen*) of the total human being. For his part, Herder uses Montaigne, Petrarch, Augustine and Cardanus as "models" of such exploration. (342)

and foremost observations taken from the real world, of which a single one often contains more value than what can be gleaned from a thousand books."[10] Moritz asks the reader to disclose – in writing – his or her innermost thoughts, and concerns: "to provide me with reports regarding their endeavors."[11] He wanted to construct a repository, an archive for astute human observations. The true observer of humanity would have to withstand the temptation to weave his or her own thoughts into the narrative, to bracket his or her own reflections off from the description of the facts; the true human observer would have to disengage him or herself from his or her own desires in order to "play" the "cold observer."[12]

However, Moritz did not shut out reflection altogether, just hasty and random judgments and thoughts that could skew or distort what was being observed. He simply wanted to gather "facts" and "data," in the form of *cases* – as many cases as possible, at which point the community of philosophically-minded physicians could begin to assemble all they had learned into a discipline – a *Seelenkrankheitslehre* as he called it – a theory and teaching of the *illnesses of the mind* proper: a diagnostics, therapeutics, and dietetics of the soul. After collecting individual cases and disseminating them in the envisioned journal, a forum for discussion and debate would be created in the *Magazin*, and the ensemble of physicians, proto-psychologists, educators and jurists would be able to order and structure this to a "purposeful totality."[13] This would be the only method, according to Moritz, by means of which "the human race, through itself, could become better acquainted with itself and bring itself to a higher degree of perfection."[14] Portraits of the self, self-observation, and self-description were to earn the greatest attention.[15]

The true human observer employs an *analogical* method according to Moritz. She takes herself as the point of departure in order to learn to read the face, gestures, language, and actions of the person to uncover the "secret

---

10 Moritz, "Vorschlag," 489: "vorzüglich Beobachtungen aus der wirklichen Welt [...] deren eine einzige oft mehr praktischen Werth hat, als tausend aus Büchern geschöpfte."
11 Moritz, "Vorschlag," 502.
12 Moritz, "Vorschlag," 492–493: "sich aus dem Wirbel seiner Begierden herauszuziehen, um den kalten Beobachter zu spielen."
13 Moritz, "Vorschlag," 489: "zu einem zweckmäßigen Ganzen."
14 Moritz, "Vorschlag," 489–490: "wie das menschliche Geschlecht durch sich selber mit sich selber bekanter und sich zu einem höheren Grad der Vollkommenheit empor schwingen könnte."
15 Moritz, "Vorschlag," 494: "Gemälde, die man sich selber von seiner eigenen Seele entwirft, verdienten die größte Aufmerksamkeit."

history" of the affliction. One must "begin with oneself," he wrote, and by attending to the totality of behavior, language, expression, and gesture learn how to analogically reason concerning other, similar cases.[16] Most importantly, such an observer must be diligent not to allow herself to fall prey to idealizations, fantasy, and dream-like projections, but rather must seek to penetrate her own real, actual world with increasing depth and scope.[17] Using one of the standard metaphors applied to the investigation of the soul of the time, the human observer of human psychology enters the "internal mechanism" that moves the individual as a kind of dissection of the soul. What distinguishes this form of observational description from the typical medical history, history of an illness, *Krankengeschichte, historia morbi*, Moritz explains, is that it seeks to see the emergence of the actions of the individual from its "first germinal seeds," employing this time an *organic* rather than a *mechanistic* metaphor. Criticizing the extant medicine and psychology of the time, he states that a merely classificatory method based on apparent characteristics or rigid universal rubrics overlooks the most essential aspects of the illness: "We do not see how the first germs of the actions of the human being develop from the deepest recesses of the soul [...] a thousand observations that one has already made in this regard have been gleaned from the surface and not from the innermost workings of the soul."[18] Observation is made *of* individuals *by* individuals. Moritz needed cases for his inauguration of the new journal which would do justice to his call for papers and the claims he made public regarding the establishment of a theory of mental illness (*Seelenkrankheitslehre*). His friend, the physician and philosopher Marcus Herz, a member of the Jewish Enlightenment or *Haskalah*, provided him with a wonderful first-person narrative case history: "Psychological description of his own illness by Dr. Markus Herz, to Sir D. J[oë]l in Königsberg" appeared in the first volume of Moritz's *Magazin* in 1783.[19] In the form of a letter to

---

[16] Moritz, "Vorschlag," 494: "von sich selber ausgehen [...]. Von der geheimen Geschichte seiner eigenen Gedanken müßte er durch Gesicht, Sprache und Handlung auf die Seele andrer schliessen lernen."

[17] Moritz, "Vorschlag," 494: "in seine eigne wirkliche Welt immer tiefer einzudringen suchen."

[18] Moritz, "Vorschlag," 493: "Wir sehen nicht, wie die ersten Keime von den Handlungen des Menschen sich im Innersten seiner Seele entwickeln [...]. Tausend Beobachtungen, die man hier schon gemacht hat, sind bloß von der Oberfläche genommen und nicht aus dem Innersten der Seele heraus gehoben."

[19] Marcus Herz, "Psychologische Beschreibung seiner eigenen Krankheit vom Herrn D. Markus Herz an Herrn D. J. in Königsberg," *Gnothi Sauton oder Magazin für Erfahrungsseelenkunde als ein Lesebuch für Gelehrte und Ungelehrte. Die Schriften in dreißig Bänden* 1, Zweites Stück (1783), ed. Petra Nettelbeck and Uwe Nettelbeck (Nördlingen: F. Greno, 1986), 121–141.

a fellow physician, Herz published a psychological case history of his illness as a set of self-observations and interpretations in the form of a diary written during and after the illness. As Carolin Kull has aptly pointed out, the letter-form as a diary, as well as the fact that it was "signed" by Herz himself, attested to the authenticity of the case, while the candid self-observations, sometimes quite critical and revealing, provided a sense of intimacy and honesty, all of which were highly celebrated in the second half of the eighteenth century.[20]

What distinguishes this case history from the classical medical case history – *Krankengeschichte, historia morbi* – which, to be sure, already had a venerable tradition and a fundamentally stable structure from Felix Platter, Thomas Sydenham, Georg Ernest Stahl and Friedrich Hoffmann to the Psycho-Physicians in Halle around 1750 – is precisely its emphatically *psychological* character. As Doris Kaufmann has pointed out: "His observations no longer describe reactions of the brain, but rather depict the struggle within the soul, in the yet unexplained part of the inner human nature."[21] Herz's "psychological description" is not merely a factual, chronological chronicle of the illness, but rather a detailed account of Herz's feelings, sense-perceptions, fantasies, dreams, and hallucinations during the illness, as well as a deferred account of the relationship of these feelings, perceptions, and hallucinations during his illness to his own life: his disposition, relations to others, fears concerning his frenetic schedule. In other words, the psychological case history imparts something like the lived-experience of the illness, and connects this experience with the actual (or perceived) life of the individual.

At the same moment, the case also objectifies and canonizes such narrative self-observations: these specifically "psychological" case histories proliferate between 1780 and 1800 to an unprecedented extent. They populate anthologies, magazines, weeklies, and journals. In these cases, it is not only a matter of self-reflexivity or self-observation, but the explicit *thematization of the intrapsychic relations* between what is experienced and the experiencing self. This is precisely what makes Herz's case history of 1783 psychological. Psychological case histories do not have to be about mental illness; it is rather the *narrative*

---

[20] Carolin Kull, "Marcus Herz: 'An Herrn Doktor J. in Königsberg'. Psychologische Beschreibung seiner eigenen Krankheit," in *Casus. Von Hoffmanns Erzählungen zu Freuds Novellen. Eine Anthologie der Fachprosagattung 'Fallerzählung,'* ed. Carsten Zelle (Hannover: Wehrhahn, 2015), 120.

[21] Doris Kaufmann, *Aufklärung, bürgerliche Selbsterfahrung und die Erfindung der Psychiatrie in Deutschland, 1770–1850* (Göttingen: Vandenhoeck & Ruprecht, 1995), 92–93: "Seine folgenden Beobachtungen beschreiben nicht mehr Gehirnreaktionen, sondern schildern den Kampf innerhalb der Seele, dem noch 'ungeklärten Teil' der inneren menschlichen Natur."

method of disclosing the internal psychological reactions and responses; processing the psychological material that emerges in the course of an illness, psychological or physical; and, finally, drawing essential connections between this experience and the history and life-circumstances of the individual. "Psychological" case histories proliferated in medical, criminal, and legal literature; we began to have an archive of psychological (self-)observations and narratives pointing to a core meaning/history that allowed the practitioners to think of something like the *modern soul*. It is this *soul* – a not yet fully secularized metaphysical entity – that was created precisely in and through such narratives.

On November 18, 1782, as a result of what he later referred to as unusual stress and a "weakening of his nerves" in the execution of his daily duties and responsibilities, and with a particular strenuous schedule between his individual patients, the Jewish Hospital, and the salon he ran with his wife, Henriette Herz de Lemos, the Berlin physician and esteemed representative of the Jewish Enlightenment Marcus Herz contracted a severe illness, which he referred to in the case history as a *Faulfieber*, a *Katarrhalfieber* or a *Nervenfieber*.[22] In the *Psychological Description of My Own Illness*, Herz divides his illness into three phases: in the first, the onset and the appearance of the first serious symptoms, Herz is conscious; in the second, he loses consciousness, but remembers specific phantasies, dreams, or hallucinations, relying on the reports and statements of his physician and friends; in the third, the period of recovery, he returns to consciousness and to himself, and is able to recollect certain events in the second, most severe phase of the illness.

The "psychological" character of the description is already evident in the first phase of the illness. Herz relates the *lived experience* of the illness, how the illness actually *felt*: "It was as if all of the nerves had been slackened, and all of the marrow from all of my bones had been dried out. I was still conscious and sensed this weakness, so that I said to my physicians and the others present: the feeling of myself was like that of a mosquito."[23] Concerning the second phase of the illness, Herz states that he has no recollection whatsoever: "These days have all utterly disappeared from the daily register of my life [...] the real objects around me, and the clarity of their effect were eradicated to an invisible

---

[22] Herz, "Psychologische Beschreibung," 122.
[23] Herz, "Psychologische Beschreibung," 127: "Es war als wenn alle Nerven auf einmal abgespannt wurden, und aller Mark aus allen meinen Gebeinen vertrocknet wäre. Ich hatte dabei mein Bewusstseyn und empfand diese Schwäche, so, daß ich zu meinen Ärzten und den Anwesenden sagte: das Gefühl meines *Ich's* gleicht jetzt dem Selbstgefühl einer Mücke."

distance."²⁴ During this phase, Herz must rely on the narration of events by his friends and his physician, yet through these little narratives and comments does recall the "fantastical images and folly" that went through his mind. Rather than dispensing with the segments of imaginings and bizarre scenes in his head, Herz is intent upon seeking to disclose their meaning and significance: "But I want to tell you about the main themes of my phantasies; there was *method in my madness*, and I am able to explain both their emergence and the connection between them very well in a *psychological fashion*."²⁵ Such an attitude or stance vis-à-vis the seemingly diffuse and inchoate material proves decisive for the psychological case; Herz recognizes that the illness has produced a physical state in which fever and delirium have clouded the capabilities of the conscious mind, yet he does not dismiss the phantasies as mere "symptoms" or "effects" of fever, but rather seeks to discover in them an inner logic.

The first instance of a psychological coordination of experienced events and internal responses is his registration of an uncanny sense of alienation, one might say paranoia, that he is no longer in his own bedroom. His friends had in fact moved him from the bedroom to his study, but he explains his own troubling sense of fear, his anguish and his sense of confusion through recourse to the disruption of the familiar routine, the displacement of the everyday:

> The absence of the usual objects, whose representation tends to accompany the soul in its activity (for one can call activity the intentional relaxation of the nerves and the suppression of lively ideas in a healthy brain), of detaching from the web of ideas, on the one hand, and the more powerful effect of new and unfamiliar objects on the other – both capture the attention of the soul, and its capacity for abstraction has to wrestle even more with difficulties [...] The nerves of my eyesight had suffered from a pressure from the very beginning: the objects of sight which otherwise could have reminded me of my home in my study had such a weak effect on my sight, I saw everything darkly, garbled, or amiss.²⁶

---

24 Herz, "Psychologische Beschreibung," 128: "Diese Tage sind gleichsam aus dem Tagesregister meines Lebens gänzlich verloschen [...]. Die wahren Gegenstände um mich, und die Klarheit ihrer Wirkung verschwanden bis zur unsichtbarsten Entfernung."
25 Herz, "Psychologische Beschreibung," 129: "Aber doch will ich Ihnen die Hauptthemata meiner Phantasien erzählen; *es war Methode in meiner Tollheit*, und ich kann mir ihre Entstehung und ihren Zusammenhang sehr gut *psychologisch erklären*."
26 Herz, "Psychologische Beschreibung," 130: "Der Mangel der gewöhnten Gegenstände, deren Vorstellung, die Seele bei ihrem Geschäft, (denn *Geschäft* kann man die willkührliche Herabspannung der Nerven und Unterdrückung der lebhaften Ideen bei gesundem Gehirn allerdings nennen) des Zurückziehens aus dem Gewebe der Ideen, zu begleiten pflegt, von der einen Seite, und die stärkere Wirkung der neuen und ungewöhnlichen Gegenstände von der anderen Seite, beides fesselt die Aufmerksamkeit der Seele, und ihr Abstraktionsvermögen hat um so vielmehr Schwierigkeiten zu überwinden [...] Meine Sehnerven haben von Anfang an einen Druck erlitten; die Gegenstände des Gesichts, die mich allenfalls auch in meiner

The sense of displacement as a lack or absence of familiar objects and the intensified presence of the unfamiliar is described with an almost phenomenological precision. Herz recognizes the weakening of his ability to see and the stressing of his nerves as a physical result of the illness, but adds another layer of description above and beyond the mere physical. The state of consciousness is not reduced to the condition of the body, in this case the inflammation of the nerves; rather, a psycho-physical explanation that takes into account the full range of experiences of the displacement is provided in which the rupture of the routine, the interruption of the everyday, is at one and the same time grasped retrospectively as a *psychological* rupture. The heightened estrangement due to his distorted and clouded perception reinforces his sense of displacement and literally exhibits the sense of the uncanny (*unheimlich*), of *not* being at home.

The second "fantasy" supports even more powerfully the constitution of a quite unique, subjective-psychological self, a self that seeks to provide reasons for the contents of the mind. It has to do solely with Herz's personality and character: "My second fantasy was that I was hated and persecuted by the entire world, all of my friends had abandoned me, all of my pateints had deserted me, and the rest of mankind dispised me, or viewed me with utter indifference."[27] Herz explains this by recourse to his specific tendency to mistrust his friends and project his own insecurity onto them in a genial transferential projection in which they become the objects of contempt:

> The cause of this fantasy was presumably that I didn't see any of my most trusted friends around me [...] And this in addition to the distrust with respect to the world that, as my friends attest to, had already been typical of me in my healthy days. Yet this fantasy was not even close to the previous one in its perniciousness. That notion instilled in me a contempt for those who despised me; a despairing calm, and an ardent wish for death as the most desirable condition.[28]

Studierstube an meine Heimat hätten erinnern können, wirkten auf das Organ zu schwach, ich sah alles dunkel, zerstümmelt oder verkehrt."

27 Herz, "Psychologische Beschreibung," 131: "Meine zweite Einbildung bestand darin, daß ich von der ganzen Welt gehasst und verfolgt wurde, alle meine Freunde haben von mir abgelassen, alle meine Kunden auf mich Verzicht gethan, und der ganze übrige Theil der Menschen mich verachtet, oder mit den gleichgültigsten Augen angesehn."

28 Herz, "Psychologische Beschreibung," 132: "Die Ursache dieser Phantasie war vermutlich, weil ich keinen von meinen vertrautesten Freunden um mich sah [...] Dies kam zu dem Mißtrauen, das, wie meine Freunde versichern, in gesunden Tagen schon mir gegen die Welt eigen war. In dessen war diese Vorstellung mir lange nicht so viel Marter als die vorige. Sie wirkte bei mir eine Gegenverachtung meiner Verächter; eine verzweifelnde Ruhe, und ein Verlangen nach dem Tode, als nach dem erwünschenswerthesten Zustande."

In retrospect, Herz not only understands that the illness itself had robbed him of his ability to actually "see" his friends as present. More significant here is the insight that mistrust and projection belonged to his normal, everyday self and that he merely was able to see this particular aspect of his personality with astonishing clarity as he analyzed the material that emerged in and through the reports concerning the period of extreme fever and inflammation. In a word, Herz explains this mistrust as a result of an unconscious, psychological illusion or conceit inherent in his character: "The cause of this mistrust was presumably a result of my aforementioned illusion, the mistrust towards the entire world."[29] The German term *Einbildung* has the specific meaning of something "invented" or "constructed," "produced" – in a word, imagined – but also connotes "vanity" and "conceit." *Einbildung* thus implicates Herz in a tendency toward both a fundamental disposition of fear and suspicion as well as a sense of *hubris*. It shifts the discourse from a purely descriptive register to an introspective psychological method of self-reflection, of how and why a self might see itself the way it does. It is thus a *psychological* concept.[30] The two *Einbildungen* described by Herz are at once material and interpretation; they constitute both the objects of his self-reflection and the medium, the *language* in terms of which such self-reflection operates.

In the final phase of the illness, that of recovery, Herz articulates his feelings, his affective state, and his perceptions/sensations, that is, the description and interpretation of "inner data." As an "observer of himself," as a self-observer, Herz becomes the role model of the philosophical physician – *der philosophische Arzt* – a doctor of the body and a doctor of the mind in late eighteenth-century Germany. Punctuated by the deictic, dyadic, binary of *weg* (gone) and *da* (here), the healing moment, the moment of recovery, is marked by an inability to sense "the entire I," a doubling of the subject (*ein ganz anderes Subjekt*), and precisely at this moment, a moment in which the "I" is not fully-present to itself, Herz has the sense of well-being, a sense of ease: "I awoke, and my illness was *gone*, my full consciousness *present*. [...] My entire *self* I could not feel, and it almost occurred to me that the one who was convalescing was another person lying next to me in bed. However, my soul was cheerful."[31] With the veil of the fever and the psychic material now lifted, Herz sees himself as another. Herz then

---

29 Herz, "Psychologische Beschreibung," 133: "Die Ursache dieses Misstrauens hing vermuthlich mit meiner ebenerwehnten *Einbildung*, dem Misstrauen gegen die ganze Welt zusammen."
30 See also Stephanie Bölts, *Krankheiten und Textgattungen: Gattungsspezifisches Wissen in Literatur und Medizin um 1800* (Berlin: de Gruyter, 2016), 214–216.
31 Herz, "Psychologische Beschreibung," 140: "Ich erwachte, und *weg* war meine Krankheit, *da* mein völliges Bewußtseyn. [...] Mein ganzes *ich* war mir nicht fühlbar, beinahe kam es mir

concludes his psychological description of his own illness with philosophical remarks that point to his position in the debate concerning the metaphysics of the soul that was taking place around 1780.

For Herz, order and disorder, coherence, and chaos are *human relational concepts*, that is, they have meaning only in the web of beliefs and in the context of human values and judgment. As Herz notes, "the greatest part of human concepts are relational concepts, order and disorder we determine according to arbitrary rules presupposed by us; in and of itself, to assume disorder in nature itself is non-sense and blasphemy."[32] In the case of the human soul and its effects, nothing is completely random or without reason; we may think that certain states or conditions of the soul are arbitrary, but, in fact, Herz argues, there are "natural laws of the soul" just as surely as there are natural laws of the heavens. Applied to his illness and its psychological description, even the most apparently mad and random appearances and imaginary projections of the delirious person have an internal logic, a distinct structure or rationale. Rather than viewing the fantasies and hallucinations experienced in the depth of illness as simply the effects of a temporarily deranged mind in the heat of fever, as anomalies of his delirium, Herz analyzes them as expressions of his personality, or as characterologically determined, thereby bringing them back into the coherence and structure of a metaphysics of the (unified) soul. His delusions during the illness were not random. In the anamnesis, the narration of the illness, Herz *reconstructs* the structure and logic of the representations and feelings, leading them back to his own sense of identity and, more generally, to generalized psychology, and anthropological assumptions concerning human nature. The narrative thus performs a mediation of the particular and the universal, the specific individual and the general. From the perspective *within* the illness, Herz brings to language what could only be perceived and recognized in an indeterminate, indistinct manner; his states of consciousness, and his innermost feelings and senses of this condition. The rupture of his everyday experience, being brought from his bedroom into the study, and his experience of dislocation and strangeness, is transformed in the final section of the description, in which he finds himself again in his beloved study, able, once again, to recognize the familiar space and its objects: "With this moment, my entire

---

vor, daß der Genesene ein ganz anderes Subjekt neben mir im Bette wäre. Meine Seele war indessen heiter."

32 Herz, "Psychologische Beschreibung," 134: "Der größte Theil menschlicher Begriffe sind Verhältnisbegriffe. Ordnung und Unordnung bestimmen wir nach willkührlich von uns vorausgesetzten Regeln, an sich ist Unordnung in der Natur anzunehmen Unsinn und Gotteslästerung."

inner feeling changed completely."³³ The transformation of his "internal feeling," a sense of being once again "at home," the end of the displacement, marks a profound psychological shift. Herz renders in great detail precisely the experience of this return, recuperation, and reintegration.

The turn towards the individual, a personality, a characterologically unique human being or person, and not simply a generalized abstraction, is traditionally understood as one of the defining features of late eighteenth-century writing. Often, perhaps all too often, it is seen, at least in its German variant, as a derivative of Pietism, that strand of inwardly-directed and often mystical, devotional religiosity associated with the figures of Philipp Jakob Spener and August Hermann Francke in Halle in the seventeenth and early eighteenth century, which is frequently credited with having "invented" the modern concept of the individual.³⁴ However, as Niklas Luhmann pointed out, the Christian concept of salvation presupposes something to be saved; an individual in the literal sense, however, is "a being with an indivisible, indestructible soul."³⁵ In an attempt to diffuse Carl Hinrichs's argument that Pietism was responsible for the modern concept of the individual,³⁶ Luhmann's systems-theory proposes two avenues for the increasing differentiation and emergence of the distinct individual in the eighteenth century: property and art. The history of the individuality of the individual does not continue beyond this point, Luhmann says. In the nineteenth century, it is codified and ideologized, according to Luhmann, as a theory of "individualism," but the basic operation undergoes no further substantial modification. However, against Luhmann, we argue that there is more to be said about the late eighteenth century with regard to this *individuality of the individual*. While Luhmann's model asserts the reduction of complexity to create and maintain identity (this is something he proposes across the board for all self-referential, auto-poetic systems), we witness, I would argue, an aberration in the

---

33 Herz, "Psychologische Beschreibung," 139: "Mit dem Augenblick änderte sich mein ganzes innres Gefühl."
34 Carl Hinrichs, *Preußentum und Pietismus. Der Pietismus in Brandenburg-Preußen als religiössoziale Reformbewegung* (Göttingen: Vandenhoeck & Reprecht, 1971), 1. See also: Gerhard Kaiser, *Pietismus und Patriotismus im literarischen Deutschland* (Frankfurt am Main: Athenaum, 1973); and, more recently, and more critically, Jonathan Sheehan, *The Enlightenment Bible: Translation, Scholarship, Culture* (Oxford and Princeton, NJ: Princeton University Press, 2005), 59.
35 Niklas Luhmann, "The Individuality of the Individual: Historical Meanings and Contemporary Problems," in *Reconstructing Individualism: Autonomy, Individuality and the Self in Western Thought*, ed. Thomas C. Heller et al. (Stanford, CA: Stanford University Press, 1986), 315.
36 Carl Hinrichs, *Preußentum und Pietismus* (Göttingen: Vandenhoeck & Reprecht, 1971).

late eighteenth-century psychological case history, namely an *increase* in complexity, an interest in the unique, the incommensurable, the *interesting*, precisely that which is not-yet known, or that which cannot be subsumed under an existing concept. And this increase in complexity is not generated merely in the service of a disciplinary surveillance that would place such individuals into a roster, a register, and in an archive of similar cases, but rather to *individualize*, to create a unique subjectivity.

From the casuistry of medical case-histories of the late seventeenth century (*historia morbi, observationes, consilia*) to the anthropological and psychological case-histories of the mid- and late eighteenth century, a decisive shift occurs. More precisely, it is in the period between 1750 and 1785 that the psychological case history with its focus on the character of the individual, no longer understood as an instance of temperament or the four humors, is born. The concern for interesting, unique cases mirrors a larger concern for the individuality of the individual that cuts across disciplinary boundaries such as philosophy, aesthetics, literature, psychology, linguistics, and anthropology.[37] This interest, taken together with the foregrounding of obscure, dark, non-distinct experience, was opened by the philosophical physicians (the "vernünftigen Ärzte" as Carsten Zelle refers to them)[38] in the mid-eighteenth century to construct a theory of *der ganze Mensch*, the "total human being" – not a generalized abstraction, but the concrete living individual, a mind-body unity, complete with all of its quirks and idiosyncrasies, its history and complex psychological constitution. Despite the apparent paradox – a *theory* of the "total human being" as an individual would erase precisely the individuality it sought to grasp – the thinkers of the late Enlightenment in Germany were steeped in precisely such a model of the human being as an historical, psycho-physical agency, unique in its specific development and trajectory. An adequate hermeneutic of such an individual would require access to and

---

37 The category of the "interesting" is one of the fascinating features of aesthetic discourse in the late eighteenth century. See: Christian Garve, "Einige Gedanken über das Interessierende" (1779), in *Philosophische Schriften über literarische, ästhetische, und gesellschaftliche Gegenstände*, ed. Kurt Wölfel (Stuttgart: Metzler, 1974), vol. 1, 161–348. On the history of this category, see: Aurel Kolnai, "On the Concept of the Interesting," in *Aesthetics in the Modern World*, ed. Harold Osborne (London: Thames & Hudson, 1968), 166–187; Kurt Wölfel, "Interesse/interessant," in *Ästhetische Grundbegriffe*, ed. Karlheinz Barck (Stuttgart and Weimar: Metzler, 2001), vol. 3, 138–174; Altrud Dumont, "Das Interessante – Theorie und narrative Praxis. Friedrich Schlegel und E.T.A. Hoffmann," *Weimarer Beiträge* 38.3 (1992): 430–447; Robert Leventhal, *The Disciplines of Interpretation: Lessing, Herder, Schlegel and Hermeneutics in Germany 1750–1800* (Berlin: de Gruyter, 1994), 260–265.
38 Carsten Zelle, ed., *Vernünftige Ärzte. Hallesche Psychomediziner und die Anfänge der Anthropologie in der deutschsprachigen Frühaufklärung* (Tübingen: Niemeyer, 2001).

careful reconstruction of the historical, developmental, "narrative" constitution of the individual.

There are numerous accounts of this emergence, all of which reduce the psychological case history to an effect, a result, or a symptom. The modern psychological case history exemplified here using Herz's text of 1782 is not simply the description of a case, or a chronicle of an illness; it does not consist solely of observations and empirical data; indeed, it is not even concerned with a psychological or mental illness – *Geistesstörung* or *Seelenkrankheit*. Rather, its psychological character lies in the way the narrative seeks to establish a personal experience by referring it back to something we would now call "personality" or "character." Neither the status of the narrator nor the psychological content itself constitutes a psychological case history. In contrast to the *monstrous*, the *anomalous*, and the *"curious"* prevalent in case histories of the fourteenth through the sixteenth centuries, the psychological case is not the representation of an uncanny instability on its way towards normative structure.[39] Nor is it simply a bourgeois oppositional figure in the class/caste battle against the rigid hierarchy of the *Ständestaat* or an effect of its dissolution. It is not an expression of "immediate intimacy" or simply the "publication of the private;"[40] not merely an ideological reflex of the program for *Bildung* ubiquitous in the 1770s and 1780s[41]; more than a "escape into the inner world"[42] or a compensation for the loss of the life-world.[43] In distinction to these explanations, one can discern a far more immediate, a far more urgent and compelling reason to write the psychological case history at precisely this time, and precisely within the culture of the late Enlightenment in Germany.

As the first narrative psychological case histories appeared in the 1780s, a stormy debate was raging in Germany concerning the human soul and, specifically, whether it had an existence independent of the physical world,

---

39 Stephen Greenblatt, "Fiction and Friction," in *Reconstructing Individualism: Autonomy, Individuality and the Self in Western Thought*, ed. Thomas C. Heller et al. (Stanford, CA: Stanford University Press, 1986), 30–52. Greenblatt treats *On Hermaphrodites* (1612) as the antipode to Jakob Burckhardt's thesis of the emergence of "Individualität" in the Renaissance.
40 Jean Marie Goulemot, "Literary Practices: Publicing the Private," in *A History of Private Life*, ed. Roger Chartier and Philippe Ariès, trans. Arthur Goldhammer (Cambridge: Cambridge University Press, 1989), vol. 3, 364–392.
41 Martin Davies, *Identity or History? Marcus Herz and the End of Enlightenment* (Detroit: Wayne State University Press, 1995), 74–75.
42 Wolf Lepenies, *Melancholie und Gesellschaft* (Frankfurt: Suhrkamp, 1972), 83.
43 Odo Marquard. "Der angeklagte und der entlastete Mensch in der Philosophie des 18. Jahrhunderts," in *Studien zum Achtzehnten Jahrhundert*, ed. Bernhard Fabian (München: Fink, 1980), vol. 2, 193–209: "Flucht in die Innerlichkeit."

specifically matter and the body. In France, a staunch naturalistic, deterministic materialism in the writings of Julian Offray de la Mettrie (1705–1751), Claude Adrien Helvétius (1715–1771), and Baron d'Holbach (1723–1789) had appeared between 1747 and 1770 that viewed the soul as a mere fabrication or invention. In England, building on John Locke's statement that substance was "something I know not what," and his denial of the soul as an immaterial substance, David Hume famously rejected the existence of a stable, persistent self in his *Treatise on Human Nature* (1739), reducing the very idea of self to simply a "bundle" of specific mental events and impressions. According to Hume, "There is no *simplicity* in it [the mind, RL] at one time, nor *identity* in different; whatever natural propension we might have to imagine that simplicity and identity."[44] This "natural propension" Hume attributed to a "union" of the various perceptions, impressions, and ideas forged in the imagination: "The identity, which we ascribe to the mind of man, is only a fictitious one, and of a like kind with that which we ascribe to vegetables and animal bodies. It cannot, therefore, have a different origin, but must proceed from a like operation of the imagination upon like objects."[45] The naturalistic materialism in France and the empirical associationism and skepticism in England challenged one of the most cherished assumptions prevalent in pietistic Germany – the existence and persistence of the soul, and its irreducibility to matter and body. In the second half of the eighteenth century, this philosophical controversy surrounding a metaphysics of the soul was increasingly being played out in the disciplines of medicine, especially physiology, and in the nascent disciplines of anthropology and of empirical psychology, which embraced a notion of the human being as the unity of mind and body, while simultaneously retaining a notion of the human soul.

With the advent of philosophical anthropology, such as Ernst Platner's *Anthropology for Physicians and Philosophers* (1772), the philosophical-psychological controversy concerning the soul is increasingly carried out with recourse to medicine, especially physiology, and the nascent empirically oriented psychology.[46] Psychological physiology, that is, the attempt to understand physical symptomology through psychological perturbation, which

---

44 David Hume, *A Treatise on Human Nature*, ed. David Fate Norton and Mary J. Norton (Oxford: Oxford University Press, 2000), 1.6.4.
45 Hume, *Treatise*, 1.6.6.
46 Michael Hißmann, *Psychologische Versuche, ein Beitrag zur esoterischen Logik* (Frankfurt and Leipzig, 1777), is a paradigmatic example of the critical, experience oriented Psychology. Influenced by Hume, he denied the existence of the self or soul. On this, see also: Nicolai Merker *Die Aufklärung in Deutschland* (München: C. H. Beck, 1982), 227–229; and Kaufmann,

had really started with Stahl in Halle at the end of the seventeenth, beginning of the eighteenth century,[47] placed the mind-body relation as on object of empirical-observational scientific research, and was directed against figures such as Moses Mendelssohn, who continued to postulate the human soul as the basis (*Grund*) and seat (*Sitz*) of the human representational-cognitive and sensory-receptive capacity; Mendelssohn in particular had always maintained that the soul was something beyond any empirical-scientific observation and scientific scrutiny. And even though Herz contradicted Haller's Irritability-Thesis,[48] he held fast to a metaphysics of the soul, like his mentor Mendelssohn. This remnant or "remainder" of Western Metaphysics was not simply a "placeholder" for these figures of the late Enlightenment in Germany in 1780. For them, it was an essential condition of human dignity, responsibility, freedom, human rights, and political-social order. One of the late editors of the *Magazin*, Kant's most astute critic the philosopher Salomon Maimon, wrote the following in 1791 in an article published in the *Magazin* entitled "Über den Plan des Magazins zur Erfahrungsseelenkunde":

> I note that, the more precise relation between the soul and the body notwithstanding, the soul also produces effects in itself, that is, brings forth modifications that have no corresponding physical modifications. Of this type we can identify the so-called "higher" powers of the soul and free-will [...] these, namely the effects of the free will are not only independent of the effects of the physical organs, but are actually directly in opposition to them [...] Health of the soul is precisely that condition of the soul in which the effects of the free-will can be exercised unhindered, just as mental illness or illness of the soul consists in exactly the opposite.[49]

Aufklärung, bürgerliche Selbsterfahrung und die Erfindung der Psychiatrie in Deutschland 1770–1850, 29–30.

47 L. J. Rather, "G.E. Stahl's Psychological Physiology," *Bulletin of the History of Medicine* 35.1 (1961): 27–49.

48 Albrecht von Haller, *De partibus corporis humani sensibilibus et irritabilus* (Zürich, 1752). On the basis of his numerous experiments, Haller demonstrated in his famous *De partibus corporis* of 1752 what he believed to be the two central properties of the living organism: *irritability* as a property unique to muscle tissue (it was virtually identical to the *contractability* of muscle fibers), and *sensibility* as a property unique to nerves.

49 Salomon Maimon, "Über den Plan des Magazins zur Erfahrungsseelenkunde," *Magazin für Erfahrungsseelenkunde* 8.3 (1791): 12: "Ich bemerke aber, daß ohngeachtet dieser genaueren Verbindung zwischen Seele und Körper, die Seele auch in sich selbst würkt, d.h. Modifikationen hervorbringt, denen keine körperliche Modifikationen entsprechen. Von dieser Art sind die Würkungen der sogenannten höheren Seelenkräfte und des freien Willens (...) Diese nämlich die Würkungen des freien Willens sind nicht nur von den Organenwirkungen unabhängig, sondern sogar denselben entgegengesetzt. (...) Seelengesundheit ist nehmlich

With Maimon, the empirical, observational method as it had been formulated by Moritz and employed as a programmatic method for the *Magazin* recedes in favor of a metaphysics of the soul which supposedly guarantees free will as the signature of the healthy soul.[50] This metaphysics of the soul remains powerful and is not squelched in the battle of mechanism and vitalism of the 1790s: *Pneuma, spiritus, die Seele* is increasingly appropriated and integrated into what was referred to as the *Prinzip des Lebens*; organic life itself "becomes a self-sufficient object of positive knowledge."[51] That is, instead of an eclipse of the soul, instead of a radical biological materialism, a rather unique transformation occurs in Germany in which the soul simply becomes the highest level of organic life, as Michael Sonntag has shown: "The organic is, from now on, that which breathes, nourishes itself, grows and propagates itself on the basis of its specific characteristics."[52] G. S. Rousseau characterized this rather unexpected and surprising rehabilitation of the soul, which had been parodied and banished by many adamantly materialist Enlightenment figures, in the following manner:

> That "mind" which the Enlightenment set out to expose as a "fiction" fought back and reasserted itself, in surprising and troublesome fashions [...] coming to recognize that lunacy was not just seated in the blood, nerves, the brain, but was an authentically mental disorder, requiring to be treated by moral means.[53]

The reference to *moral treatment* here indicates a distinctly therapeutic-psychological, rather than purely materialistic approach to mental illness. Mental illness is not simply a disease of the brain, of the nerves, or of the fluids, of hot and cold, of dry and wet; rather it is also, precisely, a *Seelenkrankheit*, an illness of the soul or mind.

---

derjenige Seelenzustand, wo die Würkungen des freien Willens ungehindert ausgeübt werden können; so wie die Seelenkrankheit in dem entgegengesetzten Zustand besteht."

50 Kaufmann, *Aufklärung*, 108–109. See also: Andreas Gailus, "A Case of Individuality: Karl Philipp Moritz and the Magazine for Empirical Psychology," *New German Critique* 79 (2000): 91: "if the sick soul is merely the healthy soul thrown off-balance, then the psychologist and his object are not so much distinct entities as individual variations arising from a shared existential ground."

51 Michael Sonntag, "Die Seele und das Wissen vom Lebenden. Zur Entstehung der Biologie im 19. Jahrhundert," in *Die Seele. Ihre Geschichte im Abendland*, ed. Gerd Jüttemann (Göttingen: Vandenhoeck & Ruprecht, 1991), 294–318: "wird selbst zum eigenständigen Gegenstand eines positiven Wissens;" "Das Organische ist von nun an das, was aus sich selbst heraus, aufgrund seiner besonderen Eigenschaften, atmet, sich ernährt, wächst, und sich fortpflanzt."

52 Sonntag, "Die Seele und das Wissen vom Lebenden," 302.

53 G. S. Rousseau, "Introduction," in *Languages of the Psyche. Mind and Body in Enlightenment Thought*, ed. Rousseau (Berkeley and Oxford: University of California Press, 1990), 33.

On the opposing side stood the advocates of a fact-driven empiricism and strict materialism. In particular, a critic of Mendelssohn and his "metaphysics of the soul" was the Professor of Philosophy at the University of Göttingen Michael Hißmann (1752–1784), who in his *Psychological Essays. A Contribution to Esoretic Logic* of 1778 wrote that the researcher should take the only correct path, "the path of experience." ("den einzig richtigen Weg, den Weg der Erfahrung"), which according to him would prevent the very idea that there is a "spiritual essence" inherent in the human being (*das dem Menschen ein geistiges Wesen innewohne*).[54] According to Hißmann, the soul was an *improbable fiction* (*unwahrscheinliche Fiktion*), a mere *invention* (*eine Erdichtung*): "No notion that has ever been thought by a human being occurs to me as being more incomprehensible and strange than the notion of a simple essence that inheres in a human being."[55] Christian Gottlob Selle, the Director of the Charité in Berlin at the time, also a critic of the metaphysics of the soul and an opponent of Herz, wrote in his *New Contributions to Natural and Medical Science* (1782–1786) that an entirely new era had dawned in medicine: the era of theory and speculation was declared ended and the era of strict observation and experiment had begun.[56] Behind this call for observation and experiment lay an unrepentant materialism. But for Herz as for his friend Moritz, the research and reporting characteristic of the psychological case-histories remained the "connection and reciprocal changes of the soul and the body: "Verbindung und wechselweise Veränderung von Seele und Körper."[57]

Platner's *Anthropology* (1772) was one of the most significant and popular books of the late eighteenth century, taking up the problem of the *commercium mentis et corporis* and seeking to provide a holistic approach to medicine, physiology, and psychology.[58] The second edition of the book (1790) specified "with special reference to physiology, pathology, moral philosophy

---

54 Hißmann, *Psychologische Versuche* (1778), quoted by Nicolai Merker, *Die Aufklärung in Deutschland* (München: C. H. Beck, 1982), 227. See also: Jutta Heinz, *Wissen von Menschen und Erzählen vom Einzelfall* (Berlin: de Gruyter, 1996), 37–38.
55 Hißmann, *Psychologische Versuche*, 249: "So kömt mir kein Gedanke, der je von einem Menschen gedacht worden, sonderbarer und unbegreiflicher vor, als der Gedanke von einem einfachen, im Menschen wohnenden Wesen."
56 Christian Gottlob Selle, *Neue Beiträge zur Natur und Arzenei-wissenschaft* (Berlin: Mylius, 1782–1786): "Es war eine Zeit, wo nichts als Theorien galten. Jetzt ist das Zeitalter der Beobachtungen."
57 Marcus Herz, *Versuch über den Schwindel* (Berlin, 1786), 1.
58 Alexander Košenina, *Ernst Platners Anthropologie und Philosophie: Der philosophische Arzt und sein Einfluss auf Johann Karl Wezel und Jean Paul* (Würzburg: Königshausen & Neumann, 1989).

and aesthetics" in its subtitle,⁵⁹ thus circumscribing the disciplinary purview of the text and placing it firmly within the anthropological discourse of *der ganze Mensch* in the late German enlightenment. Platner was the first to use the German term *Anthropologie* in the title of a book.⁶⁰ His textbook cemented the relation between Stahl's psychologically oriented medicine, the "philosophical physicians" around 1750, and "philosophical anthropology" of the last quarter of the eighteenth century.⁶¹ For Platner, as for every other philosophically-minded physician of the second half of the eighteenth century, the mind-body problem itself had become an obstacle to a more integrative conception of man and a holistic therapeutics. Against Nicolas Malebranche's occasionalism, Stahl's animism, Leibniz's theory of pre-established harmony, the stark materialism of Helvétius and La Mettrie, and Herman Boerhaave's strict empirical-experimental method, Platner developed a theory of *psychophysical reciprocity*.⁶² Contrary to an idealist conception of the self, Platner argued that the soul could only be known through experience (*Erfahrung*), not through reason alone. And opposed to the string-theory according to which the life-spirits were determined by the tension of the nerve-tubes, Platner suggested it was the flow of blood, and the system of canals in which the blood was transported, that determined the degree of the body's quality and capability of feeling. Finally, he located the soul in the brain, the *Gehirnmark*, more specifically, in that part of the brain which, if destroyed or injured, resulted in a confusion of the understanding, in mental derangement, or death.⁶³

---

59 Ernst Platner, *Neue Anthropologie für Ärzte und Weltweisee. Mit besonderer Rücksicht auf Physiologie, Pathology, Moralphilosophie und Ästhetik* (Leipzig: Crusius, 1790).
60 The Latin term *Anthropologia* had of course been used in numerous texts since the Renaissance.
61 See Hans F. Vermeulen, *Before Boas: The Genesis of Ethnography and Ethnology in the German Enlightenment* (Lincoln and London: University of Nebraska Press, 2015), 363–364.
62 Alexander Košenina, "Ernst Platner," in *Neue Deutsche Biographie* (*NDB*), ed. Historical Commission at the Bavarian Academy of Sciences (Berlin: Duncker & Humblot, 2001), vol. 20, 513–514. Cf. also Alexander Košenina: *Ernst Platners Anthropologie und Philosophie. Der 'philosophische Arzt' und seine Wirkung auf Johann Karl Wezel und Jean Paul* (Würzburg: Königshausen & Neumann, 1989); and the articles in Guido Naschert and Gideon Stiening, eds., *Ernst Platner (1744–1818). Konstellationen der Aufklärung zwischen Philosophie, Medizin und Anthropologie* (Hamburg: F. Meiner, 2007), special issue, *Aufklärung 19*.
63 Ernst Platner, *Anthropologie für Ärzte und Weltweise* (Leipzig: Dyckischen Buchhandlung, 1772), 47: "Derjenige Theil im Gehirnmark, dessen Verletzung den Tod, oder Verwirrung des Verstandes nach sich ziehet, ist der Sitz der Seele."

In his review of Ernst Platner's *Anthropology for Physicians and Philosophers* (1772), a book, according to Herz, which attempted to examine "body and soul in their reciprocal relations, limitations, and connections,"⁶⁴ Herz wrote:

> Herr Platner in our view goes too far when he maintains that apart from the relation to the body, all thinking and willing would cease. The body is totally dispensable for the inner consciousness of our self, for the idea that each one of us has of our own "I."⁶⁵

Platner located the soul in the brain and attributed dreams and fantasies as well as deviant representations to the soul,⁶⁶ but still held on to a notion of the soul as a *real, existing* entity, not simply as some representation or idea itself, and employed the terms "Ich," "Identität," and "Bewusstseyn" as synonyms. In his *Anthropology*, Platner stated that "what is conscious of itself is my soul – the I and the soul are identical."⁶⁷ The soul was a particular *type of substance* for Platner, but could not be totally divorced from the corporeal world: the soul had to stand in a relation to the body, more precisely, it was (1) dependent on the quality of the condition of the brain; (2) dependent on the ability of the body to receive and process sense-data; and (3) it existed in an empirically verifiable relationship to external reality.⁶⁸ Herz was not the only late Enlightenment figure who read – or rather misread – Platner's book and criticized his anthropology. Johann August Unzer, one of the famous psychological physicians in Halle, cut to the core of the matter when he wrote in a review of 1771:

---

64 Platner, *Anthropologie für Ärzte und Weltweise*, Vorrede, xvi: "Das, was sich bewusst ist, dies meine Seele [...] Ich und Seele sind einerley."
65 Marcus Herz, Review of *Anthropologie für Ärzte und Weltweise*, by Dr. Ernst Platner (Leipzig, 1772), *Allgemeine Deutsche Bibliothek* 20.1 (1773): 38–39: "Herr P[latner] scheint uns hierin offenbar zu weit zu gehen, wenn er behauptet, daß außer der Verbindung mit dem Körper alles Denken und Wollen aufhören müßte. Zu dem inneren Bewußtsein unserer Selbst, zu der Idee, die ein jeder von seinem eigenen Ich hat, scheint der Körper ganz entbehrlich zu seyn."
66 Platner, *Anthropologie für Ärzte und Weltweise*, Par. 501, 165. Interesting in this regard is that Platner groups all such "representations" (dreams, fantasies) together and designates them as "pathological" (*krankhaft*).
67 Platner, *Anthropologie für Ärzte und Weltweise*, 16.
68 See Rita Wöbkemeier, *Erzählte Krankheit. Literarische und Medizinische Phantasien um 1800* (Stuttgart: Metzler, 1990), 163–165. Compare also the most recent work on this by Udo Thiel, "Das Gefühl 'ich': Ernst Platner zwischen empirischer Psychologie und Transzendentalphilosophie," in *Aufklärung: Interdisziplinäres Jahrbuch zur Erforschung des 18. Jahrhunderts* (Hamburg: F. Meiner, 2007), vol. 19, 139–161.

> In addition, how can one really question that the soul could do something without being conscious of it? That the soul has an influence on the movements of the heart, even if it does not have rulership over such movements through will alone? Don't passions change these movements of the heart, and aren't passions in the soul?[69]

Platner's psycho-physical reciprocity did not resolve the mind-body dilemma for everyone. According to Herz, in stark contrast to Platner, there is, in the human soul, a consciousness of oneself that contributes to the inner character of the person – what he refers to as "the consciousness of itself, which determines the character of the human being" – and, for Herz, this constituted the basic condition of the possibility of distinct cognition: "It is only through consciousness alone that we are capable of distinct cognition."[70] Herz thus remained a staunch believer in the independence of the soul even as he supported a strong interaction between the mind and the body. Here we see exactly where the battle lines were being drawn. Platner's anthropology made the human soul and consciousness dependent on having some relation to a body, to the material experience of sensations, and to what he believed to be "the real world." For Moritz, Herz, and Mendelssohn, by contrast, it was all about the autonomous human soul, its distinctive conceptual cognition, its ability to freely and willfully *construct* its world, to constitute it rationally, not to make sense *out of it* as much as to *invent* systems that effectively deal with difficulties and gaps. This is a significant philosophical difference, one that would continue to haunt epistemology up until our time.

The psychological case history around 1780 opened up the possibility of a new, fully secularized metaphysics of the soul with an empirical-scientific rhetoric; it possessed a claim of precise human observation (*Beobachtung*)

---

69 Johann August Unzer, Review of "Briefe eines Arztes an seinen Freund," by Ernst Platner, *Allgemeine Deutsche Bibliothek* 14.1 (1771): 86: "Zu dem, wie kann man wohl in Zweifel ziehen, daß die Seele etwas thun könne, ohne sich dessen bewußt zu seyn? Daß die Seele einen Einfluß in die Bewegungen des Herzens habe, ob sie gleich durch den Willen keine Herrschaft darüber hat? Verändern nicht alle Leidenschaften die Bewegung des Herzens, und sind wohl die Leidenschaften nicht in der Seele?"
70 Herz, Review of *Anthropologie für Ärzte und Weltweise*, by Dr. Ernst Platner, 38: "Das Bewusstsein ihrer selbst, was den Charakter des Menschen ausmacht[...]Vermittels des Bewusstseins allein sind wir der deutlichen Erkenntnis fähig." It is clear that Herz does not do full justice to Platner's book and the theory of self-consciousness contained therein. The best work on Platner is by Udo Thiel, "Das Gefühl 'Ich'. Ernst Platner zwischen Empirischer Psychologie und Transzendentalphilosophie," *Aufklärung* 19 (2007): 139–161; and Werner Euler, "*Commercium mentis et corporis*? Ernst Platners medizinische Anthropologie in der Kritik von Marcus Herz und Immanuel Kant," in *Aufklärung: Interdisziplinäres Jahrbuch zur Erforschung des 18. Jahrhunderts* (Hamburg: Meiner, 2007), vol. 19, 21–68.

and advocated amassing case-histories for the purpose of eventually developing a system of diseases and illness of the soul (*Seelenkrankheit*) – mental illness. What is important was not whether the *Magazin* lived up to its programmatic assertions, which it certainly did not, but rather what it *claimed to be doing*. It was an attempt at a metaphysics of the soul by other means, with scientific validity and empirical precision.[71] Such a metaphysics fulfilled a number of different functions: first, it perpetuated a continuity and coherence of the self, the required confirmation of a non-physical soul in the confrontation with both physical and mental illness. Thus, Herz always underscored the individuality of the illness due to the difference in personality and character, the ability to withstand adversity, to deal with extreme situations, and to adapt to new conditions. So the new metaphysics of the soul guaranteed the responsibility, predictability, and competence of the individual human being. It created, second, at the same moment, a new system of knowledge, new types of subjectivity, new caretakers and monitors, and a public documentation and communication network which sought to grasp the enigmatic, the elusive "interior" of the human being, to get at the *individual case* empirically, that means, for both Herz and Moritz, through observations captured in narratives. At a later point and at another level, a *system of knowledge* of the human being, specifically a generalized science of the sick or unhealthy souls, could gradually be constructed, continually open to discussion and debate, Moritz will emphasize, so that all of the assertions could be criticized and tested. This *Seelenkrankheitslehre,* or theory of "mental illness," as he names this sub-discipline that was a section in practically every issue of the *Magazin zur Erfahrungsseelenkunde*, would provide the scientific-discursive forum for scholars, writers, philosophers, priests and preachers, schoolteachers and child caretakers, and finally physicians and jurists to

---

71 In his essay on Friedrich Schiller's *Verbrechen aus verlorener Ehre*, Alexander Košenina has profiled the "human soul" as a discursive object of what he terms the psychological case-history. See: Alexander Košenina, "'Tiefere Blicke in das Menschenherz': Schiller und Pitaval," *Germanisch-romanische Monatsschrift* 55.4 (2005): 391. In the case of Schiller, however, as Košenina emphasizes, it is always a matter not of the individual case itself, but of the universally valid knowledge of humanity as such, in a word, the assumption, according to Košenina, "daß dabei die Einheit der Menschennatur außer Frage steht." My thesis of the relevance of "Psyche" or the soul ("Seele") is also supported in the contribution of Harald Neumeyer, "'Schwarze Seelen'. Rechts-Fall-Geschichten bei Pitaval, Schiller, Niethammer und Feuerbach," *Internationales Archiv zur Sozialgeschichte der deutschen Literatur* 31.1 (2006): 101–132. The importance of the reception of the Pitaval in Germany through Schiller's edition and translation has only been recognized in research recently, above all in the work of Wolfgang Riedel.

present interesting cases, discuss etiology and symptomatology, diagnosis and prognosis, treatment and cure.

The psychological case history that emerges definitively around 1780 was not simply an "example" or "instance" of an already generalized theory, as was the case in the casuistic medical thinking and practice of the late seventeenth and early eighteenth century. Nor was it merely a set of *observationes*, an accumulation of odd and curious conditions, as it was for Platter and much of early modern European medicine. Rather, as we see yet again and as Moritz's conception of case makes even clearer, the psychological case history represents a truly distinct modern writing and communication medium of a nascent empirical psychology attempting to break the hegemony of generalized and universal approaches to mental illness and its treatment and to focus rather on the distinctive nature of an illness as a unique psycho-physical event.

Moritz's concept of an empirical psychology and of a science of illnesses of the soul can perhaps best be determined *ex negativo*. What must be avoided are rigid, intractable systems and blanket approaches or treatments that do not sufficiently take into account the individuality of the illness and the individual herself: "All anxious working towards a rigid system must be utterly avoided,"[72] he wrote, "one must take this system to be as unstable as possible."[73] General remedies, "Universal medication of all illness of the soul"[74] without consideration of the specificity of the individual case; empty speculation (*leere Spekulationen*[75]), unfounded hypotheses, hasty judgment, religious prejudice, and moral condemnation must all be avoided. The new science of illness of the soul was supposed to circumvent all of these pitfalls. As it is articulated in the *Vorschlag* of 1782, "all of these observations should be made before all reflection regarding them, until a critical mass of facts is present, so that at the end everything is ordered into a useful totality."[76]

In addition to the functions mentioned above, the psychological case history also fulfilled an important *pastoral* role – in the sense developed by Michel

---

[72] Moritz, "Grundlinien," *Werke*, vol. 1, 812: "Alles ängstliche Hinarbeiten aber auf ein festes System muss dabei gänzlich vermieden werden."
[73] Moritz, "Vorschlag," *Werke*, vol. 1, 799: "man muß dieses System auch so schwankend wie möglich nehmen."
[74] Moritz, "Vorschlag," *Werke*, vol. 1, 794: "Universalarznei aller Krankheiten der Seele."
[75] Moritz, "Vorschlag," *Werke*, vol. 1, 798: "Diese Wissenschaft würde sich auf diese Weise allmählich selber bilden, und wie fest würde dies Gebäude werden, wo die Lücken nicht durch leere Spekulationen zugestopft, sondern durch Tatsachen ausgefüllt werden."
[76] Moritz, "Vorschlag," *Werke*, vol. 1, 796–797: "alle diese Beobachtungen, nicht eher Reflexionen angestellt, bis eine hinlängliche Anzahl Fakta da sind, und dann am Ende dies alles einmal zu einem zweckmäßigen Ganzen geordnet."

Foucault in his writings on governmentality – by introducing readers to the guidance or direction of the soul. The psychological case history was therefore not merely an "example" or "instance" of an already generated theory or context of explanation. Nor was it simply an empirical procedure for the observation of individuals and their anomalies, as much as Moritz himself insisted on careful observation, rigorous description, and precise narration of events. If we consider its *function* rather than its *intention*, how the psychological case history *worked* rather than merely how it was *conceived* and *proposed*, that is, its discursive effect as a determinant of a milieu, it distinguishes itself as a medium that Foucault sought to characterize in his lectures on pastoral power. It allowed the milieu to look into the dark, hidden, secret recesses of the soul of the Other and "see," even or precisely in the most wayward actions or behaviors, the full "human being" in its totality.[77] The psychological case history therefore fulfilled, we might say, an important pastoral function in the last quarter of the eighteenth century: Foucault's "individualizing power of the pastoral"[78] states exactly that "all the dimensions of terror and force or fearful violence [...] disappear in the case of the shepherd."[79] Here, it is not a matter of coercion or force, but of guiding the wayward sheep back onto the correct path, of gently counseling, guiding, and directing them in the manner of the teacher, the pastor. Foucault referred to this as the direction of conscience or *Gewissensleitung*.[80]

---

[77] In the supressed preface to *Die Räuber*, in his reception and edition of the French Pitaval, and in the preface to *Der Verbrecher aus verlorener Ehre* (1786; 1792) Schiller attempts to determine the guiding knowledge-interest and the knowledge-transfer and – gain through the publication and dissemination of such psychologically-minded case-histories. Schiller was interested first and foremos no in unqieness and individualty, but rather knowledge of the entire human being, as he puts it, "die geheimen Bewegsursachen menschlicher Handlungen." See Alexander Košenina: "'Tiefere Blicke in das Menschenherz': Schiller und Pitaval," 388–392.
[78] Michel Foucault, *Geschichte der Gouvernementalität I: Sicherheit, Territorium, Bevölkerung. Vorlesung am College de France 1977–1978*, ed. Michel Senellart, trans. Claudia Brede-Konersmann and Jürgen Schröder (Frankfurt: Suhrkamp, 2004), 191–193.
[79] Foucault, *Security, Territory, Population*, 128.
[80] Compare Carsten Zelle, "Erfahrung, Ästhetik und mittleres Maß: Die Stellung von Unzer, Krüger und E.A. Nicolai in der anthropologischen Wende um 1750," in *Reiz – Imagination – Aufmerksamkeit*, ed. Jörn Steigerwald and Daniela Watzke (Würzburg: Königshausen & Neumann, 2003), 214–215. Zelle sees the convergence of Baumgarten, Meier, Krüger and Bolten in the fact "dass die Affekte [...] nicht unterdrückt, sondern vielmehr geleitet werden sollen," und, quoting Baumgarten, "eine sichere Führung nötig haben" (215). Zelle draws attention to the "Hinwendung zum Einzelfall und zur Fallgeschichte, d.h. den Einbezug narrativer bzw. literasiernder Verfahren in die Anthropologie als Diskurselement" (209), but does not go into this any further.

German Pietism in the eighteenth century provided a fertile field for such an intimate, dyadic, supposedly "peaceful" mentorship. In reality, such guidance was often anything but peaceful. The psychological case history as a published narrative record and account of the wayward sheep, the anomalous event, and the perturbed soul transformed the "case" or "event" into a logic and order of the soul, made it comprehensible, lent it sense and meaning. It became something that could be described and analyzed, treated, and even cured. Philosophical physicians and pastors, officers, councilors, teachers and schoolmasters, professors, and mothers could became part of the project to retrieve such souls and return them to the bourgeois order precisely through the publication, distribution, and reading of these identity-forging stories of confusion, criminality, madness, and destruction. In this sense, we still glimpse something of the old moral-theological casuistry at work, but transformed and appropriated for a totally different context. Here, the task is not to subsume, through rendering judgment, the individual case under an existing moral-theological precept, but rather, first, the construction and production of keen human observers, trained judges, and astute mentors, caring educators who would above all recognize in the case a possibility of *themselves*, and second, gently set the deviant soul back onto the correct path, by an individualizing process of treatment and therapy.[81]

To understand how this model is then transformed from one of the psychological narrative of the case to the psychiatric case history of the nineteenth century, a far more formal, less narrative genre, and how the central concepts of "norm" and "deviation" become established as psychiatric categories, we need only to consider the writings of Johann Christian Reil (1759–1813) at the turn of the century, whose *Rhapsodies on the Use of Psychological Therapies for the Mentally Disturbed* (1803),[82] according to Robert J. Richards, was the "most influential work in shaping German psychiatry before Freud."[83] Moritz's *Erfahrungsseelenkunde* and case-histories become standard references, and Herz's psychological case history of Moritz's illness (1793)[84] is cited and quoted

---

[81] The diagnostic, therapeutic, and curative aspects of this process are discussed in a later chapter.
[82] Johann Christian Reil, *Rhapsodieen über die Anwendung der psychischen Curmethode auf Geisteszerrüttungen* (Halle, 1803; Zweite Ausgabe 1818).
[83] Robert J. Richards, *The Romantic Conception of Life: Science and Philosophy in the Age of Goethe* (Chicago: University of Chicago Press, 2010), 263.
[84] Marcus Herz, "Etwas Psychologisch-Medizinisches. Moriz Krankengschichte," *Journal der praktischen Arzneykunde und Wundarzneykunst* 5.2 (1798): 259–321.

as a paradigmatic example. Reil coined the term "psychiatry" in 1808.[85] While an original psychological thinker who altered the way medicine conceived of psychological illness, Reil used existing psychological case-histories from Immanuel David Mauchart's *General Repertory for Empirical Psychology* (1792).[86] Mauchart was a pastor, proto-psychologist, and educator who had contributed to Moritz's *Magazin* and viewed his *General Repertory* as a continuation of the project of empirical psychology. In the *Rhapsodies*, Reil wrote: "Psychical cures are effects upon the soul [...] they are therefore derived from the practical empirical psychology [...] for the soul has illnesses like the body, and they stand in a steady reciprocal relation to one another."[87] In paragraph §9 of this most influential work, the title of which is "Selbstbewusstsein, Besonnenheit, Aufmerksamkeit," Reil writes of the inherent instability and vulnerability of the soul:

> Nevertheless this I, which endures in our consciousness with so much persistence, is in actuality a highly variable thing.[88]
>
> For consciousness, insofar as it expresses itself by means of a synthesis of all of our relations into the unity of a person, can deviate from the norm. The personality of the soul gets lost as does the individuality of the body.[89]

And precisely here, on the decisive spot where he is writing about the fragility and variability of the "I," Reil quotes from Herz's psychological case history of

---

85 Johann Christian Reil, "Ueber den Begriff der Medicin und ihre Verzweigungen besonders in Beziehung auf Berichtigung der Topik der Psychiaterie," In *Beyträge zur Beförderung einer Curmethode auf psychischem Wege*, by Johann Christian Reil and Johann Christoph Hoffbauer (Halle: Curtschen Buchhandlung, 1808), 153–160. On the invention of the term, see also: Otto M. Marx, "German Romantic Psychiatry. Part 1," *History of Psychiatry* 1 (1990): 351–381.
86 J. D. Mauchart, *Allgemeines Repertorium für empirische Psychologie und verwandte Wissneschaften*, ed. J. D. Mauchart and others (Nürnberg: in der Felseckerschen Buchhandlung, 1792). On Mauchart, see Peter Sindlinger, *Lebensearahrung(en) und Erfahrungsseelenkunde oder wie der Württemberger Pfarrer Immanuel David Mauchart die Psychologie entdeckt* (Nürthingen and Frickenhausen, Sindlinger-Burcharzt, 2010).
87 Reil, *Rhapsodieen*, 38: "Psychische Curen sind Wirkungen auf die Seele [...] sie sind also aus dem Gebiet der praktischen Erfahrungsseelenkunde entlehnt. [...] Dann hat sie Seele Krankheiten wie der Körper, die mit einander in einer beständigen Wechselwirkung stehen."
88 Reil, *Rhapsodieen*, 59: "Dennoch ist dieses Ich, das in unserem Bewußtsein mit so vieler Beharrlichkeit fortdauert, in der Wirklichkeit ein höchst veränderliches Ding."
89 Reil, *Rhapsodieen*, 78: "Dann kann noch das Bewußtsein, sofern es sich durch ein Zusammenfassen aller unserer Verhältnisse zur Einheit einer Person äußert, von der Norm abweichen [...] Die Persönlichkeit der Seele geht wie die Individualität des Körpers verloren."

1783.⁹⁰ Thus, possibly the first psychological case history itself becomes an example or case, as a model for the writing, reporting and publishing of such cases, now of course with the new vocabulary of "deviation" and "norm." Deviation (*Abweichung*) was a term Herz and Moritz well understood, but it was in opposition to a *human nature* understood as something universal and ahistorical. The proto-statistical discourse of "norm" and "normativity," and the notion of "deviance" as the outlier within a range of what was considered to be "normal" behavior, had not yet arrived. In 1800, Reil represents one of the first instances of the explicit emergence of *normativity*, an instance of thinking the self as a spectrum of states of unity and disunity, a normative area outside of which falls the *deviant*, the *aberrant*, and the *anomaly*.

In his book *Rewriting the Soul*, Ian Hacking wrote a genealogy of the sciences of memory in which he offered the provocative thesis that in the years 1874–1886 "knowledge about memory" becomes "a surrogate for *spiritual knowledge of the soul*."[91] In other words, in the third quarter of the nineteenth century, the eighteenth-century model of "spiritual knowledge of the soul" is definitively eclipsed: the "sciences of memory" displace such spiritual knowledge of the soul and its operations. In Wilhelm Wundt's psychological laboratory at the University of Leipzig (1879), students could be trained in introspection with objective results, actual measurements of conscious life. If this is the case, then the psychological case history – born exactly one hundred years earlier – might be viewed as the discursive precursor to Hacking's "sciences of memory."[92] In late eighteenth-century Germany, the soul became not something pre-existing and assumed, but an individual self whose history could be charted; it had a historical-contextual density that could be unfolded and explicated through empirical observation, experience, and narrative. Such knowledge of the soul was systematically linked to a "soft," non-disciplinary, pastoral apparatus of guidance, understanding, and therapeutic care. The "individualization" of the modern psychological individual – historicizing the soul and rendering it a concrete, individual "human being" – is of a piece with this system. As a practice of "truth-telling," of getting at causes that could only be disclosed through careful observation and experience, as a mechanism of recording instances of variance and irregularity, and as

---

90 Reil, *Rhapsodieen*, 79, 84, 86.
91 Ian Hacking, *Rewriting the Soul: Multiple Personality and the Sciences of Memory* (Princeton, NJ: Princeton University Press, 1995), 197; emphasis mine.
92 Hacking, *Rewriting the Soul*, 199, where Hacking lists the three "sciences of memory": "a. the neurological studies of the different types of memory; b. experimental studies of recall; c. what might be called the psycho-dynamics of memory." "Memory," Hacking writes, "already regarded as criterion of personal identity, became a scientific key to the soul" (198).

part of a network of publication, reception, and application, collections of psychologically-minded case-histories provided a discursive form of evidence, a repository of experience-based, "empirical" researches. The modern psychological subject becomes equally the *subject* and the *object* of this new constellation of knowledge and discourse, using pre-existing cases and reports as evidence and example, instance and corroboration. With the advent of this new *ensemble* of practices, protocols, therapeutics, and mechanisms of recording, writing, and dissemination emerging around 1780, traditional religious and medical discourses were revised or upended. Traditional "types" and their afflictions were transformed into modern "psychological subjects" and their idiosyncratic illnesses, and new forms of caregivers and caretakers – above all, the *philosophical physician* – were to consult, participate, and allocate responsibility for care not only in the guidance and direction, but also the registration and categorization of souls. A milieu of therapeutic care, correction, and cataloging was created in which the *individuality of individuals*[93] became the stuff of science, scholarship, learning, political concern, and public discourse.[94]

---

[93] I explicitly use Niklas Luhmann's vocabulary (Luhmann, "Individuum, Individualität, Individualismus," in *Gesellschaftsstruktur und Semantik* [Frankfurt: Suhrkamp, 1989], vol. 3, 149–258), but eschew his purely functionalist stance, inasmuch as the reciprocal information flow between patients and their guardians, as between the case-histories and their publics present us with a far more nuanced, rich history than Luhmann's functional account would suggest or allow. Luhmann analyzes this emergence solely as a mechanism of modernity's self-reproduction: the "the society of society" and its endlessly "individuating" individuals.

[94] By the term "public" I simply mean a greater circle of the literary public sphere hearing about, reading about, and discussing such cases, their subjects and "states" beyond the limits of the rather narrow set of academic experts. The discrepancies between more "learned," "scientific," "academic" and more "popular," sensationalistic discourses/publics would be the subject of another study.

6 Friedrich Schiller: The Juridical-Psychological Case History as a Literary Work of Art

> The healing art and dietetics, if the physicians are really honest, have collected their best discoveries and the most curative precepts directly faced with those who are ill and at the foot of deathbeds. Dissections, hospitals and asylums have shed the greatest light in the area of physiology. The theory of the soul, morality, and the legislative power of the state should charitably follow this example, and similarly get their teachings from prisons, courts, and criminal files – the autopsies of vice.   Schiller, *Criminal of Lost Honor* (1786) [1]

An engraving by Carl Arnold Gonzenbach and Wilhelm von Kaulbach of the Saxon Art Society from 1847 "On the Narrative 'The Criminal because of Lost Honor,' by Schiller," some sixty years after the publication of Friedrich Schiller's text, commands our interest *not* because it tells us something new, but because it rehearses something that, by 1847, had been firmly established in the popular imaginary. It stages in effect what had become by the eve of the revolutions of 1848 a commonplace: *the individual case history*. In the engraving, we see a scene from Schiller's tale *Criminal of Lost Honor* (1786) where the poacher and murderer Christian Wolf is brought before the magistrate after being captured for the second time. All the elements of the modern juridico-disciplinary apparatus bear down on the deviant individual: in the center, the judge; behind him, a bailiff, with the irons used to restrain the criminal; before them, the perpetrator himself making an impassioned plea and the kneeling mother, perhaps begging for mercy; behind them, the militia/police and the tracking hound. The signature of the engraving's modernity, however, occurs in none of these traditional figures, but in direct center, along the periphery, and in the space of the arraignment itself. The scribe is writing an account or protocol of the case, a case history. The ancillary figures are all engaged in lively discussion of what is transpiring, looking at and referring to other,

---

[1] Friedrich Schiller, "Verbrecher aus verlorener Ehre," in *Sämtliche Werke*, by Schiller, ed. Gerhard Fricke and Herbert Göpfert (München: Carl Hanser Verlag, 1967), in 5 vols. (except where noted, all references to Schiller are from this edition using the abbreviation *SW*, volume and page; all translations are my own). Schiller's text first appeared as "Verbrecher aus Infamie eine wahre Geschichte," in *Thalia* 2.1 (1786): 20–58. See *SW*, 5:1066: "Die Heilkunst und Diätetik, wenn die Ärzte aufrichtig sein wollen, haben ihre besten Entdeckungen und heilsamsten Vorschriften vor Kranken und Sterbebetten gesammelt. Leichenöffnungen, Hospitäler und Narrenhäuser haben das hellste Licht in die Physiologie angezündet. Die Seelenlehre, die Moral, die gesetzgebende Gewalt sollten billig diesem Beispiel folgen, und ähnlicherweise aus Gefängnissen, Gerichtshöfen und Kriminalakten – den Sektionsberichten des Lasters – sich Belehrungen holen."

Figure 10: "On the Narrative 'The Criminal because of Lost Honor,' by Schiller," by Carl Arnold Gonzenbach and Wilhelm von Kaulbach, Saxon Art Society, 1847. Courtesy and with permission of the Staatliche Kunstsammlungen Dresden, Kupferstich-Kabinett, A1889-131. Photo: Herbert Boswank.

perhaps similar cases; and behind them all, the archive, the scriptural repository of cases, registers of proceedings, past protocols, warrants and judgments, summaries and sentences they might consult as analogous cases. By 1847, this engraving of Schiller's story, itself based, as we shall see, on the actual case history of Friedrich Schwan from the second half of the eighteenth century, merely reiterates what had already become a fully institutionalized, scriptural order of discourse and practice, a writing mechanism and a disciplinary apparatus that – to paraphrase Michel Foucault – at once designated, individualized, and controlled the deviant and criminal subject. What is less apparent in this image are the multiple ways in which the individual is constructed in their individuality through the psychological case history, and how such a construction forms part of a socio-cultural practice of "care of the self" within a modern pastoral apparatus which, in the late 18th and early nineteenth century, displaces, to a large extent, the terror of explicit disciplinarity and the more direct, visceral anatomo-politics of the body present in this engraving.

In Foucault's genealogy of modernity, the "case" appears as one of several bio-political techniques of power in the second half of the eighteenth century. Foucault gives this emergence two different, yet complimentary descriptions. First, in *Discipline and Punish*, he wrote that the case "is no longer, as in casuistry or jurisprudence, a set of circumstances defining an act and capable of modifying a rule; it is the individual as he may be described and judged, measured, compared with others, *in his very individuality.*"[2] Later, in his writings on governmentality, Foucault placed the "case" alongside "security," "danger," "risk" and "crisis" as components of what he termed the *pastoral* apparatus, an "individualizing power" (*individualisierende Macht*) concerned not merely with singling out the individual, but also with the guidance of the (individual) human soul (*Gewissensleitung, Seelenführung*).[3] Foucault's genealogy is well-supported by the emergence of a "science of the state" or *Polizeywissenschaft* in the late eighteenth century.[4] For our purposes here, however, we are more interested in the proliferation particularly of psychological-juridical case histories in the second part of the eighteenth century in the wake of François Gayot de Pitaval's (1673–1743) *Causes célèbres et intéressantes*. As a component of the pastoral apparatus and a "method" for collecting, organizing, and classifying pathologies and disorders, the "case" and its construction, elaboration, and distribution forge an educative-scientific regime for the ordering, classification, and understanding of individual anomalies. In the last quarter of the eighteenth century, as Holger Dainat demonstrated, the presumed or presupposed harmony, balance, and rationality of the human soul was called into question or, stated in another way, one recognized how little was necessary to disrupt or destroy this enlightened construct of the individual.[5] Contingency, circumstance, and internal (psycho-physiological) and external (social-economic) conditions became determinants in criminal behavior.

What is not as evident and what has been overlooked in such an account of the juridical case (*Rechtsfallgeschichte*), however, is precisely what I refer to as the aesthetic function of the case, that is, how the "case" also became an

---

2 Michel Foucault, *Discipline and Punish* (New York: Pantheon, 1979), 191; emphasis mine.
3 Michel Foucault, *Geschichte der Gouvernementalität I: Sicherheit, Territorium, Bevölkerung. Vorlesung am College de France 1977–1978* (Frankfurt: Suhrkamp, 2004), 191–192.
4 Johann Peter Frank, *System einer vollständigen medizinischen Polizey* (Frankenthal: im Verlag der Gegelischen Buchdruckerey und Buchhandlung, 1779–1793), especially the chap. "Einleitung zur medizinischen Polizey," 42–152, where Frank specifies the increase in illnesses of the nerves as an effect of modernization.
5 Holger Dainat, "Der unglückliche Mörder: Zur Kriminalgeschichte der deutschen Spätaufklärung," *Zeitschrift für deutsche Philologie* 107 (1988): 524.

aesthetic-cultural object and an interactive, interdisciplinary medium operating between authors, physicians, teachers, philosophers, psychologists, legal theorists, scientists of the state, or practitioners of the newly emergent *Polizeiwissenschaft*, and literature. This is particularly relevant in the case of Schiller, who, in 1780, made his debut in "medical anthropology,"[6] trained as a physician, edited and translated Pitaval's texts, and transformed several psychological "cases" into literary texts, the most famous of which is his aforementioned early narrative *Criminal of Lost Honor*.[7] This transformation of the psychological-medical-legal case into a literary text is itself an *aesthetic act*, and, as such, a social practice. It constructs the case in question as a literary-aesthetic text which is not merely supposed to be interesting and edifying, but to contribute to a knowledge of humankind, to advance a certain conception of what it means to be human, and to promote a certain effort to be "concerned," or "caring." Such a transcription of a case becomes an aesthetic act insofar as it also serves to mediate between the sensuous and the rational cognitive aspects of human being, a key function of aesthetic experience in Schiller's philosophical aesthetic and in the second half of the eighteenth century more generally. Such "care" for the "entire human being" (*der ganze Mensch*) is to be evoked through the empathetic consideration of the history, state, condition, mindset, and circumstances of the individual as mitigating factors in the emergence of mental illness and criminal action.

Schiller's medical studies at the Karlsschule confronted him with several cases of narrated and actual mental illness.[8] Through his teacher and psychological-philosophical mentor, Jacob Friedrich Abel (1751–1829),[9] Schiller became acquainted with contemporary medical science, dietetics, and the theory and therapeutics of mental illness. Abel used Shakespeare's plays as "case studies" of psycho-pathology, a method Schiller found at first to be disquieting, as he himself admitted: "I was not yet ready to understand nature straight from the material itself. I could only bear an image of nature that had undergone reflection through the understanding and set right by a rule."[10]

---

6 Jutta Heinz, *Wissen vom Menschen und Erzählen vom Einzelfall. Untersuchungen zum anthropologischen Roman der Spätaufklärung* (Berlin and New York: de Gruyter, 1996), 26–30.
7 Schiller, "Verbrecher aus verlorener Ehre," in *SW*.
8 For a more complete assessment, see: Kenneth Dewhurst and Nigel Reeves, eds., *Friedrich Schiller. Medicine, Psychology, Literature* (Berkeley and Los Angeles: University of California Press, 1978).
9 On Abel, see: Walther Killy, "Abel, Jacob Friedrich (1751–1829)," in *Killy Literaturlexikon. Autoren und Werke des deutschsprachigen Kulturraums*, ed. Wilhelm Kühlman and Achim Aurnhammer (Berlin and New York: de Gruyter 2008), vol. 1, 5–7.
10 *SW*, 5:713: "Ich war noch nicht fähig, die Natur aus der ersten Hand zu verstehen. Nur ihr durch den Verstand reflektiertes und durch die Regel zurecht gelegtes Bild konnte ich ertragen."

But he eventually came to grips with the difficult task of "dissecting the human soul," to undertake what he referred to as a "autopsy of vice" – a *Leichenöffnung* or, as he also referred to it, a *Sektionsbericht des Lasters* – using the medical-anatomical metaphor in the introductory remarks to the earliest version of the novella and case history *Verbrecher aus Infamie*, which braided together psychological, medical, and moral-political discourses.¹¹ He also had first-hand experience dealing with psychological cases, as for example when he was given the task of writing the protocol of a mental illness in a report concerning his fellow Cadet at the Karlsschule Grammont, who suffered from severe depression and suicidal ideation.¹²

Schiller diagnosed Grammont's affliction as a case of melancholic hypochondria. According to Schiller, deep-thinking, ruminative, and sensitive individuals, and especially academics, were especially prone to this affliction. He wrote in his first report of 26 June 1780:

> The entire illness is in my view nothing other than a case of true hypochondria, the unfortunate condition of a human being in which the person becomes the pitiable victim of the precise sympathy between the abdomen and the soul, the illness of deep-thinking, sensitive minds and most of the great scholars. The powerful connection between body and soul make it extremely difficult to discover the first source of the malady and whether it is to be sought in the body or the soul.¹³

Schiller was quite specific in his explanation of Grammont's melancholy. As others during the late Enlightenment, Karl Philipp Moritz among others, he placed the blame for the depression in pietistic inwardness and the pathogenic suppression of feeling, which had gone to the extreme. Such strenuous pietistic regimen had made Grammont hypersensitive to all matters of virtue and religion and susceptible to conceptual confusion. The study of metaphysics at the Karlsschule in its labyrinthine complexity had then rendered him suspicious of all philosophical truth. The collision of pietism and metaphysics had essentially severed the Cadet's healthy relation to reality.

---

11 *SW*, 5:10. Peter Andre-Alt, *Schiller: Leben, Werk, Zeit* (München: C. H. Beck, 2009), 518.
12 Friedrich Schiller, "Über die Krankheit des Eleven Grammont," in *SW*, 5:268–280.
13 *SW*, 5:268–269: "Die ganze Krankheit ist meinen Begriffen nach nichts anders als eine wahre Hypochondrie, derjenige unglückliche Zustand eines Menschen, in welchem er das bedauernwürdige Opfer der genauen Sympathie zwischen dem Unterleib und der Seele ist, die Krankheit tiefdenkender, tief empfindenden Geister und der meisten grossen Gelehrten. Das genaue Band zwischen Körper und Seele macht es unendlich schwer, die erste Quelle des Übels ausfindig zu machen, ob es zuerst im Körper oder in der Seele zu suchen sei."

Pietistic sentimentality appeared to have created the basis for the malady which followed. It sharpened his conscience, made him extremely sensitive to all things having to do with virtue and religion, and confused his thinking. The study of metaphysics made him suspicious of all truth and pulled him over to the other extreme [...] In this way the path to the horrible melancholy was set.[14]

What is particularly interesting about Schiller's protocol-like report is the therapeutic method he recommends for dealing with a severely depressed patient. One must attend to the language of the patient, Schiller observes, and try to gain the trust of the patient by using the patient's very language to gain access to the core of the illness. The physician, in other words, must adopt the very terms of the hypochondriac in order to achieve a connection to the patient and thus to the underlying illness. This was for Schiller the guiding thread for their treatment of Grammont: "The trust of the patient can only be obtained surreptitiously if one uses his very language, and this general rule was also the guiding principle of our treatment of him."[15] In a double and doubling move, the physician appropriates the language of the patient to gain his trust, but also to enter into the labyrinth of the illness. The psychologically-minded medical student Schiller at the Karlsschule already intuits the necessity of following the threads in and of language and using this understanding in the therapeutic process to arrive at the underlying causes of the mental disturbance.

Schiller's translation and edition of Pitaval's *Sonderbare und merkwürdige Rechtsfälle*[16] is evidence of his interest in and passion for the narrative framing of mental illness and its consequences. In Abel's teachings, he received the sense of psychology as an empirical undertaking, one which begins with careful observations of symptoms as appearances and gradually moves to more general laws. In his *Introduction to the Theory of the Soul* of 1786, Abel wrote:

---

14 *SW*, 5:269: "Pietistische Schwärmerei schien den Grund zum ganzen nachfolgenden Übel gelegt zu haben. Sie schärfte sein Gewissen und machte ihn gegen alle Gegenstände von Tugend und Religion äusserst empfindlich und verwirrte seine Begriffe. Das Studium der Metaphysik machte ihn zuletzt alle Wahrheit verdächtig und riss ihn zum anderen Extremo über [...] Auf diese Art war der Weg zu der fürchterlichen Melancholie gebahnt."
15 *SW*, 5:279: "Das Vertrauen eines Kranken kann nur dadurch erschlichen werden, wenn man seine eigene Sprache gebraucht und diese Generalregel war auch die Richtschnur unserer Behandlung."
16 Friedrich Schiller's text edition and translation is *Merkwürdige Rechtsfälle, als ein Beytrag zur Geschichte der Menschheit. Nach dem franz. Werke des Pitaval* (Leipzig: Crusius, 1792–1795), in 4 parts.

The method of the human sciences is identical to that of the research of nature: First, to collect individual instances, and from these to construct general laws and finally to use these, partly to explain the individual instances and partly for the discovery of new rules, through whose application new products can be produced [...] Even the spirit of the psychologist is the same as that of the researcher of nature. But because the psychologist observes what has occurred in himself, and the study of the human mind contains concepts which are not easily testable by means of more nuanced and difficult experiments as in the case of the human body, the education of the psychologist is even more difficult, but also more important.[17]

Abel's analogy of the psychologist and *Naturforscher* involves the collection of individual instances (*individuelle Erscheinungen*) in the construction of general laws, which are then utilized both to explain psychological phenomena and to craft new practical rules. But the difference between the two is also significant: researchers of nature have testable experiments at their disposal, whereas psychologists only have their experience, observations of what occurs in themselves, the insights afforded by introspection, and the ability to discern – judgment.

As aesthetics emerges as a discipline in the second half of the eighteenth century, it is first and foremost a science of sensible knowledge (*scientia cognitionis sensitivae*), and only in a derivative sense a theory of art and the beautiful. The psychologically-minded physician Johann Christian Bolten remarked in his *Concerning Psychological Cures* of 1751:

> Aesthetics is a science of sensuous knowledge and of the significaation of the same. To intuit something according to the lower knowledge faculties is the same as knowing something sensuously. Aesthetics will therefore adduce the laws and rules of the lower or sensuous powers of knowledge far more precisely and extensively than psychology. One must therefore master aesthetics in order to be able to perform psychological cures.[18]

---

17 Jacob Friedrich Abel, *Einführung in die Seelenlehre* (Stuttgart: Metzler, 1786; repr. Hildesheim, Zürich, New York: Georg Olms, 1985), Vorrede: "Die Methode der Menschenlehre ist die bey Erforschung der Natur überhaupt gewöhnliche: Erst individuelle Erscheinungen zu sammeln, dann aus denselben allgemeine Gesetze zu bilden und endlich diese theils zu Erklärung der Erscheinungen, theils zu Erfindung neuer Regeln, durch deren Anwendung aufs neue gewisse Produkte hervorgebracht werden sollen, anzuwenden.[...] Auch der Geist des Psychologen ist also überhaupt der Geist des Naturforschers. Nur da der Psychologe das in ihm selbst Vorgegangene beobachtet, und die Menschenlehre unbildliche, feinere, schwerere und durch künstliche Proben nicht so leicht prüfbare Begriffe als die Körperlehre enthält, so ist die Bildung des psychologischen Geistes schwerer, aber auch viel wichtiger."
18 Johann Christian Bolten, *Gedancken von den psychologischen Curen* (Halle: Carl Hermann Hemmerde, 1751), 59: "Die Ästhetick [...] ist eine Wissenschaft von der sinnlichen Erkenntnis und der Bezeichnung der selben überhaupt. Etwas nach den untern Erkenntniskräften einsehen ist einerlei mit dem, etwas sinnlich erkennen. Die Ästhetick wird uns also die Gesetze und

Aesthetics in the mid-eighteenth century meant above all to have insight, to intuit, or to see into something, to know something directly and sensuously (*sinnlich*). While the analysis and diagnosis of the illness might well be discursive and conceptual, the cure is not; it is a *sinnlich* or sensible knowledge and craft, to modulate the sensuous apparatus of the patient, and this is, according to Bolten, the sphere of the aesthetic. Aesthetics as it was conceived by the psychologically-minded physicians at Halle around 1750, derived from the aesthetic theory Alexander Baumgarten and his disciple Georg Friedrich Meier, but their appropriation of it had less to do with art and beauty than with a particular form of cognition that is *insightful sensible knowledge*. It neither appeals to nor relies on conceptual, distinct analytical knowledge; it provides a form of immediate, direct cognition – we might think of this as insight, intuitive understanding, or sensuous knowing – particularly suited to the treatment of mental illness. Such a form of cognition is decisive for the psychological case studies in two ways: first, the case study serves as representational medium for precisely such insight or intuition into the underlying causes of mental illness and its psychological treatment. It offers, in discursive form, the content delivered by sensuous knowledge. Second, as Georg Lukács observed, the *particular* (*das Besondere*) in its particularity that is the object of such a direct, unmediated sensuous cognition is not simply a *token*. Rather, it is the quintessential category of aesthetics and, one could add, of modern literature itself.[19] The psychological case history of the late eighteenth century provided a unique genre of mediation and problematization of the relation between the particular and the general, sensuous and conceptual knowledge. Arguing convincingly in this direction, Alexander Košenina has articulated the anthropological shift that occurs in Schiller to what he calls a new aesthetic of performative signification: lively intuition (*lebendige Anschauung*) into the "inner history of the human being" rather than just discursive historical knowledge. The focus on the specificity of the patient's own expressions imparts psychological insight into the illness or crime and induces the reader to form their own judgment.[20]

Regeln der untern oder sinnlichen Erkenntniskräfte genauer und weitläufiger anführen und erklären, als es in der Psychologie geschehen kann. Man muss also die Ästhetick inne haben, um psychologische Curen verrichten zu lernen."

19 Georg Lukács, *Das Besondere als Kategorie der Ästhetik* (Neuwied: Luchterhand, 1967), 209. Of course, in literary modernism, the category of the *Besondere* becomes more problematical, as it comes to mean both the *typical* and the *particular*, as in Kafka, where the "everyday" and the "anomaly" intersect.

20 Alexander Košenina, "'Tiefere Blicke in das Menschenherz': Schiller und Pitaval," *Germanisch-Romanische Montasschrift* 55.4 (2005): 391–92.

While aesthetics as the theory of the beautiful gains the upper hand as its narrative continues, its driving force was, as Andrew Bowie has stated, "to do justice to the immediacy of the individual's sensuous relationship to the world."[21] Aesthetics seeks not simply to recuperate the individual, but to *create* the space for furthering the uniqueness of the individual in what Schiller perceived as an era of the increasing reduction of humanity, instrumentality, fragmentation, violence, terror, uniformity, and the leveling of difference. The maintenance and expansion of such uniqueness, of *Eigentümlichkeit*, an essential condition of actualizing the aesthetic state, requires for Schiller recognition of the entwinement of the particular individual in fluctuating circumstances and conditions, both internal and external. This raises the question of the status of the individual case in Schiller, in the multiple sense of the particularity, the uniqueness of the individual, as an irreducible person, but also, the legal-juridical-psychological "case" as a literary genre and discourse-medium. It stood at the center of the late eighteenth century's and Schiller's interests, from his early case history regarding his fellow-student Grammont's depression at the Karlsschule to *Criminal of Lost Honor: A True Story*, based on the true case history of the criminal Friedrich Schwan (1729–1760), to his translation and edition of Pitaval's *Merkwürdige Rechtsfälle als ein Beitrag zur Geschichte der Menschheit* (1792).[22]

Recent works on Schiller have gone a long way towards dispelling certain calcified preconceptions and fixed interpretations of Schiller's aesthetic theory; they have also shown another dimension of Schiller, a stark realist intention of his work, which almost certainly derived from his early medical, anatomo-physiological studies at the Karlsschule. Rüdiger Safranski's 2004 book *Friedrich Schiller oder die Erfindung des Deutschen Idealismus* goes to great lengths to emphasize and trace the importance of Schiller's medical studies for the development of his psychologically astute dramas. With detailed knowledge of the context, Safranski is able to show how Schiller the medical student undergoes a transformation in 1778, throwing himself into his medical studies with an intensity and tenacity he had lacked up that point. Through Jacob Friedrich Abel and his most influential medical Professor Consbruch, who taught him neurophysiology, Schiller is influenced by what Safranski refers to as the turn, around 1775, to *anthropological empiricism*, in which the texts of Bacon, Locke, Shaftesbury, Platner,

---

21 Andrew Bowie, *Aesthetics and Subjectivity from Kant to Nietzsche* (Manchester: Manchester University Press, 1990), 4.
22 Recently republished as: Friedrich Schiller, *Schillers Pitaval: Merkwürdige Rechtsfälle als ein Beitrag zur Geschichte der Menschheit, verfaßt, bearbeitet und herausgegeben von Friedrich Schiller*, ed. Oliver Tekolf, with intro. Hans Magnus Enzensberger (Frankfurt: Eichborn, 2005).

Herder and especially Ferguson's *Institutes of Moral Philosophy*, which was translated by Christian Garve into German in 1775, assume particular importance. It is indeed *der ganze Mensch*, the "whole person," the human being as a sensuous and rational being which emerges here as the point of departure for all human science. Safranski also points to the significance of the emergence of *Erfahrungsseelenkunde* and the publication of the first journal of "empirical psychology," *Gnothi Sauton. Magazin zur Erfahrungsseelenkunde* (1783–1793); the meticulous observation of individual cases, detection of the specific origins of mental dysfunction and criminality, and a sense of humanity were key forces in the production of this journal.[23] Safranski writes: "Schiller, who must learn to do autopsies, becomes, as regards the human soul, a vivisecting and experimental psychologist. His work on *Die Räuber* which he begins in 1777 serves precisely such a human psychology."[24]

According to Safranski, Schiller read the cadet Grammont's case as a philosophical, one might even say, existential crisis culminating in a nihilistic depression resulting from the disastrous convergence of the rigid discipline of the Karlsschule, the new empiricism, speculative metaphysical philosophy, and the persistence of excessive pietistic sentimentality or *Schwärmerei*. Safranski even goes so far as to suggest that Grammont's "illness" is in effect Schiller's, except that Schiller had the mental and emotional reserves to be able to stand up to the affliction, essentially sublimating and transforming his own spiritual crisis into a form of literature[25] – his protocol of Grammont's demise.

Frederick Beiser's *Schiller as Philosopher: A Re-Examination* (2005) presents a forceful re-interpretation of the *Aesthetic Letters* as "an essentially political work." For Beiser, Schiller's text "stands in the modern republican tradition of Machiavelli, Rousseau, Montesquieu, and Ferguson."[26] In contrast to older

---

[23] Rüdiger Safranski, *Friedrich Schiller oder die Erfindung des Deutschen Idealismus* (München and Wien: Carl Hanser Verlag, 2004), 76: "Aber die Begeisterung des Ausdrucks soll die Kraft zur analytischen Distanz nicht mindern. Die Seele mag sich ausdrücken, doch soll sie nicht die Disziplin einer 'Erfahrungsseelenkunde' – eine Bezeichnung, die Abel von Karl Philipp Moritz übernimmt – scheuen."

[24] Safranski, *Friedrich Schiller*, 76: "Schiller, der lernen muss, Leichen zu öffnen, wird, was die Seele betrifft, zum sezierenden und experimentierenden Psychologen. Seine Arbeit an den *Räubern*, mit der er 1777 beginnt, dient solcher Seelenkunde."

[25] Safranski, *Friedrich Schiller*, 96–98. As Schiller reports on the Cadet, the authorities become suspicious of Schiller and suspect him of complicity; they even go as far as to tell Grammont that he cannot trust Schiller. Together, in a sense, they are placed under surveillance.

[26] Frederick C. Beiser, *Schiller as Philosopher: A Re-Examination* (Oxford: Oxford University Press, 2005), 120.

readings that claim that Schiller's text merely codifies Kantian autonomy aesthetics and buries all individuality in the species-being of "mankind" and thus neglects what is most personal and communicative about the aesthetic experience itself, Beiser asserts:

> It is of the first importance to note that Schiller thinks that it is the task of culture to preserve the realm of individuality and variety as much as that of universality and unity [...] the importance of the realm of individuality – its intrinsic value and status as an end in itself – is stressed in an essentially political context in Letter IV. It is in this insistence upon the intrinsic value of individuality that Schiller begins to take one of his more important steps beyond Kant, and anticipate the later romantic ethic of Schlegel and Schleiermacher.[27]

This rehabilitation of individuality can be traced, I would suggest, to Schiller's concern for the particular case in his earliest medical studies, for it is in this context that Schiller first encounters the difficult negotiation between the individual psycho-physiological human being and the laws of nature and the state, between the particular and the general; it is here that the conflict between what ought to be and what actually is, the ideal and the real, becomes most pressing.

Despite the fine contributions of Harald Neumeyer,[28] Košenina,[29] and others in recent years on the legal-medical-psychological case in Schiller's work and the *Spätaufklärung* more generally, the aesthetic dimensions of Schiller's concern, that is, how the case figures in the overall structure of his aesthetic thought, the unique aesthetic merits and potentiality of the case, have not received the attention they deserve. This is all the more curious since Schiller's aesthetic and medical-psychological interests are clearly fused in such dramatic works as *The Robbers* (1781), as has been forcefully shown in the work of Wolfgang Riedel. According to Riedel, the "soul" in late eighteenth century had been transformed into a stage of radical heteronomous forces, "into a being that is relegated almost helplessly to the instincts and the affects (the 'dark ideas,' '*ideae obscurae*') and to the body (the brain and the nervous-

---

[27] Beiser, *Schiller as Philosopher*, 140.
[28] Harald Neumeyer, "'Schwarze Seelen': Rechts-Fall-Geschichten bei Pitaval, Schiller, Niethammer und Feuerbach," *Internationales Archiv der Sozialgeschichte der deutschen Literatur* 31.1 (2006): 101–132.
[29] Košenina, "Tiefere Blicke in das Menschenherz," 383–395. On Schiller, see also: Klaus Oettinger, "Schillers Erzählung 'Der Verbrecher aus verlorener Ehre,'" *Jahrbuch der deutschen Schillergesellschaft* 16 (1972): 266–276; Dainat: "Der Unglückliche Mörder," 517–541; and Gonthier-Louis Fink, "Théologie, psychologie et sociologie du crime. Le conte moral de Schubart à Schiller," *Recherches germaniques* 6 (1976): 55–111.

system)."³⁰ Riedel is clear about the effects of such dependency and contamination: "In all of these 'heteronomies of the soul' it is a matter of things that could not be adequately described within the framework of 'rational psychology,' namely, the interactions and entanglements of soul and body, psychology and physiology."³¹ Finally, in a decisive article,³² Košenina has countered the deeply entrenched view in German literary history since Büchner that Schiller had operated with idealized types, not with – as Büchner in his realistic excavation of the madness of Lenz – "human beings of flesh and blood."³³ The irony is that Büchner's critique of idealist aesthetics in *Lenz* would have surely gained the praise of the realist Schiller, who, in the preface to *The Robbers* of 1782, demanded that (dramatic) literature show "vice together with its entire inner mechanism," to "catch the soul in its most secret operations," to reveal "evil in its naked heinousness."³⁴ As Košenina so aptly demonstrates, Schiller makes the shift from a merely mimetic, descriptive practice of depicting the crime to signifying the internal world of the person in their own words – "the passions and most secret movements of the heart in the person's own utterances" – as he states in the repressed preface of 1781.³⁵

In the following, using these recent re-evaluations of Schiller as my basis, I argue that Schiller's sustained concern for the specificity and uniqueness of the case has been marginalized in the discussion of his aesthetics, and that conversely discussions of the "case" in Schiller have underestimated the properly aesthetic aspects of the "case" – the "case" as the bearer of another, more direct, immediate, and more individualized form of cognition focused on the

---

[30] Wolfgang Riedel, "Die anthropologische Wende: Schillers Modernität" in: *Friedrich Schiller. Die Realität des Idealisten,* ed. Hans Feger (Heidelberg: Universitätsverlag Winter 2006), 42: "in ein Wesen, das nahezu hilflos der Triebe und Affekte, des Unbewussten (der 'dunklen Ideen,' 'ideae obscurae') und des Körpers (des Gehirns und des Nervensystems) ausgeliefert ist"; emphasis mine.

[31] Riedel, "Die anthropologische Wende: Schillers Modernität," 43: "In all diesen 'Heteronomien der Seele' geht es um etwas, was im Paradigma der 'rationalen Psychologie' nicht konsistent beschreibbar war, nämlich um Interaktionen und Verschränkungen von Seele und Körper, von Psychologie und Physiologie."

[32] Alexander Košenina, "Schiller und die Tradition der (kriminal)psychologischen Fallgeschichte bei Goethe, Meißner, Moritz und Spieß," in *Friedrich Schiller und Europa: Ästhetik, Politik, Geschichte,* ed. Alice Staskova (Heidelberg: Winter, 2007), 119–139.

[33] Georg Büchner, "Brief an die Familie vom 28. Juli 1835," in: *Sämtliche Werke, Briefe und Dokumente,* ed. Henri Poschmann (Frankfurt: Deutsche Klassiker Verlag, 1999), 411.

[34] Friedrich Schiller, *Werke und Briefe in zwolf Bänden,* ed. Otto Dann et al. (Frankfurt: Suhrkamp/Insel, 1992–2004), vol. 8, 59–72.

[35] Košenina, "Schiller und die Tradition der (kriminal)psychologischen Fallgeschichte bei Goethe, Meißner, Moritz und Spieß," 123.

particular – even in the recent literature that presents the new "realist" Schiller. I will seek through some textual examples to show why the case is highly significant for Schiller's aesthetic theory and conversely, how aesthetic concerns impinge on the *literary* presentation of the case history. Specifically, I suggest that it turns on a notion of justice, and in a double sense: first, of doing justice to the uniqueness of the individual person, and further, Schiller's enduring concern of ensuring legal-political justice for the individual human being – namely the sympathetic understanding of the mitigating circumstances and events that create the conditions for violence, crime, and madness in any individual instance or situation. This latter concern, motivated and guided by a moral and juridical intent to reform society and the state, is also latent in the transformation Schiller articulates with respect to the aesthetic state in the *Aesthetic Letters*. In a sense, the case becomes an incommensurable example of the aesthetic as it is the individual and individualizing instance for which we have, as in Immanuel Kant's critique of aesthetic judgment, no adequate concept, rule, or law. In Kant, however, the aesthetic experience must be disinterested and disengaged from all worldly and mundane concerns and turns solely on the representational powers of the subject in order to guarantee the maximum free play of the imagination. And while Kant offered a possible argument to bridge the aesthetic and the moral in the famous Paragraph 59 of the *Critique of Judgment* – the aesthetic gives us a "symbolic hypotyposis" or *sensuous example of the morally good* – Kant stated that this occurred "without too violent a leap,"[36] and much of post-Kantian philosophy can be read as an attempt to mend the fissure Kant himself had opened up.[37]

For Schiller, there is a decidedly moral and juridical interest or concern that enters into any consideration of the individual case. The aesthetic "presentation" of the case, the transformation of the case into literature, an aesthetic object, and its reception, therefore cannot be entirely "free" or "autonomous" in the strict sense, and this for two reasons: first, the case itself, even as it resists easy categorization or classification, seems to call out for understanding or a way to make sense out of it. Second, the reader of the individual case responds to it not only cognitively, expanding their knowledge of human thought and action, but also viscerally, feeling the affliction of the other, and translating this into empathy and into a deeper and fuller understanding of the pitfalls of the human condition. Here resides the actual aesthetic import of the case: its

---
[36] Immanuel Kant, *Kritik der Urteilskraft*, in *Werke in zwölf Bänden* (Frankfurt a.M.: Suhrkamp, 1977), 297: "ohne einen zu gewaltsamen Sprung."
[37] Most recently Michel Chaouli, *Thinking with Kant's Critique of Judgment* (Cambridge, MA: Harvard University Press, 2017), 98.

"reality" or the force of the "real" within it should effect a more textured sense of who and what we are, of the discrepancy between the existing law and true justice, and the psycho-physiological and socio-historical determinants of human action and behavior.

To establish the centrality of case from the aesthetic – and not merely psychological, epistemological, or legal – point of view, we begin at the end, with the *Letters on the Aesthetic Education of Man* (1795), and work backwards. We can, using the basis provided by Beiser's reading of the *Aesthetic Letters*, make the case that the fourth letter of Schiller's text is essentially an attempt to recapture or rehabilitate the individuality of the individual. It states that every individual person harbors the ideal human being within them, the absolute unity of form and material; to fully actualize this, Schiller says, is nothing less than the task (*Aufgabe*) of human existence. This actualization of this mediation of matter and form is, if we follow the argument, the State (*Staat*). If it is to be legitimate and truly just in the sense of fully recognizing both the individual as well as humankind, the state must do justice to both the objective/generic and the subjective/individual character – the specificity of the individual. As Schiller writes, "it should also honor the subjective and specific character in the individuals."[38] Schiller distinguishes between the *mechanical*, the (merely) aesthetic and the pedagogical-political artist; only the latter is truly capable of achieving the highest task (*Aufgabe*) of art. Only in the reciprocity and the balance of objective and subjective, generic and specific, law and inclination, can the true unity of the State be sought; if this is achieved, Schiller argues, "he will be able to preserve this uniqueness (individuality) however much he may universalize his conduct."[39] As Benjamin Bennett has cogently argued: "What is at stake [...] is whether we human beings shall be able to have in the first place, each of us, his or her own relatively unfettered, personal, particular, individual being."[40] For Schiller, the task of aesthetics is to not merely to *restore*, but to create the conditions of the individuality of the individual—as Schiller states it, "the individuality of the case" (*die Individualität des Falls*),[41] i.e., to produce a state in which our irreducible singularity (*Eigenthümlichkeit*) can be

---

38 *SW*, 5:577: "er soll auch den subjektiven und spezifischen Charakter in den Individuen ehren."
39 *SW*, 5:578: "so wird sich auch bei der höchsten Universalisierung seines Betragens seine Eigentümlichkeit retten."
40 Benjamin Bennett, "The Irrelevance of Aesthetics and the De-Theorizing of Self in 'Classical' Weimar," in *The Camden History of German Literature. The Literature of Weimar Classicism*, ed. Simon Richter (Rochester: Camden House, 2001), vol. 7, 298.
41 *SW*, 5:866.

preserved and even enhanced, precisely in the face of "universal social and moral claims on us."[42] The entwinement of the physical and the mental, of body and soul, and of medicine and literature is so powerful in the emergence of aesthetics that any attempt to grasp the case history outside of this dual configuration of singularity and universality is bound to fail. For Schiller, as for the later eighteenth century as a whole, aesthetics is a child of a psychophysiological mode of experiencing unclear and obscure impressions and sensations, and somehow bringing these to consciousness and representation without succumbing to the analytical dissection of the understanding, so that they can be processed in such a way as to preserve the manifold sensuous content.[43] It is not a matter of making them clear and distinct, but of allowing them their own, peculiar indeterminacy and not trying to subsume them under an already existing concept.

We might say, with other words, if this particularity – the individuality of the individual – is injured, subsumed, or lost, the state will have lost its legitimacy, that is, its ability to function as the true and real *Representant* of the full human being. The preservation of *particularity* – not abstract, theoretical subjectivity – but the unique pairing of *Person* and *Zustand* in the specific individual appears here as the *sine qua non* of justice and the foundation of any truly representative, legitimate state.

Fast forward now to Letters 11 and 12 of the *Aesthetic Letters*, just before the infamous formal splitting or stylized rupture of the instincts or *Triebe*, and Schiller's famous positing of the third term – free-play (*freies Spiel*) – to reconcile form and matter, freedom and necessity. Here, Schiller again underscores the requirement of the individuality of case as a vital component of the true, actual, full human being: distinguishing between the *Person*, which is what endures (*das Bleibende*), and the *conditions* (*Zustand*) of the person, which is always in flux (*das Wechselnde*). Brought to the precision of Schiller's formulation, we arrive at the distinction between freedom, the absolute self-grounding of the person as the persistent self on the one hand, and condition, particularity, temporality, as the power of changing representations on the other hand:

> Every condition, every particular entity emerges in time, and the human being, as a phenomenon, must have a beginning, even though the pure intelligence in him is eternal. Without time, that is, without becoming, the human being would never become

---

[42] Bennett, "Irrelevance of Aesthetics," 298.
[43] David E. Wellbery, *Laocoon: Semiotics and Aesthetics in the Age of Reason* (Cambridge: Cambridge University Press, 1984).

a particular person; his personality would exist as a disposition, but not as an actual fact. Only in the series of his representations does the persistent "I" itself become a particular phenomenon and achieve appearance.[44]

Schiller's "resolution" of this opposition is that the persistent "I" must actively form the material, give structure to the world, actively maintaining and positing the "I" precisely in the face of the ever-shifting demands of reality. This, we might say, is the "healthy" or "normal" response to the challenge of existence; if one does not ascend to the level of actively forming time and reality, one remains a mere object, simply a part of the world, passive material to be determined: "As long as the human being simply senses, and desires, and acts according to this desire, it is nothing more than a part of the world."[45] In the psychological case, the human being is not grasped in the sphere of freedom, of actively forming the world, but as a piece of the world, subject to the alternating circumstances of reality.

Schiller recognizes that the opposition of the *Triebe* also involves an accentuation or emphasis of cases: "If the first [instinct] only provides cases, the other provides laws."[46] Mediation of the individual case with the law means that neither is negated and that both will somehow be "preserved." Not by chance does Schiller mention insanity and madness precisely at this point as the loss of the *Person*, which he names in the text explicitly: *ausser sich sein*. Being "outside of oneself," is the exceptional "case," the anomaly, in which the individual as *Person*, as that which remains and endures behind the ever changing situation or condition of existence, must be reconciled with the law. This is where Schiller's mediation must prove its mettle. If such individuality is not simply to be buried under the iron law, subsumed under a concept, or subjugated to a universal, some form of mitigation or reconciliation between the demands of the law and the dignity of the specific individual must occur in order for there to be "true justice."

In Letter 14, the "case" appears again, but now as important individual *instances* that, in a striking similarity to Kant, must provide a *sensible intuition* of actualized humanity: "If there were cases in which the human being could

---

[44] *SW*, 5:602: "Aller Zustand aber, alles bestimmte Dasein entsteht in der Zeit, und so muss also der Mensch, als Phänomen, einen Anfang nehmen, obgleich die reine Intelligenz in ihm ewig ist. Ohne die Zeit, das heißt, ohne es zu werden, würde er nie ein bestimmtes Wesen sein; seine Persönlichkeit würde zwar in der Anlage, aber nicht in der Tat existieren. Nur durch die Folge seiner Vorstellungen wird das beharrliche Ich sich selbst zur Erscheinung."
[45] *SW*, 5:603: "Solange er bloß empfindet, bloß begehrt, und aus bloßer Begierde wirkt ist er noch weiter nichts als Welt."
[46] *SW*, 5:605: "Wenn der erste [*Trieb*] nur *Fälle macht*, so gibt der andere Gesetze."

have this double experience, in which it could simultaneously be aware of and sense its freedom and its concrete, temporal existence, it would have in such cases, and unfortunately only in such cases, a complete intuition of its own humanity."[47] Only in the individual cases do we get the tangible intuition of the full sense of humanity; only in individual cases do we experience the concrete sense of the complete human being in its humanity. Here, the existence of individual "cases," not as mere isolated *particulars*, but as actual historico-temporal experiences of mediation, are requisite as instances of precisely the envisioned aesthetic state in which individuality and universality, inclination and law, and material and form are continually mediated with one another.

We shall now turn to the epistemic priority and advantage of the case history in Schiller. In the *Preface* to the edition he produced of Pitaval's *Causes célèbres et interessantes* (1734–1743), titled *Merkwürdige Rechtsfälle als ein Beitrag zur Geschichte der Menschheit* of 1792,[48] and in the introductory paragraphs of the case history *Der Verbrecher aus verlorener Ehre* (1786),[49] one can discern the rudiments of Schiller's aesthetics of the case. First, consider Schiller's *Preface* to his edition of Pitaval's *Merkwürdige Rechtsfälle*. Schiller stresses both the pragmatic and epistemological value of writing and reading case-histories; it is a narrative that entertains, one which "contains a good deal of reality for the understanding," "it distributes seeds of useful knowledge and serves to direct the reflection of the reader to valuable purposes"[50];

---

47 *SW*, 5:612: "Gäbe es aber Fälle, wo er (der Mensch) diese doppelte Erfahrung zugleich machte, wo er sich zugleich seiner Freiheit bewusst würde und sein Dasein empfände, so hätte er in diesen Fällen, und schlechterdings nur in diesen eine vollständige Anschauung seiner Menschlichkeit."
48 Now available in a separate edition: Tekolf, ed., *Schillers Pitaval*.
49 According to existing scholarship, the consensus is that Schiller heard the tale of the Sonnenwirth from his teacher at the Karlsschule Jacob Friedrich Abel, who himself edited a collection of case histories *Sammlung und Erklärung merkwürdiger Erscheinungen aus dem menschlichen Leben* (1787), including the case Schiller used for his story. Abel had first hand knowledge of the case since his father was actually the magistrate who arrested and charged the perpetrator Christian Wolf. While Schiller might have heard the story from Abel in the course of his studies, Minor's hypothesis that Schiller's literary version was based on Abel's was shown to be false; rather, Abel seems to have borrowed from Schiller's version in *Thalia* 1.2 (1786): 20–58, as one of his textual bases. See: Helmut Koopmann, *Schiller-Kommentar* (München: Winkler, 1969), vol. 1, 255. See also: Jacob Friedrich Abel, *Karlsschul-Schriften. Eine Quellenedition zum Philosophieunterricht an der Stuttgarter Karlsschule (1773–1782). Mit Einleitung, Übersetzung, Kommentar und Bibliographie*, ed. Wolfgang Riedel (Würzburg: Königshausen & Neumann, 1995), 620.
50 *SW*, 5:865: "streut es den Samen nützlicher Kenntnisse aus, dient dazu, das Nachdenken des Lesers auf würdige Zwecke zu richten."

"One gets a glimpse of the human being in the most intricate situations, which tense the expectation, and whose resolution provides the reader's power of divination with a pleasant activity"[51]; "The secret play of passion unfolds right in front of our eyes."[52] Case histories therefore have pedagogic, epistemological, and moral-political-juridical value; they awaken our interest and confront us with a question and enjoin the reader on the interesting task of having to "resolve" an issue, a question, or a problem. The case history is an analogue to the criminal trial, both in its manner of presentation as well as the way in which it engages the reader, and superior to even the most complete historical narrative (*Geschichtserzählung*):

> Add to this the fact that the more intricate and laborious juridical procedure is far more capable of bringing to light the hidden motivational causes of human action than is the case in other instances, and while the most complete historical narrative often leaves us dissatisfied concerning the true motives and the final reasons of the acting players, the *criminal trial* often reveals to us the innermost thoughts and the most obscure fabric of malice.[53]

Schiller also mentions knowledge of the law and jurisprudence gained through the study of such cases: "This important victory for human knowledge and the treatment of human beings is made even more powerful by the increased insights into the law which are strewn throughout them, and which gain clarity and interest through the individuality of the case in which one sees them applied."[54] Finally, and perhaps most importantly, Schiller attributes a political significance to the case. He sees in the elucidation of the individual case the performance of a "republican freedom of the reader" (*republikanische Freiheit des Lesers/des lesenden Publikums*), that is, the right of the readers themselves

---

51 *SW*, 5:865: "Man erblickt den Menschen hier in den verwickeltesten Lagen, welche die ganze Erwartung spannen, und deren Auflösung der Divinationsgabe des Lesers eine angenehme Beschäftigung gibt."
52 *SW*, 5:865: "Das geheime Spiel der Leidenschaft entfaltet sich vor unseren Augen."
53 *SW*, 5:866; emphasis in the original: "Dazu kommt, dass der umständlichere Rechtsgang die geheimen Bewegursachen menschlicher Handlungen weit ins Klare zu bringen fähig ist, als es sonst geschieht, und wenn die vollständigste Geschichtserzählung uns über die letzten Gründe einer Begebenheit, über die wahren Motive der handelnden Spieler oft unbefriedigt lässt, so enthüllt uns oft ein *Kriminalprozess* das Innerste der Gedanken und bringt das versteckteste Gewebe der Bosheit an den Tag."
54 *SW*, 5:866: "Dieser wichtiger Gewinn für Menschenkenntniss und Menschenbehandlung [...] wird um ein Großes noch durch die vielen Rechstkenntnisse erhöht, die darinn ausgestreut werden, und die durch die Individualität des Falles, auf den man sie angewendet sieht, Klarheit und Interesse erhalten."

to evaluate, judge, and decide.⁵⁵ It is therefore not merely a matter of the interesting and valuable content, and how the cases are presented, that is, the *Behandlungsart*, but the performative force of the case. In the *Vorrede* to *Merkwürdige Rechtsfälle*, Schiller insists that the authors have maintained "the dubiousness of the decision, which often puts the judge on the spot, and communicate this to the reader by mobilizing for each of the opposing parties the same care and the same great art."⁵⁶ In other words, they have not determined the outcome in advance (*vorgreifen*); doubt, ambiguity, and multi-perspicacity have been preserved; the reader themself is placed not merely in the double role of perpetrator and victim,⁵⁷ but rather in multiple roles of sympathetic reader, thoughtful citizen, witness, victim, the public, advocate, judge, and jury. The full complexity and multi-dimensionality of the case is crucial to this form of narrative and its aesthetic force to induce the public to become more careful readers and more sensitive, sympathetic judges, and this in a time, as has often been noted, when motive and circumstances were supposedly irrelevant, at least for the state and juridical apparatus, to the execution of the law, which was traditionally simply the application of a rule to a specific case.⁵⁸ At this historical moment, however, the focal emphasis of psychologically minded physicians, jurists, and reformers shifts from the deed itself to the perpetrator of the deed, and the accountability (*Zurechnungsfähigkeit*) and criminal responsibility (*Schuldfähigkeit*) of the alleged perpetrator. The juridical case sought to establish not merely *what* had occurred, but the motive and the circumstances of the delinquent.⁵⁹ Schiller is emblematic for this transformation, interested precisely in the etiology of pathology, the determination of the conditions, or the causes, of the idiosyncratic turn towards psychological dissolution, criminality, and transgression.

The introductory remarks of *Criminal of Lost Honor* focus in on the disclosure of the *conditions and causes* of the particular act, not on the abstract value of the aesthetic experience of the occurrence or the deed *per se*, but rather on the specific conditions, circumstances, and influences of and on the soul. As Schiller writes in the introductory remarks to the early version published in *Thalia*, the researcher of the human soul is interested not so much in

---

55 See Kosênina, "'Tiefere Blicke in das Menschenherz': Schiller und Pitaval," 392–393.
56 *SW*, 5:866: "die Zweifelhaftigkeit der Entscheidung, welche oft den Richter in Verlegenheit setzt, auch dem Leser mitzuteilen, indem sie für beide entgegengesetzte Parteien gleiche Sorgfalt und gleich grosse Kunst aufbieten."
57 Košenina, "'Tiefere Blicke in das Menschenherz,'" 393–394.
58 Neumeyer, "'Schwarze Seelen,'" 102.
59 Harald Neumeyer, "'Schwarze Seelen,'" 121–130.

the deed itself, but the thoughts of the deed, and even more importantly, the origins of those thoughts: "For us, there is far more in his thoughts than in his deeds, and even still more of value in the origins of those thoughts than in the consequences of those deeds."[60] It is only in the annals of the aberrations (*Verirrungen*) of human beings, how they, quite specifically, have deviated from the "norm" or become the subjects of cases, that the real lessons of morality, psychology, and the power of the state and the limits of such power can be learned according to Schiller. The central opposition here as in the introductory remarks to his edition of the *Pitaval* is between the "usual" or traditional method of treatment in history, which opens up a gap between the turbulent emotions of the historical subject or protagonist and the calm disposition of the reader, and thus cuts off every possibility of analogy and comparison, and a scientific, analytical approach that clearly traces all of the contributing factors of the crime. The criticized "historical" approach leads to the reduction of effect to mere curiosity or *Neugier*, the creation of dreamers, and a "usurpation" of the republican freedom of the reading public; and it is complicit in the bourgeois fiction of a radical discontinuity between virtue and vice, justice and injustice, good and bad, and right and wrong – a distinction that Schiller wishes to undermine.

Five distinct features of Schiller's aesthetics of case can thus be noted. First, the *Vorrang* or primacy of the case history over historical writing in Schiller's view. History is written in order to sway the emotions (*durch hinreissenden Vortrag*): "a gap remains between the historical subject and the reader...which excludes the possibility of comparison or analogy."[61] In this way, the connection between the reader and the subject is severed. Second, in a transformative movement away from the mute materiality of the deed, we are focused in the case instead on the thoughts, or, more precisely, on the "sources" of the thoughts (*Quellen seiner Gedanken*) and, even more to the point, "the constitution and placement of matters, as they surrounded the individual" (*die Beschaffenheit und Stellung der Dinge, welche einen solchen umgaben*).[62] Third, critics have often quoted the first part of Schiller's statement concerning the unchanging structure of the human soul, providing ammunition to the idealist reading that Schiller was indeed only concerned with the generalized species-being, but have failed to

---

60 Schiller, "Verbrecher aus Infamie," *Thalia* 1.2 (1786): 23; emphasis mine: "An seinen Gedanken liegt uns unendlich mehr als an seinen Thaten, und noch weit mehr an den Quellen dieser Gedanken, als an den Folgen jener Thaten."
61 *SW*, 5:14: "es bleibt eine Lücke zwischen dem historischen Subjekt und dem Leser...die alle Möglichkeit einer Vergleichung oder Analogie abschneidet."
62 *SW*, 5:15.

cite the rest of the sentence, or citing it incorrectly,[63] which is focused on the individual case, its particular instance and signature. This forms a direct link to Schiller's distinction, in Letter 11 of the *Aesthetic Letters*, between *Person* and *Zustand*, and the necessity of preserving *both* the self *and* the specificity of its ever-fluctuating conditions, its finite determinations, for any aesthetic mediation. Fourth, such a method or *Behandlungsart* would, according to Schiller, decrease the contempt, arrogance, and the proud and false sense of security with which, he says, the self-righteous look down upon the accused, thinking they are made of different blood; such a consideration would diminish the false distance between the judge, the public and the fallen, the virtuous and the criminal, the reader and the historical subject, and allow us to learn to see, to paraphrase the prefatory remarks to *Verbrecher*, "wisdom and folly, vice and virtue in *one* cradle together."[64] Fifth, cases are based on real individuals and real events. The narrative *Verbrecher* is subtitled "a true story" (*eine wahre Geschichte*)[65] – a true story – and in opposition to the drama and the novel, as Schiller notes in the Preface to *Merkwürdige Rechtsfälle*, cases have the advantage or *Vorzug* of historical truth – "historische Wahrheit"[66] – over fiction and drama. Of course, what this does not address is precisely the question of what occurs when an actual, historical case history is taken up, appropriated, and transformed into an aesthetic work, a work of *literature*.

A brief comparison of Abel's "actual" case history *Life-History of Friedrich Schwan*[67] and Schiller's literary rendition of the same case in *Criminal of Lost Honor* might be useful to discern the specifically aesthetic features of the literary stylization in the sense we have presented at the outset of this essay: namely, the preservation, even furtherance, of a sense of the uniqueness and foregrounding the individuality of the individual in the face of increasing reduction and subsumption under general rules and laws which, for Schiller, was symptomatic of modernity.

---

63 Košenina's otherwise fine analysis (2005) stumbles here: he cites the passage, but gets the second part wrong. The sentence reads: "Er [der Menschenforscher, RL] sucht sie in der unveränderlichen Struktur der menschlichen Seele und in den *veränderlichen* (emphasis mine) Bedingungen, welche sie von aussen bestimmten" (*SW*, 5:15), not, as Košenina cites, "*unveränderlichen* Bedingungen." See: Košenina, "Tiefere Blicke," 393.
64 *SW*, 5:15: "Weisheit und Torheit, Laster und Tugend in *einer* Wiege beisammen."
65 *SW*, 5:14.
66 *SW*, 5:865.
67 Abel, *Eine Quellenedition zum Philosophie unterricht an der Stuttgarter Karlsschule (1773–1782)*.

The first significant difference to note is that Schiller invents a new early history of the Sonnenwirth. His father is dead,[68] and Wolf must assist the mother in the hopeless family business. In Abel's more "reality-based" case history, we witness an original, extreme aggressivity and belligerence in the young boy, especially within the small, but intact familial context, and more specifically towards the father. In Abel's case history, recourse is made several times to an inherent, intrinsic corruption of the soul (*Verderbnis der Seele*): "To this day a number of examples are told in the place of his birth about this early vitiation of his soul"; "Yet even in such a vitiated soul a new vice could only strike roots slowly and gradually."[69] In the place of this assumption of an inherent propensity to crime, Schiller, similar to the way in which he depicts Franz Moor in *The Robbers* as being physically disfigured and repulsive,[70] focuses on Schwan's bodily deformity and his awkward, compensatory gestures and behaviors, and his exclusion or pariah status: "Nature had failed with respect to his body. A small, non-descript figure, nappy, unpleasantly dark hair, a flat-pressed nose and a swollen upper lip, which in addition had been jarred out of place by the kick of a horse – this all gave him a contrary look that repulsed all women and gave plenty of ammunition for the jokes of his comrades."[71]

The shift from an inalterable, inherent corruption or depravity of the soul (*Verderbnis der Seele*) – in some sense still according to the traditional attribution of an original sin, a basic spiritual flaw or error irreparably engraved in the soul – to the externality of "chance" appearance, to awkward and misguided behaviors, and the attendant social consequences of exclusion and rejection is significant: it makes the criminal a victim of a social world. In Abel's case history, based on eyewitness interactions with the author and the reports of several "reliable" men, the worsening of Schwan's situation was a necessary outgrowth of a fundamentally disturbed soul.

---

68 *SW*, 5:16.
69 Abel, *Eine Quellenedition zum Philosophie unterricht an der Stuttgarter Karlsschule (1773–1782)*. All quotes of Abel from this edition. "Noch werden in seinem Geburtsort eine Menge von Beyspielen erzählt, die diese frühe Verderbnis seiner Seele erweisen"; "Indessen konnte (zur Freude jedes Menschenfreundes schreibe ich diese Beobachtung nieder) auch in einer so verdorbenen Seele ein neues Laster doch nur langsam und allmählig sich einwurzeln."
70 See Riedel, "Die anthropologische Wende: Schillers Modernität," 35–60.
71 *SW*, 5:16: "Die Natur hatte seinen Körper verabsäumt. Eine kleine unscheinbare Figur, krauses Haar von einer unangenehmen Schwarze, eine plattgedrückte Nase und eine geschwollene Oberlippe, welche noch überdies durch den Schlag eines Pferdes aus ihrer Richtung gewichen war, gaben seinem Anblick eine Widrigkeit, welche alle Weiber von ihm zurückscheuchte und dem Witz seiner Kameraden eine reichliche Nahrung darbot."

In Schiller's narrative, by contrast, Wolf is ruthlessly pursued by the apprentice of the Förster, Robert, who also happens to be the suitor of the girl Wolf had fallen in love with. The decisive transformation occurs when the Sonnenwirth is incarcerated for the third time, sentenced to hard labor in a fortress. The Sonnenwirth becomes a *true* criminal. Schiller marks this transformation in the soul of the perpetrator with great intensity and precision, and it is here that we receive a first-person narrative, which allows the standpoint of the protagonist himself to emerge for the first time:

> The mandate against poaching required a solemn and exemplary retribution, and Wolf was sentenced, with the sign of the gallows burned into his back, to three years hard labor at the fortress [...] This time also passed, and he departed the fortress – but a very different person than as he had arrived. Here, a new era in his life begins; one can listen to him, as he himself confessed to his spiritual council and before the court: "I entered the fortress," he said, "as a confused person and left it as a criminal; I had still retained something in the world that was of value to me, but now my pride bent under the disgrace. When I was brought to the fortress, they locked me in with twenty-three other prisoners, among whom there were two murderers, the rest alleged thieves and vagrants. I was mocked and ridiculed [...] the work was hard and tyrannical, my body became sickly, I needed compassion, and if I were to say it honestly, I needed sympathy, and this I had to purchase with the last remnant of my conscience. And so I got used to the most depraved and abominable, and in the last quarter-year, I had surpassed my mentors."[72]

The difference between Abel's case history and Schiller's literary-aesthetic rendition of the story could not be more profound: Abel explains Schwan's criminality through an original, fundamental, inborn flaw in his soul. His acts are a natural and necessary outgrowth of a naturally disturbed mind, a corrupted soul. Schiller, in contrast, clearly seeks to trace the origins of this criminality to

---

[72] *SW*, 5:18: "Das Mandat gegen die Wilddiebe bedurfte einer solennen und examplarischen Genugtuung, und Wolf ward verurteilt, das Zeichen des Galgens auf den Rücken gebrannt drei Jahre auf der Festung zu arbeiten [...] Auch dies Periode verlief, und er ging von der Festung – aber ganz anders, als er dahin gekommen war. Hier fängt eine neue Epoche in seinem Leben an; man höre ihn selbst, wie er nachher gegen seinen geistigen Beistand und vor Gericht bekannt hat. 'Ich betrat die Festung', sagte er, 'als ein Verirrter und verliess sie als ein Lotterbube. Ich hatte noch etwas in der Welt gehabt, das mir teuer war, und mein Stolz krümmte sich unter der Schande. Wie ich auf die Festung gebracht war, sperrte man mich zu dreiundzwanzig Gefangenen ein, unter denen zwei Mörder und die übrigen alle berüchtigte Diebe und Vagabunden waren. Man verhöhnte mich [...] Die Arbeit war hart und tyrannisch, mein Körper kränklich, ich brauchte Beistand, und wenn ich es aufrichtig sagen soll, ich brauchte Bedaurung, und diese musste ich mit dem letzten Ueberrest meines Gewissens erkaufen. So gewöhnte ich mich endlich an das Abscheulichste, und im letzten vierteljahr hatte ich meine Lehrmeister übertroffen.'"

the absence of any empathetic understanding, the death of the father, the harsh labor of the *Festung*, the deterioration of the body, an implied self-prostitution (*diese musste ich mit dem letzten Ueberrest meines Gewissens erkaufen*) and, perhaps most importantly, being, quite literally, a "marked" man – "the sign of the gallows branded into his back."[73] The act and meaning of literally being marked and branded as a criminal is repeated as the Sonnenwirth returns to his town, only to be mocked by the children, excluded and banned by the populace: "Am I perhaps marked on my forehead," he asks himself; "The contempt shown to me by this young boy hurt me more that my three years of hard labor."[74] Schiller's genetic, historical-psychological method, focused on the marking that occurs in the interaction between the social world, the punishment system, and the internal psychological transformation of the Sonnenwirth, is diametrically opposed to Abel's presupposition of an original, inalterable mental dysfunction, a primordially deformed or corrupt soul: in Schiller's literary narrative, the external conditions become the internal state or *Zustand*. The consequences for aesthetics suggest that there is a dynamic interaction between the various causal agencies – social, political, and psychological forces must converge – in order to bring about the type of reflection Schiller aims at. Bringing the physical and the psychological, the moral, political, and social co-determinants into play as Schiller does heightens the reader's interest while pointing to important historical conditions. By contrast, Abel's assumption of an inalterable, original corruption of the soul *diminishes* the energy of conflicting forces, arresting the imagination of the reader in the fixity of a blind determinism.

Schiller's aesthetics has often been depicted as an idealist aesthetics of autonomy – idealizing both in its tendency to sublate the real conflicts and oppositions inherent in the real world, and idealizing in so far as it supposedly opts for the universal, the generic, the objective, and ultimately, the lawfulness of objective morality at the cost of the particular, the specific, the transitory, and the fluctuating. Our cursory look at some of the textual examples from 1786 until 1795 has shown, at the very least, that no account of Schiller's aesthetic is possible without sufficient note of the importance of case: to be precise, not the individual, but the particular admixture of *Person* and *Zustand* that inhabits each and every case. Using close reading, we were also able to point out two questionable assumptions regarding Schiller's aesthetic theory of the case:

---

[73] *SW*, 5:18: "das Zeichen des Galgens auf den Rücken gebrannt."
[74] *SW*, 5:19: "Bin ich denn irgendwo auf der Stirne gezeichnet? [...] Die Verachtung dieses Knaben schmerzte mich bitterer als dreijähriger Galiotendienst."

first, that it is aimed solely at the unchanging structure of human being, considered ahistorically and apart from all vicissitudes; and second, that the actual cases or experiential instances of the fleeting intuition of the mediation of form and material are not peripheral, but actually a condition of aesthetic experience without which we would have no tangible idea of the aesthetic process of mediation.

Neumeyer has argued that, from 1734 and Gayot Pitaval's *Causes célèbres* to 1811 and Anselm Feuerbach's collection of case-histories, the "souls of criminals" are "not 'produced,' nor do they 'develop.'"[75] That might hold true for the classical juridical case history (*Rechtsfallgeschichte*) and for the historical, legal-juridical apparatus, which still considered criminality as the necessary consequence of an originally corrupt, sinful soul. What is at stake in Schiller's aesthetics of case, however, is nothing less than the rupture of such a theory: for Schiller, cases are made, dark souls constructed. They are a function of complex constellations of character, circumstance, societal and economic conditions, and chance. Writing, reading, disseminating, and discussing them serve three decisive functions; aesthetic, epistemic, and legal-political. Aesthetics *per se* hinges on the preservation of the individuality of case. Without sufficient understanding of the specifics of case, a decisive element of aesthetic education is lost, its putative mediating power diminished. Epistemically, the individual case produces a specific form of knowledge superior to that of mere history. Finally, the case does justice to the individuality of the individual by grasping the societal and political conditions of the subjectification of the self.

Can we establish an *aesthetics* of the literary psychological-juridical case history? Would not such a theory subsume the case under a category or concept, and thereby contradict its very individuality, precisely what Schiller was advocating? Here I can only sketch the most rudimentary elements of such an aesthetics in Schiller's writings. The literary case history engenders first and foremost a knowledge of a particular individual that is at once sensuous and empathetic, combining both feeling (sympathy) and understanding, empathy for the perpetrator, and cognitive and conceptual recognition of the objective, material conditions, the law and the political power of the state. Second, the case induces a multi-perspicacity or requires the reader to occupy different stances or positions vis-à-vis the actual case. Such variability of perspective incites the reader to become more completely human, Schiller would argue, as we expand our field of judgment, perception, and sensibility. Third, the

---

75 Neumeyer, "Schwarze Seelen," 102: "schwarze Seele, sind von allem Anfang an einfach 'da' – in ihrer ganze Dichte, in ihrer ganzen Unhintergehbarkeit."

pedagogical impulse of aesthetic education – we cannot forget that Schiller understood this, not as mere abstract theory, but as a cultural-historical project – is advanced not merely in the careful and nuanced narration and edition of such cases, but in the thinking and feeling, the curiosity and moral self-reflection, the reading and discussion that such cases would spawn. Without the individual case, we would erroneously view, as Schiller writes in the prefatory remarks to the *Criminal*, "the unfortunate person, in the moment in which he performed the deed, as well as the one in which he atones for it [...] as a creature of a strange species, whose blood circulates differently than ours, whose will obeys different rules than ours."[76] With and through the case history, quite simply, we are able to see the accused as a "human being, just like ourselves."[77] The anthropological empiricism of *der ganze Mensch*, in the transmission and reading of the individual psychological case history was successfully translated into a hermeneutic aesthetics in which the human being has an expanded sense of humanity and a wider field of judgment precisely as a result of the exposure to the demands made by the specificity of the individual case. It concurs with the aesthetic as an educational and political project by assisting us to see the mentally ill and the criminally accused both as full human beings rather than as demons, monsters, or merely criminals, and as being "marked" socially and politically. The case thereby allowed the reader to realize an aspect of their individual humanity which, according to Schiller, was threatened in the increasing mechanization of society and law and the subjugation of the individual to the state.

Returning to Foucault's prescient description of modern governmentality and the "pastoral apparatus" that emerge in the second half of the eighteenth century, Schiller's narrative occurs precisely at the moment of the origins of the forensic medicine and the nascent *psychological* codification of mental illness. In the end, the Sonnenwirth Christian Wolf presents himself to the judicial apparatus, "comes to terms" with his deed, and, as Karl Moor in *The Robbers*, *rec*, recognizes the "law" as the higher instance of morality: the closing statement, delivered by free choice (*aus freier Wahl*), melds freedom and contingency, *Person* and *Zustand* in the declaration of self-identity: "I am the Sonnenwirth" (*Ich bin der Sonnenwirth*).[78] Discursively, this simple assertion states both the factual identification with what he has done and who he has

---

[76] *SW*, 5:14: "den Unglücklichen, der doch in eben der Stunde, wo er die Tat beging, so wie in der, wo er dafür büßet, [...] für ein Geschöpf fremder Gattung an, dessen Blut anders umläuft als das unsrige, dessen Wille anderen Regeln gehorcht als der unsrige."
[77] *SW*, 5:14: "Mensch war wie wir."
[78] *SW*, 5: 34.

become, but it also claims the acquiescence to the law as a self-realizing and autonomous decision. And the perpetrator, as was the case with Karl Moor in Schiller's *Robbers*, is "guided back into the path of the law" (*Der Verirrte tritt wieder in das Geleise des Gesetzes*), as Schiller expresses it in the Preface to the drama.[79] In both instances, the aberration, the anomaly, the outsider is brought back into the pastoral fold, "reconciled" with – or should we say relegated to? – his history, his fate, and the law. The conflict between the individual case and the juridical state apparatus is staged to underscore the inescapability of judgment, ours or otherwise.

At the end of the eighteenth century, such criminal psychological casehistories emerged as the "evidence" of forensic theory; they were included in or appended to textbooks and to theoretical works as "examples"; they became the equivalent of observations, and to a certain extent, experimentation, in the natural sciences. The psychological-juridical case history was a highly ambiguous genre of truth-telling, real history, empathy, education, control and surveillance, pastoral guidance and example; its aesthetic function was not merely to teach and move the reader, but to provide significant insight – in both the positive, edifying and specular, bio-political sense – into the "hidden mechanisms" of the human psyche, and to articulate the social and political determinants and construction of deviance and of criminality. By activating the capacity of judgment in the reader, and placing the reader in various positions, it sought to elevate and expand the discourse of and on those who had, through a combination of misfortune, suffering, socio-economic circumstances and bad choices, fallen between the cracks.

---

79 *SW*, 1:57.

7 A Doctor's Worst Fear: Marcus Herz's Case History of Karl Philipp Moritz *Etwas Psychologisch-Medizinisches. Moriz Krankengeschichte* (1793)

> In certain circumstances, fear and terror can bring some degree of solace for the patient.
> Stahl, *Concerning the Manifold Influence of the Movements of the Mind* (1695)[1]

> The hypochondriacs always believe they are dying, but they never quite get around to it.
> Unzer, *Der Arzt* (1769)[2]

Hysteria has its origins in the Sanskrit term for belly (*udarum*), the Proto-Indo-European *udero* (abdomen, womb, stomach), and the Greek *hystera* (womb). Since Hippocrates and Galen, it was understood as an illness or condition of women, imagined as a "wandering womb" as a result of a disturbance (childbirth), or the uterus becoming light and dry due to a lack of fluids that could be alleviated through a regular regimen of sex.[3] With the advent of Christianity, this movement of the womb became a manifestation of evil, a sign of the possession of the Devil.[4] In the Renaissance, Paracelsus, Johann Weyer and other scientifically-minded physicians sought to reclaim the disease from such demonization and show that hysteria was a "medical pathology" with natural causes that could be demonstrated just like any other illness.[5] When, in the second half of the seventeenth century, autopsies were performed on women who were thought to

---

[1] Georg Ernst Stahl, "Über den mannigfaltigen Einfluss der Gemüthsbewegungen auf den menschlichen Körper," in *Sudhoffs Klassiker der Medizin* (Leipzig: Johann Ambrosius Barth, 1961), vol. 36, 33.
[2] Johann August Unzer, ed., *Der Arzt. Eine medicinische Wochenschrift* (Leipzig: Berth, 1769), vol. 1, 346.
[3] Helen King, "Once Upon a Text: Hysteria from Hippocrates," in *Hysteria beyond Freud*, edited by Sander L. Gilman et al. (Berkeley and Los Angeles: University of California Press, 1993), 3–90.
[4] Marc S. Micale, *Approaching Hysteria: Disease and Interpretations* (Princeton, NJ: Princeton University Press, 1995), 20.
[5] Micale, *Approaching Hysteria*, 21–22. Annemarie and Werner Leibrand suggested in 1975 that Paracelsus had in fact issued in a "Copernican Revolution" in the understanding of hysteria: Annemarie Leibrand and Werner Leibrand, "Die 'kopernikanische Wende' des Hysteriebegriffs bei Paracelsus," in *Paracelsus: Werk und Wirkung*, ed. Sepp Domandl (Wien: WGO, 1975), 125–132.

suffer from the affliction and no uterine pathology could be found, a neuropsychological model of hysteria emerged in the writings of physicians like Thomas Willis (1621–1675) and Thomas Sydenham (1624–1689). Willis wrote a treatise in 1670 on the causes of hysteria and hypochondria, dismissing the notion of the "wandering womb," and locating the cause of hysteria in the brain.[6] Willis was also the first to observe that men could also be subject to hysteric fits and distemper. Sydenham in particular was the first great early modern physician to demand strict, natural scientific observation and clinical practice in the identification and treatment of hysteria. Contrary to Willis, a mechanist for whom animal spirits were "vaporized," the blood circulating the "animal liquor" or nervous fluids flowing through tubes to the brain, hysteria was for Sydenham "a farrago of disorderly and irregular phenomena,"[7] an imbalance of the mind-body relationship, whereby the animal spirits would leave their proper station and invade or possess a vulnerable site such as the stomach, the throat, the eyes, or the limbs; hysteria was "a faulty disposition of animal spirits," another term for the nerves.[8] The profound difference between Willis and Sydenham has been summarized beautifully by Jeffrey Boss: "Sydenham asserts that medicine is to be learnt only through its practice and exercise. This reverses the sequence of Willis, who proceeds from anatomy to inferences on pathology, and from these to clinical speculation."[9] Sydenham also explicitly rejected the sexual-gender encoding of hysteria and related the illness instead to class: the well-born, idle, those with a delicate constitution, or those sexually or socially dissatisfied were thought to be particularly prone to this disease. By transforming the illness from an effect of vague and elusive vapors or an imbalance of the humors, Sydenham explained the disorder as one of hypersensitivity and over-excitation of the nerves. Sydenham's theory was to exercise a decisive influence on eighteenth-century thinking and writing concerning hysteria.[10]

---

6 Thomas Willis, *Affectionum quae dicunter hystericae et hypochondriacae* (London: Allestry, 1670).
7 Thomas Sydenham, "Epistolary Dissertation to Dr. Cole," cited by Elisabeth Bronfen, *The Knotted Subject: Hysteria and its Discontents* (Princeton, NJ: Princeton University Press, 1998), 110.
8 Sydenham, "Epistolary Dissertation to Dr. Cole," cited in Bronfen, *The Knotted Subject*, 110. Natural (veins) and (arterial) vital spirits of Galenic physiology had been dispelled by William Harvey's discovery of blood circulation in 1628, but the belief in "animal spirits" (in the form of "the nervous system") persisted.
9 Jeffrey N. M. Boss, "The Seventeenth-Century Transformation of the Hysteric Affection and Sydenham's Baconian Medicine," *Psychological Medicine* 9.2 (1979): 226.
10 See Micale, *Approaching Hysteria*, 22; G. S. Rousseau, "'A Strange Pathology': Hysteria in the Early Modern World, 1500–1800," in *Hysteria beyond Freud*, ed. Sander L. Gilman et al. (Berkeley and Los Angeles: University of California Press, 1993), 158; Bronfen, *Knotted Subject*, 111; Michel Foucault, *Madness and Civilization* (London and New York: Routledge, 2001),

The eighteenth century, particularly in England but also in France and Germany, witnessed a veritable avalanche of texts and theories concerning hysteria: John Purcell's *A Treatise of Vapours, Or, Hysterick Fits* (1707) is quickly followed by Bernard Mandeville's *Treatise of the Hypochondriak and Hysterical Passions* (1711), Richard Blackmore's *A Treatise of the Spleen and Vapours* (1725), George Cheyne's *The English Malady, Or, A Treatise on Nervous Diseases of All Kinds* (1758), Robert Whytt's *Observations on the Nature, Causes, and the Cure of the Disorders which have been commonly called Nervous, Hypochondriac or Hysteric* (1764), and James Boswell's *The Hypochondriak*, published between 1777 and 1783.[11] In Germany, physicians such as Gustavus Becker, C. G. Burghart, Georg Clasius, C. G. Gross, J. F. Isenflamm, and J. C. Stock inherit, adopt, and comment on such theories of hysteria.[12] While the theory of hysteria at the beginning of the eighteenth century is still marked by a strong reliance on the vaporal theory of the physician to the French King Martin Lange (*Traité des Vapeurs, leur Origin, leurs Effets et leurs Remedes*, 1689), the gradual demise of vaporal theory and the Galenic theory of the four humors, especially after 1750, required a new explanation: hysteria as a disorder of the nerves and the nervous system. As Michel Foucault argued, "There were thus two essential lines of development in the classical period, for hysteria and hypochondria: one united them to form a common concept which was that of a 'disease of the nerves'; the other shifted their meaning and their pathological basis [...] and tended to integrate them gradually into the domain of diseases of the mind, besides mania and melancholia."[13] Whether they were conceived as a disease of the nerves or an illness of the mind, hysteria and hypochondria formed a Janus-faced pathology which profoundly influenced the development of dynamic psychology and psychiatry.[14]

137–139; and Diana Faber, "Hysteria in the Eighteenth Century," in *Brain, Mind and Medicine: Essays in Eighteenth-Century Neuroscience*, ed. Harry Whitaker et al. (New York: Springer, 2007), 321–330, on Sydenham see 322.

11 On this history, see: Ilza Veith, *Hysteria: The History of a Disease* (Chicago: University of Chicago Press, 1965); John Mullan, "Hypochondria and Hysteria: Sensibility and the Physicians," *Eighteenth Century: Theory and Interpretation* 25.2 (1984): 141–174; Lucien Israël, *L'hysterique, le sexe, et le medicin* (Paris: Masson, 1976); and G. S. Rousseau, "Strange Pathology," 91–227.

12 G. S. Rousseau, "Strange Pathology," 168.

13 Foucault, *Madness and Civilization*, 131.

14 According to Henri F. Ellenberger, *The Discovery of the Unconscious: The History and Evolution of Dynamic Psychiatry* (New York: Basic Books, 1970), the history of modern dynamic psychiatry originated with the study of hysteria.

In addition to the medical theory and teachings, the eighteenth century witnesses a dramatic increase in narrative observations of patients with hysterical afflictions. As Sabine Arnaud has written, "in the late eighteenth century physicians became increasingly interested in narrating their patients' disorder – identifying the pathology in the process of narrating it, and thereby instituting it as an object of knowledge."[15] Narrative observations of hysteria were published in medical and more popular journals in France, England, and Germany. In France, the *Journal de Médicine, Chiurgie, Pharmacie* founded by Nicolas Bertrand et Grasse in 1754 included a number of such narrative "observations" of hysterical cases, as did Joseph-Jacques de Gardanne's *Gazette de santé* for a more popular audience. As Arnaud shows, the *Société Royale de Médicine* even issued prize-essay competitions for the best treatise on hysteria.[16] Even French physicians dedicated to a nosological approach to medicine concerned more with the classification of disorders often appended narrative observations to their treatises as paradigmatic examples of their classifications.[17] These narrative observations, rather than simply "represent" or "narrate" a medical-psychological phenomena, actually structured and shaped the prevalent medical and popular understanding of hysteria. At the same time, as Arnaud argues, the physicians' narratives of hysteria existed in a "predetermined field of enunciation," in which physicians sought to establish "a discipline that will restore the subject's control of his or her body in order to cure hysteric afflictions."[18] Thus, we are justified in speaking of a casuistry of hysteria especially in the second half of the eighteenth century in Europe, of a reciprocal relation between the narrative observations and cases and the constitution of an object of medical-psychological knowledge.

The flood of writings on hysteria and hypochondria begins in the second half of the eighteenth century in the German territorial states. Writing in Johann August Unzer's journal *Der Arzt* in 1769, the anatomical physician Albrecht von Haller described hypochondria as an affliction of the digestive system, with gas, bloating, cramping, alternating constipation, and diarrhea, often accompanied by compression and pain in the head.[19] The central

---

15 Sabine Arnaud, *On Hysteria. The Invention of a Medical Category between 1670 and 1820* (Chicago: University of Chicago Press, 2015), 176.
16 Arnaud, *On Hysteria*, 178.
17 Arnaud, *On Hysteria*, 176, 178.
18 Arnaud, *On Hysteria*, 180.
19 Albrecht von Haller, "Piece No. 25," *Der Arzt: Eine Medicinische Wochenschrift* 1 (1769): 336–351, here 338: "Alles dieses trug sich bey dieser Krankheit nur allein im Unterleibe zu. Zu gleicher Zeit aber war auch die Brust beklommen, und gespannt, als wenn ein Band darum gelegt wäre; das Luftschöpfen ward beschwerlich; man fühlte oft Stiche in der Brust [...] Im Kopf empfand man bald hinten, bald vorn, reissende, spannende, drückende, stechende Schmerzen."

"theater" of hypochondria, he argued, was the abdomen, where a "corrupted digestive system," caused by a sedentary lifestyle, led to a weakening of the nerves and the obstruction of the blood.[20] Ernst Platner, author of the first philosophical anthropology, sought a more psychological explanation for hypochondria in his *Some Considerations regarding Hypochondria* of 1786:

> The hypochondrist feels 1) his life-power much weaker than it is in reality; suffers 2) from disorder, which causes an disproportional degree of uneasiness and pain in the body and then 3) when exaggerated feelings of weakness and uneasiness begin to affect him, unwarranted anxieties of death.[21]

According to Platner, the basis of hypochondria is self-deception or illusion (*Täuschung*). If the hypochondrist had an appropriate sense of their own life-power (*Lebenskraft*) and were not susceptible and sensitive to every sensation, they would be capable of discerning between actual and merely imagined illness. Platner underscored the highly variable and mobile nature of hypochondria already noted by previous physicians. An anonymous author writing in the *Neues Hamburgisches Magazin* in 1781 cautioned against attempting to identify one single cause of hypochondria, because "persons with very different ways of life very different from one another with various mistakes in the way they lead their life all complain of the same hypochondriacal attacks."[22] The hypochondria "hysteria" in Germany reached such a pitch that a weekly – *Der Hypochondrist, eine holsteinische Wochenschrift* – was published briefly in 1762, which featured a hypochondrist who made fun of himself and his many ailments, pains, and woes. We even have self-reporting ego-documents of hypochondria such as F. Schulz's *History of my Hypochondria. A Contribution to the Study of the Soul* (*Geschichte meiner Hypochondrie. Ein Beytrag zur Seelen-Naturkunde*), which appeared in the *Der teutsche Merkur* of 1786.[23] In this case

---

20 von Haller, "Piece No. 25," 338.The view that hysteria was linked to an obstruction of blood flow was advanced by Herman Boerhaave and Thomas Sydenham.

21 Ernst Platner, "Einige Betrachtungen über die Hypochondrie," in *Versuch über Verrichtungen und Krankheiten des menschlichen Verstandes, nebst einigen Bermerkungen über die Hypochondrie von D. Ernst Platner*, by Johann Friedrich Dafõurs (Leipzig: Wegandische Buchhandlung, 1786), 307: "Der Hypochondrist fühlt 1) seine Lebenskraft weit schwächer, als sie wirklich ist; leidet 2) von Unordnung, welche seine Maschine entsteht einen ganz unverhältnismäßigen Grad der Unruhe und des Schmerzes, und dann 3) wann übertriebene Gefühle von Schwachheit und Unruhe zugleich auf ihn wirken, unbegründete Beängstigungen des Todes."

22 Anonymous, "Von den Ursachen der Hypochondrie," *Neues Hamburgisches Magazin* 20.120 (1781): 494–495.

23 F. Schulz, "Geschichte meiner Hypochondrie. Ein Beytrag zur Seelen-Naturkunde," in *Der teutsche Merkur* 1 (1786): 152–169.

history, a writer tasked with producing a text under great pressure from his publisher loses his appetite, suffers severe writers-block, palpitations and shortness of breath, and begins to fantasize that he is being poisoned by the ink, and that his bed is on fire.

> It was the ink, the ink! I was (one has to think of my terror in its full power), I had been lethally poisoned – poisoned, I screamed, poisoned, poisoned! And this thought hit me at midnight [...] My friend the physician didn't understand my state, and could not advise me, not to mention help me. From me he only heard the one word: Ink! Ink! As I pointed to my tongue with my finger.[24]

The hysterical signs reproduce the illness – ink as the corrupt, thick blood threatening circulation, and destroying the digestive function – and the illness reproduces the inevitable rhetoric of the individual "symptoms" in a fierce feedback loop. In the end, it is a chance encounter with a young boy with a bloody nose that frees our writer from his delusional malady.

Hypochondria was not only viewed an individual illness of the nerves due to a sedentary lifestyle, overstimulated fantasy as a result of reading fiction, and a general weakening of bodily powers. It was also a threat to the health of the community, a security risk for the general welfare of society and the state, and therefore a matter for the *medizinische Polizei*, which was named in 1764 by Wolfgang Thomas Rau as the discipline concerned with public hygiene and the health of the population.[25] In what was the first general reference work and compendium of the new discipline in German speaking central Europe, Johann Peter Frank (1745–1821) underscored the danger posed by this "new" illness in his *System of a Complete Medical Policy*, which was published in nine massive volumes between 1779 and 1821, and became the standard-bearer for public health in the late eighteenth and early nineteenth centuries. In his introduction, Frank singled out hypochondria, which he clearly coupled with hysteria, as an important new illness of the nerves (*Nervenkrankheit*). Citing Johann Georg Zimmermann's *Von der Erfahrung* (1764) and Samuel André Tissot's

---

24 Schulz, "Geschichte meiner Hypochondrie," 162–163: "Die Tinte war es, die Tinte! Ich war (denke man sich mein Schrecken in seiner ganzen Größe), ich war tödlich vergiftet – Vergiftet, schrie ich, vergiftet, vergiftet! Und dieser Gedanke packte mich um Mitternacht [...] Mein Freund der Arzt begriff meinen Zustand nicht, und wußte nicht zu rathen, noch zu helfen. Von mir vernahm er nichts als das Wort: Tinte! Tinte! indem ich mit dem Finger auf die Zunge deutete."
25 Wolfgang Thomas Rau, *Gedanken von dem Nutzen und der Nothwendigkeit einer medicinischen Policeyordnung in einem Staat* (Ulm: Gaumische Handlung, 1764).

Traité des Nerfs (1778–1780), hypochondria was, according to Frank, a *class* issue, a disease of the scholarly and the educated:

> Hypochondria constitutes, as Zimmerman has correctly maintained, half of all chronic illnesses, and these as well as the nervous illnesses that are increasing in all regions, are necessary consequences of the sensitivization of our body as well as the disproportionate tension of the powers of our soul [...]. Indigestion, bloating, increased irritability, cramps, spitting blood, stroke, weakening are a unique illness of scholars and the educated, whose number, as everyone knows, is in every community quite considerable.[26]

Frank thus transformed hypochondria from an aberration or anomaly to a societal health risk and a public danger, a particularly "modern" illness of the population (*Bevölkerung*) that threatened the very security of the state.[27]

In the writings on hysteria in the eighteenth century, it was acknowledged that males suffered from a specific form of hysteria – hypochondriasis. Blackmore had identified hypochondria and hysteria as one and the same disease with merely different expressions,[28] and stated that hypochondriacal men are "endowed with a great share of understanding and judgment, with strong and clear Reason, a quick apprehension and vivacity of fancy and imagination,"[29] while Cheyne classified himself and his good friend Samuel Richardson as "hysterical types" – "serious, virtuous valetudianarians."[30] By mid-century, the learned, sensitive literary male was identified as a hysteric type who often

---

26 Johann Peter Frank, *System einer vollständigen medizinischen Policey* (Frankenthal: Verlag der Gegelischen Buchdruckerei und Buchhandlung, 1779–1793), vol. 1, 67–68: "Die Hypochondrie macht bey uns, wie Zimmermann mit Recht behauptet hat, den halben Theil aller chronischen Krankheiten aus, und diese sowohl, als die in allen Gegenden anwachsenden Nervenkrankheiten, sind nöthige Folgen sowohl der Verzärtlung unseres Körpers, als der übermäßigen Anspannung unserer Seelenkräfte. [...] Unverdaulichkeit, Blähungen, vermehrte Reizbarkeit, Krämpfe, Blutspeyen, der Schlagfluss, das Auszähren sind eine eigene Krankheit der Gelehrten und Halbgelehrten, deren Anzahl, wie man weiß, in jedem Gemeinwesen sehr ansehnlich ist."
27 In the introduction to his *System*, Frank defines "medizinische Polizey" as having to do with the "innere Sicherheit des Staates," (3) to regulate the population through specific rules and principles for the general welfare and health of all (4).
28 Foucault, *Madness and Civilization* (1961), 137; Michel Foucault, *History of Madness*, ed. Jean Khalfa, trans. Jonathan Murphy and Jean Khalfa (London and New York: Routledge, 2006), 278.
29 Richard Blackmore, *A Treatise of the Spleen and Vapours, Or, Hypocondriacal and Hysterical Affections: With Three Discourses on the Nature and Cure of the Cholick, Melancholy, and Palsies* (London: Pemberton, 1725), 24.
30 George Cheyne, *The English Malady, Or, A Treatise on Nervous Diseases of All Kinds* (1758) cited by Mullan, "Hypochondria and Hysteria," 146.

suffered from extreme anxiety, "alienations of the mind," somatizations, and melancholy. Since Robert Burton's *The Anatomy of Melancholy* of 1621, hysteria had been related to melancholia, or understood as a *form* of melancholia. In the eighteenth century, however, the relation between learnedness or pursuits of the mind and hypochondriasis became a steady figure in popular literature. Robert James's *A Medical Dictionary* of 1743–1745, in the entry on mania, stated "Men, Poets, Philosophers, and those charmed with the more deep and abstruse parts of mathematics and algebra are subject to melancholy,"[31] while the entry on hysteria defines the disorder as "a spasmodico-convulsive affection of the nervous kind proceeding from a retention and corruption of lymph, of blood, in the uterine vessels which influences all of the nervous parts of the body." By 1750, the linkage between hysteria and sensibility, sensitivity, learnedness, scholarly pursuits, studiousness, and the reading and writing of poetry had become a literary commonplace. The most emphatic critic was the physician Tissot, whose *On the Health of Scholars*, published in German in Zürich in 1768, argued that the weakness of the nerves due to immobility, the strain and exertion on the mind, loss of sleep, and the bad air around books and manuscripts inevitably leads to a variety of "illnesses of the nerves."[32]

While Sydenham's scientific approach wrested hysteria from the demonization characteristic of the Church prior to the early modern period, one still sees the vapours making their reappearance in certain medical treatises on hysteria of the early eighteenth century. However, by the second half of the eighteenth century, due to the advances in physiological medicine, and the ascendancy of knowledge of the nervous system, hysteria had become first and foremost *an illness of the nerves*. As early as 1733, Friedrich Hoffmann had theorized in his *Medicina rationalis systematica* that the spasmodic affections experienced by hypochondriacs and hysterics have their seat in the nervous tissue, and above all in the membranes of the stomach and intestines, from where they are communicated by the intercostal nerves to the head, the chest, the kidneys, the liver and the other principal organs of the body. As the locus of the illness shifted from the vapors to the nerves and the psyche – following Sydenham, Cheyne and other enlightened physicians of the eighteenth century who attributed all mental disorders to the nerves – the stage was set for the physicians to shift their close attention to the *mind*, the "mental state" of the patient, to the bodily symptoms, and to record, with great specificity, the

---

[31] Cited by Mullan, "Hypochondria and Hysteria," 152–153.
[32] Samuel André Tissot, *Von der Gesundheit der Gelehrten* (Zürich: Füßlin und Compagnie, 1768), 249.

individual case in all of its vicissitudes. As the late Roy Porter put it so eloquently:

> A physician henceforth had to pay close attention to the patient's mind. An indication of this change lies in the proliferation of detailed case histories taken and published in the late 18th and early 19th centuries: in sharp contrast to earlier works, some of the books appearing at this time consisted entirely in the accumulation of case histories.[33]

In the following, my aim is to analyze Marcus Herz's case history of his friend and patient, the aesthetician, novelist, and critic Karl Philipp Moritz, who suffered and died from tuberculosis. The case is unique in that a real medical condition underlay Moritz's frenzied, volatile state. Yet as the case amply demonstrates, Herz's interest was in the tumultuous affective state and mental suffering of his patient, and the challenges this posed for the physician, not the underlying organic disease.

In contrast to the still dominant model of the "vapors" and the bodily vicissitudes of humoral pathology in the seventeenth century, a "modern" discourse and the corresponding media of hysteria emerge in the eighteenth century. The neuro-psychological model of disease that becomes visible at the end of the seventeenth century and the shift in thinking regarding the anatomical "seat" of hysteria – the rejection of the notion that this was a female illness of the womb – had created the conditions of the possibility of a specification and scientific semiotics not merely of hysteria in general, but that of male hysteria in particular: hypochondria.[34] As Mark Micale has noted: "Although male hysteria had been clinically identified since the seventeenth century, physicians had hidden it under such euphemistic diagnoses as neurasthenia, hypochondria, phthiatism, neurospasia, eleorexia[...]."[35] In the mid-eighteenth century, male hysteria – specifically in the form of hypochondria – comes into its own. Historians have noted the turn from the "humoral to a neural model of the body," indeed, to an entire "mythology of the nerves."[36] The ubiquity of the

---

33 Roy Porter, *Flesh in the Age of Reason: The Modern Foundations of Body and Soul* (New York and London: W. W. Norton, 2003), 313.
34 Micale, *Approaching Hysteria*, 161–168.
35 Elaine Showalter, *Hystories. Hysterical Epidemics and Modern Media* (New York: Columbia University Press, 1998), 64.
36 Albrecht Koschorke, *Körperströme und Schriftverkehr: Mediologie des 18. Jahrhunderts* (München: W. Fink, 1999), 54–112; and Koschorke,"Poiesis des Leibes: Johann Christian Reills romantische Medizin," in *Romantische Wissenspoetik: Die Künst und die Wissenschaften um 1800*, ed. Gabriele Brandstetter and Gerhard Neumann (Würzburg: Könighausen & Neumann, 2004), 52.

discourse on and about nerves led G. S. Rousseau to even speak of a "nerve culture" during this period.[37] The pervasiveness of such a culture of nerves can be shown using the example of Herz's *Essay on Vertigo* (1786), where Herz speaks of the "communication between the nerves and the soul" (*die Mitteilung der Nerven und der Seele*).[38] We can say that, during this time, the concept of hysteria not only decoupled itself from the female body, to which it had formerly been tied; it became, according to Foucault, a "disease of the nerves [...] a pathology of the mind."[39] In distinction to female hysteria, male hysteria was viewed either as a result of actual physical trauma, or having some basis in actual organic illness, whereas female hysteria continued to be viewed as a psychic-emotion, as a purely *mental and imaginary* illness. In general, to be sure, hypochondria is the name given for masculine hysteria in the eighteenth century.[40] However, at the end of the eighteenth century, we can see a less-gender specific differentiation between hypochondria and hysteria appear: according to an anonymous book *Über die Hypochondrie* which appeared in 1777, hysteria proper is hysteria with a material basis (*mit Materie*), while hypochondria is seen as a form of hysteria without any material basis (*ohne Materie*), irrespective of the gender of the patient.[41] As this passage from Unzer's popular journal *Der Arzt* of 1769 reveals, the concern in the second half of the eighteenth century is directed at the *psychological* aspects of the malady, not the gender.

> The mind of the hypochondriac is burdened with an anxious sadness and a susceptible imagination [...] The sadness makes these people depressive, cowardly, small-minded and generally fearful. They view their illness as being far more dangerous than it really is. The constantly believe they are dying, but they never actually get around to it.[42]

---

37 G. S. Rousseau, "Strange Pathology," (1993), 91–221.
38 Marcus Herz, *Versuch über den Schwindel* (Berlin, 1786), esp. 216–232, where Herz cites both Christian Wolff and Georg Ernest Stahl, and makes his case for a reciprocal relation of the body and the soul.
39 Foucault, *Madness and Civilization*, 151, 158.
40 Mark S. Micale, "Hysteria and its Historiography: The Future Perspective," *History of Psychiatry* 1 (1990): 33–124.
41 Anonymous, *Über die Hypochondrie* (Dresden: in der Hilscherschen Buchhandlung, 1777), 7.
42 Unzer, ed., *Der Arzt*, 346: "Das Gemüth des Hypochondristen ist mit einer ängstlichen Traurigkeit und schwindlichten Einbildungskraft beschweret [...] Die Traurigkeit macht diese Leute schwermüthig, feige, verzagt, kleinmüthig, furchtsam. Sie sehen ihre Krankheiten für weit gefährlicher an, als sie sind. Sie glauben immer zu sterben, und können doch nie dazu kommen."

As the historiography of hysteria shows, the difficulty of a precise conceptual determination of hysteria is matched only by the variability and elusiveness of the affliction itself. This was noted by Purcell early in the eighteenth century: "Vapours, otherwise called Hysterick Fits, or Fits of the Mother, is a Disease which more generally afflicts Humane Kind, than any other whatsoever; and Proteus-like, transforms itself into the shape and representation of almost all Distempers."[43] In *Madness and Civilization,* Foucault famously wrote: "Hysteria is indiscriminately mobile or immobile, fluid or dense, given to unstable vibrations or clogged by stagnant humors."[44] In other words, hysteria is the enigmatic, the mobile, fleeting, indeterminate enactment of itself, with its own variability and instability, eluding the grasp of both patient and physician. More radically, Manfred Schneider characterizes the imaginary status of the disorder as a fiction created by and in literature: "Die Hysterie hat es immer schon *nicht* gegeben!" – "There was always already never any such thing as hysteria!"[45] As a textual condition or as a function of literature or the literary itself, it tends to evade definite description. Finally, the historian of hysteria Micale has more recently argued that an encompassing, overarching definition of hysteria might well be impossible, that perhaps the best we can hope for is to be able to clearly articulate historically specific discourses of *Hysteria.*[46]

However, despite the imperative of historicization and the avoidance of anachronistic assumptions, I think it is possible to discern, in fact, certain general features of hysteria – real or imagined, a medical condition or an imagined illness – that span the period from the mid-eighteenth century to Freud's time, and perhaps beyond. First, one can argue that at least since the eighteenth century, hysteria has always involved a *blurring of the boundary* between body and soul, between the physical and the mental; the difficulty in clearly "situating" it in either realm injects an irreducible indeterminacy into the discussion of hysteria. Second, a constant in the historical research concerning hysteria has been the process of *somatization*, the literal embodiment of a psychological disturbance, a materialization, as both Breuer and Freud and, after them, Sandor Ferenczi observed, of unresolved psychological conflict, or later "trauma."[47]

---

43 John Purcell, *A Treatise of Vapours, Or, Hysterick Fits* (London: Edward Place, 1707), 9.
44 Foucault, *Madness and Civilization,* 142.
45 Manfred Schneider, "Hysterie als Gesamtkunstwerk," in *Ornament und Askese im Zeitgeist des Wien der Jahrhundertwende,* ed. Alfred Pfabigan (Wien: C. Brandstaetter, 1985), 212.
46 Micale, *Approaching Hysteria,* 285.
47 Sigmund Freud and Joseph Breuer, *Studies in Hysteria,* trans. James Strachey (London: Hogarth Press, 1955), 220–223; and Sandor Ferenczi, "The Phenomenon of Hysterical Materialization" (1919), in *Further Contributions to the Theory and Technique of Psychoanalysis,*

Third, even though the putative origin of hysteria in the womb had already been definitely rejected in the eighteenth century, a bodily locus of hysteria, the *globus hystericus* was transformed first into the *clavis hystericus* (the nail being driven through the head) and then a *locus hystericus* and understood as an essential component of hysterical illness: for example, paralysis of a part of the body, a raging gut, or hysterical blindness. Fourth, the literature of and on hysteria reiterates the idiopathic and slippery, mobile, transient, and ever-changing character of hysteria, its essentially *protean* nature. This has as its consequence that hysteria or hysterical illness challenges or contests the capabilities of both the rational physician and scientific medicine itself. Finally, and for our purposes here most importantly, a very strong counter-transferential relationship develops between the physician and the patient. The patient seeks to entwine the physician in the hysterical illness, to either draw the physician into the web of symptoms, or, in some instances, to make the physician somehow "responsible" for persistent or worsening symptoms, either because of a perceived lack of understanding, lack of competence, or an inability to grasp the severity of the illness. As Lucien Israël has keenly observed: "Hysteria as a subject of medical history or the history of medicine mirrors back to its interpellators and analysts precisely the same gesture of indecision, complicity and duplicity that the hysteric's desire also sets in motion."[48] Hysteria often entails a deeply problematic "identification" between the analyst and the patient, as Elisabeth Bronfen has argued.[49] The mobility and variability of the symptoms contests the attempts of the physician, who tries – often unsuccessfully – to pin it down. As Manfred Schneider points out: "Through the medium of the doctor-patient relationship in the circular movement of symptomology and diagnosis, the pathological semiotics of the poets, theologians, and physicians enters into self-contained feedback-loop."[50]

This "structure" of hysteria – mirroring other afflictions, mobility, somatization, localization, counter-transference – certainly holds sway in the late eighteenth century. The case history presented here by Marcus Herz concerning his friend Karl Philipp Moritz was published in 1793 in the *Journal der praktischen Arzneikunde und der Wundarzneykunst*, edited by the eminent physician C. W. Hufeland (1762–1836), professor of medicine at Jena, physician to Goethe, Schiller and Herder, and ultimately chair of pathology and therapeutics at the

---

by Ferenczi, trans. Jane I. Suttie (London: Hogarth and the Institute for Psycho-Analysis, 1926), 89–104.
48 Israël, *L'hystérique, le sexe, et le médicin*, 3.
49 Bronfen, *Knotted Subject*, 106.
50 Schneider, "Hysterie als Gesamtkunstwerk," 217.

University of Berlin.[51] Herz calls his case history of Moritz *Etwas Psychologsich-Medizinisches*, or "Something Psychological-Medical," and with this disciplinary couplet, and the pointedly indeterminate "something" (*Etwas*), he deliberately underscored the ambiguity and ambivalence of the affliction itself and obliquely his own "position" and that of the illness on the border or boundary between psychology and medicine. Written after his friend's death, the case history not only describes the "implicated" physician as he is drawn into the displacements and projections of the patient, it is also a self-reflexive document that tells us as much about the challenges of the physician and his confrontation with the limits of his "art" as it does about the illness and the patient himself.[52] Moritz was, to be sure, hypochondriacal, but he did in fact suffer from tuberculosis, which ultimately caused his death. In this case, therefore, we also have an actual organic illness combined with a hysterical-hypochondriacal sensibility, a tendency toward hysterical hyperbole, overpowering literary enthusiasm, and a strong transference to his friend and physician Herz. This, I argue, is precisely what makes this case history a psychological case in the true sense, that is, an enigmatic, unique *Fall* that does not strictly conform to definition and established norm, simply an example of theory, even that of the dominant image of the hysteric. Moritz's "case" is very much about the way in which patient and physician are caught up in a therapeutic relationship, regardless of outcome or prognosis. And it is most perceptive concerning the way in which human beings must confront their own mortality and finitude, and the choices every human can make as they deal with the harsh reality of their inevitable demise.

The case history begins with a philosophical preface about the influence of various "states of mind" (*Gemüthszustände*) on the health of the body, and a reference to Herz's study *Essay on Vertigo*, in which he had written a "history of an illness" without naming the patient – the philosopher, novelist, and editor of the first journal of "empirical psychology" Moritz. Herz states that he will offer an "extensive narration of the case" (*ausführliche Erzählung des Falles*) that he deemed to be necessary and valuable to the medical art and its practitioners. For the latter, Herz specifies his wish to direct the attention of his colleagues to the "study of psychology," the knowledge of the human soul, and

---

51 Marcus Herz, "Etwas Psychologisch-Medizinisches," *Journal der praktischen Arzneikunde und der Wundarzneykunst* 5.2 (1798): 3–73.
52 This point is brought home in Jörg Steigerwald, "Ideenzirkulation und Zirkulation von Ideen. Zur empirischen Psychologie der Berliner Spätaufklärung (am Beispiel Marcus Herz)," in *Gedächtnis und Zirkulation. Der Diskurs des Kreislaufs im 18. und 19. Jahrhundert*, ed. Harald Schmidt and Marcus Sandl (Göttingen: Vandenhoeck & Ruprecht, 2002), 39–64, esp. 57–61.

the theory of the passions from a very important angle, namely *therapeutics*: "Namely this, in order to stimulate their attention for the study of psychology and to place before their eyes the knowledge of the human soul and the path of the passions from the most important side, the *therapeutic* side."[53] While Herz acknowledges that the expressions of the soul had been extensively explored in the teachings of medical semiotics, and that many forms of the disruption or ruin of the faculties of the soul had been described in great detail, the profession had still not given sufficient thought to the healing of bodily infirmities and ailments by artificial changes and directions of the capacities of the soul. Herz laments the unfortunate lack of any systematics concerning the "healing of bodily ailments through the artificial transformations of the capabilities of the soul" (*Heilung körperlicher Gebrechen durch künstliche Veränderungen und Richtungen der Seelenfähigkeiten*): "A considerable class of psychic curative remedies is still completely lacking in our medical literature."[54] The difficulties with developing such a systematics are clear: the individuality and sensitivity of the forms of psychic cures and the deviation and variability of specific individuals. Unlike the mechanical and chemical laws of the body, the changes of the human psyche are subject to a different set of laws; the rules are of such a fine and complicated weave (*von einem so feinen, verwickelten Gewebe*), because of a highly interrelated manifold (*wegen ihrer zu verwickelten Mannigfaltigkeit*) that the philosophical physician can only gradually and though "assiduous observation" (*emsiges Beobachten*) and "cautious experiments" (*behutsame Versuchen*) arrive at the systematic structure of a complete "medical science of the soul" (*vollständigen medizinischen Seelenlehre*). One should be familiar with the unique nature of the individual – what is refered to as "the psychical knowledge of the individual human being" (*die psychische Kenntnis des einzelnen Menschen*) and "the individual constitution of his mind and of the specific influences of its expressions and alterations upon his bodily condition" (*die individuelle Beschaffenheit seines Gemüths und des besonderen Einflusses von dessen Äusserungen und Veränderungen auf seinen körperlichen Zustand*) – which represents both the basic condition of the case as well as the most serious obstacle for its resolution.[55] The physician should attempt and

---

[53] Marcus Herz, "Etwas Psychologisch-Medizinisches," 4; emphasis in the original: "*Diesen, um ihre Aufmerksamkeit auf das Studium der Psychologie zu reizen und ihnen die Kenntnis der menschlichen Seele und des Ganges der Leidenschaften von der wichtigsten Seite, von der therapeutischen, vor Augen zu legen.*"
[54] Herz, "Etwas Psychologisch-Medizinisches," 5: "Eine förmliche Klasse von psychischen Heilmitteln fehlt überall in unserer *Materia medica* noch gänzlich."
[55] Herz, "Etwas Psychologisch-Medizinisches," 16–17.

document such attempts at "psychical cures" without concern about its contribution to any future system.

In 1782, Moritz returned from a trip to England with a chronic, severe cough and what he described as tightness in his chest. Herz tried in vain to get his friend and patient to accept a formal cure and the appropriate medications, which would have included a bloodletting and cold baths, but Moritz rejected all of Herz's therapeutic suggestions. Several days later, Herz was called to the Scharnstrasse in Berlin, where Moritz had collapsed, coughing up blood. Herz "flew" to the scene and found Moritz in the room of a wound-doctor "drenched in blood." Herz prescribed the appropriate bed-rest and quiet, but contrary to Herz's orders, as he arrives at Moritz's house the very next day, he is told by his household staff that Moritz had gotten up, dressed, and went off to deliver a lecture at the Gymnasium where he was Professor, followed by a lunch with councilor Büsching. Herz ordered further requisite medicines, and observed a slight improvement on the following day. But a couple of weeks later, Herz is called once again to his friend's house, where he finds Moritz in the most miserable state: severe, persistent cough, difficulty breathing, fast pulse, and a high fever. Herz wrote: "a consumptive in an advanced state" (*ein Schwindsüchtiger im ansehlichen Grade*).[56] Herz clearly recognizes the organic symptoms and the probable cause of the illness immediately, but what is significant for him is Moritz's psychological state and mindset. The first hysterical-hypochondriacal signs appear: "The most serious of the symptoms, however, was the stormy disquiet in his soul as a result of an exaggerated fear of death. Constantly with his fingers on his pulse, he leapt up, or when there was a pause between pulse beats, which he took as a sign of *a polyp on his heart*" (*das er für das Zeichen eines Polypen im Herzen hielt*).[57] After several weeks Moritz suffered yet another precipitous decline accompanied by a rampage in his soul (*Toben in seiner Seele*). Despite Herz's friendly and caring attempts to calm him, "Moritz ran around his room, railed in magnificent hexameter against his immanent death, against art, and scoffed at me [Herz] and my optimistic hopes" (*lief er [Moritz] wild in der Stube umher, schimpfte in prächtigen Hexameter auf seinen Tod, auf die Kunst und höhnte [Herz] mit [seinen] schmeichelnden Hoffnungen*). In this manner, Moritz tormented and berated his friend and physician for months, failing to comply with Herz's recommendations and scoffing at the medical profession. *Herz* the friend and physician was thus transformed, displaced, condensed into a large polyp on his heart (*Herz*). Hysterical conversion or

---

56 Herz, "Etwas Psychologisch-Medizinisches," 21.
57 Herz, "Etwas Psychologisch-Medizinisches," 22; emphasis mine.

materialization is confirmed precisely through this metonymic condensation of the illness to this polyp on/of the *Heart*.⁵⁸ Herz's complicity and entwinement in the illness, the gradual knotting of physician and patient, causes frustration, resentment, even antipathy:

> The fever, which had its source more in the mind than in the body, could not be stopped, and I saw it rubbing out the machine in a short time. I found myself in the worst of circumstances. Moritz was my friend, whom I loved dearly, he was my patient who had placed his utmost trust in me, and I was certain that I could cure this illness in anyone else, but because of the hindrances that he himself placed in my way, I was unable to achieve this joy of the healing art. I recommended another physician, but he would have nothing of it. I threatened to leave him, but then he would become sad, promised me everything and only held himself to what we had agreed on for a couple of hours. Finally, I became annoyed and querulous; I visited him reluctantly, often did not speak a word with him, and responded to his declamations with sighs and a shrug.⁵⁹

In modern psycho-analytic terms, one would employ the term counter-transference to describe Herz's increasing resistance and antipathy to Moritz and his illness. In fact, Herz's reaction suggests that he fully acknowledges he has been enlisted or recruited in this developing drama; Moritz not only defies Herz's attempts to soothe and calm him, but mocks his medical expertise and indeed medical science as a whole. The "illness" is as much a case of tuberculosis as it is a struggle against Herz, the art of healing, fear that he will be abandoned, and the anxiety of an impending death. The agitation and rage in Moritz's soul enact or act-out precisely the sense of helplessness and loss that he experiences in view of his rapid decline, and the projection of this helpless and loss onto his friend and physician.

---

58 A preliminary discussion of this condensation/displacement was made by Arnold Huttmann, "Eine imaginäre Krankheit: Der Polyp des Herzens," *Medizinhistorisches Journal* 18. 1–2 (1983): 43–51.

59 Herz, "Etwas Psychologisch-Medizinisches," 24: "Das Fieber, das seine Quelle mehr im Gemüthe als im Körper hatte, war nicht zu bekämpfen, und ich sah es mit Gewissheit in kurzer Zeit die Maschine aufreiben. Ich befand mich in einer der misslichsten Lagen. Moritz war mein Freund, den ich sehr liebte, er war mein Kranker, der das auffallende Vertrauen in mich setzte, ich hielt mich versichert, dieselbe Krankheit bey jedem anderen überwinden zu können, und musste gerade bey ihm wegen der Hindernisse, die er selbst mir in den Weg legte, auf diese Künstlerfreude Verzicht thun. Ich schlug ihm einen anderen Arzt vor, davon wollte er nichts wissen; ich drohte ihn zu verlassen, dann bat er wehmütig, versprach alles und hielt das geringste kaum einige Stunden. Endlich war ich verdrüsslich, missmuthig, machte meine vergeblichen Besuche mit Widerwillen, sprach oft bey ihm fast gar nicht und beantwortete seine Deklamationen blos mit Seufzern und Achselzucken."

In view of this worsening condition of his patient and his continued resistance against every form of treatment and care, Herz decides on a radical form of treatment. In one of their encounters, the hysterical Moritz screams:

> It's horrible (*das ist schrecklich!*) [...] one beat different from the next, the blood is being blocked by this large polyp and it will be, it must soon be over! [...] O, Herz knows it and must indeed know it even better. He can't cure a polyp on the heart, why doesn't he just say it straight out? Why does he treat me as a child [...] It's not a polyp he always says. But just feel my pulse! *Ha ha*, just feel it![60]

Now Herz develops his rather bold, cunning psychological-therapeutic plan to "tear" Moritz out of his state by force (*mit Gewalt*). Herz now seeks to convince Moritz of his imminent, certain death and to destroy in him every hope of recovery. In a word, Herz attempts to "shock" Moritz out of his hysterical obstinacy through *terror* – by admitting to him that it is indeed a polyp, that it is obstructing his respiration, that he is unable to help him, and that he will indeed succumb to the illness. As Moritz sits up, holds out his arm, and asks Herz to feel his pulse again, the following dialogue ensues, which I reproduce in its entirety and with the German text:

> **He:** So, how is it?
>
> (Herz) I shrugged my shoulders without uttering a sound.
>
> **He:** Won't it get better soon? In a few weeks the phlegm will certainly be gone from my chest! –
>
> You're annoyed, or even angry?
>
> (Herz) I sighed deeply, went to the window and took on the same posture.
>
> **He:** Strange that the illness doesn't seem to want to go away.
>
> **I:** (with a small smile) Strange? To be sure, very strange that there are illnesses that cannot be cured at all.
>
> **He:** (somewhat terrified) Cannot be cured? – you mean to say my illness cannot be cured?
>
> (Herz) I remained at the window, very still and immersed in thought.
>
> **He:** (after a long pause) And you said always so nicely: just be calm, it will be alright.

---

60 Herz, "Etwas Psychologisch-Medizinisches," 29.

I: (cold and calm) I did believe that if you *had* been calm, it *would* have been alright.

He: (after a loud, bitter laugh) I should have believed you and remained calm when I had an intermittant pulse, with my coughing and the heart palpitations dashing every attempt at calm?

(Herz) I remained unperturbed in my position. After a long pause, as Moritz gesticulated wildly with his hands like a madman, without uttering a sound, he finally screamed: now what do you say? What are you thinking?

I: (still in the previous tone) I'm thinking the last thought of the possibility of your recovery, and now I am finished even with that.

He: Huh? (terrified) What? How can that be?

I: Even the thought of a recovery has now disappeared. It's over. I think this way and that, in vain. You cannot be saved.

He: (terrified) What? How can that be?

I: My art, the medical art, is finished. Nothing more can be done.

He: I must die? Have to die?

I: (as i raised my head high and shook my head) Indeed, you must die.

He: (after a short interlude jumping up with intensity) That is unheard of!

Er: Nun, wie ist es?

Ich zuckte die Achsel ohne einen Laut vor mir zu geben.

Er: Wird es nun nicht bald besser werden? In einigen Wochen muss doch endlich der Schleim von der Brust weg! – Sie sind wohl verdrüsslich, oder gar böse?

Ich holte einen tiefen Seufzer, ging wieder an das Fenster und nahm meine vorige Stellung an.

Er.: Wunderbar, dass es mit der Krankheit gar nicht fort will!

Ich: (mit einem kleinen Lächeln) Wunderbar? Ja, freylich sehr wunderbar, dass es Krankheiten giebt, die gar nicht geheilt werden können [...]

Er: (etwas erschrocken) nicht geheilt werden können – also meine Krankheit kann nicht geheilt werden?

Ich stand immerfort ganz stille vertieft am Fenster.

Er: (nach einer langen Pause) Und Sie sagten doch immer so hübsch: seyn Sie nur ruhig, es wird schon gehen.

Ich: (kalt und gelassen) Ich habe es geglaubt, und *wären* Sie ruhig gewesen, es *wäre* gegangen.

Er: (nach einer lauten bitteren Lache) ich hätte Ihnen glauben und ruhig seyn sollen, da mein intermittierender Puls, mein Husten, mein Herzklopfen jede beginnende Ruhe zerstiebten?

Ich blieb gelassen in meiner Stellung. Nach einer langen Pause, während Moritz wie ein halb Wahnsinniger mit den Händen heftig gestikulierte, ohne einen Ton hervorzubringen, schrie er endlich: nun was sagen Sie? Woran denken Sie?

Ich: (immer im vorigen Tone) An dem letzten Gedanken von der Möglichkeit ihrer Geneseung, und eben bin ich mit ihm fertig geworden.

Er: Nun? (erschrocken) Wie? Was?

Ich: Auch dieser ist endlich verschwunden. Es ist vorbey, ich denke hin, ich denke her, umsonst, Sie sind nicht zu retten.

Er: (erschrocken) Wie? Was?

Ich: Meine Kunst, die Kunst überhaupt ist zu Ende, es ist nichts mehr zu machen.

Er: Ich muss also sterben? Muss sterben?

Ich: (indem ich meinen Kopf in die Höhe richtete, und die Achsel zuckte) Ja wohl, Sie müssen sterben.

Er: (nach einer kurzen Zwischenzeit mit Heftigkeit aufspringend) Das ist doch unerhört![61]

The drama enacted here, complete with gesticulation directives, as if for stage direction and *mise-en-scène*, repeats the inner struggle in Moritz and the transference and counter-transference of the physician-patient relationship in hysteria. Herz distances himself from Moritz, assumes a cold and resigned demeanor, and enacts precisely what Moritz had been accusing him of. By informing Moritz that his medical "art" has been exhausted and that he must die, Herz performs and affirms Moritz's fear of death. Moritz's reaction signifies precisely what makes him unable to properly deal with his illness: it is "unheard

---

61 Herz, "Etwas Psychologisch-Medizinisches," 31–32.

of" (*unerhört*), meaning not merely that which is unbelievable or cannot be grasped, but that he has literally never heard such a thing before (the death sentence that he must die). Herz then delivers the final blow:

> **I:** (with some vehemence) Unheard of? How so? Unheard of, that someone can die of a serious illness that cannot be cured? That you could die of this is certainly unheard of up to now; when you have died of it it will be unheard of in view of those around you [...].
>
> **He:** (suddenly thinking deeply and walking around the room) But that is horrendous!
>
> **Ich:** (gleichfalls mit einiger Heftigkeit) Unerhört? Wie so? Unerhört, dass jemand an einer unheilbaren Krankheit stirbt? Dass Sie daran sterben ist freylich biz jezo unerhört; wenn Sie daran gestorben seyn werden, wird es in Ansehung Ihrer unerhört seyn [...].
>
> **Er.:** (gleichsam tief nachdenkend in der Stube herumlaufend) Das ist doch schrecklich![62]

Herz compares his technique with Moritz to that of a surgeon or wound-doctor: cutting into the flesh of the patient, working with laser-like focus toward the final goal of repairing what has been torn asunder, resisting the strong feeling that threatens to make his hand shake. He breaks off from the dialogue with Moritz and returns to a strict narrative mode, describing how he had sought to remain in the posture of concern and care regarding his friend and patient. The disease, Herz writes, had encompassed them both, entangled them in the greatest tension and tumult: "Day and night his image and the image of his condition did not leave my soul, it enveloped now the physician, now the friend, and maintained both of us in the greatest tension, to try to remedy the vexatious malady."[63] As Herz provides the therapeutic antidote – "You cannot be saved [...] my art, every art is exhausted, there is nothing further to be done [...] You must die" – he waits for the precise moment to carry out the death-sentence in even greater detail with emphasis: "I am now convinced that the lungs are filled with pus and that a *polyp-like growth in the heart* has formed that will soon bring the already difficult blood circulation to a complete halt."[64] In response to Moritz's admission that he has not *lived wisely*, Herz advises him to *die wisely* – *weise zu sterben*.

---

[62] Herz, "Etwas Psychologisch-Medizinisches," 33.
[63] Herz, "Etwas Psychologisch-Medizinisches," 41: "Tag und Nacht entwich sein und seines Zustandes Bild nicht aus meiner Seele, bald umfasste es den Arzt, bald den Freund, und erhielt beide in der größten Spannung, dem leidigen Übel abzuhelfen."
[64] Herz, "Etwas Psychologisch-Medizinisches," 43–44.

With this death-sentence from his friend Herz, the hoped-for rupture in Moritz's obstinacy, resistance, rage and belligerence toward Herz occurs and the bedside scene changes totally. Moritz shifts from his recalcitrant, even hostile and contemptuous mood, breaks down, and begs his friend not to abandon him in his time of need. The case history ends with a series of reciprocal, chiastic phrasings. Moritz once again finds in Herz the physician as friend, and the friend as physician; Herz, for his part, is able to continue to practice his medical art, but more importantly, to teach Moritz an invaluable lesson on how to conduct one's life, no matter the circumstance. Moritz's temporary recuperation allows him the decision to "live wisely," and the two continue their friendship by greeting each other on the streets of Berlin: "Live wisely!" – to which the other would respond "so one dies wisely!" Herz's case history of Moritz is thus far more than a classical "history of an illness" (*Krankengeschichte*) with its typical structure and features such as *anamnesis, present status, diagnosis, prognosis, therapy/prescription, course of the illness* and *epicrisis*.[65] Herz provides a thoroughly psychological account of Moritz's illness quite apart from the material basis – the tuberculosis that was to eventually kill him some ten years later; he identifies Moritz's hypochondriacal-hysterical mindset, the disavowal and resistance, illusion and deception that block Moritz's capacity to trust and respect Herz and his medical expertise. Above all, Herz's case-study narrates the precise moment in which the trust and respect between the friends is temporarily suspended, and Herz's radical, psychological intervention that breaks the hold of the hysterical reactivity and enacts in the end a reconstitution of the reciprocity and symmetry of friendship.

It is a sign of hysterical signs that the physical symptoms or somatic disturbances are sublated in and through crisis leading to a psychological catharsis. As Manfred Schneider has suggested: "The therapy attempts to make all the 'signs' disappear."[66] As the case history shows, what is required is a kind of psychological cunning, a trick, a deception or lie, in order to bring the hysterical illness out into the open, in order to make it finally disappear. As Gabriele

---

65 Stefan Goldmann, "Kasus – Krankengeschichte – Novelle," in *"Fakta, und kein moralisches Geschwätz". Zu den Fallgeschichten im Magazin zur Erfahrungsseelenkunde (1783–1793)*, ed. Sheila Dickson et al. (Göttingen: Wallstein, 2011), 33–64, wishes to caution about the use of the term *Fallgeschichte* with regard to the case-studies presented in Moritz's *Magazin*, which he maintains are classical *Krankengeschichten*. It should be pointed out that while the precise term *Fallgeschichte* – case history – is not used in the German eighteenth century, a discourse of unique, individual case-studies as the basis of medical-psychological knowledge confirms a profound shift in thinking about and writing in cases in the second half of the century.
66 Schneider, "Hysterie als Gesamtkunstwerk," 217.

Dürbeck has noted: "What is required of the physician is not merely psychological knowledge, but also the application of wit, cunning, and tricks in order to heal the original imaginary through yet another one."[67] This process of bringing the hysterical pathology into the light, allowing the imaginary to appear as such, swapping out one idea for another through the narrative and dialogue may even induce us to speak of the *beauty* of hysteria, an aesthetics or transfiguration of hysteria.[68] The conciliatory *resolutio* reinstates knowledge, equilibrium, and reciprocity. The displacement of the disease onto a *globus hystericus* – in this case the polyp on the heart – the condensation and somatization of the fear and anxiety, the heightening of the crisis through the cunning strategy of the physician, and finally the revelation, confession, and recognition (*anagnorisis*) imbue this psychological case history with a dramatic, aesthetic, and rhetorical structure. Herz's psychological case history of Moritz follows the hysterical structure outlined at the beginning of this chapter, and the "psychical cure" performed by Herz only affirms precisely this structure and its effects.

All of the structural elements mentioned at the beginning of the chapter concerning hysteria find their rhetorical expression in the narrative of the case history: the blurring of the mind-body or the physical-psychic distinction; hysterical *conversion* or materialization and/or somatization; the *globus hystericus* (here, the metonymic condensation of the polyp located, appropriately, on the heart/*Herz*); the contestation of the physician's ability; the transferential (Moritz's sense of helplessness projected onto Herz) and counter-transferential (Herz's stinging death-sentence) relationship between patient and physician; and finally, the psychological "breakthrough" or recognition, in which the patient is able to work-through, in language, the hysterical symptom. I have invoked this revised "rhetoric" of hysteria embodied in the psychological case history of 1793 in order to show that Herz follows the hysterical logic to its conclusion, operating in and within the terms of the hysterical structure. However, the question remains whether or not we are warranted, as some have suggested, to assert that hysteria is *nothing other than* its own literary or semiotic self-production, or, as Manfred Schneider has argued "nothing more than its

---

[67] Gabriele Dürbeck, "Physiologischer Mechanismus und aesthetische Therapie: Ernst Anton Nicolais Schriften zur Psychopathologie," in *Vernünftige Ärzte. Hallesche Psychomediziner und die Anfänge der Anthropologie in der deutschsprachigen Frühaufklärung*, ed. Carsten Zelle (Tübingen: Niemeyer, 2001), 112: "Von dem Arzt ist nicht nur psychologische Kenntnis gefordert, sondern auch die Anwendung von Witz, List und Tricks, um eine Einbildung durch eine andere zu heilen."

[68] Schneider, "Hysterie als Gesamtkunstwerk," 219.

literary affect."⁶⁹ To be sure, this early psychological case history presented here is not merely literature in the sense that it forms a discursive element in the literary-medical archive of the eighteenth century; it is also structured at once as drama, with the staging of conflict, epicrisis, and resolution/recognition, and uses a rhetorical device (chiasm) as the key to the reconstitution of reciprocity and friendship between patient and physician. As Schneider suggests, the poetry of the hysterical sign derives, at least in part, from the literary discourse and theory of its scriptural "history" in western culture since Hippocrates.

I would contend, however, that hysteria is no less a reality as a result. Even if hysteria is, to speak with Bronfen, an "illness of representation," or, as Schneider argues, "nothing more than its literary effect," it nevertheless wreaks havoc on the patient, the physician, and all who surround them; it often drives them into despair, terror, and hopelessness, all of which are quite "real." As a genre of psychological illness, it has been powerful enough to form the basis for literally hundreds of studies and papers; one can justifiably speak of a discourse of hysteria ranging from the eighteenth century into the early twentieth century and beyond.⁷⁰ In this early psychological case history we can recognize the linkage between psycho-pathological phenomenology – the description of the emergence, course, and experience of the illness – and a "history of suffering" which Freud identified as a central characteristic of hysteria. Hysteria is indeed a psychological-medical or a medical-psychological hybrid, a double or a twin located on the border between medicine and psychology.⁷¹ In the double-play of the title of Herz's case history of Moritz, in the "something" (*Etwas*) – for what is this *Etwas* if not indeterminable and undecidable? – as also in the dash that separates the terms "psychological" und "medical" in its title – we can already read the powerful ambivalence of this modern phenomenon in its nascent phase at the end of the eighteenth century. It was precisely the ambivalence, the indeterminacy and the conflicted nature of hysteria that made it so compelling for the physicians of the time, profiled it as a special area of concern for the philosophical physicians of the late eighteenth century. As a "nervous illness" or an illness simultaneously of the mind and the body, it operated on a hotly contested boundary and articulated anxieties on three levels. First, regarding the new

---

69 Schneider, "Hysterie als Gesamtkunstwerk," 219.
70 For more contemporary iterations of hysteria, and how hysteria and mass hysteria can be and have been constructed through media representation, see: Elaine Showalter, *Hystories: Hysterical Epidemics and Modern Media* (New York: Columbia University Press, 1998).
71 Petra Rau, "The Poetics of Pathology: Freud's *Studien über Hysterie* and the Tropes of the Novella," *German Life and Letters* 59.1 (2006): 62.

anthropological-materialist conception of medical science, we note a fear about its (in-)ability to explain illnesses situated on this tenuous borderline, or, conversely, the threat such illnesses represented to "materialist" empirical medicine. Second, hysteria stages what I would refer to as an "anxiety of feminization," insofar as male hysteria constructed the male body as "feminine," as "meager, thin, and unmuscular; of a pale, livid, and saturnine complexion,"[72] subject to powerful emotional shifts and somatizations. And third, more generally, and very much in line with the previous point, hysteria performs anxieties about a culture of "sensitive reading" and psychological introspection now increasingly prone to, as we quoted at the beginning of this chapter, "anxious sadness and a susceptible imagination."[73]

Culturally, hypochondria became a "fashionable" illness of educated literary types who somehow felt more deeply the contradictions of enlightenment and, as Porter explained, had sufficient leisure time to dwell on their pains and sufficient knowledge of illness, the limits of medicine, and the physiology of the body to become "expert" at fantasizing the workings of the disease.[74] It thus represented the "faddish enculturation of sickly sensibility" that allowed the patient to enter into a psychological struggle with the physician, enacting a script of victimhood and passivity while in fact empowering and enabling the hysteric as they resisted all treatment and care. As the pathological other of Enlightenment individualism and rationality, hypochondria literalized the mind-body connection, but in stark contrast to the philosophical anthropology of the time that idealized the seamless and reciprocal exchange between the two, it revealed the possibility of a disturbed and disproportionate relation controlled by what we might refer to now as masochistic and narcissistic self-indulgence and anxiety.

On a more philosophical level, such anxieties concerning an overpowering imagination, somatizations, and the reading of imaginative literature (the novel) are most explicitly focused on the loss of the freedom of the will. The philosopher Salomon Maimon, the last editor of Moritz's *Magazin zur Erfahrungsseelenkunde*, the first journal of "empirical psychology," wrote in 1791:

> I note that even aside from this precise relation between the body and the soul, the soul also has an independent power, that is, brings forth modifications that do not correspond to any bodily modifications. Of this type are the effects of the so-called higher powers of the soul and the free will. These precisely are not only independent of the effects of the

---

72 Blackmore, *Treatise of the Spleen and Vapours*, 15.
73 Unzer, ed., *Der Arzt*, 346.
74 Porter, *Flesh in the Age of Reason*, 401–402.

organs, they are directly juxtaposed to them. Health of the soul is the state in which the free will can be expressed without hindrance, whereas mental illness (*Seelenkrankheit*) is the exact opposite.[75]

Ten years after Herz's psychological case history of Moritz, Johann Christian Reil's *Rhapsodies Concerning the Application of the Psychical Cure Method on Mental Illness* (1803), perhaps the most important medical text in the German speaking world of the time, also expressed this anxiety concerning the loss of freedom of the will due to illnesses of the mind or soul:

> These connections of the components of the soul among themselves are based on such a specific distribution of powers in the brain and the entire nervous system [...] If this delicate relation is disturbed, these powers cannot express themselves in a way that is consistent with the freedom of the will.[76]

It is one of the interesting ironies of German intellectual and cultural history during this period around 1800 that, precisely as the philosophy of German Idealism – specifically the post-Kantian systems of Johann Gottlieb Fichte and Friedrich Schelling – dazzled the cultural scene with its unconditional and original positing of the absolute "I" and human freedom, the construction of the world in and through the constituting power of human subjectivity – as Niklas Luhmann put it, "the individual is the world in the particular I. The individual is the subject of the world"[77] – the disciplines of medicine, anthropology, psychology, and literature struggled with deep-seated anxieties about the mind-body divide, the threat of a feminization of the male body, the all-too-sensitive

---

[75] Salomon Maimon, "Über den Plan des Magazins zur Erfahrungsseelenkunde," *Magazin für Erfahrungsseelenkunde* 8.3 (1791): 12. "Ich bemerke aber, daß ohngeachtet dieser genaueren Verbindung zwischen Seele und Körper, die Seele auch in sich selbst würkt, d.h. Modifikationen hervorbringt, denen keine körperliche Modifikationen entsprechen. Von dieser Art sind die Würkungen der sogenannten höheren Seelenkräfte und des freien Willens [...] Diese nämlich die Würkungen des freien Willens sind nicht nur von den Organenwirkungen unabhängig, sondern sogar denselben entgegengesetzt [...] Seelengesundheit ist nehmlich derjenige Seelenzustand, wo die Würkungen des freien Willens ungehindert ausgeübt werden können; so wie die Seelenkrankheit in dem entgegengesetzten Zustand besteht."
[76] Johann Christian Reil, *Rhapsodieen über die Anwendung der psychischen Curmethode auf Geisteszerrüttungen* (Halle, 1803; Zweite Ausgabe 1818), 46: "Diese Beziehungen der Theile des Seelenorgans unter einander sind auf eine so bestimmte Vertheilung der Kräfte im Gehirn und dem gesamten Nervensystem gegründet [...] Wird das Verhältnis gestört, [...] können sie sich nicht mehr der *Freiheit des Willens* gemäß äussern."
[77] Niklas Luhmann, "Individuum, Individualität, Individualismus," in *Gesellschaftsstruktur und Semantik. Studien zur Wissenssoziologie der modernen Gesellschaft*, by Luhmann (Frankfurt: Surhkamp, 1993), vol. 3, 207.

reading practices, and the elusive disturbances of the soul, all of which inform the hybrid discourse of hysteria-hypochondria at the end of the eighteenth century. Marcus Herz's case history of his friend Karl Philipp Moritz allows us to see, in a detail and self-reflexivity often lacking in other descriptions and case-presentations, one instance of the entwinement, somatization, transference, and condensation of hysteria in the eighteenth century "from below," from the points of view of the practicing physician and his patient.

8 The Case History, Therapeutics, and the Dietetics of the Soul: Aesthetics and Empirical Psychology in the Work of Karl Philipp Moritz

> And even assuming that no immediate use for actual life could be shown from these considerations, nevertheless this point of view would still always serve to ennoble the circle of human thought in general, to beautify, and to give all other things in life more interest and value.
> Moritz, "Concerning the Objective of the Magazine for Experiential Psychology"[1]

> We should not constitute a continuous history of the *gnothi seauton* whose explicit or implicit postulate would be a general or universal theory of the subject, but should, I think, beginning with an analytics of the forms of reflexivity, inasmuch as it is the forms of reflexivity that constitute the subject as such.
> Foucault, *Hermeneutics of the Subject*[2]

The first epigraph quoted above by the aesthetician, journalist, critic, novelist, professor of art and linguistics, and member of the Berlin-Brandenburg Academy of Sciences Karl Philipp Moritz (1756–1793) signals the ambivalent tension that inhabits the considerations (*Betrachtungen*) and observations (*Beobachtungen*) that were collected in the ten year run of the first journal of empirical-experiential psychology edited by him, *ΓΝΩΘΙ ΣΑΥΤΟΝ oder Magazin zur Erfahrungsseelenkunde* (1783–1793).[3] These observations appeared in the form of individual case-histories, more or less extensive narratives of individual, concrete cases. On the one hand, this passage from 1791 indicates striving for the correct point of view (*Gesichtspunkt*), in this case, the appropriate objective, non-moralistic search for *Fakta*, actual observations and true experiences to be supplied by teachers, pastors, guardians, civil administrators, physicians, and jurists – the new bourgeois reading public – regardless of their moral implications and their possible

---

[1] Karl Philipp Moritz, "Über den Endzweck des Magazins zur Erfahrungsseelenkunde," in *Gnothi Sauton oder Magazin zur Erfahrungsseelenkunde*, ed. Karl Philipp Moritz (Berlin: August Mylius, 1791), vol. 8, 2.
[2] Michel Foucault, *Hermeneutics of the Subject: Lectures at the Collège de France, 1981–82*, ed. Frédéric Gros, trans. Graham Burchell (New York: Picador, 2001 or Palgrave Macmillan, 2005), 462.
[3] An earlier version of this chapter was published in German as Leventhal, "Die Fallgeschichte zwischen Ästhetik und Therapeutik," in *"Fakta, und kein moralisches Geschwätz." Zu den Fallgeschichten im Magazin zur Erfahrungsseelenkunde (1783–1793)*, ed. Sheila Dickson, Stefan Goldmann, and Christof Wingertszahn (Göttingen: Wallstein Verlag, 2011), 65–83.

conclusions. On the other hand, Moritz specifically warned against any immediate instrumentalization, any direct application in real life (*das eigentliche Leben*) of the knowledge and insights achieved in and through the observations, experiences, and case-histories offered in the journal. The statement is absolutely clear that this special point of view achieved through this form of communication medium – the exchange and publication, reading and discussion of these observations and case-studies – would have an edifying, humanizing, even aesthetic effect on its readers. The use of the term *verschönern* – to beautify or to improve – is particularly significant in this regard. In addition, this unique point of view refers to the intimate relation between two components, sub-disciplines of the journal's four key mission areas – the theory of illness of the soul (*Seelenkrankheitskunde*) and the theory of a therapeutics of the soul (*Seelenheilenkunde*)[4] – and the function of the publication and reading of such accounts. As Moritz stated in 1791, "to ennoble the circle of human thought in general, to beautify, and to give all other things in human life more interest and value."

The designation of a special *Gesichtspunkt* or "point of view" to be achieved in empirical psychology shows the close relationship between this emerging field of the empirical study of the individual human soul and the discipline of philosophical aesthetics, not simply as a theory of the beautiful and aesthetic experience, but more generally as a theory of (perfected) sensate cognition.[5] At the University of Halle around 1750, Alexander Baumgarten (1714–1762) and Georg Friedrich Meier (1718–1777) forged aesthetics as a science of sensate cognition and as a method of guiding the so-called lower cognitive faculties to perfection. As shown in chapter 1, the vital connection between empirical psychology and aesthetics was achieved in the writings of Johann Christian Bolten (1727–1757), Professor of Medicine at the University of Halle and a member of the constellation of psychologically-minded physicians there, whose *Thoughts Concerning Psychological Cures* (1751)[6] made the case for an aesthetic (in the sense of a theory of guidance and direction of sensate cognition) approach to psychological illness. Bolten took his cue in particular from Baumgarten's student and assistant Meier,[7] whose theory of the aesthetic as

---

4 The German term *Kunde* can mean "theory," "field," "area" of study, or "studies."
5 Hans Rudolf Schweizer, *Ästhetik als Philosophie der sinnlichen Erkenntnis: Eine Interpretation der "Aesthetica" A.G. Baumgartens mit teilweiser Wiedergabe der lateinischen Textes und deutscher Übersetzung* (Basel and Stuttgart: Schwabe, 1973), 114: "Aesthetices finis est perfectio cognitionis sensitivae."
6 Johann Christian Bolten, *Gedanken von psychologischen Curen* (Halle: Carl Hermann Hemmerde, 1751), 62, 69.
7 Bolten, *Gedanken von psychologischen Curen*, 60, where he mentioned in particular the usefulness of Meier's *Anfangsgründe aller schönen Wissenschaften* (1748–1750), specifically the chapter on *Arzneigelahrtheit*.

a general theory of the guidance and development of human sensate cognition informed his thinking about psychological cures. The purpose of what he called *philosophical pathology* for Bolten lay precisely in the governance of the "lower" or "sensate" powers of knowledge, or how one could stimulate, suppress, modulate, and transform affects, passions, movements of the mind (*Gemüthsbewegungen*), and the contents of the imagination; this was the job of aesthetics.[8] Let us recall Bolten's statement from the *Gedanken*: "Aesthetics will better be able to provide and explain the laws and rules of the lower or sensible cognitive faculties than psychology [...] one must therefore master aesthetics in order to learn how to bring about psychological cures."[9] Bolten's aesthetic approach to psychological medicine, however, was concerned with pathology, the identification and correction of disequilibrium, disharmony, and imbalance. It had to do neither with the requisite, appropriate point of view of the observer, nor did it contain any methodological procedure for the actual application of those "laws and rules" of the lower or sensible cognitive faculties. On practical matters of his proposed *philosophical pathology*, Bolten was notoriously vague. In this sense, he differed markedly from Moritz, who, thirty years later, was keenly interested in the procedure, method, and function of empirical psychology, in particular, a therapeutics of the soul (*Seelenheilkunde*): how to treat, cure, and heal mental illness.

Serious questions regarding the nature and function of *Erfahrungsseelenkunde*, many of which have been the subject of considerable debate, become acute in Moritz's *Concerning the Final Objective of a Magazine for Experiential Psychology* of 1791: first, how are the many reports, narratives, case-histories and studies, anecdotes and reflections, and commentary and explanations collected and published in the journal supposed to move beyond a mere aggregation, beyond the mere archive of interesting and thought-worthy individual observations, toward empirical psychology as a systematic scientific discipline or *Wissenschaft*? Second, how does experiential psychology (*Erfahrungsseelenkunde*) differ from previous empirical psychology and from pietistic conceptions of *Seelensorge* in its methods and aims? Third, how can such a discipline remain autonomous in its claims for unedited, unprejudiced, "real" experience (*Erfahrung*), and empirical observation (*Beobachtung*) of the individual human being, free from moral and theological dogma and metaphysical speculation? How, if at all, can the theoretical and practical aspects of such a discipline of *Erfahrungsseelenkunde* be reconciled, given that

---

8 Bolten,*Gedanken von psychologischen Curen*, 86–87.
9 Bolten,*Gedanken von psychologischen Curen*, 59–60: "Die Ästhetik wird uns also die Gesetze und Regeln der untern oder sinnlichen Erkenntniskräfte genauer und weitläufiger anführen und erklären, als es in der Psychologie geschehen kann [...] man muss also die Ästhetik inne haben, um psychologische Curen verrichten zu lernen."

it eschewed immediate, direct application in real life (by which we mean the unreflective, generalized use of a specific "cure" discussed in a case history) and advocated for a gradual and continual process of knowledge accumulation and transfer, discussion, debate, and verification? How, precisely, is the correct or appropriate *Gesichtspunkt* to be achieved by any individual observer, and wherein does such a point of view consist? Finally, what is the precise relation between Moritz's aesthetics and his plan for empirical psychology?

The title of this chapter may raise some eyebrows or even appear to be fundamentally misguided. How could the observations, remarks, and commentary contained in the over one hundred case histories presented in the *Magazine* over the ten years of its existence possibly have a bearing on aesthetics, both as a theory of sensate cognition and as a theory of the beautiful? After all, most of the case histories in the *Magazine* were presented in the section of the journal on mental illness and its treatment (*Seelenkrankheitskunde*), and therefore concerned psychopathological subjects and topics, often horrible and terrifying acts and events (*Kindermord, Selbstmord, Massenmord*), and extreme forms of mental disturbance (mania, hypochondria, melancholia, madness) – subjects that, at first sight at least, hardly elicit an *aesthetic* response or feeling.[10] And, concerning the form of the contributions, the observations and case-histories presented are anything but "complete unto themselves" (*in sich selbst vollendet*), the fundamental condition of any properly aesthetic work according to the aesthetics of autonomy put forth by Moritz.

As regards the second term in my title, therapeutics, one has reason to be even more skeptical. Moritz explicitly warned against reading and thinking about the case-histories presented in the *Magazin* simply as examples to be converted directly into praxis. To be sure, Moritz did not reject any therapeutic value of such stories out of hand, but repeatedly insisted that one must first research the "sources and causes" of the particular illnesses, specifically "how they emerge from the disruption of the balance between the various powers of the soul."[11] The psychologically-minded physician should not jump to conclude anything from a case history presented in the journal, but should rather undertake investigations

---

10 It is important to note that Moritz thematized, in addition to and just as important as the traditional forms of mental illness, what we, after Freud, would refer to as a psychopathology of everyday life: indolence, envy, fear, pride, arrogance, denial, rage, humiliation, obsession, and other neurotic states and behaviors. See his "Revision der drei ersten Bände dieses Magazins," *MzE* 4.1 (1786): esp. 5–9.
11 Moritz, "Revision der drei ersten Bände dieses Magazins," 2: "wie sie aus der Aufhebung des Gleichgewichts zwischen Seelenkräften entstehen."

"concerning the specific condition of the ill person from time to time, and concerning the inner nature and constitution of the illness itself."[12] However, a general, therapeutic interest in the sense of a concern for the well-being of the soul (*Seelensorge*), a care of the *self* enunciated by philosophically-minded physicians of the period, can be gleaned from Moritz's writings in connection to the aesthetics of Baumgarten and Meier, and to Bolten's teaching of the direction and guidance of sensate cognition.[13]

In the following, my aim is not to evaluate the case-histories presented in Moritz's *Magazin* in terms of their literary or aesthetic qualities, to view them as aesthetic texts, or, as Nicolas Pethes has aptly shown, to demonstrate how the new orientation toward the individual case emerged as an aesthetic phenomenon in the second half of the eighteenth century.[14] Rather, my aim is to examine Moritz's programmatic writings concerning the purpose and value of empirical psychology – essays and brief texts – as to their underlying structural discourses and patterns of argumentation, specifically, in their suggestion of the particular method of observation (*Beobachtung*), the establishment of the correct point of view (*Gesichtspunkt*), and attention to or concern for the self (*Aufmerksamkeit*). The second interest is to try to discern to what degree Moritz's claims for the type of knowledge to be attained and disseminated in *Erfahrungsseelenkunde* reveal a structural similarity with the form of aesthetic experience – specifically, autonomy and disinterestedness – as it was formulated in the late-enlightenment anthropological project of a reconstitution of whole human being (*der ganze Mensch*). Third and finally, this chapter seeks to trace the classical tradition of *gnothi sauton* – know thyself – appropriated by Moritz as the title for his journal, as a form of *therapeuein* in the sense of a concern for and care of the soul (*Seelensorge; epimeleia heautou*), as this has been discussed by Foucault in his writings on the history of care of the self, and

---

12 Moritz, *Vorschlag zu einem Magazin einer Erfahrungsseelenkunde*, in *Werke in zwei Bänden*, by Karl Philipp Moritz, ed. Heide Hollmer and Albert Meier (Frankfurt: Deutsche Klassiker Verlag, 1997–1999), 1:794 (hereafter cited as *Werke*, with volume and page number): "über den jedesmaligen Zustand des Kranken, und über die innere Natur und Beschaffenheit der Krankheit."
13 Compare Carsten Zelle, "Sinnlichkeit und Therapie. Zur Gleichursprünglichkeit der Ästhetik und Anthropologie um 1750," in *Vernünftige Ärzte. Hallesche Psychomediziner und die Anfänge der Anthropologie in der deutschsprachigen Frühaufklärung*, ed. Zelle (Tübingen: Niemeyer, 2001), 5–24.
14 Nicolas Pethes, "Ästhetik des Falls. Zur Konvergenz anthropologischer und literarischer Theorien der Gattung," in *"Fakta, und kein moralisches Geschwätz." Zu den Fallgeschichten im Magazin zur Erfahrungsseelenkunde (1783–1793)*, ed. Sheila Dickson et al. (Göttingen: Wallstein Verlag, 2011), 13–32.

embed this in a more general pastoral apparatus.[15] It is not a matter of defining the aesthetic characteristics of the case history in Moritz's programmatic writings on the discipline of *Erfahrungsseelenkunde*, or the direct therapeutic utility of specific case-studies. Rather, I situate empirical psychology and its privileged form, the psychological case history, historically and disciplinarily between two "discourses" – therapeutics and dietetics on the one hand; knowledge of and concern for the soul on the other – in order to demonstrate common patterns of argumentation and similar discursive strategies governing empirical psychology and the discipline of aesthetics.

Moritz wanted real facts (*wirkliche Fakta*)[16] to form the basis of the new discipline, or, as he stated in the preface to the journal in 1783: "Facts, and no moral drivel, no novel, and no dramatic comedy"[17] he advised: not "inventions" (*Erdichtungen*), but rather observations from the real world (*Beobachtungen aus der wirklichen Welt*).[18] The strict boundary constructed here between the case-histories or studies to be presented to the journal and literature meant that narratives should be based in actual experience and observation; they should be grounded in empirical fact, not imagination; and, most importantly, they should be void of any aesthetic embellishment and moral posturing. One might say that such an imperative was part of the Enlightenment project of discerning clearly and distinctly between truth and falsehood. However, the subjective nature of experience (*Erfahrung*) and the demand for facts based on observation (*Beobachtung*) raised the question of precisely how much reflection and interpretation the authors of such case-histories should engage in. Moritz is far from clear on this. In some of his assertions in the programmatic writings, he insists that the writer of such case-histories ought to resist the temptation of weaving reflections into the narrative (*der Versuchung widerstehen, Reflexionen einzuweben*),[19] in other words they are to describe the case as precisely and as objectively as possible, instead of interpreting it or seeking to explain it. In other statements, however, Moritz assumes

---

15 Foucault, *Hermeneutics of the Subject* (2005).
16 Moritz, *Vorschlag*, in *Werke*, 1:797.
17 Moritz, *Vorrede zum Magazin zur Erfahrungsseelenkunde*, in *Werke*, 1:811: "Fakta, und kein moralisches Geschwätz, keinen Roman, und keine Komödie,"
18 Moritz, *Vorschlag*, in *Werke*, 1:796. In an earlier version of the *Vorschlag*, Moritz states: "Dann müßten aber schlechterdings nur wirkliche Fakta darinn abgedruckt werden, und wer sie einsendete, müßte der Versuchung widerstehen, Reflexionen einzuweben." Karl Philipp Moritz, *Aussichten zu einer Experimentalseelenlehre* (Berlin: August Mylius, 1782), 12.
19 Compare Yvonne Wübben, "Traum, Wahn und Wahnwissen. Karl Philipp Moritz als Sammler psychologischer Erfahrungsberichte," in *Kulturen des Wissens im 18. Jahrhundert*, ed. Ulrich Johannes Schneider (Berlin and New York: de Gruyter, 2008), 426–430.

a less rigid, more dialectical, gradualist position: "Even this magazine could grow through [the integration of] important reflections and significant facts."[20] This connotes a more developmental, incremental approach, in which one begins with the facts and slowly mounts second-order statements based on those facts, as he stated in the *Basic Guidelines for the Project of an Experiential Psychology*: "In a magazine of experiential psychology, especially at the beginning, there must be as few inserted reflections as possible. As it develops and grows, more and more significant reflections and important facts can reciprocally come to one another's assistance."[21] In 1791, looking back on eight years of the journal, Moritz summarized his position in the following manner: "experiences should be guided by reflection, but reflection should also be reciprocally corrected through experiences."[22] Such a reciprocal, dialectical, probative procedure of experience and reflection would allow the researcher of the human soul to gradually achieve knowledge of a more general nature. Experience and analogical reasoning from cases through reflection, commentary, and discussion would construct a scientific apparatus of the soul: a theory and semiotics, as well as a theory of therapeutics of mental illness.

Moritz's concept and plan for empirical psychology and a specific discipline for the diagnosis and treatment of mental illness (*Seelenkrankheitskunde*) in particular can perhaps best be described *ex negativo*. The guiding principle was always that mental illness was not a religious or moral sin, or a purely physical, organic dysfunction or imbalance, but a *disturbance of the individual psyche* that must be understood and treated as such. The project of *Erfahrungsseelenkunde* was to be fueled by reports, observations, and experiences submitted by people from all walks of life, but there was also a more esoteric interest in the depth-psychological mechanisms of a nascent psychopathology, one which, as Wolfert von Rahden has observed, should be "extricated from the pre-interpreted moral and religious semantics" that had governed such writing previously.[23] To be avoided in the writing

---

20 Moritz, *Vorschlag*, in *Werke*, 1:797: "Selbst dieses Magazin könnte wechselsweise durch wichtige Reflexionen und wichtige Fakta wachsen."
21 Moritz, *Vorschlag*, in *Werke*, 1:797: "In einem Magazin der Erfahrungsseelenkunde müssen, insbesondre anfänglich, der eingestreuten Reflexionen so wenige als möglich sein. In der Folge kann es immer mehr durch wichtige Reflexionen und wichtige Fakta wachsen, die sich wechselseitig einander zu Hülfe kommen."
22 Moritz, "Ueber den Endzweck des Magazins zur Erfahrungsseelenkunde," *MzE* 8.1 (1791): 3–4: "die Erfahrungen sollen freilich durch Nachdenken geleitet, das Nachdenken aber auch wechselseitig durch Erfahrungen berichtigt werden."
23 Wolfert von Rahden, "Sprachpsychonauten. Einige nicht-institutionelle Aspekte der Entstehung einer 'Sprachbetrachtung in psychologischer Rücksicht' im letzten Drittel des 18. Jahrhunderts am Beispiel der Diskurskonkurrenz zwischen Immanuel Kant und Karl Philipp

of such case-histories was the rush toward a fixed, complete system, as Moritz argued: "All anxious working towards a rigid system must be avoided completely."[24] Also excluded from the new discipline were universal remedies of any kind – "Universalarznei aller Krankheiten der Seele"[25] – without focused consideration of and attention to the unique character of each individual case. Moritz eschewed any form of speculation, ungrounded hypotheses, hasty judgment, religious prejudices, and any hint of moral judgment: "This science would in this way gradually emerge in and through itself, and how sturdy this edifice will become, in which gaps are not simply filled in through empty speculation, but with real facts."[26] He specifically cautioned against viewing the study of empirical psychology as a mere casuistic enterprise, a mere accumulation of cases without any direction, plan, or systematic trajectory. The cases were to be collected, disseminated through the journal, ordered under specific rubrics; the journal was to provide the discursive medium or archive of discussion and argument, a repository for reflections and emendations, until gradually an edifice of systematic knowledge would emerge: "All of these observations ought to be collected under specific rubrics in a journal devoted to them, and reflections avoided until a sufficient quantity of facts are present, and then finally all of this ordered into a purposeful totality. What an important work for humanity this could be!"[27] A gradualistic, inductive-empirical, one might say "analytical" procedure, derived from the empirical scientific models of the seventeenth and early eighteenth centuries, beginning with experience and observation and slowly generating increasingly refined and general knowledge, and eventually establishing certain laws while rejecting speculation and hypotheses, informed Moritz's methodological plan for empirical psychology.[28] In this regard, Bacon's *Novum Organon* (1620) was a watershed moment, as it advanced the view of the gradual evolution of scientific knowledge using

---

Moritz," in *Sprachwissenschaft im 18 Jahrhundert. Fallstudien und Überblicke*, ed. Klaus D. Dutz (Münster: Nodus, 1993), 111–141.
24 Moritz, "Grundlinien zu einem ohngefähren Entwurf in Rücksicht auf die Seelenkrankheitskunde," in *Werke*, 1:812.
25 Moritz, *Vorschlag*, in *Werke*, 1:794.
26 Moritz, *Vorschlag*, in *Werke*, 1:794: "Diese Wissenschaft würde sich auf diese Weise allmählich selber bilden, und wie fest würde dies Gebäude werden, wo die Lücken nicht durch leere Spekulationen zugestopft, sondern durch Tatsachen ausgefüllt werden."
27 Moritz, *Vorschlag*, in *Werke*, 1:796: "Alle diese Beobachtungen erstlich unter gewisse Rubriken in einem dazu bestimmten Magazine gesammelt, nicht eher Reflexionen angestellt, bis eine hinlängliche Anzahl Fakta da sind, und dann am Ende dies alles einmal zu einem zweckmäßigen Ganzen geordnet. Welch ein wichtiges Werk für die Menschheit könnte dieses werden!"
28 Mark Boulby makes the case that the empiricism of the *Vorschlag* derived from the Göttingen empiricist Michael Hissmann, but Moritz's empiricism is grounded in the

observation and experimentation and informed the "empirical turn" of medicine in the seventeenth century. As mentioned previously, Moritz changed the name of the journal and the proposed discipline from *Experimentalseelenkunde* (experimental psychology) to *Erfahrungsseelenkunde* (empirical psychology) on the suggestion of Moses Mendelssohn, who had argued that the very idea of experiments on the human soul ran counter to the idea of the dignity of the human being. Moritz should be placed in a long line of experimental-empirical thinking including Bacon, Boyle, Newton and, in German medicine, Friedrich Hoffmann, Georg Ernest Stahl, the psychologically minded physicians at the University of Halle and Johann Georg Zimmermann[29] in the mid-eighteenth century, all of whom prized the unique value of the individual results of specific case-histories that could furnish proof of a theory or a natural law.[30] The case-histories themselves were to serve as the evidentiary basis of the new science of empirical psychology, analogous to the experiment in physiology.[31] Moritz's *Magazin zur Erfahrungsseelenkunde* was to become more than simply "a large body of individual cases;"[32] as a journal dedicated to psychology, it was to serve science, education, and humanity as a whole.

*

Aesthetics as a discourse that emerged in the eighteenth century concerning the so-called lower faculties of the human being, what was referred to as "sensate cognition" – sensation, perception, feeling, and emotion – was already at the very

---

assumption of a soul, which Hissmann rejected. See Mark Boulby, *Karl Philipp Moritz: At the Fringe of Genius* (Toronto: University of Toronto Press, 1979).

29 Consider Zimmermann's definition of medicine as "durch die wohl gemeinte und wohl überlegte Beobachtungen und Experimente erlangte Fertigkeit in der Kunst den Menschen vor Krankheiten zu bewahren." Johann Georg Zimmermann, *Von der Erfahrung in der Arzneykunst* (Brugg and Zürich, 1763–1764), 46.

30 See Johanna Geyer-Kordesch, "Medizinische Fallbeschreibungen und ihre Bedeutung in der Wissensreform des 17. und 18. Jahrhunderts," *Medizin, Gesellschaft, Geschichte* 9 (1990): 10–11.

31 Karl Philipp Moritz, "Vorrede zum Magazin für Erfahrungsseelenkunde," in *Karl Philipp Moritz. Die Schriften in dreißig Bänden*, ed. Petra Nettelbeck and Uwe Nettelbeck (Nördlingen: F. Greno, 1986), vol. 1, 8: "Nach dem Vorschlage des Herrn Moses Mendelssohn werde ich die Eintheilungen in der Arzneiwissenschaft auf die Erfahrungsseelenkunde anzuwenden suchen."

32 Hans Adler, "Fundus Animae – Grund der Seele. Zur Gnoseologie des Dunklen in der Aufklärung," *Deutsche Vierteljahrsschrift für Literaturwissenschaft und Geistesgeschichte* 62.2 (1988): 209: "ein Fundus einzelner Fälle."Adler draws an interesting connection between Johann Georg Sulzer and Karl Philipp Moritz in the call for the exact description and collection of individual cases.

beginning closely related to medicine, in particular the burgeoning interest in psycho-physiology.[33] Specifically, certain forms of aesthetic representation and practice were linked metaphorically to "infection" and "contagion," especially the theater and the reading of novels. As Alexander Košenina has remarked in his monograph on Moritz: "The contagious power of the theatrical play becomes precisely the measure of success of reception-aesthetics. The medical advances in the area of epidemiology, especially the recently developed vaccinations, continue right into the metaphors of the aestheticians."[34] But it was not merely a metaphorical fear of infection or contagion that traveled from medicine to aesthetics and forged a link between the two. The constellation of aesthetics and psychology in Halle around 1750 had already introduced a therapeutics aimed at the regulation of the affects; Baumgarten had situated aesthetics within psychology, and the psychologically-minded physicians – especially Nicolai and Bolten – argued for the aesthetic modulation of psychological perturbances. A deep-seated concern for the psycho-physiological unity of the human being was also clearly at work. Aesthetics was understood as a sphere and medium in which the entire human being – the soul and the body, *der ganze Mensch* – could experience this profound connection directly and intuitively. The theory of soul-healing (*Seelenheilkunde*) was aimed precisely at bringing the two into a harmonious equilibrium. Two key thinkers in Germany prior to Moritz and the publication of the *Magazin* already circumscribed the close relation between aesthetics, both as a theory of sensate cognition and as a theory of the beautiful, and psychology: Johann Georg Sulzer and Mendelssohn.

Johann Georg Sulzer (1720–1779) was a Swiss mathematician who eventually became head of the philosophical section of the Berlin Academy of Sciences after the death of Pierre-Louis Moreau de Maupertuis (1698–1759). He published extensively on the origin of the arts and sciences, morals, aesthetics, psychology, and poetics. In 1751–1752, he published his *Investigation into the Origin of Pleasurable and Unpleasurable Sensations* (*Untersuchung über den Ursprung der angenehmen und unangehmen Empfindungen*), which he re-worked and re-published again in

---

33 Simon Richter, *Laocoon's Body and the Aesthetics of Pain. Lessing, Herder, Moritz and Goethe* (Detroit: Wayne State University Press, 1991), esp. 139–163. More recently, see: Barbara Thums, "Das feine Gewebe der Organisation: Zum Verhältnis von Biologie und Ästhetik in Karl Philipp Moritz Kunstautonomie Ornamenttheorie," *Zeitschrift für Ästhetik und allgemeine Kunstwissenschaft* 49.2 (2004): 237–260; and Martin Davies, "Moritz und die aufklärerische Berliner Medizin," in *Karl Philipp Moritz und das 18. Jahrhundert*, ed. Martin Fontius and Anneliese Klingenberg (Tübingen: Max Niemeyer, 1995), 215–226.
34 Alexander Košenina, *Karl Philipp Moritz. Literarische Experimente auf dem Weg zum psychologischen Roman* (Göttingen: Wallstein, 2006), 124.

1762 under the title *Theory of Pleasant and Unpleasant Sensations* (*Theorie angenehmen und unangehmen Empfindungen*) – a treatise situated on the boundary between aesthetics and psychology that sought to deduce the principles underlying the human experience of pleasure and displeasure. According to Sulzer, the fundamental, inherent power of the soul is representation (*Vorstellung*). The soul experiences *pleasure* in the representation of perfection, and *displeasure* at the representation of imperfection. However, in the experience of pleasurable representations, the soul cannot be overwhelmed or overpowered by a barrage of such representations. The representations cannot be overly complex or obscure if they are to give rise to pleasure and thus to produce the feeling of perfected sensate cognition – the beautiful. If the cognitive apparatus is barraged with noisy and disparate perceptions without any unifying structure, the human being experiences imperfection and thus *displeasure*. We require unity and coherence in order to have representations that are pleasing to the soul. There must be what Sulzer refers to as a certain ease or effortlessness (*Leichtigkeit*),[35] and an absence of all coercion and force (*Zwang*).[36] Perfection (*Vollkommenheit*) according to Sulzer was simply a harmonious multiplicity that refers to a unity and effortlessly brings forth a pleasurable sensation in the soul. As he wrote later in his *General Theory of the Beautiful Arts* (*Allgemeine Theorie der Schönen Künste*, 1771–1774), this unity, coherence, and harmony is the basis of all perfection and beauty:

> Therefore unity is the basis of perfection and beauty; for perfection is that which is complete and without flaw, that which is how it should be; beauty is that whose perfection one can feel or sense. And for this reason nothing can please us that has no unity, or whose unity we are not able to recognize, because in this case we cannot judge whether or not the object is what it should be.[37]

---

[35] J.G. Sulzer, *Theorie der angenehmen und unangenehmen Empfindungen* (Berlin: bey Friedrich Nicolai, 1762), 60–62.

[36] The political rhetoric is unmistakable. *Zwang* is a pejorative term in the second half of the eighteenth century in Germany; it refers to the arbitrary, capricious and illegitimate use of force or coercion by political authorities. On this, see Hans-Wolf Jäger, *Politische Kategorien in der Poetik und Rhetorik der Zweiten Häfte des 18. Jahrhunderts* (Stuttgart: Metzler, 1970).

[37] Johann Georg Sulzer, *Allgemeine Theorie der schönen Künste* (Leipzig: Weidmanns, Erben, and Reich, 1771), vol. 1, 302: "Also ist die Einheit der Grund der Vollkommenheit und der Schönheit; denn vollkommen ist das, was gänzlich und ohne Mangel, das ist, was es seyn soll; schön ist das, dessen Vollkommenheit man sinnlich fühlt oder empfindet. Daher also kommt es, daß uns von Gegenständen unsrer Betrachtung nichts gefallen kann, darin keine Einheit ist, oder dessen Einheit wir nicht erkennen, weil wir in diesem Fall nicht beurtheilen können, ob die Sache das ist, was sie seyn soll."

In the encounter with sensuous perfection, and in its representation in the soul, one experiences an easing of the demands of attentiveness on the soul because, Sulzer argued, we can always count on there being an overarching unity of or within the multiplicity of the perceptions. The question then was precisely the provenance of this "unity," how it emerges and where it is to be situated, in human cognition, in the object itself, or in some combination or meeting of the two. For Sulzer, this perfect harmony of unity and multiplicity as the condition of beauty was ontologically rooted in the object itself.[38] Nature, according to Sulzer, afforded humanity with the requisite unity as the very ground of perfection and beauty.

Mendelssohn's *On the Sensations* (1755) agreed with Sulzer regarding the necessity of a unifying structure (*Einheit*). Paraphrasing Sulzer, Mendelssohn wrote: "It [the soul] will be able to survey the manifold concepts as it were from a single viewpoint."[39] But Mendelssohn strongly disagreed with Sulzer's account of beauty as a form of perfected sensate cognition with its basis not in the mind but in nature, in the object itself, and predicated on the idleness, an ease or laxity of the soul. Sulzer had suggested that the unity of the sensate multiplicity of experience could be found within experience itself, and unburdened the soul by allowing it a certain repose from arduous striving, giving rise to the feeling of pleasure. Mendelssohn objected that such a view was utterly incompatible with the formative, striving power of the soul, and the secondary pleasure the mind derives from experiencing its own power, for it emphasized in Mendelssohn's thinking a weakness or privation of the soul's representational powers. The experience of the unity in multiplicity is not due to or a result of a relaxation or the passivity of the representing powers; rather, such an experience is a direct result of the mind's representational power and the very ground of beauty. Experiencing the unity in multiplicity is for Mendelssohn a function of experiencing the soul's great representational capacity, and can be perceived by the mind with ease as long as the mind is not distracted by the minute particulars and as long as the object itself is

---

[38] Paul Guyer, "18th Century German Aesthetics," *Stanford Encyclopedia of Philosophy* (Winter 2016), ed. Edward N. Zalta, first published 16 January 2007; substantive revision 3 March 2014, https://plato.stanford.edu/archives/win2016/entries/aesthetics-18th-german/ (accessed 22 January 2017): "Thus the experience of beauty becomes the sensation or sentiment (*Empfindung*) caused by the perfection of the object, rather than a clear but indistinct cognition of that perfection. The real object of pleasure then becomes the activity of one's own representational state, manifested in the form of sentiment, that is caused by the perfection of the beautiful object."

[39] This is Mendelssohn's paraphrase of Sulzer in *Über die Empfindungen*. On Sulzer, see Ernst Stöckmann, *Anthropologische Ästhetik: Philosophie, Psychologie und ästhetische Theorie der Emotionen im Diskurs der Aufklärung* (Berlin: de Gruyter, 2009), 201–250.

not fraught with completely disparate aspects. Our enjoyment and pleasure according to Mendelssohn is predicated upon a hybrid apprehension of the object as simultaneously multiple and unified. As Theocles writes in Letter 5 of *On the Sensations*: "Here your soul will become intoxicated from the ecstasy, here you will attain intuitive knowledge of an authentic perfection, a pleasure that depends *not on your weakness*, but on the rational striving for representations grounded in one another."[40]

The close connection for Moritz between aesthetics and empirical psychology has been recognized by a number of scholars. In 1980, the Germanist Hans-Joachim Schrimpf formulated the relation in the following manner:

> If one considers the dominant categories of the Moritzian aesthetic as a whole, its anthropological and socio-psychological orientation becomes clearly recognizable [...] the rigoristic autonomy-postulate of Moritz' aesthetic appears as an emancipatory regulative Utopia, one which the autobiographer, the empirical psychologist and the anthropologist does not internalize in an attempt to flee the world, but rather places over and against the dreary contemporary reality, with an enlightened claim to publicity demanding social change.[41]

According to Schrimpf, aesthetics and *Erfahrungsseelenkunde* operated hand in hand for Moritz: an emancipatory regulative utopia aimed at change and reform of the contemporary reality of the *deutsche Misere* informed both the aesthetics of autonomy and the therapeutic project of soul-healing (*Seelenheilkunde*) within empirical psychology.[42] The tensions between Moritz's concept of art as autonomous, as transforming suffering into beauty, and the casuistic, empirical approach of *Erfahrungsseelenkunde*, uncovering the wayward paths of the human soul Schrimpf explained as Moritz rejecting any attempt to harmonize reality or to resolve the rupture between ideal beauty and the actuality of human suffering. Such a gap was constitutive for Moritz. Jutta Osinski quickly questioned Schrimpf's postulate, pointing out the apparent inconsistencies between Moritz's aesthetic program and the project of empirical psychology: the open-ended, aggregating procedure of the latter, its concentration on individual cases seemed to contradict

---

40 Moses Mendelssohn, "On the Sentiments," in *Philosophical Writings*, by Mendelssohn, ed. Daniel O. Dahlstrom (Cambridge: Cambridge University Press, 2000), 24; emphasis mine.
41 Hans-Joachim Schrimpf, *Karl Philipp Moritz* (Stuttgart: J. B. Metzler, 1980), 116: "Stellt man die dominierenden Kategorien der Moritzschen Ästhetik zusammen, so wird ihre anthropologische und soziopsychologische Orientierung deutlich erkennbar [...] Das rigoristische Autonomie-Postulat der Moritzschen Ästhetik erscheint als eine emanzipatorische regulative Utopie, die der Autobiograph, Erfahrungsseelenkundler und Anthropologe nicht weltflüchtig verinnerlicht, sondern mit aufklärerischem Öffentlichkeitsanspruch, soziale Veränderung fordernd, der schlechten zeitgeschichtlichen Wirklichkeit entgegensetzt."
42 Schrimpf, *Karl Philipp Moritz*, 54.

the containment, closure, and perfection attributed to the aesthetically beautiful.[43] Using Moritz's psychological novel *Anton Reiser* (1785–1790), Osinski argues that the narrator is not a psychologically-minded physician (*philosophischer Arzt*) in his treatment of Anton's suffering and pathological wanderings,[44] and that the implicit aesthetic claim of the "work" and its empirical-psychological interest both *fail* due to its fragmentary inconclusiveness and the absence of any truly valuable insight into or correction of Reiser's persistent going-awry. In a word, in Osinski's view, the potential of formative education (*Bildung*) and the reform-critical impulse of both aesthetics and empirical psychology break down in the novel and in Moritz's work as a whole. More recently, Barbara Thums has elucidated several further *aporias* in Moritz's theory of self-observation, many of which touch directly on the connection between aesthetics and empirical psychology: the demand for disinterestedness/autonomy on the part of the observer of human souls (as detachment from external vestments and agendas) in contrast to the profound, clearly very interested attention (*Aufmerksamkeit*) to small details (*das Kleinscheinende*).[45] The paradox of what Thums calls an "inattentive attention" (*unaufmerksame Aufmerksamkeit*) is precisely that it constitutes an aesthetic form of intuition (*ästhetische Anschauung*) that makes possible the self-observation crucial to the practice of empirical psychology.[46] It is therefore anything but "disinterested." Finally, Klaus Becker has demonstrated the further development of Moritz's psychological-anthropological interest within his aesthetic writings,[47] although, as Yvonne Wübben has correctly pointed out, Moritz himself never fully theorized the precise entwinement of the two in a systematic fashion.[48] While one must take

---

43 Jutta Osinski, "Psychologie und Ästhetik bei Karl Philipp Moritz," in *Karl Philipp Moritz und das 18. Jahrhundert. Bestandaufnehmen, Korrekturen, Neuansätze*, ed. Anneliese Klingenberg and Martin Fontius (Tübingen: Niemeyer, 1995), 201–214.
44 The position of Lothar Müller, *Die kranke Seele und das Licht der Erkenntnis. Karl Philipp Moritz' Anton Reiser* (Frankfurt: Athenaeum, 1987).
45 Barbara Thums, *Aufmerksamkeit. Wahrnehmung und Selbstbegründung von Brockes bis Nietzsche* (München: Wilhelm Fink, 2008), 94: "Deutlich wird hier bereits ein Konflikt zwischen dem allseitigen Interesse einer im Dienst der mikroskopischen Introspektion stehenden Aufmerksamkeit aufs Kleinscheinende einerseits und dem ebenfalls der Selbstbeobachtung dienenden, von den sinnlichen Wahrnehmungen abstrahierenden Desinteresse andererseits."
46 Thums, *Aufmerksamkeit*, 96.
47 Klaus Becker, *Von der Kraft, den rechten Gesichtspunkt zu treffen. Ein spätes Echo auf Karl Philipp Moritz und einige seiner Zeitgenossen – In einem Briefwechsel aus jüngerer Zeit* (Hannover: Wehrhahn, 2005), 205.
48 Wübben, "Traum, Wahn und Wahnwissen," 428.

seriously the tensions and inconsistencies between the two disciplines in Moritz's work pointed out by Osinski's, Thums, and Wübben, certain discursive or deep-structural connections between Moritz's aesthetics and empirical psychology, however "inconsistent," need to be fleshed out. In the following, I attend to precisely these tensions and questions in Moritz's programmatic writings.

Even though the experience of the beautiful and a theory of the beautiful work of art increasingly claimed priority as the discussion concerning aesthetics advanced in the second half of the eighteenth century, let us recall the mainspring of aesthetic experience remained, as Andrew Bowie has stated, "to do justice to the immediacy of the individual's sensuous relationship to the world."[49] This impetus to profile the individual's unique, immediate, sensuous world-experience should not be thought of merely as a "compensatory" or reactive gesture in the face of increasing civilizing moral and social forces, as Odo Marquardt has suggested,[50] but positively and constructively as a realm of experience in which precisely the irreducibility and unique experience of every individual would not only be maintained, but pushed forward and expanded, demarcating a unique realm of a special kind of experience.[51] As Benjamin Bennett has argued:

> the task of aesthetics is, accordingly, to restore the self, to restore a condition in which our strict *Eigentümlichkeit*, the unrepeatable particularity of our being ourselves, can be preserved even in the face of universal moral and social claims on us, and restore us to a condition in which we, like the Greeks, will be at once "individual and genus," namely representatives of the human genus or "Repräsentanten der Gattung."[52]

Bennett's argument concerning aesthetics in the eighteenth century introduces a tension between irreducible individuality and the representation of what is essentially "human." However, an even more powerful dissonance exists at the

---

[49] Andrew Bowie, *Aesthetics and Subjectivity: From Kant to Nietzsche* (Manchester: Manchester University Press, 1990), 4.
[50] Odo Marquard, "Several Connections between Aesthetics and Therapeutics in Nineteenth-Century Philosophy," in *The New Schelling*, ed. Judith Norman and Alistair Welchman (New York: Continuum, 2004), 13–29.
[51] Niklas Luhmann, *Art as Social System*, trans. Eva M. Knodt (Stanford, CA: Stanford University Press, 2000), 277: "From Baumgarten to Kant, efforts to understand art led straight into the field of cognitive theory. ›Aesthetics‹ thought of itself as cognitive possibility, as a philosophical science whose task was to demarcate and interrogate its own terrain."
[52] Benjamin Bennett, "The Irrelevance of Aesthetics and the De-Theorizing of Self in 'Classical' Weimar," in *The Camden History of German Literature*, ed. Simon Richter (Rochester, NY: Camden House, 2001), vol. 7, 295–321.

very heart of the aesthetic project: the very articulation of the "theory" or the abstract principles of a "discipline" of aesthetics seems to contradict the very individuality it purports to guarantee. As Terry Eagleton has pointed out:

> With the birth of the aesthetic, the sphere of art begins to suffer something of the abstraction and formalization of modern theory in general; yet the aesthetic is nevertheless thought to retain a charge of irreducible particularity [...]. Aesthetics is thus always a contradictory, self-undoing sort of project, which in promoting the theoretical value of its object risks emptying it of exactly that specificity or ineffability.[53]

The very moment we attempt to theorize the aesthetic experience, it loses precisely its sensuous, immediate, intuitive force, as well as its critical juxtaposition to the discursive concepts and norms it purports to circumvent.

Bearing these more general paradoxes or tensions in mind, we turn to the case of Karl Philipp Moritz. In his work, there appears at first to be a sharp divide between his theory of aesthetic autonomy and the project of an empirical psychology: the aesthetic experience of a work of art that is in itself "complete" and "perfect" – by which he means is not contingent upon nor beholden to any real-life interest or agenda – seems at first to be completely at odds with a discipline of the soul and its pathologies. However, as I will seek to show in the following, the two intersect and overlap in surprising ways – we might call them disciplinary border-crossings or transgressions – that have yet to be articulated in the existing scholarship. In terms of the *object* of their respective purviews itself, both are concerned first and foremost with the "lower" faculties of cognition as they were thought of at that time, the "dark" (*dunkle*) or "indistinct" (*undeutliche*) representations of the soul. More interestingly, at the level of the apprehension of the object, both the aesthetic experience and pathologies of the soul are, in each case, fundamentally individual; they are individual "cases" that cannot be readily subsumed under an existing concept, rubric, or rigid determination; they defy categorization and discursive categories. Finally, at the level of the subject position, both require an astonishingly similar subjective posture or attitude: to lift oneself (or, as the case may be, be elevated) beyond the narrow confines of the self, to transcend the mundane, everyday natural attitude, instrumental agendas and interests, and achieve a universally human point of view whose communication is the very ground of the experience. The self-overcoming Moritz demands of the human observer (*Menschenbeobachter*) in matters of the research into the soul in experiential psychology bears a stunning similarity to the transcendence of the self in the aesthetic experience

---

[53] Terry Eagleton, *The Ideology of the Aesthetic* (Oxford: Oxford University Press, 1990), 2.

of the beautiful. Both promise, one could say, a transformative potential – what Schrimpf referred to as an "emancipatory regulative utopia" – whereby suffering (*Leiden*) is transformed into empathy (*Mitleiden*), destruction and death into education and self-formation, individuality into that which is, at least at the end of the eighteenth century, "essentially" and universally human: the human being in its unique entirety (*der ganze Mensch*) as being somehow exemplary for humanity in general.

In 1785, Moritz published *Essay on the Unification of All Beautiful Sciences under the Concept of that which is Complete unto Itself* (*Versuch einer Vereinigung aller schönen Wissenschaften unter dem Begriff des in sich selbst Vollendeten*) in the form of a letter to Mendelssohn in the *Berlinische Monatsschrift*, one of the most important journals of the late Enlightenment in Germany. This text is rightly considered to be one of the founding documents of "the aesthetics of autonomy" which achieves its most precise and famous formulation in Immanuel Kant's *Critique of Judgment* (1790).[54] In a word, the aesthetics of autonomy states that the work of art is not subservient to any determinate concept or specific use; that the pleasure we experience in the encounter with it is not based on any fixed rubric, and is not merely simple pleasure or enjoyment, but is grounded in an implicit communicative universal judgment that others would or could, in principle, find the object beautiful as well, apart from any utility or application. In the *Essay on the Unification of All Beautiful Sciences*, Moritz developed the thesis that the beautiful work of art can only be designated as such on the basis of its unique, internal completion and perfection, its individual constitution and irreducibly *particular* value, and, perhaps most importantly, its lack of any external utility.[55] To be sure, the work of art has a sense of what Moritz calls *inner purposiveness* (*Zweckmäßigkeit*), but it lacks any actual determinant purpose, any external functionality or concrete utility:

> In cases where an external use or purpose is lacking, this must be found in the work itself if it is to awaken our pleasure; or, I must find in its individual parts so much purposiveness that I forget to ask what the whole point is. This means, in other words: I must find pleasure in a beautiful object *solely for its own sake*, and to this end, the lack of external purpose must be replaced by an internal purposiveness; the object must be something perfected in itself.[56]

---

[54] Kant certainly read Moritz's essay, as he was a regular reader of and contributor to the journal, and in fact had an essay published in the same issue.
[55] Moritz, *Werke*, 2:944.
[56] Moritz, "Versuch einer Vereinigung aller schönen Künste und Wissenschaften unter dem Begriff des in sich selbst Vollendeten," *Berlinische Monatsschrift* 5.3 (1785): 231; emphasis mine: "Wo also bei einem Gegenstand ein äußerer Nutzen oder Zweck fehlt, da muß dieser in dem

Moritz distinguishes, in the case of our encounter with that which is aesthetically beautiful, the pleasurable forgetting of our self (*das angenehme Vergessen unsrer selbst*).[57] More precisely, Moritz writes of a loss of self (*Selbstverlust*) in our experience of the beautiful:

> Even this sweet astonishment, the pleasurable forgetting of ourselves in the consideration of a beautiful work of art, is proof of the fact that our pleasure in this instance is secondary [...]. As the beautiful places our consideration fully on itself and detaches it from us, it creates a situation in which we appear to lose ourselves in the beautiful object, and precisely this loss, this forgetting of our self, is the highest degree of pure and disinterested pleasure, which the beautiful affords us. We sacrifice in this moment our individual, finite existence to a form of higher being.[58]

Disinterested pleasure is the key phrase here and in the aesthetics of autonomy in general. Moritz isolates a form of enjoyment/pleasure in the aesthetic experience of the beautiful object that is not contingent upon any external interests. As such, it frees the individual from its finite particularity and the concrete realm of specific dependencies and purposes that typically govern instrumental, means-ends thinking. Such a transcendence of the individual self is required both in the creation and in the reception of the beautiful work of art according to Moritz. For the true artist, it is neither a particular purpose or interest, approval or critical reception that is at stake in the creation of true art, but the inner perfection and unique unity of the work itself, the emergence of a harmonic totality that is complete unto itself (*in sich selbst vollendet*). On the side of reception, the subject does not seek to subsume the beautiful object under an already existing determinate concept; nor does one try to instrumentalize the object for a specific

---

Gegenstand selbst gesucht werden, sobald derselbe mir Vergnügen erwecken soll; oder; ich muß in den einzelnen Theilen desselben so viel Zweckmäßigkeit finden, daß ich vergesse zu fragen, wozu nun eigentlich das Ganze soll? Das heißt mit anderen Worten: ich muß an einem schönen Gegenstand nur um sein selbst willen Vergnügen finden; zu dem Ende muß der Mangel der äußern Zweckmäßigkeit durch eine innere Zweckmäßigkeit ersetzt sein; der Gegenstand muß etwas in sich selbst Vollendetes sein."
57 Moritz, "Versuch einer Vereinigung," 229; also in *Werke*, 2:945.
58 Moritz, "Versuch einer Vereinigung," 229; also in *Werke*, 2:945: "Auch das süße Staunen, *das angenehme Vergessen unserer selbst* bei Betrachtung eines schönen Kunstwerks, ist ein Beweis, daß unser Vergnügen hier etwas Untergeordnetes ist [...] Während das Schöne unsere Betrachtung ganz auf sich zieht, zieht es sie von uns selber ab, und macht, daß wir uns in dem schönen Gegenstand zu verlieren scheinen; und eben dies Verlieren, dies Vergessen unsrer selbst, ist der höchste Grad des reinen und uneigennützigen Vergnügens, welches uns das Schöne gewährt. Wir opfern in dem Augenblick unser individuelles eingeschränktes Dasein einer Art von höherem Dasein auf."

purpose, to assign it any particular goal. In fact, the subject moves beyond itself and its particular sphere of ends.

One decisive aspect of Moritz's theory of aesthetics is the role of judgment in the aesthetic experience – more specifically, whether the judgment of the beautiful comes before or after the pleasure experienced by the subject. In paragraph 9 the *Critique of Judgment*, Kant famously argued that in order for one to experience truly *disinterested* pleasure, the act of judgment (*Beurteilung*) – in particular, the universal judgment that others, too, could, at least in principle, find the object beautiful and take pleasure in it – must in fact *precede* the feeling of pleasure; indeed, it is the implicit act of judgment that makes the particular form of pleasure associated with the beautiful at all possible according to Kant. It is, as Kant states, the key to a critique of taste. If the pleasure or enjoyment one derives were to *precede* the judgment of the universal communicability of such pleasure, this would reduce such pleasure to the merely pleasant (*das Angenehme*), which is decidedly interested, subjective, and contingent. Kant wishes to show that the particular pleasure we experience in reference to the beautiful is in fact *a result* of the judgment of its universal communicability, the idea that others, too, would or could experience the object as beautiful.[59]

> If the pleasure in the given object precedes, and it is only its universal communicability that is to be acknowledged in the judgment of taste about the representation of the object, there would be a contradiction. For such pleasure would be nothing different from the mere pleasantness in the sensation, and so in accordance with its nature could have only private validity, because it is immediately dependent on the representation through which the object *is given*. [...] Hence, it is the universal capability of communication of the mental state in the given representation which, as the subjective condition of the judgment of taste, must be fundamental, and must have the pleasure in the object as its consequent.[60]

---

[59] Immanuel Kant, *Kritik der Urteilskraft*, in *Werke in zehn Bänden*, ed. Wilhelm Weischedel (Darmstadt: Wiss. Buchgesellschaft, 1983), vol. 5, 216–217: "Ginge die Lust an dem gegebenen Gegenstande vorher, und nur die allgemeine Mitteilbarkeit derselben sollte im Geschmacksurteile der Vorstellung des Gegenstandes zuerkannt werden, so würde ein solches Verfahren mit sich selbst im Widerspruche stehen. Denn dergleichen Lust würde keine andere, als die bloße Annehmlichkeit in der Sinnenempfindung sein, und daher ihrer Natur nach nur Privatgültigkeit haben können, weil sie von der Vorstellung, wodurch der Gegenstand gegeben wird, unmittelbar abhinge. Also ist es die allgemeine Mitteilungsfähigkeit des Gemütszustandes in der gegebenen Vorstellung, welche als subjektive Bedingung des Geschmacksurteils, demselben zum Grunde liegen, und die Lust an dem Gegenstande zur Folge haben muß."
[60] Immanuel Kant, *Kant's Critique of Judgement*, trans., with intro. and notes by J. H. Bernard, 2nd ed. rev. (London: Macmillan, 1914), para. 9; emphasis mine.

Moritz makes the exact same claim regarding the order of pleasure and judgment:

> "Is therefore the enjoyment not itself a purpose?" – I respond: what is this enjoyment, or how does it emerge, other than out of the intuition of purposefulness. If there were something for which enjoyment itself was the purpose, then I could judge the usefulness of the thing simply from the enjoyment itself that arises from it. My enjoyment itself must, however, emerge in the first place *from this judgment*; otherwise it would have to exist before it existed.[61]

When Moritz avers that the enjoyment is not primary and must emerge out of the specific intuition of purposiveness, and that the enjoyment occurs as a result of the judgment (*Beurtheilung*), he is stating exactly that judgment is required for the feeling of enjoyment or pleasure, and therefore must precede it. Moritz, in other words, had already grasped the necessity of the communicable judgment of the beautiful *prior to* the pleasure we experience, indeed as being the basis of such pleasure – though he had not put it precisely in the terms of "universal communicability" (*allgemeine Mitteilbarkeit*) and "purposivity without a (distinct) purpose" (*Zweckmäßigkeit ohne Zweck*) as Kant did – five years before the publication of the Kant's *Critique of Judgment*.

As Joachim Jacob has perceptively argued, a strong parallel exists between Moritz's notion of a self-contained artwork, considered free from all external purposes and interests, its inability to be subsumed under an extant concept, and the irreducibility of the individual "case," the scriptural form of the experiences and observations.[62] I would like to push Jacob's insight even further and claim that the "true observer" in Moritz's outline of empirical psychology or *Erfahrungsseelenkunde* of 1782 must similarly undergo such a self-transcendence, or a sacrifice of the self in order to achieve what Moritz referred to as the correct or appropriate point of view (*Gesichtspunkt*) in the practice of empirical psychology. In his aesthetic, Moritz advocates the purification of every trace of self-interest not only in order to achieve a higher, disinterested,

---

61 Moritz, "Versuch einer Vereinigung," 235; emphasis mine: "Also ist das Vergnügen gar nicht Zweck?" – Ich antworte: was ist Vergnügen anders, oder woraus entsteht es anders, als aus dem Anschauen der Zweckmäßigkeit. Gäbe es nun etwas, wovon das Vergnügen selbst allein Zweck wäre; so könnte ich die Zweckmäßigkeit jenes Dinges bloß aus dem Vergnügen beurtheilen, welches nur daraus erwächst. Mein Vergnügen selbst aber muß ja erst aus dieser Beurtheilung entstehen; es müßte also da sein, ehe es da wäre."

62 Joachim Jacob, "Das Besondere des Falles. Zur ästhetiktheoretischen Vorgeschichte der Fallstudie im 18. Jahrhundert," in *Fallstudien: Theorie – Geschichte – Methode*, ed. Johannes Süßmann et al. (Berlin: Trafo Verlag, 2007), 257.

human perspective, but to bring about a transformation of the affective content of experience. In *On the Educative Representation of the Beautiful*, Moritz characterizes this transformation as "pulling the individual outside of itself,"[63] as transfiguring "individual suffering in the presentation" into "sublime empathy,"[64] "the most bitter suffering through sublime empathy concerning the individuality" (*das bitterste Leiden, durch das über die Individualität erhabne Mitleid*) flowing into "the sweetest melancholy" (*die süsseste Wehmut*), and "that which is most damaging in reality" (*des höchst Schädlichen in der Wirklichkeit*) transmuted into the "notion of the highest beauty" (*in den Begriff des höchsten Schönen*).[65] In the aesthetic condition, the human being transcends its own peculiarity, and is able to experience a premonition of the great harmony in which self-formation and destruction exist side by side (*ein Vorgefühl von jener grossen Harmonie, in welche Bildung und Zerstörung einst Hand in Hand, hinüber gehn*).[66] Precisely through the persistent destruction of the individual, the continual dissolution of our own individual finitude and unique essence (*immerwährende Zerstörung des Einzelnen,*[67] *immerwährende Auflösung unsres eigenen Wesens*),[68] the human being gets a glimpse of the unity or convergence of construction and destruction, individuality and genus, particularity and universality, reality and appearance that is constitutive of the aesthetic state.

Precisely such an overcoming of self is also required in the case of the practice of empirical psychology according to Moritz, a vital component of which is *self-observation*, or the capacity to reflect on how one is positioning onself vis-à-vis the case under investigation. A condition of the possibility of self-observation as well as the observation of others, and writing a narrative case history of onself or of another individual, is the task of lifting oneself beyond the self, as well as beyond the pre-judgments, normative thinking, and instrumental reasoning that often accompanies the self, so that one can reflect on one's own dissatisfaction (*über sich selbst erheben, dass man über seine eigne Unzufriedenheit reflektiert*).[69] The striving toward a disinterested, an "unpartisan" second-order observation

---

[63] Moritz, *Über die bildende Nachahmung*, in *Werke*, 2:986: "das Individuum [sich] selbst aus seiner Individualität herausziehend,"
[64] Moritz, *Über die bildende Nachahmung*, in *Werke*, 2:985: "[das] individuelle Leiden in der Darstellung."
[65] Moritz, *Über die bildende Nachahmung*, in *Werke*, 2:986.
[66] Moritz, *Über die bildende Nachahmung*, in *Werke*, 2:990.
[67] Moritz, *Über die bildende Nachahmung*, in *Werke*, 2:989.
[68] Moritz, *Über die bildende Nachahmung*, in *Werke*, 2:990.
[69] Moritz, *Vorschlag*, in *Werke*, 1:800.

and level of reflection clarifies Moritz's vision of an experimental holism based on the accumulation and evaluation of experiences (*Erfahrung*). As he states in the *Vorschlag*, the "facts" which are sent to the editors in the form of case-studies could confirm a proposition that had previously seemed questionable, limit another, or completely overthrow a third that had been erroneously accepted as truth.[70] Thus, at a structural or discursive level, the self-distancing or – overcoming – elevating oneself beyond self-interest and exisiting prejudicial preconceptions and discursive categories – forms the prescriptive basis for how the observer of the human soul is to proceed with respect to the material presented in experience and written down in the case history. Such a disengagement from pre-existing discursive, conceptual thinking is the *sine qua non* of astute psychological observation and attention.

It should not surprise us, then, that the programmatic writings of Moritz are unconsciously saturated by an aesthetic rhetoric of the work of art, even though he explicitly eschewed any contamination of the imagination in the presentation of the "facts." Painting and theater in particular are the two "aesthetic" genres that govern Moritz's outline of the true human observer. As he writes in the *Recommendation*: "True portraits (*Gemälde*) that one makes of one's own soul always earn the greatest attention."[71] Moritz explicitly compares the case (*Fall*) with a drama (*Schauspiel*), a psychological observer of the human soul and the observer (*Zuschauer*) or audience of a play as another instance of medial transgression or boundary-crossing between psychology and aesthetics. In the *Recommendation*, the temperature of the observer is cold: he demands "Coldness and cheerfulness of the soul" (*Kälte und Heiterkeit der Seele*),[72] a cold observer[73] (*kalten Beobachter*) who views everything like a dramatic play with "cold-blooded attention" (*mit kaltblütiger Aufmerksamkeit*).[74] Extending the dramatic metaphor further, Moritz recommends the following for the observer of the soul: they must see through the curtain (*Vorhang*) of the so-called moral way of life, through the curtain of

---

70 Moritz, *Vorschlag*, in *Werke*, 1:797: "einen bisher zweifelhaften Satz endlich bestätigen, oder einen andern einschränken, oder wiederum einen fälschlich behaupteten ganz aufheben."
71 Moritz, *Vorschlag*, in *Werke*, 1:800: "Getreue Gemälde, die man sich selber von seiner eignen Seele entwirft, verdienen immer die größte Aufmerksamkeit."
72 Moritz, *Vorschlag*, in *Werke*, 1:800.
73 Moritz, *Vorschlag*, in *Werke*, 1:800.
74 Moritz, *Vorschlag*, in *Werke*, 1:800. On the *kalter Blick* of the human self-observer, see Birgit Nübel, "Karl Philipp Moritz: Der kalte Blick des Selbstbeobachters," in *Karl Philipp Moritz zu ehren. Beiträge zum Eutiner Symposium im Juni 1993*, ed. von Wolfgang Griep (Eutin: Struve Verlag, 1993), 31–53.

wisdom (*Lebensklugheit*), through the curtain of smugness, and wanting to be liked by others before they can truly enter the innermost regions of the heart.[75] The tension involved in such a call to cutting through the assumptions and pretensions of moral life become evident in the precise phrase Moritz employs to characterize the movement of the self – *von sich selber ausgehend* – which means both taking the self as the point of departure as well as parting from or moving beyond the self. Only by means of such extradition can the human observer learn to truly understand the language and actions of others: "To place oneself above this earth, and above oneself, almost as if one were a different being than what one is, one that smiles in a higher region – and in this way smiles at one's own complaints and grievances – what bliss, what an elevation to the all-encompassing creator of the universe!"[76] The implicit pleasure or enjoyment (signaled by the terms *lächeln* [to smile] and *Wonne* [bliss])to be derived from adopting such a stance, as well as the more forceful identification with the all-encompassing creator of the universe of course contradicts the "coldness" indicated above. However, the disinterested form of this specific pleasure links it to aesthetic experience and the pleasure involved in the encounter with beautiful works of art.

If we now abstract from the apparent disciplinary and medial differences between aesthetics and empirical psychology, an unmistakable discursive constant emerges that gives warrant to the claim of a shared methodological isomorphism, of a profound intersection between the two disciplines. The transcendence of specific interests or purposes, desire and will, moving beyond existing concepts and rubrics informs both disciplines with regard to their putative procedure and aim. The human observer in *Erfahrungsseelenkunde* as the aesthetic subject in the encounter with the beautiful deflect from all concrete instrumentalization and all generalizing theory, and direct their attention to the unique individuality of the case before them. Similarly, the aesthetic object is the object of a disinterested pleasure, an object for which there is no determinant concept, just as the individual case history presents a highly unique case that cannot be subsumed under the existing categories, concepts and rubrics of psychology. In this sense, the case study approximates Johann Wolfgang Goethe's famous dictim in his conversations with Johann Peter Eckermann of

---

75 Moritz, *Vorschlag*, in *Werke*, 1:803.
76 Moritz, *Vorschlag*, in *Werke*, 1:802: "sich hinaus versetzen über diese Erde, und über sich selber, gleichsam als ob er ein andres von sich selber verschiedenes Wesen wäre, das in einer höhern Region aller dieser Dinge lächelt – und auf die Art über sich selber, über seine eignen Klagen und Beschwerden – lächeln [...] – welche Wonne, welch eine Erhebung zum alles umfassenden Schöpfer des Weltalls!"

1827 concerning the Novella as the narrative of an *unerhörte Begebenheit* – an "unheard of event."[77]

Turning the tables, it can also be shown how aesthetics itself, or a misprision of wherein the true aesthetic experience actually consists, often becomes a fateful problem, even a form of trauma or psychopathology in case histories. As an exemplary case of such an abuse or distortion of true aesthetics, or its degradation into mere pleasure or indulgence, Moritz's case history *From K...s Papers* (*Aus K...s Papieren*) can serve to alert us to the dangers and even psychopathology of the failure to recognize the true essence and boundaries of the aesthetic. Although this case history was not published in the *Magazin*, but rather in the collection edited by Moritz and Karl Friedrich Pockels titled *Denkwürdigkeiten, aufgezeichnet zur Beförderung des Edlen und des Schönen*[78] of 1786, this psychological narrative of the young student K. has all of the generic attributes of a narrative psychological-literary case history.[79] *From K...s Papers* contains a belated frame-narrative in which the editor of the papers of the deceased student K. collects the literary remains of K. along with other documents and biographical annotations concerning his demise. K. suffered precisely from a fixation on, even an addiction to, sensual knowledge, more precisely the sensual pleasure derived from such knowledge. Keeping in mind what has been said about the pleasure in the aesthetic experience being derivative of the judgment and not itself fundamental, Moritz had clearly subordinated the pleasure in aesthetic experience to a judgment concerning its elevating potential. K., by contrast, remained cathected to the taking of pleasure in itself (*Genuss*), pleasure for its own sake, failing to recognize the more lofty underpinning of such pleasure or its true purpose. K.'s downfall is an excess of such unfettered *Genuss*.[80] The editor remarks on K.'s inability to move beyond the momentary enjoyment of pleasure: "Even assuming

---

[77] Stefan Goldmann, "Kasus – Krankengeschichte – Novelle," in *"Fakta, und kein moralisches Geschwätz." Zu den Fallgeschichten im Magazin zur Erfahrungsseelenkunde* (1783–1793), ed. Sheila Dickson et al. (Göttingen: Wallstein Verlag, 2011), 58: "Krankengeschichte und Novelle behandeln mit unterschiedlichen Mitteln und unterschiedlichem Erkenntnisinteresse dieselben problematischen und rätselhaften Fälle."

[78] *Denkwürdigkeiten, aufgezeichnet zur Beförderung des Edlen und des Schönen*, ed. Karl Philipp Moritz and Karl Friedrich Pockels (Berlin: Johann Friedrich Ungar, 1786).

[79] On this characterization, see: Košenina, *Karl Philipp Moritz*.

[80] Such a downfall in the surfeit of sensual pleasure is a commonplace of literature at this time. On this, see: Adler, "Fundus Animae – Grund der Seele," 197–221. See also: Christopher Wild, "Theorizing Theater Antitheatrically: Karl Philipp Moritz's Theatromania," *MLN* 120.3 (2005): 516, where he notes the several cases of young men who have been befallen by a pathological tendency toward the theater.

that his soul had never been trained in abstract, metaphysical thought, but rather had the tendency to sensuous, intuitive cognition, and to lead everything back to the moment of the actual pleasure."[81] The phrase "sensuous, intuitive cognition" alludes precisely to the aesthetic state and its effects. However, the subject's immersion in this form of "mere pleasure" or *Genuss* never advances to the actualization of the truly aesthetic, which requires a disengagement from interest, a supercession of empirical considerations, and the possibility of universal judgment.

At the end of *Aus Ks...Papieren*, we are provided with K.'s last essay, written in what is referred to by the editor as a severe fever (*heftiger Fieberparoxysmus*), in which he attempts to come to terms with the fact that the world is given over to the three hammers of fate – disease, war, and death. Demarcated by a *ceasura*, and with the title "beautiful" in bold type, K. delivers a short discourse on aesthetics:

> **Beautiful!**
> Is this beautiful to you? – Beautiful to me is that which coincides with my essence; beautiful to you is that which agrees with your essence.
>
> For me, multiplicity, life, and movement are beautiful. – Why? – Because my essence is multiplicity, life, and movment.
>
> If your essence is uniformity, idolence, inactivity, then life, movement, and multiplicity cannot be beautiful.[82]

K.'s unabashed relativism with respect to his false aesthetic – beautiful is that which simply suits the individual – disavows the very possibility of the key element Moritz had identified in his aesthetic theory as the very ground of true aesthetic experience: judgment (*Beurtheilung*), which requires a projected agreement or consensus. Furthermore, K. embraces multiplicity to the exclusion of any unity whatsoever, constant movement to the exclusion of all structuring, formative stability. The radical departure from

---

81 Moritz, *Aus K...s Papieren*, in *Werke*, 1:690: "Gesetzt noch dazu, dass seine Seele nie im abstrakten, metaphysischen Denken geübt worden ist, sondern den Hang hatte, alles auf sinnliche, anschauende Erkenntnis, und auf den Moment des wirklichen Genusses zurückzuführen."

82 Moritz, *Aus K...s Papieren*, in *Werke*, 1:693; emphasis in the original: "**Schön!** Ist euch das schön? – Schön ist mir, was mit meinem Wesen übereinstimmt; Schön ist euch, was mit eurem Wesen übereinstimmt. Mir ist Mannigfaltigkeit, Leben, Bewegung schön. – Warum? – Weil mein Wesen Mannigfaltigkeit, Leben, Bewegung ist. Ist euer Wesen Einförmigkeit, Trägheit, Untätigkeit; so kann euch ja Leben, Bewegung, und Mannigfaltigkeit nicht schön sein."

all substantial thought-structures and objective judgment, combined with indulgence in fleeting pleasures, paves the way for a fall into dissolution and death. K.'s psycho-physical illness thus crosses the boundary between medicine, psychology, and philosophy, emphasizing the dangers of an unregulated and wanton aestheticism; K. lives as what one might call the *false* "aesthetic" man, consumed in the momentary "life" of pure pleasure or mere enjoyment (*Genuss*), thereby alienating himself from family, friends, and community, and incapable of creating anything of lasting value or substance. The case history of K. traces this ever-widening gap between him and humanity in what can only be termed a pathological addiction to the immediacy of the pleasurable moment. In other words, K. completely mistakes the true formative-substantive function of the aesthetic, to produce something that is complete and perfect unto itself, and to experience a perfection that resides beyond the transient moment and the individual subject and can be, at least subjunctively, appreciated by all. By losing himself in the immediacy of the fleeting moment, K. thus misapprehends the very conditions of the aesthetic; on the productive side, the creation of a a work that is complete unto itself; and on the receptive side, transcendence beyond the individual, purely subjective and momentary pleasure to one that it is formative (*bildend*), communicative, and enduring. This is confirmed by the editor's remark as to the title he would give to the collection of K.'s papers: "If I were to give these papers a title, I would call them the last efforts of a debilitated capacity of action."[83] *Tatkraft* – which roughly translates as the power of action – is the most essential and indispensible quality of the *truly* aesthetic human being, as Moritz states in his *On the Educative Representation of the Beautiful*: "The sense for the greatest beauty in the harmonious construction of the whole, which does not encompass the representational power of the whole, lies immediately in the *active principle itself*, which cannot rest until that which slumbers within it has at least approached the representational power."[84] Debilitated power of action, while particularly destructive to the true, formative aesthetic posture, also means the absence of a proportional agreement and harmony of all of the capacities of the soul, which Moritz in the *Basic Guidelines* defined as mental illness (*Seelenkrankheit*).[85] *From K...s Papers* documents the case of a downfall into a life of transient and fleeting

---

[83] Moritz, Aus K...s Papieren, in Werke, 1:680: "Der Sinn aber für das höchste Schöne in dem harmonischen Bau des Ganzen, das die vorstellende Kraft des Ganzen nicht umfaßt, liegt unmittelbar in der **Tatkraft** selbst;" "Wenn ich diesen Papieren eine Überschrift geben sollte, so würde ich sie die letzten Anstrengungen *einer gelähmten Tatkraft* (emphasis mine) nennen."
[84] Moritz, Über die bildende Nachahmung des Schönen, in Werke, 2:970.
[85] Moritz, Grundlinien zu einem ohngefähren Entwurf in Rücksicht auf die Seelenkrankheitskunde, in Werke, 1:812.

sensual pleasure, failed aesthetic *Bildung*, and the incapacity to structure or form anything of lasting value – in a word, *madness*. For Moritz, aesthetic *Bildung* is not an optional or ancillary capability alongside other functions of the human soul. It is absolutely essential to the human being. The investigation into its failure became the stuff of a psychological case history.

For all of the close filiations between aesthetics and *Erfahrungsseelenkunde*, important differences have been noted as well. The most significant distinction concerns the focus and attention of observation in the study of empirical psychology. In order to characterize the requisite form of attuned observation (*Beobachtung*) in Moritz's program for empirical psychology at the end of the eighteenth century, it may be useful to draw on the register developed by Lorraine Daston and Peter Galison in their incisive book *Objectivity*. Daston and Galison distinguish three major stages of objectivity in Western scientific thought: "truth-to-nature," "mechanical objectivity," and what they refer to as "trained judgment" and "informed observation."[86] Moritz's demand for *Fakta* over speculation, hypothesis, moral and religious-theological prejudice, his claim concerning attentive observation of gesture, language, behavior, history, diet, climate, and affect clearly falls into Daston and Galison's third stage of objectivity – trained judgment and informed observation. But whereas in the experience of empirical psychology the observer is counseled to delve always deeper into the real world (*in die eigne wirkliche Welt immer tiefer einzudringen*),[87] aesthetic experience makes claim to a very different sort of "objectivity," one which coincides rather with the sublation of the specific individual in the species and the transfiguration of suffering in the creative formation of an *ideal* harmonious whole, complete unto itself. While the aesthetic realm certainly holds therapeutic promise as a medium in which the disparate and fragmented real world can be momentarily transformed, thus mitigating the damaging effects of isolated individuality and leveling uniformity, the observation key to empirical psychology and psychological case-narratives begins concretely and analytically, its aim always to describe, in sufficient detail, the particulars of a given case based on an assessment of the entire human being (*der ganze Mensch*).

The human observer of empirical psychology must be, first and foremost, an observer of themselves. Such self-observation (*Selbstbeobachtung*) might be difficult and even at first disturbing, but the overall effect according to Moritz is consolation (*Trost*). Moritz stated in the *Recommendation*: "Under no

---

86 Lorraine Daston and Peter Galison, *Objectivity* (Cambridge: Cambridge University Press, 2007).
87 Moritz, *Vorschlag*, in *Werke*, 1:801.

circumstance is the observation of onself and the people around us something unpleasant or arduous. Rather, it is much more a consolation."[88] The term *Trost* – comfort, solace, consolation – belongs to a pastoral vocabulary of pietist/quietist provenance in the eighteenth century, one that is closely connected to the notion of *therapeutics*, not in the sense of the *consilia* or *consultatoria* – physicians' concrete prescriptions, medications, and directions – common to the case-studies of late seventeenth and early eighteenth centuries, for example in those of the physicians in Halle Hoffmann and Stahl. Rather, it refers here to therapeutics in a more general and classical sense of *therapeuiein*, the sense of a care of and for the self (*epimeleia heautou*), which indicates a certain relation to the self, an individual concern for the self pervasive in the culture of classical antiquity with which Moritz was intimately familiar. It is no coincidence that the main title of his journal of empirical psychology was the famous *gnothi seauton* – know thyself! – the imperative of the Delphic oracle at the Temple of Apollo and the rallying cry of the late German *Aufklärung*, slightly transformed, revitalized, and made famous in Kant's *Groundwork of the Metaphysics of Morals* as the first command of self-regulating duties, and as *Sapere aude* – dare to know! – in Kant's essay *What is Enlightenment?* of 1784.

In his *Hermeneutics of the Subject*, Foucault showed the close connection between the Delphic imperative *gnothi seauton* and the more general attitude or posture of a care for and of the self:

> When this Delphic precept (this *gnothi seauton*) appears, it is coupled or twinned with the principle of "take care of yourself" (*epimeleia heautou*). I say "coupled, or twinned." In actual fact, it is not entirely a matter of coupling. In some texts [...] there is, rather, a kind of subordination of the expression of the rule "know yourself" to the precept of care of the self. The gnothi seauton ("know yourself") appears, quite early and in a number of significant texts, within the more general framework of the *epimeleia heautou* (care of oneself) as one of the forms, one of the consequences, as a sort of concrete, precise, and particular application of the general rule: You must attend to yourself, you must not forget yourself, you must take care of yourself.[89]

Epimeleia heautou according to Foucault was a "fundamental principle for describing the philosophical attitude through the Greek, Hellenistic, and Roman culture."[90] However, in Epicurus and with the Epicureans, this care

---

88 Moritz, *Vorschlag*, in *Werke*, 1:803: "In keinem Verhältnisse des Lebens ist die Beobachtung seiner selbst und der Menschen um uns her etwas Unangenehmes oder Beschwerliches. Es ist vielmehr ein Trost."
89 Foucault, *Hermeneutics of the Subject* (2001), 4–5.
90 Foucault, *Hermeneutics of the Subject*, 8.

of the self is stated by and framed within the verb *therapeuein*, which subsequently came to mean "to take care of" with special reference to care of and for the soul.[91] What emerges from Foucault's extended discussion of the genealogy of this notion of *epimeleia heautou* or "caring for the self" is the subjectification, if one will, which is of course always a form of *subjection*, of the soul. As Foucault writes: "care of the self becomes concerned with the soul as subject" and "not at all with the soul as substance."[92] Not, to be sure, in the sense of subjugation or discipline from without or above, but a guidance, direction, a self-transformational care of the soul and, above all, a unique relation of the self to itself. For in the very prescription to "take care of oneself," two important corollaries appear: this "self" that one ought to take care of, and manner in which or the techniques through which it is to be "taken care of."

In *Hermeneutics of the Subject*, Foucault did not extend his analysis of the imperative *gnothi sauton* and the reflexive *epimeleia heautou* (care of oneself) into the modern period, except for a highly suggestive, yet very brief and skeletal interpretation of Goethe's *Faust*,[93] one that deserves closer consideration. For our purposes here, however, it is sufficient to take Foucault's twinning of *gnothi sauton* and *epimeleia heautou* as an interpretive lever and discover how "care of and for the self by the self" manifests itself as a form of therapeutics in Moritz's project of empirical psychology. We must be mindful, however, of the specific context within which Moritz employs the vocabulary of care (*Sorge*) and the physician of the soul (*Seelensorger; Seelenarzt*). With regard to the Halle constellation of psychologically-minded physicians around 1750 – Unzer, Krüger, Nicolai, and Bolten – Carsten Zelle has persuausively shown how Bolten in particular polemicizes against any pietistic ethos of *Seelensorge*, which he equated with priests and pastors using empty phrases to bring about the salvation of the soul. Bolten insisted rather on the medical model of *influxus* and on the reciprocal mind-body relationship as the basis of his "psychological cure," and rejected Stahl's thesis of the absolute primacy of the soul in all matters relating to the human organism.[94] The psychologically-minded physicians in Halle had combined the new emphasis on sensibility (*aisthesis*) of Baumgarten and Meier with an anthropological concern for the human being in its totality (*der ganze Mensch*). Zelle fully acknowledges, however, a *reinvention* of the very notions of therapeutics and care in Bolten's *Gedanken von*

---

91 Foucault, *Hermeneutics of the Subject*, 9.
92 Foucault, *Hermeneutics of the Subject*, 57.
93 Foucault, *Hermeneutics of the Subject*, 308–311.
94 Zelle, "Sinnlichkeit und Therapie," in *Vernünftige Ärzte*, 18.

psychologischen Curen of 1751, essentially recasting the traditional pietistic notion of *Sorge* with one based on experience, observation, diagnostics, and therapeutics: "In general, Bolten wishes to provide in his demonstration the diagnostic and therapeutic knowledge in order for the physician or caretaker of the soul could discover the 'mental state of the patient' through skillful questioning, while also acquiring the capability of applying the aesthetic rules of setting the mind into motion."[95] We therefore have to be attentive to the various uses and valences of terms such as *Sorge* and *Seelensorge*, as they, too, shift from one discursive and institutional context to another.

Specifically, in 1780, thirty years after the work of the psycho-physicians in Halle, fully aware of the dangers of pietistic upbringing and enforced or coerced inwardness, Moritz mobilizes the pietistic-pastoral concern for/of the soul (*Seelensorge*) as a form of care of and for the self (*Selbstsorge*) in his program for empirical psychology. The "practice" or "exercise" of *gnothi sauton* (know thyself!), Moritz argues, must always be the heuristic idea and the point in which all experiences and observations of an empirical psychology converge.[96] Such "care of and for the self" cuts both ways; the philosophical physician must cultivate a self-concern and care in order to be able to care for and to treat the mentally ill patient; a care for the self is the first and highest imperative of the human being in regulating feelings and emotions to attain an equilibrium of the soul's powers. On the side of the patient, such a position or attitude of *Selbstsorge* must be cultivated to break through the various screens of dissimulation and illusion. In the *Recommendation* of 1782, Moritz begins with the *desideratum* that man has not directed the requisite attention (*Aufmerksamkeit*) to himself: "Among all of the various things that human beings concern themselves with, the attention that the human being directs to itself has held the least value."[97] The figure of the *Seelensorger* – one who cares for the soul[98] – appears alongside the judge, the physician,

---

95 Zelle, "Sinnlichkeit und Therapie," in *Vernünftige Ärzte*, 19: "Insgesamt will Bolten durch seine Ausführungen diagnostische und therapeutische Kenntnisse an die Hand geben, damit der Seelenarzt bzw. der Seelesorger sowohl durch geschickte Fragen den 'Gemüthszustand des Patienten' entdecken könne, als auch die Fertigkeit erhält, 'die ästhetischen Regeln anzuwenden, die Gemüter in Bewegung zu setzen.'"
96 Moritz, "Revision der drei ersten Bände dieses Magazins," 3.
97 Moritz, *Vorschlag*, in *Werke*, 1:794: "Unter allen übrigen Dingen hat der Mensch sich selber seiner eignen Aufmerksamkeit vielleicht noch am aller wenigsten werth gehalten."
98 The figure of the *Seelensorger* has a long history in pietistic literature dating back to the end of the seventeenth and beginning of the eighteenth centuries in Germany. At the end of eighteenth century, it denotes one who is interested in illnesses of the mind, their care and therapy, usually, but not always, with a pastoral, pietistic intent. See: Jacob Friedrich Abel,

and "especially" the writer as those for whom the *Magazin zur Erfahrungsseelenkunde* would be indispensible: "And simply the Magazine of this science itself would be a project that would be indispensible for those concerned with care of the soul, the judge, the physician, and, perhaps most of all, the writer."[99] *Seelensorge* entails a specific relation to the self to itself as something to be concerned with and cared for, and this in turn requires a special capacity for self-observation, the techniques of which Moritz elucidates in several passages of his programmatic writings on *Erfahrungsseelenkunde*. The astute human observer (*Menschenbeobachter*), it will be remembered, has to be able to see through the many veils of flattery, self-importance, vanity, prestige, and wanting to be liked in order to develop a true sense of the uniqueness of the soul and its vicissitudes. Genuine self-observation (*Selbstbeobachtung*) presupposes an enhanced freedom from destructive emotions and passions, a "dietetics of the soul," which in turn increases one's capacity for focused self-observation and the careful observation of others.[100] Only through rigorous self-observation can the moral, psychologically-minded physician or *Seelensorger* transfer "care of the self" to another, and truly comprehend specific instances of mental illness and develop the means to intervene, to treat, and to heal. In the *Basic Guidelines*, Moritz describes the task of the *Seelensorger* in the following words:

> He must seek to repair, whenever possible, the injured relation between the capacities of the soul. He must know how to blot out destructive ideas and to illuminate others appropriately. He has to effect the proper degree of connection within the entire system of ideas and, when necessary, penetrate the deepest interstices of the all-to-rigid system of such ideas.[101]

Erläuterungen wichtiger Gegenstände aus der philosophischen und christlichen Moral, besonders der Ascetik durch Beobachtungen aus der Seelenlehre (Tübingen: Heerbrandt, 1790), 103: "Vor allererst muß der Seelsorger die wahre Beschaffenheit und den wahren Werth solcher Menschen kennen; nur dies allein macht ihn fähig, ihre wirklich oft grossen Fehler zu tragen, und ihre, oft sehr miskannten, und doch wahrhaftig grossen und schätzbaren Tugenden zu lieben und hochzuschätzen, vorzüglich aber den einzigen sicheren Weg zu ihrer Besserung einzuschlagen."
99 Moritz, *Vorschlag*, in *Werke*, 1:798: "Auch das bloße Magazin dieser Wissenschaft würde auf die Art schon ein Werk sein, das dem Seelsorger, dem Richter, dem Arzt, und vorzüglich dem Schriftsteller des menschlichen Herzens unentbehrlich wäre."
100 Barbara Thums has argued similarly and effectively with regard to Moritz's *Beiträge zu einer Philosophie des Lebens* (1780). See Thums, *Aufmerksamkeit*, 93.
101 Moritz, *Grundlinien zu einem ohngefähren Entwurf in Rücksicht auf die Seelenkrankheitskunde*, in *Werke*, 1:815: "Er muß das verletzte Verhältnis zwischen den Seelenfähigkeiten, wo möglich,

Reparation of injury, dismantling destructive ideas, and probing the interconnectedness of a rigid system of belief belong to a therepeutics aimed at restoration of a balance of all of the powers of the soul. If we recall that aesthetics in the eighteenth century was not merely a *theory* of the beautiful work of art and aesthetic experience, but a *medium* of formative life-direction or a *life-practice*, and that its origins lie in the guidance, direction and regulation of the so-called lower faculties, it is clear that *Seelensorge* requires the steerage of attention and concern to the repair of the disequilibrium of the soul's powers. The philosophical physician is tasked first with a particular type of attention directed at oneself (*Selbstsorge*) to cut through the many veils and dangers of self-delusion discussed above – dissimulation, disguise, pretense – and then the achievement of that specific point of view and attention – *Gesichtspunkt* and *Aufmerksamkeit* – in order to be able to fulfill empirical psychology's reparative function. Moritz thus proposed, allbeit without systematic rigor or completion, an *aesthetic therapeutics* of the soul, based on experience (*Erfahrung*), observation (*Beobachtung*), attention (*Aufmerksamkeit*), and, most importantly, care and concern for the soul, one inextricably linked to both the aesthetic-anthropological project of restoration and formative-education of the total human being, and the self-regulation of the emotions. In both instances of the philosophical physician and the patient, it is this concern and care for the human being that constitutes the anthropological knowledge-interesest of empirical psychology: "What is more important to man than man himself?" – "Was ist dem Menschen wichtiger, als der Mensch?"[102]

The most explicit articulation of such a therapeutics centered around the care of and concern for the self appears in Moritz's statements on the dietetics of the soul (*Seelendiätetik*), one of the four sub-disciplines of empirical-experiential psychology. The aim of such a dietetics of the soul is, according to Moritz, "to maintain all of the capacities of the soul, in relational balance to one another, in the highest condition of perfection."[103] And he continues:

---

wieder herzustellen suchen. Er muß schädliche Ideen zu verdunkeln, und andre wieder gehörig zu erhellen wissen. Er muß den gehörigen Grad des Zusammenhangs zwischen dem ganzen System der Ideen bewürken, und wieder in die innersten Fugen des allzufesten Zusammenhangs derselben, wenn es nötig ist, eindringen können." In the translation, I have used "system" here because Moritz's use of *Zusammenhang* in this second instance refers to an entrenched imbalanced or dysfunctional system or structure that must be adjusted or recalibrated.

102 Moritz, "Einleitung," in *MzE* 1.1 (1783), 2.
103 Moritz, "Zur Seelendiätätik," in" *MzE* 1.1 (1783): 111: "alle Seelenfähigkeiten, verhältnismäßig gegeneinander, in dem möglichst vollkommenen Zustand zu erhalten."

> Dietetics of the soul teaches either how to maintain the healthy condition of the soul, or how the sick condition of the soul can be mitigated or eliminated, and in this last case it enters into the discipline of soul-healing (*Seelenheilkunde*), from which it differentiates itself only in that this latter field emphasizes the healing of illnesses with actual efficacious means, whereas the former stresses the law of abstinence in view of the inappropriate or disorderly use of any single faculty of the soul.[104]

Each human being has its own, unique state of the "health of the soul" according to Moritz, its own balance of the capacities of the soul (*Seelenfähigkeiten*). Therefore, a dietetics of the soul must be an individual calibration of the most perfect equilibrium of the faculties of the soul in any given individual.

> Because each human being has its own individual state of health of the soul, a dietetics of the soul presupposes a knowledge of this unique condition of the health of the soul in any individual case. Whoever wishes to be continuously happy has to abstract his or her own dietetics of the soul by and by from careful observations concerning him or herself, and seek to become ever more perfect in this salutary discipline.[105]

While the care exhibited in this dietetics of the soul is in each case an individual practice, Moritz suggests that it might be possible to gradually arrive at more general principles of such a dietetics. Precisely through the reciprocal communication of various experiences (*Erfahrungen*) and observations (*Beobachtungen*) gleaned from the case-studies published in the *Magazin*, the aim was to discover more general principles of such a dietetics that might prove useful in individual instances: "and in this way it is perhaps not impossible to invent some more general rules for the soul, which would have a certain effect in each individual subject."[106] This bottom-up approach of gathering the

---

104 Moritz, "Zur Seelendiätätik," 112: "Die Seelendiätätik lehrt entweder, wie der gesunde Zustand der Seele erhalten, oder der kranke Zustand derselben zum Theil gemildert oder gehoben werden kann, und in diesem letztern Falle schlägt sie in das Fach der Seelenheilkunde, wovon sie sich nur darin unterscheidet, das die letzere sich zur Heilung der Krankheiten reeller würkender Mittel, die erstre aber vorzüglich nur des Gesetzes der Enthaltsamkeit, in Ansehen des zweckwidrigen oder unordentlichen Gebrauchs irgend einer Seelenfähigkeit betont."
105 Moritz, "Zur Seelendiätätik," 112: "Weil jeder Mensch seinen eigen individuellen Seelengesundheitszustand hat, so setzt die Seelendiätetik eine genaue Kenntnis desselben voraus. Wer also fortdauernd glücklich zu seyn wünscht, muß sich aus sorgfältigen Beobachtungen über sich selber, nach und nach seine eigene Seelendiätetik abstrahieren, und in dieser heilsamen Wissenschaft immer vollkommener zu werden suchen."
106 Moritz, "Zur Seelendiätätik," 113: "so ist es vielleicht nicht unmöglich, einige allgemeinere Regeln für die Seele zu erfinden, welche bei jedem einzelnen Subjekt ihre gewisse Wirkung hat."

experiences and observations presented in the case-studies, inviting further reflection, discussion, and commentary, and developing guiding principles is for Moritz juxtaposed to a rigid system of universal remedies imposed from above.

As it emerged in the Halle-constellation around 1750 in the work of Baumgarten and Meier, aesthetics served not merely as a theory of the beautiful and the experience of beauty as perfected sensate cognition, but as a specific way of regulating or directing the so-called "lower," non-rational, pre-distinct, pre-semiotic cognitive functions of sensation, feeling, emotion, intuition, and imagination. As aesthetics develops after Baumgarten and Meier as a theory of aesthetic experience, the key question becomes how the unity of such experience arises from the manifold of sensuous content. This question was addressed first by Sulzer in 1759, who reasoned that there was an original natural beauty in nature and natural objects, that the mind mimetically repeats such unity in the apprehension of the beautiful object, and that the mind delights and experiences perfection in the unity which is ontologically grounded in the beauty and unity of the object itself. Mendelssohn took issue with Sulzer, arguing that such a view was incompatible with the representational power of the human soul. As we saw in chapter 6, Schiller's aesthetics of the case attempts to do justice to the individual human being as conditioned being of flesh and blood, with a unique story that is both edifying and adjudicative, calling the reader's response to the fore. Moritz, who took many cues from Mendelssohn,[107] identified beauty as an internally complete whole, with the judgment concerning beauty being *prior to* the actual experience of the beautiful. In the first explicit document of "autonomy aesthetics," Moritz theorized the unique, disinterested nature of the experience of the beautiful, its detachment from any external interest or specific usage. In order to attain such a perspective or stance, the aesthetic subject first had to emancipate itself from the web of material entanglements and purposes, wrest itself from the empirical self, and achieve a position of disinterested pleasure. This "loss" or "forgetting" of the empirical, material self and its web of specific interests and agendas paved the way for a "pure" experience of the beautiful object: the self-contained, complete totality. The beautiful object itself was also "emancipated" from any specific interest or purpose; its aesthetic value was utterly divorced from any fungible aim or plan.

---

107 Moritz, *Vorschlag*, in *MzE* 1.1 (1783): 503: "Herr Moses Mendelssohn hat mir selber seine Gedanken über den Plan zu diesem Werke mitgeteilt, und die Veränderung der Benennung Experimentalseelenlehre, welche ich anfangs gewählt hatte, in Erfahrungsseelenkunde angerathen." Moritz had still used *Experimentalseelenlehre* in his earlier announcement of the journal in his *Aussichten einer Experimentalseelenlehre* (1781).

Empirical psychology (*Erfahrungsseelenkunde*) was the title given to an emerging discipline in the eighteenth century which sought to do justice to the entire human being (*der ganze Mensch*) as a unity of mind and body, reason and sensation, thought and feeling, and understanding and emotion. In the programmatic writings of Moritz for the *Magazin zur Erfahrungsseelenkunde*, it required the acquisition of a particular point of view (*Gesichtspunkt*), a commitment to observation (*Beobachtung*), a specific form of mindful attention (*Aufmerksamkeit*), and, above all, a working-through and casting aside of the various self-inflicted obstacles, prejudices, particular moral or theological interests, and agendas that could obscure the unfettered experience (*Erfahrung*) of mental illness and its discursive inscription in narrative case-histories. Of the many qualities a human observer of the soul should possess, Moritz emphasized the ability to detach onself from the tumult of the passions: "He must take the time to describe the history of his thoughts, and to make himself the object of his sustained observations [...] to pull himself out of the tumult of his own desires, in order to play the cold observer for a certain time."[108]

Through the ongoing, reciprocal coupling of observation, experience, attentiveness and reflection, thoughtful consideration and mutual communication, empirical psychology would prove beneficial to the individual and to society. Moritz instituted the first journal of empirical psychology in 1783 as an archive, repository, and medium of public contributions to and discussions of the nature of the human soul, mental health and illness, interesting and compelling cases worthy of reflection, therapeutics and a dietetics of the soul. Such a project would have been unthinkable without earlier empirical psychology, the decisive contributions of the psychological physicians in Halle around 1750, and the emergence of the discipline of aesthetics as the theory of guiding, directing, and regulating the so-called lower faculties of the soul. Empirical psychology and aesthetics both required a disengagement from the immediate interests and specific purposes of the individual, a stance beyond the quotidian immersion in purely means-ends living, a disinterestedness as the condition of the possibility of an elevated, "pure" point of view that, in each case, created the basis for a distinct mode of human experience. In empirical psychology, this meant the ability to lift the various illusions and see oneself as fundamentally human and as an Other, susceptible to all sorts of mental imbalances and incongruities, but most importantly to become the detached, "cold" observer,

---

108 Moritz, *Vorschlag*, in *MzE* 1.1 (1783): 492: "Er müßte sich Zeit nehmen, die Geschichte seiner Gedanken zu beschreiben, und sich selber zum Gegenstande seiner anhaltendnen Beobachtungen zu machen [...] sich plötzlich aus dem Wirbel seiner Begierde auszuziehen, um eine Zeitlang den kalten Beobachter zu spielen."

attentive to the individual and its unique history and condition. In aesthetics, this demanded the sacrifice or elision of the individual self and its myriad dependencies and interests to enter into the medium of aesthetic experience and the sensuous cognition of a perfectly complete, harmonious, beautiful object. Both are derivatives of the anthropological project of the second half of the eighteenth century in Germany: placing the entire human being (*der ganze Mensch*) as an object of theoretical and practical concern.

9 Towards an Epistemology of the Individual Case: Stance and Deviation in the Philosophy of Marcus Herz

> We think of so many things as being of one kind that, if experience were to one day reveal their hidden differences to us, they would simply collapse into different kinds.
>
> Herz, "Über die analogische Schlussart"[1]

> Thus, it can happen that a physician or judge or statesman has many fine pathological or juridical or political rules in his head, and is even able to teach them well, and yet stumbles in applying them, either because he is short of the natural power of judgment (though not of understanding); he understands the universal in the abstract but can't tell whether a given concrete case falls under it; or because he hasn't been trained well enough for this act of judgment, through examples and actual practice.
>
> Kant, *Critique of Pure Reason*[2]

Marcus Herz was the paradigmatic example of the "philosophical physician," an invention of the eighteenth century.[3] Though his work has been analyzed in earlier parts of the book, we should recall his origins and development before turning to his variant of medical psychology or psychological medicine. Born 17 January 1747 into a religious family in Berlin – his father was a Torah scribe – he was enrolled in the *Ephraimstift,* where he received a classical Talmudic education. At the age of fifteen years, he was sent to Königsberg to pursue a career in business, but soon realized he was interested in medicine and philosophy. With the financial assistance of the Jewish community of Königsberg, Herz was matriculated in the medical faculty in 1766. While at the *Albertina*, Herz attended Immanuel Kant's lectures in philosophy – metaphysics, ethics, anthropology, psychology, and anthropology. Herz was held in such high regard by Kant that the philosopher designated the young Jewish student as his respondent in the defense of Kant's inaugural dissertation of 1770 *On the Forms and Principles of the Sensible*

---

[1] Marcus Herz, "Über die analogische Schlussart," *Berlinische Monatsschrift* 2 (1784): 246–251, here 251.
[2] Immanuel Kant, *Critique of Pure Reason*, trans., with intro. and notes by J. H. Bernard, 2nd ed. revised (London: Macmillan, 1914), B173.
[3] This designation was made famous by Melchior Adam Weikard: *Der philosophische Arzt* (Frankfurt, Hanau, and Leipzig: Weickard, 1773–1775).

and Intelligible World (*De mundi sensibilis atque intelligibilis*).[4] Herz was in regular communication with the leading intellectuals of his time: Moses Mendelssohn, Kant, Karl Philipp Moritz, and Salomon Maimon. Herz was also a major contributor to and supporter of Moritz's journal of empirical-experiential psychology *Magazin zur Erfahrungsseelenkunde*. Raised in a strict Talmudic household in which short stories, fables, parables, sayings, legends, and tales were commonplace,[5] not to mention the *Urszene* of the psychological case history in the Old Testament, the Book of Job, it is not strange that the young physician showed an inclination toward and a remarkable talent for narrative. Not unlike the psychologically-minded physicians at Halle, where Herz achieved his doctorate in medicine in 1774 after leaving Königsberg, Herz developed an extremely rare interdisciplinary approach to medicine that combined Psychology, Philosophy, the nascent discipline of Anthropology, and most importantly for our purposes, the detailed construction of case histories which he argued were essential for any inquiry into "the causes of human suffering." Especially the narrative of the inner experiences of the subject (the *innere Erlebnisse*, as he wrote about them), of the passions and feelings, and of the fantasies and images of the patient subject were of paramount importance if the physician wished to gain a full understanding of the emergence of mental illness.

In 1777, Herz began lecturing on Kant's emerging critical philosophy in the salon he shared with his young wife Henriette Herz de Lemos, based on notes he was receiving on a regular basis from students of Kant in Königsberg. According to some scholars, he became Kant's "disciple" or "representative" in Berlin. This was not the case.[6] Herz had already significantly departed from his mentor, and was clearly able to both lecture on Kant's philosophy *and* develop his own, distinct philosophical views in sharp contrast to Kant's.[7] In 1782, Herz

---

[4] On the relationship between Herz and Kant, see my "The Jewish Physician as Respondent, Confidant, and Proxy: The Case of Marcus Herz and Immanuel Kant," in *On the Word of the Jew: Religion, Reliability, and the Dynamics of Trust*, ed. Nina Caputo and Mitchell Hart (Bloomington: Indiana University Press, 2019), 222–244.

[5] Jeffrey L. Rubenstein, *Talmudic Stories: Narrative Art, Composition, and Culture* (Baltimore: Johns Hopkins University Press, 1999); and Jeffrey L. Rubenstein, *Rabbinic Stories* (New York and Mahwah, NJ: Paulist Press, 2002).

[6] See Leventhal, "The Jewish Physician as Respondent, Confidant, and Proxy," 228–230.

[7] Lewis White Beck, "Kant's Letter to Marcus Herz, February 21, 1771," trans. Arne Unhjem, in *Studies in the Philosophy of Kant*, by Beck (Minneapolis and New York: Bobbs-Merrill, 1965), 55, who claims that Herz was Kant's "ambassador in Berlin." For a corrective of this view of Herz merely as Kant's delegate in Berlin, see my "The Jewish Physician," 222–244.

became the director of the famous Jewish Hospital of Berlin, and in 1787, Friedrich Wilhelm II named him Professor of Philosophy, even though there was no university in Berlin at the time and Herz had no academic institutional affiliation. Although he was nominated to the Berlin Academy of Sciences, Herz was rejected because of his Jewish origins. As Martin Davies has observed, Herz can be considered the center of the empirical-therapeutic medical culture of Berlin medicine in the latter part of the eighteenth century.[8]

Today, with few exceptions,[9] the theories and texts of Herz have not been given an adequate profile, either in Philosophy, the History of Ideas, or the History of Medicine. In Thomas Broman's study of the history of medicine in Germany 1750–1820, for instance, Herz is mentioned only twice.[10] In much of what has been written about him, he is often read either as the disciple or student of Kant or as Kant's "representative" in Berlin, or he is viewed as a "mediator" between the *Maskilim* (advocates of the Jewish Enlightenment or

---

8 Martin Davies, "Moritz und die aufklärerische Berliner Medizin," in *Karl Philip Moritz und das 18. Jahrhundert*, ed. Martin Fontius and Anneliese Klingenberg (Tübingen: Max Niemeyer, 1995), 215–217.
9 Martin Davies, *Identity or History: Marcus Herz and the End of Enlightenment* (Detroit: Wayne State University Press, 1995); Doris Kaufmann, *Aufklärung, bürgerliche Selbsterfahrung und die Erfindung der Psychiatrie in Deutschland 1770–1850* (Göttingen: Vandenhoeck & Ruprecht, 1996), 92–93: "Seine folgenden Selbstbeobachtungen beschreiben nicht mehr Gehirnreaktionen, sondern schildern den Kampf innerhalb der Seele." See also: Mark Boulby: "Marcus Herz the Psychologist," *Jahrbuch für internationale Germanistik* 8.4 (1980): 327–331; Gernot Huppmann, "Marcus Herz (1747–1803): Arzt, Philosoph und Medizinischer Psychologe," *Zeitschrift für medizinische Psychologie* 1 (1992): 90–95; Mary Lindemann, "The Enlightenment Encountered: The German *Physicus* in His World, 1750–1820," in *Medicine in the Enlightenment*, ed. Roy Porter (Amsterdam: Rodopi, 1995), 181–198; Jörn Steigerwald, "Ideenzirkulation und Zirkulation von Ideen. Zur empirischen Psychologie der Berliner Spätaufklärung (am Beispiel Marcus Herz)," in *Gedächtnis und Zirkulation. Der Diskurs des Kreislaufs im 18. und 19. Jahrhundert*, ed. Harald Schmidt and Marcus Sandl (Göttingen: Vandenhoeck & Ruprecht, 2002), 39–64; Matthew Bell: *The German Tradition of Psychology in Literature and Thought, 1700–1840* (Cambridge: Cambridge University Press, 2005), 94; Christoph Maria Leder, *Die Grenzgänge des Marcus Herz. Beruf, Haltung, und Identität eines jüdischen Arztes gegen Ende des 18. Jahrhunderts* (München: Waxmann, 2007); Stefanie Buchenau, "Markus Herz. Kritik und Religion," in *Aufklärung und Religion. Neue Perspektiven*, ed. Michael Hofmann, Carsten Zelle (Hannover: Wehrhahn, 2010), 223–242; and Bettina Stangneth, "Der Arzt der Philosophen," in *Marcus Herz: Versuch über den Schwindel. Mit beiden Ergänzungen von 1797 und 1798, Einleitung, Werkverzeichnis und Anmerkungen*, ed. Stangneth (Hamburg: F. Meiner, 2019), vii–lxxxi.
10 Thomas Broman, *The Transformation of German Academic Medicine, 1780–1820* (Cambridge: Cambridge University Press, 2002).

Haskalah) and the German intellectuals of the late Enlightenment in Berlin.[11] In any case, intensive, precise readings of his texts, interpretations of his fascinating contributions to medicine, aesthetics, and epistemology, and his path-breaking case histories remain an urgent task for German literature, the History of Medicine, and German philosophy of the late eighteenth century. Davies's monograph on Herz of 1995 did reveal decisive differences to Kant,[12] but his thesis that Herz remained firmly within the confines of rationalist metaphysics,[13] and the major distinction he attributed to Herz between philosophy as the "objective" basis of the arts and sciences, and medicine as merely the "subjective" basis, does not adequately capture the profound interpenetration of philosophy and medicine in Herz's work.[14] Davies's conclusion that Herz was not a truly original thinker, but rather derivative of the Leibniz-Wolffian school of physico-theology,[15] or that his aesthetics is one based entirely on rationalistic principles *a priori*, within the tradition of Alexander Gottlieb Baumgarten and his student Georg Friedrich Meier – "Herz's solution is to attempt to turn aesthetics into an exact science."[16] – does not withstand a rigorous study of Herz's texts. Davies does recognize that Herz placed what he referred to as a "psychopathological limit" on the capacity of reason (*Vernunft*) in his study of 1786 *Versuch über den Schwindel*, but he never interrogates the contours of that limit, nor does he explore precisely how Herz veers from a strictly rationalistic position.[17]

Similarly, the research on Herz has not done justice to the significant role of experience (*Erfahrung*) and the importance of unique individuality in his corpus. In the second letter of the first volume of the *Letters to Physicians* (1777; 1784), for instance, directed to Christian Andreas Cothenius, one of the renowned physicians of the period, Herz emphasizes the inability of reason alone to determine the limit of medical "art."

> In a word, that we would be able to draw the limits of our art so that, in every case that appeared before us, we would know whether it falls within our purview or not? – This is a difficult circumstance in many other sciences, and in ours perhaps the most difficult. By means of reason alone it is impossible to attain this, as it would require a more

---

[11] Schmuel Feiner, *The Jewish Enlightenment*, trans. Chaya Naor (Philadelphia: University of Pennsylvania Press, 2011), 206–213.
[12] Davies, *Identity or History*.
[13] Davies, *Identity or History*, 44.
[14] Davies, *Identity or History*, 98.
[15] Davies, *Identity or History*, 128.
[16] Davies, *Identity or History*, 53.
[17] Davies, *Identity or History*, 53.

complete knowledge of both, namely the human body as well as all of the therapeutic means, than we can ever hope to achieve.[18]

The limits of the medical physician cannot be determined *a priori*, Herz argues, for this would presuppose a more complete knowledge of both the body and the therapeutic means than is possible or practical. The individual illness and diseases are of such complexity, and in every individual case so varied, that we cannot, through reason alone, determine the limits of medical knowledge. However, it is not only reason that proves to be ineffective in the determination of this boundary. The way of experience (*Erfahrung*) itself is also beset by problems with regard to this boundary determination: "What concerns the path of experience, this too is in our case far more difficult than in every other. For, in the first place, the differences and small variations of illness are infinite, as are the healing means with the multiplicity of natural products through which an illness can be remedied."[19] The multiplicity and variability of illness can be traced back to the irreducible individuality of an illness in each individual case, where it can suffer, as Herz calls it, a unique disposition (*eine eigene Disposition*)[20]: the minute, unique circumstances or situation that often determine whether an illness is within the reach of the physician or not. As Herz argues, the medical art is "always subject to doubt as to whether there is some miniscule difference in the present individual case that was not present in one that had come before, one that might be sufficient to make this particular illness receptive to a cure. We cannot venture to say with certainty how great the influence of this small particular individuality is with respect to the illness."[21] In the *Letters to Physicians*, the smallest, hardly noticeable circumstance of the

---

18 Marcus Herz, *Briefe an Ärzte* (Berlin: Voss, 1784), 155: "mit einem Worte, dass wir die Gränzlinien unserer Kunst genau bezeichneten, damit jeder vorkommende Fall erkannt werden könne, ob er in ihren Umfang gehöre oder nicht? – Dieses ist ein schwieriger Umstand in mancher andern Wissenschaft, und in der unsrigen vielleicht der schwierigste. Durch die blosse Vernunft ist es unmöglich dahin zu gelangen, dieses würde eine vollständigere Kenntnis beyder, des menschlichen Körpers so wohl als der Heilungsmittel, voraus setzen, als wir je zu Erlangen hoffen dürfen. . . ."
19 Herz, *Briefe an Ärzte*, 157: "Was aber den Weg der Erfahrung betrifft, so ist dieser in unserm Falle gleichfalls ungemein schwieriger als in jedem andern. Dann erstlich sind von der einen Seite die Verschiedenheiten und kleine Abänderungen der Krankheiten eben so unendlich, als es von der Seite andern Seite die Mannigfaltigkeit der Naturprodukte ist, wodurch die Krankheiten gehoben werden können."
20 Herz, *Briefe an Ärzte*, 157.
21 Herz, *Briefe an Ärzte*, 157: "So muss doch jedesmal [. . .] ein Zweifel in uns entstehen, ob nicht in einem einzelnen Fall ein kleiner unmerklicher Umstand sich findet, der bey aller vorhergeganenen nicht war, und der vielleicht allein hinreichend seyn mag, in diesem Fall die

individual case that differs from all previous cases might indeed be the factor that proves decisive in rendering the illness curable.

Even though Herz could not go along with the "transcendental turn" of his teacher and mentor Kant, his interest was always directed at the inherent limits of reason, the transgression of the usual disciplinary boundaries between philosophy and psychology, philosophy and medicine, and, above all, the irreducible individuality of the case in epistemology. Herz forged an interdisciplinary approach to illness and disease on the threshold or boundary between philosophy, medicine, physiology, and psychopathology.[22] Herz sought to modify a strict rationalistic methodological procedure by showing the limited validity of analogical reasoning in comparing and contrasting specific cases in an article he contributed to the *Berlin Monthly* in 1784.[23] Directed against his colleague Christian Gottlob Selle, who had maintained in a previous issue that *analogy* was simply another name for causal connection, Herz insisted that the analogical form of reasoning differed from causal thinking; as a mode of probabilistic reasoning, and concerned with *qualities* rather than cause and effect, it could only be applied in individual cases in a probative manner until experience taught us differently.[24] His entire conception of philosophical medicine culminates in what he referred to as *physiological psychology*; under the influence of the aesthetics of his time, he named the system of nerve-channels and nervous fluid a *sensorium communis*, and placed the center of this system in the human brain.[25] For Herz, the human being could only be considered as a whole,

---

Krankheit der Heilung fähig zu machen [...] Wir können es nicht wagen mit Gewißheit zu bestimmen, wie gross der Einfluss dieser geringen Individualität auf diese Krankheit sein mag."

22 Davies, *Identity or History*, 93: "The metaphor of patrolling borders describes his way of putting Enlightenment ideas into practice by mediating between metaphysical speculation and empirical application." It is not clear why Davies chose the term "patrolling." Herz employed the expression "Umherwandeln in den Gränzorten," which literally means "to wander around in the borderlands."

23 Herz, "Über die analogische Schlussart," 246–251. It was a response to Christian Gottlob Selle's "Von der analogischen Schlussart," *Berlinische Monatsschrift* (1784), 185–186.

24 Herz, "Über die analogische Schlussart," 250: "Die Analogie gilt immer nur so lange, bis die Erfahrung uns vom Gegentheil überzeugt." Analogical thinking is essential to "thinking in cases." See John Forrester, "If p, then what? Thinking in cases," *History of the Human Sciences* 9.3 (1996): 1–25.

25 Herz's physiological-psychology epitomizes the shift from a humoral to a nueronal model of the human being traced by Albrecht Koschorke, *Körperströme und Schriftverkehr. Mediologie des 18. Jahrhunderts* (München: W. Fink, 2003); and in his essay "Physiological Self-Regulation: The Eighteenth-Century Modernization of the Human Body," *MLN* Vol. 123.3 (2008): 469–484.

a unity of mind and body. In this respect he was very much a product of the anthropology of the late Enlightenment in Germany.

In the following I will attempt to tease out the aesthetic and epistemological dimensions of Herz's philosophy, especially as these bear on Herz's thematization of the individual case and its scriptural and discursive genre, the psychological case history. Throughout his life, Herz was concerned with the diversity and variability (*Verschiedenheit*) exhibited by human beings, their divergent tastes, and the distinct forms of madness from which they suffer. In a first step, I will examine Herz's argument of the origin of this difference in his work *Essay on Vertigo* (1786; 1791). Then, I will be chiefly concerned with his theory of "deviation" (*Abweichung*) as it is articulated in his *Considerations of Speculative Philosophy* (1771), and what I see as the central concept of his philosophy, the notion of *Haltung* – position or stance – a notion he appropriated from the work of Johann Georg Sulzer,[26] but transformed in a decisive way in his *Treatise on Taste and the Reasons for its Diversity* (1776). For Sulzer, *Haltung* was primarily corporeal; it had to do chiefly with the stances or gestures of the body.[27] "Deviation" (*Abweichung*) for Herz is, by contrast, the manner in which the unique individuality of the individual is expressed. "Stance" (*Haltung*) refers to the unique way in which a manifold becomes, in each individual case, a unity; how the disparate parts, in any singular instance, unite to become a whole, both objectively and subjectively, to constitute meaningful experience within the human being. Taken together, what we might call three fundamental epistemological figures – difference, deviation and stance – inform Herz's writing and thought about the significance of the individual case and the importance of the genre of the case history in his overall philosophy.

In the ninth chapter of the *Essay on Vertigo*, Herz confronts the decisive question of how, even though the soul is fundamentally a representational power that seems to be uniform and universal for all human beings,[28] the representations themselves (*Vorstellungen*) can differ so widely in one and the same subject from time to time, and across different subjects. Herz recognizes at the outset that such

---

26 Johann Georg Sulzer, *Allgemeine Theorie der schönen Künste* (Leipzig: Weidmanns Erben, and Reich, 1773), vol. 1.
27 Sulzer, *Allgemeine Theorie*, vol. 1, 460: "Haltung des Körpers. (Schöne Künste). Wir verstehen hier durch dieses Wort das, was man gemeiniglich durch das französische Wort *Maintien* ausdrückt, die charackteristische Art, wie ein Mensch bey verschiedenen Stellungen und Gebehrden sich trägt, oder hält."
28 Herz, *Versuch über den Schwindel* (Berlin: Voss, 1791), 37: "Das ganze Wesen der menschlichen Seele besteht in Vorstellungen. Alle ihre Fähigkeiten und Äusserungen müssen, so wie die Eigenschaften jedes andern Dinges, auf dessen Wesen, auf dieses ihr Grundvermögen, *Vorstellungen zu haben*, zurückgebracht werden können."

differences in the rapidity and ease with which some subjects are able to grasp connections between ideas are not merely the result of habit and exercise or drill; there seem to be fundamental differences in the power of representation itself. Such differences also obtain in one and the same subject in various states of mind (*Gemüthszustände*) and moods (*Laune*): "All capacities of the soul are subject to mood and the shifts in the mind."[29] The vast differences of physical strength and ability can be explained more easily, whereas the basis of the different capabilities of the power of representation is much harder to account for. The soul is a simple substance (*eine einfache Substanz*), according to Herz, without extension or resistance, i.e., its power cannot be described or defined in the physical vocabulary we use in talking about physical objects. It would stand to reason then that a general "law" of the soul would be that frequent practice and exercise, constant application would ensure a certain easiness or facility in representation. But this is not the case, and Herz poses this as a basic, psychological question – namely, how does one explain the difference (*Verschiedenheit*) of the representational power among various human beings? Even assuming there is one and the same basic human representational power (*Anlage*), how can one account for the profound differences in this power and the differences in the representations themselves? Because we cannot discern the cause of such difference immediately within the soul – the soul itself and the representational flow do not and indeed cannot provide the answer to that question – we must look according to Herz to what he refers to as the mediate (*mittelbare*) causes. Herz answers this by advancing a theory of "parallelism" according to which every change or shift in the soul can only occur under the condition of a corresponding change or shift in the body:

> We have to assume (and this we can do with almost demonstrative certainty) that every change in the soul, that is, every expression of its power, can only occur under the condition of a change in the body, more precisely, in that part of the body, with which the connection is closest, namely in the brain and in the nerves [...] With every representation A. in the soul the movement in brain a. must arise; with every representation B. the movement b. and so forth.[30]

---

[29] Marcus Herz, *Versuch über den Schwindel*, 129–130: "Allen Seelenfähigkeiten sind dem Launen und Gemüthswechsel unterworfen."

[30] Herz, *Versuch über den Schwindel*, 134: "Wir müssen annehmen (und dies können wir beynahe mit demonstrativer Gewissheit), dass jede Veränderung der Seele, d.i. jede Ausserung ihrer Kraft, nur unter der Bedingung einer entsprechenden Veränderung im Körper geschehen kann, und zwar in demjenigen Theile des Körpers, mit welchem ihre Verbindung die nächste ist: in dem Gehirne und in den Nerven[...]. Bey jeder Vorstellung A. in der Seele muss im Gehirn die Bewegung a. entstehen; bey jeder Vorstellung B. die Bewegung b."

Unlike David Hume and his advocate in Göttingen, Michael Hissmann,[31] who decried the soul as a metaphysical ghost and dismissed any psychology concerned with anything other than the connection between ideas and their associations as mere speculation, Herz remained convinced that one could not reasonably speak of such representations without assuming the soul as the fundamental and irreducible representational power. Otherwise, Herz argued, philosophers would find themselves in a vicious circle, an infinite regress, always seeking to find the basis for one representation through another *ad infinitum*, and therefore never arriving at the foundation or absolute condition of such representation. The psychology of the strict empiricists such as Hissmann who denied the existence of the soul could never get beyond the series of representations themselves, unable to explain how such representations could arise in the first place, and the particular constitution (*Beschaffenheit*) of such representations. Nor would they be able to provide a theory for the variability of representations across or within various subjects.[32]

Differences between representations and sensation were to be explained according to Herz either as natural (*natürlich*), which had to do with the basic disposition of the human being, age, temperament, character, type, relation, and the subject's general ability to discern things (*Absonderungsgeschäft*).[33] Or they were to be explained through what Herz referred to as *widernatürlich* or detrimental organic/physical differences that affected the body such as an increased or decreased viscosity of the nervous fluid (*Nervensaft*), obstruction or blockage of the nerve channels or tubes (*Kanäle*), the relative thickness and circulation of the blood, an altered condition of the brain, and so forth. As Albrecht Koschorke has argued, in the second half of the eighteenth century, the gradual dissolution of the Cartesian self issues in a double contingency: on the one hand, a multiplication of representations in the mind and the modes of such representation, and on the other hand, a new complexity and arbitrariness of physiological and nervous "alterations" or "deviations" in the determination of the "state" or "condition" of the neuronal human organism.[34] The psychophysiology of Herz stands precisely under Koschorke's "double contingency."

---

31 Herz mentions both Hume and Hissmann in *Versuch über den Schwindel*, and it is quite clear he is seeking to set up an alternative to their particular form of empiricism in the text.
32 It is remarkable to note the similarity of Herz's argument in the *Versuch* to the later argument by J.G. Fichte in his First *Introduction to the Science of Knowledge* (1794). On Fichte's fundamental distinction, see Dieter Henrich, "Fichte's Original Insight," trans. David Lachterman, *Contemporary German Philosophy* 1 (1982): 15–53.
33 Herz, *Versuch über den Schwindel*, 147.
34 Albrecht Koschorke, "Wissenschaft des Arbiträren. Die Revolutionierung der Sinnesphysiologie und die Entstehung der modernen Hermeneutik um 1800," in *Poetologie des Wissens um 1800*, ed. Joseph Vogl (München: Fink, 1999), 32.

Such differences and such variations of those differences he believed were also at work in certain medical conditions and in different types of mental illness (*Verrückung*). In the ninth chapter of *Essay*, Herz inserts two case histories (*Krankengeschichten*) in footnotes that he had also published in Moritz's *Magazin zur Erfahrungsseelenkunde* as examples of the key differences he is interested in. The first concerned an artillery officer who experienced a paralysis of the tongue, hands, and feet after an illness and received treatment that restored feeling and movement in the hands and feet, as well as the ability to utter words, but only when he *read* something; the free, intentional use of speech continued to elude him.[35] Herz sought to explain this as a disrupted relationship between the language organs and the representational power, which required a certain degree of reflexivity in order to produce the requisite "intention" and "facility" of unrehearsed speech.

> In order to place our language organs into motion for the expression of a word, it is necessary that the representation of this, whether it comes from within us or through some kind of external cause, must be present in our soul previously, which then incites our freedom and determines it to move the nervous fluid into the nerves of the language muscles in such a way that is demanded for the expression of the corresponding word.[36]

One could easily see such an explanation as a physical-mechanical account of arbitrary (i.e., unrehearsed or undetermined, free) language usage. The crucial point is, however, that Herz identifies "presence within the soul" as a condition of such expression; in other words, we must on some level be aware of what we wish to say, and be able to consciously enact a connection with the organs of language, in order to freely express ourselves without a pre-existing text or script.

The second case history inserted in the footnote by Herz told the story of a deeply melancholic woman who, out of unrequited love, would not speak a word. She, too, when given a text and called upon to read, could do so with the normal facility of a healthy human being. Herz reasoned that because of the singular focus on the lost love-object, the brooding attention to this one representation to the exclusion of all others, the normal effect of any other representation

---

[35] Marcus Herz, "Wirkung des Denkvermögens auf die Sprachwerkzeuge," *Magazin zur Erfahrungsseelenkunde* 8.2 (1791): 1–6.
[36] Herz, *Versuch über den Schwindel*, 138: "Um unsere Sprachwerkzeuge zur Hervorbringung eines Wortes in Bewegung zu setzen, ist es nothwendig, dass dessen Vorstellung, sie mag nun von selbst, oder durch aeussere Veranlassung in uns entstehen, vorher in unsere Seele gegenwärtig sey, welche alsdann unsere Willkühr rege macht, und sie bestimmt, in die Nerven der Sprachmuskeln den Nervensaft gerade so hin zu bewegen, wie es die Aussprache des ihr entsprechenden Wortes erfordert."

was so diminished, and the representational power therefore so debilitated, that the will could not be transformed into actual activity. On a physiological level, the movement of the nervous fluids halted any transmission from the representational power to the speech-organs causing the incapacity to speak freely.

Herz concluded this chapter of *Essay on Vertigo* with a summary of the "most important circumstances that are responsible for the different behaviors (*Verhalten*) of the soul with respect to the lasting exercise of the soul's representation power."[37] He spelled out his theory (*Lehre*) which he said constitutes the basis of all psychology,[38] praising John Locke for having made an important start in this direction. Here, we are concerned with Herz's seventh argument, which, he believed, provided the answer to the question of the basis of the differences and divergences in representations. The natural and unnatural circumstances (*Umstände*) that obtain under various conditions (*Bedingungen*) are so different among human beings and, in various situations, even in and across the range of an individual's experience, that one must conclude that there is a particular progression of representations unique to each individual, which is itself subject to deviation:

> Seventh: but these circumstances are, as we have seen, among human beings in general, and in each individual human being, under many conditions, different; for this reason there has to be a particular progression of ideas that is unique to each human being, but also subject to a deviation from her usual measure according to the difference of the circumstances.[39]

The three terms that stand out in his effort to explain the variability of representations among human beings and even within a single person are diversity (*Verschiedenheit*), uniqueness (*eigenthümlich*), and deviation (*Abweichung*). To be sure, the three terms are not identical according to Herz. Diversity (*Verschiedenheit*) refers specifically to the difference of *circumstances* for Herz, while unique (*eigenthümlich*) signifies the manner in which representations are usually connected to one another in any single person, who also at times can

---

37 Herz, *Versuch über den Schwindel*, 149: "Dies sind die wichtigsten Umstände, worauf es bey dem verschiedenen Verhalten der Seele in Ansehung der anhaltenden Ausübung ihrer Vorstellungskraft ankommt."
38 Herz, *Versuch über den Schwindel*, 150: "welche die Grundlage der ganzen Psychologie ausmacht."
39 Herz, *Versuch über den Schwindel*, 152: "*Siebentens:* diese Umstände sind aber, wie wir gesehen haben, unter den Menschen überhaupt, und bey jedem einzelnen unter manchen Bedingungen verschieden; daher muss zwar ein bestimmter Fortgang der Vorstellungen jedem Menschen eigenthümlich, aber nach Verschiedenheit der Umstände auch der Abweichung von seinem gewöhnlichen Masse unterworfen seyn."

experience deviation (*Abweichung*) from their usual or typical way of representing something, depending on natural (*natürlich*) or unnatural/pathological (*widernatürlich*) circumstances or conditions. Attention to these factors is absolutely critical in the practice of medicine and the understanding of illness.

According to Herz, illness and disease are – as they were for Thomas Sydenham and Herman Boerhaave before him – a state contrary to nature, one which arises from a loss or destruction of the natural and "healthy" equilibrium of the natural forces within the human being.⁴⁰ Medicine, according to this view and explicitly stated in Herz's *Considerations concerning Philosophy* of 1771, is nothing other than the art, science, and capability of the physician to ascertain the cause of this disequilibrium, and to restore the balance and harmony of the natural forces.⁴¹ This "art" (*Kunst*), according to Herz, requires medical theory and knowledge of anatomy and physiology, heightened awareness and precise observation, and an adept application of the analogical method of drawing conclusions from similar cases, but it requires something else as well: *Genius*. As Herz states: "The application of these on an individual case is the work of genius" (*Anwendung dieser auf individuelle Fälle* [...] *ist lediglich Werk des Genies*).⁴² One might well ask why this supplement of genius is even necessary. The answer is that, for Herz, reason itself is absolutely and fundamentally limited. At the end of *Essay on Vertigo*, Herz writes that reason, precisely that faculty of the human being that "measures worlds and presses into the very essence of the infinite, is unfamiliar with its own area and instruments!"⁴³ This inherent limitation or "lack" of reason – its inability to understand its own abode and operations – renders the element of *Genius* indispensable for the art and science of medicine.

---

40 Stangneth, "Der Arzt der Philosophen," XXIV: "Krank ist ein Mensch dann, wenn er aus seinem natürlichen Gleichgewicht geraten ist. Medizin ist die Lehre der Methode, den Menschen wieder in seinen natürlichen Zustand zu versetzen. Darum kann der Arzt dabei auf die Hilfe der Natur hoffen, denn Krankheit ist wesentlich der Versuch der Natur, das Widernatürliche zu beseitigen." I am grateful to Bettina Stangneth for making her valuable introduction available to me before the publication of her text.
41 Marcus Herz, *Betrachtungen aus der spekulativen Weltweisheit*, ed. Elfriede Conrad et al. (Hamburg: F. Meiner, 1990), 2.
42 Herz, *Grundriß aller medizinischen Wissenschaften* (Berlin: Voss, 1782), 2–4. On this, see Broman, *Transformation of German Academic Medicine*, 118.
43 Marcus Herz, *Versuch über den Geschmack* [zuerst: Leipzig u.a. 1776]. 2., verm. u. verb. Auflage (Berlin: Voss, 1790), 448: "die Welten misst und bis in das Wesen des Unendlichen dringt, gerade ihre eigene Wohnstätte und ihre unmittelbaren Werkzeuge am wenigsten kennt."

In most of the research on Herz, the overarching rationalistic tenor of his work has been emphasized to the detriment of other facets of his thought that deserve our attention.[44] And, to be sure, Herz makes claim to and relies on the basic principles of reason in his argumentation. But this belief in the underlying validity of the precepts of human reason did not deter Herz from advancing a powerful critique of the absolute applicability and usefulness of reason (*Vernunft*), specifically in his digressions,[45] in his theory of difference (*Verschiedenheit*) in human representation and taste, and in his theory of deviation (*Abweichung*) in the text *Concerning the Contradictions in Human Nature*.[46] Herz's text, which appeared in 1773 in *Der teutsche Merkur*, signals a truly transformative moment in the history of medicine. Not reason alone, but experience, honed by the capacity of judgment and sharpened through the encounter with individual cases, attention to the individuality of the case, and empirical knowledge gained from both direct and others' experience (*Erfahrung*), distinguish the genuinely "philosophical physician." Such a physician operates in the "borderlands" between philosophy and medicine, reason and practical experience: "wandering about in the border regions of the two lands, philosophy and medicine,"[47] or, as he also puts it, "dwelling near the borders."[48] Borders and borderlands imply thresholds, and indicate movements away from the center towards the periphery. Deviation (*Abweichung*) for Herz, which also implies a centrifugal movement away from the center, is an essential ingredient of human nature, and must become the object of scientific inquiry; what we might see as contingency (*Zufall*) and peculiarity are not themselves random or fortuitous. Distance from the ideal – perfection, harmony, and beauty – tell us more about the individual human being than the conformity to any idealized image or preconceived notion. It is precisely through such deviations that we understand disease and illness, and can assist the individual in its specific striving to overcome the inherent contradictions in its nature.

---

44 Above all Davies, who sees in Herz's *Betrachtungen* simply a rationalistic reformulation of Kants Dissertation *De mundi sensibilis atque intelligibilis*. See Davies, *Identity or History*, 60–65. John Efron, *Medicine and the German Jews: A History* (New Haven, CT: Yale University Press, 2008), 93, 98. Like Davies, Efron sees Herz as the consummate rationalist.
45 Herz, *Betrachtungen*, 23. Compare Davies: *Identity or History*, 50–53, on "the first digression."
46 Marcus Herz, "Über die Widersprüche in der menschlichen Natur," *Der Teutsche Merkur* 1 (1773): 144–163.
47 Letter of Marcus Herz to Immanuel Kant, 27 February 1786, in *Gesammelte Schriften*, ed. The Prussian Academy of Sciences (Berlin: G. Riemer, 1902), vol. 10, 431–432: "das Umherwandeln in den Gränzorten der beyden Länder, der Philosophie und der Medizin."
48 Herz, *Betrachtungen*, 40: "das Verweilen bey den Grenzen."

> Every individual deviates from his kind, and to the degree that it deviates, it becomes more or less imperfect. These deviations do not prove disorder in nature but are rather in accordance with her laws, on the basis of which an individual has a reason for the changes which take place, and are necessary, as long as such laws themselves are necessary.[49]

Herz's theory of deviation does not remain at the level of the individual, nor does it idealize or essentialize deviation for its own sake as some sort of abstract, metaphysical construct. Deviation and difference serve a significant sociocultural and historical function as well. In seeking to comprehend the effects of the mixture of races (*Mischung*), Herz hypothesizes that with increasing commerce, exchange, and the interrelation of various peoples and ethnicities, the various forms of deviations will be eliminated (*aufheben*), each form will push others to the extremes to which they are destined, and will in effect ultimately cancel each other out, leading to an ever greater degree of perfection.

> The more all peoples of the earth mix through encounter and action, the more their deviations will cancel each other out; with opposing forces such that each will pull the other towards the extremity to which it itself tends.[50]

In this view of global human history – that exchange, commerce, and intermarriage would gradually ameliorate the stark deviations and differences between peoples, moving them from their unique "extremes" to a more fully human "middle" – Herz demonstrated a degree of cosmopolitanism consonant with the most progressive Enlightenment ideals of his time.

Moreover, the individuality of the individual is a result precisely of such deviation or *Abweichung*: the distance from the ideal, the particular organization and circumstances, makes a person what they are. What deviates from the ideal and the rational is contingency or chance – *Zufall* – and distance or deviation from perfection is contingent (*zufällig*), exactly what makes the individual unique. However, deviation is not an end in itself. Rather, it spurs the individual on, serves as an impetus to strive toward perfection; it is therefore for Herz

---

49 Herz, "Über die Widersprüche," 151: "Jedes Individuum weicht aber von den seinigen ab, und in dem Grade, dass es abweicht, wird es mehr oder weniger unvollkommen. Diese Abweichungen beweisen nicht Unordnung in der Natur, sie sind vielmehr ihren Gesetzen, vermöge welcher ein Wesen den Grund enthält von den Veränderungen, die in dem anderm vorgehen, gemäß, und so lange diese Gesetze notwendig dieselben bleiben, notwendig."
50 Herz, "Über die Widersprüche," 162: "Je mehr alle Völker der Erde durch den Umgang und Handlung sich vermischen werden, je mehr werden ihre Abweichungen einander aufheben, mit gegen einander wirkenden Kräften wird jede die andere zu der Extremität hinziehen, zu der sie sich selbst neigt."

"*eine bildende Kraft*" – a formative, educative force, pushing the individual toward ever greater power, perfection, harmony, equilibrium, and happiness.

In his review of Ernst Platner's *Anthropologie* (1772),[51] Herz criticized Platner's failure to recognize the influence of the mind on the body: "Least of all can it be understood how the author of this Anthropology can deny the influence of spiritual life on the mechanical. Wherein should the connection between soul and body consist otherwise?"[52] Against what was for Herz a physical-physiological reduction of the soul and the sense of self in Platner, Herz argues for a reciprocal, dynamic relation between the soul and body, and for the totality of the human being:

> the physician can never leave out of consideration the concept of *connection* (*Verknüpfung*) which obtains between the soul and the body. Two entities that are connected to one another and constitute a whole must be of a specific composition, that each contains the basis of everything that is in the other, and therefore that there can be no change in the state of one without there being a corresponding change in the state of the other, and this refers to the idea of *nexus*, which must be considered in all explanations. A circumstance that is all too often neglected by the psychologists as well as the medical doctors, through which the basis is prepared for many false hypotheses and systems.[53]

Nexus and *Verknüpfung* (connection, conjunction, linkage) refer to the interrelatedness of mind and body for Herz, which is always determined (*bestimmt*) in a specific way depending on the individual case. Unlike the theory of *influxus* advocated in the early eighteenth century by Stahl and continued, with some degree of modification, by the psychologically-minded physicians at the Universität

---

51 Marcus Herz, Review of *Anthropologie für Ärzte und Weltweise*, by Dr. Ernst Platner (Leipzig, 1772). *Allgemeine Deutsche Bibliothek* 20.1 (1773): 25–51; repr. Marcus Herz, *Philosophisch-Medizinische* Aufsätze, ed. Martin Davies (St. Ingbert: Röhrig, 1997), 7–23.
52 Herz, Review of *Anthropologie für Ärzte und Weltweise*, by Dr. Ernst Platner, 12: "Am wenigsten lässt es sich begreifen, wie der Verfasser einer Anthropologie den Einfluß des geistigen Lebens auf das mechanische leugnen kann, worinn besteht sonst die Verknüpfung zwischen Seele und Körper?" See also Hans Peter Nowitzki, *Der wohltemperierte Mensch. Aufklärungsanthropologien im Widerstreit* (Berlin: de Gruyter, 2003), 203f.
53 Herz, Review of D. Ernst Platner, 50; emphasis mine. Compare also Herz, *Briefe an Ärzte. Zweite Sammlung* (Berlin: Voss, 1784), 231: "der Arzt [darf] in seiner Theorie nie den Begriff der Verknüpfung außer Acht lassen, welche zwischen der Seele und dem Körper stattfindet. Zwei Dinge, die mit einander verknüpft sind, und ein Ganzes ausmachen, müssen von der Beschaffenheit seyn, dass ein jedes von Ihnen den Grund von allen denjenigen enthält, was in dem anderen vorhanden ist, und daher kein Zustand des einen verändert werden kann, wenn der Zustand des andern derselbe bleiben soll, dieses liegt in der Idee des *Nexus*, worauf bey allen Erklärungen Rücksicht genommen werden muss. Ein Umstand, der von den Psychologen sowohl als von den Arzeneygelehrten nur zu oft vernachlässigt wird, wodurch aber der Grund zu vielen falschen Hypothesen und Systemen gelegt wird."

Halle at mid-century, Herz rejected a rigid determinism from either side of the mind-body divide, and consistently argued for the dynamic and reciprocal influence of mind and body, always inflected in each individual instance: the specific valence of difference, deviation, nexus, and stance in the particular case. Above all, Platner's mechanistic-materialistic account of the relation between body and soul cannot account for representations (*Vorstellungen*), because, as Herz argues, changes or movements in the brain do not constitute representations, even though for every such representation there must be a "corresponding" movement in the brain. Representations occur as a function of the soul, not the brain; and while the parallelism postulated by Herz dictated a certain isomorphism between psychic and physiological events, he did not collapse the two.

Herz's *Considerations concerning Philosophy* (1771) was supposed to be simply an exposition of Kant's dissertation of 1770, *De mundis sensibilis atque intelligibilis et principiis*,[54] and it has often been viewed as such, with some minor alterations. However, a close analysis of the text reveals a number of decisive "digressions" or deviations from Kant. These digressions and deviations in fact signal a profound departure from Kant's rigorous rationalism and his insistence on *a priori* formal conditions in the determination of varying empirical content. In his letter to Kant of 9 July 1771, excusing himself as not having actually planned to veer away from Kant's argumentation, Herz tells Kant that he had Kant's dissertation fully in view when he wrote the text, but that – "here and there" as he put it – he had made some "digressions" – Herz actually uses the term *Digreßionen* – that had occurred to him during the actual writing of the text: "I have had your text before me, followed the thread of your thoughts, and only made slight digressions here and there which occurred to me while I was working on the book, and without my having planned them beforehand."[55] In reality, these "digressions" actually constitute a significant criticism of what Kant had written in the dissertation. Later in the same letter, Herz refers to this as an *Auschweifung* (digression) concerning the principles of the beautiful which had allowed him to prove the existence of the soul. Herz had, in his own words, only made "a small movement – placing the foot just a bit farther"[56] – but the divergence from and advance beyond Kant's fundamental

---

[54] Immanuel Kant, *De mundis sensibilis atque intelligibilis et principiis* (Königsberg: Jacob Kanter, 1770).
[55] Herz to Kant, *AA*, vol. 10 124: "Ich habe bloß Ihre Schrift vor Augen gehabt, den Faden Ihrer Gedanken gefolgt, und nur hie und da einige Digreßionen gemacht, die mehr im Arbeiten einfielen als daß ich sie vorher mit im Plane gebracht habe."
[56] Herz to Kant, *AA*, vol. 10, 124: "eine kleine Bewegung [...] den Fuß etwas weiter su setzen."

position was both evident and fundamental. The term *Auschweifung* connotes both diversion, divergence, and departure, but also a transgression from the norm, excess and even indulgence, so that Herz's admission of a digression from Kant's argument rings both of *clinamen*, misprision, guilt, going "astray," and the pleasure of self-empowerment in differing from the master's theory. Indeed, much more was at stake than a mere digression concerning aesthetics and the "beautiful" in Herz's comments on Kant in the *Betrachtungen*.

The first "digression" in the *Considerations*, at the same time a decisive swerve from Kant's philosophy, occurs right at the beginning of the text. Herz attempts to elucidate "the subtle difference between the subjective and the objective of sensible knowledge in terms of both the form and the matter of such knowledge."[57] By introducing the issue of sensuous knowledge (*sinnliche Erkenntnis*), a commonplace for aesthetics in the second half of the eighteenth century, and by raising the question of the differential between the form and the content of such knowledge, Herz deliberately interjects the problem of aesthetics directly into the domain of epistemology. This was clearly in and of itself a significant transgression against Kant's insistence on a clear division between the three central faculties: reason, the understanding, and judgment. Herz emphasizes the "subjective moment" of every cognition and – unlike Kant – traces this into the very *form of the cognition itself*, not simply the content, as Kant had suggested. As he was unfolding his transcendental-critical philosophy, Kant insisted that the *forms* of actual and possible cognition themselves must remain identical *a priori*, while the content is constantly shifting. In a word, according to Herz, *the very form itself* is inflected, we might say "contaminated," by the individual case.[58] Due to the importance of this argument, I quote from the two paragraphs in the *Considerations* at length in order to allow the full force of Herz's deviation or digression from Kant to become legible:

> I distinguish in the cognition of the beautiful, as in sensuous cognition in general, the *material* from the *form*. The objective [content] in the material is the impression itself,

---

57 Herz, *Betrachtungen*, 20: "den subtilen Unterschied zwischen dem Subjektiven und Objektiven der sinnlichen Erkenntnis, insofern die *Form* und insofern die *Materie* derselben betrachtet wird."
58 Jason Michael Peck's dissertation on Herz, *From the Transcendental to the Particular: German-Jewish Philosophy at the End of the Eighteenth Century*, PhD diss., University of Minnesota, 2006, argues that Herz "attempts to reconcile the subjective experience of the senses with the ability to objectively cognize objects outside of us" (45). Davies, *Identity and History*, 55–57, argues that Herz "put a revisionistic gloss on what was Kant's revolutionary initial formulation" (55), that Herz "elides" the personal and the objective (56), and thereby also misses the incisive move made by Herz.

which the senses receive from the object, or the alteration of the circumstance which the soul suffers as a result. The exact determination of this objective content, however, is dependent on what is *unique to the individual subject*, and must therefore be *different in different subjects*. The form is constituted by the universal principles which aesthetics discerns, which are objective to the degree that they are present within the soul as necessary laws according to which the soul is able to judge the beauty or ugliness of any given sensuous object. *But because these principles in any particular determination must be applied to a very specific material, and this contains within itself something subjective, therefore the particular form is not something objective, but will contain something subjective, as it is mixed with the material, to which the form is applied.*⁵⁹

Now if everything that has objective reality is also universally valid, the material and the form of the beautiful will not be subject to any strife as long as they are considered undetermined (*unbestimmt*), for the impressions of the object itself as well as the laws which are prescribed to us in any judgment must be found without any differentiation in all subjects. *But as soon as the form is determined and applied to an individual case, it becomes subjective, insofar as something subjective is contained in the material itself and therefore can be applied differently in different subjects or in one and the same subject under different circumstances.*⁶⁰

Herz's strong deviation and departure from Kant is very clear in the passages I have emphasized by using italics. First, Herz introduces aesthetics into a discussion of epistemology, thereby questioning the rigid borders and limits

---

59 Herz, *Betrachtungen*, 21–22; emphasis mine: "Ich unterscheide in der Erkenntnis des Schönen, gleichwie in der sinnlichen Erkenntnis überhaupt, die *Materie* von der *Form*. Das Objektive in der Materie ist der Eindruck, den die Sinne von dem Gegenstand empfangen, oder die Veränderung des Zustandes, welche die Seele dadurch leidet. Die genaue Bestimmung desselben hingegen hängt von demjenigen ab, was jedem Subjekt besonders eigen ist, und muss daher in verschiedenen Subjekten verschieden sein. Die Form machen die allgemeinen Grundsätze aus, welche die Ästhetik auseinandersetzt, die wiederum insofern objektiv sind, als sie der Seele als notwendige Gesetze beiwohnen, nach denen allein sie die Schönheit oder Hässlichkeit irgendeines sinnlichen Gegenstandes beurteilen kann. *Da diese Grundsätze aber bei der genauen Bestimmung auf die genau bestimmte Materie angewendet werden müssen, und diese etwas Subjektives in sich enthält, so wird auch die bestimmte Form nicht bloß Objektives sein, sondern ebenso viel Subjektives enthalten, als mit der Materie, auf welche sie angewandt wird, untermischt ist.*"

60 Herz, *Betrachtungen*, 22; emphasis mine: "Wenn nun alles, was eine objective Wirklichkeit hat, auch allgemein gültig ist, so werden notwendig die Materie und die Form des Schönen, solange sie als unbestimmt betrachtet werden, keinem Streit unterworfen sein können, denn sowohl die Eindrücke des Gegenstandes als auch die Gesetze, welche uns in Beurteilung desselben vorgeschrieben sind, müssen sich ohne Unterschied in allen Subjekten finden. *Sobald aber die Form bestimmt und auf einen besonderen Fall angewandt werden soll, so wird sie insofern subjektiv werden, als in der Materie Subjektives enthalten ist und daher in verschiedenen Subjekten oder in ein und demselben Subjekt unter verschiedenen Umständen auch verschiedentlich angewandt werden.*"

Kant had always insisted on between the different faculties (reason, understanding, judgment) and the various functions of these faculties. This itself performs a transgression or boundary-crossing. Second, Herz interjects aesthetics precisely at the beginning of his study in a discussion of epistemology to underscore the unavoidability, indeed the absolute necessity of a specific application (*Anwendung*) in individual cases. To be sure, general principles always have to be applied in any individual case, but the individual case brings something to the fore that demands judgment and cannot simply be subsumed under a general concept. In this moment of application, according to Herz, there is something irreducibly subjective, unique, and individual. Aesthetics is thus not conceived as a "special application" or instance of sensuous knowledge, but is itself the very model of how the subjective moment of the individual case is determinant in the experience of the individual, notwithstanding general "principles" of the judgment of the beautiful. Only in this manner, according to Herz, can we account for the fact that the same subject will perceive something differently at different times, or that various subjects will perceive something differently at the same moment. While Kant had persuasively argued both in his precritical phase as well as in the *Critique of Pure Reason* that the material or content itself shifts while the *form* of such cognition must remain universal, objective, and unchanging, Herz introduces an important difference with regard to the very *form* of sensuous cognition itself.[61]

In a letter to Kant of 25 November 1785, Herz circumscribed the specific problem of practicing medicine; what is smooth and rounded-out by reason appears in the actual application, in individual cases, to have "corners" and "rough spots": "The practical medical life is the most uneasy and most exhausting for the mind and the body. The art [of medical healing] remains still very far away from allowing pure reason find repose there. What reason so carefully levels and rounds out appears in the application full of sharp corners and unevenness."[62] Herz had already seized on this difficult relation between pure reason and theory, and the

---

61 In contrast to Davies, *Identity or History*, 52–53, who asserts: "Herz uses Kant's distinction between matter and form in perception to try to resolve the crucial and intractable issues of the eighteenth century [...] whether beauty is a purely subjective judgment or arises in conformity with absolute logical criteria" (53). This misses Herz's point entirely. Herz is clearly concerned with more than beauty in these passages.
62 Marcus Herz to Immanuel Kant, 25 November 1785, in *Gesammelte Schriften*, by Kant, ed. Preußischen Akademie der Wissenschaften, vol. 10, 425–426: "Das praktische medicinische Leben ist das unruhigste und beschwerlichste für Geist und Körper. Die Kunst ist noch lange nicht dahin, dass die reine Vernunft sich daran laben könnte. Was diese noch so sorgfältig glättet und ründet erscheint in der Anwendung nur zu oft voller Ecken und Rauhigkeiten."

actual cases he was confronted with in the early 1770s. In the *Considerations* and in a short text of the same period, "Concerning the Contradictions in Human Nature," Herz developed nothing short of a theory of the *individual case* – an epistemologically and medically-based sense of the irreducible individuality of each individual. In the case of individuals, the "deviations" from the generalized notion of the "human" actually make a person what he or she actually is; such deviations or *Abweichungen*, the organization and circumstances (*Organisation und Umstände*), that individuate each human being (*zu dem machen, was er ist* [63]) are also, however, the sources of diseases and particular "errors" in the constitution: "afflictions of the body" (*Gebrechen des Körpers*) and "certain mistakes in the organization" (*gewisse[r] Fehler in der Organization*) as Herz refers to them.[64] Above all, they are the causes of illness – "verursachen sie Krankheiten"[65] – that befall the individual. Such "deviations" and the differential they inscribe between the individual and the natural and moral perfection of the human being drive the individual to abandon the undesirably contingencies – Herz writes this as an "Ablegung des Zufälligen"[66] – to overcome contingency and to *approach* "the perfection of universal human nature."[67] Herz's notion of such perfection did not prescribe an absolute; rather, it defines an asymptotic process of approximation to a projected regulative idea in Kant's sense – something that assists human beings in their rational orientation within the world.

Herz developed his aesthetics in his *Essay on Taste and the Reasons for Its Diversity* (1776). The key concept is *Haltung*,[68] a term exceedingly difficult to translate: stance, position, attitude, or orientation. It originated in the visual

---

[63] Herz is referring here to temperament, climate, the emotions and passions, societal standing, and other "external" circumstances and situational factors that have an effect on the individual.
[64] Herz, "Über die Widersprüche," 158.
[65] Herz, "Über die Widersprüche," 156.
[66] Herz, "Über die Widersprüche," 160.
[67] Herz, "Über die Widersprüche," 158: "Vollkommenheit der allgemeinen menschlichen Natur."
[68] In the first edition of *Versuch über den Geschmack* (1776), Herz actually believed he had coined this concept. In the second edition of 1790 he recognizes that Sulzer had applied this concept not merely to painting, but more generally in aesthetics. Compare Herz, *Versuch*, 38; Davies, *Identity or History*, 106, translates the term *Haltung* alternately as *coherence, proportion, disposition*. See also Leder, *Grenzgänge des Marcus Herz*, 146. On the origin of the aesthetic concept of *Haltung*, see finally: Hans Joachim Dethlefs, "Ästhetisches Glücksversprechen. *Haltung* in der Kunstanschauung von Johann Heinrich Merck," *Das achtzehnte Jahrhundert* 32.1 (2008): 74–95.

arts, and was employed by Sulzer 1771 in his *General Theory of the Beautiful Arts*[69] for his aesthetic own theory. In the *General Theory* of 1771, Sulzer wrote:

> One says of a painting that it has particular stance (*Haltung*) when each part, with respect to the depth of the space or the distance of the eye, distinguishes itself from the one standing next to it, so that the things near appropriately come to the fore, and the distanced ones recede more or less according to the measure of the distance. It is by the effect of stance that a flat table can represent a deep space, that a painted ball does not appear as a circular-round surface, just as a round tower in the distance appears as a flat wall. Accordingly, the stance is that which gives life and true nature to the painting; because with it no object can appear as actual body, but would remain merely a shadow-image.[70]

Haltung designated for Sulzer a distinction or differentiation (*Absonderung*) of a particular element of a work that gives it its unique contour and form. Sulzer admits the difficulty of a strict definition of *Haltung*, but approaches the concept in the following way: "As impossible as it is to describe what actually belongs to stance, its effect for the sophisticated connoisseur is clear and certain. It is one of the means through which the soul is made visible."[71] *One of the means of making the soul visible*; by discerning the central focal point or the specific profile of the subject, *Haltung* for Sulzer constitutes an element intrinsic to the artwork itself, placed there by the artist, in order to guide and lead the view of the spectator or reader towards the very center of the artwork, or, as the case may be, the soul of the other.

Sulzer was one of the great forerunners of the understanding of the human unconscious, and his perceptive recognition of the "obscure (*dunkle*) effects" of

---

69 Sulzer, *Allgemeine Theorie*, vol. 1, 507–509: "Der Begriff der Haltung muss nicht bloss auf die Werke der zeichnenden Künste eingeschränkt werden; er erstreckt sich auf alle Werke der Kunst." See also Davies, *Identity or History*, 183.

70 Sulzer, *Allgemeine Theorie*, vol. 1, 507: "Man sagt von einem Gemählde es habe Haltung, wenn jeder Theil in Ansehung der Tiefe des Raumes, oder der Entfernung vom Auge, sich von den neben ihm stehenden merklich absondert, so daß die nahen Sachen gehörig hervortreten, die entfernten, nach Maaßgebung der Entfernung, mehr oder weniger zurück weichen. Es ist die Würkung der Haltung, daß eine flache Tafel einen tiefen Raum vorstellt, daß eine gemahlte Kugel nicht wie eine zirkelrunde Fläche, sondern wie ein dicker Körper erscheinet. Hingegen macht der Mangel der Haltung alles flach, so wie ein runder Thurm von Ferne als eine flache Mauer erscheinet. Demnach ist die Haltung das, was eigentlich dem Gemählde das Leben und die wahre Natur giebt; weil ohne sie kein Gegenstand als ein würklicher Körper erscheinen kann, sondern ein bloßes Schattenbild ist."

71 Sulzer, *Allgemeine Theorie*, vol. 1, 302: "So unmöglich es auch ist, das was zur Haltung gehört, zu beschreiben, so klar und gewiß ist doch ihre Würkung auf den feinen Kenner. Sie ist eines der Mittel, wodurch die Seele sichtbar gemacht wird."

the soul and the possibility of such effects leaving "traces" that can be known by the conscious mind might have been precisely what attracted Herz to his theory of stance or positionality. For Sulzer, psychology was the "science of the human soul," and, following Christian Wolff, Sulzer divided the study of psychology into rational and empirical. Empirical psychology won special status, as it contained for Sulzer distinct and exact descriptions of everything that is known to us about the soul through experience.[72] Without empirical psychology, Sulzer claimed, it would be impossible to achieve the correct knowledge of the soul. Sulzer's argumentation here led him to a theory of displaced consequences of these "obscure effects":

> For even though many effects of the soul show themselves distinctly, there are also others that are so obscure and occur so suddenly that they can escape the attention of the soul. Some of these effects are so constituted that a person would not perceive them in the depths of the soul if they didn't discover traces of their existence through remote changes that resulted from them.[73]

Sulzer himself never made the connection between stance or positionality (*Haltung*), which he discussed only within the discipline of aesthetics, and empirical psychology, which demands a particular *Haltung* on the part of the observer. Herz, however, created the explicit link; *Haltung* became the objective as well as the subjective basis for the mediation between aspect and whole, part and unity, the particular and the general, so essential to aesthetic experience as well as the reflective knowledge concerning the dark and obscure recesses of the soul.

Like most of his contemporaries, Herz conceived of beauty (*Schönheit*) as a "clearly [but not distinctly!] represented perfection" (*klar vorgestellte Vollkommenheit*) that consisted of a manifold which achieves a harmonious unity (*in der Mannichfaltigkeit, welche zur Einheit übereinstimmt*).[74] For Herz, this raised the essential question of precisely how this manifold as an integrated, coherent *unity*, not as panoply of *disparate particulars* – "as a collective

---

72 Johann Georg Sulzer, *Kurzer Begriff aller Wissenschaften und anderer Theile der Gelehrsamkeit* (Leipzig: Johann Christian Langenheim, 1759), 157.
73 Sulzer, *Kurzer Begriff aller Wissenschaften*, 157–158: "Denn wiewohl viele ihrer Würkungen sich deutlich zeigen, so sind hingegen andre so dunkel und geschehen so plötzlich, dass sie der Aufmerksamkeit sehr leichte entgehen. Einige dieser Würkungen sind so beschaffen, dass man die in der Tiefe der Seele nicht würde gewahr werden, wenn sie nicht durch entfernte Veränderungen, die von ihnen herrühren, Spuren ihres Daseyns entdeckten."
74 Herz, *Versuch*, 7, 30.

totality, not as disparate particulars"[75] – actually obtains. *Haltung* is for Herz, in contradistinction to Sulzer, not an element of the work itself, not simply an objective property of the aesthetic object, but rather the specific, always *unique* relation between the manifold elements, their appropriate constellation and relation to the unity, and the resultant unity itself. It is at once subjective *and* objective: subjective insofar as the imagination of the subject creatively binds the various elements particulars together into a meaningful totality, and objective insofar as such a possibility must be, at least to some extent, already present or latent within the work itself. In this process, the imagination of the subject plays a decisive role; it is the "indispensable support of reason"[76]; the imagination holds the spatially and temporally disparate moments of the manifold together in a coherent whole. Thus Herz did not merely appropriate the concept of *Haltung* from Sulzer; he was able to demonstrate how *Haltung* – the positionality or stance of each subject – provides the glue or binding power to bring the manifold into a harmonious whole (*Ganzes*) which constitutes a unity (*Einheit*). He succeeds in showing the validity of his theory of *Haltung* by providing evidence that the manifold of the disparate moments actually contributes more to beauty than the resultant unity.[77] His argument represents a departure from the aesthetic theory that had preceded him (Gotthold Ephraim Lessing, Mendelssohn, Sulzer) insofar as it is the *manifold*, and the process of unification, and not the resultant constituted unity itself, which makes the specific, unique aesthetic experience what it is:

> According to my argument, the reason why the manifold actually contributes more to beauty than the unity itself is easy to see. For to the degree that there is more of a manifold than constitutes the whole, there emerges a double moment of beauty: first, the enlargement of the entire effect, in proportion to the degree of the manifold, of

---

[75] Herz, *Versuch*, 34: "als ein collectives Ganzes, nicht als disparate Einzelheiten."
[76] Herz, *Versuch*, 35: "die unentbehrliche Stütze der Vernunft."
[77] Herz, *Versuch*, 46: "die Mannigfaltigkeit *mehr* zur Schönheit als die Einheit [beiträgt]." In this argument, Herz was undoubtedly influenced by Moses Mendelssohn's *Concerning the Sensations* (*Über die Empfindungen*, 1755; 1761), which takes Sulzer to task for not giving the human imagination enough credit and power in the constitution of beauty: Perfection according to Sulzer was a harmonious multiplicity that refers to a unity: "The multiplicity promises the soul something that will occupy its attentions and engage its efforts" (20). Mendelssohn objects that placing so much in the work itself is utterly incompatible with the power of the soul, for it emphasizes the weakness of the soul's representing powers, the need of a crutch. The experience of the unity in multiplicity is not due to or a result of a weakness: it is the very ground of beauty. For a more detailed analysis of the difference between Mendelssohn and Sulzer, see chapter 3.

course; and second, the stance (*Haltung*), or the perfection that emerges from the proportional accord of the individual effects with their cause.[78]

The priority of the manifold and constructive process over the achieved unity initiates what Herz refers to as a "double moment" of beauty (*ein doppeltes Moment der Schönheit*): first, the greater the manifold, the greater the resultant overall effect, and second, the perfection in the unity that does emerge is proportionate to the degree of manifold contained in the experience. In other words, the human being experiences a double or intensified, heightened sense of perfected sensuous experience in the aesthetic: the fullness of the experience itself – rich, complex, diverse, textured – and the tremendous accomplishment of the soul's representational power in the formation of the unity from such teeming and vibrant sensate cognition.[79] Thus, it is not *simply* the relation of part and whole, or cause and effect, that is at stake in the notion of *Haltung*, but rather a *proportional relation* such that the greater, richer, more replete the manifold, the greater the aesthetic effect. Such a connection (*Verknüpfung*) depends in each case on the particular (*das Besondere*). And, as was the case in his aesthetic-epistemological digression in the *Betrachtungen*, there must be a direct correlation between the subjective and objective moments of the aesthetic: the subject-centered powers of the soul – reason, imagination, and sense of *Haltung* on the subjective side – correspond, in power and proportion, to the unity, multiplicity, and *Haltung* on the objective side. The appropriate (*angemessene*) relation, the proportional integration of the manifold to the totality, the felicitous (*treffende*) agreement of the manifold elements and their successful effect defines the mediating position of *Haltung*; it positions itself on the border between the subjective and objective and is always bound to the unique, individual instance. There can be no general formula valid for all instances. Herz explains the infinite variability of the aesthetic – the fact the beauty can take on

---

[78] Herz, *Versuch*, 46: "Nach meiner Entwickelung läßt sich der Grund dieser Erscheinung, warum die Mannigfaltigkeit mehr zur Schönheit beyträgt, als die Einheit, leicht einsehen. Denn durch einen jeden Grad Mannichfaltigkeit, der zum Ganzen hinzukommt, erwächst diesem ein doppeltes Moment der Schönheit, erstlich die Vergrößerung der gesammten Wirkungen [der Elemente] *b.d.f.h.* um einen Grad, und zweytens die Haltung (*l.*) oder die Vollkommenheit, die aus der proportionirten Übereinstimmung dieser einzelen Wirkung mit ihrer Ursache, die sie hervorbringt, entspringt."

[79] Herz is clearly in dialogue with Sulzer's *Theorie der angenehmen und unangehmen Empfindungen* (1751); and the aesthetics of his friend Mendelssohn, who in his *Über die Empfindungen* (1755; 1761) argued against Sulzer and underscored the necessity of a vibrant manifold – the *"rational striving for representations grounded in one another"* – rather than a single, unified viewpoint in the constitution of aesthetic experience.

so many different forms as there are possible "appropriate" or "felicitous" compositions of the manifold – through the possibilities of *Haltung*: "The diversity of the manifolds that are employed in creating a congruence is the very basis of the difference between the beautiful arts and sciences."[80]

Three aspects of Herz's aesthetics give us warrant to speak of a theory of the significance of the individual case in his epistemology. First, the specific stance, orientation, or attitude (*Haltung*) implicit in each iteration of aesthetic experience prioritizes the manifold as the determinant factor over the resultant unity and renders the moment of specific individuality indispensable. The manifold endows aesthetic experience with its rich texture, complexity, and depth, and provides the sensual basis for what is unique, different, and *interesting*. Second, the multiplicity of possible combinations of the manifold elements in various *Realitäten*, as Herz calls them, undergirds and guarantees the multiple possibilities of such experience. Third, the individuality and variability of *Haltung* and the subjective orientation of *Haltung* in each individual case explains how, in a particular instance, the manifold comes together into a distinct, meaningful unity for a particular individual at a particular time under specific circumstances. The guiding epistemological and aesthetic interest in Herz's texts is therefore not a strict *a priori* determination of fixed rationalistic principles,[81] or an extension of the pre-critical Kant, as some scholars have suggested, but rather the reciprocal interpenetration of the subjective and objective moments of experience based upon the nuances and peculiarities of the individual instance. Precisely by linking the subjective moment of *Haltung* to the experience of the manifold, Herz contributes to the emerging discussion concerning the status of the *interesting* (*das Interessante*) and its role in aesthetic discourse visible in the 1770s, and departs from the aesthetics of autonomy as it was enunciated by Moritz and Kant, discussed previously.[82] For something to be beautiful, according to Herz, it must contain something that *interests* us; it

---

80 Herz, *Versuch*, 31: "Die Verschiedenheit der Mannigfaltigkeiten die zur Übereinstimmung verwendet werden, macht die Grundlage der Verschiedenheit der schönen Künste und Wissenschaften."
81 Davies, *Identity or History*, 53: "Herz's solution is to attempt to turn aesthetics into an *exact science*."
82 Christian Garve, "Einige Gedanken über das Interessierende" (1779), in *Philosophische Schriften über literarische, ästhetische, und gesellschaftliche Gegenstände*, ed. Kurt Wölfel (Stuttgart: Metzler, 1974), vol. 1, 161–348. On the history of this category, see: Aurel Kolnai, "On the Concept of the Interesting," in *Aesthetics in the Modern World*, ed. Harold Osborne (London: Thames and Hudson, 1968), 166–187; Kurt Wölfel, "Interesse/interessant, " in *Ästhetische Grundbegriffe*, ed. Karlheinz Barck (Stuttgart and Weimar: Metzler, 2001), vol. 3, 138–174; Altrud Dumont, "Das Interessante – Theorie und narrative Praxis," *Weimarer*

must have a unique quality that draws us in, and this derives in large measure from the manifold of experience we encounter and the particular stance, attitude, or orientation (*Haltung*) we bring to bear on it. Using the anatomical-metaphor of "strings" – along with the model of "tubes" one of the central ways of conceiving of the nervous-system at the end of the eighteenth century – Herz develops what one might refer to as a physiological-psychological aesthetic:

> Through the disturbance of a single inclination all of the others of the same tone are put into motion; and in this manner there emerges an always-changing play of the various strings in the soul, which in turn heightens its own sense of self (*Selbstgefühl*) and allows for the soul to sense the reality of its own existence in the most gentle manner. And one understands nothing other than this when one speaks about *interest* in objects of taste, precisely this connection between one inclination and others. The work of art lacks a decisive element in order to please if it is not *interesting*, that is, if the manifold or the unity of the whole has as its object inclinations that only stand in very limited relation to others.[83]

Not only does the aesthetic experience entail a "shock" or "tremor" (*Erschütterung*) that sets the various inclinations into motion, having an aesthetic experience in the first place is the correlation of or communication between these various inclinations; this is what makes something *interesting* or compelling in the first place. The work of art must be *interesting*, that is, it must provoke, as Herz states, "an always-changing play of the various strings in the soul," which in turn allows the soul to experience the fundamental and irreducible reality of its own existence – or, as we might say, using Luhmann, the *individuality of the individual*.

Herz was not a systematic philosopher, and did not create a clear guiding thread that can be followed throughout his many writings on aesthetics, medicine, psychology and philosophy. Nevertheless, we have attempted in this chapter to discern core elements of his epistemology and aesthetics that bear directly on the irreducible uniqueness of the individual, and, by extension, the absolutely central

---

Beiträge 38.3 (1992): 430–447; Robert Leventhal, *The Disciplines of Interpretation* (Berlin: de Gruyter, 1994), 260–265.

83 Herz, *Versuch*, 163–164; emphasis mine: "Durch die Erschütterung einer einzigen [Neigung; R.L.] werden alle mit ihr gleichtönigen in Bewegung gesetzt; und so entsteht ein abwechselndes Spiel unter verschiedenen Saiten in der Seele, das ihr Selbstgefühl ungemein erhöht, und sie die Realität ihres Daseyns auf die sanfteste Weise empfinden lässt. Und nichts anders versteht man unter dem Begriff *Interesse* bey Gegenständen des Geschmacks, als eben diese Verknüpfung zwischen einer Neigung und mehreren. Dem Kunstwerke [...] fehlt ein wesentliches Ingredienz um zu gefallen, wenn es nicht genugsam *interessant* ist, d.i. wenn die Mannichfaltigkeit oder die Einheit des Ganzen solche Neigungen zum Gegenstande hat, die nur mit wenigen andern in Verbindung stehen."

role of the individual case history. Beginning with the *Essay on Vertigo*, we attempted to reconstruct Herz's response to the question of the difference and divergence of human representations, especially given that the soul as representational power underlies and makes possible representation in general. On the basis of a correspondence theory in which every representation (*Vorstellung*) of the soul is at the same time a movement of the body (for Herz, in this case, an alteration or movement of the brain [*Gehirn*]), the nerve-channels (*Nervenfaser*), and nervous fluids (*Nervensäfte*), Herz argues for a seamless connection (*Verknüpfung; Nexus*) between mind and body which is always subject to the vicissitudes of circumstance, deviation, and unique condition. Such a general "theory" is always subject to the natural and counter-natural differences and deviations in both the representational apparatus as well as the bodily constitution, physiology, and "condition" of the distinct individual. How a disturbance in the soul's representational power can effect bodily function, the language-organs in particular, was shown in two individual case histories (*Krankengeschichten*) presented by Herz, themselves interesting and revealing "deviations" from what might be considered a healthy interaction between mind and body.

Moving to the *Considerations*, we identified Herz's powerful, self-proclaimed "digression" from Kant; by interjecting aesthetics into a discussion of epistemology, Herz accomplished both a blurring of the borders and limits of faculties and disciplines as well as a stunning critique of the universal validity of the *form of cognition*. Herz did not repudiate the notion of cognitive form per se, but argues that in the process of a *determinant* cognition, that is, whenever cognition operates in a specific instance, the very *form of cognition* itself takes on something subjective and unique: "*as soon as the form is determined and applied to an individual case, it becomes subjective, insofar as something subjective is contained in the material itself and therefore can be applied differently in different subjects or in one and the same subject under different circumstances.*"[84] The precise valence or instantiation of the form in the individual application is decisive. The identification of a subjective, unique moment in the *form* of cognition itself opens the path to a sense of the irreducible individuality of representations and experience. Otherwise, Herz argues, one simply could not account for the difference and disparity between human representations of one and same object. Finally, with Herz's appropriation of Sulzer's concept of *Haltung* in his *Essay on Taste and the Reasons for Its Diversity* (1776), Herz was able to mobilize this notion to account for both the subjective and objective ways in which a manifold, in any particular instance, is able to achieve the

---

[84] Herz, *Betrachtungen*, 22; emphasis mine.

unity required for coherent experience. At the "objective" pole, *Haltung* is already present in the work of art (and experience in general!) through the interconnection and agreement between part and whole, with one element or a set of elements achieving particular profile or "distinction" or standing out as being central to the representation of the whole. The "subjective" correlate of this, that is, the requisite subjective *Haltung* on the part of observer/reader, is the art of attention to the nuances and specificity of the relation between part and whole. When achieved maximally, the unity of the objective and subjective aspects of *Haltung* results in the perfected mediation or mediated perfection of manifold and unity that is art itself. The manifold and particular way it becomes unified in any individual case is what for Herz makes such a mediation *interesting*, a basic condition of aesthetic experience.

Herz deviated from the widely held rationalistic, objectivistic self-understanding of the late *Aufklärung* – its presupposition of universality and uniformity – by insisting on the subjective, unique, individual inflection in each experience: *Haltung*, or stance. Whether in the sphere of aesthetics, medicine, or psychology, difference and deviation (*Abweichung*) supplied for him the necessary condition of the possibility of coherent experience, and an account of how individual human beings can have very different experiences and representations of the same object, or how a single individual can have varying experiences and representations over time, depending upon mental state, physical condition, and environment. In order to understand how, in any individual case, such unique experience and representation obtains, Herz employed time and again the case history or case study (*Krankengeschichte*) as the textual medium or genre to detail such divergence and difference, the form apt for the articulation of the specific stance or *Haltung*. For Herz, the case history was the form *par excellence* for plumbing the depths of specific deviations and their origins, for narrating illness, and for drawing connections between the mind and the body. It was the basis of philosophical medicine. The case history was for him, as Gianna Pomata has argued in a different context and with no reference to Herz, a truly *epistemic genre*: its function was to articulate, at both an individual and a sociocultural level, how individuals are constituted, how they end up who and what they are, how their experience and cognition are conditioned through internal and external factors, and to communicate this in a manner that could be understood by the literate public.[85] Rather than merely providing

---

[85] Gianna Pomata has developed the theory and practice of the observation and case history as epistemic genre in a number of articles, most seminally in "Sharing Cases: The *Observationes* in Early Modern Medicine," *Early Science and Medicine* 15 (2010): 193–236.

exemplary cases to shore up existent theory, case studies and case narratives opened up avenues of research yet to be explored, interesting or compelling events that might prove useful to the practicing physician and help to further medical science. Such case studies were to be written up (and down), published in journals and collections (*Sammlungen*), and disseminated, read, and discussed by physicians, *Seelensorger*, academics, and civil servants concerned with health science (*Gesundheitswesen*) in the burgeoning public sphere in order to achieve a better understanding of the individuality of the individual, the specific nature of an illness, its etiology, diagnosis, and possible therapeutics. They also served as the evidentiary basis and knowledge repository to further medicine and psychology as disciplines on their way to becoming *Wissenschaft*.[86] If medicine became indeed the new (though hardly uncontested) "philosophy" of the late Enlightenment, claiming an unprecedented significance in everyday life as well as in the policy and the "science" of the state, the case history was surely the genre that embodied its empirical-scientific project.

---

[86] That this was very much in question can be gleaned from the scathing critique offered by the skeptic J. B. Erhard, "Ueber die Medicin. Arkesilas an Ekdemus," *Der neue Teutsche Merkur* 8 (1795): 337–378, who argued that medicine in particular, because it had no firm grounding in reason and was relegated to case-by-case treatments and the particularities of individual instances of illness, could never achieve the status of *Wissenschaft*. To get a sense of the powerful effect of this critique, see the physician C. W. Hufeland's response: "Ein Wort über den Angriff der razionellen Medicin im N.T. Merkur. August 1795," *Der neue Teutsche Merkur* 3 (1795): 138 – 155, and Wieland's editorial note, which sought to justify the publication of Erhard's article in the journal.

Conclusion: Becoming a Culture of Individual Cases

> The case [...] Everything that occurs, or can occur, insofar as it occurs or can occur, every event, condition or state, or circumstance that is the object of a discourse or a sentence, according to the model of the Latin *casus* or the French *cas*.
> Johann Christoph Adelung, "Der Fall"[1]
>
> The exception is a kind of exclusion. What is excluded from the general rule is an *individual case*.
> Giorgio Agamben, *Homo Sacer*[2]
>
> Cases may occur, situations present themselves, that no amount of ingenuity could possibly make worse, it would seem.
> Imre Kertész, *Fatelessness*[3]

When Christian Wolff published his *Psychologia Empirica* in 1732, he not only differentiated a scientific discipline, wresting it from the rulership of theoretical, rational psychology and according it a unique and indeed fundamental role in the construction of the science of psychology. He single-handedly created the scholarly-scientific framework for the experiential psychology of the later eighteenth century. As Robert J. Richards has stated:

> Empirical psychology, while not neglecting observations of external behavior, has as its primary method the mind's direct introspection of its own activities, either by catching on the wing its normal operations or by contriving experiments in order to elicit particular acts. Wolff details two sets of assumptions, one regarding the structure of perceptual experience and the other its certitude, that make the introspective method of empirical psychology possible.[4]

The method of direct introspection of the mind's representational activities, the notion that a specific form of apperception was available to the human being to

---

[1] Johann Christoph Adelung, *Grammatisch-kritischen Wörterbuches der hochdeutschen Mundart* (Leipzig, 1774–1786), vol. 5, entry "Der Fall": "Alles, was geschiehet oder geschehen kann, so fern es geschiehet oder geschehen kann, eine jede Begebenheit, Zustand oder Umstand, so der Gegenstand einer Rede oder eines Satzes ist, nach dem Muster des Latein. casus, und Franz. Cas."
[2] Giorgio Agamben, *Homo Sacer: Sovereign Power and Bare Life*, trans. Daniel Heller-Roazen. (Stanford, CA: Stanford University Press, 1998), 19.
[3] Imre Kertész, *Fatelessness*, trans. Tim Wilkinson (New York: Vintage/Random House, 2004), 171.
[4] Robert J. Richards, "Christian Wolff's Prolegomena to Empirical and Rational Psychology: Translation and Commentary," *Proceedings of the American Philosophical Society*, 124.3 (1980): 228.

experience its own thought processes and thus be able to analyze them in a rational manner, remained latent in Leibniz and Spinoza to the extent that neither spelled out a definitive discipline or procedure for such an investigation.[5] Wolff's contribution was to make this explicit and lay out the specific methodological requirements for such a scientific discipline. Wolff wrote: "In empirical psychology the characteristics of the human soul are established through experience; but we experience that of which we are aware (*cognoscimus*) by attending to our perceptions."[6] Hence we come to know the subjects dealt with in empirical psychology by "*attending to those occurrences in our souls of which we are conscious.*"[7] The method put forth by Wolff is a *habit* of "referring what is experienced to accurate definitions and determinate propositions. And it is clear that this habit can be acquired."[8] Not only does empirical psychology supply the principles of rational (theoretical) psychology according to Wolff, the method or procedure of becoming aware of what one is experiencing, and how to refer such experiences to "accurate definitions and determinate propositions" is something that can and must be *learned*. According to Wolff, the method of introspection is to be learned from *experience*. Wolff likens the study of empirical psychology to experimental physics: to get clear about the physical mechanisms we observe in the world, they must be referred to rational definitions and specific propositions. To get clear about what we experience in ourselves, we have to learn how to identify and discern the various activities and dispositions of the soul with rigor and repeated attention. Wolff's method

---

[5] Leibniz referred to the unconscious perceptions of the mind in the *New Essays on Human Understanding* as *petites perceptions*: "there is at every moment an infinity of perceptions in us, unaccompanied by awareness and unaccompanied by reflection; that is, an infinity of changes in the soul itself of which we are not aware." *Leibniz: New Essays on Human Understanding*, trans. and ed. Peter Remnant and Jonathan Bennett (Cambridge: Cambridge University Press, 1996), 53. Spinoza developed a theory of self-consciousness in Part 2 of the *Ethics* (1677), where he states in P22 "the human mind perceives [*percipit*] not only the affections of the body, but also the ideas of these affections," and a sophisticated and exhaustive theory of the emotions, what he refers to as *affects* and *passions*, in parts 3 and 4. See Spinoza, *Ethics* (1677). Edited and translated by Edwin Curley (Princeton: Princeton University Press, 1985).
[6] Wolff, *Philosophia rationalis sive Logica*, 664: "We are said to experience whatever we are aware of (cognoscimus) by attending to our perceptions. Cognition of what is evident only by attending to our perceptions is called experience," translated in Richards, "Christian Wolff's Prolegomena to Empirical and Rational Psychology," 231.
[7] Wolff, *Psychologia Empirica*, Par. 2, translated in Richards, "Christian Wolff's Prolegomena to Empirical and Rational Psychology," 231; emphasis mine.
[8] Wolff, *Psychologia Empirica*, para. 3, translated in Richards, "Christian Wolff's Prolegomena to Empirical and Rational Psychology," 231.

of introspection and the analysis of the representational activities of the mind or soul was one of the key elements in the development of experiential psychology of the second half of the eighteenth century, but it was not sufficient. Pathbreaking work in medicine – specifically the influxionist, vitalist, animist program of Georg Ernest Stahl during his tenure at the University of Halle, 1693–1734 – paved the way to think of the mind/soul as determinate in the etiology of illness.

Stahl's program combined rigorous observation with the basic idea that the mind or soul was decisive in determining the health or disease of the body. Eschewing speculation and the influence of theological prejudice, Stahl identified what he referred to as a fundamental life force operating in all things. Now this was nothing new; it can be traced back to Aristotle and, in early modern medicine, such a theory would find its chief adherent in the work of William Harvey.[9] But Stahl made the more profound psychological assertion – his detractors would say leap – that the mind/soul was in fact *identical* with this basic life force, and that mind thus understood pervaded and determined all matter. To properly understand illness and pathology, one would have to understand how the specific constitution of the mind-soul-life force had gone awry, had deviated from the natural, healthy path. Mechanistic explanations would always fall short, Stahl argued, for they failed to make the vital connection between the material cause and effect relations and the determinant state and condition of the soul. Stahl's inaugural disputation *De passionibus animi corpus humanum varie alterantibus* (1695), which charted the various influences of the soul on the human body, in fact gave birth to a new discipline – Medical Psychology or *medizinische Psychologie*. And, as Gernot Huppmann has pointed out, Stahl was not alone in identifying the mind/soul as a decisive element in the formation of illness, disease, and pathology. His colleague and sometimes opponent Friedrich Hoffmann at Halle, who opted for an iatro-chemical, materialist-mechanistic model, similarly argued for an empirically-based, observationally informed science of the influence of the mind on the body in his inaugural dissertation of 1699 *De animi sanitatis et morborum fabro*.[10] Mental activity, specifically imagination, feelings, passions, and the emotions, became crucial to the study of the etiology, treatment, and prognosis of disease and illness. Thus, despite profound

---

9 As was recognized by Stahl's advocates in the early nineteenth century in psychiatry, who often refer to William Harvey's *Exercitationes de Generatione Animalium* (London: Typis Du-Gardianis; Impensis O. Pulleyn, 1651), as the forerunner to Stahl's animistic-vitalistic model.
10 On this aspect of Hoffmann, see Gernot Huppmann, "Marginalien zur medizinischen Psychologie des Stahlantipoden Friedrich Hoffmann (1660–1742)," *Schriftenreihe der deutschen Gesellschaft für die Geschichte der Nervenheilkunde* 3 (1997): 95–103.

differences on almost every other issue of medical theory and practice – pulse rate, whether inflammation was in the blood or the nerves, the origin of fevers – Hoffmann and Stahl were both pietists and physicians for whom the soul constituted an irreducible, axiomatic principle as the basis for all medical-scientific theory. Stahl persisted in his animist account of the influence of the soul on the body, while Hoffmann remained a disciple of the iatro-mechanical school of Robert Boyle (1627–1691).[11]

The long reach of Wolff's empirical psychology and Stahl's medical psychology has been traced in this book by looking at the psychologically-minded physicians centered at the University of Halle around 1750, all of whom were profoundly influenced by Alexander Baumgarten and his student Georg Friedrich Meier, especially Meier's *Theoretical Knowledge of the Movements of the Mind* of 1744.[12] Johann August Unzer, Johann Gottlob Krüger, Ernst Anton Nicolai, and Johann Christian Bolten combined an anthropological understanding of *der ganze Mensch* as a mental-physical unity with a robust empirical scientific model of rigorous observation and experience, a desire to understand how the mind/soul could initiate bodily transformation and, perhaps most importantly, how one could mobilize all of the soul's representational capacities to effect salutary changes for the well-being of the entire human being. Beginning in the late 1740s, Krüger began publishing a series of books that sought to bring mind and body, soul and mechanism into a genuine, unified experimental scientific study. This culminated in his *Attempt at an Experimental Theory of the Soul* (1756), which attempted to elevate Wolff's empirical psychology to the level of a *physics of the soul*. Krüger's argumentation went beyond an explanation of the reciprocal relation between sensation, feeling, stimulation of the nerves and the thoughts, and representations and imaginings of the mind. He developed a sophisticated model of psychological cure in his *Naturlehre* (1748) in which the patient would be guided back to the state of an overpowering sensation or *Empfindung*, and, through rational means, shown how the pathological imaginative content had gained the upper hand, revealing the contradiction between what was originally perceived and what the imagination had constructed. The patient would thus be

---

[11] Francesco Paolo de Ceglia, "Hoffmann and Stahl: Documents and Reflections on the Dispute," *History of Universities* 22 (2007): 98–140.

[12] The pioneering work of Carsten Zelle, *Vernünftige Ärzte. Hallesche Psychomediziner und die Anfänge der Anthropologie in der deutschsprachigen Frühaufklärung* (Tübingen: Niemeyer, 2001), opened up this fascinating constellation in Halle. More generally on Halle at this time, see the excellent overview by Jürgen Helm, "Hallische Medizin zwischen Pietismus und Frühaufklärung," in *Universitäten und Aufklärung*, ed. Notker Hammerstein (Göttingen: Wallstein, 1995), 63–95.

returned to the true, natural, real sensation or perception; the pathological imaginary would be expelled.[13]

All of the psychologically-minded physicians at Halle were influenced by the emergence of the discipline of philosophical aesthetics as a theory of the beautiful and as a study of the so-called lower faculties as it was being articulated by Baumgarten and Meier in Halle. But Nicolai and Bolten forged a particularly strong intellectual alliance with the emerging discipline of aesthetics in their writings. Nicolai's theory of "medical-philosophical pathology" in his *Effects of the Influence of the Soul on the Body* of 1744 identified the imagination (*Einbildungskraft*) as one of the key sources of mental illness. Bolten built on Nicolai's insights and, profoundly influenced by Meier's aesthetic theory, published his theory of "philosophical pathology" in his *Thoughts concerning Psychological Cures* in 1751. Mental illness was a matter of the disturbed lower faculties of the soul – feeling, sensation, emotion, the imagination – and *aesthetics* as the guiding discipline for these faculties taught how one could modulate and suppress certain detrimental representations of the soul and incite or encourage others. Bolten's "philosophical pathology" drew on aesthetics, but sought to elaborate a comprehensive psychological practice of healing or "cure." As we noted in chapter 1, this turned out to be something quite different from what we today think of as a psychological therapy; nevertheless, Bolten's explicit *plaidoyer* for a "psychological cure," using the principles of aesthetics, was proof that the disciplines of medicine, psychology, and aesthetics were indeed inextricably intertwined, that they constituted the basis for an experimental psychology and ways of treating and healing mental illnesses. Guiding the passions, directing the soul, modulating strong emotions, binding the imagination – this was the goal of Bolten's "philosophical pathology," a paradigmatic example of Michel Foucault's pastoral power – at least in theory – in the German *Aufklärung* in the mid-eighteenth century. The philosophical physicians at the University of Halle around 1750 were all in some manner disciples of Stahl's medical psychology, but they were also critical of Stahl's theoretical bias and his failure to actually demonstrate what he had postulated. Unzer's review "Considerations concerning Herr Councilor Stahl's Theoretical Foundation of Medical Science" in the *Hamburg Magazine* of 1753 took Stahl to task for not having provided strong empirical evidence for much of his theoretical work, and for failing to recognize

---

[13] As Gabriele Dürbeck has shown, the imagination was seen as capable of both arousing, inciting and also moderating the affects, influencing perception and bringing forth the past, and was therefore held to be both dangerous and salutary in its capability to affect the soul. See her *Einbildungskraft und Aufklärung um 1750* (Tübingen: Niemeyer, 1998).

that matter and the causal relations obtaining therein were also animated by the same life-force Stahl had identified with the soul.

In the work of Johann Georg Sulzer and Baumgarten, the positionality and stance of the body became singularly determinant in the activity of the mind and the representations of the soul. The soul's intimate relation to a body in each case constitutes in a quite positive sense the condition of the way in which the soul grasps the world, yet at the same time restricts the knowability of the soul precisely because of the perspectival and transient nature of bodily stance or positionality – referred to as *Haltung* – a notion later appropriated by Marcus Herz. The notion of the *self* defies clear and distinct cognition and remains obscure precisely because of an ever-changing, multiple, variable bodily perspectivity. To counter the constant fluctuations of the soul and the variability of *Haltung*, and to support empirical psychology in its struggle to ascertain a degree of certainty and clarity, Baumgarten and Sulzer proposed different, yet analogous solutions that would empower the mind to focus on and analyze its own activity. In his *Metaphysics* (1739), which went through four editions between its original publication and 1779, Baumgarten put forth his idea of a *nexus* – interconnectedness – of representational ideas and perceptions, making the vital connection between the two the very basis of an empirical psychology. One can attend to the particular *nexus* in any individual case. Marcus Herz employed precisely this notion of *nexus* or interconnectedness in his theory of psychological medicine. According to Baumgarten, this *nexus* would be the cornerstone of any empirically-based psychology. Like Wolff, Baumgarten distinguished between rational psychology and empirical psychology, but conceived of the relation between the two differently. Rational psychology for Baumgarten was concerned with the "human soul" (*anima humana*), the universal forms of representation shared by all human beings, whereas empirical psychology concerned itself with "my soul" (*anima mea*), the subjective conditions of individual representation and the specific manner in which sensate cognition operates in any individual. As a part of empirical psychology, aesthetics as "perfected sensate cognition" affirmed the irreducible individuality of sensation and imagination.[14] In his *Concerning Consciousness and Its Influence on Our Judgments* (1757), Sulzer argued for a distinct *discipline or science of the soul*, whereby one could consciously attend to such shifts in perspective and position, thematize the representations and their connection to various sensations, and observe the mind's operations as they were unfolding. In his aesthetics, Sulzer appropriated Baumgarten's conception of *Haltung* – stance or positionality – which Herz later

---

14 Baumgarten, *Metaphysics*, §501, §505.

utilized in his epistemology in order to bridge the gap between the subjective and objective aspects of cognition. Both Baumgarten and Sulzer sought to give content and specificity to Wolff's the underlying procedure of his empirical psychology – introspection or apperception, the ability of the soul to *observe itself* in the process of its subjective representational activity.

Johann Georg Zimmermann refined the very notion of experience (*Erfahrung*) by underlining the difference between experience, observation, and experiment in his influential *On Experience in the Art of Medicine* (1763–1764). For Zimmermann, experience was derived from sound observations and experiments; it was a capability to draw from various observations, experiments, and case histories so as to be better able to prevent disease. Zimmermann, who according to Horst Thomé and Lorna Martens influenced Christoph Martin Wieland and the psychological style demonstrated in Wieland's novel *Geschichte des Agathon* (1766–1767),[15] which Christian Friedrich von Blanckenburg praised as shifting the interest and focus of the novel from plot to character in his *Theory of the Novel* of 1774,[16] greatly enhanced the conversation around the very notion of *Erfahrung* in two decisive ways: first, by imbuing it with a hermeneutical understanding – experience presupposed some form of understanding or *Verstehen* to be true experience, not just perception or sensation – and, second, by historicizing it. This extended even to *case histories* written by others according to Zimmermann, which offered a form of experience to the practicing physician that could often exceed and expand the knowledge offered by his own experience and could inform his practice. But whereas Zimmermann widened the notion of experience itself, his notion of psychology remained fairly traditional, holding fast to the belief in universal psychological laws which governed all human beings. He decided the vexing question of the relation between the typical, uniform and the singular, individual in human behavior in favor of the former. In this sense, he can be seen as remaining within the discursive framework

---

15 Horst Thomé, *Roman und Naturwissenschaft: Eine Studie zur Vorgeschichte der deutschen Klassik* (Frankfurt: Peter Lang, 1978), 119–120, and 199–201, claims that Zimmermann was Wieland's chief "mentor" in matters psychological. Lorna Martens expands on this to show precisely how Wieland implements psycho-narration in order to get at the interior of Agathon's inner feeling and emotion in her "Constructing Interiority in Eighteenth-Century Narrative Fiction: Wieland's Geschichte des Agathon," *German Quarterly* 81.1 (2008): 49–65, esp. 56. Martens sees Wieland's novel as the first instance of a representation of human psychology in Germany, edging away from universal psychological laws and towards individual psychology, pushing the novel form toward the purely psychological-individual *Werther*.

16 Christian Friedrich von Blanckenburg, *Versuch über den Roman* (Leipzig und Liegnitz: David Siegerts Witwe, 1774); repr. in *Romantheorie. Dokumentation ihrer Geschichte in Deutschland 1620–1880*, ed. E. Lämmert (Köln and Berlin: Kohlhammer, 1971), 5–6.

of an earlier Enlightenment assumption of *human nature* with its universal and inalterable laws. While Wieland and Zimmermann were on the cusp of the articulation of a unique, singular individuality with its own pathological logic, this real breakthrough was the great achievement of the young Johann Gottfried Herder and Johann Wolfgang von Goethe. Perhaps this is why, as we noted in chapter 1, Andreas Elias Büchner's manual on the writing of case histories of 1765 appears to us somewhat baroque in its structure and form, as belonging to a past era, and, except for its insistence on *narrative* (*Erzählung*), as a remnant of an antiquated practice a bit out of step with the psychological advances of its time. However, Büchner's thematization and underscoring of *narrative* over mere chronicle, description, nosology – "die Geschichte einer Krankheit bestehet ordentlicher Weise in einer deutlichen und zusammenhangenden Erzählung" – pushes us, I would argue, beyond the traditional *historia morbi* or *Krankengeschichte*.[17] Büchner and Zimmermann concurred that "experience" also consists of the well-written and well-observed case histories of other credible and respected physicians.

With subtle interpretation, we might discern in European literature and letters prior to 1770 texts that seem to institute what I am referring to as the invention of unique, singular individuality, and even Herder himself offers us a genealogy of this invention; he names Petrarch, Augustine, Cardanus, Montaigne, and Rousseau as authors who provide us with a glimpse into the hidden recesses of the individual human soul. Indeed, contemporary theorists of the self find no difficulty in attributing at least one strain of modern individualism to the Renaissance or to Montaigne.[18] But no interpretive subtlety is required to recognize the new sensibility of unique individuality after 1770; Herder leaves nothing to the imagination (or interpretation) and spells out this new interest and focus in exquisite detail in his writings of the early 1770s, but perhaps most eloquently in his *On Knowledge and Sensation in the Human Soul* (1774, 1775, 1778). In short, the typical, uniform, and universal are effaced to make room for what is individual, unique, and singular. Herder cited three types of textual documents in particular through which could get to know "the

---

17 Andreas Elias Büchner, *Der in schweren und verwirrten Krankheiten vernünftig rathende und glücklich curirende Medicus, oder Gründlicher Unterricht, wie in solchen wichtigen Fällen besonders von jungen Ärzten Consilia medica am sichersten können theils eingeholet, theils auch fürnemlich nach Hofmannischen und Boerhaavischen Grundsätzen klüglich ertheilet werden* (Erfurt: Weber, 1762–1765), in 2 vols., §5.

18 Charles Taylor, *Sources of the Self: The Making of the Modern Identity* (Cambridge: Cambridge University Press, 1992), 181–182; Nannerl O. Keohane, "Montaigne's Individualism," *Political Theory* 5.3 (1977): 364–366.

most entangled pathology of the human soul," to be able to discern "the deepest particularities" of a personal individual life, the "dark indications" of a unique human being: life-descriptions or autobiographies, written observations (*Bemerkungen*) of physicians and friends of those afflicted with illness, and literature, what he referred to as the "prophecies of the poets." Already for Herder, in other words, "individuality" was not simply a new idea among others in the history of thought, a "new semantics" as we might say in current parlance, but a *textual condition*, made possible by the convergence of sciences or *Wissenschaften* – medicine, psychology, anthropology – specific modes of writing, and literature itself. Herder understood as few before him that these discourses, disciplines, and sciences were shot through with history, and that the individual itself could only be thought as a specific combination, intersection, convergence of various discursive forces. Only by understanding the particular ensemble of such forces and discourses could we begin to plumb the true essence of the individual in its individuality.

The case history of a young Jewish woman thought by her parents and a Rabbi to be suffering from a case of hysterical possession in Schaumburg-Lippe in 1744 might appear to be an exception in the genealogy of the case history within the parameters of empirical psychology. But the case of Grendel presented in chapter 4 beautifully demonstrates that alongside a strong enlightenment culture of rational adjudication, painstakingly accurate protocol, and what they certainly believed was "humane" treatment, Grendel remained a total enigma to the rabbis, priests, physicians, privy counselors, and civil administrators, and even the Duke himself, all of whom struggled to understand the causes and the nature of her affliction. No amount of reasonable interrogation of all the parties involved or the examination of the surrounding context and facts seemed to offer any assistance in solving the "case." Grendel was, as it were, not a pathological case to be situated somewhere along the spectrum of possible human cases, but outside all reason, understanding, and resolution. The protocol itself – a "case history" of some length marked by a diligence which reveals the degree to which the State had become interested in such matters – produces a series of conflicted reactions and stances; first thought to be malingering, when no *dolus* or *impostura* can be reasonably established, the incomprehensibility of her illness assumes center stage as the entire pastoral apparatus of family, community, medicine, religion, state administration, and the law unflinchingly press for a clear diagnosis and a reasonable outcome. Neither can we detect what Grendel truly experienced *an-und-für-sich*, in-and-for itself, nor does her "case" remain a mere token of enlightened absolutist power, a subaltern voice submerged by the authorities who are tasked with the consideration of the case. What makes this case so interesting is precisely the liminal space it occupies at a turning point in the psychological understanding of mental pathology during the German *Frühaufklärung*. Academic, theoretical debates and treatises that were circulating at the time espousing a rational, scientific, and humane approach to mental illness had seeped so thoroughly into the "practices of everyday life," to speak with Michel de Certeau, had so permeated the "common sense" about pathology. The Duke himself repeatedly calls for a rational, humane procedure and treatment of her illness, for Grendel to be brought to the castle and cared for in an effort to prevent any further influence of the clearly superstitious and perhaps even fanatical Jewish community. Despite the enlightened attitude of the authorities and insistence on a "rational" resolution, the physicians and councilors simply did not have the medical-psychological sensibility, vocabulary, or knowledge to be of any real assistance in resolving the case. The juridical, civil, and medical authorities involved in Grendel's case, influenced by the Enlightenment's demand of rational explanation and reasonable treatment, had dispensed with the notion of possession by evil demons, but they did not yet possess any idiom within which to understand Grendel's mental illness. They elected to allow the planned exorcism by the Rabbi to move forward, stating that it was a matter for the Jewish community to decide as no criminal act had been committed. The protocol of Grendel is a wonderful example of a pre-modern *narrative* case, which cannot be subsumed within the contemporary rational discourse of and on the soul. As such, it is a suitable foil for the psychological narrative case histories which definitively emerge in the experimental or experiential psychology of the 1780s. In 1744, as Meier's treatise *Theoretische Lehre von den Gemüthsbewegungen überhaupt* clearly shows, the theory of the movements of the mind was in its infancy, a theory of the movement of the soul – a *Seelenlehre* – more a propaedeutic or projected discipline than an actuality. First with the psychologically-minded physicians in Halle around mid-century, surely influenced heavily by Stahl's animism – do we find a body of anthropological-medical literature aimed squarely at the aberrations of the soul and their effects on the condition of health of the individual, and a distinctly *psychological* mode of understanding, describing, and treating mental illness.

Herz's *Psychological Description of my Own Illness* (1783) was not only a response to Karl Philipp Moritz's call for interesting case histories to populate his newly found journal *Gnothi Sauton oder Magazin zur Erfahrungsseelenkunde*; it is, to my knowledge, the first instance of a case history or history of an illness (*Krankengeschichte*) in which the term "psychological" is explicitly used in the title. Written primarily in the first-person, Herz had to rely on the reports of friends regarding what happened in the most acute phase, of which he had no memory. Now we can say that there were indeed other case histories circulating at the time which explored the inner connection between forms if illness – mental or physical – and psychological states of mind, inner feelings, and emotions, the psychological history of the patient and what factors might have led up to the crisis. But the use of the descriptor "psychological" in Herz's title is still highly significant. Herz, intimately familiar with the psychological, medical, and philosophical literature of the eighteenth century, interested precisely in the connection between the mind and the body, and dissatisfied with the genre of the classical *historia morbi*, was probing new territory. What made Herz's case history of his own illness so novel, what differentiated it from the traditional *Krankengeschichte*, we argued, was precisely the way in which it connected the illness to his own psychological tendencies (his frenzied, ambitious, one might say obsessive-compulsive drive, his hubris and conceit); how it explored his dreams, fantasies, and hallucinations during the illness as a function of his particular personality and character; and, finally, how the illness is narrated in a highly nuanced, psychological fashion, always seeking to elucidate the specific content of thoughts and perceptions during the illness in terms of his memories, projections (as when they moved the bed into another room, or his penchant to see the world as inimical), and fears. What is most salient perhaps is his interest in understanding the illness as a *psychological*, rather than as a purely *medical, physical phenomenon*. The feedback loop of the call for papers and Herz's case history should alert us to the media-specific event-character of this emergence: if Herz's case exhibited the first fully explicit semiology of the individual case, it is no less the case that the case history itself and a journal dedicated to the collection and dissemination of such case histories produced the media-specific conditions under which the invention of this type of case history and the singular, unique individual first became possible. While the construction and representation of an individual and pathological interior had certainly been underway in literature since the publication of Goethe's Werther (1774), it was all too easy to dismiss such wayward deviation in fiction. Herz, a highly respected, genial physician and philosopher, created a psychological account of his illness, making his own experience explicit, real, self-referential, and accurately historical in a way which literature alone could not. And yet his psychological "description" – we might even sense an irony here – is very much *literature*: Herz's use of rhetorical figures and phrases, the first-person psycho-narration of his innermost sensations, feelings and thoughts, rendering a certain transparency of the mind, is not sufficiently captured within the simplistic notion of empirical "description" or mimetic representation. The language of his text in a sense "suffers" the illness itself, memory and fantasy intersect and merge, description submits to the figuration of metaphor as we read Herz struggling to find an adequate idiom for what was a very new way of writing the human soul. As Carolin Kull has thoughtfully remarked: "[Herz] begins to derive the emergence and the connection of his fantasies psychologically [...] by narrative means he opens up an insight into psychological as well as medical modes of consideration, procedure, and treatment."[19]

In chapter 7, Herz's case history of his friend and patient Moritz (1793), a psychological-medical hybrid as the subtitle *Etwas Psychologisch-Medizinisches* suggests, charts a hysterical-hypochondriacal affective disorder in Moritz as he comes to understand the gravity of his very real illness and grapples with his demise. Herz was concerned in this posthumously published case not with the underlying medical, physical illness (tuberculosis), but with the mental torment and psychological instability in Moritz that was surely adding to his suffering and exacerbating his symptoms. More importantly, Herz engages the transferential relationship between patient and physician, the resistance of the patient, and the specific metaphorical displacement and metonymic condensation present in Moritz's identification of a *fatal polyp on his heart* with the physician Herz (*heart*) as the cause of his impending death. Moritz's real illness and suffering notwithstanding, this case history explores one of the most celebrated psychological afflictions of the eighteenth century, and how the philosophical physician is able, through language, to turn the situation around and transform the knotted, grinding, horrified patient into a wise man better able to deal with his own finitude. This was no simple case of hysteria. The existence of a real organic illness complicated matters, as Herz well understood. Moritz enacts the abandoned child whom the physician father is unable to cure and denigrates both Herz and the medical profession. In his cunning move – "you are not to be saved ... my medical art cannot do anything more ... you must die!" – Herz shocks Moritz into grasping his mortality, and brings him back into the fold of the reciprocal patient-physician relationship so Herz can ease his burden as he lives out his life. The case employs the reciprocal rhetorical repartee "Live wisely – Die wisely!" that brings both Herz and Moritz into a more intimate understanding of their relationship and effectively ends Moritz's hysterical-affective acting out. On the level of literature, the wonderful *mis-en-scéne* at the moment of crisis stages for us the "knot" of the hypochondriacal affliction, while the chiastic rhetoric of

---

19 Carolin Kull, "Marcus Herz: "An Herrn Doktor J. In Königsberg. Psychologische Beschreibung seiner eigenen Krankheit," in *Casus. Von Hoffmanns Erzählungen zu Freuds Novellen. Eine Anthologie der Fachprosagattung 'Fallerzählung,'* ed. Carsten Zelle (Hannover: Wehrhahn, 2015), 121–123: "beginnt die Entstehung und den Zusammenhang seiner Phantasien psychologisch herzuleiten [...] Durch narrative Mittel eröffnet der Text Einblicke in psychologische sowie medizinische Betrachtungs-, Vorgehens- und Behandlungsweisen."

the final reconciliation itself accomplishes the restorative pairing of patient and physician. Classical features of hysterical hypochondriasis were played out here: the imaginary *globus hystericus*, the entwinement of patient-doctor, and the dread of an imminent death. However, what distinguished Herz's nuanced narrative of Moritz's illness and what made it more than just another instance of male hysteria was the dynamic, intersubjective, even playful tension between physician and patient; the empathetic doctor at his wits' end to try to help his ailing friend; Herz's decisive *epicrisis* and, finally, Moritz's *anagnorisis* as he realizes the limits of medicine, the fact that there are diseases which cannot be cured, his very own human fragility, and most importantly, the unceasing dedication and commitment of his friend Herz.

Friedrich Schiller's beginnings at the Karlsschule, his fascination with psychological and juridical cases, and his famous short narrative literary case history *Criminal of Lost Honor – A True Story* (1786) have been the subjects of a vast research literature, and we owe it to Wolfgang Riedel to have documented, in great detail, not only Schiller's own psychological education and the multiple influences on his psychological thinking, but the impact of the discipline of psychology on his literary work and philosophical program. My contribution in chapter 6 on Schiller and the psychological-juridical case history was aimed at pointing out the as yet obscure relation between this genre and Schiller's aesthetics. On the one hand, showing how profoundly Schiller departs from the caricature of idealism so often presented, his burning concern for the individual, material human being and how cases are *made*, not simply given, and, perhaps most importantly, on the other hand, how Schiller's case history à clef aesthetically transposes the actual case history of the *Sonnenwirth* with the distinct interest of showing how Christian Wolf comes to be the robber and murderer he is made out to be; how the forces of society combine with inner trauma and tragedy to produce a criminal *from lost honor*. The task was also to demonstrate Schiller's aesthetic concern for the case history as a particularly modern genre capable of producing pedagogical, epistemological, and moral-legal reflection. We did this using the *Preface* to the edition Schiller produced of Pitaval's *Causes célèbres et interessantes* (1734–1743), titled *Interesting Cases as a Contribution to the History of Mankind* (*Merkwürdige Rechtsfälle als ein Beitrag zur Geschichte der Menschheit*) of 1792, as well as in the introductory paragraphs of the case history *Criminal of Lost Honor* (1786). It was observed how Schiller elevated the case history beyond the genre of historical narrative, which remained bound to the *species facti* and the chronological depiction of facts and events, and opened up a specific *republican freedom of the reader,* who would henceforth be able to decide for him or herself what s/he thought about the case, to adjudicate it, as it were, through an empathetic understanding of the individual and their history, circumstance, and the forces of society and the state. What is beautifully underscored in Schiller is the shift underway in the late eighteenth century from the *act itself, the deed*, to the *motivation, intention*, and *causes of the act*, as Schiller put it in the version of *Criminal of Lost Honor* he published in his journal *Thalia* in 1786: "For us, it much more a matter of his thoughts than his deeds, and still more on the very spring of his thoughts than the consequences of his actions."[20] In a word, Schiller structured the case history of the Sonnenwirth, transfigured it to become a case of someone who becomes literally and figuratively marked by society, literalizing the metaphor and enacting, through narrative, the process of how criminals are not simply given as "dark souls" destined to do evil, born of a corrupted soul, but systematically *made, constructed, invented*.

The work of Karl Philipp Moritz, in particular his programmatic writings of the 1780s on empirical-experiential psychology occupies an absolutely central position in the emergence of the psychological narrative case history. The journal he founded in 1783 *ΓΝΩΘΙ ΣΑΥΤΟΝ or Magazine for Experiential Psychology* (1783–1793) has been rightly called the beginning of modern psychology, a key forerunner to the psychiatry of the nineteenth century, and even a precursor to psycho-analysis in its concern for childhood memory, past trauma, and what Moritz referred to as *Seelenkrankheitskunde*, a comprehensive theory of the diseases of the soul.[21] In its ten year run, over one hundred individual cases were presented, many with a psychological interest or narrating psychological conditions. In his *Recommendation of a Magazine of Experiential Psychology* published in the *Deutsches Museum* of 1782, Moritz stated he wanted *real facts*, presented in the form of actual case histories, from educators, jurists, clergy, physicians, civil administrators, and the educated public at large to begin his journal and to build a library or repository of psychological knowledge which would prove beneficial to mankind, edifying to the individual, and useful for the development of an experiential science if the soul. In an *Announcement of the Appearance of a Magazine for Experiential Psychology* that appeared in the *Allerneueste Mannigfaltigkeiten* of the same year (1782), Moritz wrote:

> In this magazine, especially at the beginning, only facts are to be taken up. The teacher, the preacher, the legal scholar, the physician, the officer can all deliver important

---

[20] Friedrich Schiller, "Verbrecher aus Infamie," *Thalia* 1.2 (1786): 23: "An seinen Gedanken liegt uns unendlich mehr als an seinen Thaten, und noch weit mehr an den Quellen dieser Gedanken, als an den Folgen jener Thaten."

[21] See Jürgen Schlumbohm, "Constructing Individuality. Childhood Memories in Eighteenth-Century Empirical Psychology and Autobiography," *German History* 16.1 (1998): 29–42.

contributions. But the facts must have to do with *individual people*, or be able to be led back to the stories of individuals, because in this magazine materials for the history of mankind are to be collected; and these facts have to be especially narrated with attention to the apparently minor circumstances.²²

The core of this passage – *the facts have to be about individual human beings* – marks the turn toward a fully individualized consideration of the unique human being in its singularity, not as a type or a token, not as exemplifying any illness or theory, but the individual in its individuality; this is the object proper of the new science of the soul. Moritz cautioned to avoid both generalization and universal therapeutics, and to resist the temptation to rush to a fixed, rigid system that, in his view, would hamper the open-ended, gradual, tentative, ever researching procedure of the journal. Eschewing all speculation, mysticism, abstraction, moral and theological judgment, and overzealous attempts to codify what was presented, Moritz envisioned the *Magazin* as an ongoing forum for the presentation, reflection, commentary, discussion, and debate about the psychological cases presented. In this manner, he urged, the scientific-learned community could gradually arrive at an ever more comprehensive science of the soul, which included a theory of mental illness, semiotics, therapeutics and care of the soul.

What interested us in particular in Moritz's programmatic writings on the function, scope and ultimate purpose of *Erfahrungsseelenkunde* was the proximity of the achievement of the proper point of view (*der richtige Gesichtspunkt*) to the discourses of aesthetics and empirical psychology, in particular the necessity of transcending one's own narrow sphere of interest to be able to play what Moritz referred to as the *cold observer*, disinterested in outcome, functionality or specific agenda. Moritz's was the originator of the aesthetics of autonomy in his *Attempt at a Unification of all beautiful Sciences under the Notion of that which is Complete unto Itself* (*Versuch einer Vereinigung aller schönen Wissenschaften unter dem Begriff des in sich selbst Vollendeten*) published in 1785 in the *Berlinische Monatsschrift* in the form of a letter to Moses Mendelssohn. The "true observer" in Moritz's outline of empirical psychology, we noted, must similarly

---

22 Karl Philipp Moritz, "Ankündigung eines Magazins für Erfahrungsseelenkunde," *Allerneueste Mannigfaltigkeiten* 1 (1782): 775–778; emphasis mine: "In dieses Magazin sollen, besonders im Anfange, bloß Fakta aufgenommen werden. Der Schulmann, der Prediger, der Rechtsgelehrter, der Arzt, der Offizier können alle sehr wichtige Beyträge dazu liefern. Nur müßen die Fakta einzelne Menschen betreffen, oder doch am Ende auf die Geschichte einzelner Menschen zurück geführt werden, weil in diesem Magazin die Materialien, zu einer inner Geschichte der Menscheit gesammelt werden sollen; auch müßen diese Fakta noch insbesondere mit Aufmerksamkeit auf kleinscheinende Umstände, die auf das Ganze einen wichtigen Einfluß haben, erzählt werden."

undergo a self-transcendence, or a sacrifice of the self, to achieve what Moritz refers to as the appropriate point of view (*Gesichtspunkt*) in the practice of empirical psychology. In his aesthetic, Moritz advocated the purification of every trace of self-interest not only in order to achieve a higher, disinterested, human perspective, but to bring about a transformation of the affective content of experience. Similarly, in the practice of empirical psychology, the observer of the human soul has to see through the veil of bourgeois, so-called "moral" life, through the arrogance of wisdom (*Lebensklugheit*), through the illusions of propriety and expectation, before one can truly "see" the innermost regions of the individual. In the aesthetic condition, as we also saw in the case of Schiller, the individual is returned into its own, yet higher individuality, freed up from functionalist definitions and the crushing force of society, morality, law and the state. At the same time, it creates through the medium of *judgment* a transcendent intersubjectivity, a universal communicability allowing the individual to experience a pleasure that could, or would be, at least in principle, experienced by all. Five years before the publication of Immanuel Kant's *Critique of Judgment*, Moritz not only circumscribes the aesthetic experience itself as the "object of disinterested pleasure," but articulates that this pleasure does not precede, but must follow the implicit judgment of the universal communicability of such pleasure: that the specific feeling of aesthetic pleasure could or would be able to be felt by all.

In a further step, the attempt was made to relate both modes or conditions of observer and judge to a care or concern for the self. Moritz's *Gnothi Sauton* in the title of the journal invokes the classical Delphic "know thyself" not merely as an epistemic imperative of empowerment, but as a modality of relating to and caring for the self. In particular, as Foucault argued in his *Hermeneutics of the Subject*, the injunction to "know thyself" was always "coupled or twinned with the principle of 'take care of yourself' (*epimeleia heautou*),"[23] and this "care" or "concern" as a way of relating to one's self harbored in it a *subjection* of the self, making the self autonomous, the double and doubling demand to become free and insightful, but in that freedom to tend to one's self precisely as a distinct, autonomous *subject*, as something that must be cared for, as the subject and object of a specific form of circumspection and concern. When this fails, when the subjection of the subject to an autonomous, self-determinant individual goes awry, one turns to the *Seelensorger*, who, as Moritz explicitly states, must "seek to repair, whenever possible, the injured relation between

---

23 Michel Foucault, *Hermeneutics of the Subject: Lectures at the Collège de France 1981–82*, ed. Frédéric Gros, trans. Graham Burchell (New York: Picador, 2001), 4–5.

the capacities of the soul. The psychologically minded physician must know how to blot out destructive ideas and to illuminate others appropriately. They must know how to recognize the proper degree of connection within the entire system of ideas and, when necessary, penetrate the deepest interstices of the all-too-rigid system of such ideas."[24] The therapeutic of concern and care for the soul of the individual came to the fore most vividly in the part of empirical psychology referred to by Moritz (and others at the time) as *Seelendiätetik*, the dietetics of the soul, which had the task of maintaining the various capabilities of a soul in the correct and proportional relation to one another. Aesthetics and empirical psychology thus conspired to direct, guide, and lead the soul in a particular salutary fashion, towards balance and equilibrium, proportion and autonomy, coherence and integrity, selfhood and an "authentic," self-realizing subjectivity *and* intersubjectivity.

Herz was fascinated by the fact that, despite the basic uniformity of representation (*Vorstellung*) as the fundamental activity of the soul, an axiom of thought in the German *Aufklärung* – human beings have ideas about the world, things in the world, other people, and abstract ideas of which they are conscious – human beings also have among themselves very different representations of one and same thing, and even a single individual can entertain very different types of representations over time, depending upon positionality, circumstance, and contingency. The range and variety of human representation is a thread that weaves through his entire corpus. What could account for the variability and diversity of such representations? In a word, how can we explain the individual uniqueness of representation? For Herz, this was not merely a philosophical but a medical-psychological question as well. How can we understand how an illness can have very different effects and outcomes in different people, or how various people react very differently to the same illness, and show greater or less resiliency? Every illness is marked by a unique disposition in each case (*eine eigene Disposition*), and the smallest difference or deviation can determine whether there will be a felicitous or grave outcome. Herz the philosopher sought to develop a theory for what Herz the physician experienced in his practice. A simplistic empiricism that denied the existence of the soul as a mere illusion as was being heralded by those influenced by David Hume or by the French determinist-materialism of Julien Offray de la Mettrie, Claude Adrien Helvetius or Paul-Henri Thiry, Baron d'Holbach would never be able to

---

[24] Karl Philipp Moritz, *Grundlinien zu einem ohngefähren Entwurf in Rücksicht auf die Seelenkrankheitskunde*, in *Werke in zwei Bänden. Dichtungen und Schriften zur Erfahrungsseelenkunde*, ed. Heide Hollmer and Albert Meier (Frankfurt: DKV, 1999), 1:815.

adequately explain such difference both among people and even at different times under different circumstances within the same person. This was, according to Herz, the result of the specific relation of mind and body in every case. Difference (*Verschiedenheit*), uniqueness (*Eigenthümlichkeit*), and deviation (*Abweichung*) provided a framework for understanding the diverse points of view, senses, and unusual or atypical ideas we encounter within ourselves and in the world. Deviation (*Abweichung*) itself can either be *natural* or *unnatural/ pathological*, depending on whether it is a slight detour from what is customary, or whether it is actually a truly deleterious, harmful, and destructive departure from what is beneficial and good. While such deviations reveal a less perfect state or condition according to Herz, it is crucial to understand them; they hold the key, for Herz, to a true understanding of illness and disease. Furthermore, such deviations function for Herz as a *bildende Kraft,* a formative, edifying power, spurring the individual on to ever greater perfection. Unlike the animist-influxionist theory advanced by Stahl and continued at least in part by the psychological physicians at Halle, which merely considered the influence of the mind on the body but not *vice versa*, Herz insisted on *Nexus* and *Verknüpfung* (connection, conjunction, linkage) of the body and mind in a constant, reciprocal relation to one another, which is always determined (*bestimmt*) in a specific way depending on the individual case.

In his *Considerations concerning Speculative Philosophy* of 1771, which was supposed to be a mere explication of his mentor Kant's inaugural dissertation *De mundis sensibilis atque intelligibilis et principiis*, we witnessed how, in chapter 9, Herz enacts three significant digressions or diversions from Kant: (1) a blurring of the strict distinction between epistemology and aesthetics; (2) a critique of the traditional distinction between form and content; and (3) exposing the subjective "moment" not merely in the ever shifting content, but in the very *form* of cognition. Although in his letter to Kant, Herz passes these off as mere "further steps" or minor emendations of what Kant had written, they in fact represent a significant shift away from his mentor's philosophy. In the discussion of epistemology, Herz launches into a subtle, nuanced discussion of aesthetics and sensible knowledge, thus transgressing a disciplinary or "faculty" boundary. As one who enjoyed "the wandering about on the borders of the disciplines of medicine and philosophy," Herz is fully conscious of his "digressions" or "deviations." He does this in order to question Kant's *a priori* bias and to problematize the relation between form and content, and to interject a subjective component into the very form of cognition itself. Any determination or application of a rational "rule," "category," or "law" is itself "subjective" to the extent that each individual case has something unique or distinct that renders the cognitive form itself subject to precisely this peculiarity. The "precise determination of the precisely determined material"[25] as Herz put it means that there is always something "subjective" not simply in the aesthetic realm of sensible knowledge and the beautiful, but in cognition in general. To understand the precise nature of this digression and the interjection of the subjective, we turned to Herz's adoption and adaptation of Sulzer's notion of *Haltung* – positionality or stance – to examine the relation between the manifold and the resultant unity in Herz's aesthetic theory in *Versuch über den Geschmack*. Herz deviates in this text from previous aesthetic theory in that he clearly prioritizes the manifold and the process by which this manifold is rendered a unity or totality rather than the resultant unity or totality itself. *Haltung* is at once the subjective *and* objective condition of the unity that is achieved through any form of human cognition; *subjective* insofar as the individual is bound to synthesize the manifold in a specific manner dependent on its particular position or stance, and *objective* insofar as the material itself has a particular predisposition or *Haltung* that lends itself to certain forms or modalities of cognitive unification. In aesthetic experience *par excellence*, but in all human cognition more generally, there must be a direct correlation between the subjective and objective moments of the relation between manifold and unity: the subject-centered powers of the soul – reason, imagination, and sense of *Haltung* on the subjective side – correspond, in power and proportion, to the unity, multiplicity and specific *Haltung* of the material itself on the objective side. The appropriate (*angemessene*) relation of subjective and objective, the proportional integration of the manifold to the totality, the felicitous (*treffende*) agreement of the manifold elements and their successful effect in rendering the unity possible is the core of Herz's epistemology. But there can be no general formula of this relation or its proportionality valid for all instances, just as there is no general story to be told about *Haltung*. In fact, Herz accounted for the infinite variability of the aesthetic – the fact the beauty can take on so many different forms as there are possible "appropriate" or "felicitous" compositions of the manifold – through the theoretically infinite possibilities of *Haltung* itself: "The diversity of the multiplicities that are brought to congruity is the very basis of the diversity of beautiful arts and sciences."[26]

In this study, we have been concerned with the emergence of a specific epistemic genre in eighteenth-century Germany and its power of subjectification: the psychological narrative case history as text-type aimed at the representation

---

[25] Marcus Herz, *Betrachtungen aus der spekulativen Weltweisheit*, ed. Elfriede Conrad et al. (Hamburg: F. Meiner, 1990), 22.
[26] Herz, *Versuch über den Geschmack*, 31: "Die Verschiedenheit der Mannigfaltigkeiten, die zur Übereinstimmung verwendet werden, macht die Grundlage der Verschiedenheit der schönen Künste und Wissenschaften."

of individual experience. As Gianna Pomata has taught us, from the early *observationes* of early modern Europe to Freud's famous case studies and beyond, the case history tells us how knowledge is organized, how experience is transformed into narrative, text, and discourse; how the dissemination and "sharing" of cases constituted a scientific culture in early modern Europe. My aim here was to make this claim more genre-, discourse-, and period-specific; to show how, in the span of about fifty years from 1750 to 1800, we became a culture of narrative psychological cases, cases that we can readily understand because they are written in the idiom of a unique individual. While it is true that the case history has a rich, well-researched history from the early *consilia* and *consultatoria*, and the *historia morbi* of early modern physicians of Europe, they served either as examples, using the traditional Galenic theory of specific four types of character, of the corruption, morbidity, unnatural waywardness of a soul; or to back up existing medical notions or theory; or finally to show the success or failure of certain forms of treatment. They lacked the specifically individual, psychological interest and focus until the second half of the eighteenth century.

In 1782, when Moritz sent out his call for papers, the time was ripe. Several disciplines (anthropology, medicine, empirical psychology itself), several important historical events and constellations (the psychological *Ärzte* in Halle around 1750), the turn toward the unique individual in literature and criticism (beginning with Wieland, but then explicitly in the young Herder, Goethe, and Blanckenburg's theory of the novel) all converged to make this unique genre possible. Specific experience (*Erfahrung*), according to J.G. Zimmermann in 1763 and A.E. Büchner in 1765, could be transmitted in case histories. A well-written case history, as the physician Büchner noted in 1765, consisted of a well-ordered *Erzählung*. Cases could serve as the surrogate for evidence, or the evidentiary basis for an empirical-experiential psychology based on "facts" and "experience." Cases ceased to be the provenance of physicians and academic medical professors alone. Moritz authorized jurists, officers, teachers, priests, rabbis, philosophers, physicians, and parents to make such cases known by sending them in for publication in his *Magazin zur Erfahrungsseelenkunde* (1783–1793), one of the most famous journals of the late Enlightenment in Germany. Case histories were not merely the medium, but the message as well: individuality could be documented, textualized, made concrete and real. They told a story of suffering, of the relation between history, memory, present and past trauma, and illness, of how individuals were made into certain kinds of subjects, of how a person could become an "interesting case," a case worthy of thought (*denkwürdig*), a case for which there was no existing category or rubric, no theory or model that could adequately explain the specific manner of alteration or deviation. As André Jolles already suggested in his study of 1930, the case posed a question, but did not answer it; "it tasks us with the duty of a decision, but does not contain the decision itself. What is realized in the 'case' is the weighing, but not the result of the weighing."[27] As Moritz emphasized, the contributors were to refrain from generalizing hypotheses and universal assertions: simply the cases and the specific "facts" they presented sufficed for beginning a new science which would gradually work toward ever more general statements and theories; an envisioned "system" was still far off, but detailed, rigorous, observant narrative case histories that recounted the inner history of an illness or crime would be the cornerstones of a future empirical psychology. The presence of the precise phrase inner history (*innere Geschichte*) of the individual human being in Blanckenburg's *Versuch über den Roman* of 1774[28] and Moritz's programmatic writings on empirical psychology attests to an historical, structural homology, a discourse on and of the individuality of the individual.[29] In *Über Thomas Abbts Schriften* (1768), Herder articulated this as *Eigenheit*, the unique, historical specificity that makes the individual what it is.[30]

Despite the materialism and determinism prevalent in the Enlightenment, especially in France, and despite the skeptical empiricism and associationist psychology that took hold in England, the soul did not simply disappear. Indeed, one can argue that it asserted itself in an ever more powerful, and for modern technologies of the self, ever more prescient manner. In Germany, as Manfred Walther has persuasively argued, the nominalist-empirical science of England the materialist-determinism in France never truly caught on in major way, because in Germany a belief in a "soul" was not viewed to be in any way inconsistent with the claims and pursuits of science or *Wissenschaft*.[31] In

---

27 André Jolles, *Einfache Formen* (Halle [Saale]: Niemeyer, 1930; Tübingen: Niemeyer, 1968), 179–191.
28 Christian Friedrich von Blanckenburg, *Versuch über den Roman*. Faksimiledruck der Originalausgabe von 1774, afterword by Nachwort von Eberhard Lämmert (Stuttgart: J.B. Metzler, 1965), 392: "Wenn die Ausbildung und Formung, die ein Charakter durch seine mancherley Begegnisse erhalten kann, oder noch eigentlicher, *seine innere Geschichte*, das Wesentliche und Eigenthümliche eines Romans ist."
29 Karl Philipp Moritz, *Anton Reiser. Ein psychologischer Roman*, ed. W. Martens (Stuttgart: Metzler, 1998), 6: "Auch wird man in einem Buche, welches vorzüglich die innere Geschichte des Menschen schildern soll, keine große Mannigfaltigkeit der Charaktere erwarten."
30 Johann Gottfried Herder, *Über Thomas Abbts Schriften. Der Torso von einem Denkmal, an seinem Grabe errichtet* (Leipzig: Hartknoch, 1768), 20.
31 Manfred Walther, "Spinozissimus ille Spinoza oder wie Spinoza zum 'Klassiker' wurde," in *Beobachter und Lebenswelt: Studien zur Natur-, Geistes- und Sozialwissenschaft*, ed. Klaus Hammacher and Helmut Reinalter (Wien and München: Thaur, 1996), 183–238.

a word, *Aufklärung* in Northern Germany with its pietistic underpinning required a rigorous, empirical investigation into the soul itself. Souls mattered, and not merely because of sin and salvation, corruption and grace. The soul (*pneuma*, breath, life) became the organic life-force itself as well as the enigmatic, elusive, and deep "container" of all sorts of dangerous and threatening ideas, dreams, illusions, memories, and emotions. And as the State became ever more interested in the health, rectitude, hygiene, stability, fertility, and productivity of its population, "souls" – their health and vitality, their rationality and integrity, and above all their educability – became, alongside populations, an important subject and unit of concern, care, treatment, and therapeutics. One can only understand the emergence written about in these pages against the backdrop of the appearance of an entire array of state, communal, provincial, parish medical, pedagogical, and juridical – in a word *pastoral* – apparatuses designed to ensure the well-being and care of their flocks – what Foucault termed "governmentality" in his later work. Cases were one of the central epistemic and power-functional "figures" in the avalanche of various forms of *Polizeiwissenschaft* – the science and theory of the policing and policy of the state – which became common in the second half of the eighteenth century. Cases became the grist of a bio-politics of mental hygiene, a crucial piece of a complex pastoral apparatus directed at the guidance and direction, the care and rehabilitation of souls as well as the more general health of the population. Johann Peter Frank's *Complete System of a Medical Policy*, which appeared in nine volumes between 1779 and 1821 and was reprinted many times during his lifetime, is only one text among many at this time concerned with public health, hygiene, and medical policy.[32] Of great concern at this time were mental illness, pregnancy and childbirth, child delinquency and criminality in particular, all of which became the object of medical and state policy, subjects of considerable discussion and concern in books, journals, and magazines of the late *Spätaufklärung* in Germany, 1780–1800. Cases were cited, republished, mentioned as exemplary, rejected as deleterious, debated, and contested. Sulzer and Herz both used cases to back up observations of aberrational thinking and behavior. Moritz sought out cases to build a new discipline. Schiller, for his part, transformed a famous case history into an even more famous case study as novella, transcribing the genre and

---

32 Others include: Johann Thedor Pyl, *Neues Magazin für die gerichtliche Arzneikunde und medizinische Poliziei* (Stendal: bei Dan. Christ, Franzen und Grosse, 1785); Zacharias Gottlieb Hußty, ed. *Diskurs über die medicinische Polizey* (Pressburg und Leipzig: Anton Löwe, 1786); Johann Dionys John, *Die medicinische Polizei und die Arzneiwissenschaft*. (Prague: bei Johann Gottfried Calve, 1798); Johann Christian Friedrich Scherf, ed., *Beiträge zum Archiv der medizinischen Polizei und der Volksarzneykunde* (Leipzig: Weygand, 1790).

showing the intersection of psychology, law, criminality and social justice. Herz transgressed disciplinary boundaries and demonstrated how the individual case is an *epistemological* as well as *aesthetic* problem.

Rather than identify any one of these historical scientific and disciplinary events, cultural developments or specific figures as being absolutely determinant in and of itself, this study has urged the convergence or co-determination of all of these forces in the emergence, codification, and institutionalization of the case history as the genre *par excellence* for the narrative representation of the individual human soul. At the moment of its birth, the self-determining, self-conscious, autonomous subject of the Enlightenment was already fraught with contradiction, caught in a double-bind. "Know thyself!" – the subtitle of Moritz's journal – was not just an epistemic injunction; it also entailed the ontological imperative to "be oneself!" But the business of being oneself, the unique individuality that one is in all cases, is always subject to and contingent upon a specific self-relation that cannot, now or in the late eighteenth century, simply be assumed or taken for granted. The subject individuates through a relation to itself and to others, and this relation is mediated through language and discourse, literary techniques and narrative styles, genres and media. From Grendel to Moritz, the individuality of the individual is always a problematic if not impossible situation seeking some form of resolution, adjudication, or explanation. If the humors and the vapors, if caste and social status, if theological precepts and rhetorical discourse forms no longer held sway, there needed to be an "anchor" for what was surely thought to be a messy, delicate, vulnerable tangle of emotions, feelings, sensations, thoughts, and ideas. The individual soul provided just such an "anchor" or "grounding" principle, a modern *a priori* that has since then never ceased to continually produce individuality in ever new, ever changing ways.

But if the narrative psychological case histories of the eighteenth century have taught us anything, it is precisely that the individuality of the individual is not simply "given," or merely a biological, corporeal "fact." It is *narrated*, subjected to and within discourse, framed in the pages of case histories, disseminated and read by individuals in precisely the same double-bind of self-invention first made explicit in the late eighteenth century: Be yourself! Be autonomous! But do so only in accordance with the norm, the milieu and habitus of community, the sociability of society, and the laws of the State! Be unique! But be unique in a way that counts as "unique," "different," and distinctive, and is viewed as such by others![33] Such narrative emplotment and framing, in the very act of

---

33 Perhaps the most explicit example of this double-bind is Kafka and his "Letter to His Father," and the best reading of the paradox in Kafka is Gerhard Neumann, "'The Judgement,'

representing the unique experience of the subject, implicates a "breach" or "rupture" of the supposedly self-same, perfectly unified and integral subject, as well as the norms and conventions of such narration, as recent narrative theory has suggested.[34] We create our "selves" only to find that the very linguistic-discursive means we use in order to instantiate and to project such individuality are themselves a function of a historical discourse that, at least for the last two hundred and fifty years, has been hell-bent on tirelessly producing and re-producing the individuality of the individual, the autonomy, integrity, dignity, coherence, and cohesion of the self. Beginning in the third quarter of the eighteenth century, the universal "soul" was transformed into the self, the "subject" of a narrative for and about irreducibly unique individuals, not merely a token or *exemplum* of an idea of what the human being is or ought to be. The narrative psychological case history created knowledge of the particular, a *unique* form of writing – in the double sense of this phrase – to narrate that which could not be subsumed under already existing concepts and knowledge. It thereby became a key genre for the invention of this unique self; through collections, magazines, journals and books, a discourse apparatus for this culture of "individuals;" and, most importantly, the scriptural medium through which such individuality could be produced, inscribed, disseminated, and archived, and thus posited as an object of knowledge.

'Letter to His Father,' and the Bourgeois Family," in *Reading Kafka: Prague, Politics, and the Fin-de-Siecle*, ed. Mark Anderson (New York: Schocken, 1989), 215–228. On "distinction" as a cultural "differential" through which individuals "distinguish" themselves, see the pathbreaking work of Pierre Bourdieu, *Distinction. A Social Critique of the Judgment of Taste* (New York: Routledge, 1986).

34 In the Introduction and throughout, we referred to the narratological work of Monika Fludernik, *An Introduction to Narratology* and Jerome Bruner, "The Narrative Construction of Reality" in this regard.

Bibliography

Primary Sources

Abel, Jacob Friedrich. *Einleitung in die Seelenlehre*. Stuttgart: Metzler, 1786. Reprint. Photmech. Nachdruck: Hildesheim, Zürich, New York: Georg Olms, 1985.
Abel, Jacob Friedrich. *Erläuterungen wichtiger Gegenstände aus der philosophischen und christlichen Moral, besonders der Ascetik durch Beobachtungen aus der Seelenlehre.* Tübingen: Heerbrandt, 1790.
Abel, Jacob Friedrich. *Karlsschul-Schriften. Eine Quellenedition zum Philosophieunterricht an der Stuttgarter Karlsschule (1773–1782). Mit Einleitung, Übersetzung, Kommentar und Bibliographie*. Edited by Wolfgang Riedel. Würzburg: Königshausen & Neumann, 1995.
Abel, Jacob Friedrich. *Sammlung und Erklärung merkwürdige Erscheinungen aus dem menschlichen Leben*. 3 vols. Frankfurt and Leipzig, 1784–1790.
Adelung, Johann Christoph. *Grammatisch-kritischen Wörterbuches der hochdeutschen Mundart*. Leipzig: B.C. Breitkopf und Sohn, 1774–1786.
Anonymous. *Über die Hypochondrie*. Dresden: in der Hilscherschen Buchhandlung, 1777.
Anonymous. "Von den Ursachen der Hypochondrie." *Neues Hamburgisches Magazin* 20.120 (1781): 493–508.
Aristotle. *The Complete Works of Aristotle. Revised Oxford Translations*. 2 vols. Edited by Jonathan Barnes. Princeton, NJ: Princeton University Press, 1995.
Bacon, Francis. *The New Organon*. Edited by Lisa Jardine and Michael Silverthorne. Cambridge: Cambridge University Press, 2000.
Baumgarten, Alexander. *Metaphysics: A Critical Translation with Kant's Elucidations, Selected notes, and Related Materials*. Translated and edited by Courtney D. Fugate and John Hymers. London, New Delhi, New York: Bloomsbury, 2013.
Bernd, Adam. *Eigene Lebensbeschreibung samt einer aufrichtigen Entdeckung und deutlichen Beschreibung einer der größten, obwohl grossen theils noch unbekannten Leibes- und Gemüths-Plage*. Leipzig: J. S. Heinsius, 1738.
Blackmore, Richard. *A Treatise of the Spleen and Vapours, Or, Hypocondriacal and Hysterical Affections: With Three Discourses on the Nature and Cure of the Cholick, Melancholy, and Palsies*. London: Pemberton, 1725.
Blanckenburg, Christian Friedrich von. *Versuch über den Roman*. Facsimile of the original edition of 1774. Afterword by Eberhard Lämmert. Stuttgart: J. B. Metzler, 1965.
Blanckenburg, Christian Friedrich von. *Versuch über den Roman*. Leipzig und Liegnitz: David Siegerts Witwe, 1774. Excerpts reprinted in *Romantheorie. Dokumentation ihrer Geshicchte in Deutschland 1620–1880*. Edited by E. Lämmert. Köln and Berlin: Kohlhammer, 1971.
Blumenbach, Johann Friedrich. "Über den Bildungstrieb (*Nisus formativus*) und seinen Einfluss auf die Generation und Reproduktion." *Göttingsches Magazin zur Wissenschaft und Literatur* 1.5 (1780): 247–266.
Boerhaave, Herman. *Sylloge Epistolarum cum responsis*. Göttingen: Vandenhoeck, 1744.
Bolten, Johann Christian. *Gedancken von den psychologischen Curen*. Halle: Carl Hermann Hemmerde, 1751.

Bourneville, Désiré-Magloire, and P. Regnard. *Iconographie photographique de la Salpêtrière, 1875–81*. Paris: Progrès médical - A. Delahaye, 1875–1881. Available online at http://char cot.bum.jussieu.fr/matiere.php?NF=7

Büchner, Andreas Elias. *Der in schweren und verwirrten Krankheiten vernünftig rathende und glücklich curirende Medicus, oder Gründlicher* Unterricht, *wie in solchen wichtigen Fällen besonders von jungen Ärzten Consilia medica am sichersten können theils eingeholet, theils auch fürnemlich nach Hofmannischen und Boerhaavischen Grundsätzen klüglich ertheilet werden*. 2 vols. Erfurt: Weber, 1762–1765.

Büchner, Georg. *Sämtliche Werke und Schriften. Marburger Ausgabe*. Edited by Burghard Dedner and Thomas Michael Mayer. Darmstadt: Wissenschaftliche Buchgesellschaft, 2000.

Büchner, Georg. *Sämtliche Werke, Briefe und Dokumente*. Edited by Henri Poschmann. Frankfurt: Deutsche Klassiker Verlag, 1999.

Büchner, Georg. *Woyzeck. Texte und Dokumente*. Edited by Egon Krause. Frankfurt: Insel Verlag, 1969.

Carus, Friedrich. *Geschichte der Psychologie*. Leipzig: Barth und Kummer, 1808.

Casper, Johann Ludwig. *Klinische Novellen zur gerichtlichen Medicin: nach eigenen Erfahrungen*. Berlin: Hirschwald, 1863.

Casper, Johann Ludwig. *Practisches Handbuch der gerichtlichen Medizin*. Berlin: Hirschwald, 1857–1858.

Cheyne, George. *The English Malady, Or, A Treatise on Nervous Diseases of All Kinds*. London: G. Strahen and J. Leake, 1758.

Clifton, Francis. *The State of Physick, Ancient and Modern*. London: W. Bowyer, 1731.

Crichton, Alexander. *An Inquiry into the Nature and Origin of Mental Derangement*. London: Cadell, Junior, and W. Davis, 1798.

Dessoir, Max. *Geschichte der neueren deutschen Psychologie*. Berlin: Carl Duncker, 1902.

The English Standard Version Bible: Containing the Old and New Testaments with Apocrypha. Oxford: Oxford University Press, 2009.

Erhard, J. B. "Ueber die Medicin. Arkesilas an Ekdemus." *Der neue Teutsche Merkur* 8 (1795): 337–378.

Ferenczi, Sandor. "The Phenomenon of Hysterical Materialization" (1919). In *Further Contributions to the Theory and Technique of Psychoanalysis*, translated by Jane I. Suttie, 89–104. London: Hogarth and the Institute for Psycho-Analysis, 1926.

Feuerbach, Paul Johann Anselm. *Merkwürdige Rechtsfälle vorgetragen und herausgegeben von Paul Johann Anselm Feuerbach*. Gießen: Tasché and Müller, 1808; 1811.

Frank, Johann Peter. *System einer vollstaendigen medizinischen Polizey*. Frankenthal: im Verlag der Gegelischen Buchdruckereu und Buchhandlung, 1779–1793.

Frank, Johann Peter. *System einer vollständigen medicinischen Polizei*. 5 vols. Wien: Carl Schaumberg, 1793–1827.

Garve, Christian. "Einige Gedanken über das Interessierende" (1779). In *Philosophische Schriften über literarische, ästhetische, und gesellschaftliche Gegenstände*, edited by Kurt Wölfel, vol. 1, 161–348. Stuttgart: Metzler, 1974.

Goethe, Johann Wolfgang. *Briefe. Historisch-Kritische Ausgabe*. 10 vols. Edited by Elke Richer and Georg Kurscheidt. Berlin: Akademie Verlag, 2008.

Goethe, Johann Wolfgang. *Sämmtliche Werke in 40 Bänden*. Frankfurt: Deutscher Klassiker Verlag, 1994.

von Haller, Albrecht. *De partibus corporis humani sensibilibus et irritabilus* in Commentarii Societatis Regiae Scientiarum Gottingensis 2 (1752)[published 1753]. 114–158.

von Haller, Albrecht. "Piece No. 25." *Der Arzt. Eine Medicinische Wochenschrift* 1 (1769): 338–351.
Harvey, William. *Exercitationes de Generatione Animalium*. London: Typis Du-Gardianis; Impensis O. Pulleyn, 1651.
Harvey, William. "Letter to Physician John Vlackveld of Harlem." In *The Works of William Harvey*, translated by Robert Willis, 614. London: Sydenham Society, 1847.
Hauska, Ferdinand. *Compendium der gerichtlichen Arzneikunde*. Wien: Braumüller, 1857; 2nd revised edition. Wien: Braumüller, 18. Wien: Braumüller, 1869.
Hegel, Georg Wilhelm Friedrich. *Vorlesungen über die Geschichte der Philosophie. Teil 4*. Edited by Pierre Garniron and Walter Jaeschke. Hamburg: F. Meiner, 1986.
Herbart, Johann Friedrich. *Psychologie als Wissenschaft, neu gegründet auf Erfahrung, Metaphysik, und Mathematik*. Königsberg: Unger, 1824.
Herbart, Johann Friedrich. *Sämmtliche Werke*. Edited by G. Hartenstein. Leipzig: Leopold Voss, 1850.
Herder, Johann Gottfried. *Über Thomas Abbts Schriften. Der Torso von einem Denkmal, an seinem Grabe errichtet*. Leipzig: Hartknoch, 1768.
Herder, Johann Gottfried. *Werke in zehn Bänden*. Vol. 2. *Schriften zur Ästhetik und Literatur, 1767–1781*. Edited by Gunter E. Grimm. Frankfurt: Deutsche Klassiker Verlag, 1994–2010.
Herder, Johann Gottfried. *Werke in zehn Bänden*. Vol. 4. *Schriften zu Philosophie, Literatur, Kunst und Altertum, 1774–1787*. Edited by Jürgen Brummack and Martin Bollacher. Frankfurt: Deutsche Klassiker Verlag, 1994–2010.
Herz, Marcus. *Betrachtungen aus der spekulativen Weltweisheit*. Edited by Elfriede Conrad, Heinrich P. Delfosse, and Birgit Nehren. Hamburg: F. Meiner, 1990.
Herz, Marcus. *Briefe an Ärzte*. 2 vols. Berlin: Voss, 1784.
Herz, Marcus. "Etwas Psychologisch-Medizinisches. Moriz Krankengschichte." *Journal der praktischen Arzneykunde und Wundarzneykunst* 5.2 (1798): 259–339.
Herz, Marcus. *Grundriß aller medizinischen Wissenschaften*. Berlin: Voss, 1782.
Herz, Marcus. *Philosophisch-Medizinische Aufsätze*. Edited by Martin Davies. St. Ingbert: Röhrig, 1997.
Herz, Marcus. "Psychologische Beschreibung seiner eigenen Krankheit vom Herrn D. Markus Herz an Herrn D. J. in Königsberg." In *Gnothi Sauton oder Magazin für Erfahrungsseelenkunde als ein Lesebuch für Gelehrte und Ungelehrte. Die Schriften in dreißig Bänden* 1, Zweites Stück (1783), edited by Petra Nettelbeck and Uwe Nettelbeck, 121–141. Nördlingen: F. Greno, 1986.
Herz, Marcus. Review of *Anthropologie für Ärzte und Weltweise*, by Dr. Ernst Planter (Leipzig, 1772). *Allgemeine Deutsche Bibliothek* 20.1 (1773): 25–51.
Herz, Marcus. "Über die analogische Schlussart." *Berlinische Monatsschrift* 2 (1784): 246–251.
Herz, Marcus. "Über die Widersprüche in der menschlichen Natur." *Der Teutscher Merkur* 1 (1773): 144–163.
Herz, Marcus. *Versuch über den Geschmack*. 2nd. ed. Berlin: Voss, 1790.
Herz, Marcus. *Versuch über den Schwindel*. Berlin: C.F. Voss und Sohn, 1786.
Herz, Marcus. "Wirkung des Denkvermögens auf die Sprachwerkzeuge." *Magazin zur Erfahrungsseelenkunde* 8.2 (1791): 1–6.
Hißmann, Michael. *Psychologische Versuche, ein Beitrag zur esoterischen Logik*. Frankfurt and Leipzig, 1777.

Hobbes, Thomas. *The Elements of Law Natural and Politic*. Edited with an introduction by J.C.A. Gaskin. Oxford: Oxford University Press, 1999.
Hoffmann, Friedrich. *De animi sanitatis et morborum fabro. Dissertatio physico-medica inauguralis*. Halle: Zeitler, 1699.
Hoffmann, Friedrich. *Medicina Consultatoria*. 12 vols. Leipzig: Halle im Magdeburg: in der Rengerischen Buchhandlung, 1721–1738.
Hoffmann, Friedrich. *De modo historias morborum recte consignandi et ad usum applicandi*. Diss., Halle: Johann Christian Zahn, 1721.
Hörisch, Jochen, ed., *Ich möchte ein solcher werden wie...: Materialien zur Sprachlosigkeit des Kaspar Hauser*. Frankfurt: Suhrkamp, 1979.
Hußty, Zacharias Gottlieb, ed. *Diskurs über die medicinische Polizei*. Pressburg und Leipzig: Anton Löwe, 1786.
Hufeland, C. W. "Ein Wort über den Angriff der razionellen Medicin im N.T. Merkur. August 1795." *Der neue Teutsche Merkur* 3 (1795): 138–155.
Hume, David. *A Treatise on Human Nature*. Edited by David Fate Norton and Mary J. Norton. Oxford: Oxford University Press, 2000.
Jacob, Joachim. "Das Besondere des Falles. Zur ästhetiktheoretischen Vorgeschichte der Fallstudie im 18. Jahrhundert." In *Fallstudien: Theorie – Geschichte – Methode*, edited by Johannes Süßmann, Susanne Scholz, and Gisela Engel, 251–264. Berlin: Trafo Verlag, 2007.
Jenisch, Daniel. *Theorie der Lebensbeschreibung*. Berlin: Frölich, 1802.
John, Johann Dionys. *Die medicinische Polizei und die Arzneiwissenschaft*. Prague: bei Johann Gottfried Calve, 1798.
Kant, Immanuel. *Anthropologie in pragmatischer Hinsicht*. In *Werke in zehn Bänden*, edited by Wilhelm Weischedel. Darmstadt: Wiss. Buchgesellschaft, 1983, 396–690.
Kant, Immanuel. *Gesammelte Schriften*. 29 vols. Edited by Preußische Akademie der Wissenschaften. Berlin: G. Riemer, 1902–.
Kant, Immanuel. *Kant's Critique of Judgement*. Translation, with introduction and notes by J. H. Bernard, 2nd revised edition. London: Macmillan, 1914.
Kant, Immanuel. *Kritik der Urteilskraft*. In *Werke in zwölf Bänden*. edited by Wilhelm Weischedel. Frankfurt a.M.: Suhrkamp, 1977.
Kant, Immanuel. *De mundis sensibilis atque intelligibilis et principiis*. Königsberg: Jacob Kanter, 1770.
Kant, Immanuel. *Werke in zehn Bänden*. 10 vols. Edited by Wilhelm Weischedel. Darmstadt: Wiss. Buchgesellschaft, 1983.
Krüger, Johann Gottlob. *Naturlehre*. Vol. 2. *Zweiter Theil, welcher die Physiologie oder Lehre von dem Leben und der Gesundheit der Menschen in sich fasset*. Halle: Carl Hemmerde, 1748.
Krüger, Johann Gottlob. *Neue Lehre von den Gemüthsbewegungen*. Halle: Carl Hemmerde, 1746.
Krüger, Johann Gottlob. *Versuch einer Experimentalseelenlehre*. 2 vols. Halle and Helmstedt: Hemmerde, 1756.
Krüger, Johann Gottlob. *Zuschrift an seine Zuhörer von der Ordnung, in welcher man Arztneygelahrtheit erlernen müsse*. Halle: Carl Hermann Hemmerde, 1752.
Lambert, Johann Heinrich. *Neues Organon*. Berlin: Akademie-Verlag, 1764.
Lange, Martin. *Traité des Vapeurs, leur Origin, leurs Effets et leurs Remedes*. Paris: Veuve Denis. Nion, 1689.

Lavater, Johann Casper. *Vermischte Schriften*. 2 vols. Winterthur: Heinrich Steiner, 1774–1781.
Leibniz, Gottfried Wilhelm. *Leibniz: New Essays on Human Understanding*. Translated and edited by Peter Remnant and Jonathan Bennett. Cambridge: Cambridge University Press, 1996.
Locke, John. *An Essay on Human Understanding*. London: Basset, 1690.
Maimon, Salomon. *Salomon Maimon's Lebensgeschichte*. Edited by Karl Philipp Moritz. Berlin: Friedrich Vieweg, 1792.
Maimon, Salomon. "Über den Plan des Magazins zur Erfahrungsseelenkunde." *Magazin für Erfahrungsseelenkunde* 8.3 (1791): 1–7, 12.
Mandeville. Bernard. *Treatise of the Hypochondriack and Hysterical Passions*. London: Dryden Leach, 1711.
Mauchart, J. D. *Allgemeines Repertorium für empirische Psychologie und verwandte Wissenschaften*. Edited by J. D. Mauchart and others. Nürnberg: Felseckersche Buchhandlung, 1792.
Meier, Georg Friedrich. *Theoretische Lehre von den Gemütsbewegungen überhaupt* (1744). Reprint: Frankfurt: Athenäum, 1971.
Mendelssohn, Moses. "On the Sentiments." In *Philosophical Writings*, by Mendelssohn, edited by Daniel O. Dahlstrom, 7–95. Cambridge: Cambridge University Press, 2000.
de la Mettrie, Julien Offray. *Man – Machine*. (1748) Translated Jonathan Bennett. *Early Modern Texts* December (2009). http://www.earlymoderntexts.com/assets/pdfs/lamettrie1748.pdf (accessed 22 May 2017.)
Moritz, Karl Philipp. "Ankündigung eines Magazins für Erfahrungsseelenkunde." *Allerneueste Mannigfaltigkeiten* 1 (1782): 775–778.
Moritz, Karl Philipp. *Anton Reiser. Ein psychologischer Roman*. Edited by W. Martens. Stuttgart: Metzler, 1998.
Moritz, Karl Philipp. *Aussichten zu einer Expermentalseelenlehre*. Berlin: August Mylius, 1782.
Moritz, Karl Philipp. *Dichtungen und Schriften zur Erfahrungsseelenkunde. Werke in zwei Bänden*. Edited by Heide Hollmer and Albert Meier. Frankfurt: Deutsche Klassiker Verlag, 1997–1999.
Moritz, Karl Philipp. *Gnothi Sauton oder Magazin zur Erfahrungsseelenkunde*. Edited by Karl Philipp Moritz, Karl Pockels, and Salomon Maimon. 10 vols. Berlin: Mylius, 1783–1793
Moritz, Karl Philipp. "Grundlinien zu einem ohngefähren Entwurf in Rücksicht auf die Seelenkrankheitskunde." In *Werke in zwei Bänden*. Vol. 1. *Dichtungen und Schriften zur Erfahrungsseelenkunde*, edited by Heide Hollmer and Albert Meier, 812–816. Frankfurt: DKV, 1999.
Moritz, Karl Philipp. *Karl Philipp Moritz. Die Schriften in dreißig Bänden*. Edited by Petra Nettelbeck and Uwe Nettelbeck. Nördlingen: F. Greno, 1986.
Moritz, Karl Philipp. "Versuch einer Vereinigung aller schönen Künste und Wissenschaften unter dem Begriff des in sich selbst Vollendeten." *Berlinische Monatschrift* 5.3 (1785): 225–236.
Moritz, Karl Philip. "Vorschlag zu einem Magazin einer Erfahrungsseelenkunde." *Deutsches Museum* 1 (1782): 485–503.
Moritz, Karl Philip. *Werke in zwei Bänden*. 2 vols. Edited by Heide Hollmer and Albert Meier. Frankfurt: Deutsche Klassiker Verlag, 1997–1999
Moritz, Karl Philipp, and Karl Friedrich Pockels, eds., *Denkwürdigkeiten, aufgezeichnet zur Beförderung des Edlen und des Schönen*. Berlin: Johann Friedrich Ungar, 1786.

Müchler, Karl. *Kriminalgeschichten. Aus gerichtlichen Akten gezogen*. Berlin: Friedrich Vieweg, 1792.
Müchler, Karl. *Kriminalgeschichten. Ein Beitrag zur Erfahrungsseelenkunde*. 4 vols. Berlin: W. Natorff, 1828–1833.
Nasse, Fredrich, ed. *Zeitschrift für psychische Aerzte*. Leipzig: Carl Cnobloch, 1818–1824.
Nicolai, Ernst Anton. *Wirkungen der Einbildungskraft in den menschlichen Körper*. Halle: Carl Hermann Hemmerde, 1744.
Oberlin, Johann Friedrich. "Der Dichter Lenz, im Steinthal," [edited by August Stöbel]. In *Georg Büchner: Werke und Briefe*, edited by Karl Pörnbacher, Gerhard Schaub, Hans-Joachim Simm, and Edda Ziegler, 63–76. München: DTV, 2001.
Pascal, Blaise. *The Provincial Letters of Blaise Pascal*. Edited O. W. Wright. Boston: Houghton, Osgood, 1880.
Platner, Ernst. *Anthropologie für Ärzte und Weltweise*. Leipzig: Dyckischen Buchhandlung, 1772.
Platner, Ernst. "Einige Betrachtungen über die Hypochondrie." In *Versuch über Verrichtungen und Krankheiten des menschlichen Verstandes, nebst einigen Bermerkungen über die Hypochondrie von D. Ernst Platner*, by Johann Friedrich Daföurs, 301–338. Leipzig: Wegandische Buchhandlung, 1786.
Platner, Ernst. *Neue Anthropologie für Ärzte und Weltweise. Mit besonderer Rücksicht auf Physiologie, Pathology, Moralphilosophie und Ästhetik*. Leipzig: Crusius, 1790.
Platner, Ernst. *Philosophische Aphorismen*. Leipzig: Schwickertschen Verlage, 1793.
Platter, Felix. *Observationes. Krankheitsbeobachtungen in drei Büchern* (1614). Translated by Günther Goldschmidt. Edited by Heinrich Buess. Bern and Stuttgart: H. Huber, 1963.
Purcell, John. *A Treatise of Vapours, Or, Hysterick Fits*. London: Edward Place, 1707.
Pyl, Johann Theodor. *Aufsätze und Beobachtungen aus der gerichtlichen Arzneywissenschaft*. Berlin: August Mylius, 1783–1791.
Pyl, Johann Theodor. *Neues Magazin für die gerichtliche Arzneikunde und medizinische Polizei*, 2 vols. Stendal: Franzen & Grosse, 1785–1787.
Rau, Wolfgang Thomas. *Gedanken von dem Nutzen und der Nothwendigkeit einer medicinischen Policeyordnung in einem Staat*. Ulm: Gaumische Handlung, 1764.
Reil, Johann Christian. *Rhapsodieen über die Anwendung der psychischen Curmethode auf Geisteszerrüttungen*. Halle: Curtschen Buchhandlung, 1803; 2nd edition 1818.
Reil, Johann Christian. "Ueber den Begriff der Medicin und ihre Verzweigungen besonders in Beziehung auf Berichtigung der Topik der Psychiaterie." In *Beyträge zur Beförderung einer Curmethode auf psychischem Wege*, edited by Johann Christian Reil and Johann Christoph Hoffbauer, 153–160. Halle: Curtschen Buchhandlung, 1808.
Reil, Johann Christian, and Johann Christian Hoffbauer. "Nachschrift der Herausgeber." In *Beyträge zur Beförderung einer Curmethode auf psychischem Weg*, by Reil and Hoffbauer, 1.1 (1808): 153–160.
Rousseau, Jean-Jacques. *Confessions*. Translated by Angela Scholar. Oxford: Oxford University Press, 2000.
Scherf, Johann Christian Friedrich, ed. *Beiträge zum Archiv der medizinischen Polizei und der Volksarzneykunde*. Leipzig: Weygand, 1790.
Schiller, Friedrich, ed., *Merkwürdige Rechtsfälle als ein Beitrag zur Geschichte der Menscheit. Nach dem französischen Werke des Pitaval durch mehrere Verfasser ausgearbeitet*. 4 parts. Leipzig: Crusius, 1792–1795.

Schiller, Friedrich. *Sämmtliche Werke*. 5 vols. Edited by Gerhard Fricke and Herbert Göpfert. München: Hanser 1958–1959.
Schiller, Friedrich. *Schillers Pitaval: Merkwürdige Rechtsfälle als ein Beitrag zur Geschichte der Menschheit, verfaßt, bearbeitet und herausgegeben von Friedrich Schiller*. Edited by Oliver Tekolf, with an introduction by Hans Magnus Enzensberger. Frankfurt: Eichborn, 2005.
Schiller, Friedrich. *Werke und Briefe in zwolf Bänden*. Edited by Otto Dann et al. Frankfurt: Suhrkamp/Insel, 1992–2004.
Schipperges, Heinrich, ed. *Geschichte der Medizin in Schlaglichtern*. Berlin: Bibliographisches Institut, 1990.
Schmid, Carl Christian Erhard. *Empirische Psychologie*. Jena: Cröckische Handlung, 1791.
Schulz, F. "Geschichte meiner Hypochondrie. Ein Beytrag zur Seelen-Naturkunde." *Der teutsche Merkur* 1 (1786): 152–169.
Schweizer, Hans Rudolf. *Ästhetik als Philosophie der sinnlichen Erkenntnis: Eine Interpretation der "Aesthetica" A.G. Baumgartens mit teilweiser Wiedergabe der lateinischen Textes und deutscher Übersetzung*. Basel and Stuttgart: Schwabe, 1973.
Selle, Christian Gottlob. *Neue Beiträge zur Natur- und Arzeneiwissenschaft*. Berlin: Mylius, 1782–1786.
Selle, Christian Gottlob. "Von der analogischen Schlussart." *Berlinische Monatsschrift* 4 (1784): 185–186.
Semler, Johann Salamo. *Johann Salamo Semlers Lebensbeschreibung von ihm selbst abgefasst*. Halle, 1781–1782.
Smith, Adam. *Theory of Moral Sentiments*. Edinburgh: Millar, Kincaid, J. Bell, 1759.
Spinoza, Baruch. *Ethics* in *The Collected Works of Spinoza. Volume I*. Edited and translated by Edwin Curley. Princeton: Princeton University Press, 1985.
Stahl, Georg Ernest. *Collegium causuale magnum*. Edited and translated by Johannes Storch. Leipzig, 1733.
Stahl, Georg Ernest. *Dissertatio inauguralis medica de medicina medicinae curiosae*. Halle: Christian Henckel, 1714.
Stahl, Georg Ernest. *De passionibus animi corpus humanum varie alterantibus*. Halle, 1695. Translated as *Über die mannigfaltigen Einfluss der Gemüthsbewegungen auf den menschlichen Körper*. In *Georg Ernest Stahl*, by Bernward Josef Gottlieb. Leipzig: Johann Ambrosius Barth, 1961.
Stahl, Georg Ernest. "Über den mannigfaltigen Einfluss der Gemüthsbewegungen auf den menschlichen Körper." In *Sudhoffs Klassiker der Medizin*. Vol. 36. Leipzig: Johann Ambrosius Barth, 1961.
Sulzer, Johann Georg. *Allgemeine Theorie der schönen Künste*. 2 vols. Leipzig: Weidmanns, Erben, and Reich, 1771; 1773.
Sulzer, Johann Georg. *Kurzer Begriff aller Wissenschaften und anderer Theile der Gelehrsamkeit*. Leipzig: Johann Christian Langenheim, 1759.
Sulzer, Johann Georg. *Theorie der angenehmen und unangehmen Empfindungen*. Berlin: Friedrich Nicolai, 1762.
Sulzer, Johann Georg. *Vermischte Philosophische Schriften*. Part 2. Leipzig: Weidmanns Erben and Reich, 1773. 307–322.
Sulzer, Johann Georg. *Von dem Bewusstseyn und seinem Einfluss in unsere Urtheile* (1757). In *Vermischte Philosophische Schriften*. Part 1. Theil. Leipzig: Weidmanns Erben and Reich, 1773.

Sydenham, Thomas. *Observationes medicae*. London: Kettilby, 1676.
Tissot, Samuel André. *Von der Gesundheit der Gelehrten*. Zürich: Füßlin und Compagnie, 1768.
Unzer, Johann August. "Betrachtungen über des eligen Herrn Hofraths Stahls theoretischer Grundsatz in der Arzneywissenschaft." *Hamburgisches Magazin* 10.4 (1753): 400–421.
Unzer, Johann August, ed. *Der Arzt. Eine medicinische Wochenschrift*. Leipzig: Berth, 1764–1769.
Unzer, Johann August. *Gedanken vom Einfluss der Seele in ihren Körper*. Halle: Hemmerde, 1746.
Unzer, Johann August. Review of "Briefe eines Arztes an seinen Freund," by Ernst Platner. *Allgemeine Deutsche Bibliothek* 14.1 (1771): 81–90.
Weikard, Melchior Adam. *Der philosophische Arzt*. 3 vols. Frankfurt, Hanau, and Leipzig: Weickard, 1773–1775.
Westphal, Carl Friedrich Otto. "Die conträre Sexualempfindung: Symptom eines neuropathischen (psychopathischen) Zustandes." *Archiv für Psychiatrie und Nervenkrankheiten* 2.1 (1869): 73–108.
Whytt, Robert. *Observations on the Nature, Causes, and the Cure of the Disorders which have been commonly called Nervous, Hypochondriac or Hysteric*. Edinburgh: T. Becket and P. A. de Hondt, 1765.
Willis, Thomas. *Affectionum quae dicunter hystericae et hypochondriacae*. London: Allestry, 1670.
Willis, Thomas. *Pathologiae Cerebri et nervosi generis specimen*. Oxonii: Excudebat Guil, 1667.
Wolff, Christian. *Gesammelte Werke*. Edited by H. Arndt and J. Ecole. Hildesheim: G. Olms, 1962–.
Wolff, Christian. *Psychologia empirica, methodo scientifica per- tractata, qua ea, quae de anima humana indubia experientiae fide constant, continentur*. Francofurti and Lipsiae: officina libraria Rengeriana, 1732, 1738.
Wolff, Christian. *Vernünftige Gedanken von den Kräften des menschlichen Verstandes und ihrem richtigen Gebrauche in Erkenntnis der Wahrheit*. Halle: Rengerische Buchhandlung, 1713.
Wolff, Christian. *Vernünftige Gedanken von Gott, der Welt und der Seele des Menschen, auch allen Dingen überhaupt [Deutsche Metaphysik]*. Halle: in der Rengerischen Buchhandlung, 1719.
Zedler, Johann Heinrich. *Grosses vollständiges Universal-Lexicon aller Wissenschaften und Künste*. Halle and Leipzig: Verlag Johann Heinrich Zedler, 1731–1754.
Zimmermann, Johann Georg. *Von der Erfahrung in der Arzneykunst*. Brugg and Zürich: bey Heidegger und Compagnie, 1763–1764.

Secondary Sources

Adler, Hans. "Fundus Animae – Grund der Seele. Zur Gnoseologie des Dunklen in der Aufklärung." *Deutsche Vierteljahrsschrift für Literaturwissenschaft und Geistesgeschichte* 62.2 (1988): 197–220.
Agamben, Giorgio. *Homo Sacer: Sovereign Power and Bare Life*. Translated by Daniel Heller-Roazen. Stanford, CA: Stanford University Press, 1998.
Alt, Peter-André. *Schiller: Leben, Werk, Zeit*. 2 vols. München: C. H. Beck, 2009.

Ameriks, Karl. *Kant's Theory of Mind: An Analysis of the Paralogisms of Pure Reason*. Oxford: Oxford University Press, 1992; 2000.
Ankerloo, Bengt, Stuart Clark, and William Monter, eds., *Witchcraft and Magic in Europe*, vol. 4. *The Period of the Witch Trials*. London: Athlone Press, 2002.
Arnaud, Sabine. *On Hysteria. The Invention of Medical Category between 1670 and 1820*. Chicago: University of Chicago Press, 2015.
Aschauer, Lucia, Horst Gruner, and Tobias Gutman, eds. *Fallgeschichten. Text- und Wissensform exemplarischer Narrative in der Kultur der Moderne*. Würzburg: Königshausen & Neumann, 2015.
Bauman, Zygmunt. "Allosemitism: Premodern, Modern, Postmodern." In *Modernity, Culture, and "the Jew*," edited by Bryan Chenette and Laura Marcus, 143–156. Cambridge: Polity Press, 1998.
Beck, Lewis White. "Kant's Letter to Marcus Herz, February 21, 1771," translated by Arne Unhjem. In *Studies in the Philosophy of Kant*, 230–238. Minneapolis and New York: Bobbs-Merill, 1965.
Becker, Klaus. *Von der Kraft, den rechten Gesichtspunkt zu treffen. Ein spätes Echo auf Karl Phlipp Moritz und einige seiner Zeitgenossen – In einem Briefwechsel aus jüngerer Zeit*. Hannover: Wehrhahn, 2005.
Behrens, Rudolf, and Carsten Zelle, eds. *Der ärztliche Fallbericht. Epistemische Grundlagen und textuelle Strukturen dargestellter Beobachtung*. Wiesbaden: Harrassowitz, 2012.
Beiser, Frederick C. *Schiller as Philosopher: A Re-Examination*. Oxford: Oxford University Press, 2005.
Bell, Matthew. *The German Tradition of Psychology in Literature and Thought, 1780–1840*. Cambridge: Cambridge University Press, 2005.
Bennett, Benjamin. "The Irrelevance of Aesthetics and the De-Theorizing of Self in 'Classical' Weimar." In *The Camden History of German Literature*. Vol. 7. *The Literature of Weimar Classicism*, edited by Simon Richter, 295–321. Rochester, NY: Camden House, 2001.
Berlant, Lauren Gail. "On the Case." *Critical Inquiry* 33.4 (2007): 663–672.
Bernheimer, Charles, and Claire Kahane, eds., *In Dora's Case: Freud, Hysteria, Feminism*. New York: Columbia University Press, 1985.
Bezold, Raimund. *Popularphilosophie und Erfahrungsseelenkunde und im von Werk Karl Philipp Moritz*. Würzburg: Königshausen & Neumann, 1984.
Bilu, Yoram. "The Taming of the Deviants and Beyond: An Analysis of *Dibbuk* Possession and Exorcism in Judaism." In *The Psychoanalytic Study of Society*. Vol. 11. *Essays in honor of Wemer Muensterberger*, edited by L. Bryce Boyer and Simon A. Grolnick, 1–32. London and Hillsdale, NJ: Analytic Press, 1985.
Black, Joel. *The Reality Effect: Film, Culture and the Graphic Imperative*. New York: Routledge, 2002.
Blank-Panitzsch, Margarete. "Eine Krankengeschichte Herman Boerhaaves und ihre Stellung in der Geschichte der Klinik." *Archiv für Geschichte der Medizin* 27.1–2 (1934): 51–86.
Böhm, Klaus, Carl O. Köhler, and Rainer Thome. *Historie der Krankengeschichte*. New York and Stuttgart: F. K. Schattauer, 1978.
Böhme, Hartmut, and Gernot Böhme. *Das Andere der Vernunft: Zur Entwicklung der Rationalitätsstrukturen am Beispiel Kants*. Frankfurt: Suhrkamp, 1983.
Bölts, Stephanie. *Krankheiten und Textgattungen: Gattungsspezifisches Wissen in Literatur und Medizin um 1800*. Berlin: de Gruyter, 2016.

Borchers, Stefan. *Die Erzeugung des 'ganzen Menschen'. Zur Entstehung von Anthropologie und Ästhetik an der Universität Halle im 18. Jahrhundert*. Berlin and Boston: de Gruyter, 2011.
Boss, Jeffrey N. M. "The Seventeenth-Century Transformation of the Hysteric Affection and Sydenham's Baconian Medicine." *Psychological Medicine* 9.2 (1979): 221–234.
Boulby, Mark. *Karl Philipp Moritz: At the Fringe of Genius*. Toronto: University of Toronto Press, 1979.
Boulby, Mark. "Marcus Herz the Psychologist." *Jahrbuch für internationale Germanistik*. Reihe A. 8.4 (1980): 327–331.
Bourdieu, Pierre. *Distinction. A Social Critique of the Judgment of Taste*. New York: Routledge, 1986.
Bowie, Andrew. *Aesthetics and Subjectivity: From Kant to Nietzsche*. Manchester: Manchester University Press, 1990.
Broman, Thomas H. *The Transformation of German Academic Medicine, 1750–1820*. Cambridge: Cambridge University Press, 1996; 2002.
Bronfen, Elisabeth. *The Knotted Subject: Hysteria and Its Discontents*. Princeton, NJ: Princeton University Press, 1998.
Bruner, Jerome. "The Narrative Construction of Reality." *Critical Inquiry* 18.1 (1991): 1–21.
Buchenau, Stefanie. "Markus Herz. Kritik und Religion." In *Aufklärung und Religion. Neue Perspektiven*, edited by Michael Hofmann and Carsten Zelle, 223–242. Hannover: Wehrhahn, 2010.
Campe, Rüdiger. "Von Fall zu Fall. Goethes *Werther*, Büchners *Lenz*." In *Was der Fall ist. Casus und Lapsus*, edited by Inka Mülder-Bach and Michael Ott, 33–55. München: Fink, 2014.
Canguilhem, Georges. *The Normal and the Pathological* (1943). New York: Zone Books, 1991.
Chajes, J. H. *Between Worlds: Dybbuks, Exorcists, and Early Modern Judaism*. Philadelphia: University of Pennsylvania Press, 2005.
Chajes, J. H. "He Said She Said: Hearing the Voices of Pneumatic Early Modern Jewish Women Author(s)." *Nashim: A Journal of Jewish Women's Studies & Gender Issues*. Jewish Women's Spirituality. 10.2 (Fall 5766/2005): 99–125.
Chaouli, Michel. *Thinking with Kant's Critique of Judgment*. Cambridge, MA: Harvard University Press, 2017.
Charon, Rita. *Narrative Medicine. Honoring the Stories of Illness*. Oxford: Oxford University Press, 2008.
Childress, James. F. "Narrative(s) Versus Norm(s): A Misplaced Debate in Bio-Ethics." In *Stories and their Limits: Narrative Approaches to Bioethis*, edited by Hilde Lindemann Nelson, 252–271. New York and London: Routledge, 1997.
Clare, Anthony. "Freud's Cases: The Clinical Basis of Psychoanalysis." In *The Anatomy of Madness: Essays in the History of Psychiatry*. Vol. 1, *People and Ideas*, edited by W. F. Bynum, Roy Porter, and Michael Shepherd, 271–288. London and New York: Routledge, 1985.
Class, Monika. "K. P. Moritz's Case Poetics: Aesthetic Autonomy Reconsidered." *Literature and Medicine* 32.1 (2014): 46–73.
Clouser, K. Danner. "Bioethics and Philosophy." *Hastings Center Report* 23.6 (1993): 10–11.
Cohn, Dorrit. "Freud's Case Histories and the Question of Fictionality." in *Telling Facts: History and Narration in Psychoanalysis*, edited by Joseph H. Smith, 21–47. Baltimore: Johns Hopkins University Press, 1992; repr. in *Oxford German Studies* 25 (1997): 1–23.

Cordemann, Claas. *Herders Christlicher Monismus. Eine Studie zur Grundlegung von Johann Gottfried Herders Christologie und Humanitätsideal*. Tübingen: Mohr-Siebeck, 2010.
Crombie, A. C. *Styles of Scientific Thinking in the European Tradition*. Vol. 2. *The History of Argument and Explanation Especially in the Mathematical and Biomedical* Sciences and Arts. London: Duckworth, 1994.
Cunningham, Andrew, and Roger French, eds. *The Medical Enlightenment of the Eighteenth Century*. New York and Cambridge: Cambridge University Press, 1990.
Dainat, Holger. "Der unglückliche Mörder: Zur Kriminalgeschichte der deutschen Spätaufklärung." *Zeitschrift für deutsche Philologie* 107 (1988): 517–541.
Danziger, Kurt. *Constructing the Subject: Historical Origins of Psychological Research*. Cambridge: Cambridge University Press, 1990.
Danziger, Kurt. *Naming the Mind: How Psychology Found Its Language*. London: Sage, 1997.
Daston, Lorraine. "Strange Facts, Plain Facts, and the Texture of Scientific Experience in the Enlightenment." In *Proof and Persuasion. Essays on Authority, Objectivity and Evidence*, edited by Suzanne Marchand and Elisabeth Lunbeck, 42–59. Brussels: Brepols, 1996.
Daston, Lorraine, and Peter Galison. *Objectivity*. Cambridge: Cambridge University Press, 2007.
Davies, Martin. *Identity or History?: Marcus Herz and the End of Enlightenment*. Detroit: Wayne State University Press, 1995.
Davies, Martin. "Moritz und die aufklärerische Berliner Medizin." In *Karl Philip Moritz und das 18. Jahrhundert*. Edited by Martin Fontius and Anneliese Klingenberg, 215–226. Tübingen: Max Niemeyer, 1995.
Davis, Lennard J. *Obsession: A History*. Chicago: University of Chicago Press, 2009.
Dear, Peter. *Discipline and Experience. The Mathematical Way in the Scientific Revolution*. Chicago: University of Chicago Press, 1995.
de Ceglia, Francesco Paolo. "Hoffmann and Stahl: Documents and Reflections on the Dispute." *History of Universities* 22 (2007): 98–140.
de Certeau, Michel. *The Writing of History*. Translated by Tom Conley. New York: Columbia University Press, 1992.
Dedert, Hartmut, Hubert Gersch, Stephan Oswald, and Reinard Spiess. "J.-F. Oberlin: Herr L. . . . Edition des bisher unveröffentlichten Manuskripts. Ein Beitrag zur Büchner- und Lenz-Forschung." *Revue des Langues Vivants* 42 (1976): 357–385.
Derrida, Jacques. *Specters of Marx*. New York and London: Routledge, 1994.
Dethlefs, Hans Joachim. "Ästhetisches Glücksversprechen. Haltung in der Kunstanschauung von Johann Heinrich Merck." *Das achtzehnte Jahrhundert* 32.1 (2008): 74–95.
Dewhurst, Kenneth, and Nigel Reeve, eds. *Friedrich Schiller. Medicine, Psychology, Literature*. Berkeley and Los Angeles: University of California Press, 1978.
Dickson, Sheila, Stefan Goldmann, and Christof Wingertszahn, eds. *"Fakta, und kein morlalisches Geschwätz": Zu den Fallgeschichten im Magazin zur Erfahrungsseelenkunde (1783–1793)*. Göttingen: Wallstein, 2011.
Didi-Huberman, Georges. *Invention of Hysteria: Charcot and the Photographic Iconography of the Salpêtriere*. Cambridge, MA: MIT Press, 2004. http://charcot.bum.jussieu.fr/matiere.php?NF=7
Diethelm, Oskar, and Thomas F. Heffernan. "Felix Platter and Psychiatry." *Journal of the History of the Behavioral Sciences* 1.1 (1965): 10–23.

Dinges, Martin. "Medizinische Aufklärung bei Johann Georg Zimmermann. Zum Verhältnis von Macht und Wissen bei einem Arzt der Aufklärung." In *Schweizer im Berlin des 18. Jahrhunderts*, edited by M. Fontius and H. Holzhey, 138–150. Oldenbourg 1996.

Dinges, Martin. "Medizinische Policey zwischen Heilkundigen und Patienten (1750–1830)." In *Polizey und frühneuzeitliche Gesellschaft*, edited by Karl Härter, 263–295. Frankfurt am Main: Vittorio Klostermann, 2000.

Dörner, Klaus. *Madmen and the Bourgeoisie: A Social History of Insanity and Psychiatry*. Translated by Joachim Neugroschel and Jean Steinberg. Oxford: Basil Blackwell, 1981.

Duden, Barbara. *Geschichte unter der Haut. Ein Eisenacher Arzt und seine Patientinnen um 1730*. Stuttgart: J. B. Metzler, 1987.

Duden, Barbara. *The Woman Beneath the Skin: A Doctor's Patients in Eighteenth-Century Germany*. Translated by Thomas Dunlap. Cambridge, MA: Harvard University Press, 1998.

Dumont, Altrud. "Das Interessante – Theorie und narrative Praxis. Friedrich Schlegel und E.T.A. Hoffmann." *Weimarer Beiträge* 38.3 (1992): 430–447.

Duncan, Bruce. *Goethe's Werther and the Critics*. Rochester NY: Camden House, 2005.

Dürbeck, Gabriele. "Aporien der Erfahrungsseelenkunde." In *Karl Philipp Moritz und das 18. Jahrhundert. Bestandsaufnahmen, Korrekturen, Neuansätze*, edited by Annaliese Klingenberg and Martin Fontius, 227–235. Tübingen: Niemeyer, 1995.

Dürbeck, Gabriele. *Einbildungskraft und Aufklärung. Perspektiven der Philosophie, Anthropologie und Ästhetik um 1750*. Tübingen: Niemeyer, 1998.

Dürbeck, Gabriele. "Physiologischer Mechanismus und aesthetische Therapie: Ernst Anton Nicolais Schriften zur Psychopathologie." In *Vernünftige Ärzte. Hallesche Psychomediziner und die Anfänge der Anthropologie in der deutschsprachigen Frühaufklärung*, edited by Carsten Zelle, 104–119. Tübingen: Niemeyer, 2001.

Dürbeck, Gabriele. "'Reizende und reizbare Einbildungskraft': Anthropologische Ansätze bei Johann Gottlob Krüger und Albrecht von Haller." In *Reiz – Imagination – Aufmerksamkeit: Erregung und Steuerung von Einbildungskraft im klassischen Zeitalter*, edited by Jörn Steigerwald and Daniela Watzke, 225–245. Würzburg: Königshausen & Neumann, 2003.

Düwell, Susanne, and Nicolas Pethes. "'Erfahrungsseelenkunde' als 'innere Geschichte des Menschen': Marcus Herz Beschreibung seiner eignen Krankheit und die Anfänge psychologischer Falldarstellungen." In *Gattungswissen. Wissenspoetologie und literarische Form*, edited by Michael Bies, Michael Gamper, and Ingrid Kleeberg, 74–95. Göttingen: Wallstein, 2013.

Düwell, Susanne, and Nicolas Pethes, eds. *Fall– Fallgeschichte – Fallstudie. Theorie und Geschichte einer Wissensform*. Frankfurt and New York: Campus, 2014.

Düwell, Susanne, and Nicolas Pethes. "Noch nicht Wissen. Die Fallsammlung als Prototheorie in Zeitschriften der Spätaufklärung." In *Literatur und Nicht-Wissen: Historische Konstellationen 1730–1930*, edited by Michael Bies and Michael Gamper, 131–148. Zürich: Diaphanes, 2012.

Dyck, Corey. *Kant and Rational Psychology*. Oxford: Oxford University Press, 2014.

Eagleton, Terry. *The Ideology of the Aesthetic*. Oxford: Oxford University Press, 1990.

Eckermann, Johann Peter. *Gespräche mit Goethe in den letzten Jahren seines Lebens*. Edited by Fritz Bergemann. Frankfurt: Insel, 1981.

Efron, John. *Medicine and the German Jews: A History*. New Haven, CT: Yale University Press, 2008.

Ellenberger, Henri F. *The Discovery of the Unconscious: The History and Evolution of Dynamic Psychiatry*. New York: Basic Books, 1970.

Ellis, John M. *Narration in the German Novella*. London and New York: Cambridge University Press, 1974.
Epstein, Julia. *Altered Conditions: Disease, Medicine and Storytelling*. New York and London: Routledge, 1995.
Euler, Werner. "*Commercium mentis et corporis*? Ernst Platners medizinische Anthropologie in der Kritik von Marcus Herz und Immanuel Kant." In *Aufklärung: Interdisziplinäres Jahrbuch zur Erforschung des 18. Jahrhunderts*, vol. 19, 21–68. Hamburg: F. Meiner, 2007.
Faber, Diana. "Hysteria in the Eighteenth Century." In *Brain, Mind and Medicine: Essays in Eighteenth-Century Neuroscience*, edited by Harry Whitaker, C. U. M. Smith, and Stanley Finger, 321–330. New York: Springer, 2007.
Faierstein, Morris M. "The *Dibbuk* in the *Mayse Bukh*." *Shofar: An Interdisciplinary Journal of Jewish Studies* 30.1 (2011): 94–103.
Feiner, Shmuel. *The Jewish Enlightenment*. Translated by Chaya Naor. Philadelphia: University of Pennsylvania Press, 2011.
Fink, Gonthier-Louis. "Théologie, psychologie et sociologie du crime. Le conte moral de Schubart à Schiller." *Recherches germaniques* 6 (1976): 55–111.
Fisch, Harold. "The Messianic Politics of Menassah ben Israel." In *Menasseh Ben Israel and His World*, edited by Yôsēf Qaplan, Richard Henry Popkin, and Henry Méchoulan, 228–239. London: Brill, 1989.
Fludernik, Monika. *An Introduction to Narratology*. Translated by Patricia Häusler-Greenfield and Monika Fludernik. London: Routledge, 2009.
Forrester, John. "If p, then what? Thinking in Cases." *History of the Human Sciences* 9.3 (1996): 1–25.
Forrester, John. *Thinking in Cases*. Cambridge and Malden, MA: Polity, 2017.
Förster, Michael. "Herder und Spinoza." In *Spinoza and German Idealism*, edited by Eckhart Förster and Yizak Y. Melamed, 59–84. Cambridge: Cambridge University Press, 2012.
Fossaluzza, Cristina. *Subjektiver Antisubjektivismus: Karl Philipp Moritz als Diagnostiker seiner Zeit*. Hannover-Latzen: Wehrhahn Verlag, 2006.
Foucault, Michel. *The Birth of the Clinic: An Archeology of Medical Perception*. Translated by A. M. Sheridan Smith. New York: Random House, 1979.
Foucault, Michel. *Discipline and Punish: The Birth of the Prison*. Translated by Alan Sheridan. New York: Random House, 1979.
Foucault, Michel. *Geschichte der Gouvernementalität I: Sicherheit, Territorium, Bevölkerung. Vorlesung am Collège de France 1977–1978*. Edited by Michel Senellart. Translated by Claudia Brede-Konersmann and Jürgen Schröder. Frankfurt: Suhrkamp, 2004.
Foucault, Michel. *Hermeneutics of the Subject: Lectures at the Collège de France, 1981–82*. Edited by Frédéric Gros. Translated by Graham Burchell. New York: Picador, 2001; Palgrave Macmillan, 2005.
Foucault, Michel. *History of Madness*. Edited by Jean Khalfa. Translated by Jonathan Murphy and Jean Khalfa. London and New York: Routledge, 2006.
Foucault, Michel. *The History of Sexuality*. Vol. 1. *An Introduction*. Translated by Robert Hurley. New York: Random House, 1978.
Foucault, Michel. *Madness and Civilization*. London and New York: Routledge, 2001.
Foucault, Michel. "Die Politik der Gesundheit im 18. Jahrhundert." Translated by Daniel Eckert and Wolfgang Neurath. *Österreichische Zeitschrift für Geschichtswissenschaften* 7.3 (1996): 311–326.
Foucault, Michel. *Power*. Edited by James D. Faubion. New York: New Press, 2000

Foucault, Michel. *Security, Territory, Population: Lectures at the College de France, 1977–1978*. Edited by Michel Senellart. New York: Palgrave MacMillan, 2007.
Foucault, Michel. "The Subject and Power." *Critical Inquiry* 8.4 (1982): 777–795.
Freud, Sigmund, "A Child is Being Beaten – A Contribution to the Study of the Origins of Sexual Perversions." *International Journal of Psychoanalysis* 1 (1920): 371–395.
Freud, Sigmund. *Studies in Hysteria*. New Tork: Basic Books, 2000.
Freud, Sigmund, and Joseph Breuer. *Studien über Hysterie*. Frankfurt: Fischer Verlag, 1991.
Freud, Sigmund, and Joseph Breuer. *Studies on Hysteria*. Translated by James Strachey. London: Hogarth Press, 1955.
Frevert, Ute. *Krankheit als Politisches Problem 1770–1880*. Göttingen: Vandenhoeck & Ruprecht, 1984.
Frey, Christiane. "Fallgeschichte." In *Literatur und Wissen. Ein interdisziplinäres Handbuch*, edited by Roland Borgards, Harald Neumeyer, Nicolas Pethes, and Yvonne Wübben, 282–287. Stuttgart: J. B. Metzler, 2013.
Frey, Christiane."'Ist das nicht der Fall der Krankheit?' Der literarische Fall am Beispiel von Goethes *Werther*." *Zeitschrift für Germanistik* 19.2 (2009): 317–329.
Gailus, Andreas. "*Anton Reiser*, Case History, and the Emergence of Empirical Psychology." In *A New History of German Literature*, edited by David Wellbery, Judith Ryan, and Hans-Ulrich Gumbrech, 409–414. Cambridge, MA: Harvard University Press, 2005.
Gailus, Andreas."A Case of Individuality: Karl Philipp Moritz and the Magazine for Empirical Psychology." *New German Critique* 79 (2000): 67–105.
Galison, Peter. "Specific Theory." *Critical Inquiry* 30.2 (2004): 379–383.
Gelfand, Toby, and John Kerr, eds. *Freud and the History of Psychoanalysis*. London and Hillsdale, NJ: Taylor & Francis, 1992.
Gemünden, Gerd. "The Enigma of Hermeneutics: The Case of Kaspar Hauser." In *Reading after Foucault: Institutions, Disciplines, and Technologies of the Self in Germany, 1750–1830*, edited by Robert S. Leventhal, 127–150. Detroit: Wayne State University Press, 1994.
Gersch, Hubert. *Der Text, der (produktive) Unverstand des Abschreibers und die Literaturgeschichte: Johann Friedrich Oberlins Bericht "Herr L..". und die Textüberlieferung bis zu Georg Büchners "Lenz"–Entwurf*. Berlin: de Gruyter, 1998.
Gessinger, Joachim. "Das Mädchen, der Arzt, und der böse Geist." *Osnabrücker Beiträge zur Sprachtheorie* 37 (1987), 161–192.
Geyer-Kordesch, Johanna. "Georg Ernest Stahl's Radical Pietist Medicine and Its Influence on the German Enlightenment." In *The Medical Enlightenment of the Eighteenth Century*, edited by Andrew Cunningham and Roger French, 67–87. Cambridge, New York, and Melbourne: Cambridge University Press, 1990.
Geyer-Kordesch, Johanna. "Medizinische Fallbeschreibungen und ihre Bedeutung in der Wissensreform des 17. und 18. Jahrhunderts." *Medizin, Gesellschaft, Geschichte* 9 (1990): 7–19.
Geyer-Kordesch, Johanna. *Pietismus, Medizin, und Aufklärung im Preußen im 18. Jahrhundert*. Tübingen: Niemeyer, 1996; new title *Das Leben und Werk Georg Ernst Stahls*. Berlin: de Gruyter, 2000.
Gilman, Sander L. *The Case of Freud. Medicine and Identity at the Fin de Siécle*. Baltimore: Johns Hopkins University Press, 1993.
Ginzburg, Carlo. "Ein Plädoyer für den Casus." In *Fallstudien: Theorie – Geschichte – Methode*, edited by Johannes Süßmann, Suzanne Scholz, and Gisela Engel, 29–48. Berlin: Trafo, 2007.

Goldish, Matt, ed. *Spirit Possession in Judaism: Cases and Contexts from the Middle Ages to the Present.* Detroit: Wayne State University Press, 2003.

Goldmann, Stefan. "Kasus – Krankengeschichte – Novelle." In *"Fakta, und kein moralisches Geschwätz." Zu den Fallgeschichten im Magazin zur Erfahrungsseelenkunde* (1783–1793), edited by Sheila Dickson, Stefan Goldmann, and Christof Wingertszahn, 33–64. Göttingen: Wallstein Verlag, 2011.

Goldstein, Jan E. *Console and Classify: The French Psychiatric Profession in the Nineteenth Century.* Chicago: University of Chicago Press, 2002.

Goulemot, Jean Marie. "Literary Practices: Publicing the Private." In *A History of Private Life*, edited by Roger Chartier and Philipe Ariès, translated by Arthur Goldhammer, vol. 3, 364–392. Cambridge: Cambridge University Press, 1989.

Greenblatt, Stephen. "Fiction and Friction." In *Reconstructing Individualism: Autonomy, Individuality and the Self in Western Thought*, edited by Thomas C. Heller, Morton Sosna, and David E. Wellbery, 30–52. Stanford, CA: Stanford University Press, 1986.

Greiner, Bernhard. "'that until now, the inner world of man has been given ... such unimaginative treatment': Constructions of Interiority around 1800." In *Rethinking Emotion. Interiority and Exteriority in Pre-Modern, Modern and Contemporary Thought*, edited by Rüdiger Campe and Julia Weber, 137–171. Berlin: de Gruyter, 2014.

Guyer, Paul. "18th Century German Aesthetics." *Stanford Encyclopedia of Philosophy* (Winter 2016), edited by Edward N. Zalta. First published 16 January 2007; substantive revision 3 March 2014. https://plato.stanford.edu/archives/win2016/entries/aesthetics-18th-german/ (accessed 22 January 2017).

Hacking, Ian. "Biopower and the Avalanche of Printed Numbers." *Humanities in Society* 5 (1982): 279–295.

Hacking, Ian. "Making Up People." In *Reconstructing Individualism: Autonomy, Individuality and the Self in Western Thought*, edited by Thomas C. Heller, Morton Sosna, and David E. Wellbery, 222–236. Stanford, CA: Stanford University Press, 1986.

Hacking, Ian. *Rewriting the Soul: Multiple Personality and the Sciences of Memory.* Princeton, NJ: Princeton University Press, 1995.

Hacking, Ian. "Styles of Scientific Reasoning." In *Post-analytic Philosophy*, edited by John Rajchman and Cornel West, 145–164. New York: Academic Press, 1985.

Hacking, Ian. *The Taming of Chance.* Cambridge: Cambridge University Press, 1990.

Hansen, Leeann. "From Enlightenment to *Naturphilosophie*: Marcus Herz, Johann Christian Reil, and the Problem of Border Crossings." *Journal of the History of Biology* 26.1 (1993): 39–64.

Hasselmeier, Hans-Heinrich. *Die Stellung der Juden in Schaumburg-Lippe von 1648 bis zur Emanzipation.* Bückeburg: Verlag Grimme, 1967.

Hatfield, Gary. "Empirical, Rational, and Transcendental Psychology: Psychology as Science and as Philosophy." In *Cambridge Companion to Kant*, edited by Paul Guyer, 200–227. Cambridge: Cambridge University Press, 1992.

Hatfield, Gary. "Psychology as a Natural Science in the Eighteenth Century." *IRCS Technical Report Series* 153 (May). 1994 http://repository.upenn.edu/ircs_reports/153 (accessed 18 January 2019).

Heinz, Jutta. *Wissen von Menschen und Erzählen vom Einzelfall. Untersuchungen zum anthropologischen Roman der Spätaufklärung.* Berlin and New York: de Gruyter, 1996.

Helm, Jürgen. "Hallesche Medizin zwischen Pietismus und Frühaufklärung." In *Universitäten und Aufklärung*, edited by Notker Hammerstein, 63–95. Göttingen: Wallstein, 1995.

Helm, Jürgen. "'observatio' and 'experientia' – Fallgeschichten in der Medizin des 18. Jahrhunderts." In *Aus Gottes Wort und eigener Erfahrung gezeiget*: *Erfahrung – Glauben, Bekennen und Gestalten im Pietismus*, edited Christian Soboth and Udo Sträter, 361–376. Halle: Harrassowitz, 2009.

Henrich, Dieter. "Fichte's Original Insight," translated by David Lachterman. *Contemporary German Philosophy* 1 (1982): 15–53.

Hess, Volker. "*Observatio* und *Casus*: Status und Funktion der medizinischen Fallgeschichte." In *Fall – Fallgeschichte – Fallstudie. Theorie und Geschichte einer Wissensform*, edited by Susanne Düwell and Nicolas Pethes, 34–59. Frankfurt and New York: Campus, 2011.

Hess, Volker, and J. Andrew Cunningham. "Case and Series: Medical Knowledge and Paper Technology, 1600–1900." *History of Science* 48.3–4 (2010): 287–314.

Heydebrand, Renate. "Innerlichkeit." In *Historisches Wörterbuch der Philosophie*, edited by Joachim Ritter and Karlfried Gründer, vol. 4, 386–388. Basel: Schwabe, 1976.

Hinrichs, Carl. *Preußentum und Pietismus. Der Pietismus in Brandenburg-Preußen als religiös-soziale Reformbewegung*. Göttingen: Vandenhoeck & Reprecht, 1971.

Hoffmann-Richter, Ulrike, and Asmus Finzen. "Die psychiatrische Krankengeschichte - eine vernachlässigte Quelle." *BIOS* 11 (1998): 280–297.

van Hoorn, Tanja. *Entwurf einer Psychophysiologie des Menschen. Johann Gottlob Krügers Grundriß eines neuen Lehrgebäudes der Artzneygelahrtheit (1745)*. Hannover-Laatzen: Wehrhahn, 2006.

van Hoorn, Tanja, and Yvonne Wübben, "Zwischen Experimentalphysik und Experimentalseelenlehre." In *'Allerhand nützlicher Versuche': Empirische Wissenskultur in Halle und Göttingen (1720–1750)*, edited by van Hoorn and Wübben. Hannover: Wehrhahn Verlag, 2009. 7–20.

Horstmann, Rolf-Peter. "Kant's Paralogismen." *Kant-Studien* 84.4 (1993): 408–425.

Huppmann, Gernot. "Marcus Herz (1747–1803): Arzt, Philosoph und Medizinischer Psychologe." *Zeitschrift für medizinische Psychologie* 1 (1992): 90–95.

Huppmann, Gernot. "Marginalien zur medizinischen Psychologie des Stahlantipoden Friedrich Hoffmann (1660–1742)." *Schriftenreihe der deutschen Gesellschaft für die Geschichte der Nervenheilkunde* 3 (1997): 95–103.

Huttmann, Arnold. "Eine imaginäre Krankheit: Der Polyp des Herzens." *Medizinhistorisches Journal* 18.1–2 (1983): 43–51.

Israël, Lucien. *L'hysterique, le sexe, et le medicin*. Paris: Masson, 1976.

Izenberg, Gerald N. *Impossible Individuality: Romanticism, Revolution, and the Origins of Modern Selfhood, 1797–1802*. Princeton, NJ: Princeton University Press, 1992.

Jackson, Stanley W. "Melancholia and the Waning of Humoral Theory." *Journal of the History of Medicine and Allied Sciences* 33.3 (1978): 367–376.

Jäger, Hans-Wolf. *Politische Kategorien in der Poetik und Rhetorik der zweiten Hälfte des 18. Jahrhunderts*. Stuttgart: Metzler, 1970.

Jannidis, Fotis. "'Individuum est ineffable'. Zur Veränderung der Individualitätssemantik im 18. Jahrhundert." *Aufklärung* 9.2 (1996): 77–110.

Jardine, Lisa. *Ingenious Pursuits: Building the Scientific Revolution*. New York: Anchor Books, 2000.

Jerusalem, Carl Wilhelm. "*...Kein Geistlicher hat ihn begleitet*": *Dokumente aus dem Nachlass von Johann Christian Kestner über den Selbstmord Carl Wilhelm Jerusalems am 30. Oktober 1772 in Wetzlar*. Edited by Michael Wenzel. Wetzlar: Michael Imhof Verlag, 2015.

The Jewish Encyclopedia. New York: Funk & Wagnalls. 1901–1906.

Jolles, André. *Einfache Formen*. Halle (Saale): Niemeyer, 1930; Tübingen: Niemeyer, 1968.
Jonsen, Albert R., and Stephen Toulmin. *The Abuse of Casuistry: A History of Moral Reasoning*. Berkeley, Los Angeles, and London: University of California Press, 1988.
Jütte, Robert. "Vom medizinischen Casus zur Krankengeschichte." *Berichte zur Wissenschaftsgeschichte* 15.1 (1992): 50–52.
Kaiser, Gerhard. *Pietismus und Patriotismus im literarischen Deutschland*. Frankfurt am Main: Athenäum, 1973.
Kaufmann, Doris. *Aufklärung, bürgerliche Selbsterfahrung und die Erfindung der Psychiatrie in Deutschland, 1770–1850*. Göttingen: Vandenhoeck & Ruprecht, 1995; 1996.
Kennedy, Margaret. *A Curious Literature: Reading the Medical Case History from the Royal Society to Freud*. PhD. Diss., Brown University, 2000.
Keohane, Nannerl O. "Montaigne's Individualism." *Political Theory* 5.3 (1977): 363–390.
Kiceluk, Stephanie. "The Patient as Sign and Story: Disease Pictures, Life Stories, and the First Psychoanlaytic Case History." *Journal of Clinical Psychoanalysis* 1.3 (1992): 333–368.
Killy, Walther. "Abel, Jacob Friedrich (1751–1829)." In *Killy Literaturlexikon. Autoren und Werke des deutschsprachigen Kulturraums*, edited by Wilhelm Kühlman and Achim Aurnhammer. 13 vols., vol. 1, 5–7. Berlin and New York: de Gruyter, 2008–2012.
King, Helen. "Once Upon a Text: Hysteria from Hippocrates." In *Hysteria beyond Freud*, edited by Sander L. Gilman, Helen King, Roy Porter, G. S. Rousseau, and Elaine Showalter, 3–90. Berkeley and Los Angeles: University of California Press, 1993.
Kitcher, Patricia. "Kant's Paralogisms." *Philosophical Review* 91.4 (1982): 515–547.
Kittler, Friedrich. "Das Subjekt als Beamte." In *Die Frage nach dem Subjekt*, edited by Manfred Frank, Gérard Raulet, and Willem van Reijen, 401–420. Frankfurt: Suhrkamp, 1988.
Klemme, Heiner F., Gideon Stiening, and Falk Wunderlich, eds. *Michael Hißmann (1742–1784): Ein materialistischer Philosoph der deutschen Aufklärung*. Berlin: Akademie-Verlag, 2013. er, 2013.
Kolnai, Aurel. "On the Concept of the Interesting." In *Aesthetics in the Modern World*, edited by Harold Osborne, 166–187. London: Thames & Hudson, 1968.
Koopmann, Helmut. *Schiller-Kommentar*. 2 vols. München: Winkler, 1969.
Koschorke, Albrecht. "Alphabetisation und Empfindsamkeit." In *Der ganze Mensch. Anthropologie und Literatur im 18. Jahrhundert*, edited by Hans Jürgen Schings, 605–628. Stuttgart and Weimar: Metzler, 1994.
Koschorke, Albrecht. *Körperströme und Schriftverkehr. Mediologie des 18. Jahrhunderts*. München: W. Fink, 1999.
Koschorke, Albrecht. "Physiological Self-Regulation: The Eighteenth-Century Modernization of the Human Body." *MLN* 123.3 (2008): 469–484.
Koschorke, Albrecht. "Poiesis des Leibes: Johann Christian Reils romantische Medizin." In *Romantische Wissenspoetik. Die Künst und die Wissenschaften um 1800*, edited by Gabriele Brandstetter and Gerhard Neumann, 259–272. Würzburg: Königshausen & Neumann, 2004.
Koschorke, Albrecht. "Wissenschaft des Arbiträren. Die Revolutionierung der Sinnesphysiologie und die Entstehung der modernen Hermeneutik um 1800." In *Poetologie des Wissens um 1800*, edited by Joseph Vogl, 19–52. München: Fink, 1999.
Koselleck, Reinhard. *Kritik und Krise. Eine Studie zur Pathogenese der bürgerlichen Welt*. Freiburg and München: K. Alber, 1959.

Košenina, Alexander. "Ernst Platner." In *Neue Deutsche Biographie (NDB)*, edited by the Historical Commission at the Bavarian Academy of Sciences, vol. 20, 513–514. Berlin: Duncker & Humblot, 2001.

Košenina, Alexander. *Ernst Platners Anthropologie und Philosophie. Der "philosophische Arzt" und seine Wirkung auf Johann Karl Wezel und Jean Paul.* Würzburg: Königshausen & Neumann, 1989.

Košenina, Alexander. "Es 'ist also keine dichterische Erfindung': Die Geschichte vom Bauernburschen in Goethes *Werther* und die Kriminalliteratur der Aufklärung." *Goethe Jahrbuch* 124 (2007): 189–197.

Košenina, Alexander. *Karl Philipp Moritz. Literarische Experimente auf dem Weg zum psychologischen Roman.* Göttingen: Wallstein, 2006.

Košenina, Alexander. *Literarische Anthropologie: Die Neuentdeckung des Menschen.* Berlin: de Gruyter, 2008.

Košenina, Alexander. "Schiller's Poetics of Crime." In *Schiller: National Poet – Poet of Nations*, edited Nicholas Martin, 241–256. Amsterdam and New York: Rodopi, 2006.

Košenina, Alexander. "Schiller und die Tradition der (kriminal)psychologischen Fallgeschichte bei Goethe, Meißner, Moritz und Spieß." In *Friedrich Schiller und Europa: Ästhetik, Politik, Geschichte*, edited by Alice Staskova, 119–139. Heidelberg: Winter, 2007.

Košenina, Alexander. "'Tiefere Blicke in das Menschenherz': Schiller und Pitaval." *Germanisch-romanische Monatsschrift* 55.4 (2005): 383–395.

Kull, Carolin. "Marcus Herz: An Herrn Doktor J. in Königsberg. Psychologische Beschreibung seiner eigenen Krankheit." In *Casus. Von Hoffmanns Erzählungen zu Freuds Novellen. Eine Anthologie der Fachprosagattung 'Fallerzählung,'* edited by Carsten Zelle, 113–123. Hannover: Wehrhahn, 2015.

Langholf, Volker. *Medical Theories in Hippocrates: Early Texts and the 'Epidemics.'* Berlin: de Gruyter, 1992.

Laqueur, Thomas W. "Bodies, Details, and Humanitarian Narrative." In *The New Cultural History*, edited by Lynn Hunt, 176–204. Berkeley: University of California Press, 1989.

Leary, David E. "The Historical Foundation of Herbart's Mathematization of Psychology." *Journal of the History of the Behavioral Sciences* 16.2 (1980): 150–163.

Leary, David E. "The Philosophical Development of the Conception of Psychology in Germany, 1780–1850." *Journal of the History of the Behavioral Sciences* 14.2 (1978): 113–121.

Leder, Christoph Maria. *Die Grenzgänge des Marcus Herz. Beruf, Haltung, und Identität eines jüdischen Arztes gegen Ende des 18. Jahrhunderts.* München: Waxmann, 2007.

Lehmann, Johannes F. "Erfinden, was der Fall ist. Fallgeschichte und Rahmen bei Schiller, Buechner und Musil." *Zeitschrift für Germanistik* 19.2 (2009): 361–380.

Leibrand, Annemarie, and Werner Leibrand. "Die 'kopernikanische Wende' des Hysteriebegriffs bei Paracelsus." In *Paracelsus: Werk und Wirkung*, edited by Sepp Domandl, 125–132. Wien: WGO, 1975.

Lepenies, Wolf. *Melancholie und Gesellschaft*. Frankfurt: Suhrkamp, 1972.

Leventhal, Robert. "Ästhetische Dimensionen der psychologischen Fallgeschichte: Zu einer Ästhetik der Abweichung und Grenzüberschreitung am Beispiel von Marcus Herz' Beschreibung seiner eigenen Krankheit (1783)." In *Kleine anthropologische Erzählformen des 18. Jahrhunderts*, edited by Alexander Košenina and Carsten Zelle, 191–228. Hannover: Wehrhahn Verlag, 2011.

Leventhal, Robert. *The Disciplines of Interpretation: Lessing, Herder, Schlegel and Hermeneutics in Germany 1750–1800.* Berlin: de Gruyter, 1994.

Leventhal, Robert. "'Eins und Alles': Herders Spinoza-Aneignung in *Gott, einige Gespräche*." *Publications of the English Goethe Society* 86.2 (2017): 67–89.
Leventhal, Robert. "Der Fall des Falls: Neuere Forschung zur Geschichte und Poetik der Fallerzählung im 18. Jahrhundert." *Das Achtzehnte Jahrhundert. Zeitschrift der Deutschen Gesellschaft zur Erforschung des 18. Jahrhunderts* 41.1 (2017): 94–102.
Leventhal, Robert. "Die Fallgeschichte zwischen Ästhetik und Therapeutik." In *"Fakta, und kein moralisches Geschwätz." Zu den Fallgeschichten im Magazin zur Erfahrungsseelenkunde* (1783–1793), edited by Sheila Dickson, Stefan Goldmann, and Christof Wingertszahn, 65–83. Göttingen: Wallstein Verlag, 2011.
Leventhal, Robert. "The Jewish Physician as Respondent, Confidant, and Proxy: The Case of Marcus Herz and Immanuel Kant." In *On the Word of a Jew: Religion, Reliability, and the Dynamics of Trust*, edited by Nina Caputo and Mitchell Hart, 222–244. Bloomington: Indiana University Press, 2019.
Leventhal, Robert. "Kasuistik, Empirie und Pastorale Seelenführung: Die Entstehung der modernen psychologischen Fallgeschichte, 1750–1800." *Jahrbuch Literatur und Medizin* 2 (2008): 13–40.
Lindemann, Mary. "The Enlightenment Encountered: The German Physicus and His World, 1750–1820." In *Medicine in the Enlightenment*, edited by Roy Porter, 181–198. Amsterdam: Rodopi, 1995.
Lindemann, Mary. *Health and Healing in Eighteenth-Century Germany*. London and Baltimore: Johns Hopkins University Press, 1996.
Lüdemann, Suzanne. "Literarische Fallgeschichten. Schillers *Verbrecher aus verlorener Ehre* und Kleists *Michael Kohlhaas*." In *Das Beispiel. Epistemologie des Exemplarischen*, edited by Jens Ruchatz, Stefan Willer, and Nicolas Pethes, 208–223. Berlin: Kulturverlag Kadmos, 2007.
Luhmann, Niklas. *Art as Social System*. Translated by Eva M. Knodt. Stanford, CA: Stanford University Press, 2000.
Luhmann, Niklas. "The Individuality of the Individual: Historical Meanings and Contemporary Problems." In *Reconstructing Individualism: Autonomy, Individuality and the Self in Western Thought*, edited by Thomas C. Heller, Morton Sosna, and David E. Wellbery, 313–328. Stanford, CA: Stanford University Press, 1986.
Luhmann, Niklas. "Individuum, Individualität, Individualismus." In *Gesellschaftsstrukur und Semantik. Studien zur Wissenssoziologie der modernen Gesellschaft*, by Luhmann, vol. 3, 149–258. Frankfurt: Suhrkamp, 1989; 1993.
Luhmann, Niklas. *Love as Passion: The Codification of Intimacy*. Translated by Jeremy Gaines and Doris L. Jones. Stanford, CA: Stanford University Press, 1986.
Lukács, Georg. *Das Besondere als Kategorie der Ästhetik*. Neuwied: Luchterhand, 1967.
Marcus, Steven. "Freud and Dora: Story, History, Case History." In *Freud and the Culture of Psychoanalysis: Studies in the Transition from Victorian Humanity to Modernity*, 42–86. Englewood Cliffs, NJ: Prentice Hall, 1987.
Mark, Zwi. "*Dybbuk* and *Devekut* in the *Shivhe ha-Besht*: Toward a Phenomenology of Madness in Early Hasidim." In *Spirit Possession in Judaism: Cases and Contexts from the Middle Ages to the Present*, edited by Matt Goldish, 257–303. Detroit: Wayne State University Press, 2003.
Marquard, Odo. "Der angeklagte und der entlastete Mensch in der Philosophie des 18. Jahrhunderts." In *Studien zum achtzehnten Jahrhundert*, edited by Bernhard Fabian, vol. 2–3, 193–209. München: Fink, 1980.

Marquard, Odo. "Several Connections between Aesthetics and Therapeutics in Nineteenth-Century Philosophy." In *The New Schelling*, edited by Judith Norman and Alistair Welchman, 13–29. New York: Continuum, 2004.

Marquard, Odo. "Über einige Beziehungen zwischen Ästhetik und Therapeutik." In *Schwierigkeiten mit der Geschichtsphilosophie*, by Marquard, 85–121. Frankfurt am Main: Suhrkamp, 1982.

Martens, Lorna. "Constructing Interiority in Eighteenth-Century Narrative Fiction: Wieland's *Geschichte des Agathon*." *German Quarterly* 81.1 (2008): 49–65.

Marx, Otto M. "German Romantic Psychiatry. Part 1." *History of Psychiatry* 1 (1990): 351–381.

Marx, Otto M. "German Romantic Psychiatry. Part 2." *History of Psychiatry* 2 (1991): 1–25.

Mauser, Wolfram. "Johann Gottlob Krüger. Der Weltweise als Arzt. Zur Anthropologie der Frühaufklärung in Deutschland." In *'Vernünftige Ärzte': Hallesche Psychomediziner und die Anfänge der Anthropologie in der deutschsprachigen Frühaufklärung*, edited by Carsten Zelle, 48–67. Tübingen: Niemeyer, 2001.

Megill, Allan. "The Reception of Foucault by Historians." *Journal of the History of Ideas* 48.1 (1987): 117–141.

Merker, Nicolai. *Die Aufklärung in Deutschland*. München: C. H. Beck, 1982.

Micale, Mark S. *Approaching Hysteria: Disease and Interpretations*. Princeton, NJ: Princeton University Press, 1995.

Micale, Mark S. "Hysteria and its Historiography: The Future Perspective." *History of Psychiatry* 1 (1990): 33–124.

Micale, Mark S. "Hysteria Male, Hysteria Female: Reflections on Comparative Gender Construction in Nineteenth-Century France and Britain." In *Science and Sensibility: Gender and Scientific Inquiry, 1780–1945*, edited by Marina Benjamin, 200–241. London: Blackwell, 1991.

Midelfort, H. C. Erik. "The Devil and the German People." In *The Witchcraft Reader*, edited by Darren Oldridge, 240–253. New York: Psychology Press, 2002.

Midelfort, H. C. Erik. "The Devil and the German People: Reflections on the Popularity of Demon Possession in Sixteenth-Century Germany." *Religion and Culture in the Renaissance and Reformation*, Sixteenth Century Essays and Studies 11 (1989): 99–119.

Midelfort, H. C. Erik. *Exorcism and Enlightenment: Johann Joseph Gassner and the Demons of Eighteenth Century Germany*. New Haven, CT: Yale University Press, 2005.

Midelfort, H. C. Erik. *A History of Madness in Sixteenth-Century Germany*. Stanford, CA: Stanford University Press, 1999.

Midelfort, H. C. Erik. "Madness and Civilization in Early Modern Europe: A Reappraisal." In *Michel Foucault: Critical Assessments*, edited by Barry Smart, vol. 4, 117–133. London and New York: Routledge, 1995.

Minter, Catherine J. *The Mind-Body Problem in German Literature, 1770–1830: Wezel, Moritz, and Jean Paul* Oxford: Clarendon Press, 2002.

Möller, Caren. *Medizinalpolizei. Die Theorie des staatlichen Gesundheitswesens im 18. und 19. Jahrhundert*. Frankfurt: Vittorio Klostermann, 2005.

Moretti, Franco. *Distant Reading*. London and New York: Verso, 2013.

Mülder-Bach, Inka, and Michael Ott, eds. *Was der Fall ist. Casus und Lapsus*. Paderborn: Fink, 2014.

Mullan, John. "Hypochondria and Hysteria: Sensibility and the Physicians." *Eighteenth Century: Theory and Interpretation* 25.2 (1984): 141–174.

Müller, Lothar. *Die kranke Seele und das Licht der Erkenntnis. Karl Philipp Moritz'* Anton Reiser. Frankfurt: Athenaeum, 1987.
Müller-Sievers, Helmut. "Reading without Interpreting: German Textual Criticism and the Case of Georg Büchner." *Modern Philology* 103.4 (2006): 498–518.
Müller-Sievers, Helmut. *Self-Generation: Biology, Philosophy, and Literature around 1800.* Stanford, CA: Stanford University Press, 1997.
Naschert, Guido. "Kurzbiographie: Johann Georg Sulzer (1720–1779)." In *Aufklärung. Interdisziplinäre Jahrbuch zur Erforschung des 18. Jahrhunderts*, vol. 19, 379–382. Hamburg: F. Meiner, 2007.
Naschert, Guido, and Gideon Stiening, eds., *Ernst Platner (1744–1818). Konstellationen der Aufklärung zwischen Philosophie, Medizin und Anthropologie*. Special issue. *Aufklärung* 19. Hamburg: F. Meiner, 2007.
Neumann, Gerhard. "'The Judgement,' 'Letter to His Father,' and the Bourgeois Family." In *Reading Kafka: Prague, Politics, and the Fin-de-Siecle*, edited by Mark Anderson, 215–228. New York: Schocken, 1989.
Neumeyer, Harald. "'Schwarze Seelen'. Rechts-Fall-Geschichten bei Pitaval, Schiller, Niethammer und Feuerbach." *Internationales Archiv zur Sozialgeschichte der deutschen Literatur* 31.1 (2006): 101–132.
Niehaus, Michael, and Hans Walter Schmidt-Hanissa, "Einleitung." In *Unzurechnungsfähigkeiten. Diskursivierungen unfreier Bewusstseinszustände seit dem 18. Jahrhundert*, edited by Niehaus and Schmidt-Hanissa, 7–13. Frankfurt: Peter Lang, 1998.
Niggl, Gunter. *Geschichte der deutschen Autobiographie im 18. Jahrhundert*. Stuttgart: Metzler, 1977.
Nowitzki, Hans Peter. *Der wohltemperierte Mensch. Aufklärungsanthropologien im Widerstreit*. Berlin: de Gruyter, 2003.
Nübel, Birgit. "Karl Philipp Moritz: Der kalte Blick des Selbstbeobachters." In *Karl Philipp Moritz zu ehren. Beiträge zum Eutiner Symposium im Juni 1993*, edited by Wolfgang Griep, 31–53. Eutin: Struve Verlag, 1993.
Oettinger, Klaus. "Schillers Erzählung 'Der Verbrecher aus verlorener Ehre'." *Jahrbuch der deutschen Schillergesellschaft* 16 (1972): 266–276.
Osinski, Jutta. "Psychologie und Ästhetik bei Karl Philipp Moritz." In *Karl Philipp Moritz und das 18. Jahrhundert. Bestandaufnehmen, Korrekturen, Neuansätze*, edited by Anneliese Klingenberg and Martin Fontius, 201–214. Tübingen: Niemeyer, 1995.
Ostermann, Eberhard. "Das Interessante als Element ästhetischer Authentizität." In *Authentizität als Darstellung*, edited Jan Berg, Hans-Otto Hügel, and Hajo Kurzenberger, 197–215. Hildesheim: Universitätsverlag, 1997.
Patai, Raphael. "Exorcism and Xenoglossia among the Safed Kabbalists." *Journal of American Folklore* 91.361 (1978): 823–835.
Paulin, Roger. *Der Fall Wilhelm Jerusalem. Zum Selbstmordproblem zwischen Aufklärung und Empfindsamkeit*. Göttingen: Wallstein, 1999.
Peck, Jason Michael. *From the Transcendental to the Particular: German-Jewish Philosophy in the Late of the Eighteenth Century*. PhD diss., University of Minnesota, 2006.
Pethes, Nicolas. "Ästhetik des Falls. Zur Konvergenz anthropologischer und literarischer Theorien der Gattung." In *"Fakta, und kein moralisches Geschwätz". Zu den Fallgeschichten im Magazin zur Erfahrungsseelenkunde (1783–1793)*, edited by Sheila Dickson, Stefan Goldmann, and Christof Wingertszahn, 13–32. Göttingen: Wallstein Verlag, 2011.

Pethes, Nicolas. *Literarische Fallgeschichten. Zur Poetik einer epistemischen Schreibweise.* Konstanz: Konstanz University Press, 2016.

Pfotenhauer, Helmut. *Literarische Anthropologie: Selbstbiographien und ihre Geschichte am Leitfaden des Leibes.* Stuttgart: Metzler, 1987.

Pilet, P. E. "Felix Platter." In *The Dictionary of Scientific Biography*, edited by Charles C. Gillispie, vol. 11, 33. New York: C. Scribner, 1975.

Pomata, Gianna. "The Medical Case Narrative: Distant Reading of an Epistemic Genre." *Literature and Medicine* 32.1 (2014): 1–23.

Pomata, Gianna. "Observation Rising: Birth of an Epistemic Genre, 1500–1650." In *Histories of Scientific Observation*, edited by Lorraine Daston and Elizabeth Lunbeck, 45–80. Chicago: University of Chicago Press, 2011.

Pomata, Gianna. "*Praxis Historialis*: The Uses of *Historia* in Early Modern Medicine." In *Historia: Empiricism and Erudition in Early Modern Europe*, edited by Gianna Pomata and Nancy G. Siraisi, 105–146. Cambridge and London: MIT Press, 2005.

Pomata, Gianna. "Sharing Cases: The *Observationes* in Early Modern Medicine." *Early Science and Medicine* 15.3 (2010): 193–236.

Porter, Roy. *Flesh in the Age of Reason: The Modern Foundations of Body and Soul.* New York and London: W. W. Norton, 2003.

Porter, Roy. *Patients and Practitioners: Lay Perceptions of Medicine in Pre-Industrial Society.* Cambridge: Cambridge University Press, 2003.

Porter, Roy. "Foucault's Great Confinement." *History of the Human Sciences* 3.1 (1990): 47–54.

Porter, Roy. *Madness. A Brief History.* Oxford: Oxford University Press, 2002.

Porter, Roy. "The Patient's View: Doing Medical History from Below." *Theory and Society* 14.2 (1985): 175–198.

Prince, Gerald. *Dictionary of Narratology.* Lincoln and London: University of Nebraska Press, 1987.

Probst, Christian. "Johann Peter Frank als Arzt am Krankenbett." *Sudhoffs Archiv* 59.1 (1975): 20–53.

Pütz, H. P. "Büchners 'Lenz' und seine Quelle: Bericht und Erzählung." *Zeitschrift für deutsche Philologie* 84 (1965): 1–22.

Quetelet, Lambert Jacques Adolphe. *Treatise on Man and the Development of his Faculties.* Translated by R. Knox. Edited by T. Smibert. Cambridge: Cambridge University Press, 2013.

von Rahden, Wolfert. "Sprachpsychonauten. Einige nicht-institutionelle Aspekte der Entstehung einer 'Sprachbetrachtung in psychologischer Rücksicht' im letzten Drittel des 18. Jahrhunderts am Beispiel der Diskurskonkurrenz zwischen Immanuel Kant und Karl Philipp Moritz." In *Sprachwissenschaft im 18. Jahrhundert. Fallstudien und Überblicke*, edited by Klaus D. Dutz, 111–141. Münster: Nodus, 1993.

Ralser, Michaela. *Das Subjekt der Normalität: Das Wissensarchiv der Psychiatrie. Kulturen der Krankheit um 1900.* München: Wilhelm Fink, 2010.

Rather, L. J. "G.E. Stahl's Psychological Physiology." *Bulletin of the History of Medicine* 35.1 (1961): 27–49.

Rau, Petra. "The Poetics of Pathology: Freud's *Studien über Hysterie* and the Tropes of the Novella." *German Life and Letters* 59.1 (2006): 62–77.

Regner, Suzanne. *Visuelle Gewalt: Menschenbilder aus der Psychiatrie des 20. Jahrhunderts.* Bielefeld: Transcript Verlag, 2010.

Remak, Henry H. H. *Structural Elements of the German Novella from Goethe to Thomas Mann.* New York, Bern, Berlin, and Frankfurt: Peter Lang, 1996.

Retzlaff, Stefanie. *Observieren und Aufschreiben. Zur Poetologie medizinischer Fallgeschichten (1700–1765).* München: Wilhelm Fink, 2017.

Richards, Robert J. "Christian Wolff's Prolegomena to Empirical and Rational Psychology: Translation and Commentary." *Proceedings of the American Philosophical Society* 124.3 (1980): 227–239.

Richards, Robert J. *The Romantic Conception of Life: Science and Philosophy in the Age of Goethe.* Chicago: University of Chicago Press, 2002; 2010.

Richter, Simon. *Laocoon's Body and the Aesthetics of Pain: Lessing, Herder, Moritz and Goethe.* Detroit: Wayne State University Press, 1991.

Riedel, Wolfgang. *Die Anthropologie des jungen Schiller: Zur Ideengeschichte der medizinischen Schriften und der 'Philosophischen Briefe.'* Würzburg: Königshausen & Neumann, 1985.

Riedel, Wolfgang. "Anthropologie und Literatur in der deutschen Spätaufklärung. Skizze einer Forschungslandschaft." *Internationales Archiv für Sozialgeschichte der deutschen Literatur* 6.3 (1994): 93–157.

Riedel, Wolfgang. "Die anthropologische Wende: Schillers Modernität." In *Friedrich Schiller. Die Realität des Idealisten*, edited by Hans Feger, 55–69. Heidelberg: Universitätsverlag Winter, 2006.

Riedel, Wolfgang. "Erkennen und Empfinden. Anthropologische Achsendrehung und Wende zur Ästhetik bei Johann Georg Sulzer." In *Der ganze Mensch. Anthropologie im 18. Jahrhundert*, edited by Hans-Jürgen Schings, 410–439. Stuttgart: Metzler, 1994.

Riedel, Wolfgang. "Erster Psychologismus: Umbau des Seelenbegriffs in der deutschen Spätaufklärung." In *Zwischen Empirisierung und Konstruktionsleistung: Anthropologie im 18. Jahrhundert*, edited by Jörn Garber and Heinz Thoma, 1–18. Tübingen: Niemeyer, 2004.

Riedel, Wolfgang. "Johann August Unzer." In *Literaturlexicon. Autoren und Werke deutscher Sprache*, edited by Walther Killy, vol. 2, 494. München and Gütersloh: Bertelsmann, 1991.

Riedel, Wolfgang. "Literarische Anthropologie: Eine Unterscheidung." In *Wahrnehmen und Handeln: Perspektiven einer Literaturanthropologie*, edited by Wolfgang Braungart, Klaus Ridder and Friedmar Apel, 337–366. Bielefeld: Aisthesis, 2004.

Roper, Lyndal. *Witch Craze: Terror and Fantasy in Baroque Germany.* New Haven, CT: Yale University Press, 2004.

Rousseau, G. S. *Enlightenment Crossings: Pre- and Post-Modern Discourses. Anthropological.* Manchester and New York: Manchester University Press, 1991.

Rousseau, G. S. "Introduction." In *Languages of the Psyche. Mind and Body in Enlightenment Thought*, edited by Rousseau, 3–44. Berkeley and Oxford: University of California Press, 1990.

Rousseau, G. S. "'A Strange Pathology': Hysteria in the Early Modern World, 1500–1800." In *Hysteria beyond Freud*, edited by Sander L. Gilman, Helen King, Roy Porter, G. S. Rousseau, and Elaine Showalter, 91–221. Berkeley and Los Angeles: University of California Press, 1993.

Rubenstein, Jeffrey L. *Rabbinic Stories.* New York and Mahwah, NJ: Paulist Press, 2002.

Rubenstein, Jeffrey L. *Talmudic Stories: Narrative Art, Composition, and Culture.* Baltimore: Johns Hopkins University Press, 1999.

Safranski, Rüdiger. *Friedrich Schiller oder die Erfindung des Deutschen Idealismus.* München and Wien: Carl Hanser Verlag, 2004.

Scheerer, Eckhart. Article "Psychologie." In *Historisches Wörterbuch der Philosophie*, edited by Joachim Ritter, vol. 7, 1599–1653. Basel: Schwabe, 1971.
Schings, Hans-Jürgen, ed., *Der ganze Mensch. Anthropologie und Literatur im 18. Jahrhundert*. Stuttgart and Weimar: J. B. Metzler, 1994.
Schings, Hans-Jürgen. *Melancholie und Aufklarung: Melancholiker und ihre Kritiker in Erfahrungsseelenkunde und Literatur des 18. Jahrhunderts*. Stuttgart: Metzler, 1977.
Schlumbohm, Jürgen. "Constructing Individuality: Childhood Memories in Eighteenth-Century Empirical Psychology and Autobiography." *German History* 16.1 (1998); 29–42.
Schmitt, Wolfram. "Psychisch Kranke und ihre Helfer am Ende des 18. Jahrhunderts. Pfarrer Oberlin und der Dichter Lenz," edited by Bettina von Jagow and Florian Steger. *Jahrbuch Literatur und Medizin* 2 (2008): 41–60.
Schneider, Manfred. "Hysterie als Gesamtkunstwerk." In *Ornament und Askese im Zeitgeist des Wien der Jahrhundertwende*, edited by Alfred Pfabigan, 212–229. Wien: C. Brandstaetter, 1985.
Schrimpf, Hans-Joachim. *Karl Philipp Moritz*. Stuttgart: J. B. Metzler, 1971.
Schrimpf, Hans-Joachim. "Das Magazin zur Erfahrungsseelenkunde und sein Herausgeber." *Zeitschrift für deutsche Philologie* 99 (1980): 161–187.
Seigel, Jerrold. *The Idea of the Self: Thought and Experience in Western Europe since the Seventeenth Century*. Cambridge: Cambridge University Press, 2005.
Sheehan, Jonathan. *The Enlightenment Bible: Translation, Scholarship, Culture*. Oxford and Princeton, NJ: Princeton University Press, 2005.
Showalter, Elaine. *Hystories: Hysterical Epidemics and Modern Media*. New York: Columbia University Press, 1998.
Sindlinger, Peter. *Lebenserahrung(en) und Erfahrungsseelenkunde oder wie der Württemberger Pfarrer Immanuel David Mauchart die Psychologie entdeckt*. Nürthingen and Frickenhausen: Sindlinger-Burcharzt, 2010.
Siraisi, Nancy. *History, Medicine, and the Traditions of Renaissance Learning*. Ann Arbor: University of Michigan Press, 2007.
Sohn, Werner. "Bio-Macht und Normalisierungsgesellschaft – Versuch einer Annäherung." In *Normalität und Abweichung: Studien zur Theorie und Geschichte der Normalisierungsgesellschaft*, edited by Werner Sohn and Herbert Mertens, 9–30. Opladen and Wiesbaden: Wesdeutscher Verlag, 1999.
Sonntag, Michael. "Die Seele und das Wissen vom Lebenden. Zur Entstehung der Biologie im 19. Jahrhundert." In *Die Seele. Ihre Geschichte im Abendland*, edited by Gerd Jüttemann, 294–318. Göttingen: Vandenhoeck & Ruprecht, 1991.
Stangneth, Bettina. "Der Arzt der Philosophen." In *Marcus Herz: Versuch über den Schwindel. Mit beiden Ergänzungen von 1797 und 1798, Einleitung, Werkverzeichnis und Anmerkungen*, edited by Bettina Stangneth. Hamburg: F. Meiner, 2019.
Steigerwald, Jörn. "Ideenzirkulation und Zirkulation von Ideen. Zur empirischen Psychologie der Berliner Spätaufklärung (am Beispiel Marcus Herz)." In *Gedächtnis und Zirkulation. Der Diskurs des Kreislaufs im 18. und 19. Jahrhundert*, edited by Harald Schmidt and Marcus Sandl, 39–64. Göttingen: Vandenhoeck & Ruprecht, 2002.
Steinberg, H. "Creation of the First University Chair in Psychiatry: Johann Christian August Heinroth in Leipzig." *Nervenarzt* 75.3 (2004): 303–307.
Steinberg, H. "Johann Christian August Heinroth (1773–1843): The First Professor of Psychiatry as a Psychotherapist." *Journal of Religion and Health* 51.2 (2012): 256–268.

Steinlechner, Gisela. *Fallgeschichten: Krafft-Ebing, Panizza, Freud, Tausk*. Wien: WUV-Universitatsverlag, 1995.
Stöckmann, Ernst. *Anthropologische Ästhetik: Philosophie, Psychologie und ästhetische Theorie der Emotionen im Diskurs der Aufklärung*. Berlin: de Gruyter, 2009.
Struve, Ulrich, ed., *Der imaginierte Findling: Studien zur Kaspar-Hauser-Rezeption*. Heidelberg: Carl Winter, 1995.
Sturm, Thomas. *Kant und die Wissenschaft am Menschen*. Paderborn: Mentis Verlag, 2009.
Sulloway, Frank. "Reassessing Freud's Case Histories: The Social Construction of Psychoanalysis." *Isis: Journal of the History of Science* 82.2 (1991): 245–275. Reprint. *Freud and the History of Psychoanalysis*. Edited by Toby Gelfand and John Kerr, 153–192. London and Hillsdale, NJ: Taylor & Francis, 1992.
Swales, Martin. *The German Novelle*. Princeton, NJ: Princeton University Press, 1977.
Taylor, Charles. *Sources of the Self: The Making of the Modern Identity*. Cambridge: Cambridge University Press, 1992.
Thiel, Udo. "The Critique of Rational Psychology." In *A Companion to Kant*, edited by Graham Bird, 207–221. New York: John Wiley, 2009.
Thiel, Udo. "Das Gefühl 'ich': Ernst Platner zwischen empirischer Psychologie und Transzendentalphilosophie." In *Aufklärung: Interdisziplinäres Jahrbuch zur Erforschung des 18. Jahrhunderts*, vol. 19, 139–161. Hamburg: F. Meiner, 2007.
Thiel, Udo."Hißmann und der Materialismus." In *Michael Hißmann (1752–1784): Ein materialistischer Philosoph der deutschen Aufklärung*, edited by Heiner F. Klemme, Gideon Stiening, and Falk Wunderlich, 25–41. Berlin: de Gruyter, 2015.
Thomé, Horst. *Autonomes Ich und 'Inneres Ausland': Studien über Realismus, Tiefenpsychologie und Psychiatrie in deutschen Erzähltexten 1848–1914*. Berlin: de Gruyter, 1993.
Thomé, Horst. *Roman und Naturwissenschaft. Eine Studie zur Vorgeschichte der deutschen Klassik*. Frankfurt: Peter Lang, 1978.
Thums, Barbara. *Aufmerksamkeit. Wahrnehmung und Selbstbegründung von Brockes bis Nietzsche*. München: Wilhelm Fink, 2008.
Thums, Barbara. "Das feine Gewebe der Organisation: Zum Verhältnis von Biologie und Ästhetik in Karl Philipp Moritz Kunstautonomie – Ornamenttheorie." *Zeitschrift für Ästhetik und allgemeine Kunstwissenschaft* 49.2 (2004): 237–260.
Toellner, Richard. "Medizin in der Mitte des 18. Jahrhunderts." In *Wissenschaft im Zeitalter der Aufklärung*, edited by Rudolf Vierhaus, 194–217. Göttingen: Vandenhoeck & Ruprecht, 1985.
Totelin, Lawrence. *Hippocratic Recipes. Oral and Written Transmission of Pharmacological Knowledge in the Fifth- and Fourth-Century Greece*. London: Brill, 2008.
Tougaw, Jason Daniel. *Strange Cases: The Medical Case History and the British Novel*. New York: Routledge, 2006.
Toulmin, Stephen. *Cosmopolis: The Hidden Agenda of Modernity*. Chicago: University of Chicago Press, 1990.
Toulmin, Stephen. "How Medicine Saved the Life of Ethics." *Perspectives in Biology and Medicine* 25.4 (1982): 736–750.
Veith, Ilza. *Hysteria: The History of a Disease*. Chicago: University of Chicago Press, 1965.
Vermeulen, Hans F. *Before Boas: The Genesis of Ethnography and Ethnology in the German Enlightenment*. Lincoln and London: University of Nebraska Press, 2015.

Vickers, Neil. "Coleridge, Moritz and the 'Psychological' Case History." *Romanticism* 13.3 (2007): 271–280.
Vidal, Fernando. "Psychology in the Eighteenth Century: A View from Encyclopaedias." *History of the Human Sciences* 6.1 (1993): 89–119.
Vidal, Fernando. *The Sciences of the Soul: The Early Modern Origins of Psychology*. Translated by Saskia Brown. London and Chicago: University of Chicago Press, 2011.
Viëtor, Karl. "La Maladie du siècle." In *Goethe: A Collection of Essays*, edited by Victor Lange, 26–32. Englewood Cliffs, NJ: Prentice Hall, 1968.
Walther, Manfred. "Spinozissimus ille Spinoza oder wie Spinoza zum 'Klassiker' wurde." In *Beobachter und Lebenswelt: Studien zur Natur-, Geistes- und Sozialwissenschaft*, edited by Klaus Hammacher and Helmut Reinalter, 183–238. Wien and München: Thaur, 1996.
Watt, Ian. *The Rise of the Novel. Studies in Defoe, Richardson and Fielding*. Berkeley: University of California Press, 1957.
Wellbery, David E. *Lessing's Laocoon: Aesthetics and Semiotics in the Age of Reason*. Cambridge: Cambridge University Press, 1984.
White, Hayden. *Metahistory. The Historical Imagination in Nineteenth Century Europe*. Baltimore: Johns Hopkins University Press, 1973.
Wiener, Dora B. "Mind and Body in the Clinic: Pinel, Crichton, Esquirol, and the Birth of Psychiatry." In *The Languages of Psyche: Mind and Body in Enlightenment Thought*, edited by G. S. Rousseau, 331–402. Berkeley and Oxford: University of California Press, 1990.
von Wiese, Benno. *Novella*. Stuttgart: J. B. Metzler, 1963.
Wild, Christopher. "Theorizing Theater Antitheatrically: Karl Philipp Moritz's Theatromania." *MLN* 120.3 (2005): 507–538.
Wöbkemeier, Rita. *Erzählte Krankheit. Medizinische und Literarische Phantasien um 1800*. Stuttgart: Metzler, 1990.
Wölfel, Kurt. "Interesse/interessant." In *Ästhetische Grundbegriffe*, edited by Karlheinz Barck, vol. 3, 138–174. Stuttgart and Weimar: Metzler, 2001.
Wübben, Yvonne. "Traum, Wahn und Wahnwissen. Karl Philipp Moritz als Sammler psychologischer Erfahrungsberichte." In *Kulturen des Wissens im 18. Jahrhundert*, edited by Ulrich Johannes Schneider, 425–431. Berlin and New York: de Gruyter, 2008.
Wuthenow, Ralph-Rainer. *Das erinnerte Ich: Europäische Autobiographie und Selbstdarstellung im 18. Jahrhundert*. München: C. H. Beck, 1987.
Zammito, John H. *The Gestation of German Biology: Philosophy and Physiology from Stahl to Schelling*. Chicago: University of Chicago Press, 2017.
Zammito, John H. *Kant, Herder, and the Birth of Anthropology*. Chicago: University of Chicago Press, 2002.
Zelle, Carsten, ed. *Casus. Von Hofmanns Erzählungen zu Freuds Novellen*. Hannover: Wehrhahn, 2015.
Zelle, Carsten. "Erfahrung, Ästhetik und mittleres Maß: Die Stellung von Unzer, Krüger und E. A. Nicolai in der anthropologischen Wende um 1750." In *Reiz – Imagination – Aufmerksamkeit*, edited by Jörn Steigerwald and Daniela Watzke, 203–224. Würzburg: Königshausen & Neumann, 2003.
Zelle, Carsten. "Experiment, Experience and Observation in Eighteenth-Century Anthropology and Psychology – the Examples of Krüger's *Experimentalseelenlehre* and Moritz' *Erfahrungsseelenkunde*." *Orbis Litterarum* 56.2 (2001): 93–105.

Zelle, Carsten. "Experimentalseelenlehre und Erfahrungsseelenkunde." In *Vernünftige Ärzte. Hallesche Psychomediziner und die Anfänge der Anthropologie in der deutschsprachigen Frühaufklärung*, edited by Zelle, 174–185. Tübingen: Niemeyer, 2001.

Zelle, Carsten. "Ey was hat der Arzt mit der Seele zu thun? Physiologie und Psychologie bei Haller und Krüger." In *'Allerhand nützlicher Versuche': Empirische Wissenskultur in Halle und Göttingen (1720–1750)*, edited by Tanja van Hoorn and Yvonne Wübben, 21–40. Hannover: Wehrhahn Verlag, 2009.

Zelle, Carsten. "'Die Geschichte bestehet in einer Erzählung': Poetik der medizinischen Fallerzählung bei Andreas Elias Büchner 1701–1769." *Zeitschrift für Germanistik* 19.2 (2009): 301–316.

Zelle, Carsten. "Sinnlichkeit und Therapie. Zur Gleichursprünglichkeit der Ästhetik und Anthropologie um 1750." In *Vernünftige Ärzte. Hallesche Psychomediziner und die Anfänge der Anthropologie in der deutschsprachigen Frühaufklärung*, edited by Zelle, 5–24. Tübingen: Niemeyer, 2001.

Zelle, Carsten, ed. *Vernünftige Ärzte. Hallesche Psychomediziner und die Anfänge der Anthropologie in der deutschsprachigen Frühaufklärung*. Tübingen: Niemeyer, 2001.

Index

Abel, Jacob Friedrich 8, 10, 16, 42–43, 104n134, 108, 137–140, 144–145, 222, 224–225, 227, 235n49, 239–242
– *Einleitung in die Seelenlehre* 138, 224
– *Sammlung und Erklärung merkwürdiger Rechtsfälle* 16, 235n49
Adelung, Johann Christoph XIII, 339
Adler, Hans 87, 281n32, 296n80
aesthetics 6, 11, 37, 73
– of autonomy 11, 242, 276, 285, 289–290, 333, 353
– in Baumgarten 8, 37, 118–119, 125, 226, 274–277, 282, 287n51, 301, 306, 312, 343
– in Bolten 126–127, 225–226, 274–277, 282, 343
– as discipline of the lower faculties 6, 8, 35, 37, 109, 127, 275, 281, 288, 304, 307, 343
– in Herz 8, 105, 312, 314–315, 324–327, 328n68, 330–332, 332n79, 333, 333n81, 334, 356–357
– and the individual 93, 95, 127, 202, 227, 229, 231–232, 235, 243, 287, 299, 344, 354
– in Kant 5, 11, 118, 231, 287n51, 289, 291, 354, 356
– in Moritz 11, 105, 333
– in Schiller VII, 105, 231, 235–236, 239, 306
– as sensate cognition 63, 119, 274, 276–277, 281–282, 306, 332
– and therapeutics 282–285, 287, 299, 302, 304 (see also Baumgarten; experience; genre; Kant; Moritz; Schiller; science; sensate cognition; Sulzer)
Agamben, Giorgio 106, 339
Ameriks, Karl 140n115
anamnesis 22, 28, 200, 267
Andre-Alt, Peter 223n11
Ankerloo, Bengt 157n31
anthropology 2, 3, 6, 64, 87, 90, 107, 117, 200, 202
– empiricism 227, 244
– Enlightenment 48, 78, 208–209, 227, 315

– Platner and 55–56, 135–137, 144–145, 208, 227
– Kant and 8–9, 107n2, 108, 143–145, 309
– medical 222, 348
– model 44
– emergent discipline of 37, 50, 78, 107n2, 108, 135, 204, 310
– as a science of *der ganze Mensch* 6, 123, 125, 136, 148, 202, 208, 228, 244, 282, 289, 301, 304, 307–308, 342
– theory 37, 60
– "turn" 6, 35n35, 108, 109n5, 111, 135, 138 (see also genre; Kant; Krüger; science)
apperception 2, 115n27, 147
– in Baumgarten 345
– in Sulzer 128, 345
– in Platner 136–137
– in Leibniz 115–116, 128, 136–137, 139–140, 339–340 (see also introspection; self-observation)
Aristotle 21–22, 40, 112, 341
Arnaud, Sabine 250
Aschauer, Lucia 47n75
Aufmerksamkeit 32, 130, 215, 277, 286, 294, 302, 304, 307
autobiography 42, 48, 60–64, 78, 98, 103, 105, 108, 134, 146, 285, 347
– genre of 6, 59
autonomy 11, 50, 54, 56, 93, 96–97, 101–102, 229, 242, 276–277, 285–286, 288–290, 306, 333, 353, 355, 362 (see also individual; self)

Bacon, Francis 23–25, 38, 40, 88, 94, 113, 227, 280–281
Bauman, Zygmunt 159
Baumgarten, Alexander 6, 8, 107–108, 120, 123n58, 141, 144, 301, 312
– *Aesthetics* 118
– association of ideas (nexus) 119, 144, 344
– and the body 119, 125, 344
– and cognition 119, 287n51, 306, 342
– and discipline of aesthetics 37, 119, 226, 274–275, 277, 282, 306

- lower faculties 6, 8, 37, 109, 343
- *Metaphysics* 118, 344
- theory of the soul 118–119, 345 (see also aesthetics; *Haltung*; nexus)

Beck, Lewis White 310n7
Becker, Klaus 286
Behrens, Rudolf 47n75
Beiser, Frederick C. 228–229, 232
Beispiel 1, 46, 66, 71
Bell, Matthew 88, 107n2
Bennett, Benjamin 232, 287
Beobachtung 36, 36n40, 40, 54, 66, 110, 130, 130n86, 138, 141–142, 192, 210, 273, 275, 277–278, 299, 304–305, 307
Berlant, Lauren Gail 28
Bernd, Adam 59, 61–63, 63n130, 63n132
Bernheimer, Charles 74n17
Bildung 64–65, 101–103, 203, 286, 299
biology 52, 105
Black, Joel VII, 75n20
Blackmore, Richard 249, 253
Blanckenburg, Christian Friedrich von 6, 64–65, 91, 91n86, 345, 358–359
Blank-Panitzsch, Margarete 26, 26n13–26n14
Blumenbach, Johann Friedrich 53
body 53
- anatomo-politics and 69, 83, 83n53, 220
- in Baumgarten 119, 125, 344
- as a distinct substance 56, 112, 134, 136–137, 141, 209
- human 35, 112, 122, 122n55, 125–126, 147, 225, 313, 341
- inhabitation/possession of 9, 119, 149–150, 153, 164
- as merely passive 121–122
- Nicolai's notion of 37, 120, 125–126, 145, 342
- in Platner 54–55, 135–137, 208–210, 251, 323–324
- relationship of mind and 28, 51, 108, 134, 137, 145, 156, 186, 204, 307, 315, 323–324, 335, 342, 356
- relationship to soul and 35–36, 52, 54, 121, 135, 158, 183, 209, 223, 230, 233, 257, 323–324

- in Sulzer 145, 315, 329, 344 (see also Baumgarten; physiology; self; soul; Sulzer, stance; system; Unzer)

Boerhaave, Herman 5, 26, 36–37, 40, 40n54, 44, 71, 88–89, 94, 108, 121, 126, 132, 155n26, 158, 208, 251n20, 320
Böhm, K. 22n5
Böhme, Gernot 143n25
Böhme, Harmut 143n25
Bolten, Johann Christian 2, 111, 120, 126, 126n71, 127, 145–146, 155, 225–226, 274–275, 277, 282, 301–302, 342–343
- *Gedanken von psychologischen Curen* 126, 274, 343
- philosophical pathology in 11, 127, 275, 343
Bölts, Stephanie 199n30
Boss, Jeffrey N. M. 248
Boulby, Mark 280n28
Bourdieu, Pierre 362n33
Bourneville, D. M. 75n23
Bowie, Andrew 227, 287
Breuer, Joseph 257
Broman, Thomas H. 108n4, 311
Bronfen, Elisabeth 258, 269
Bruner, Jerome 12–13
Buchenau, Stefanie 311n9
Büchner, Andreas Elias 2, 26, 37–41, 43–45, 132, 346, 358
Büchner, Georg 17, 32, *33*, 104–105, 230

Campe, Rüdiger 29, 103
Canguilhem, Georges 18n47
care 2, 31, 96, 183–184
- medical 184
- and mental illness 183, 185–186, 222, 263, 270, 302
- and responsibility of the state 58–59, 158
- of the self 3, 11, 277, 300–304, 354
- of the soul 83, 186, 216–217, 277, 301, 303–304, 353, 355, 360
- therapeutic 216–217, 300–301, 302n98, 355 (see also pastor; physiology; religion; *Seelensorge*; soul)
case (-study, -history) VII, XIII-XIV, 1–3
- classification system 1, 5, 28, 89, 93, 221, 231

Index — 393

- dissemination of 6n16, 18, 27, 48, 58, 78, 105–106, 133, 154, 213n77, 349, 358
- educational use 92, 106, 155, 232, 243–244, 281
- as epistemic genre 4, 70, 89, 93, 96, 133, 154n23, 336, 336n85, 357
- epistemology of 2, 309–337, 312, 334
- framework 4, 38, 64, 70, 89
- -history VII, XIII, *31, 33, 146, 170*
- juridical 1, 9–10, 16, 16n41, 27, 34, 40, 48n76, 59, 78n32, 87, 92, 106, 219, 221–222, 227, 231, 236–237, 243, 245, 348, 351
- interpretation of 3, 15, 21, 76, 98, 195, 278, 312
- medical 1, 4, 8, 22–23, *24*, 25, 27–28, 34, 38, 43–45, 57, 70n7, 71, 76, 88n72, 89, 94, 195, 202
- as medium of learned and/or scholarly exchange 1–3, 10, 19, 36, 47, 59, 77, 80, 99–101, 105, 133, 146, 212, 222, 226–227, 274, 280, 307, 358, 362
- narrative XIV, 9, 16, 18, 45, 74, 76, 85, 194, 293, 307, 348, 359
- pastoral use/function 1–3, 9, 11, 57, 83, 84, 86–87, 105, 212–213, 220–221, 245, 277–278
- psychological VII, 1–17, 14, 21, 27–28, 37, 64, 70, 72, 76–77, 78, 86, 96, 103–106, 108, 195–197, 202–203, 207, 210, 212–216, 220, 226, 229, 234, 244–245, 268–269, 299, 310, 315, 358, 362
- publication of 3, 14n34, 16–17, 48, 57n108, 77–78, 80n38, 94, 152, 203, 213n77, 217, 228, 274, 292, 344, 349, 354, 358
- state/civil use 3–4, 9, 17–18, 70, 84, 86, 105–106, 158, 219, 229, 231, 237, 238, 273, 337, 347, 352, 354 (see also *Erfahrung*; *Erfahrungsseelenkunde*; Foucault; Freud; genre; hysteria; literature; medicine; moral; Moritz; narrative; novel; observation; pastor; psychology; Schiller; science; Stahl; Sulzer; system; therapeutics)

Casper, Johann Ludwig VII, 18

casuistry 1, 14, 26–27, 29, 37, 40, 45, 69, 81–82, 202
- Kant on 21
- system of moral-theological 27, 45, 58, 81, 214, 212, 250 (see also Ginzburg; Jonsen; Pascal; Toulmin)

de Ceglia, Francesco Paolo 158n36
de Certeau, Michel 151, 348
Chajes, J. H. 149
Chaouli, Michel 231n37
Charcot, Jean-Martin 75–76
- Hacking on 76
- and hysteria 75
- iconography 75n23
Cheyne, George 249, 253–254
Childress, James. F. 82n49
Clifton, Francis 88, 94
Cohn, Dorrit 74n18
Cordemann, Claas 134n97
Crichton, Alexander 14n35, 41
Crombie, A. C. 79n37
Cunningham, Andrew 113n19

Dainat, Holger 221
Danziger, Kurt 6n17, 14, 73n16, 110
Daston, Lorraine 36n39, 133, 133n95, 299
Davidson, Arnold 69
Davies, Martin 311–312, 314n22
Dear, Peter 133, 133n95
deviation 4, 59, 145, 192, 260, 358
- in Herz (*Abweichung*) 12, 216, 309, 315, 317, 319–328, 335–336, 349, 355–356
- and norm 18, 66, 68, 71, 214, 216
Dewhurst, Kenneth 222n8
Diätätik (see dietetics; *Seelendiätätik*; *Seelenheilkunde*; therapeutics)
Dickson, Sheila VIII
Didi-Huberman, Georges 75n23
dietetics 83n53, 219, 222, 273, 303–304, 307, 355
- of the soul 11, 193, 273, 278, 303–305, 307, 355
- and therapeutics 193, 222, 307 (see also care, of the soul; *epimeleia hautou*; *Seelendiätätik*; *Seelensorge*; therapeutics)
Dörner, Klaus 41n56

Duden, Barbara 43, 44n66, 94, 152n19
Dumont, Altrud 72n14
Duncan, Bruce 29n21
Dürbeck, Gabriele 37, 122n58, 123–124, 268, 343n13
Düwell, Susanne 22n7

Eagleton, Terry 288
Eckermann, Johann Peter 295
Efron, John 321n44
Einbildungskraft 37, 62, 125, 343
Ellenberger, Henri F. 249n14
Ellis, John M. 77n29
emotion 6–7, 42, 44, 50, 108–109, 116, 124, 127–128, 144–146, 228, 238, 270, 281, 302–304, 306–307, 328n63, 340n5, 341, 343, 345n15, 349, 360–351
– inner world of 1, 42, 73
– and women 151, 158, 180, 256
Enlightenment 6, 36n39, 52–53, 158, 184, 186, 188, 270, 278, 300, 314n22, 347–348, 359, 361
– early 9, 63, 147, 154, 185–186, 189, 346
– German 48, 51, 61, 63, 77–78, 94, 107, 109, 119n45, 137, 185–186, 202–203, 205, 208, 289
– late 2–3, 47, 60, 77, 94, 111, 202–203, 205, 208–209, 223, 277, 289, 312, 315, 322, 337, 358
– and medical science 186
– notions of 49
– philosophy of 37
– and the soul 109, 137, 206
– values of 9 (see also anthropology; Jew; Kant)
epimeleia heautou 277, 89, 300–301, 354
Epstein, Julia 88, 94
Erfahrung 35, 275, 278, 294
– and case histories 358
– distinction between experiment and 191n2
– meaning/notion of 35–36, 45–46, 130n86, 131, 345
– and medicine 108, 113, 130, 312–313, 321
– of mental illness 307
– and the soul 136–137, 144–145, 208, 304 (see also *Beobachtung*; experience; observation; *Wahrnehmung*)

Erfahrungsseelenkunde 8, 15, 17, 35, 87, 107, 111, 111n14, 146, 228, 275–277, 279, 285, 292, 295, 299, 303, 307, 353
– and case histories 14, 16, 65, 214, 278
– definition/translation of XIII 6, 191n2
– practitioners of 15 (see also psychology, empirical, empirical-experiential)
Erzählung (see narrative)
etiology 4, 35, 41, 61–62, 76, 76n26, 90, 114, 158, 212, 237, 337, 341
experience 1–2
– actual 36, 117, 150–151, 278, 306
– aesthetic 5, 72, 95, 222, 229, 231, 243, 274, 277, 287–291, 295–297, 299, 304, 306, 308, 330–331, 332n79, 333–334, 336, 354, 357
– and Büchner's two principles 38–39
– direct 22, 26, 51, 94, 110
– in early modern Europe 26, 358
– first hand 223
– individual 7n21, 8, 357–358
– in Herz 196–197, 199, 201
– lived 4, 68, 152, 195–196
– memory of 12, 41, 352
– notion of 36n39, 45, 131, 345
– personal/own 41, 129, 132, 203, 345, 349
– transformation of 133, 133n95
– scientific 36, 46
– unique 8, 336, 362
– in Zimmermann 2, 45–46, 108, 111, 113, 130–132, 145, 345–346(see also *Erfahrung*; Moritz; narrative; observation; Platner; psychology, empirical-experiential; science; Unzer; Wolff)
Euler, Werner 55–56

Fallgeschichte (-*studie*, -*erzählung*) VIII, XIII, 29, 38, 66, 70, 70n7 (see also case; *Krankengeschichte*)
Feiner, Shmuel 312n11
Ferenczi, Sandor 257
Feuerbach, Paul Johann Anselm 17, 243
Fink, Gonthier-Louis 229n29
Fisch, Harold 149
Fludernik, Monika 12, 362n34
Forrester, John 2, 27, 56, 79–82, 87, 110
Förster, Michael 134n97, 241

Foucault, Michel 1, 99, 185–186, 249, 256
- *Birth of the Clinic* 41, 84–86, 92
- and the case 2, 2n3, 41, 69–70, 80–82, 85–87, 221
- care of the self 11, 220, 227, 277, 300–301, 303
- *Discipline and Punish* 45, 69, 80, 82–83, 86, 92, 221
- and *epimeleia heautou* 89, 277, 300–301, 354
- and *gnothi sauton* 273, 300–301
- and governmentality 11, 82–84, 86, 188, 213, 221, 244, 360
- *Hermeneutics of the Subject* 273, 300–301, 354
- *History of Madness* 109, 185, 253n28
- *The History of Sexuality* 69–70
- and the history of subjectivization 4, 64, 106
- *Madness and Civilization* 257
- and the Pastoral 2, 57–58, 83, 83n53, 84, 86, 105, 188, 213, 221, 244, 343
- *Security, Territory, Population* 188, 191
- "The Subject and Power" 4n11, 106n140
Frank, Johann Peter 28, 252–253, 253n27, 360
- and medical policy 28, 59n113, 94, 106, 252, 253n27, 360
- significance of the case in 94, 106
Freud, Sigmund VII, 13, 57, 214, 257, 269, 276n10
- the case-history in 17–19, 73–76, 358
- and Charcot 75–76, 76n26
- the novella and 69, 76–77, 104
- *Studies in Hysteria* 69, 74, 76
- use of narrative 19, 57, 73–74, 74n18, 75–77, 358
Frey, Christiane 29n23

Gailus, Andreas 47n76, 78n32, 91–92
Galen 9, 40–41, 44–45, 49, 107, 112, 153, 155, 247, 248n8, 249, 358
- medicine 49, 153
Galison, Peter 299
Garve, Christian 60, 72, 138, 202n37, 228
Gemünden, Gerd 104n137
genre 5–6, 34, 42, 77n29, 92–93, 349, 358

- aesthetic 294, 351
- anthropological-psychological 2–3, 70
- of the case-history 1–2, 10, 17, 21, 28, 46, 47n76, 48, 57, 68, 70, 77–78, 78n32, 79, 86, 90, 214, 226, 269, 315, 337, 361
- and deviance/demonic 87, 151, 214
- epistemic 4, 70, 89–90, 93, 96, 133, 336, 336n85, 357
- Freud's use 57, 73–74
- and individuality 3, 3n7, 7, 18, 64, 100, 105, 315
- medico/al-philosophical 10–12, 16
- and the narrative 6, 17–19, 68, 72, 76, 90, 214, 351
- and the novel/novella 59, 76–77, 88, 100–101, 105, 360
- psychological-juridical 10, 227, 245, 351
- and the self 64, 98, 101, 362
- theoretical 47, 358 (see also autobiography; case)
Gersch, Hubert 31n31
Gesichtspunkt 273–274, 276–277, 292, 304, 307, 353–354
Gessinger, Joachim VII, 157, 182n67
Geyer-Kordesch, Johanna 35n36, 113n19
Gilman, Sander L. VII
Ginzburg, Carlo 5
Goethe, Johann Wolfgang 6–7, 7n23, 37, 98, 105, 298, 301, 346, 349
- concept of self 42, 101–103
- *Conversations with Eckermann* 295–296
- *The Sorrows of Young Werther* 7, 28–29, 29n22, 30, *31*, 102
- theory of the Novella 73, 77, 91, 358
- *Wilhelm Meisters Lehrjahre* 101–103
Goldish, Matt 150n12
Goldmann, Stefan VIII, 70n7
Goldstein, Jan E. 74n17, 185n76
Goulemot, Jean Marie 49n81
Gnothi sauton 2, 10–11, 42, 191, 228, 277, 301–302, 348, 354
Greenblatt, Stephen 49n80, 203n39
Greiner, Bernhard 45n67
Guyer, Paul 15n36

Hacking, Ian VII, 18, 69, 76, 216, 216n92
- "Biopower and the Avalanche of Printed Numbers" 18n49
- dynamic nominalism in 69
- on the emergence of social statistics 18
- "Making up People" 69
- *Rewriting the Soul* 1-2, 216
- the role of the soul according to 2
- "Styles of Reasoning" 79n37, 111n13
- *The Taming of Chance* 18n48, 79n37
- two vectors of power in 69
von Haller, Albrecht 26, 37, 40n54, 45, 121, 205, 250
Haltung 11-12, 183, 315, 328, 328n68, 329-336, 344-345, 357
Harvey, William 21-22, 50, 147, 154, 248n8, 341
Hasselmeier, Hans-Heinrich 157n31
Hatfield, Gary 15n36
Hauska, Ferdinand 67-68
Heffernan, Thomas F. 24n12
Hegel, Georg Wilhelm Friedrich 101, 114
Heinz, Jutta 48n78
Helm, Jürgen 155n25, 342n12
Henrich, Dieter 99
Herbart, Johann Friedrich 15-16, 65
- *Psychologie als Wissenschaft* 15
Herder, Johann Gottfried 8, 133-134, 137, 145, 228, 258, 346-347
- and autobiography (life-descriptions) 60-61, 134
- concept of self 42, 101-103
- and the expressivist self 97, 101
- monism 134, 136-137, 145
- on psychology 37, 135, 144, 192n9
- and the soul 51, 54, 60, 107, 134, 136
- *Über Thomas Abbts Schriften* 107, 358-359
- *Vom Erkennen und Empfinden der menschlichen Seele* 60, 134 (see also indvidual)
Herz, Marcus VIII, 2, 8
- *Abweichung* in 11-12, 215-216, 315, 319-323, 336, 356
- *Betrachtungen aus der spekulativen Weltweisheit* 320n41, 321n44, 325-326, 335, 357
- on the border between medicine and philosophy 259, 314n22, 321, 326-327, 356
- *Briefe an Ärzte* 312-313, 313n18
- departure from Kant 310-315, 324-325, 325n58, 326-327, 327n61, 335-356
- and epistemology 2, 210, 309-337, 344-345, 356-357
- *Essay on Vertigo* (*Versuch über den Schwindel*) 256, 259, 312, 315, 317n31, 319-320, 335
- *Etwas Psychologisch-Medizinisches. Moriz Krankengeschichte* VIII, 214n84, 259, 247-272, 350
- *Grundriß aller medizinischen Wissenschaften* 320, 320n42
- *Haltung* in 11-12, 315, 328-336, 344-345, 357
- *On the Forms and Principles of the Sensible and Intelligible World* 309-310
- *Psychologische Beschreibung seiner eigenen Krankheit* 194, 194n19
- *Über die analogische Schlussart* 309, 314n23
- *Über die Widersprüche in der menschlichen Natur* 321, 321n46
- *Versuch über den Geschmack* 328, 328n68, 357 (see also aesthetics; deviation; Jew; Kant; Moritz; Platner; soul, natural law; therapeutics)
Hess, Volker VII, 22
Heydebrand, Renate 41n58
Hinrichs, Carl 201
Hippocrates 21-22, 94, 107, 247, 269
Hißmann, Michael 53, 207
- *Psychological Essays* 53, 207
Hoffbauer, Johann Christian 13-14, 14n35, 65
Hoffmann, Friedrich 33, 34, 36-37, 40, 43-44, 71, 113-114, 122, 125, 133, 148, 155, 155n26, 158, 195, 254, 281, 341-342
Hoffmann-Richter, Ulrike 74n17
von Hohenheim, Theophrastus Bombastus (Paracelsus) 22
Holmes, Oliver Wendell 27-28
van Hoorn, Tanja 122

Hörisch, Jochen 104n136
Horstmann, Rolf-Peter 140n115
Hufeland, C. W. 258, 337n86
Hume, David 53, 107n2, 122n58, 204, 317, 355
humor (-s, -al) 9, 40–41, 44–45, 49–50, 124, 147, 153–155, 186, 202, 248–249, 255, 257, 314n25, 361 (see also Galen)
Huppmann, Gernot 341
hypochondria 11, 24, 92, 185, 247–256
– hysterical- 11, 50, 92, 185, 248–250, 259, 261, 267, 272, 350–351
– melancholic 50, 62, 185, 223–224, 249, 276 (see also hysteria)
hysteria 50, 92, 268–269, 269n70
– and the brain 248
– case studies 250, 268
– and class 248
– and females 185n78, 247–248, 255–256, 270
– Freud and 69, 73–76
– history of 189n82, 247, 249–251, 257–258
– inclusion of males 253, 255–256, 270
– medicine and psychology 269
– and melancholy 254
– Moritz 247, 258, 265, 272, 350–351
– and the nervous system 249, 252, 254, 256
– and possession 150, 185, 189n82, 247, 254
– theory 249
– and treatment 248 (see also hypochondria)

individual (-ity) VII, XIII-XIV, 1–3, 7
– concepts/notion of 3, 3n7, 50, 91–92, 201
– construction of 3, 7, 92
– Hacking and VII, 2, 18, 69
– history of 64, 201
– "I" 64, 98, 113n18, 129–130, 199, 215, 234, 271
– ideology of 102
– Luhmann and 2–3, 42, 49n84, 94–95, 95n99, 147, 201, 217n93, 271, 334
– model/modeling of 3n7, 4, 44, 72, 93, 96, 201–202
– modern 3, 7, 105, 346

– and the unique 1, 3, 3n7, 41, 59, 102n130, 295, 312, 315, 346, 349, 358, 361–362 (see also aesthetics; experience; Foucault; genre; Moritz; novel; Seigel; Schiller; self; soul; Taylor; Watt)
influxion 35, 51, 113, 120–121, 147, 341, 356
interdisciplinarity 2, 48, 78, 222, 310, 314 (see also field of study; theory)
introspection 2, 8, 15–16, 42, 49, 73, 110–111, 111n14, 113–115, 117–118, 145, 147, 192, 216, 225, 270, 339–341, 345
– Kant's critique of 15, 142–144 (see also self-, observation)
Israël, Lucien 258
Izenberg, Gerald N. 102n130

Jackson, Stanley W. 155n25
Jacob, Joachim 292
Jäger, Hans-Wolf 283n36
Jannidis, Fotis 41n58
Jardine, Lisa 3n8
Jenisch, Daniel 61
Jerusalem, Carl Wilhelm 30, *31*
Jew (-ess, -s, -ish) 51, 150, 158–159, 178–181, 196, 309–311
– and allosemitism 159
– Enlightenment 194, 196, 311
– and exorcism 149–150, 157, 159–163, 167–168, *170*, 177, 178–182, 187, 348
– and the Jewish community 9, 157–162, 179–180, 184, 187–189, 309, 348
– Herz as 194–196, 309
– prejudices 181, 187
– protected (*Schutzjude*) 158–160
– in Schaumburg-Lippe 9, 157, 157n31, 161, 167, 179, 189, 347
– "wandering Jew" 149n10
Jolles, André 5, 46–47, 64, 184, 358–359
Jonsen, Albert R. 27

Kant, Immanuel 5, 11, 101, 229, 271, 289n54, 333
– *Anthropology from a Pragmatic Point of View* 8, 143, 145
– critique of casuistry 16, 21
– *Critique of Judgment* 231, 289, 291–292, 354

- *Critique of Pure Reason* 113, 118, 115n140, 309
- dissertation 309, 321n44, 324, 356
- and empirical psychology 8–9, 65, 108, 113n18, 140, 140n114, 141–145
- and Herz 12, 120, 310–315, 324–325, 325n58, 326–327, 327n61, 335–356
- on inner sense 144
- on knowledge and science (*Wissenschaft*) 15, 140–142
- and Maimon 51–52, 205
- on mental illness 144
- *Metaphysical Foundations of Natural Science* 8, 113n18, 140, 142
- *The Metaphysics of Morals* 21, 300
- philosophy of 14–15, 137–138, 231, 309–310, 325
- and science 142–143, 145
- and the self 101
- on self-observation 142–144
- and the soul 107, 113n18, 138, 141, 144
- theory of self-consciousness 118
- and the three central faculties 325, 327
- *What is Enlightenment?* 300 (see also aesthetics; anthropology; autonomy; casuistry; introspection; mind; Moritz; observation; science; self, -transcendence; system; Wolff)

Kaufmann, Doris 109, 195
Kennedy, Margaret 88, 93
Keohane, Nannerl O. 346n18
Kiceluk, Stephanie 41
Killy, Walther 222n9
Kittler, Friedrich 81n46
Köhler, C. O. 22n5
Kolnai, Aurel 72n14
Koopmann, Helmut 235n49
Koschorke, Albrecht 314n25, 317
Koselleck, Reinhard 58n112
Košenina, Alexander VII, 56n106, 90–91, 93, 111, 211n71, 226, 229–230, 239n63, 282
Krankengeschichte VIII, XIII, 1, 4, 26, 29, 40, 44–45, 66, 70, 70n7, 71, 74, 194–195, 247, 267, 267n65, 318, 335–336, 346, 348–349
Krüger, Johann Gottlob 2, 10n24, 34, 120, 123n62, 124–126, 155, 301

- and the active soul 35–36
- and anthropological psychology 122, 125, 342
- and the brain/mind 123n62, 124, 136, 342
- and empirical psychology 122–123
- and experimental psychology 35–36, 111, 111n14, 123n59
- and observation 36, 36n40, 111, 111n14
- *Naturlehre* 124, 342
- *Neue Lehre von den Gemüthsbewegungen* 124
- and the soul 122–124, 342
- *Versuch einer Experimentalseelenlehre* 35, 122 (see also *Erfahrung*)

Kull, Carolin 195, 350

Lambert, Johann Heinrich 18n48
Lange, Martin 249
Langholf, Volker 21n4
Laqueur, Thomas W. 88
Lavater, Johann Caspar 29, 29n23, 45, 59, 134, 192
Leary, David E. 15n39
Lebensbeschreibung 6, 59–61, 192, 192n9 (see also autobiography; Bernd, Adam)
Leder, Christoph Maria 311n9
Leibniz, Gottfried Wilhelm 38, 101, 110, 116, 119, 119n45, 128, 136–137, 139–141, 148, 208, 312, 340, 340n5
Leibrand, Annemarie 247n5
Leibrand, Werner 247n5
Lepenies, Wolf 49n82
Leventhal, Robert 14n35, 48n77, 93n91, 103n132, 119n45, 155n27, 202n37, 310n6, 334n82
Lindemann, Mary 82n49
literacy 1, 23, 27, 58, 70n7, 153, 156, 336
literature 2, 60, 74, 105, 108–109, 192, 226, 228, 230, 296n80, 349–351, 358
- and case histories/studies 2, 17, 30, 41, 73, 87, 93, 95n99, 104, 106, 134, 196, 231, 239, 269, 278
- and crimes 93
- European 346
- and fact and fiction 33
- German 29, 41, 73, 77, 302n98, 312

– and medicine 21, 43, 202, 222, 233, 260, 271, 347–349
– and psychology 111, 254, 271, 347, 349
– and rabbinic 149–150, 162n42
– Western 21, 31 (see also autobiography; case)
Locke, John 38, 40–41, 88, 97–99, 107n2, 108, 110, 122n58, 145, 204, 227–228, 319
Luhmann, Niklas 2, 41–42, 49n84, 94–95, 147, 201–202, 217n93, 271, 334
Lukács, Georg 226

Maimon, Salomon 51–52, 59, 64, 205–206, 270–271, 310
Mandeville, Bernard 249
Marcus, Steven 74n17
Mark, Zwi 150
Marquard, Odo 287
Martens, Lorna VII, 345, 345n15
Marx, Otto M. 13n30
Mauchart, J. D. 17, 215
– *Allgemeines Repertorium für empirische Psychologie und verwandte Wissenschaften* 17
Mauser, Wolfram 35n35
medicine (-al) 2, 4, 12–13
– art 12, 22, 259, 264, 267, 313, 350
– classification 1, 6, 28, 89, 250
– early modern 1, 4, 8, 22, 24, 26, 43, 71, 89, 108, 112, 122, 133, 154, 136, 212, 248, 341, 358
– ethics and 82
– forensic VII, 18, 18n50, 67, 244
– Galen and 9, 41, 44–45, 49, 112, 153, 155, 247, 248n8, 249, 358
– history of 4, 22, 44, 46, 71, 88, 152, 152n19, 258, 311–312, 321
– Hippocrates and 21–22, 94, 107, 247, 269
– nosology 6, 28, 40, 84–86, 250, 346
– nosography 6, 28, 85, 86n65, 111
– philosophy and 11–12, 15, 37, 40, 48, 78, 122, 298, 309–314, 321, 334, 356
– psychology and 4, 6, 15, 86n65, 108, 194, 259, 269, 309, 337, 341–343
– psycho-dynamic model of 108, 111, 113–114, 216n92

– and psychopathology 126, 276n10, 314 (see also anthropology; care; case-history; Enlightenment; *Erfahrung*; Frank; genre; Herz; hysteria; literature; narrative; observation; psychology; physician; science; Stahl; system; therapeutics)
Megill, Allan 185n76
Meier, Georg Friedrich 6, 8, 37, 125–126, 144, 226, 274, 277, 301, 306, 312, 342–343, 348
Mendelssohn, Moses 10n24, 35–36, 45, 51, 53–54, 108, 111n14, 191n2, 205, 207, 210, 281–282, 284–285, 289, 306, 310, 331, 331n77, 332n79, 353
Merker, Nicolai 51n86
metanarrative (see narrative)
metaphysics 5, 5n15, 35, 56, 87, 117–118, 133, 210, 223–224, 300, 309, 312, 344
– and the German Enlightenment (*Aufklärung*) 51
– opposition to 53–54, 71–73
– of the soul 50–52, 56, 113, 118, 138, 200, 204–207, 211
– uncritical 141
– Western 51, 205 (see also Baumgarten; Kant; Wolff)
de la Mettrie, Julien Offray 53, 204, 208, 355
Micale, Mark S. 255, 257
Midelfort, H. C. Erik 150, 150n13, 151–152, 152n18, 153, 156
mind (the) 1–2
– activities of 115, 115n27, 116, 339, 341
– constitution of 39, 68, 119, 260, 341
– contents of 198, 275
– function/processes/operation of 8, 10, 13, 46, 111, 116, 135, 139, 144, 158, 187, 193, 204
– illness/disease of 23, 28, 50, 62, 65, 143, 156, 158, 186–187, 192–193, 206, 211, 249, 256, 271, 341
– and Kant 9, 15, 65, 113n18, 140n115
– mental state 40, 56, 67, 254
– movement/fluctuations of 124, 127, 137, 247
– and the nervous system 64, 254, 256
– notion of 118

– power of 148
– and Reil 13
– representation of 2, 8
– and the senses 41, 117, 119, 129–131, 200, 234, 325n58, 356
– study of 15, 65 (see also body; hypochondria; hysteria; soul; system)
moral (-ity) 1, 7–8, 21, 27, 53, 61, 83, 96, 159, 233, 273, 282, 287, 295, 328
– and case history 58, 133, 223
– casuistry 27, 45
– claims 287
– and empathy 91
– impairment/sin 58, 152n18, 279
– judgment 56, 231, 280, 353
– -juridical 10, 231, 236
– law 101, 242, 244, 351, 354
– and modernity 96
– philosophy 135, 207–208, 228
– and psychological treatment 206, 307
– reasoning 27
– and the self 41, 60, 96, 100, 244, 300, 303
– and the soul 127, 212, 294, 354
– and the state 59, 219, 238, 354
– -theological 27, 40, 58, 60, 81, 87, 214, 275, 299 (see also Kant; Moritz)
Moretti, Franco 89–90
Moritz, Karl Philipp 4
– and asethetics 11, 105, 333
– "Ankündigung eines Magazins für Erfahrungsseelenkunde" 353n22
– *Anton Reiser* 42, 59, 64, 73, 102, 191, 286
– *Aus K . . . s papieren* 90, 296, 297
– and case histories 14n35, 17, 48n76, 56, 71, 90, 193, 207, 212, 354
– *Denkwürdigkeiten, aufgezeichnet zur Beförderung des Edlen und des Schönen* 296
– and empirical psychology 110, 212, 273–308
– and experiential psychology 35, 111, 111n14
– *Gnothi Sauton oder Magazin zur Erfahrungseelenkunde* VIII, 2, 10, 11, 16, 42, 51–52, 86, 88, 91, 92, 191, 193, 205, 211, 228, 270, 273, 276, 281, 303, 307, 308, 310, 318, 348, 352–353, 358

– *Grundlinien zu einem ohngefähren Entwurf in Rücksicht auf die Seelenkrankheitskunde* 86n66, 280n24, 298n85, 303n101, 355n24
– Herz's case-history of 92, 247–272, 350
– and hysteria 247, 258, 265, 272, 350–351
– illness and death of 11, 214, 267, 350–351
– and individuality 135, 361
– influence on Kant 11
– journal of empirical-experiential psychology 10–11, 16, 78n32, 86, 91, 206, 310, 352–353, 359
– "Know thyself!" 361 (see also *gnothi sauton*
– and the narrative 11, 16, 193, 211, 352
– and "norm" 216
– and the observer 193, 213, 353
– psychological novel 6, 42, 64, 73, 191
– and scientific approach to psychology 16
– and the self 42
– and the soul 5, 11, 51, 54, 87, 91, 191–192, 194, 206, 210, 304–305, 355
– *Über den Endzweck des Magazins zur Erfahrungsseelenkunde* 273n1
– *Über die bildende Nachahmung des Schönen* 298n84
– *Versuch einer Vereinigung aller schönen Wissenschaften unter dem Begriff des in sich selbst Vollendeten* 289, 353
– *Vorrede zum Magazin für Erfahrungsseelenkunde* 35n39, 278n17
– and Zimmerman as a bridge 130, 130n86, 131 (see also hysteria; therapeutics)
Müchler, Karl 17
Mülder-Bach, Inka 29n24
Mullan, John 249n11
Müller, Lothar 286n44
Müller-Sievers, Helmut 32

narrative (*Erzählung*) XIII-XIV, 1–2, 38, 40, 44, 81, 88, 214, 259, 275
– autobiographical 59, 61, 63
– distinguished from chronicles/notes/stories 12–13, 71, 75–76, 239, 278, 346
– and dialogue 266, 268, 332n79
– and experience 12, 37, 68, 108, 132, 189, 358

- features of 12–13, 193, 358
- and fiction/novel 31, 71, 98, 239, 296
- in first person 44, 71, 97, 194, 241, 348–349
- and Freud 57, 73–74, 74n18, 75–77, 358
- function or purpose of 73, 216
- historical 61, 236, 351
- on illness 38–40, 57, 65, 90, 179, 200, 224, 250, 310, 350, 359
- medical case histories 1, 6, 27–28, 44n66, 71, 78n32, 86n65, 88, 126, 222, 244, 337
- meta- 3, 63, 96–97, 99–100, 103
- moral 61
- as psychology case histories XIV, 1–19, 28, 45, 47n76, 64–67, 72, 76–77, 90, 108, 111, 203, 296, 299, 348, 352, 361
- religious/spiritual 61–62, 105
- and scientific elements 18, 71, 106
- of self 193–196, 203, 293
- shifts in content and genre 59–61, 78n32, 346
- and the soul 56, 109, 203, 214, 352, 361
- theory 12, 74n18, 126, 362
- in third person 97
- writing of 37, 40, 85, 94, 145, 235, 266, 278, 361–362 (see also Bruner; Fludernik; genre; Moritz; observation; Schiller)

Naschert, Guido 128n77
Nasse, Friedrich 14, 65–66
- *Zeitschrift für psychische Ärzte* 14, 65
Naturphilosophie 13, 15
nerves 45, 50, 53, 114, 183, 185–186, 196–198, 205n48, 206, 221n4, 248–249, 251–252, 254–256, 316, 318, 342
Neumann, Gerhard 361n33
Neumeyer, Harald 221n71, 229, 243
Nexus (nexus) 119–120, 144–145, 323–324, 335, 344, 356
Nicolai, Ernst Anton 2, 34, 37, 45, 111, 120, 125–127, 145, 155, 282, 301, 342–343
- *Gedancken von den Würckungen der Einbildungskraft in den menschlichen Körper* 37
Niggl, Gunter 61n122

novel 3, 59, 93n91, 239, 270, 278, 282
- Blanckenburg's theory of 6, 64–65, 91, 91n86, 345, 358
- and case histories 29–30, 64–65, 88, 103, 255, 259
- dangers for women 185n78
- epistolary 100, 104n134
- as genre of modern individuality 3, 7, 98, 101, 105, 108, 146, 345n15
- Goethe and 28–29, *31*, 98
- psychological 6, 28–30, *31*, 42, 48, 73, 78, 102, 191, 286, 345
- romance 49
- Seigel and 3n7, 7, 100–101
- Taylor and 3n7, 7, 98–100
- theory of 6, 73, 345, 358
- Watt's theory of 7, 7n21, 98–99
- in distinction to case 18 (see also autobiography)
Novella (novella) 10, 32, *33*, 67, 69, 73, 76–77, 81, 104, 223, 296, 360
Nowitzki, Hans Peter 323n52
Nübel, Birgit 294n74

Oberlin, Johann Friedrich 31–32, 32n31, *33*
observation 24, 34, 46, 51–52, 54, 83, 142, 147
- accuracy of 26, 40, 73, 99, 148, 155, 216, 320
- and case histories 12, 57, 67, 132, 154, 273–276, 305–306, 336n85
- direct 63, 115, 132
- documentation/recording of 22–23, 28, 57, 94, 109, 134, 347
- elements of 25, 123
- and empirical psychology 1, 3, 8, 14–15, 73, 89, 113, 116, 118, 130, 141–142, 154, 187, 205, 216, 224, 275, 292, 299, 307, 342
- and experience 26, 36, 56, 63, 86, 114–115, 130–132, 225, 273, 304, 345
- and experimentation 36, 111n14, 207, 245, 278
- and facts 85, 193, 278–280
- Hippocrates 22
- human XIII, 193, 210, 286, 288, 294–295
- and human dignity 36n40

– as methodology 23, 105, 117, 192, 280
– of mental illness 65–67, 70, 115, 203, 248, 257
– vs. notes/narratives/stories 75, 86n65, 211, 250, 359
– objectivity and validity of 143, 194, 293–294, 299
– and perception/point of view 36, 275, 277, 307
– by physicians/medical 22, 43–44, 89, 131–132, 159, 202, 260, 281
– physiological- psychology 107, 123n58
– scientific method 25, 94
– selective attention 89
– self- 108, 112n17, 113, 139, 143, 192–193, 195–196, 199, 286, 293, 303
– subjective 142
– visual method 67 (see also *Beobachtung*; *Wahrnehmung*; self-, observation)
Oettinger, Klaus 229n29
Osinski, Jutta 285–287
Ostermann, Eberhard 72n14
Oswald, Stephan 31n31
Ott, Michael 29n24

Pascal, Blaise 27
pastor (-al) 4, *33*, 59, 86, 148, 168, 245, 273
– apparatus 1–3, 11, 58, 83, 87, 105, 216, 220–221, 244, 278, 300, 347, 360
– care 183–184, 186, 302n98
– and case history 57, 86, 105, 212
– and demonic possession 9, 178
– history of 84
– power 57, 83, 83n53, 84, 188, 191, 213, 343
– and the soul 18, 83, 86, 214, 301–302 (see also care, of self; Foucault; Mauchart; Oberlin)
Patai, Raphael 149n6
Peck, Jason Michael 325n58
Pethes, Nicolas 90, 92–93, 277
Pfotenhauer, Helmut 59n115
physiology 13, 22, 133, 135, 139, 192n9, 219, 230, 270, 314, 323–324
– anatomo- 50, 227
– contributions 22, 155, 248n8, 254

– and experimentation 6n17, 36, 73n16, 123, 147, 281
– holistic approach 206–207
– of internal sense 143
– and mental illness 23, 40–41, 155
– and metaphysics 50, 204–205
– neuro- 155, 227, 248n8, 254, 314n25, 317, 319
– and observation 107n2, 123n58, 205
– and psychology 39–40, 51, 56, 60, 93, 108, 134–137, 158, 221, 229, 232–233, 281, 314, 317, 334
– theory 56, 105, 112, 158, 320, 335 (see also anthropology; Herz; Stahl)
Pietism 6, 63, 73, 201, 214, 223
Pilet, P. E. 24n12
Pitaval, François Gayot de 2, 16–17, 42, 56n106, 57n108, 78, 93–94, 211n71, 213n77, 221–222, 224, 227, 235, 239, 243, 351
– *Causes célèbres* 2, 10, 42, 93–94, 221, 235, 243, 351
Platner, Ernst 8, 55n101, 108, 209n66
– and anthropology 55–56, 135–137, 144–145, 208, 227
– *Anthropology for Physicians and Philosophers* (*Anthropologie für Ärzte und Weltweisen*) 54, 135, 204, 207, 209
– as dualist 136–137
– Herz's critique of 54–55, 55n104, 210, 210n70, 323
– and hypochondria 251
– *Philosophische Aphorismen* 136
– the role of experience in 208
– and the self 136, 323
– and the soul 55–56, 136, 140, 208–210, 324
– and theory 208
– Unzer's critique of 55, 209–210 (see also anthropology)
Platter, Felix 5, 23, *24*, 43, 71, 153–154, 195, 212
Pockels, Karl Friedrich 17, 296
Pomata, Gianna 4, 70, 89, 96n101, 133, 155, 184, 336, 336n85, 358
Porter, Roy 4, 44n66, 70–71, 255, 270
possession 9, 147–189

- de Certeau on 151
- demonic 9, 147–148, 148n4, 149–154, 157, 178–179, 181–186, 188
- as distinct from witchcraft 152–153
- and exorcism 148–149, 149n7, 150, 154n23, 161
- and the female womb 247
- hysterical 157, 347
- Midelfort on 150, 150n13, 151, 152n18, 153, 153n20, 156, 178, 185
- rejection of as explanation for mental illness 154, 154n24, 348
- Roper on 153, 153n20 (see also hysteria; Jew, and exorcism)
Prince, Gerald 12n27
Probst, Christian 28n20
psychologia empirica 8, 115–117, 339 (see also Wolff)
psychology
- associationist 108, 359
- critique of 14, 65, 135, 140n114, 143, 145
- empirical XIII, 1, 5, 8–9, 16, 36, 45, 47, 50, 65, 73, 77, 87, 106, 107n2, 108–115, 115n27, 116–118, 120, 122–123, 128, 133, 137–138, 140, 140n114, 141–145, 147, 204, 212, 215, 228, 259, 273–281, 285–288, 292–293, 295, 299–302, 304, 307, 330, 339–340, 342, 344–345, 347, 358–359
- empirical-experiential XIII, 2, 10, 66, 86, 106, 115, 191, 273, 304, 310, 352, 358
- European 112
- German (eighteenth century) 50, 107, 107n2, 109, 113
- human 110, 194, 228, 345n15
- medical 6, 15, 86n65, 309, 341–343
- modern (nineteenth century) 352
- philosophical 115, 314
- rational 14, 107n2, 115, 117–118, 140, 140n115, 141–142, 144–145, 230, 239, 344
- scientific 14–16, 18, 65, 110, 339 (see also Baumgarten; genre; Herder; Herz; Kant; Krüger; Moritz; narrative; observation; science; Stahl; Sulzer; Universität Halle; Wolff)

psychopathology 6n17, 33, 73n16, 116, 126, 276n10, 279, 296, 314 (see also *Seelenkrankheitslehre*)
Purcell, John 249, 257
Pütz, H. P. 32n31
Pyl, Johann Theodor 350n32

Quetelet, Lambert Jacques Adolphe 18

von Rahden, Wolfert VII, 279
Ralser, Michaela 84n59
Rather, L. J. 114
Rau, Petra 269n71
Rau, Wolfgang Thomas 252
Reeve, Nigel 222n8
Regnard, P. 75n23
Regner, Suzanne 76n24
Reil, Johann Christian 11, 13–14, 14n35, 65, 214–216, 271
- *Beyträge zur Beförderung einer Curmethode auf psychischem Wege* 13
- *Rhapsodies Concerning the Application of the Psychical Cure Method on Mental Illness* 11, 13, 214–215, 271
Remak, Henry H. H. 77n29
Richards, Robert J. 13, 214, 339
Richter, Simon 232n40, 282n33
Riedel, Wolfgang 100, 111, 137, 211n71, 229–230, 351
Roper, Lyndal 153
Rousseau, G. S. 52–53, 206, 256
Rousseau, Jean-Jacques 42, 59–60, 97–98, 134, 192, 228, 346
Rubenstein, Jeffrey L. 310n5

Safranski, Rüdiger 227–228
Scheerer, Eckhart 112n15
Scherf, Johann Christian Friedrich 360n32
Schiller, Friedrich 17, 42, 66, 90, 93, 111, 351
- and Abel 10, 104n134, 145, 222, 224–225, 227, 235n49, 239, 241–242
- advantage of case with respect to historical narrative 10, 57n108, 104, 236, 239, 351
- aesthetics and/of the case VII, 105, 231, 235–236, 239, 306

– and the *Causes célèbres* 2, 10, 42, 93–94, 221, 235, 243, 351
– *Criminal of Lost Honor* 2, 10, 43, 77, 100, 219, 220, 222, 227, 237, 239, 351–352
– as editor/translator 2, 10, 94, 211n71, 222, 224, 227, 231
– epistemological significance of the case 10, 57n108, 64, 232, 235–236, 351
– and individuality 135, 213n77, 229, 232, 234, 244, 354
– *Letters on the Aesthetic Education of Man (Aesthetic Letters)* 10, 228, 231–233, 239
– and patient trust 224, 228n25
– and realism 227, 230–235
– *Die Räuber (The Robbers)* 10, 42, 57n108, 213n77, 228–230, 240, 244–245
– the significance of individuality in 135, 229, 232–236, 239
– and the soul 51, 56n106, 238, 241
– *Unerhörte Kriminalfälle: eine Sammlung berühmter und merkwürdiger Kriminalfälle* 17
– *Über die Krankheit des Eleven Grammont* 10, 42, 223, 224, 227–228
Schings, Hans-Jürgen 109n5, 111, 135
Schlumbohm, Jürgen 352n21
Schmitt, Wolfram 32n31
Schneider, Manfred 257–258, 267–269
Schrimpf, Hans-Joachim 285, 289
Schulz, F. 251
Schwärmerei 49, 143–144, 228
Schweizer, Hans Rudolf 274n5
science 15, 37, 127, 280, 312, 320
– and aesthetics 119, 127–128, 225, 274, 289, 312, 333, 333n81, 353, 357
– anthropology as 2, 50, 78, 105, 109, 111, 135–138
– and case histories/studies 69–71, 74–75, 79, 360
– clinical 81, 84
– of empirical/experiential psychology 110, 11n14, 113, 117, 132–133, 135, 141–142, 147, 281212, 228, 341, 352, 359
– forensic 65
– history of 2, 4, 46, 70, 79, 282
– Kant's critique of psychology as 21, 142–145
– and use of Latin 94, 112
– of medicine 21, 23, 54, 88n72, 186, 192, 207, 222, 262, 270, 312, 320, 336, 343
– of memory 2, 216, 216n92
– and mental illness 50, 192
– natural 8, 111n14, 113n18, 123, 125, 138, 207, 245
– psychology as 15, 60, 65, 81, 155, 335
– of sensate cognition 8, 63n132, 119, 274–277, 281–284, 306, 332, 344
– of the soul 1–2, 18, 106, 109–110, 113, 117, 123, 127, 130, 135–136, 139, 212, 260, 303, 330, 344, 353
– of the state 70, 158, 221, 337
– and systematic knowledge (*Erkenntnis*) 14, 130, 142, 211, 325
– as *Wissenschaft* (Kant) 13, 15, 140, 142, 191n2, 275, 347, 359
Seelendiätätik 11, 305, 355 (see also dietetics)
Seelenkrankheitslehre 191–194, 211 (see also psychopathology)
Seelenheilkunde 275, 282, 285, 305 (see also therapeutics; dietetics)
Seelensorg(-er) 11, 275, 277, 301–302, 302n98, 303–304, 337, 354
Seigel, Jerrold 3, 3n7, 7, 96, 99–103
self 1–7, 11
– and the body 54, 145, 209
– care for/of 11, 220, 222, 277–278, 300–304, 354
– -consciousness 55, 118, 136–137
– -determination 56
– -formation 64, 100–103, 203, 286, 289, 293, 299
– -identity 47, 58, 97–98, 106, 136, 145, 200, 216n92, 244
– -knowledge 97, 113n18
– loss of 234, 290
– -narration 98
– notion of modern 96–98, 100
– -observation (*Selbstbeobachtung*) 143, 192–193, 195, 286, 293, 299, 303
– -realization 96, 102
– -reflection 100, 108, 113, 199
– sense of 80n38, 96–97, 128–130, 136–137, 323, 334

– and the soul 97, 136, 204n46, 208, 211, 278, 323
– -transcendence 288, 295, 298, 234
– unique 1, 362 (see also autonomy; *Bildung*; Foucault; *gnothi sauton*; Hacking; individuality; Luhmann; Seigel; *Selbstsorge*; Taylor)
Selle, Christian Gottlob 54, 207, 314
Semler, Johann Salamo 59–60, 134, 192
sensate cognition 8, 63n132, 119, 274–277, 281–284, 306, 332, 344
Sheehan, Jonathan 201n34
Showalter, Elaine 255n35
Sindlinger, Peter 215n86
singularity 1, 37, 79, 89, 232–233, 353
Siraisi, Nancy 72n13
Smith, Adam 100
Sohn, Werner 18n47
Sonntag, Michael 52, 206
soul (human) 1–2, 5–8, 15
– according to Abel 137–139, 145, 240–241
– according to Platner 54–56, 135–138, 144, 208–210, 230, 323–324
– body and 35–36, 54, 121, 135, 158, 183, 209, 223, 233, 257, 324
– corruption of 192, 240, 242, 358, 360
– critique of (Hißmann) 50n86, 53, 207
– dietetics of 11, 193, 273, 278, 303–305, 307, 355
– direction of/guidance of (*Gewissensleitung, Seelenführung*) 2, 28, 83, 86, 106, 121, 127, 188, 191, 213–214, 217, 221, 260, 301, 304, 360
– discipline of 8, 130, 145, 288, 301, 305, 344
– dissection of 10, 194
– existence of 118, 317, 324, 355
– and free will 52, 205–206, 270–271
– heath of 52, 55, 205, 271, 305
– and hierarchical society 2–3, 58
– illnesses of 52, 87, 126–127, 191–192, 211–212, 274
– individual 7, 28, 49n85, 50, 57–58, 105, 188, 191, 361
– knowledge of 56n106, 113n18, 137, 216, 330

– metaphysics of 50–52, 56, 113, 118, 138, 200, 204–207, 211
– natural laws of (Herz) 200
– and observation 35, 83, 86, 113, 206, 216, 341–342
– representations of 137, 144, 288, 343–344
– science of 2, 18, 106, 109–110, 123, 142, 260, 344, 353 (see also Baumgarten; care; Enlightenment; *Erfahrung*; Hacking; Herder; Krüger; moral; Moritz; narrative; pastor; observation; self; *Seelenheilkunde*; *Seelenkrankheitslehre*; *Seelensorge*; Sulzer; therapeutics; Unzer; Wolff)
Spiess, Reinard 31n31
Stahl, Georg Ernest 34, 122n55, 155n26, 247
– and animism 35, 50, 113–114, 120, 122, 208, 341n9, 342, 348, 356
– and case histories/studies 37, 44, 71, 300
– and Hoffmann 5, 34, 37, 113, 122, 133, 148, 155–156, 158n36, 208, 341–342, 348, 356
– inaugural disputation 341
– influxionism 35, 51, 113–114, 120–121, 123, 147, 301, 323, 341, 356
– and observation 35–36, 43, 205
– psycho-dynamic account of illness and disease 108, 111, 113–114, 341
– psychological medicine 35, 108–109, 111–114, 158, 195, 208, 343
– and string model of the nerves 114
– at the Universität Halle 34, 51, 108, 113n19, 120, 155–156, 205, 281, 341
– and Unzer 34–35, 120–122, 343
Stangneth, Bettina 311n9
Steigerwald, Jörn 35n35
Steinberg, H. 14n34
Steinlechner, Gisela 74n17
Stiening, Gideon 51n86
Stöckmann, Ernst 284n39
Struve, Ulrich 104n137
Sturm, Thomas 31, *33*
Sulloway, Frank 74n17–74n18
Sulzer, Johann Georg 8, 45, 60, 72, 108
– and aesthetics 128, 306, 328n68, 329–331, 332n79, 344–345

– *Allgemeine Theorie der Schönen Künste* 283
– case-histories 129–130, 360
– definition of apperception 128–129
– and empirical psychology 108, 114, 128, 330, 345
– *Kurzer Begriff aller Wissenschaften* 128
– Mendelssohn's critique of 284–285, 306
– the self and body 130, 145
– and the soul 51, 130, 284, 330–331, 331n77, 335, 344
– and stance 315, 329–330, 344–345, 357
– *Theorie der angenehmen und unangenehmen Empfindungen* 283n35, 332n79
– theory of consciousness 128, 329
– *Untersuchung über den Ursprung der angenehmen und unangehmen Empfindungen* 282–283
– *Von dem Bewusstseyn und seinem Einfluss in unsere Urtheile* 128–130
Swales, Martin 77n29
Sydenham, Thomas 5, 24–25, 28, 43, 50, 71, 94, 155n26, 195, 248, 251n20, 254, 320
system 2, 42, 109, 127, 260, 304n101, 323, 352, 359
– and case histories 2, 6n16, 21, 28, 70, 88, 211, 280
– circulation (of the body/blood) 147, 208
– classificatory 2, 88
– digestive 250–251
– and Kant 142, 271
– and knowledge 70, 142, 211, 216, 280
– of medical policy (Frank) 28, 94, 106, 252, 253n27, 260, 360–361
– moral theological casuistry 27
– nervous (and the mind) 41, 50, 64, 124, 155–156, 229–230, 248n8, 249, 254, 271, 314, 334
– procedures 94
– and psychology 275
– and rationality 120, 210, 254
– rigidity of 212, 280, 303–304, 306, 353, 355
– social 2, 28, 242
– and theory 14n35, 78, 94, 142, 201–208

Taylor, Charles 3, 3n7, 7, 80n38, 96–101
therapeutics 11, 72, 273, 276, 282, 337
– care of self 300–302, 304
– and case history 88, 217
– and Herz 258–259
– holistic 208
– and medicine 22
– and Moritz 353
– pastoral 183–184, 300
– of the soul 274–275, 278, 304, 307, 353
– and theory 259, 279
– and treatment for deviation/mental illness 145, 193, 222, 279, 307, 360
– types of 59 (see also aesthetics; dietetics; care; soul; *Seelenheilkunde*)
Thiel, Udo 51n86
Thomasius, Christian 148, 154
Thomé, Horst 345
Thome, R. 22n5
Thums, Barbara 286–287, 303n100
Tissot, Samuel André 252–254
Toellner, Richard 114n21
Tougaw, Jason Daniel 88, 93
Toulmin, Stephen 23, 27

Universität Halle VIII, 2, 8, 10n24, 34, 36, 37, 73, 108, 113n19, 126, 130, 130n86, 144, 201, 282, 301, 306, 342n12
– founding of 113, 155
– Hoffmann and 34, 40, 113, 125, 195, 300, 341
– and the psychological physicians 2, 8, 10n24, 36, 37, 55, 108, 111, 120, 122, 125–126, 130n86, 144–145, 148, 155, 191, 226, 274, 281, 301–302, 307, 310, 323–324, 342–343, 348, 356, 358
– Stahl and 34, 51, 108, 112–113, 113n19, 158, 195, 205, 209, 300, 341 (see also Halle)
Unzer, Johann August 2, 34, 120, 126, 155, 301, 343
– *Der Arzt* (journal) 120, 247, 250, 256
– *Betrachtungen über des heiligen Herrn Hofraths Stahls theoretischer Grundsatz in der Arztneywissenschaft* 120
– experiential psychology 111

- *Gedanken vom Einfluß der Seele in ihren Körper* 35, 120–121
- idea of self 145
- and metaphysics 35
- and observation 35–36, 342
- and Platner 55, 209–210
- rejection of soul and body 35, 120–122

vapors 9, 41, 45, 49–50, 147, 153–154, 248, 254–255, 361
Veith, Ilza 249n11
Vickers, Neil 56n107
Vidal, Fernando 5–6, 72–73, 109–110
Viëtor, Karl 29n21

Wahrnehmung 36
Walther, Manfred 359
Watt, Ian 3n7, 7, 7n21, 98–99
Weikard, Melchior Adam 309n3
Wellbery, David E. VII
Westphal, Carl Friedrich Otto VII, 18, 67
White, Hayden 13, 63n131
Whytt, Robert 249
Wild, Christopher 296n80
von Wiese, Benno 77n29
Willis, Thomas 50, 155n29, 156, 248
Wingertszahn, Christof VII-VIII
Wöbkemeier, Rita 87
Wölfel, Kurt 72n14
Wolff, Christian 1–2, 8, 38, 107, 117n33, 120, 122, 148, 154, 312
- and Baumgarten 118–119, 123n58
- discussion of senses and feelings 116–117
- empirical psychology 1–2, 107, 107n2, 108, 113, 115, 117, 123n58, 139, 339–340, 345

- empirical-experiential psychology 115, 117, 125, 144
- and habit 340
- and Kant 113n18, 141, 144
- notion of "apperception" 115–116, 128, 136–137
- *Philosophia rationalis sive Logica* 340n6
- *Psychologia empirica* 8, 115–117, 339
- and rationality 115, 117, 120, 140, 144, 339–340, 344
- the role of empirical psychology in 339–340
- and the soul 113–115, 117, 123, 136, 139–140, 256n38, 330, 340, 342
- *Vernünftige Gedanken von Gott, der Welt und der Seele des Menschen, auch allen Dingen überhaupt [Deutsche Metaphysik]* 117n33
Wübben, Yvonne 286–287
Wunderlich, Falk 51n86
Wuthenow, Ralph-Rainer 59n114

Zammito, John H. 107n2, 122n55, 122n58, 123n58
Zedler, Johann Heinrich 21
Zelle, Carsten VII, 35, 36n40, 38n46, 39n50, 40, 43, 58n111, 111, 126n71, 130n86, 202, 213n80, 301–302
Zimmermann, Johann Georg 2, 8, 37, 45–46, 108, 111, 113, 130, 130n86, 131–132, 145, 252, 281, 281n29, 345, 345n15, 346, 358
- *Concerning Experience in Medicine (Von der Erfahrung in der Arzneykunst)* 45n67, 46, 111, 113, 130

About the Author

Robert S. Leventhal is Associate Professor and Director of the Program in German Studies at William & Mary, Williamsburg, Virginia. He is the author of *The Disciplines of Interpretation: Lessing, Herder, Schlegel and Hermeneutics in Germany, 1750–1800* (Walter de Gruyter, 1994) and editor of the volume *Reading after Foucault: Institutions, Disciplines, and Technologies of the Self in Germany, 1750–1830* (Wayne State University Press, 1995). He has published articles on eighteenth century German literature, intellectual history and the history of disciplines, Early German Romanticism, and Spinoza and Spinozism in Germany.

www.ingramcontent.com/pod-product-compliance
Lightning Source LLC
Chambersburg PA
CBHW031411230426
43668CB00007B/271